OXFORD MONOGRAPHS IN
PRIVATE INTERNATIONAL LAW

GENERAL EDITOR: P. B. CARTER QC
Emeritus Fellow of
Wadham College, Oxford

INSOLVENCY IN PRIVATE INTERNATIONAL LAW

OXFORD MONOGRAPHS IN
PRIVATE INTERNATIONAL LAW

The aim of the series is to publish work of quality and originality in a number of important areas of private international law. The series is intended for both scholarly and practitioner readers.

ALSO IN THIS SERIES

Autonomy in International Contracts
PETER NYGH

Intellectual Property and Private International Law
JAMES J. FAWCETT and PAUL TORREMANS

Foreign Law in English Courts
Pleading, Proof and Choice of Law
RICHARD FENTIMAN

Declining Jurisdiction in Private International Law
JAMES J. FAWCETT

INSOLVENCY IN PRIVATE INTERNATIONAL LAW

National and International Approaches

IAN F. FLETCHER

MA, LLM, MCL, PhD, LLD
of Lincoln's Inn, Barrister
Professor of Commercial Law and Director of the
Centre for Commercial Law Studies, Queen Mary and Westfield College,
University of London

CLARENDON PRESS · OXFORD
1999

Oxford University Press, Great Clarendon Street, Oxford OX2 6DP
www.oup.co.uk

Oxford New York
Athens Auckland Bangkok Bogotá Buenos Aires Calcutta
Cape Town Chennai Dar es Salaam Delhi Florence Hong Kong Istanbul
Karachi Kuala Lumpur Madrid Melbourne Mexico City Mumbai
Nairobi Paris São Paulo Singapore Taipei Tokyo Toronto Warsaw

and associated companies in
Berlin Ibadan

Oxford is a registered trade mark of Oxford University Press

Published in the United States
by Oxford University Press Inc., New York

First published 1999

British Library Cataloguing in Publication Data
Data available

Library of Congress Cataloging in Publication Data
Fletcher, Ian F.
Insolvency in private international law: national and international approaches / Ian F. Fletcher.
(Oxford monographs in private international law)
Includes bibliographical references and index.
1. Conflict of laws—Bankruptcy. I. Title. II Series.
K7510.F555 1999 340.9'78—dc21 98–51383
ISBN 0–19–825864–X

1 3 5 7 9 10 8 6 4 2

Typeset in Palatino
by Hope Services (Abingdon) Ltd.
Printed in Great Britain
on acid-free paper by
Bookcraft Ltd., Midsomer Norton, Somerset

For Letitia,
Daniel and Julian

General Editor's Preface

Traditionally each nation, and sometimes each constituent State or Province of a federal nation, has been treated as having its own system of private international law. At the same time the trans-border nature of the subject-matter and of underlying policy considerations has given rise to significant similarities in some areas of the subject. And, of course, as between common law countries there are as usual fundamental similarities and affinities.

However, a pressing need for a much more radical departure from tradition has emerged relatively recently in the law relating to cross-border insolvency. Various attempts have been made, and are being made, to meet that need. These have taken the form, not only of judicial ingenuity and creativity and of statutory innovation, but also of substantial, if often unavoidably complex, transnational cooperation. The process is continuing. In Part I of this book Professor Fletcher surveys the background against which contemporary and possible future development must be viewed. He also analyses in great and illuminating detail the ways in which problems relating to cross-border insolvency in respect of corporations and individuals have been, and are being, approached by national courts. The author compares the English approach with that taken in some other jurisdictions, such as Canada, Australia and the USA. In Part II Professor Fletcher analyses the various international and regional conventions and agreements, such as the EU Insolvency Convention and the UNCITRAL Model Law on Cross-Border Insolvency, that have been under negotiation in response to the difficult problems created by transnational insolvency. Finally the author addresses possible future developments.

The book will appeal not only to insolvency experts but also to international commercial lawyers more generally. Moreover, it can be seen as a good example of achievement of the aim of the Series, *Oxford Monographs in Private International Law*. That aim is to publish works of quality and originality in a number of important and developing areas of private international law.

Wadham College, Oxford
1 November, 1998

P. B. CARTER

Preface

The invitation to contribute a volume devoted to the subject of Insolvency in Private International Law to this series of Oxford monographs presented me with a welcome opportunity to combine several interests into a single scheme of treatment. I was also aware that the task would be a challenging one. The fusion of such specialised branches of study entails a certain risk with regard to the amount of knowledge which the reader should be assumed to possess about the fundamental characteristics of each discipline. On the other hand, to engage in a lengthy discourse upon the general principles of insolvency law, and those of private international law, seemed likely to overtax the patience of the majority of potential readers. I have therefore limited such material as much as possible, save where I felt the need to ensure that the underlying reasons for some otherwise obscure or confusing proposition might be insufficiently clear.

Part I of the book is mainly devoted to an examination of the body of rules and practice that has evolved in England, during the past two and a half centuries, for dealing with cases of insolvency in which more than one jurisdiction has some legitimate interest in relation to the issues that are involved. The historical dimension, while important, should not be supposed to predominate, however: a most exciting phase of development has been taking place in recent years, characterised by judicial activism and a measure of statutory innovation, in which a new spirit of international cooperation has emerged. Parallel, and in many ways similar, developments have taken place in other jurisdictions whose laws are the subject of comparative discussion throughout Part I, namely Australia, Canada, and the USA.

The themes of international regulation of cross-border insolvency, and of recognition and assistance pursuant to internationally concluded arrangements, are explored in Part II. During the period in which the writing of the book was taking place, several important initiatives were passing through crucial stages of elaboration. These developments, undertaken under the respective auspices of the European Union, the Council of Europe, and UNCITRAL, are explored in detail in Chapters 6, 7 and 8. Although the texts of these three instruments have become finalised, certain questions remain unresolved with regard to the possibility of their entry into effect. Every effort has been made to provide an updated assessment of the situation as at the latest practicable time while the book was going through the press. Subject to this, the contents of this book are based on material available to me in August 1998.

I am profoundly indebted to many persons and institutions for their indispensable assistance in my efforts to produce this book. Although I have elected not to attempt to mention all of them here by name, there are several friends and colleagues whose counsel and support over the years has been such that it would be not only uncivil, but also unethical, to refrain from acknowledging their intellectual and spiritual contribution to the finished work. These include: Ron Harmer, Bruce Leonard, Eamon Murphy, Nick Segal, Philip Wood, Neil Cooper, Professor Roy Goode, Professor Jacob Ziegel, Professor Robin Morse, Michael Crystal QC, Gabriel Moss QC, and David Graham QC. I am especially grateful to Professor Jay L. Westbrook for his wise advice, unstintingly and frequently given, and for his being instrumental in enabling me to spend several weeks as Visiting Scholar at the Law School of the University of Texas at Austin. In that scholarly haven, and with the exceptional resources of the Tarlton Law Library at my disposal, the writing of the second part of the book gained crucial momentum. Not for the first time, I must record my appreciation of the fine service provided to me by Jonathan Pratter and David Gunn of the Tarlton Library, under the presiding genius of Professor Roy Mersky. Needless to say, none of the foregoing are to be deemed accountable for any defects in the book itself, for which I alone am responsible.

The period of gestation of this book was extended far beyond my original intentions, largely due to circumstances beyond my control. In addition to the fluctuating fortunes of the international developments mentioned above, which made it expedient to delay embarking upon the task of writing any critique or commentary until the texts at least were finalised, the growing burden of my administrative responsibilities in recent years was a further obstacle to progress. I am therefore deeply appreciative of the fact that my College granted me formal leave for the academic year 1997–1998 to enable me to devote my energies to research and writing. I also extend my thanks to my colleagues in the Centre for Commercial Law Studies for enabling me to relinquish my duties as Director during that time. This arrangement ensured that I was finally able to fulfil my commitment to the Oxford University Press, and to the General Editor of this series. It is fitting that I should pay tribute to Peter Carter for his patience and loyalty, and above all his calmness, in the face of so many postponements of the date for completion, and for his meticulous scrutiny of the final product, whereby I was spared numerous retrospective blushes. Finally, throughout the long years of planning and preparing for the writing of the work, and during the intensely busy months of its actual execution, I have been sustained, consoled and encouraged by my wife and by our two sons. Without their tolerance and support, the motivation to complete the project would have withered on the vine. To them belong my unbounded thanks.

IAN F. FLETCHER

Centre for Commercial Law Studies
Queen Mary & Westfield College
University of London
August 1998

Summary of Contents

Contents

Table of Latin Terms and Expressions

The Latin language has supplied many technical terms and expressions which continue to be used in English legal discourse. This is particularly true of the subject of private international law, where Latin terms provide a convenient shorthand for many concepts which are mentioned with great frequency, and which generally require many more words to state fully and precisely in English. The following is a list of the Latin terms and expressions which are frequently used throughout this book, with their English meaning alongside.

Forum:	The law district or country in which a case was, is being, or may be heard; hence, also, the court by which a legal action or application is, or was, heard.
Forum concursus:	The court within whose jurisdiction an insolvency proceeding is currently taking place, or formerly took place.
Lex fori:	The legal system, and rules of law, in force in the country where the *forum* sits.
Lex concursus:	The system and rules of insolvency law in force in the country where an insolvency proceeding takes place.
Forum non conveniens:	A plea or defence alleging that the forum is inappropriately selected and should refrain from exercising jurisdiction.
Lex causae:	The legal system whose substantive rule governs the matter in issue, as selected by the private international law of the forum.
Lex domicilii:	The law of the place where the person is domiciled.
Lex loci(—actus; —contractus; —celebrationis; —delicti; —solutionis; etc.):	The law of the place where (—the act is performed; —the contract is made; —the marriage is celebrated; —the wrong is committed; —the contract is to be performed, or the debt is due to be paid; etc.).
Lex patriae:	The law of the State of which the person possesses nationality.
Situs:	The place where a thing (i.e. an item of property) is situate.

Lex situs (alternatively: *lex loci rei sitae*):	The law of the place where the property is situate.
Lis alibi pendens:	Plea that the defendant is currently being sued by the same plaintiff before some other forum on the basis of the same cause of action.
Res judicata:	Plea that the matter in issue has already been the subject of a final adjudication by a court of competent jurisdiction.
Par est condicio omnium creditorum:	(Literally: 'The condition of all creditors is equal'). This maxim is widely employed to express the principle of equality of treatment and status to be accorded to all creditors generally. It is a principle which admits of numerous exceptions, which vary according to the provisions contained in the laws of the various countries.
Pari passu:	(Literally: 'On an equal footing', hence, proportionately). The principle of distribution of an insolvent estate, based upon the notion of equality of treatment of creditors (see above), whereby the creditors receive a payment of their debts in shares proportioned to the value of their respective claims.
Vis attractiva concursus:	(Literally: 'The attractive force of the bankruptcy proceeding'). A rule of jurisdiction, based on the premise that the court in which bankruptcy proceedings are taking place should exercise jurisdiction over any related or concurrent proceedings concerning the same debtor. The doctrine is not universally accepted, and is applied in variable degrees, and subject to numerous exceptions, in those systems (principally civil law countries) by which it is accepted.[1]

[1] The doctrine is closely associated with France, where bankruptcy courts were accorded exclusive jurisdiction over all matters in any way related to the bankruptcy proceedings by Art. 635 of the Commercial Code of 1838. For a comparative survey, and copious references, see J.H. Dalhuisen, *Dalhuisen on International Insolvency and Bankruptcy* (2 vols., looseleaf, last updated 1986), § 2.04[4].

Table of Cases

Australia

Ireland

New Zealand

Scotland

South Africa

U.K.

U.S.

Table of Statutes

Australia

Canada

EC

France

Ireland

Italy

Japan

Jersey

Netherlands

Scotland

U.K.

U.S.

Table of Treaties and Conventions

Part I

INTERNATIONAL INSOLVENCY: NATIONAL APPROACHES

1

Theory and Principle in Cross-Border Insolvency

1.1 INTRODUCTION: INSOLVENCY AND ITS INTERNATIONAL DIMENSION

The concept of insolvency—and indeed its reality—may be said to form part of the common experience of organised human society. With the evolution of such notions as property, obligation, credit, and commercial exchange, the elements are in place from which individuals may manipulate their affairs with a view to enhancing the sum total of their material wellbeing. In a portion of cases, whether through misfortune, miscalculation or mismanagement (or some combination of these) the outcome will be less satisfactory. The hoped-for gains may fail to materialise; or losses may emerge which more than cancel out such gains as may accrue. In due course, the debtor's situation declines to a point where the combined total of the outstanding liabilities exceeds the measurable value of all assets. This unenviable state of negative net worth is what is traditionally understood as 'insolvency'. More precisely, in modern parlance it represents the condition known as 'balance-sheet' insolvency,[1] since it is based upon assessed valuations of the totality of assets and liabilities associated with the patrimony of a given debtor. In the developed societies of the present Age, the debtor may be a natural, or a legal, person: the essential principle is one and the same.

While the traditional concept of insolvency has very ancient roots, and continues to supply the basis of social and legal responses to this phenomenon, an alternative, and more sophisticated, concept has been developed in recent times as a reflection of the pervasive role of credit in the increasingly complex and interdependent conditions of social and commercial existence. This parallel concept is variously referred to as 'short-term', or 'practical', or 'cash-flow' insolvency, and is associated with the debtor's inability to command sufficient liquidity of resources to enable debts to be paid as they fall due.[2] Even if the debtor's underlying financial circumstances, measured on the 'balance sheet' basis, remain in surplus assuming that time were to be allowed for the realisation of assets at

[1] Also referred to as 'absolute' insolvency.

[2] Hence the condition is sometimes termed a 'liquidity crisis'.

something approaching their optimum value, the present reality is one of default occasioning adverse consequences for those creditors whose debts are currently mature and exigible. In many countries nowadays this fact can be invoked as a ground for initiating formal insolvency proceedings against the debtor concerned. This amounts to recognition of the erosion of general confidence in the credit system that would result from a state of affairs where unpaid creditors were compelled to await their debtor's descent into absolute insolvency before any collective satisfaction could be sought. From this development, the enlightened perception has gradually emerged in a number of countries that it may sometimes be possible by timely intervention in a debtor's financially troubled affairs to bring about a restoration of equilibrium and prudent governance that may avert the ultimate fate of balance sheet insolvency altogether, or otherwise diminish the scale on which it takes place, thereby accomplishing worthwhile results. Thus there has evolved the notion of the 'rescue culture', with a further range of complementary procedures whose purpose is to facilitate the reorganisation of the business and affairs of a debtor at or close to the point of insolvency.

Diversity of national insolvency laws

Although it is possible to describe the factual attributes of insolvency in terms which may be universally recognised and understood, national attitudes towards the phenomenon of insolvency are extremely variable, as are the social and legal consequences for the debtors concerned. Since, by definition, insolvency impacts upon the entire patrimony of the debtor, the range of legal interests which are in some way affected is very extensive. This ensures that there is a profound and intimate correlation between insolvency—whether individual or corporate—and the very wellsprings of policy and social order from which national law ultimately draws its inspiration. For this reason, despite numerous general resemblances, national insolvency laws and procedures differ from one another almost infinitely in ways both great and small. The variations range from such fundamental matters as the underlying philosophy of the law—including the key question of whether its sentiments are inclined towards the alleviation of the debtor's predicament, or towards the amelioration of the creditors' exposure to loss[3]—to the more specific questions of detail concerning the manner in which proceedings are conducted, and the contents of rules of substance or procedure which bear upon a particular set of facts. Although some of these differences appear relatively minor, it can

[3] For a graphic illustration of the global differentiation between insolvency laws that are broadly pro-debtor or pro-creditor (with some intermediate groupings), see Philip R. Wood, *Maps of World Financial Law*, 3rd edn. (Allen & Overy Global Law Maps: World Financial Law, 1997).

readily be appreciated that the outcome for any party in interest can be materially different, depending upon which country's law is applied in the circumstances of a given case. Of course, if all material elements, and all interested parties, belonging to the case happen to be connected exclusively with one and the same country, the hypothetical alternatives that might result from the application of a different system of law are essentially of academic interest only: all legitimate expectations may be said to rest, naturally and properly, on the one body of law that has been constantly in play at all relevant times. However, not all cases can be so conveniently and hermetically contained within the confines of a single geopolitical entity and its associated system of law. Even from the earliest recorded times—and increasingly so in the modern world—interaction between parties belonging to different countries and legal systems generates the potential for insolvencies to occur in which the debtor's affairs are in some way connected with more than a single jurisdiction. It is in such circumstances that an insolvency may be said to raise issues belonging to the realm of private international law.

The essence of a cross-border case

Many different factors are capable, either singly or in combination, of imparting a cross-border dimension to a case of insolvency. The debtor may have had dealings with one or more parties from other countries, or may own or have interests in property not all of which is exclusively within the jurisdiction of a single state. Liabilities may be owed to parties whose forensic connections are predominantly with a different country to that with which the debtor is associated; or the relevant obligations may be governed by foreign law, may have been incurred outside the debtor's home country, or may be due to be performed abroad. The diversified state of the debtor's affairs and activities may be such that the conditions for opening insolvency proceedings are simultaneously met with regard to more than one country, giving rise to the possibility of multiple proceedings in different jurisdictions. In any of the foregoing ways, a cross-border case may come into being. Where this is so, the conceptual matrix of private international law can be applied so as to identify the issues which may have to be resolved. These are, first, in which jurisdictions may insolvency proceedings be opened? Secondly, what country's rules of law should be applied with respect to those aspects of the case in which elements of diversity are present? And thirdly, what international effects will be accorded to proceedings conducted at a particular *forum* (including where necessary the granting of enforcement to any judgment or order affecting persons or property involved in the proceedings)?

Because of the complex, and comprehensive, nature of insolvency the practical difficulties encountered in a cross-border case may be considerably greater than those found in the more usual context of international litigation between solvent parties. Although many of the issues of principle are essentially the same, the close identification between insolvency law and public policy can introduce additional considerations of a quite fundamental character into the approach that will be adopted by national courts when presiding over an international insolvency matter. Unfortunately, the collateral victims of the prevailing state of disharmony are the parties whose misfortune it is to be ensnared in an insolvency having transnational elements: creditors who are already fated to receive only a fractional return upon their unsatisfied claims may well experience a further diminution of the value eventually transmitted to them, due to the additional costs, and systemic inefficiencies, associated with the administration of such cases. On the other hand, some creditors may discover that they can exploit the existing legal fragmentation to personal advantage, and may achieve a better rate of recovery through individual acts of diligence than would have been forthcoming to them via the insolvency processes on which the majority must perforce rely. What must be remembered, however, is that such private opportunism takes place, inevitably, at the expense of the less advantageously positioned majority. No one should pretend that this provides a basis for anything resembling a system of justice.

The quest for order and rationalisation

The foregoing observations help to explain why the private international law aspects of insolvency have long been regarded as an arcane and rarified area of specialisation, and at the same time have been castigated for their arbitrary and capricious impact upon private and commercial interests alike. Over the past two decades, the frequency and magnitude of the cases which have confronted courts and practitioners have exposed the limitations of the existing body of law, nationally and internationally.[4] The long-familiar paradox of the subject of private international law has once again been on prominent display, namely that the rules which have been developed within each system of law for the very purpose of accommodating the conflicting effects of different national laws have somehow contrived to perpetuate, albeit at a different level and in a different way, the syndrome of diversity which originally inspired them. Just as national systems of law differ from one another in their provisions and effects, so too do the national systems of private international law. When one examines those portions of each country's private international law which are concerned with insolvency, the divergent—and often irreconcilable—

[4] For accounts of some of the *causes célèbres* of international insolvency, see Becker (1976) 62 A.B.A.J. 1290; the same author, (1981) 29 A.J.C.L. 706; Riesenfeld (1976) 24 A.J.C.L. 288; Nadelmann (1977) 52 N.Y.U.L.Rev. 1; Fletcher (1993) 2 I.I.R. 7; Bradley (1994) 3 I.I.R. 89.

positions are even more deeply entrenched, and fervently defended, than in the case of other types of conflict of laws. The increased awareness in recent times of the negative consequences of such international fragmentation of policy and approach to cross-border insolvency issues has fuelled the quest for improved solutions. Various initiatives have been pursued, as will be discussed in the later chapters of this book. These include, in some cases, reform of national laws with a view to engendering a more 'international' approach on the part of courts and officials.[5] At the same time a number of multilateral treaties or conventions have been concluded, to provide a harmonised body of rules in place of the individualised responses developed by each national system.[6] Presently, most of these initiatives have yet to attain their intended objectives, and the lack of an internationally-agreed framework for resolving cross-border problems remains a matter to be deplored.[7] One of the principal aims of this book is to provide an account of the current state of these various developments, indicating both their virtues and also their shortcomings, in the hope that a clearer picture will thereby emerge of what is needed and what can realistically be achieved under prevailing conditions of governmental willingness to enter into international commitments in this field.

1.2 DOMINANT PRINCIPLES OF DOMESTIC AND INTERNATIONAL INSOLVENCY LAW

In a cross-border context, insolvency law draws upon a blend of principles, some of which are referable to the general approach to be followed in cases of insolvency, while others address the special questions that result from the international dimension within the instant case. As already stated, the traditional differences between the laws of independent, sovereign countries render it somewhat dangerous to speak in terms of concepts and principles as though they enjoyed some kind of standardised application throughout the world. However, some common features can be cautiously identified within the make-up of many of the individual systems that have been studied comparatively, and hence a limited degree of generalisation may be justified in terms of the structures and processes encountered within domestic laws. Just as legal systems can be arranged into groupings which represent various traditions, or 'families', within the global community of nation states, so do they appear to form themselves into a number of 'sub-sets' in terms of their allegiance to certain principles which influence their approach to the international aspects of insolvency,

[5] See Chapter 4 below.
[6] See Chapters 5 to 8 inclusive below.
[7] See the sentiments expressed, extrajudicially, by Sir Peter Millett in (1997) 6 I.I.R. 99, esp. at 108–113.

although the membership of the groupings at this level is by no means co-extensive with the respective legal 'families' in the realm of domestic laws.[8]

General principles in domestic law

Despite the wide variation between legal systems in terms of policy and approach towards insolvency, extending across the gamut from pro-debtor to pro-creditor,[9] at least one fundamental principle appears to command universal acceptance (although the exact circumstances and mode of its application can vary). This may be termed 'the principle of collectivity', and amounts to a recognition that insolvency constitutes an example of the so-called 'common pool problem', which arises whenever conditions are such that more than one person has rights over the same, finite fund of resources.[10] By regarding all those with claims against the insolvent debtor as members of a collectivised entity, the law transforms what were originally multiple relationships between each creditor and the debtor into a unified whole for the purpose of administering and distributing such value as remains in the debtor's estate. One notable consequence of this process of transformation is that the chronological order in which the original liabilities were incurred ceases to be of relevance. An important aspect of the concept of collectivity is the *pari passu* principle of distribution, whereby all debts of equivalent rank are subject to an arithmetical process of abatement, based upon the relative proportions of the collective mass of claims belonging to that ranking class, and the total size of the fund available to pay those claims: the dividend payable to the holder of each separate claim is then calculated on a *pro rata* basis, applying this proportional formula, so that the scale of abatement is identical in every case.[11] The essential notion of equality of treatment of creditors is sometimes expressed by means of the Latin maxim: *par est condicio omnium creditorum*.

In terms of the insolvency procedures provided under individual national laws, which vary from one another in countless ways, the princi-

[8] For comparative surveys, based on extensive but by no means comprehensive assessments of the world's legal systems and traditions, see Nadelmann (1943–4) 5 Un. Tor. L.J. 324; J.H. Dalhuisen, *Dalhuisen on International Insolvency and Bankruptcy* (1980–1986, looseleaf), Part II; Fletcher in I.F. Fletcher (ed.), *Cross-Border Insolvency: National and Comparative Studies (Reports delivered at the XIII International Congress of Comparative Law, Montreal 1990)* (1992), Part II, p.269 *et seq.*

[9] See *supra*, n.3 and text thereto.

[10] See the classic exposition of the common pool problem as it relates to bankruptcy law in T.H. Jackson, *The Logic and Limits of Bankruptcy Law* (1986), esp. chs. 1 and 2.

[11] For example, if the total funds available amount to £1,000, and the aggregate of claims ranking for dividend is £100,000, the arithmetical proportion is 1:100 (also expressible as 1%). Hence a creditor whose claim is valued at £100 will receive £1; one whose claim is for £1,000 will receive £10; and one whose claim is for £10,000 will receive £100.

ple of collectivity is a common denominator which is capable (within limits) of transcending the conceptual and structural distinctions between systems that are an inescapable reality at present, and for the foreseeable future. All systems generally provide at least one main procedure whereby an insolvent debtor's entire patrimony (apart from some permitted exemptions in the case of individuals) can be subjected to a process of liquidation and schematic distribution in accordance with the principle of collectivity. A further type of procedure which is widely encountered is one which offers an alternative to outright liquidation by means of a binding composition or arrangement concluded between the debtor and the general body of creditors. The principle of collectivity is also a standard feature of composition procedures in that, while it is often permissible for an agreement to acquire binding force through being accepted by a prescribed majority of creditors, and so become binding upon the dissenting minority, the latter are entitled to full parity of treatment under the terms of the scheme of distribution that can be imposed upon them.[12]

One further issue which is of fundamental importance is the extent to which rights arising under general law, and which were duly acquired and perfected prior to the commencement of insolvency, are recognised as surviving the onset of formal insolvency proceedings. The principle of respect for such pre-bankruptcy rights is widely accepted by national laws, even if the nature of such rights and the conditions attaching to their creation are by no means uniform throughout the world. Broadly speaking however, the precedence enjoyed by proprietary over personal and contractual claims under general law is replicated under the regime of insolvency law, with the consequence that security interests and other rights *in rem* which have been created prior to the commencement of insolvency remain intact, and are thus enabled to accomplish their intended purpose of insulating the creditor from full exposure to risk of loss in the event of the debtor's default. Hence the fully-secured creditor is enabled to stand outside the collective process of administration of the debtor's unencumbered assets, while the partially-secured creditor is placed in the position of having to rely on that process in respect of the unsecured balance of his claim.[13] The ability of creditors to base their expectations on this principle, and to create appropriate arrangements to suit their particular needs, is one of the vital elements in the system of credit in both the domestic and the international context. Where such international arrangements break down, or encounter uncertainty, due to the differences between the rules of the domestic laws of the countries concerned, the

[12] The concept of binding a dissenting minority, provided the terms imposed are not unfairly discriminatory, is sometimes referred to as 'cram-down'.

[13] For a comparative survey of various kinds of real security, considered in the context of international insolvency, see Fletcher, *supra* n.8, at pp.289–291.

destructive impact upon commercial confidence can be especially acute, and the sensitive deployment of private international law techniques offers perhaps the last line of defence.[14]

Rival principles of international insolvency

Even though it is possible to discover an underlying concurrence between domestic insolvency laws with regard to some of the most fundamental matters of principle, it must be acknowledged that the dissimilarities are so numerous, and so substantial, as to oblige the realist to accept that the world essentially consists of separate, self-contained systems. When confronted by a case of insolvency containing international elements, national systems have responded by developing their rules of private international law, employing traditional techniques and concepts, to determine issues of jurisdiction, choice of law and international recognition in conformity with locally accepted norms of decision. The ensuing diversity has been unusually intense, even by the standards of private international law, with the result that the quest for unifying principles has so far proved to be elusive. What can be discerned is an historic struggle between opposing principles, espoused at various times by different schools of thought whose global influence has fluctuated. In so far as a prevalent tendency seems to be emerging at the current time, the rate of progress is slow and the results uneven.

Doctrinal argument—and the relevant principles associated with the respective camps of opinion—can be broadly divided into two pairs of antithetical propositions. One pairing juxtaposes the principle of 'Unity of Bankruptcy' with its diametrical opposite—an acceptance of the possibility of plurality of proceedings, to be determined by the circumstances of the instant case. In support of the principle of unity, it is urged that for every given debtor there should logically be a unified process of administration of the estate in the event of insolvency, with all interests and claims being channelled into the one process. This theory seems initially to be in fullest harmony with the principle of collectivity, and the equal treatment of all creditors on a global basis. While it may be conceded that this appears to represent the ultimate ideal towards which we should be progressing, present reality suggests that its implementation would give rise to major difficulties, and real injustice. Since it is an inherent part of the doctrine of Unity that the process is opened at the place with which the debtor's affairs, interests and general circumstances have their closest affinity, and that the administration is conducted in accordance with the

[14] See, however, the less than satisfactory approach of the English court to the problems generated by irreconcilable national approaches to the *pari passu* principle (as applicable to the doctrine of set-off), in *Re Bank of Credit and Commerce International S.A. (No.10)* [1996] 4 All E.R. 796, discussed in Chapter 2 at 2.3 below.

insolvency law of that place,[15] this raises the spectre that parties in other jurisdictions, whose dealings with the debtor may have been conducted mainly or exclusively with reference to their local law, may experience a defeat of their legitimate expectations due to the imposition of a different regime of law upon the occasion of the debtor's insolvency. Moreover, the practical difficulties of dealing with property located in one jurisdiction from a distant operational base in another country may be such that it would be more cost-efficient to conduct a local administration in accordance with local law and procedure. Above all, it must be recognised that States are averse to allowing foreign laws to operate with extraterritorial effect in relation to property located within their jurisdiction. In the absence of specific treaty relationships formed out of established ties of trust between the States concerned, local rules of jurisdiction are likely to be deployed so as to enable local assets to be administered in accordance with the provisions of domestic law. In practice, therefore, the pragmatic attractions of plurality are likely to prevail over the more idealistic claims of the principle of Unity. What then remains is the task of discovering some framework within which the concurrent proceedings can be best coordinated in the interests of avoiding other forms of injustice such as discriminatory treatment of different groups of creditors dispersed among different countries. Some of the ways in which this challenge has been met, even if imperfectly, are explored later in this book.[16]

The second pairing of antithetical propositions addresses the issue of the effects of insolvency proceedings opened under the law of a given State, and places the principle of 'Universality of Bankruptcy' in opposition to that of 'Territoriality'. The former, as may readily be inferred, advances the claim that such proceedings enjoy worldwide—hence, 'universal'—effect over all property and interests of the debtor wheresoever these may be found. Such transcendent ambitions encounter the same basic objections as the principle of Unity, namely that States do not concede that foreign laws can bring about extraterritorial effects as of right, and they are extremely cautious about committing themselves to allow such consequences to take place, even pursuant to the terms of a treaty. Thus, while it is not uncommon to find the national law expressed in terms which declare that the insolvency proceedings of that system shall enjoy universal effect, it is the author's experience that no State has yet adopted, freely and unilaterally, a policy of according matching effect to insolvency

15 The difficulties of determining the whereabouts of this 'centre' in a given case, and even the problems of selecting the criteria to be used for that purpose, should not be underestimated.

16 For nationally developed responses to the problem of coordinating plural proceedings see Chapter 2, at 2.8 below; Chapter 3, at 3.9 below; and Chapter 4 generally. International initiatives pursued by means of treaties or conventions, and other international instruments, are explored throughout Part II of this book.

proceedings conducted under the laws of foreign States. This is especially true in the case of immovable property located within the State in which such effects would be experienced.[17] The converse principle, that of Territoriality, argues that the effects of insolvency proceedings are confined to such property as is located within the territorial jurisdiction of the country in which the proceedings are opened, and carries no consequences with respect to foreign assets of the debtor. In some rare instances—as in the case of Japan in former times—the principle of territoriality was strictly maintained in both outward and inward modes of operation, so that no extraterritorial effect was claimed on behalf of proceedings opened inside the country, and no effect was conceded within the domestic legal order as a result of proceedings opened under foreign law.[18] The more usual approach however has been one whereby the State regards its own, domestic bankruptcy laws as producing universal effects, particularly if the debtor's relationship with the country is a close one which enables the case to be classified as a 'domiciliary' proceeding. On the other hand, the notion of territoriality is applied towards foreign proceedings involving debtors with property or other interests which lie within the jurisdiction of the State in question: by denying the capability of the foreign proceedings to produce any effects regarding that part of the debtor's patrimony, the way is left open for local actions to be taken by any party with standing to exercise rights over it.[19] Thus it may be observed of the Territoriality principle that, while based upon the generally accepted view that the laws of each sovereign country cannot, of themselves and as of right, produce effects within the territory of another sovereign and independent jurisdiction, it provides an unsatisfactory foundation for approaching the special problems generated by a cross-border insolvency. Since States cannot be persuaded to subscribe to the tenets of the Universality doctrine in its fullest and purest form, a middle way must be found.

A pragmatic approach: the internationalist principle

It is possible that a workable compromise can be devised through a pragmatic combination of elements from all four of the leading doctrines which have just been considered, namely Unity, Plurality, Universality and

[17] Cf. the approach of English law (which is otherwise among the most liberal in terms of willingness to accord extraterritorial effects to foreign bankruptcy proceedings), concerning the effect of foreign proceedings in relation to land in England: see Chapter 2 at 2.6.1(b); Chapter 3 at 3.7.1(b) below.

[18] See Makoto Ito in Fletcher, *supra* n. 8, ch. 9, esp. at pp.180–183; cf. Matsushita (1997) 6 I.I.R. 210 at 212–18, 221–222.

[19] See the account of the position under the law of The Netherlands provided by Dalhuisen in Fletcher, *supra,* n.8, ch. 10, esp. at pp.187–188, 196–198; also the report on Swedish law by Bogdan, *ibid.*, ch. 11, esp. at pp. 206–214.

Territoriality. It may be termed 'the Internationalist Principle', since it is predicated upon the truism that an international insolvency requires a collaborative response on the part of every State whose legal or material interests are somehow involved within the fabric of the case. First, the integrity of each system and its concerns must be properly respected, by recognising that any process which takes place under the auspices of the legal system of one country can only produce effects within another country with the latter's concurrence. In the absence of a special treaty, cross-border effects can take place only through the active interplay of rules of private international law. To that extent, the essence of Territoriality is conceded, but only up to a certain point. It is submitted that, in a world where States allow their citizens—including companies formed under their laws—the freedom to have dealings and relationships which transcend national frontiers, and to own and transfer property between jurisdictions with relative ease, it becomes incumbent upon all States to play a responsible part in constructing rules of private international law that are in harmony with the realities of such cross-border activity. Under these circumstances, it is not appropriate for legal systems to maintain an insular detachment from the consequences of a multi-jurisdictional insolvency: law and practice must be modified where necessary, to enable the courts and other institutions of the State to respond in a positive way, even while upholding the essential values of the system to which they belong.

The second component of the proposed internationalist principle involves a modification of the doctrine of Universality so that it complements, rather than negates, the concept of Territoriality. What is required is that, at the culmination of the global operation to administer the insolvent debtor's estate, there shall have been sufficient coordination between the various component parts of the administration that it amounts to *de facto* universality. This eschews the unattainable dogma associated with the traditional notions of Universality, which argue for extraterritorial effects to take place on a *de iure* basis. In place of this, the pragmatic approach aspires to work via the rules and processes of private international law and cross-border cooperation (between courts, and also between office holders in insolvency proceedings). By this means, the net outcome can be one in which the worldwide estate is completely administered, with all creditors having the right of participation at some point, and with the principle of collectivity supplying the ultimate basis of the solutions which are arrived at.

Thirdly, the renunciation of cherished fundamentals also applies towards the Unity *versus* Plurality antithesis: neither of these should be allowed to occupy a dominant place in the approach to a cross-border case, but each should be regarded as a potential option to be employed, according to circumstances. Thus, if the distribution of the debtor's affairs is such that it would not be cost-efficient to conduct multiple proceedings, each administered according to the rules of local law, then it is demonstrably in the best interests of creditors, regarded as a whole, that a unitary proceeding should take place, thereby maximising the value available for distribution. This is dependent upon there being sufficient flexibility within the law of the State in which the unitary proceedings are centred—including that State's rules of conflict of laws—to enable suitable account to be taken of the localised interests of foreign creditors whose expectations have legitimately been based upon the provisions of some other State's law. Conversely, if the logical conclusion, derived from an assessment of the pattern of dispersal of assets and claims and also of the complexity of the administrative process, is that the goals of convenience and efficiency will best be realised through plural administrations, then this should be preferred subject to the proviso that the laws of the States concerned are furnished with provisions to enable proper coordination and communication to take place between the respective administrations. The model which has become increasingly favoured in recent times is one which utilises the concept of 'primary' and 'secondary' bankruptcy administrations which are linked by means of complementary sets of rules to ensure that a kind of *de facto* universality of administration is attained.[20]

The Internationalist principle is therefore one which aspires to realise, as faithfully as is practicable in any given case of international insolvency, the ideals of collectivity, equality of treatment for all creditors, and the respect for previously acquired rights, which as we have seen provide a unifying theme within the diversity of domestic insolvency laws. To achieve that objective, flexibility and pragmatism must be substituted for the dogmas so beloved of former Ages. This entails a vital role for the judges within each State concerned, since it is only through their activism and initiative that the system can respond to the particular challenges posed by the circumstances of a live case.[21] There is an established tradition among judges within the common law legal 'family' of extending international cooperation to each other in the name of the doctrine of 'comity'. The underlying spirit which infuses that approach is also an integral part of the principle of Internationalism which is here advocated as a suitable approach towards the treatment of international insolvency in the early years of the Third Millennium.

[20] See Hanisch (1993) 2 I.I.R. 151; Trautman, Westbrook and Gaillard (1993) 41 A.J.C.L. 573; Balz (1996) 70 Am. Bankr. L. J. 485, esp. at 519–527.

[21] See Millett, *supra* n.7.

1.3 HISTORIC ANTECEDENTS—THE INTERNATIONALIST TRADITION IN ENGLISH LAW

English law is usually considered to have remained largely impervious to the development of the study and practice of private international law until the second half of the eighteenth century.[22] Then, thanks largely to the judicial activism of Lord Mansfield, a belated awakening took place via the practice of citation of Continental scholars' writings during the course of arguing cases before the English courts.[23] This was eventually matched, almost a century later, by the development of an indigenous tradition of writings and commentaries on the conflict of laws for which the foundations were laid by Westlake,[24] and later by Dicey.[25] Among the judicial decisions of this formative period of English conflict of laws, several were concerned with cross-border insolvency. Many of these decisions are referred to in subsequent parts of this book, where they continue to serve as the basis of the present law.[26] The observation that can be made at this point is that these early decisions contain the seeds of what can be justly acclaimed as an internationalist tradition spanning more than two centuries of English judicial development of international insolvency. For example, as early as 1764 the English court was prepared to rule that a foreign bankruptcy could have direct extraterritorial effect upon the bankrupt's movable property situate within the jurisdiction of the English court.[27] Other decisions dating from the same period establish the foundations of the doctrine of 'Hotchpot', whose purpose is to counteract the exploitation by individual creditors of any opportunities to obtain a relative advantage, at the expense of the general body of creditors, due to the dispersal of the debtor's assets across several jurisdictions.[28] Judicial concern that the debtor's estate should be administered for the benefit of all

[22] For accounts of the historic development of private international law, see M. Wolff, *Private International Law*, 2nd edn. (1950), ch. 3; C.M. Schmitthoff, *The English Conflict of Laws*, 3rd edn. (1954), ch. 2; Cheshire and North, *Private International Law*, 12th edn. (1992), ch. 2; Sack, in *Law: A Century of Progress 1835–1935*, (1935), vol. 3, pp.342–354; Lipstein (1972) *Hague Recueil des Cours*, vol. I, pp.104–166.

[23] See the landmark case of *Robinson v. Bland* (1760) 2 Burr. 1077, 97 E.R. 717; 1 Wm. Bl. 234, 96 E.R. 129 and 141. See also *Mostyn v. Fabrigas* (1774) 1 Cowp.161, 98 E.R. 1021; *Holman v. Johnson* (1775) 1 Cowp. 341, both seminal decisions presided over by Lord Mansfield.

[24] The first edition of Westlake's *Private International Law* was published in 1858. A 7th edition was published in 1925.

[25] The first edition of Dicey's *The Conflict of Laws* was published in 1896. The current, 12th edition was published in 1993 under the General Editorship of Dr Lawrence Collins.

[26] See e.g. Chapter 2 at 2.4, 2.6, 2.7 below.

[27] *Solomons v. Ross* (1764) 1 Hy. Bl. 131n, 126 E.R. 79: this and other decisions from the same period are referred to in Chapter 2 at 2.6.1(b)(i) below.

[28] See e.g. *Neale v. Cottingham* (1764) 1 H. Bl. 132n, 126 E.R. 81; *Sill v. Worswick* (1791) 1 H. Bl. 665, 126 E.R. 379. The doctrine of Hotchpot is discussed in Chapter 2, section 2.4.

creditors on a worldwide basis has been a motivating factor which has inspired many important initiatives over the years.

The case of Odwin v. Forbes (1814–1817)

If one were to select a single case to demonstrate the intuitive judicial affinity with the principle of internationalism, the proceedings in the case of *Odwin v. Forbes* have a strong claim to be chosen for this purpose. The case was originally decided in 1814 by the Court of Demerara and Essequibo, under the Presidency of Jabez Henry, whose judgment was subsequently confirmed by the Privy Council, sitting at the Cock Pit in London on 31 May 1817.[29] The central issue in the case was the international effect of a certificate of discharge obtained through bankruptcy proceedings in England, by a debtor who subsequently went abroad and settled in the foreign and independent jurisdiction of Demerara.There he was sued by creditors whose debts had been provable in the English bankruptcy, and who had refrained from lodging proof of their claims despite having had notice of the proceedings. The defendant pleaded that the discharge obtained in England was a good and complete defence to the action in Demerara; the plaintiffs argued that English law had no force in the colony, due to the special arrangements for maintenance in force of the Dutch laws when the colony became a British possession.[30] The Court unanimously concluded that the English discharge could not command the same direct force in Demerara as in its country of origin: though purporting to be of universal effect, it could only attain that objective in other jurisdictions on the basis of comity accorded by the foreign court under the authority of its own law. It was therefore necessary to investigate the provisions of Dutch law as the mother law of the colony, to determine whether it was the practice of the Dutch courts to give effect to foreign judgments. As those courts were disposed to take account of the extent to which their own determinations were accorded comity on a reciprocal basis by the courts of the other country, the Demerara court's researches also included an appraisal of the jurisprudence of the English courts during the preceding half century, paying particular regard to the enforcement of judgments originating from Holland.[31] Having satisfied itself that

[29] *Odwin v. Forbes* (1817) 1 Buck. 57 (PC). The appeal was decided by Lord Chancellor Eldon, sitting with Vice-Chancellors Plumer and Leach. 'The Cock Pit' was the sobriquet applied to the block of buildings on the site of the former cockpit at Whitehall, used for governmental purposes. Hence, in early nineteenth century usage, the term was a synonym for the Judicial Committee of the Privy Council, which used to meet in the building.

[30] Demerara had formerly been a Dutch colonial possession, where the system known as Romano-Dutch law was administered. The Dutch laws had been retained in force in the articles of capitulation at the time of surrender of the colony to the English.

[31] The case of *Solomons v. Ross* (*supra* n.27) was a notable example of the according of extraterritorial effects in England to a Dutch bankruptcy judgment. A near-contemporary decision in which the English court had granted supportive remedies at the instance of

the state of the authorities in both jurisdictions was favourable to the exercise of comity, the court decided that it was bound to exercise similar comity towards the English discharge, and the plaintiffs' action failed.

The decision in *Odwin v. Forbes* was remarkable in many ways. The reasoning process on which the judgment of the first instance court was based has a maturity, and breadth of vision, that seems far ahead of its time. The sensitive recourse to the principle of comity is especially striking, and may be contrasted with the prevailing insularity of approach on the part of courts of the USA during the early nineteenth century when disposing of similar issues. Indeed, in the case of *Ogden v. Saunders*, decided by the United States Supreme Court in 1827, just ten years after the Privy Council had affirmed the judgment of the Court of Demerara, it was held that a foreign discharge in bankruptcy was no defence to an action by a creditor residing in the USA unless the creditor consented to the foreign court's exercise of jurisdiction over the claim.[32] Besides the intrinsic merits of the decision itself, the case of *Odwin v. Forbes* furnished the inspiration for the President of the Court, Jabez Henry, to undertake extensive scholarly research into the subject of international bankruptcy. This resulted in two significant publications which constitute the doctrinal foundation of the English tradition in this field. In 1823 he published in London a full account of the judgment of the Court over which he had presided in 1814, accompanied by copious accounts of the English and foreign authorities referred to in the course of the proceedings.[33] The work comprises some 295 printed pages and offers a classic account of the spirit of approach for which the English courts at this period can justly take credit. Although extant copies are a considerable rarity, the book deserves an honoured place among the landmarks of the literature of cross-border insolvency.

Jabez Henry continued to reflect upon his experiences in presiding over such a fascinating case of cross-border insolvency, and upon the lack of an agreed framework for courts to follow when dealing with such issues. In about 1825 he published a 14-page tract entitled *Outline of Plan of an*

Dutch-appointed curators of an Amsterdam merchant was *Jollet v. Deponthieu* (1769) 1 Hy. Bl. 132n, 126 E.R. 80.

[32] *Ogden v. Saunders* , 25 U.S. (12 Wheat.) 213 (1827). See also *Harrison v. Sterry*, 9 U.S. (5 Cranch) 289 (1809). For a critical survey of the early American case law, see Riesenfeld (1976) 24 A J.C.L. 288 at 290–295. The Supreme Court, albeit by a bare majority, was eventually persuaded to endorse the doctrine of comity in *Hilton v. Guyot*, 159 U.S. 113, 40 L.Ed. 95, 16 S.Ct. 139 (1895).

[33] J. Henry, *The Judgment of the Court of Demerara in the case of Odwin v. Forbes, to which is prefixed A Treatise on the Difference between Personal and Real Statutes, and its effect on foreign judgments and contracts, marriages and wills* (London, 1823). The judgment occupies Part II of the book (pp.86–178).

International Bankrupt Code for the Commercial States of Europe.[34] His proposal was largely motivated by the desire to overcome the frequent incidence of frauds practised upon 'foreign and unrepresented creditors and absentees, by the facility and dispatch in obtaining a certificate and discharge, and the undue preference afforded in many cases'.[35] Henry also perceived the benefits that an international, uniform code of bankruptcy could impart in the realm of trade and commerce, where certainty and predictability would place all participants on a footing of equality as to their rights, and would 'enable every man, when trading with a foreigner, to know his risk and his remedy'.[36] The fundamental principle of the proposed code was that the judge of the bankrupt's domicile would be universally regarded as having competence to impose a forcible assignment of his property, wheresoever situate, and to grant a release from all liabilities that was co-extensive and co-effective with the divesting of his property. Henry was clearly drawing upon the lessons learnt in *Odwin v. Forbes* when he wrote that 'to strip the bankrupt of his foreign property, and yet leave him exposed to the demands of his foreign creditors if he changes domicile, is certainly unjust: yet the English and other bankrupt laws affect to do this'.[37] Henry's proposal was that by an international treaty concluded by the major European commercial powers,[38] certain aspects of bankruptcy could be divorced from their location in national law, and placed on an international footing so that they would provide fixed rules applicable to every case. He listed a total of twenty-one 'chief points', of which the following may be mentioned here:

(a) to determine what should constitute an act of bankruptcy, and its effect, to the divesting of the property out of the bankrupt by operation of law by this act, so as to render void all acts of ownership or dominion exercised afterwards;[39]
(b) to avoid undue preference by any local mode of proceeding, as by arrest, attachment, extents in aid, or otherwise, as is the case in some countries: and to make the arresting or attaching creditor, after an act of bankruptcy, a mere trustee for the others; he being, nevertheless, preferent for his costs;[40]

34 Published in London, printed by Cox and Baylis, Great Queen Street (hereafter: '*Outline of Plan*'). The pamphlet bears no date, but was published some time between 1823 and 1827. The copy held by the British Library bears the hand-written inscription: 'To Jeremy Bentham Esq. with the author's best respects'. For an appraisal, see Nadelmann (1961) 10 I.C.L.Q. 70.

35 *Outline of Plan, supra* n.34, at p.3.

36 *Ibid.*, p.11.

37 *Ibid.*, p.12. This insight by Henry is a most prophetic one, as was subsequently to be confirmed by the decision of the Court of Appeal in *Gibbs & Sons v. La Société Industrielle et Commerciale des Métaux* (1890) 25 Q.B.D. 399, critically discussed in Chapter 2 at 2.7 below.

38 Holland, France and England were regarded by Henry as the key participants in his proposed treaty.

39 *Outline of Plan, supra* n.34, Point 2 (p.4).

40 *Ibid.*, Point 3 (p.4).

(c) release and discharge of the bankrupt on a *bona fide* conformity to the bankrupt laws of his domicile. The duties and conduct required of the bankrupt to be defined on general principles, and rendered as nearly uniform in each state as possible;[41]

(d) to allow no trader to obtain a release by a fraudulent change of domicile;[42]

(e) a curator for foreign and unrepresented creditors and absentees to be appointed by the government of each state, as a public officer, with power to examine the bankrupt's books and the bankrupt himself, as to his foreign debts and engagements, and to issue the notices to foreign creditors by advertisements in the gazettes of their respective states;[43]

(f) fugitive bankrupts to be given up by each state.[44]

The unmet challenge of international insolvency

Jabez Henry envisaged that, through the adoption of his proposed treaty, those engaged in international trade would become, in effect, quasi-subjects of every state of Europe to which their dealings extended, and which were parties to the treaty. Thereby, the commercial and economic deployment of their property and interests would be complemented by the legal regime applicable to them. It is respectfully submitted that, more than 170 years after the publication of these prescient ideas, the essential problems await a satisfactory resolution by concerted action among the commercially significant states of Europe and the world beyond. In later chapters of this book we will examine a number of such initiatives which have been pursued at the European level, and even globally.[45] The fact that, at the time of writing, these initiatives have not yet given rise to any treaty that is currently in force for the majority of European States obliges us to admit

[41] *Ibid.*, Point 5 (p.4).

[42] *Ibid.*, Point 5 (p.4). It may be noted that in his own published report of his judgment in *Odwin v. Forbes* (1814) (*supra*, n.33), Henry had found that the debt in that case, and the whole amount of the plaintiff's claim and demand, originated in London, which was also the agreed place of payment, so that London was both the place of contracting and the place of performance. Moreover, the defendant's domicile at the time of incurring the debt, and also at the time of his English bankruptcy, was in England (see pp.164–165). Henry makes the telling observation that 'this is not the case of a man, who after contracting debts in one country removes to another and there obtains his discharge' (see p.170). In Forbes' case, England was, by intention and in fact, 'the seat of his affairs and fortunes' (*sedes rerum ac fortunarum*) (p.165). Henry's conceptualisation of the debtor's 'seat of affairs' anticipates by some 150 years the work of the authors of the conventions produced by the Council of Europe and by the European Union, and also the UNCITRAL Model Law on Cross-Border Insolvency. These are considered in Chapters 6, 7 and 8 below.

[43] *Outline of Plan*, *supra* n.34, Point 7 (p.5); see also Points 10–12 (p.6). The idea of a network of public officials responsible for ensuring that the debtor's international estate is secured, and that creditors' interests are properly safeguarded, is one which it would be worthwhile to revive for consideration under present-day conditions.

[44] *Ibid.*, Point 20 (p.8).

[45] See Chapters 5 to 8 inclusive below.

that the challenge of international insolvency has still to be fully met. Despite this, it is submitted that the account of the English approach to cross-border insolvency which is contained within this book demonstrates that, for all its faults and imperfections (and they are many) it can be fairly claimed of English law that it is essentially internationalist in its spirit and orientation.

2

Insolvency of Individuals

PRELIMINARY

In this chapter the issues to be considered are those arising from the insolvency of individuals. Strictly speaking, English law reserves the term 'bankruptcy' for the procedure whereby the estate of an individual debtor is liquidated and distributed among the bankrupt's creditors according to a predetermined, statutory regime. Where the insolvent debtor is a legal person—such as a company formed and registered under law—the quite distinct procedure known as winding up (also termed 'liquidation') is employed.[1] In observing this dichotomy between individual and corporate insolvency, and in maintaining separate procedures for each, English law keeps company with a number of other common law jurisdictions, including those of Australia and New Zealand and (less strictly) Canada. On the other hand, under the approach adopted by the USA since the nineteenth century, the concept of bankruptcy is treated as equally applicable to individuals and corporations, and the principal procedures established under the Bankruptcy Reform Act 1978 (as amended) are applicable to both types of debtor. Under the present-day insolvency law of England and Wales there are a limited number of alternative procedures to outright bankruptcy, including the Individual Voluntary Arrangement and compositions or arrangements concluded under the protective shield provided by the IVA (or in other circumstances, independently of such protection). Although most of the litigious activity in the area of individual, cross-border insolvency has tended to be concerned with bankruptcy, some of the same issues of principle can arise in cases of compositions or arrangements as in cases of bankruptcy, and accordingly these will be considered below.

From the standpoint of private international law, the issues of principal interest in relation to personal bankruptcy are: (1) Jurisdiction—under what circumstances can bankruptcy proceedings take place in a given

[1] Under the law of England and Wales, a partnership has no legal personality separate from its members. Until 1986, partnership insolvency was dealt with under the law of bankruptcy. Under the Insolvency Act 1986, s.420, a special insolvency regime for partnerships has been implemented, allowing an insolvent partnership to be wound up as an unregistered company, either in conjunction with bankruptcy proceedings involving the partners, or as a free-standing procedure. See Insolvent Partnerships Order 1994 (S.I. 1994 No. 2421).

jurisdiction, in relation to a given debtor? (2) International Effects of Bankruptcy—the extent to which a bankruptcy adjudication is capable of taking effect in relation to property of the debtor situate in foreign jurisdictions outside the forum of bankruptcy; (3) Choice of Law—the principles to be applied in determining the governing law for the main process of the bankruptcy itself, and in resolving subsidiary or incidental questions arising in the context of the main proceedings, and affecting claims or parties in interest; (4) Treatment of Creditors and Claims in the bankruptcy process—which creditors' claims are admissible, and on what terms are they enabled to participate in the process of distribution? What measures may be invoked to restrain creditors from taking individual action in foreign jurisdictions, or to correct any distortion to the distributional process that may ensue from such foreign recoveries? (5) International Effects of Discharge—where the process of bankruptcy (or a composition with creditors) results in the debtor being discharged from further liability upon the bankruptcy debts according to the *lex concursus*, to what extent is that effect recognised and given effect under the laws of other countries, and by those countries' courts? (6) Recognition of Foreign Bankruptcies—under what circumstances will recognition be accorded to insolvency proceedings involving an individual debtor which take place under the laws of a foreign country? To what extent will a foreign bankruptcy be recognised as having effect in relation to property situate in the recognising state? (7) Recognition of the Effects of a Foreign Discharge—to what extent will a debtor's discharge consequential upon a foreign bankruptcy or composition furnish a bar to further attempts by creditors to enforce their claims in other jurisdictions? and (8) Concurrent Bankruptcies and Auxiliary Proceedings—what doctrines have been evolved to facilitate the management of parallel proceedings in different jurisdictions, in the interests of fairness and justice to the extent that these goals may be attainable?

The themes stated above will be examined in the sequence indicated. In each section, the current English law and its background will be described, followed by a survey of the ways in which this approach has either been followed, modified or disavowed in the other common law jurisdictions selected for purposes of comparison (chiefly, Australia, Canada and the USA).The aim is to formulate a critique of the solutions offered under the developed law and practice of the systems surveyed. Where appropriate, each section will include an assessment of the need for reform or adjustment of the English approach. Save where some particular rule or process of domestic insolvency law is of special relevance to the appreciation of the impact of private international law in the context of the point being discussed, no attempt will be made to provide a systematic exposition of the internal rules and procedures of the various systems themselves. For more detailed information about the content and operation of the domestic insolvency laws of the jurisdictions referred to in the course of discussion, the reader is referred to the specialised literature of the countries in question. A selective bibliography can be found in Appendix VII to assist with such investigations.

2.1 JURISDICTION

Since the late sixteenth century, the English law of bankruptcy has been based upon statutory provisions contained in successive Parliamentary enactments which, until the most recent reforms of the late twentieth century, bore the title 'Bankruptcy Act'. Although the current statute bears the freshly-coined title 'Insolvency Act 1986', to reflect the new approach whereby the law and procedures concerning both individual and corporate insolvency are comprised within a single, principal statute, the historic legacy of the English law of bankruptcy has by no means been erased or suppressed. While a deliberate attempt was made in 1986 to harmonise and integrate the two branches of insolvency law so far as practicable,[2] the Act is so structured that certain of its Parts apply exclusively to the insolvency of individuals, and certain procedures—including bankruptcy itself—are applicable only to debtors who are individuals.[3] The necessary starting point for an exploration of the jurisdictional rules of English law is therefore the 1986 Act, whose provisions in this respect embody many features from earlier bankruptcy statutes, albeit a considerable amount of remodelling and redrafting is to be noted, reflecting important structural changes that were introduced as part of the overhaul of the procedure of bankruptcy itself. These include a number of elements that had previously been of significance with respect to the law's operation in an international context, and which can be said to have played a vital part in shaping the courts' decisions in some of the past cases which, as we shall see, continue to dominate the English judicial approach to certain questions of fundamental importance. Such concepts as the commission of an act of bankruptcy by the debtor as an essential prerequisite to the court's ability to exercise jurisdiction, and the associated doctrine of

[2] See the Report of the Insolvency Law Review Committee (the Cork Report), Cmnd.8558 (June 1982). The Committee's terms of reference are reproduced at p. iii of the Report. For the tortuous process by which the Report's recommendations were partly adopted in the Insolvency Acts of 1985 and 1986, see Fletcher [1983] J.B.L. 94–104, 200–217; [1984] J.B.L. 304–307; [1987] J.B.L. 365–376.

[3] See Insolvency Act 1986, Parts VIII–XI inclusive, ('The Second Group of Parts') which apply exclusively to the insolvency and bankruptcy of individuals. Parts XII–XIX inclusive ('The Third Group of Parts') are of general application, and bear upon both company and individual insolvency.

relation back of the title of the trustee in bankruptcy to the date of the earliest available act of bankruptcy on which the adjudication could be founded, were dominant themes in many cross-border bankruptcy cases until the reforms of 1986 swept them from the statute.[4] The full implications of these changes, including any consequential adjustment of approach to the operation of English law in an international setting, still await an extensive judicial exploration, although it is submitted that the recasting of the law in 1986 has left the way open to the courts to reconsider such questions in an atmosphere that is largely free from the usual constraints imported by the doctrine of binding precedent.

2.1.1 'A debtor'

The Insolvency Act 1986 follows the drafting practice of previous legislation in referring consistently to the person who is the subject of individual insolvency proceedings as ' the debtor'. Therefore, to determine whether insolvency proceedings can be commenced in England it is necessary to establish that the person who is to be the subject of those proceedings meets the criteria for being 'a debtor' within the meaning of the Act. The Act itself provides a rather limited, and prosaic, definition of the term ' the debtor' for the purposes of those Parts of the statute which deal with the insolvency of individuals. Section 385(1) states that it means (a) in relation to a proposal for an individual voluntary arrangement, the individual making or intending to make that proposal, and (b) in relation to a bankruptcy petition, the individual to whom the petition relates. Neither of these statements is of any assistance in ascertaining the circumstances under which an individual is to be taken to be within the ambit of the Act so as to be subject to the jurisdiction of English insolvency law. The relevant question, which courts have sought to answer on those occasions when their own jurisdictional competence was a material issue for determination, is whether a given individual may properly be regarded as 'a debtor' for the purposes of the application to him or her of the provisions of the current Bankruptcy Act in force in England and Wales. Such an approach unfortunately runs the risk of employing a circular course of reasoning, because successive statutes (including the current one) have failed to express clearly and completely the

[4] The concept of the act of bankruptcy remains part of the law of bankruptcy in both Australia and Canada, and in those jurisdictions it is still a central part of any discussion of the exercise of bankruptcy jurisdiction to examine which of the various types of act of bankruptcy can be committed abroad, and which cannot. See, e.g. J.-G. Castel, *Canadian Conflict of Laws* , 3rd edn. (1993), ch. 30, at p. 521 *et seq.* (hereafter: 'Castel'); P. E. Nygh, *Conflict of Laws in Australia*, 6th edn. (1995), ch. 34, at p. 525 *et seq.* (hereafter: 'Nygh'); E. I. Sykes and M. C. Pryles, *Australian Private International Law*, 3rd edn. (1991), ch. 23, at p. 781 *et seq.* (hereafter: 'Sykes and Pryles'). By contrast, the bankruptcy law of the USA does not utilise the concept of the act of bankruptcy.

intention of Parliament with regard to this most basic of concerns. Traditionally, the courts have adopted a pragmatic, two-stage approach to matters touching upon the limits of application of the bankruptcy statutes. First, the individual's status as 'a debtor' is explored from the standpoint of whether it is technically appropriate to regard him or her as a debtor according to the natural, commonsense meaning of that expression. This may be characterised as the court's attempt to establish the 'actuality' of the individual's status as 'a debtor', consistently with reason and good sense. Secondly, if satisfied that they are dealing with someone who may properly be termed 'a debtor', the courts have gone on to consider the implications of those provisions of the legislation which impose limits to the exercise of jurisdiction. These provisions—now mostly contained in section 265 of the 1986 Act—can be rationalised as disclosing a Parliamentary intention to confine the exercise of insolvency jurisdiction to those cases where the nexus between the debtor and this country is sufficiently substantial to satisfy traditional English notions as to the appropriate limits of exercise of jurisdiction. Once again, however, the potential for circularity of reasoning must be noted.

(a) The 'actuality' of the status of the debtor

On closer investigation, this proves to be a compound of different elements, partly expressive of the logical necessity for it to be demonstrable that the person in question owes unsatisfied liabilities, which English law recognises as enforceable by means of legal process, to one or more persons whose right to invoke the process of English law is also recognised. Thus, the existence of any vitiating circumstances which preclude enforceability by the party to whom a debt is alleged to be due, such as the expiry of the requisite period under the Limitation Act 1980 for the bringing of proceedings to enforce the liability in question, or the operation of some rule of the general law of contract, or of a regulatory statute,[5] whose effect is to preclude enforcement of a liability on grounds such as illegality, fraud or mistake, or the violation of public policy, may produce the consequence that the apparent 'debtor' cannot be regarded as falling within the ambit of the Insolvency Act on the basis of claims of this kind alone.

Further ways in which the status of 'debtor' may be removed are through the process of discharge brought about by a bankruptcy or composition recognised by English law as embracing the debt or liability in question, so that it is rendered unenforceable in the eyes of English law. Such discharge may be the product of earlier proceedings in England itself, or may have come about under the operation of some foreign law

[5] See, e.g., Consumer Credit Act 1974, Part II, esp. ss.25–26, 29, 32, and 39–40, and also Part IX, esp. ss. 127, 137–138.

whose effects English law will recognise under rules to be considered below.[6] Thus it may be seen that the attribution of the status of being 'a debtor' within the meaning of the Insolvency Act can, under some circumstances, require reference to rules of domestic law, or to rules of private international law, in order to confirm the indispensable premise that a cognisable debtor-creditor relationship subsists so as to furnish a basis for invoking the processes of insolvency law. In the parlance of private international law, such questions assume an 'incidental' character, and may involve a subsidiary excursion into the realm of choice of law in order to furnish an answer to the question whether an enforceable liability exists. So, if the alleged debt arises under a contract whose international character necessitates the determination of its governing law in order to confirm the enforceability of that obligation, an English court would apply the relevant provisions of the Rome Convention of 19 June 1980 to ascertain the governing law of the contract, and then consult the internal rules of that law to establish enforceability or otherwise.[7]

(b) The nexus between the debtor and the territorial domaine of English law

Insolvency proceedings are unique in many respects. Because of their collective and comprehensive character, and also because of their potential consequences in terms of the legal status of the debtor, they must be regarded as fundamentally different to the orthodox types of civil or commercial litigation pursued on a party-to-party basis. It is appropriate, therefore, to assess the principles for exercise of insolvency jurisdiction in an independent manner, without necessarily adopting any rule or policy from the realm of general international litigation unless it can withstand further scrutiny under the more exacting standards that should attend the operation of insolvency jurisdiction in an international context. Unfortunately, it must be conceded that there is a lack of internal evidence, in the successive statutory enactments that have borne upon the matter of jurisdiction and its limits, of any systematic or principled approach to these problems on the part of the Legislature. If anything, the ambit of the operation of our bankruptcy laws has been designed in such a way as to endow the law with an exceedingly wide reach in terms of distance, time and circumstance. It has been left to the courts, utilising the broad powers of discretion which they traditionally enjoy in the operation of insolvency

[6] See at 2.5 and 2.7 below.

[7] See the Convention on the Law Applicable to Contractual Obligations (Rome, 19 June 1980), incorporated into English law with effect from 1 April 1991 by the Contracts (Applicable Law) Act 1990. Uniform rules for determining governing law are contained in Title II of the Convention (Articles 3–22 inclusive. See especially Articles 3–7). If the challenge to contractual enforceability is on the basis that the alleged contract was not validly concluded, the provisions of Articles 8 and 9, concerning material and formal validity respectively, may be of relevance.

law, to furnish safeguards against the exercise of jurisdiction in an exorbitant manner.[8] In practice, despite the near-ubiquitous use of the permissive 'may' throughout the statutory provisions dealing with the courts' powers and their sphere of application, there has been only a limited indication until very recent times of any judicial disposition towards restraint in the exercise of jurisdiction where an individual is found to fulfil the statutory criteria that are about to be discussed.

In the case of a bankruptcy petition, section 264 of the Insolvency Act 1986 maintains the traditional position whereby English law has allowed bankruptcy to operate on either a voluntary or an involuntary basis, from the debtor's point of view. Paragraphs (a) and (b) of subsection (1) provide that a petition for a bankruptcy order to be made against an individual may be presented to the court by one of the individual's creditors (or jointly by more than one of them), or by the individual himself. A further possibility, which entered the law for the first time in 1986, arises under section 264(1)(c), whereby a bankruptcy petition may be presented by the supervisor of (or by any other person who is for the time being bound by) a voluntary arrangement concluded by the individual under Part VIII of the Act. Since this third possibility arises out of a pre-existing procedure to which the debtor has already become, as its name indicates, a voluntary party, it seems unlikely that any substantial questions of jurisdictional competence would present themselves at this stage. In the case of a petition for a bankruptcy order presented under paragraphs (a) or (b), however, there could well be instances where the amenability of the debtor to undergo adjudication under English law may become a material issue. Here, the provisions of section 265 must be carefully considered. That section is to the following effect:

Section 265 (1) A bankruptcy petition shall not be presented to the court under section 264(1)(a) or (b) unless the debtor—
- (a) is domiciled in England and Wales,
- (b) is personally present in England and Wales on the day on which the petition is presented, or
- (c) at any time in the period of 3 years ending with that day—
  - (i) has been ordinarily resident, or has had a place of residence, in England and Wales, or
  - (ii) has carried on business in England and Wales.

(2) The reference in subsection (1)(c) to an individual carrying on business includes—
- (a) the carrying on of business by a firm or partnership of which the individual is a member, and
- (b) the carrying on of a business by an agent or manager for the individual or for such a firm or partnership.

[8] See further the discussion below on *Abstention and forum non conveniens.*

Before examining the contents of the above section in detail, certain general points should be noted. First, there is no trace of any legislative concern to include the factor of the debtor's nationality among the connecting factors capable of founding jurisdiction in bankruptcy. This is in keeping with the long-established tradition under English law whereby, with only a few special exceptions touching upon the realm of public law, no significance is attached to the nationality, or citizenship rights, of an individual for purposes of applying rules of private international law, including rules of jurisdiction and choice of law.[9] Neither in the 1986 Act, nor in its lineal antecedents, is there any provision to the effect that the possession of United Kingdom nationality constitutes either a necessary or even a sufficient connecting factor for the purposes of rendering the individual amenable to be made the subject of a bankruptcy order, although the courts in former times were inclined to adopt a different approach.[10] By the same token, the total silence of the statutory provisions with regard to the matter of nationality means that it is equally of no relevance that a person may be a citizen of some foreign country, provided that he or she fulfils at least one of the criteria that are specified in section 265.[11] Secondly, it can be observed that there is nothing in section 265 to suggest that a person can be made bankrupt in England on the basis only of having assets in this country. The position in the case of individual debtors is in contrast to that which has evolved in relation to the winding up of foreign corporations for which, as will later be seen, judicial initiatives in the later twentieth century have resulted in a 'presence of assets' test being applied to enable English courts to take jurisdiction, subject to certain conditions.[12]

[9] For a succinct explanation of the rationale underlying English law's historic aversion to the use of nationality as a connecting factor in its approach to private international law, see *Dicey and Morris, The Conflict of Laws*, 12th edn. (1993), at pp. 163–166.

[10] The judicial disposition, prior to 1986, to regard the bankruptcy legislation as applying to English citizens resident abroad was reviewed by the Court of Appeal in *Re Tucker* [1990] Ch. 148. The very much changed position under the modern law is revealed, e.g. in *Re Seagull Manufacturing Co. Ltd.* [1991] 4 All E.R. 257 (Mummery J.), affd (CA) [1993] B.C.C. 241; *Bishopsgate Investment Management Ltd. v. Maxwell* [1993] Ch. 1 (CA); and *Re Paramount Airways Ltd.* [1993] Ch. 223 (CA). See also Fletcher [1988] J.B.L. 168, 341.

[11] Cf. *Re Artola Hermanos* (1890) 24 Q.B.D. 640 (CA), where the five partners against whom bankruptcy proceedings were successfully brought in England were stated to be 'Spaniards by birth'. See also *Re Pascal* (1876) 1 Ch.D. 509 (CA) (where the debtor was of Peruvian nationality). In cases decided under pre-1986 bankruptcy legislation, when it was a legal requirement that the debtor must have committed an available act of bankruptcy according to English law, reference can sometimes be found to the factor of nationality. This tends to occur when considering if the debtor should be treated as 'subject to English law', and whether an act of bankruptcy was committed by conduct which either took place abroad or in the course of departing from this country. See *Re Crispin* (1873) L.R. 8 Ch.App. 374; *Ex parte Blain* (1879) 12 Ch.D. 522; *Re Pearson* [1892] 2 Q.B. 263; *Re A.B.& Co.(No.2)* [1900] 2 Q.B. 429 (all CA); *Cooke v. C.A.Vogeler Co.* [1901] A.C. 102 (HL). These cases continue to be of some relevance in those countries—including Australia and Canada—where acts of bankruptcy retain their traditional role under the law.

[12] See Chapter 3 at 3.2.2 below. Under the Bankruptcy Act of the USA, a 'presence of

Turning to the contents of section 265 itself, it is at once apparent that each of the alternative connecting factors mentioned within the section is sufficient of itself to fulfil the requirement that there should exist some recognised nexus between the debtor and this country. However, with the possible exception of one of the factors mentioned in section 265(1)(c), namely the debtor's having been ordinarily resident in England and Wales at some time within the period of three years ending with the day on which the petition is presented, there is no overt concern with the quality or intensity of the debtor's actual involvement with England, either in some absolute sense or in relative terms when set in the total context of the debtor's personal way of conducting his life and affairs. For the purposes of section 265, therefore, it suffices merely for it to be demonstrable that any one of the possible criteria is satisfied in fact, and in that event the requirements of English law with regard to its own jurisdictional competence are duly established. Since no formal directions are included in the statute to require the court actively to consider whether it is appropriate to exercise jurisdiction in any particular case, and since the terms of section 265 itself suggest that the Legislature was desirous of giving wide scope for the potential exercise of bankruptcy jurisdiction, it is perhaps unsurprising to discover that there are very few instances in which English courts have been disinclined to make a bankruptcy order when any of the requirements of section 265 (or its former equivalent) was in fact met.[13] These requirements will next be examined in the sequence in which they are mentioned in the section itself.

(i) 'Domiciled in England and Wales'. The concept of domicile, as evolved and applied under traditional rules of English common law, has numerous features which differ not only from the concept of domicile as used by countries belonging to the civil law tradition, but also from the concept of domicile that has been developed in modern times by other independent countries belonging to the common law 'legal family' itself. Modern legislative reforms in England have indeed effected important changes to the way in which the traditional common law of domicile operates in relation to different kinds of person,[14] and there have been successive proposals for the further reform and simplification of the law, so far not enacted by

assets' test is included among the alternative grounds of jurisdiction established by s.109(a), which bears the heading 'Who may be a debtor', and contains the provision that: 'only a person that resides or has a domicile, a place of business, or property in the United States, or a municipality, may be a debtor under this title' (11 U.S.C. s.109; Bankruptcy Reform Act 1978, as amended).

[13] For such rare examples of judicial abstention from adjudication as are found in the reported cases, see at 2.1.3 below.

[14] This is especially the case with married women and dependent children: see the Domicile and Matrimonial Proceedings Act 1973.

Parliament.[15] An additional element of complication was introduced into English legal parlance from 1 January 1987, with the implementation of the Brussels Convention of 27 September 1968 on Jurisdiction and the Enforcement of Judgments in Civil and Commercial Matters.[16] The seeds of terminological and conceptual confusion were sown at this point in time, because the Brussels Convention utilises a concept of domicile which is fundamentally different from the traditional common law concept. Consequently, two different concepts of domicile co-exist within the sphere of operation of English law, so that it is essential to make a clear identification of the context in which the term 'domicile' is being used, in order to gain an accurate understanding of the rules and principles to be applied. For our present purposes, however, it must suffice to observe that the Brussels Convention by its own express provision is precluded from having any application to insolvency proceedings.[17] Therefore, in speaking of 'domicile' in relation to the bankruptcy jurisdiction of English courts we must be understood to refer exclusively to the traditional, common law concept of domicile as it continues to be applied by English law for all purposes except in those statutorily defined cases to which the Brussels Convention is applicable.

Although it is outside the scope of this book to provide a detailed account of the English law of domicile,[18] some discussion of the essential aspects of the doctrine is necessary in order to give an indication of the potential scope of its operation as one of the bases for exercise of bankruptcy jurisdiction. As developed by the English judiciary, especially from the second half of the nineteenth century onwards, the concept of domicile has an elusive, almost spiritual quality which can become the cause of uncertainty and confusion under some circumstances. The central paradox concerning the concept itself is that it is said to be based upon the notion of 'home', in the sense of 'that place which constitutes a person's permanent home',[19] yet there is no necessary correlation between the place of domicile (as determined by English law by means of this ultimately subjective test) and the person's current pattern of life and

[15] See the Report of the English and Scottish Law Commissions, *The Law of Domicile*, Law Com. No. 168; Scot. Law Com. No. 107, Cm.200 (1987). The Commissions' previously published Working Paper No. 88/63, bearing the title *Private International Law; The Law of Domicile* (1985) is also an excellent source of critical and informed insight into the law and its working.

[16] Civil Jurisdiction and Judgments Act 1982, Part I.

[17] Article 1(2) of the Brussels Convention states that the Convention shall not apply to: 'bankruptcy, proceedings relating to the winding-up of insolvent companies or other legal persons, judicial arrangements, compositions and analogous proceedings'.

[18] For detailed treatment of the subject, see *Dicey and Morris, The Conflict of Laws*, 12th edn. (1993), ch.7; P. M. North and J. J. Fawcett, *Cheshire and North's Private International Law*, 12th edn. (1992), ch.9, together with the Law Commissions' publications mentioned *supra*, n.15.

[19] Cf. *Whicker v. Hume* (1858) 7 H.L.Cas. 124, 160, per Lord Cranworth.

residential associations, which are the objective factors most likely to be accessible to other parties. Indeed, under some circumstances it is possible that English law may hold a person to be domiciled in a country which is not, and never has been, the location of any actual, physical home, and it can even be the case that a person may never have visited the country of domicile, or may not have revisited it for many years since emigrating and resettling abroad.[20] Therefore, in marked contrast to the position under many systems of law which use the term 'domicile' to signify the current, main place of residence, the English concept of domicile is as 'an idea of law . . . the relation which the law creates between an individual and a particular locality or country'.[21] Domicile has reference to the territory over which a single system of law operates, and is therefore not necessarily co-extensive with the international boundaries of a particular State. In the case of a State comprised of several internal legal units—such as the United Kingdom, or the USA, Canada or Australia—it is to the internal unit that the attribution of domicile is made. Thus, a person would have a domicile in England or Scotland; in California or Delaware; in Ontario or Quebec; in Victoria or New South Wales, as the case may be.

According to the English doctrine, every person must at all times have a domicile, and no person can at the same time and for the same purpose have more than one operative domicile.[22] Every person receives at birth a domicile of origin, determined according to the circumstances obtaining at the time of birth: a legitimate child born during the lifetime of its father has its domicile of origin in the country in which the father was domiciled at the time of the birth, whereas a legitimate child not born in the lifetime of its father, or an illegitimate child, has its domicile of origin in the country in which its mother was domiciled at the time of the birth.[23] The domicile of origin is particularly tenacious and, while capable of being displaced through the acquisition of a domicile of choice by a person who has attained independence, has a character somewhat akin to a dormant volcano in that the doctrine of revival will cause the domicile of origin to reactivate whenever the current domicile of choice is lost or abandoned without a new domicile of choice being acquired. Following revival, the domicile of origin will continue until such time, if ever, as a fresh domicile of choice is validly acquired. A further rule bearing upon the process of ascertaining a person's domicile as at any particular point in time is that it is presumed that an existing domicile, of whatever kind, continues until a new domicile is proved to have been validly acquired, the onus being

[20] Cf. *Re O'Keefe* [1940] Ch.124; *Nelson v. Nelson* [1925] 3 D.L.R. 22 (Alta.).

[21] *Bell v. Kennedy* (1868) L.R. 1 Sc. & Div. 307, 320, per Lord Westbury.

[22] *Udny v. Udny* (1869) L.R. 1 Sc. & Div. 441 at 457, per Lord Westbury; *Bell v. Kennedy, supra.* n.21.

[23] *Udny v. Udny, supra* n.22.

upon the party alleging that a change of domicile has occurred to establish that this is the case.[24] To acquire a domicile of choice, a person must be independent and of full mental capacity, and must establish a residence in the country of intended domicile, accompanied by the intention of permanent or indefinite residence there. Both the fact of residence and the requisite mental intention must demonstrably coincide, in order for the law to recognise that a change of domicile has come about. Even a very lengthy period of residence in a country cannot suffice by itself to bring about the acquisition of a domicile of choice there, unless the vital element of intention can be established.[25] Similarly, mere intention alone, however strong and unequivocal, cannot effect the gaining of a new domicile if the requirement of residence in the country in question is not fulfilled.[26] A person abandons a domicile of choice by ceasing to reside in the country of domicile and by ceasing to intend to reside there permanently or indefinitely: once again, both the factual and mental elements must be established and must coincide. While the abandonment of a domicile of choice can be operative from the moment of departure from the country in question, the more tenacious quality of a domicile of origin causes it to subsist until such time as a new domicile is validly acquired.

From the above summary of the salient features of domicile as operative under English law, it will readily be appreciated that a person may be held to have an English domicile in circumstances where there is no present, functional association with this country and its economy. Indeed, factors traceable to the parental situation at the time of the person's birth, coupled with later developments in the course of his lifetime, could result in the sustained retention of an English domicile of origin, or in its re-emergence due to the operation of the doctrine of revival. As we have seen, merely to depart from this country with the fixed intention of abandoning an English domicile, while capable of terminating a domicile of choice, will not bring about this consequence if the domicile happens to be the domicile of origin. Thus the English domicile might endure, even in defiance of the subject's own intentions and expectations, while other factors could conspire to prevent the valid acquisition of a fresh domicile of choice. Conversely, it must be borne in mind that the complex interplay of subjective and objective factors under the English approach means that outward appearances—such as many years' residence in this country—may be unreliable in forming an estimation of a person's domicile according to

[24] *Bell v. Kennedy supra* n.21; *Udny v. Udny , supra* n.22; *Winans v. Attorney-General* [1904] A.C. 287; *Ramsey v. Liverpool Royal Infirmary* [1930] A.C. 588; *Re Fuld's Estate (No. 3)* [1968] P. 675.

[25] Cf. *Winans v. A-G; Ramsey v. Liverpool Royal Infirmary*, both *supra* n.24.

[26] *Bell v. Kennedy, supra* n.21, at 319, per Lord Chelmsford.

English law.[27] Set alongside this is the practical consideration that the person who presents a bankruptcy petition needs to be sure of the jurisdictional ground, and would be unwise to risk incurring the costs of an unsuccessful petition where the only available basis for the English court's jurisdiction rests upon the possibility that a non-resident debtor, who satisfies none of the alternative criteria offered by section 265, might be shown to have a current domicile here. The onus is on the petitioning creditor to prove that the debtor's domicile is in England, which at the very least entails the introduction of *prima facie* evidence that would, unless disproved by contrary evidence from the debtor's side, establish this assertion.[28]

It may perhaps be the case that the inclusion of domicile among the connecting factors mentioned within section 265 is nowadays for the largely symbolic reason that it commemorates the historic identification of bankruptcy as a process intimately bound up with personal status, and hence (in the view of English law) properly to be conducted by the courts of the person's domicile, and in accordance with the law of that country. Occasionally, the fact that an English domicile can prove to be a remarkably durable attribute may serve as a useful means of asserting jurisdiction over a debtor who has sought to take refuge from his creditors by withdrawing offshore, although the creditor is best advised,in a doubtful case, to seek for any indications that one of the more objectively established grounds—such as the carrying on of business—could be used as the basis for meeting the requirements of section 265. Nevertheless, even though the practical role of domicile may nowadays be minimal in comparison to the other connecting factors mentioned elsewhere within section 265, it may prove difficult to dislodge this quintessentially English connecting factor from the statutory listing. In reality, however, it would seem appropriate to maintain a sense of proportion with regard to its potential use as an instrument for the exercise of exorbitant or oppressive jurisdiction over debtors who otherwise lack any meaningful connection with England and its system of insolvency law.

(ii) Personal presence of the debtor on the day on which the petition is presented. Section 265(1)(b) enables bankruptcy proceedings to take place in this country on the basis of the debtor's personal presence in England and Wales on the day on which the petition is presented. No further requirement is imposed concerning the quality or extent of the debtor's connections with this country that give rise to a personal presence on the day in question. A temporary presence, unconnected with the proceedings or

[27] See *Re Duleep Singh* (1890) 7 Morr. 228 (CA), for a particularly vivid illustration.

[28] *Re Mitchell, ex parte Cunningham* (1884) 13 Q.B.D. 418 (CA), explained in *Re Barne* (1886) 16 Q.B.D. 522 (CA).

with any of the other interested parties, would therefore suffice for the purposes of this provision. It may be inferred, by analogy with the established law relating to the commencement of civil litigation by means of a writ served upon the defendant during a temporary presence in the jurisdiction,[29] that the presence of the debtor must be voluntary, that is to say not procured by fraudulent enticement, nor by the use of unlawful force. If such impropriety can be shown to have taken place, it may be expected that the court would have recourse to its discretionary powers in refusing to make a bankruptcy order against the debtor.[30]

Where the debtor presents his own petition for adjudication pursuant to section 264(1)(b) of the Act, this may be thought of as tantamount to an act of voluntary submission to the bankruptcy jurisdiction of this country. If, in such a case, the only basis upon which the condition imposed by section 265 can be fulfilled is the factor of presence within the jurisdiction, care should be taken to ensure that the requirement of *personal* presence is in fact met, since there is nothing in paragraph (b) itself, nor elsewhere within the section or the Act, to suggest that this condition can be satisfied by means of an agent or representative authorised to represent a debtor who is in reality absent abroad on the day in question. The filing of the petition in court by an attorney acting on the debtor's instructions cannot, it is submitted, be safely assumed to obviate the need for the debtor's personal presence within the jurisdiction to be capable of confirmation, in the event of any challenge on this point.

What has been stated above with regard to the need to demonstrate the debtor's personal whereabouts on the day the petition is presented is equally applicable in the case of involuntary proceedings commenced by means of a creditor's petition presented under section 264(1)(a). Since the debtor's cooperation cannot be relied upon in such cases, care should be taken to confirm that the debtor is physically within the jurisdiction for at least some part of the relevant day. Bankruptcy proceedings differ from those species of civil proceedings which are commenced by means of a writ, in that it is not necessary for the petition to be served upon the debtor personally in order to establish the jurisdiction of the English court. A bankruptcy petition is presented to the court by filing it in the office of the court with jurisdiction to receive it.[31] Thereafter, it is required that a copy of the petition be served personally on the debtor, and that the fact of such service should be verified by affidavit filed in court.[32] However, substi-

[29] See, e.g., *Colt Industries Inc v. Sarlie* [1966] 1 All E.R. 673 (CA); *Maharanee of Baroda v. Wildenstein* [1972] 2 Q.B. 283 (CA).

[30] Cf. *Watkins v. North American Land and Timber Co. Ltd.* (1904) 20 T.L.R. 534 (HL) (not a bankruptcy case).

[31] Insolvency Rules 1986 (S.I. 1986 No. 1925, as amended), rr.6.10(1), 6.12(1); Forms 6.7–6.9.

[32] *Ibid.* rr.6.14, 6.15; Form 6.17.

tuted service may be authorised if the court is satisfied that the debtor is keeping out of the way to avoid service of the petition, and there are further powers vested in the court to give leave for service of a bankruptcy petition outside England and Wales, and to order service outside the jurisdiction where any process or order of the court, or other document, is required to be served on a person who is not in England and Wales.[33] Thus, if the debtor departs abroad before service of the petition can be effected, the bankruptcy proceedings can continue provided he can be shown to have been personally present in this country on the day the petition was presented.

(iii)(A) The debtor's residential connection with England and Wales. Section 265(1)(c)(i) offers the possibility that bankruptcy proceedings can be based upon the fact that the debtor, at any time in the period of three years ending with the day on which the petition is presented, has been ordinarily resident, or has had a place of residence, in England and Wales. These are expressed as alternative criteria, so that it will suffice if either one of them can be established on the evidence available. Moreover, the paragraph is so drafted as to be conspicuously wide in its potential application, for it will suffice if it can be shown that either one of these criteria was satisfied even for some portion of time, however brief, falling within the three-year period of backwards reference. It is noteworthy that this reference period was actually lengthened by a factor of three at the time of enactment of the Insolvency Act 1986, the previous legislation having specified a period of just one year culminating in the date of the petition.[34] Furthermore, there is no requirement as to the length of time for which the debtor must have been ordinarily resident, or have had a place of residence, in this country in order to give rise to this nexus. In an extreme case, therefore, a person who for a brief period has fulfilled either of these residential criteria remains potentially subject to English bankruptcy jurisdiction until a clear interval of three years has elapsed since the ending of the connection in question.

The technical meaning of each criterion also merits some explanation:

Ordinarily resident. The concept of 'ordinary residence' has been part of the terminology employed in English legislative drafting for more than a hundred years. Despite the widespread use of the term as a key component in various statutes concerned with a range of matters including taxation, social security and immigration, no consistent official or statutory definition has been provided, so that it has been left to the judiciary to invest the term with legal meaning, according to the context. Further want of certainty has been caused through the use in other statutory provisions

[33] *Ibid.*, rr.6.14(2),(3), 12.12 (2),(3); Forms 6.15, 6.16.

[34] See e.g. Bankruptcy Act 1914, s.4(1)(d); Bankruptcy Act 1883, s.6(1)(d) (both repealed).

of the expressions 'residence' and 'habitual residence', giving rise to some debate as to the appropriate distinctions, if any, that may be intended to be drawn between the three terms. While it may be reasonable to infer that the use of the adjectives 'ordinary' and 'habitual' indicates a qualitative distinction of some kind, in contrast to the simple term 'residence', the courts appear to have reached a position where the expressions 'ordinary residence' and 'habitual residence' are regarded as virtually synonymous,[35] although the established practice of using one or other of them in a particular statutory context, depending upon the subject matter, may ensure that there will remain a degree of uncertainty as to the extent to which cases decided with reference to the one term can be drawn upon in construing statutes which specify the other.

The judicial view of the meaning of 'ordinary residence' was expressed long ago at the highest level on the basis that it 'connotes residence in a place with some degree of continuity and apart from accidental or temporary absences'.[36] Nevertheless, in determining whether a given person can be regarded as ordinarily resident in this country for the purposes of the tax legislation, the House of Lords in 1928 confirmed that a person may for some purposes at least be ordinarily resident in two or more countries simultaneously, having regard to the pattern and circumstances of his life. It was held that a person who lived in Ireland, but who spent about one week each month in England where he came on business and lived in various hotels during those periods, was resident and ordinarily resident in England as well as in Ireland, and so was assessable here for taxation purposes.[37] In a more recent, unanimous decision of their Lordships' House, Lord Scarman, delivering the sole speech, affirmed that: 'Unless . . . it can be shown that the statutory framework or the legal context in which the words are used requires a different meaning, I unhesitatingly subscribe to the view that "ordinarily resident" refers to a man's abode in a particular place or country which he has adopted voluntarily and for settled purposes as part of the regular order of his life for the time being, whether of short or long duration'.[38]

The courts have consistently taken the view that the determination of a person's ordinary residence is a question of fact and degree in each case, and that it is possible to be ordinarily resident in a country without having any single or fixed address at which to reside.[39] The nature, purpose and motivation of a person's visits to this country can be material factors

[35] *R v. Barnet London Borough Council, ex parte Nilish Shah* [1983] 2 A.C. 309 (HL).

[36] *Levene v. I.R.C.* [1928] A.C. 217, 225, per Lord Cave.

[37] *I.R.C. v. Lysaght* [1928] A.C. 234 (HL). This approach is consistent with that of the Court of Appeal in the bankruptcy case *Re Norris* (1888) 4 T.L.R. 452; 5 Morr.111.

[38] *R v. Barnet London Borough Council, ex parte Nilish Shah* [1983] 2 A.C. 309, 344.

[39] *I.R.C. v. Lysaght; Re Norris*, both *supra* n.37; *Re Bright* (1901) 18 T.L.R. 37 (CA), reheard and reaffirmed (1903) 19 T.L.R. 203, 47 Sol. Jo. 253.

in the court's final assessment of the legal consequences of a given pattern of conduct, however. Thus, a series of visits for purposes of business, or to participate in litigation or arbitration of a protracted nature, may produce the conclusion that the person is ordinarily resident here during the period in question,[40] whereas an intermittent series of visits, even using lodgings at the same address, or a visit to stay with a relative for perhaps several consecutive weeks, may be held to lack the qualitative features that would justify a finding of ordinary residence.[41] Provided that the qualitative aspect is established to the court's satisfaction, the status of being ordinarily resident can be acquired after a relatively short period of time. Judges have been careful however to refrain from specifying any precise, threshold test for this purpose (apart from occasional, non-specific observations to the effect that a period of just two or three days would be plainly insufficient).[42]

Place of residence. The alternative way of satisfying the residential connecting factor is if the debtor has had a place of residence in England and Wales at any time within the previous three years. The expression 'place of residence' was employed for the first time in the 1986 Act as part of the modernisation and redrafting of the terms of section 265. Previous legislation had made use of the term 'dwelling-house' to signify the debtor's amenability to the jurisdiction through having residential premises here.[43] Conceptually, there was a tendency for the rather quaint-sounding term 'dwelling-house' to generate the impression that it was necessary for the debtor to have residential facilities here of a fairly substantial character, even if the exact nature of the qualifying title was left unspecified. In reality, the judicial approach when construing the term 'dwelling-house' in relation to various forms of residential arrangements effected by debtors, who were seeking to contest the issue of jurisdiction, was both broad and liberal. In one case, a set of five, furnished rooms rented by the debtor for the use of himself and his family was held to constitute a dwelling-house for the purposes of the then-current Bankruptcy Act.[44] Conversely, in other cases involving the same statutory provision the Court of Appeal were resistant to the suggestion that a room in an hotel, even if reserved and paid for by the debtor for an extensive period, could constitute a 'dwelling-house' in this context.[45] However, in one of the last reported cases turning on the application of the pre-1986 legislation, the Court of Appeal asserted, albeit by way of *obiter dicta*, that it was not necessary for

40 See cases cited *supra*, n.39.
41 *Re Erskine* (1893) 10 T.L.R. 32 (CA).
42 *Re Bright* (1903) 19 T.L.R. 203, 204, per Collins M.R.
43 e.g. Bankruptcy Act 1914, s.4(1)(d) (repealed).
44 *Re Hecquard* (1889) 24 Q.B.D. 71 (CA), decided under the Bankruptcy Act 1883, s.6(1)(d).
45 *Re Norris* (1888) 4 T.L.R. 452 (CA); cf. *Re Bright* (1901) 18 T.L.R. 37 (CA).

the debtor to have a legal or equitable interest in the alleged dwelling-house, and that consequently it might suffice if the debtor were shown to be merely a licensee.[46]

It is submitted that a number of technical niceties have been eliminated as a result of the substitution of the less specific expression 'place of residence' in the modern version of this legislative provision. Arguably, a person who has made arrangements for accommodation to be available on a standing or regular basis, according to need and inclination, has thereby secured a 'place of residence', even if the reservation relates to but a single room in an hotel, or in other premises capable of being occupied for residential purposes. Further than this, it is perhaps debateable whether the fact of ownership of residential property can of itself amount to having 'a place of residence' for the purposes of section 265(1)(c)(i), if the debtor has no intention of using it as a personal residence and has in fact made no such use of it at any time within the previous three years. Although it seems clear, and would be consistent with past judicial thinking, that there is no actual requirement that it be shown that the debtor has actually occupied the place of residence at any time during the relevant period, it would be reasonable to construe the provision as embodying the basic notion that the property or accommodation should have the intended function of supplying to some extent the current, or potential, residential needs of the debtor personally (including, perhaps, the needs of his family or those intimately associated with him). If that personal, residential nexus has never been established, or if it has long ago been abandoned through a conscious alteration in the debtor's mode of life, it would involve a somewhat artificial reading of the language of section 265(1) to hold that 'the debtor . . . has had a place of residence in England and Wales' within the requisite period of time.[47] While modern judicial authority on the scope and meaning of the provision is lacking, it is appropriate to point out that English law has no past tradition of utilising a 'presence of assets' test as a basis for exercising jurisdiction in bankruptcy, and that no such test is introduced under the present legislation. Accordingly, there is no basis for treating the ownership of immovable property here as sufficient in itself to make the owner amenable to the bankruptcy law, even if the property is capable of being used for residential purposes. Provided that any persons who do make residential use of the property are unconnected with the debtor in a personal, as opposed to a commercial, sense, there would seem to be no justification for regarding

[46] *Re Brauch* [1978] Ch. 316, 334, per Goff L.J.

[47] Cf. *Re Nordenfelt* [1895] 1 Q.B. 151 (CA) (in which the debtor had abandoned the dwelling-house, which he had formerly had, before the commencement of the period of reference, and was held not to have had a dwelling-house in England for the purposes of the Bankruptcy Act 1883, s.6(1)(d)).

the debtor as having 'a place of residence' in England, although the separate question may perhaps arise, if the property is leased to other persons, regarding the possibility that the debtor is carrying on some form of business, as considered below. Lastly, it may be noted that this paragraph of section 265(1) is so formulated that it is the fact of having a place of residence (provided it can properly be so described), rather than the act of residing in it for any given period of time, or even at all, that supplies the qualifying condition. Provided that the condition was fulfilled for some measurable time falling within the overall reference period of three years prior to the presentation of the petition, the requirements of the section are satisfied.[48]

(iii)(B) The debtor has carried on business in England and Wales. The last of the alternative conditions listed in section 265(1) of the 1986 Act is expressed in paragraph (c)(ii), which enables a bankruptcy petition to be presented if at any time within the period of three years ending with the day on which the petition is presented the debtor has carried on business in England and Wales.[49] Once again, the provision is so drafted as to enable this condition to be met if it can be shown that a business was being carried on here by the debtor for any measurable period falling within the three-year time frame, without imposing any further requirement as to the duration of that activity. Moreover, there is no necessity that the business should continue to be carried on at the time the proceedings are commenced. The vital question is whether a business was being carried on at some time within the qualifying period. This in turn raises the questions of what constitutes the carrying on of a business, and what events or characteristics serve to mark its commencement and cessation?

No statutory definition of the expression 'to carry on business' is supplied by the Insolvency Act 1986. Even with respect to the meaning of the term 'business' the Act is only moderately informative, since section 436 merely states that it 'includes a trade or profession'. Legislative reticence as to the technical meaning of this key expression has been matched by the judiciary, who over the years have also shown themselves averse to attempting a full and exhaustive definition of what is meant by the carrying on of a business for the purposes of this provision or its statutory predecessors. The preferred approach has been to treat the carrying on of

[48] Cf. *Re Hecquard* (1903) 19 T.L.R. 203, 204, per Lord Esher M.R. (concerning the analogous position under the provision in the Bankruptcy Act 1883, s.6(1)(d), in which the qualifying nexus was the debtor's having a dwelling-house in England at any time within the previous year).

[49] The alternative, business-related criterion of the debtor's having 'a place of business' in England was omitted from the conditions listed in s.265 when it was revised as part of the reforms enacted in 1985–1986. For comparison, see e.g. Bankruptcy Act 1914, s.4(1)(d) (repealed).

business as a concept capable of determination according to a commonsense appraisal of the facts in a given case, coloured by the notion that 'a business' represents a sustained and systematic means of attempting to generate an income or livelihood for those who conduct it.[50] This provides a pragmatic basis of distinguishing certain isolated, or non-systematic, transactions which happen to yield a profit, but which do not represent a planned or regular activity whose objective is the realisation of gains.[51] A pragmatic and commonsense approach to assessing whether or not a person is carrying on business has much to recommend it, since it allows the courts to avoid becoming impeded by mere formulations of language when confronted by novel types of entrepreneurial activity to which it may be difficult even to ascribe a name at the point of first encounter.[52] The courts have also adopted the view that the business carried on by the debtor must be *his* business, as opposed to being that of some other person by whom he is employed or controlled, or on whose behalf he functions.[53] This may sometimes give rise to difficulties in terms of evaluation of the evidence, and there may be additional complexities in cases where a person has made use of the device of incorporation of one or more companies to undertake his business activities. Since it is possible for a person to be simultaneously the controlling shareholder of a company and also to be its employee, an entire mode of conducting business may be so structured as to generate the impression that the individual is acting as a mere employee or agent of the company, rather than carrying on his own business, when transactions are entered into in this country. Once again, the pragmatic approach of the courts has the advantage that it enables a realistic and comprehensive view to be taken of the business operation, having regard to such matters as the ultimate controlling interest and the lines of command and initiative that are identifiable, so as to reach a conclusion as to who is the party who can properly be said to be carrying on business within the jurisdiction.[54]

The meaning and scope of the business-based connecting factor referred to in subsection (1)(c)(ii) is considerably expanded by the provisions of section 265(2), to the effect that the reference to an individual carrying on business includes (a) the carrying on of business by a firm or partnership

[50] Cf. *Re Dagnall* [1896] 2 Q.B. 407, 410, per Vaughan-Williams J.; *Re Worsley* [1901] 1 Q.B. 309 (CA); *Re a Debtor (No. 3 of 1926)* [1927] 1 Ch. 97 (CA); *Re Brauch* [1978] Ch. 316 (CA). See also *Re Williams' Will Trusts* [1953] 1 Ch. 138.

[51] *Re Mutton, ex parte Board of Trade* (1887) 19 Q.B.D. 102 (CA); *Re Wallis* (1885) 14 Q.B.D. 950.

[52] *Re Clark* [1914] 3 K.B. 1095 (CA); *Re Brauch, supra* n.50, where particularly instructive passages are to be found in the judgments of Goff and Buckley L.J.J. at [1978] Ch. 330 and 336, respectively.

[53] *Graham v. Lewis* (1888) 20 Q.B.D. 780; aff'd 22 Q.B.D. 1 (CA).

[54] See *Re Brauch, supra* n.50, especially the passages referred to in *supra*, n.52.

of which the individual is a member, and (b) the carrying on of business by an agent or manager for the individual or for such a firm or partnership. Although these provisions are apt to bring within the catchment of English jurisdiction many of those persons who utilise a variety of commercial arrangements to enable them to do business at long range, and who in some cases may never visit this country at any relevant time, it is always necessary to demonstrate that business is being carried on *in* this country by whomsoever has been entrusted with the conduct of affairs on the debtor's behalf. In this context, there is a degree of uncertainty about the extent to which it is possible for the rules of contract and agency law to be manipulated so as to enable the debtor to argue that no business is being done *in* England because his representative is precluded from making binding contracts in dealing with parties here. English courts have long been accustomed to making a distinction, in cases concerned with the exercise of jurisdiction over foreign corporations for the purpose of initiating *inter partes* litigation, between foreign corporations which do business *in* England and those which merely do business *with* parties in this country.[55] It is submitted that there is no compelling necessity for this distinction to be applied in relation to the exercise of bankruptcy jurisdiction over individuals, and that it is more in keeping with the general policy of the bankruptcy law to have regard to the underlying realities of the debtor's method of conducting his business affairs: if the net result of the chosen *modus operandi*—however sophisticated and circuitous—is that business revenue is being generated through dealings with parties in England, it should be possible to form the conclusion that the debtor is carrying on business here, even though the place of technical formation of contracts may be offshore, and matters are so arranged that the contracts themselves are governed by foreign law.[56]

With regard to the determination of the commencement and cessation of business, the courts' readiness to take a realistic view is again to be noted. While prepared to accept that a 'one-off' transaction need not be treated as necessarily denoting the carrying on of a business, it is equally recognised that every business must have a beginning, so that there is in principle no reason why a single transaction should not be regarded as indicative that business is being carried on, provided that the appropriate intentions on the debtor's part can be shown to exist. Once a debtor has commenced carrying on business here, the vital question is under what

[55] See, e.g., *Okura & Co. Ltd. v. Forsbacka Jernverks Akt.*[1914] 1 K.B. 715; *Saccharin Corpn. Ltd. v. Chemische Fabrik von Heyden Akt.* [1911] 2 K.B. 516, *The World Harmony* [1967] P. 341.

[56] See, e.g the landmark decisions of the U.S. Supreme Court: *International Shoe Co. v. State of Washington*, 326 U.S. 310, 66 S.Ct.154, 90 L.Ed. 95 (1945), in which a 'minimum contacts' test for state court jurisdiction over out-of-state corporations was formulated; and *Asahi Metal Industry Co. Ltd. v. Superior Court of California, Solano County*, 480 U.S. 102, 107 S. Ct. 1026, 94 L. Ed. 2d 92 (1987).

circumstances will English law regard that state of affairs as having come to an end, so that the three-year 'catchment' period begins to run? The answer is that, according to a long-established doctrine applied by the English courts, a business is regarded as continuing to be carried on so long as any debts incurred in the course of the business remain unpaid.[57] The concept of 'debts of the business' is a broad one, and extends from the debts or liabilities incurred towards customers or suppliers, to such debts as may be due to the Crown or to public authorities in respect of taxation on profits of the business, or other fiscal liabilities or social contributions to which the business is assessable, and which are referable to the period when the debtor was in control of it. Thus, a debtor's attempt to sever his business ties with this country by disposing of his business, or by purporting to close it down, will be unavailing unless all trade debts are shown to have been paid in full. Only when this precondition is fulfilled does time begin to run according to the terms of section 265(1)(c)(ii), so that not until a minimum interval of three years has elapsed since the date of cessation of business will this nexus cease to be operative for the purposes of commencing bankruptcy proceedings in England.

2.1.2 Other preliminary conditions for opening bankruptcy proceedings

Under further provisions of the Insolvency Act 1986, certain conditions are required to be satisfied in order for it to be competent for a bankruptcy petition to be presented to the court. Although these conditions do not raise any special issues from a private international law standpoint, they will be briefly mentioned here for the sake of providing a more complete indication of what are the requirements of English law for the opening of bankruptcy proceedings.[58]

In the case of a debtor's petition, the Act imposes no qualifying condition as to the minimum amount of unsecured indebtedness which needs to be shown in order that a debtor may apply for a bankruptcy order to be made. All that is required, according to section 272(1), is that the petition must declare that the debtor is unable to pay his debts, in support of which assertion it is required by section 272(2) that the petition must be accompanied by a statement of the debtor's affairs conforming to prescribed requirements, containing particulars of the debtor's creditors and of his

[57] *Re Dagnall* [1896] 2 Q.B. 407; *Re Worsley* [1901] 1 Q.B. 309 (C.A.); *Theophile v. Solicitor-General* [1950] A.C. 186 (HL); *Re Bird* [1962] 1 W.L.R. 686, [1962] 2 All E.R. 406 (CA). See also *Re a Debtor (No. 784 of 1991)* [1992] Ch. 554 (in which Hoffmann J. confirmed that the same approach is operative under the Insolvency Act 1986).

[58] For a more detailed account of the matters referred to in this section, see I.F. Fletcher, *The Law of Insolvency*, 2nd edn. (1996), ch. 6.

debts and other liabilities, and also of his assets and means, including any form of income.[59] Despite the absence of any explicit 'threshold' requirement to enable a debtor to invoke the bankruptcy process, the courts have maintained a degree of discipline by interpreting the provision concerning the debtor's inability to pay his debts as referring to such debts as are currently due and payable.[60] Thus (in contrast to the regime for company insolvency), it is not open to an individual debtor to apply for a bankruptcy order on the basis of a 'balance sheet' test of insolvency in which contingent and future liabilities are included in the calculation of net deficiency: if the debtor is able to pay current debts as they fall due, he is ineligible to present his own petition. Further judicial control of the use of the debtor's petition is exerted using the court's discretion to dismiss a petition which it considers to be an abuse of the right of petition, or to rescind or annul an order made in response to a petition which is retrospectively perceived to have been improperly presented. One recognised form of impropriety is where the debtor attempts to make repeated use of the device of presenting his own bankruptcy petition as a means of escaping from the claims of his creditors.[61] Although English law regards bankruptcy as a legitimate means of enabling a debtor to extricate himself from an inexorable burden of indebtedness, it is resolutely averse to any exploitation of the procedure by cynical or feckless persons.

In the case of a creditor's petition, special conditions are laid down by section 267 of the 1986 Act to control the right to make use of this process. The essence of these restrictive conditions is that a creditor's petition must be presented in respect of a debt or debts which constitute what is traditionally termed a 'good petitioning creditor's debt', as determined by applying several key criteria. First, the amount of the debt, or the aggregate amount if several debts are used as the basis for the petition, must be equal to or exceed a prescribed level known as 'the bankruptcy level', which is currently set at £750.[62] Secondly, the debt, or each of the debts, must be for a liquidated sum payable to the petitioning creditor, or to one or more of the petitioning creditors, either immediately or at some certain, future time, and the debt must be unsecured.[63] Thirdly, the debt, or each

[59] See also Insolvency Rules 1986 (S.I. 1986 No. 1925, as amended), rr.6.37–6.42; Forms 6.27, 6.28.

[60] *Re a Debtor, ex parte The Debtor v. Allen (No. 17 of 1966)* [1967] Ch. 590.

[61] *Re Bond* (1888) 21 Q.B.D. 17; *Re Betts* [1901] 2 K.B. 39; cf. *Re Painter* [1895] 1 Q.B. 85; *Re Dunn* [1949] 1 Ch. 640, 647, per Lord Evershed M.R.

[62] Insolvency Act 1986, s.267(2)(a),(4)

[63] *Ibid.*, s.267(2)(b). A partly secured creditor is eligible to present a bankruptcy petition provided the unsecured balance of the debt is at least £750, since in such circumstances s.269(2) treats the debt as two separate debts. A secured creditor also has the option of stating in the petition his willingness to give up his security for the benefit of all the creditors generally, in the event of a bankruptcy order being made: s.269(1)(a) provides that such a statement overcomes the need for a petitioning creditor's debt to be unsecured.

of the debts, must be a debt which the debtor appears either to be unable to pay or to have no reasonable prospect of being able to pay.[64] Section 268 of the Act provides alternative ways for the petitioning creditor, who may well have no means of knowing the complete state of the debtor's financial affairs, to take procedural steps which, if the debtor cannot respond in a satisfactory way, will demonstrate an insufficiency of means which the law will regard as meeting this third requirement. In the case of a debt which is payable immediately, the procedural options are twofold. The first is for the creditor to serve on the debtor a formal demand for payment or satisfaction, known as a statutory demand. Thereafter, if at least three weeks have elapsed without the debtor complying, either through payment of the debt or through securing or compounding for it to the satisfaction of the creditor, and provided the statutory demand itself has not been set aside upon any challenge mounted by the debtor, the debtor's apparent inability to pay is established.[65] It is noteworthy that the statutory demand can be employed without the need for any prior judgment or order to be obtained against the debtor. On the other hand, if there is such a judgment or order of any court in favour of the petitioning creditor, the alternative option can be employed of issuing execution or other process of enforcement in respect of the debt. If the enforcement process is subsequently returned unsatisfied in whole or in part, the debtor's apparent inability to pay is duly established.[66]

In the case of a debt not immediately payable, a different form of statutory demand must be employed, whereby the debtor is subjected to the requirement that within three weeks from the date of service he establishes to the satisfaction of the creditor that there is a reasonable prospect that he will be able to pay the debt when it falls due, failing which the third condition, concerning the debtor's inability to pay, is established.[67] Thus, a duly qualified creditor may petition for the debtor's bankruptcy even though the debt is not payable until some time in the future. Such preemptive petitions are somewhat rare in practice, but they can be resorted to where it is evident that a debtor's financial situation is deteriorating rapidly, so that any delay in opening bankruptcy proceedings will be especially detrimental to the prospects for ordinary, unsecured creditors to receive any return on their debts by way of dividend. As there is no restriction on the right of petition either in the case of foreign creditors, or in the case of creditors whose debts are governed by a law other than English law, they may avail themselves of the procedure for presenting a bankruptcy petition, in the same way as domestic creditors.

[64] Insolvency Act 1986, s.267(2)(c). [65] *Ibid.*, s.268(1)(a). [66] *Ibid*, s.268(2)(b).
[67] *Ibid*, s.268(2).

The proper court for bringing proceedings

In England and Wales, jurisdiction in cases of individual bankruptcy is allocated to the High Court and, outside London, to certain County Courts. For this purpose, groups of County Court districts are arranged under the presidency of designated County Courts, to constitute a special network of Insolvency Districts covering the entire country.[68] When exercising jurisdiction in insolvency matters a County Court has all the powers and jurisdiction of the High Court, and orders of the County Court are enforceable accordingly. To determine the appropriate court in which to present a bankruptcy petition it is necessary to ascertain the whereabouts of the debtor's domestic address or, if the debtor carries on a business, the place where that business is carried on. A reference period of six months, immediately prior to the date of presentation of the petition, is applicable. The following rules of jurisdiction apply:

(1) The petition must be presented to the High Court:
   (a) in cases where the petition is presented by a Minister of the Crown, or by a government department;
   (b) in cases where the debtor has resided or carried on business within the London Insolvency District for the greater part of the six-month reference period, or for a longer period in those six months than in any other insolvency district;
   (c) if the debtor is not resident in England and Wales; or
   (d) if the petitioner is unable to ascertain the residence of the debtor, or his place of business.[69]

(2) In any other case, the petition must be presented to the County Court for the Insolvency District in which the debtor has resided or carried on business for the longest period during the six-month reference period.[70] In cases where the debtor's residential address and his place of business are located in different insolvency districts, the connecting factor based upon place of business predominates, and if during the reference period the debtor has carried on business in more than one insolvency district, the petition must be presented to the court for the insolvency district in which is, or has been for the longest period within those six months, his principal place of business.[71] Where a

[68] *Ibid.*, ss.373(1), 374; Civil Courts Order 1983 (S.I. 1983 No. 713), (as amended); Insolvency Rules 1986 (S.I. 1986 No. 1925), Sch. 2, as substituted by the Insolvency (Amendment) Rules 1987 (S.I. 1987 No. 1919).

[69] Insolvency Act 1986, s.373(3)(a); Insolvency Rules 1986, rr. 6.9(1), 6.40(1). The London Insolvency District comprises the County Court districts of sixteen metropolitan County Courts, corresponding approximately to the Greater London Area: see Insolvency Act 1986, s.374(4)(a); Civil Courts Order 1983, *supra* n.68, Sch. 3 (as amended).

[70] Insolvency Act 1986, s.373(3)(b); Insolvency Rules 1986, rr.6.9(2), 6.40(2).

[71] Insolvency Rules, rr. 6.9(3),(4), 6.40(2)(b),(c).

bankruptcy petition is presented against a debtor for whom there is already in force an individual voluntary arrangement under Part VIII of the Insolvency Act, a special, overriding rule of jurisdiction is applicable. This requires the petition to be presented to the court to which the nominee's report under section 256 of the Act was presented, in fulfilment of the preliminary conditions to the convening of a creditors' meeting at which such a voluntary arrangement may be concluded.[72] This is designed to ensure continuity and consistency in the judicial supervision and control of insolvency proceedings involving a given debtor.

The rules of jurisdiction are drafted with the intention that they provide clear guidance as to the proper court to which a petition is to be presented. They are also expressed in mandatory terms. However, difficulties may sometimes arise in applying the rules to a case where the debtor's circumstances or conduct may cause confusion, and it is also possible for an unintentional error to be made by a petitioner even where the relevant facts are not in doubt. Where it transpires that proceedings have been commenced in the wrong court, rule 7.12 of the Insolvency Rules 1986 supplies a flexible and discretionary power to enable the court either to order the transfer of the proceedings to the court in which they ought to have been commenced, or to order that they be continued in the court where they have been commenced. A third possibility, which could be utilised in cases where the petitioner has acted irresponsibly, or even oppressively, in bringing proceedings in the wrong court, is that the proceedings may be struck out. It may be observed that rule 7.12 is concerned with the internal management of insolvency jurisdiction as between different courts in England and Wales, where the conditions for commencement of insolvency proceedings in this country are otherwise satisfied. A quite separate issue arises where, despite it being the case that the court is properly seised of the matter, the submission is advanced that the court should nonetheless decline to exercise its jurisdiction on the ground that the insolvency proceedings should take place in some other country which is alleged to be a more appropriate or convenient forum for this purpose. This issue is addressed in the section next following.

2.1.3 Jurisdictional abstention: *forum non conveniens*

Up to this point, we have been concerned with the requirements which, under the law of England and Wales, must be fulfilled in order for the

[72] Insolvency Rules 1986, rr.6.9(4A),6.40(3A). An individual voluntary arrangement (IVA) is a procedure whereby a debtor may attempt to avert personal bankruptcy by concluding a composition or scheme of arrangement with his creditors. See at 2.5.1 below. On the preliminary steps towards concluding an IVA, see the Insolvency Act 1986, ss. 256, 257.

courts of this country to have jurisdiction to make a bankruptcy order against an individual debtor. In keeping with the international focus of this book, special attention has been paid to cases where the rules of jurisdiction enable a bankruptcy order to be made even where the debtor's connections with this country are currently less substantial than those which serve to establish ties with one or more foreign countries. In such circumstances, it is highly probable (although not inevitable) that the debtor could be simultaneously amenable to the bankruptcy laws of several countries. The possibility of multiple bankruptcy proceedings, taking place concurrently under the laws of different countries, is not merely a theoretical one, and we will examine the ways in which English law has attempted to deal with the problems generated by parallel insolvencies in section 2.8. below, and also in Chapter 4 below. Before concluding this account of the rules of jurisdiction however it is appropriate to consider whether there are any circumstances under which an English court may elect not to make a bankruptcy order despite having jurisdictional competence to do so.

The practice whereby a court, at its discretion, may abstain from exercising a jurisdiction which otherwise exists is generally known as the doctrine of *forum non conveniens* (inappropriate forum), although this is in fact but one of several possible grounds on which an English court may stay or strike out proceedings which it is otherwise competent to entertain.[73] Until comparatively recent times, English law was resistant to the development of a general doctrine of *forum non conveniens*, although it was accepted that a court might exercise its discretion to stay an English action which was 'oppressive and vexatious' to the defendant, provided that the latter could show that such a stay would not cause injustice to the plaintiff. The circumstances under which the defendant would have the strongest prospects of persuading an English court to grant a stay were those where the same cause of action was simultaneously being litigated between the same parties in another jurisdiction (*lis alibi pendens*), where there was also evidence that the plaintiff was exploiting the tactical opportunities resulting from the bringing of multiple proceedings, with a view to weakening the defendant's capability to maintain an effective defence

[73] In civil or commercial litigation between parties who are subject to a contract containing a valid jurisdiction clause whereby all disputes between them are to be referred to the exclusive jurisdiction of a foreign court or tribunal, an English court will abstain from exercising jurisdiction unless the plaintiff can show that the interests of justice require it to do otherwise. However, private contractual arrangements between parties cannot prevail over the exercise of bankruptcy jurisdiction, which belongs to the realm of public policy, serving a wider spread of interests including, ultimately, those of society at large. Cf. *National Westminster Bank Ltd. v. Halesowen Presswork and Assemblies Ltd.* [1972] A.C. 785, at 809 per Lord Simon and at 824 per Lord Kilbrandon; and *Re Bank of Credit and Commerce International SA (No. 10)* [1996] 4 All E.R. 796, 812 per Scott, V.C. (affirming that no arrangement is permissible whereby the mandatory rules of set-off in bankruptcy are by-passed or modified).

in each set of proceedings.[74] From 1974 onwards however the judicial approach to the subject of *forum non conveniens* underwent a revolutionary change, resulting in a modernised doctrine which is more liberal and international in character, thanks to the renunciation of the restrictive and chauvinistic policy towards jurisdictional abstention which was previously maintained.[75] The current approach, which corresponds closely to that which has been followed by the courts in Scotland since the nineteenth century,[76] is expressed in a celebrated passage of the speech of Lord Goff in *Spiliada Maritime Corpn. v. Cansulex Ltd.*,[77] in which he affirmed that English proceedings may be stayed if the court is satisfied that there is some other available forum, having competent jurisdiction, which is the appropriate forum for trial of the action, because the case may be tried there more suitably for the interests of all the parties and the ends of justice.[78]

While recognising the importance of this transformation of the English law approach to the declining of jurisdiction, concerning both the principles to be followed and the spirit of their application by the courts, it is necessary to keep in mind that the leading cases in this jurisprudential saga were concerned with classic types of international litigation between directly interested parties, in which questions of insolvency law were not immediately involved. Some caution is therefore appropriate when any attempt is made, by way of an extrapolation from these cases, to postulate a modern restatement of the principles of jurisdictional abstention which English courts might be expected to apply in cases of international insolvency. The collective nature of such proceedings, together with the broader spread of interests and policy considerations that must be taken into account when administering insolvency law in either a domestic or an international context, militate against an unqualified extension of the approach which has evolved in relation to litigious actions conducted on an *inter partes* basis. Nevertheless, the welcome infusion of a more magnanimous, and inter-

[74] See, e.g. *The Atlantic Star* [1974] A.C. 436 (HL); cf. *MacShannon v. Rockware Glass Ltd.* [1978] A.C. 795 (HL).

[75] See the cases cited *supra*, n.74, together with the subsequent, leading decisions of the House of Lords: *The Abidin Daver* [1984] A.C. 398, and *Spiliada Maritime Corpn. v. Cansulex Ltd.* [1987] A.C. 460. For detailed accounts of the transformation of this aspect of English law, and the present position, see: *Dicey and Morris on the Conflict of Laws*, 12th edn. (1993), ch. 12; *Cheshire and North's Private International Law*, 12th edn. (1992), ch. 12; J.G. Collier, *Conflict of Laws*, 2nd edn. (1994), ch. 8; J.J. Fawcett (ed.), *Declining Jurisdiction in Private International Law* (1995). A detailed analysis of the case law on jurisdictional abstention in relation to bankruptcy is contained in P. Smart, *Cross-Border Insolvency* (1991), ch. 2.

[76] See *Sim v. Robinow* (1892) 19 R.(Ct. of Sess.) 665, 668 per Lord Kinnear.

[77] See *supra* n.75.

[78] [1987] A.C. 460, at 476. The same principle is followed in relation to the exercise of judicial discretion to refuse leave to the plaintiff to serve the writ on the defendant outside the jurisdiction (under the rules contained in Order 11 of the Rules of the Supreme Court). The *Spiliada* case itself was an example of application under Ord.11 R.S.C. by a plaintiff seeking to commence proceedings against a defendant absent abroad.

nationally sensitive spirit of approach towards the exercise of international jurisdiction by English courts, from the highest level downwards, since 1974 could not fail to exert some influence upon the mode of decision when questions concerning the exercise of insolvency jurisdiction arise in subsequent cases. Before attempting to assess the impact of this development, it is appropriate to examine the extent to which rules of abstention had already been established by past case decisions, bearing in mind that these mostly date from the heyday of that ethos of 'judicial chauvinism' which has been openly disavowed by the courts in recent times, to be replaced by the espousal of the spirit of 'judicial comity'.[79]

At the core of the judicial approach to the exercise of jurisdiction in insolvency matters is the jealously guarded tradition of upholding the ultimate discretion of the court to exercise its statutory (and also its inherent) powers according to its view of what will best serve the ends of fairness and justice. This view in turn has been powerfully influenced by the historic involvement of the Chancery judges in the administration of insolvency law. Even when applying statutory provisions drafted in unqualified, and seemingly mandatory terms (as exemplified by such expressions as 'the court shall . . . make an order'), the courts have been at pains to insist that they retain the power to refuse to make the order in question (or to rescind an order that has been made) if the circumstances are such that the court is persuaded that this is the correct course from the standpoint of all the relevant interests with which an insolvency court has to be concerned.[80] These range from the individual interests of the debtor, and perhaps also certain of the creditors singled out by circumstance, to the collective interests of all creditors involved in the debtor's insolvency, and the wider public concerns of society at large, including the maintenance of confidence in the integrity of the legal process itself. Since such interests are both infinitely variable from case to case, and are also capable of conflicting with one another in any given case, this can involve the court in a delicate process of evaluation and discernment. Much care has been taken by the higher courts to sustain the role of the judge at first instance in exercising his discretion after a careful consideration of all the elements presented in the course of the live proceedings conducted before him, and it has become axiomatic that appellate courts will only interfere with the exercise of discretion by a lower court where there is clear and compelling evidence that the latter has mishandled its powers, or has reached a decision which is manifestly wrong.[81]

[79] See the celebrated *dictum* of Lord Diplock in his speech in *The Abidin Daver* [1984] A.C. 398 at 411.

[80] Cf. *Re Bond* (1888) 21 Q.B.D. 17; *Re Betts* [1901] 2 K.B. 39.

[81] See, e.g., *Re Payne, ex parte Castle Mail Packets Co.* (1886) 18 Q.B.D. 154; *Re Stainton* (1887) 4 Morr. 242; *Re Smith* [1947] 1 All E.R. 769, 771 *et seq.*, per Lord Greene M.R.

In the course of time, a somewhat limited number of examples have emerged of the ways in which judicial discretion may be employed in relation to the exercise of jurisdiction in insolvency cases with international aspects.

(a) Absence of assets

English courts have on some occasions declined to make an adjudication order against a debtor who otherwise fulfils the criteria making him or her amenable to the bankruptcy jurisdiction, upon it being demonstrated to the court that the debtor has no assets in this country which would be capable of being administered for the benefit of the creditors.[82] The courts' stated view, that to make an adjudication order in such circumstances would be 'a vain thing', brings to mind the Chancery maxim that 'Equity does nothing in vain', but it is important to note that there must be cogent evidence to establish not merely the absence of assets currently, but also the absence of any prospect that assets may come into existence in the future, so that it can correctly be asserted that the only result of an adjudication would be a wastage of money in costs. It is not sufficient cause for the court to decline to make an adjudication order if it can merely be established that the debtor *apparently* has no assets for distribution among his creditors: the rigorous investigative processes of the bankruptcy itself may well reveal the existence of assets which have been either concealed or overlooked during the earlier phase of the proceedings.[83] If the court is in any doubt about the full facts of the case, it may conclude that the safest course is to allow the bankruptcy to commence so that the true picture may subsequently emerge. Even if it is alleged that all the assets are abroad, and are destined to be administered abroad in proceedings commenced under foreign law, the English court may elect not to relinquish its jurisdictional hold over the matter until it can be completely satisfied that no evasive tactics are being deployed, particularly by a debtor who may have revealed a propensity for seeking refuge from existing creditors by moving to a jurisdiction where presently no debts are outstanding.[84]

(b) Existing bankruptcy elsewhere

It is certainly not the case that the mere fact that a debtor has already undergone adjudication in some foreign jurisdiction constitutes, of itself and without more, a ground for the non-exercise by the English courts of their jurisdiction to make a bankruptcy order.[85] If it should later transpire

[82] *Re Robinson* (1883) 22 Ch.D. 816 (CA); *Re Otway* [1895] 1 Q.B. 812 (CA); *Re Somers* (1897) 4 Mans. 227; *Re Betts* [1897] 1 Q.B. 50 (CA).

[83] *Re Leonard* [1896] 1 Q.B. 473 (CA).

[84] Cf. *Re Pascal* (1876) 1 Ch.D. 509 (CA).

[85] *Re McCulloch* (1880) 14 Ch.D. 716 (CA); *Re Artola Hermanos* (1890) 24 Q.B.D. 640 (C.A.); *Re a Debtor (No. 199 of 1922)* [1922] 2 Ch. 470 (CA); *Re a Debtor (No. 737 of 1928)* [1929] 1 Ch. 362 (CA). Cf. *Re Robinson supra* n.82.

that the foreign proceedings are taking place in what can sensibly be regarded as the appropriate, central forum in which the debtor's assets can be conveniently and properly administered in a way which meets the requisite standards of fairness to all interested parties, the English courts have given indications in past cases that they might later stay proceedings in this country and allow a unitary process of distribution to be centred, for example, in the debtor's country of domicile.[86] Concrete examples of such an outright surrender of proceedings into the control of a foreign forum are lacking in the reported cases, however.

(c) Abuse of legal process; fraud on creditors

Courts are likely to be more receptive to arguments in favour of jurisdictional abstention where they can be convinced that the utilisation of English bankruptcy law amounts to an abuse of legal process, either on the part of a creditor seeking to harass or oppress the debtor, or by the debtor who is perhaps hoping that an English adjudication, followed by discharge, may somehow serve as a barrier to immunise his future property from being seized by or on behalf of unpaid creditors whose claims are comprised in foreign insolvency proceedings from which the debtor remains undischarged.[87] While necessarily keeping in mind that one of the accepted purposes of individual insolvency law is to provide a controlled regime whereby a debtor may be freed from the burden of debt, and gain a fresh start for the future, courts must be ever-vigilant to the possibility that some debtors may take advantage of the law's beneficent policy, by exploiting the protective facilities of a statutory moratorium and subsequent discharge in such a way as to perpetrate fraud on their creditors. One such misuse of the law takes the form of serial filings by the debtor at relatively short intervals, thereby seeking to initiate a fresh bankruptcy while still undischarged, or only recently discharged, from the previous adjudication. Where this course is pursued in England itself, it has in the past been countered by the use of the court's discretion to refuse to make a bankruptcy order in response to the most recent petition. Under the modern law there is the further possibility that such practices may be countered using the provision in section 279(1)(a) of the Insolvency Act

[86] See e.g. *Re Pascal*, *supra* n.84, and *Re Artola Hermanos*, *supra* n.85. See also *Re a Debtor (No. 737 of 1928)*, *supra* n.85, at 370, for less specific hints by Lord Hanworth M.R. as to the court's willingness to deal with difficulties caused by concurrent proceedings, as and when they arose.

[87] See *Ex parte Gibson* (1865) 34 L.J.Bkcy. 31 (where the debtor's attempt to gain 'asylum' in England from creditors in his country of domicile was not detected until it was technically too late for Lord Westbury L.C. to annul the English adjudication. The judicial response following the belated discovery of the true facts, using the discretionary powers attaching to the English rules of discharge, as well as its powers regarding the award of costs where other parties had contributed to the previous misapplication of the law, is particularly instructive). See also *Re Betts* [1901] 2 K.B. 39 (not an international case).

1986, which withholds the benefits of the automatic discharge provisions, available under that section, in any case where the debtor had been an undischarged bankrupt at any time in the period of fifteen years ending with the commencement of the current bankruptcy. In such a case, discharge can only be obtained by an order of the court upon successful application by the bankrupt, who is not allowed to apply for discharge until a minimum of five years have elapsed from the date of commencement of the bankruptcy.[88]

Typically, examples of serial filings take place within the same jurisdiction, but it is also possible for a debtor to move between countries while perpetrating his evasive strategy. If timely detection can be achieved, we have seen that the English court can simply exercise its discretionary power to refuse to make a bankruptcy order. Where the true picture does not emerge until some later stage in the proceedings, recourse may be had to the court's power to annul the bankruptcy order under section 282(1)(a) of the Act on the basis that, due to the grounds existing at the time the order was made, it ought not to have been made. In this way, a retrospective response can be sought in the light of the debtor's improper use of legal process. Either of these responses, it is submitted, could be employed in a case where the debtor's previous bankruptcies have taken place in other jurisdictions. It is somewhat debateable whether a debtor who has previously been made a bankrupt in some foreign country can be regarded as coming within the ambit of section 279(1)(a), so that any English adjudication will only be discharged through an order made upon application to the court. The definition of 'bankrupt' in section 381(1) contains no reference to the possibility that the bankruptcy order from which the status of bankrupt is derived may have been made in any other jurisdiction outside England and Wales (including other parts of the United Kingdom). Hence it would seem probable that a debtor who has undergone successive adjudications, first in another country and then in England, would have to be treated as a 'first-time' bankrupt for the purposes of the provisions in section 279(2) of the Insolvency Act which bring about an automatic discharge and rehabilitation within a maximum of three years from the commencement of bankruptcy.[89] On the other hand, it may be possible for an interpretative gloss to be applied when considering the term 'bankrupt' in relation to a person who has previously been adjudged bankrupt by a court whose jurisdictional competence is recog-

[88] Insolvency Act 1986, s.280(1). For the court's powers regarding the granting of discharge, see *ibid.*, s.280(2),(3).

[89] In cases where a summary administration certificate is issued, by reason of the relatively small total value of the unsecured debts, the period of time for the gaining of an automatic discharge is reduced to two years: Insolvency Act 1986, s.279(2)(a). See also ss. 273 and 275 of the Act. The 'small bankruptcies level' is currently prescribed at £20,000: S.I. 1986 No. 1996.

nised according to English private international law,[90] as would certainly be the case where the previous bankruptcy took place upon a petition (or filing) made by the debtor personally. This possibility remains untested as far as the author is aware, but would certainly be worth exploring in view of the ease of mobility enjoyed by individuals nowadays.

The modern approach of English courts

The full impact of the revised doctrine of *forum non conveniens*, as proclaimed by the House of Lords in the landmark decisions already referred to,[91] upon the exercise of jurisdiction in insolvency matters will not be apparent for some time, due to the unpredictability of the emergence of cases in which such issues have to be resolved. Because of the complex nature of insolvency, combined with the collective character of a bankruptcy administration, the application of *Spiliada*-based principles to determine whether or not an English bankruptcy order should be made will be neither easy nor straightforward. Even if it is possible, at the time when the hearing of the petition is taking place, to ascertain the whereabouts of all the various assets, and to identify the locality of each creditor and the associated claim against the estate, it may be far from obvious that there is any one jurisdiction which can properly be considered as the 'most appropriate' centre in which the proceedings should be concentrated. Even if such a forum can be identified, further considerations remain on account of the public aspects of insolvency law, including the need to ensure that the fundamental policy goals of English law are not compromised or sacrificed by the act of declining jurisdiction. There is thus considerable temptation to follow a cautious approach and to retain control over the proceedings for as long as possible. However, this can entail considerable wastage of value through the duplication of costs in parallel proceedings, and in the interest of avoiding such consequences it is advisable to provide the court with the clearest picture of the relative advantages offered by the alternative lines of action that are in prospect. While it would be unwise to offer any dogmatic assertions about the possible response of the court in any hypothetical situation, the greatly changed atmosphere of judicial consensus with regard to the exercise of jurisdiction in cases with international elements, since the *Spiliada* decision, does at least make it reasonable to submit that cases may occur in which, despite the fact that there are assets in England, and also creditors whose claims arose here, the ends of justice and fairness can best be served by allowing a single administration to be conducted in a foreign country which happens to be the most appropriate forum for bankruptcy. Provided it is demonstrable that no legitimate interests of parties in this country are

[90] See at 2.6 below.

[91] See *supra* nn. 75 and 78 and text thereto.

likely to be unduly prejudiced through their being obliged to participate in bankruptcy proceedings conducted in a foreign country and in accordance with its law,[92] a 'best interests' argument may be constructed, showing that the elimination of the extra costs that would be incurred in a parallel administration is likely to result in an improved return to creditors by way of dividend, and that English creditors will share in the ensuing benefits. Under such conditions, an English court could conceivably be persuaded to refrain from making a bankruptcy order, in the interests of securing the optimum application of the principle of *pari passu* distribution of the available funds.

2.1.4 Selected comparisons

Australia.[93] The statutory provisions governing the exercise of bankruptcy jurisdiction are contained in the Bankruptcy Act 1966 (Cth). The ancestral roots of this statute are very evident, with many close affinities between the provisions currently in force in Australia and those which were included in the Bankruptcy Acts previously in force in England prior to the reforms enacted in 1986 (and, in many respects, still found in the English law of today). Notably, the Australian procedure continues to embody the requirement that an act of bankruptcy must have been committed by the debtor during the six months immediately preceding the presentation of a bankruptcy petition.[94] This has the consequence that it continues to be a live issue for jurisdictional purposes to establish whether the particular act of bankruptcy which the debtor is alleged to have committed is one which, according to the terms of the relevant statutory provision, is capable of being committed outside Australia. The latter possibility is signified by the insertion of the phrase 'in Australia *or elsewhere*' in the provision which specifies the nature of the conduct or event which constitutes the act of bankruptcy.[95] In addition, it is necessary to establish that at the time of committing an available act of bankruptcy the debtor satisfied at least one of the recognised criteria which establish a nexus with Australia that is sufficiently substantial to justify the exercise of bankruptcy jurisdiction over him or her. The qualifying connections are

92 Material factors for the English court to take into account would include: additional delays due to the reduced levels of speed and efficiency of the foreign insolvency process; additional costs or disadvantages for English creditors due to the physical remoteness of the other jurisdiction, plus any special factors such as translation and related costs; relative prejudice to the creditors' prospects of recovery, including difference in the priority to be accorded to any claim or security rights as compared to the treatment under English law.

93 See P.E. Nygh, *Conflict of Laws in Australia*, 6th edn. (1995), ch. 34; E.I. Sykes and M.C. Pryles, *Australian Private International Law*, 3rd edn. (1991), ch. 23. For a clear and concise account of the Australian law of bankruptcy, see A.R. Keay, *Insolvency*, 2nd edn. (1994), ch. 2.

94 Bankruptcy Act 1966 (Cth), ss.43(1)(a), 44(1)(c).

95 (Emphasis added in text). See Bankruptcy Act 1966 (Cth), s.40(1)(a),(b),(c) and (g).

listed in section 43(1)(b) as: (a) being personally present or ordinarily resident in Australia; (b) having a dwelling-house or place of business in Australia; (c) carrying on business in Australia, either personally or by an agent or manager; or (d) being a member of a firm or partnership carrying on business in Australia. One notable contrast with English law in this respect is the omission from the 1966 Act of the connection based upon the debtor's domicile in Australia.[96] Nevertheless, the potential catchment of the rules of jurisdiction is very wide, and is extended still further by a judicial interpolation of the nexus based upon the carrying on of a business, whereby a business is still regarded as being carried on despite its ostensible closure, and even despite the debtor's departure from the jurisdiction, if debts incurred by the business remain unsatisfied.[97]

Australian law allows a bankruptcy petition to be presented by a duly qualified creditor (or by two or more acting as joint petitioners), to whom an unsecured debt of not less than AUS$1,500 is due, or by the debtor himself.[98] In the latter event, although section 55 of the 1966 Act imposes no requirement that the debtor must be resident in Australia, the courts have shown a readiness to scrutinise the motives of a non-resident debtor whose current connection with Australia (apart from owing substantial debts there) was limited to fulfilling the technical requirement of being present in the country on the day of presenting his own petition. In *Re Coote*[99] Northrop J. observed that, while the statutory conditions attaching to a debtor's petition were less exacting than those necessarily imposed in the case of a creditor's petition, the court must be alert to the possibility that a debtor may have recourse to bankruptcy proceedings in circumstances which perpetrate a fraud upon creditors. In such cases, the court may utilise its discretion to reject the petition and thus deny the debtor the opportunity to exploit the law nefariously.[100]

Canada.[101] The governing statute currently is the Bankruptcy and Insolvency Act, most recently amended in 1992 and 1997.[102] While the

[96] Cf. the Insolvency Act 1986, s.265(1)(a), discussed at 2.1.1(b) above.

[97] *Re Vassis* (1986) 9 F.C.R. 518; 64 A.L.R. 407. Cf. *Theophile v. Solicitor-General* [1950] A.C. 186 (HL), discussed at 2.1.1(iii)(A) above.

[98] Bankruptcy Act 1966 (Cth), ss.44(1)(a), 55. In the case of a creditor's petition, the debt must be a liquidated sum payable immediately or at some certain, future time (i.e. not subject to some contingency), and must exist in liquidated form both at the date of commission of the act of bankruptcy and at the date of petition: *ibid.*, s.44(1)(b). This dual-reference test was formerly a feature of English bankruptcy law, prior to the abolition of the concept of acts of bankruptcy in 1986. See, e.g., *Re a Debtor (No. 20 of 1953)* [1954] 3 All E.R. 74 (CA).

[99] (1993) 120 A.L.R. 134.

[100] *Ibid.*, at 136–141.

[101] See J.-G. Castel, *Canadian Conflict of Laws*, 3rd edn. (1993), ch. 30; J.G. McLeod, *The Conflict of Laws* (1983), ch. 5. For a concise account of the Canadian bankruptcy law, see E. Bruce Leonard, *Guide to Commercial Insolvency in Canada* (1988), Part I. More detailed treatment may be found in L.W. Houlden and G.B. Morawetz, *Bankruptcy and Insolvency Act*, 3rd edn. (1992), 2 vols., looseleaf, with 1998 Annotated Companion Volume.

[102] SC 1992, c.27; SC 1997, c.12.

origins of the Canadian system are to be found in the English bankruptcy legislation of the early twentieth century, the pace of revision and reform has accelerated in recent years, producing a more individualised system that nevertheless retains many familiar characteristics. As with Australia, so too the Canadian law retains the requirement that a debtor must have committed an act of bankruptcy within six months preceding the petition, in order that an involuntary proceeding can be commenced.[103] As with Australia, the possibility that some acts of bankruptcy may qualify as 'available' even though they took place outside Canada is selectively provided for by the use of the drafting formula 'in Canada *or elsewhere*'.[104] However, it is also necessary that the person against whom bankruptcy proceedings are to take place must satisfy the definition of being 'a debtor' as defined in section 2 of the Act, which requires that the insolvent person must either reside or carry on business in Canada, and owe unpaid liabilities to the petitioner of at least CAN$1,000. The requirement of a residential or business nexus thus precludes the commencement of bankruptcy proceedings against a foreign debtor who happens to commit what corresponds to an act of bankruptcy during a temporary presence in Canada. Even where the requisite nexus with Canada is established, the courts retain a full discretion to stay or dismiss a petition in the light of a balanced evaluation of the overall merits of the case. Where the greater portion of the debtor's assets are located in Canada, this may incline the Canadian court to exercise its jurisdiction even where the petitioning creditor's debt was incurred elsewhere.[105] As in England, a proven absence of assets in Canada is one recognised reason for dismissal of a petition, while the fact that the debtor has already been adjudged bankrupt in a foreign country does not deprive the Canadian court of jurisdictional competence, although it is a factor which may be taken into account in deciding whether a concurrent bankruptcy will serve any useful purpose.[106] A strong concern of the court will be to inquire what are the interests of local creditors in having a further set of bankruptcy proceedings take place in Canada.[107] Section 49(1) of the Act allows a voluntary proceeding to be initiated by an insolvent debtor through the expedient of making an assignment of all his property to the official receiver for the general benefit of his creditors.

USA. The governing bankruptcy legislation is Federal, as authorised by Article 1(8) of the United States Constitution. The substantive law cur-

[103] Bankruptcy and Insolvency Act, s.42(1).

[104] *Ibid.*, s.42(1)(a),(b),(c),(d) and (g). (Emphasis added in text). The other acts of bankruptcy listed in s.42(1) do not operate extraterritorially.

[105] *Sugarman v. Rainbow Plastics Ltd. and Archambaut* [1963] Que.Q.B. 546 (CA).

[106] *Re E.H. Clarke & Co* [1923] 1 D.L.R. 716 (Ont.).

[107] *Re Commonwealth Savings Plan Ltd.* (1969) 4 D.L.R. (3d) 423 (BCCA).

rently in force is gathered in Title 11 of the United States Code, 'Bankruptcy', and is based upon the Bankruptcy Reform Act of 1978 (effective from 1 October 1979) which, however, has been much amended since that date, most notably by the Bankruptcy Reform Act of 1994. Moreover, further reforms are in prospect following completion in 1997 of the work of the National Bankruptcy Review Commission, established under the 1994 Act.[108] In addition to the 'Bankruptcy Code' contained in Title 11 U.S.C., jurisdictional provisions relating to bankruptcy are found in Title 28, U.S.C., 'Judiciary'.[109]

The definition of 'debtor' as currently expressed in section 109(a) of the Bankruptcy Code comprises 'a person that resides or has a domicile, a place of business, or property in the United States'.[110] The fourth of these alternative criteria enables bankruptcy jurisdiction to be based upon the presence of assets alone, regardless of the debtor's nationality, domicile, residence or place of business. No quantitative threshold is specified as to the value or proportion of the debtor's property which must be situate in the USA. Potentially this could threaten to give rise to American bankruptcy proceedings involving a debtor whose nexus with the USA, based purely on the proprietary factor, is minimal by comparison to the contacts with some other country or countries. The counter to possible misuse of the broadly-drawn jurisdictional rules lies in the well developed doctrine of abstention, based on the courts' desire to uphold the aims of justice and fairness. The doctrine of *forum non conveniens* may therefore be deployed to bring about the dismissal of filings that are abusive or oppressive, or which are perceived to be not in good faith, or which are otherwise inappropriately brought before the American court. Section 305 of the Code provides for the dismissal of a bankruptcy case, or the suspension of all proceedings therein, at any time if, after notice and a hearing, the court decides that the interests of creditors and the debtor would be better served thereby. Even where the debtor's connections with the USA are of a sufficiently substantial character to warrant the opening of bankruptcy concurrently with other proceedings based overseas, American courts are apt to invoke the doctrine of international comity as a basis for declining to exercise jurisdiction over some matter arising during the course of the proceedings—such as an action to avoid preferences previously given by the debtor—where the inherent features of the transaction in question

[108] See Report of the National Bankruptcy Review Commission, established under the Bankruptcy Reform Act 1994. The N.B.R.C. Report, entitled *Bankruptcy: The Next Twenty Years*, was filed in Congress on 20 October 1997.

[109] See E.F. Scoles and P. Hay, *Conflict of Laws*, 2nd edn. (1992), ch. 23, Part II.

[110] 11 U.S.C. s.109(a), as amended 1984. Note that neither American nationality, nor mere physical presence in the USA, is sufficient of itself to confer jurisdiction over an insolvent debtor: one of the four specified connecting factors must be established.

indicate that the more appropriate forum for its determination is the centre from which the debtor's main business affairs were conducted.[111]

American bankruptcy law provides for both voluntary and involuntary proceedings, in the case of both liquidation proceedings, under Chapter 7 of the Code, and reorganisation proceedings under Chapter 11. One structural feature which differentiates the American system of bankruptcy from the approaches followed by Australia, Canada and England is that the procedures under Chapters 7 and 11 are applicable to all types of eligible debtor, irrespective of whether the debtor is an individual or a corporation.[112] A voluntary filing (which is by far the most common circumstance) may be initiated at any time by the debtor without the need to satisfy any financial test to establish a state of current or prospective insolvency.[113] No adjudication is necessary, although the act of filing places the debtor and his estate under the regime of the bankruptcy law, and the control and supervision of the bankruptcy court is a prominent feature of the ensuing process. An involuntary proceeding may be commenced by any creditor except one whose claim is contingent (in the sense that it is dependent upon an event which is not certain to occur), or whose claim is *bona fide* disputed.[114] A petition may be presented by one or more creditors, but if the debtor has more than eleven creditors (excluding certain connected persons or employees), section 303(b)(1) of the Code requires that a minimum of three must join in the petition. In every case, the total amount owed to the petitioning creditor(s) must be at least $5,000 over and above the value of any security they hold. Finally, there must be evidence of a need for bankruptcy proceedings, either because the debtor is generally not paying his debts as they become due, or because a general assignee for the benefit of creditors or a general receiver has taken charge of the debtor's property within the previous 120 days.[115]

[111] See, e.g., *Re Maxwell Communications Corporation plc*, 170 BR 800, 801–807 (Bankr SDNY 1994) (Judge Brozman); affd. 186 BR 807, 812–815 (SDNY 1995) (Scheindlin, USDJ); affd. 593 F3d 1036 (2nd Cir 1996) (Cardamone, Circuit Judge); Note (Fletcher) [1997] J.B.L. 476–480. See also *Re Berthoud* 231 Fed. 529 (1916); *Hilton v. Guyot*, 159 U.S.113 (1895), at 164.

[112] Other chapters of the Bankruptcy Code apply exclusively to particular types of debtor: Chapter 9 governs adjustment of debts of a municipality; Chapter 12 the adjustment of debts of a family farmer with regular income; and Chapter 13 the adjustment of debts of an individual with regular income.

[113] B.C. s.301.

[114] B.C., s.303(b).

[115] B.C., s.303(h).

2.2 INTERNATIONAL EFFECTS OF AN ENGLISH ADJUDICATION

2.2.1 Generally

In terms of the broad distinction drawn between the territorial and the universalist theories of international bankruptcy,[116] it can be affirmed that English law's espousal of the universalist doctrine is an especially prominent feature of the approach towards questions concerning the international effects of its own adjudications. However, we must note that it is one thing to lay claim to universality of effect for legal proceedings generated under a particular system of law, and quite another thing for those claims to be accorded extraterritorial acceptance, notably within any foreign country in which property of the debtor happens to be situated. It is a long established principle of private international law that questions affecting title to property, whether movable or immovable, are referred to the law of the *situs* at the relevant time.[117] This means that the ultimate destiny of any property of the debtor that is located outside England is dependent on the interaction between the laws of the countries concerned. Whatever English law may presume to say about the consequences of a bankruptcy adjudication that takes place here, these cannot immediately enter into force in the real world except with respect to those items of property currently to be found within the territorial jurisdiction over which English law enjoys sovereign application. Everywhere else, the net outcome is determined by the law of the *situs*, with particular emphasis on the rules of private international law that are operative in that country, together with any rules of its domestic law which are derived from international treaties or other arrangements which are applicable in matters concerning insolvency. Both components of this interactive process must therefore be examined.

First, it is necessary to scrutinise the exact terms in which the English law is formulated, in order to confirm the true substance of its claimed effects over a bankrupt's property. In this context, the key sections of the Insolvency Act 1986 are sections 283, 306, 314(8), 426 and 436. Section 283 is a detailed provision whose purpose is to define the composition of the bankrupt's estate for any purposes concerned with the working of the Act. In addition to identifying such items of property as are exempted from the effects of adjudication,[118] the section declares that the bankrupt's estate

[116] See Chapter 1 at 1.2 above, at pp. 10–12.

[117] *Cammell v. Sewell* (1860) 5 H.& N. 728, 157 E.R. 1371; *Nelson v. Bridport* (1846) 8 Beav. 547, 50 E.R. 207; *Luther v. Sagor* [1921] 3 K.B. 532 (CA); *Bank voor Handel en Scheepvaart v. Slatford* [1953] 1 Q.B. 248; *Winkworth v. Christie, Manson and Woods Ltd.* [1980] Ch. 496.

[118] See the Insolvency Act 1986, s.283(2),(3),(3A).

comprises: (a) all property belonging to or vested in the bankrupt at the commencement of the bankruptcy, and (b) any property which by virtue of any of the subsequent provisions in Part IX of the Act is comprised in that estate or is treated as falling within paragraph (a). The full significance of this provision is only apparent when read in conjunction with the definition of 'property' supplied by section 436, which states:

> '**property**' includes money, goods, things in action, land and every description of property *wherever situated* and also obligations and every description of interest, whether present or future or vested or contingent, arising out of, or incidental to, property. (Emphasis added).

The inclusion of the vital phrase 'wherever situated' has the effect of superimposing on the law's scheme of operation the claim to have worldwide application in relation to any property of the debtor, regardless of its actual *situs*. Hence, the universalist aspirations of English bankruptcy law are revealed through the combined effects of sections 283 and 436. Further confirmation of this is supplied by section 314(8), which declares that nothing in the Act is to be construed as restricting the capacity of the trustee in bankruptcy to exercise any of his powers outside England and Wales. The final element of the picture is derived from section 306, which governs the process of transmission of title to the bankrupt's estate to his trustee in a manner that is both instantaneous and automatic. It provides that the bankrupt's estate shall vest in the trustee immediately on his appointment taking effect or, in the case of the official receiver, on his becoming trustee, and it further provides that where any property which is, or is to be, comprised in the bankrupt's estate vests in the trustee it shall so vest without any conveyance, assignment or transfer.

The above provisions of the Insolvency Act 1986, taken together, advance the claim on behalf of English law that any bankruptcy adjudication that is the product of English proceedings has the effect of an automatic assignment to the trustee in bankruptcy of the totality of the debtor's estate, both movable and immovable, on a worldwide basis. Although, as has already been stated, the accepted canons of private international law render it impossible for such an effect to take place extraterritorially as the direct product of the operation of English law, this assertion of universality of effect is by no means an empty or futile gesture. In the first place, it establishes a vital basis for the internal application of remedies and sanctions against the debtor, and also as against any creditors who are personally subject to the jurisdiction of the English court. Such persons may be held accountable for any actions they take affecting property situate abroad.[119] Secondly, it operates as a signal to every foreign legal system where assets may be located, or where parties' interests may come before

[119] See at 2.4 below.

the courts, of the *aspiration* of English bankruptcy law to be accorded universal effect. Thus, it may trigger the processes of recognition and the giving of effect to foreign proceedings that are a part of the private international law of the States concerned. In the absence of a clear indication of the universalist position of English law, it would be open to the foreign system to conclude that any property over which it has control is unaffected by the English bankruptcy proceedings, thus leaving the way open for other parties to take steps locally to assert their claims by any means available under the law of the *situs*.[120] This is the position encountered with respect to the relatively small number of countries, whose number however currently includes Japan, which have chosen to follow a strictly territorial approach to bankruptcy law, so that their adjudications expressly disclaim any effect over the bankrupt's foreign property.[121]

Excepted property: the 'subject to equities' doctrine

Before considering the extent to which English law's universalist ambitions are accorded a positive response by other legal systems, it is as well to take note of the limitations and exceptions to the automatic divesting of the bankrupt's property which are an accepted part of the English law itself. First, as observed above, certain items or categories of property are exempted from forming part of the bankrupt's estate for distribution among creditors.[122] The exemptions are conceded in the interests of according the bankrupt and his family the elements of clothing, bedding, furniture and household equipment and provisions necessary for satisfying their basic domestic needs, and to allow the bankrupt to continue to earn a livelihood by retaining such tools, books, vehicles and other items of equipment as are necessary for use personally by him in his employment, business or vocation. No monetary limit is placed upon the maximum value of the property capable of benefiting from this exemption in any given case, although the qualifying conditions have been carefully drafted with a view to avoiding abuse. It is also possible for the trustee to claim for the estate any item of exempt property whose realisable value happens to be substantial, and for which a reasonable replacement can be substituted at lower cost, so that the surplus value may be made available to the creditors.[123] Secondly, it is one of the fundamental principles of English bankruptcy law that the trustee in bankruptcy takes the

[120] Cf. *Ex parte Melbourn* (1870) L.R. 6 Ch.App. 64, at 69–70, per Mellish L.J. See also *Orient Leasing Ltd. v. The 'Kooei Maru'* (1978) 94 D.L.R. (3d) 658.

[121] For Japan, see Bankruptcy Act, Law No.71, 25 April 1922, Art. 3(1); Makoto Ito in I.F. Fletcher (ed.) *Cross-Border Insolvency, National and Comparative Studies* (1992), (Montreal Congress Reports, 1990), ch. 9, at pp. 180–181. For indications of potential change in the Japanese position, as signalled by trends in recent case law, see J. Matsushita [1997] 6 I.I.R. 210.

[122] Insolvency Act 1986, s.283(2),(3),(3A), see *supra* n.118.

[123] *Ibid.*, s.308.

bankrupt's property 'subject to equities', in the sense that any imperfections in that title, and any valid and subsisting claims arising from the property or any security rights previously effected in relation to it, are transmitted intact so as to be exercisable against the trustee as the new owner.[124] It is essential that the liability or incumbrance must be enforceable against the property itself: any equity which is merely personal in character—in that it is enforceable against the debtor in person—falls outside the ambit of this doctrine.

In an international context, the 'subject to equities' rule retains its significance, but the manner of its application follows the usual principles of private international law concerning the law of property, namely that there must be a reference to the law of the *situs* to discover what claims or charges are recognised as affecting the property to which the trustee claims to have become entitled.[125] A further relevant factor is that the third party's claim or charge over the property must have been perfected prior to the time at which the title of the trustee in bankruptcy first accrued, so that it can be said that, at that time, the bankrupt could not have effected a voluntary assignment in favour of the trustee free of the incumbrance in question. We have seen that section 306 of the Insolvency Act provides for the vesting of the bankrupt's estate in the trustee to take place immediately (and automatically) on his appointment taking effect, which is an event that happens at a time subsequent to the making of the order of adjudication itself, usually following the convening of a general meeting of the bankrupt's creditors. The convening of such a meeting is a task which the official receiver is required to carry out as soon as practicable in the period of twelve weeks from the date of the bankruptcy order.[126] However, if the official receiver concludes that no useful purpose would be served by convening a creditors' meeting, or if a meeting is held but does not proceed to appoint a trustee from the private sector, other statutory provisions are brought into play whose net effect is that the official receiver becomes trustee in the bankruptcy, as will also be the case if any vacancy occurs in the tenure of the office of trustee during the incumbency of a practitioner from the private sector.[127] Thus the precise date on which the bankrupt's estate vests in the trustee by virtue of section 306(1) will vary according to

[124] *Johnson v. Smiley* (1853) 17 Beav. 223; 51 E.R.1019; *Re Mapleback* (1876) 4 Ch.D. 150; *Re Garrud* (1880) 16 Ch.D. 552, at 531 per James L.J.; *Re Beeston* [1899] 1 Q.B. 626, at 630 per Lindley M.R.; *Re Eastgate* [1905] 1 K.B. 465.

[125] *Re Somes* (1896) 3 Mans. 131; *Re Sykes* (1932) 101 L.J.Ch. 298; *Murphy's Trustee v. Aitken* 1983 S.L.T. 78. Cf. the unsatisfactory outcome in *Galbraith v. Grimshaw* [1910] A.C. 508 (HL), criticised at 2.6 below, where the title of a trustee under a Scottish sequestration was held to be relegated, in respect of a debt due to the bankrupt from a creditor in England, to that of a judgment creditor who had garnished the debt before the date when the trustee's title was held to have taken effect.

[126] Insolvency Act 1986, s.293(1).

[127] *Ibid.*, ss.293(2),(3), 294–296, 300.

circumstances, but may possibly not occur until after the elapse of some weeks from the date of the adjudication. This temporal hiatus may give rise to some confusion in cases where third parties invoke the 'subject to equities' rule in respect of an interest which was only perfected during the period following the making of the bankruptcy order. For internal purposes, the rights of such parties are affected by a range of statutory provisions which deprive the bankrupt of the capacity to manage or dispose of his estate with effect from the making of the order against him, by constituting the official receiver as receiver and manager of the estate until such time as it vests in a trustee.[128] This is reinforced by provisions invalidating any disposition of property made by the bankrupt in the period between the presentation of the petition for the bankruptcy order and the date of vesting of his estate in a trustee and, in a case where any judgment creditor was engaged in the process of enforcing his claim by execution or attachment when the bankruptcy commenced, depriving the creditor of the benefit of the enforcement process unless it was completed before the commencement of the bankruptcy.[129] These provisions may be of limited assistance to a trustee who is in the position of asserting title to property whose *situs* lies within the jurisdiction of a foreign court, in competition with claims of other parties. Even where the foreign law is disposed to recognise, in principle, the status of the trustee to claim the property on behalf of the general body of the bankrupt's creditors, it is probable that the formal date of accrual of that title will be treated as marking the operative date against which to measure the claim of any other party to have perfected an interest to which the law of the *situs* accords priority as against that of the trustee. Although it may be open to the trustee to argue that the formal vesting of his title merely completes a process of mandatory divestment of the bankrupt's property that commenced with the making of the bankruptcy order, the absence of any formal statement to that effect within the statutory provisions contained in the current Insolvency Act may prove an obstacle to gaining acceptance for that proposition in a foreign forum.[130] This is a matter to which legislative

[128] *Ibid.*, s.287. See also *ibid.*, s.286 concerning the possibility of an interim receiver being appointed before a bankruptcy order has been made.

[129] *Ibid.*, ss. 284, 285, 346. The date of commencement of bankruptcy is the day on which the bankruptcy order is made: *ibid.*, s.278(a). This has displaced the rule in force prior to 1986 whereby the trustee's title was declared to relate back to the date of commission of the act of bankruptcy on which the receiving order was made which resulted in the adjudication of bankruptcy (see Bankruptcy Act 1914, s.37(1), repealed). Although the doctrine of relation back ceased to be operative in England after the enactment of the Insolvency Act 1986, it remains a feature of the laws of Australia and Canada (see at 2.2.1 below).

[130] There would be a degree of poetic justice about such an outcome, in the light of the approach followed by the House of Lords in its heavily criticised decision in *Galbraith v. Grimshaw* (*supra* n.125), to the detriment of the claim by a Scottish trustee in competition with that of a creditor who obtained attachment in England after the date to which the doctrine of

attention ought to be addressed, since it is a notorious fact that the onset of insolvency proceedings is frequently accompanied by an intensification of the efforts of creditors to safeguard their own interests through pursuit of individual remedies wherever assets of the debtor are known to be located.[131] English courts have themselves recognised that where proceedings in a foreign court result in an *in rem* judgment in favour of the winning party relating to property of the debtor lying within that court's jurisdiction, the effect is to remove that property from the *corpus* of the debtor's available estate, even where the date of the foreign judgment is later than the date of an order of the English court which marks the point of commencement of the debtor's insolvency according to English law.[132]

Effects within the United Kingdom

Although both Scotland and Northern Ireland are separate countries from England and Wales, and from each other, in the special sense of private international law, they are subject to the legislative authority of the United Kingdom Parliament. Consequently, coordinated provisions can be made within the insolvency laws in force in each of these countries, so as to enhance the effects enjoyed by a bankruptcy order made in any part of the United Kingdom for any purpose falling under the jurisdiction of the laws of either of the other parts.This is currently achieved by means of provisions within section 426 of the Insolvency Act 1986, which are extended to Scotland and to Northern Ireland by sections 440(2)(c) and 441(1)(a) respectively. Section 426(1) provides that an order made by a court in any part of the United Kingdom in relation to insolvency law shall be enforced in any other part of the United Kingdom as if it were made by a court exercising the corresponding jurisdiction in that other part.[133] The modern legislation has adopted a more sensitive approach than that formerly found in Bankruptcy Acts down to and including that of 1914, which imperiously sought to extend the proprietary effects of an English bankruptcy to the rest of the United Kingdom with automatic effect.[134] Diplomatically, section 426(2) now emphasises that nothing in subsection (1) requires a court in any part of the United Kingdom to enforce, in relation to property situated in that part, any order made by a court in any other part of the

relation back would have caused the trustee's title to take effect, according to Scots law. (See further at 2.6 below).

131 See the discussion of the potential operation of the European Union Convention on Insolvency Proceedings, in Chapter 6 below.

132 *Minna Craig Steamship Co. v. Chartered Mercantile Bank* [1897] 1 Q.B. 460 (CA) (a case concerning company liquidation).

133 For the meaning of the term 'insolvency law', see the Insolvency Act 1986, s.426(10), as explained by the Court of Appeal in *Hughes v. Hannover Ruckversicherungs-A.G.* [1997] 1 B.C.L.C. 497, discussed in Chapter 4, at 4.1.1 below.

134 *Cf.* Bankruptcy Act 1914, ss. 18, 53 and 167 (repealed).

United Kingdom. Thus, the integrity of the principle of the sovereign authority of the courts of the *situs* of property is maintained even as between the component parts of the United Kingdom itself.[135] However, should the need arise, an office holder may utilise the provision in section 426(4), whereby the courts having jurisdiction in relation to insolvency law in any part of the United Kingdom are subject to the mandatory obligation to assist the courts having the corresponding jurisdiction in any other part of the United Kingdom, or in 'any relevant country or territory'. Normally, cooperation under section 426(4) must be sought on a court-to-court basis, hence obliging the office holder to apply to the court from which his appointment is derived, asking it to request the necessary assistance from the other court. However, section 426(6) enables a person who is a trustee or assignee under the insolvency law of any part of the United Kingdom and who is claiming property situated in any other part to make a direct submission of that claim to the court of the *situs*, whereupon the same obligation to assist arises as in the case of a request made to that court under subsection (4). Further provisions governing the mode of assistance to be given by the court to which the request is made are included in subsection (5), which states that the latter court is authorised to apply, in relation to any matters specified in the request, the insolvency law which is applicable by either the requested court, or the court for the jurisdiction from which the request is made, in relation to comparable matters falling within its jurisdiction. This broadly-framed power of assistance is buttressed by the proviso that in applying its discretion under the subsection 'a court shall have regard in particular to the rules of private international law'. By this rubric, the requested court is reminded that it must adhere to the established principles for resolving issues involving a conflict of laws, so that the ultimate selection of the law to be applied may be made with reference to the law by which any relevant transaction is governed, as well as to the law of the *situs* of the property in question.[136]

Effects outside the United Kingdom

Outside the territorial limits of direct constitutional authority exercisable by the Westminster Parliament, the extent to which an English bankruptcy can produce external effects depends upon the degree to which, and the manner in which, the established principles of private international law

[135] Enabling powers are conferred by s.426(3) of the 1986 Act to allow Ministerial orders to be made for the purpose of securing that a trustee or assignee under the insolvency law of any part of the U.K. has (subject to any necessary modifications) the same rights in relation to property situated in another part of the U.K. as he would have in the corresponding circumstances if he were a trustee or assignee under the insolvency law of that part. To date, no orders have been made pursuant to this provision.

[136] The effects of *ibid.*, s.426(4) and (5) are further considered at 2.6 below, and in Chapter 4, at 4.1 below.

are observed within the legal system of any country in which the issue of recognition and enforcement of the English bankruptcy may arise. Such capacity as is accorded to the trustee to claim property on behalf of the general body of creditors is a matter over which the law of the *situs* retains full control, and cannot be asserted as a matter of right based on the authority of English law alone. Nevertheless it is the case that, partly for reasons of history and partly as a consequence of more modern forces conducive towards international cooperation, there are certain jurisdictions in which an English adjudication is likely to be accorded a more assured reception, and the trustee be more readily assisted in carrying out his allotted tasks, than would be the case elsewhere. Of these, the first group to be noted consists of the Channel Islands and the Isle of Man. These do not form part of the United Kingdom, being constitutionally distinctive in that as self-governing Crown dependencies they enjoy a large degree of internal autonomy while their external relations are the responsibility of the United Kingdom. Reflecting this close relationship, section 426 of the Insolvency Act 1986 is made applicable to the Channel Islands and the Isle of Man by their express inclusion in the definition of 'relevant country or territory' in section 426(11)(a), thereby extending to the courts of those islands the judicial assistance of the courts of all parts of the United Kingdom that is available under subsections (4) and (5) of the section (see above). Reciprocal arrangements have been adopted in the insolvency laws in force in the various islands, so that the assistance of the local courts can be sought in an analogous way by an office holder appointed under the insolvency law in any part of the United Kingdom.[137]

A second, albeit diminishing, constituency of territories in which an English adjudication continues to enjoy virtually automatic effectiveness consists of the overseas colonies and dependent territories over whose internal affairs the United Kingdom continues to exercise sovereign dominion, with the consequence that legislative arrangements are locally maintained to ensure a close coordination between the legal system of each territory and that of the Mother country, including judgments and orders made in the context of insolvency proceedings. This is matched by reciprocal provision to enable courts in the remaining colonies to seek assistance from their counterparts in the United Kingdom, using the procedure under section 426 of the Insolvency Act already mentioned.[138]

[137] See, e.g. Bankruptcy (Désastre) (Jersey) Law 1990, Art. 48, discussed by M. Wilkins [1994] 3 I.I.R. 72 at 76–78. The text of the Jersey law is reproduced at [1994] 3 I.I.R. 183 *et seq.*

[138] See at 2.6 below. The following colonies and dependencies are included in the list of countries and territories designated as 'relevant' for the purposes of s.426 of the 1986 Act, by statutory instrument made under subsection (11)(b): Anguilla, the Bahamas, Bermuda, Cayman Islands, Falkland Islands, Gibraltar, Montserrat, St Helena, Turks and Caicos Islands, and the Virgin Islands (Co-operation of Insolvency Courts (Designation of Relevant Countries and Territories) Order 1986 (S.I. 1986, No. 2123)).

Within these colonies and dependencies, the doctrine of external effectiveness of an English adjudication, as formerly enunciated during the heyday of the British Empire, could still be said to apply with something approximating to its erstwhile force. To that extent at least, cases decided during that era may be cautiously regarded as still expressive of the position obtaining in the remaining British dependent territories.[139]

However, in the far more numerous, and populous, association of former British colonies and dominions which have become fully independent and sovereign countries in their own right, and which now belong to the Commonwealth, an English bankruptcy order, like any other product of the working of our legal system, can no longer claim to produce direct effects within the territory of what are politically and legally autonomous States. Such effects as are accorded to an English bankruptcy adjudication in those countries are the result of the standard processes of private international law whereby one legal system determines to what extent it will recognise and give effect to legal orders and processes originating elsewhere. The legacy of history, and the continuing ties of association, are likely however to prove advantageous in facilitating a more ready and comprehensive response on the part of Commonwealth countries than might be forthcoming in States with no comparable links to this country and its legal tradition. Not only does it remain true in most instances that the insolvency laws of most Commonwealth countries bear a close resemblance to those of England itself (on which they were generally modelled), but it was also one of the usual features of the independence-granting process itself that legislative provisions were left in place that would enable the accrued body of colonial legislation to continue in force until repealed or amended, and as part of that 'dowry' there would usually be provisions that embodied a formal obligation to act in aid of other 'British' courts, and to accord local effect to an English bankruptcy over both movable and immovable property.[140] These residual provisions have in most cases been revised during the years since full independence was gained, and local practice towards the giving of assistance to an English trustee is now far from being a standardised matter. Nevertheless, there are a

[139] See, e.g., *Gill v. Barron* (1868) L.R. 2 P.C. 157 at 175–176 per Kelly L.C.B.; *Ellis v. M'Henry* (1871) L.R. 6 C.P. 228 at 234 *et seq.* per Bovill C.J.; *Callender, Sykes & Co. v. Colonial Secretary of Lagos* [1891] A.C. 460 PC. Contrast *New Zealand Loan and Mercantile Agency Co. Ltd. v. Morrison* [1898] A.C. 349 (PC).

[140] See, e.g. India (Consequential Provisions) Act 1949, s. 1; Republic of the Gambia Act 1970, s.1. For the contrasting responses of the courts in a former Dominion, before and after the gaining of self-government, en route to full independence, see the Canadian cases of *Re Eades Estate* (1917) 33 D.L.R. 335 (with extensive review of authorities at 337–363, per Mathers C.J.); *Re Graham* [1928] 4 D.L.R. 375 at 376 per Taylor J.; but *cf. Re Graham (No. 2)* [1929] 3 D.L.R. 353. As an example of the reciprocal approach to judicial cooperation under modern conditions, see the sentiments voiced by the Court of Session in *Home's Trustee v. Home's Trustees* 1926 S.L.T. 214, 216 per Lord Ashmore.

number of Commonwealth countries where the level of cooperation in legal matters continues to reflect the sustained, special relationship with the United Kingdom, albeit the modern basis for this is reciprocity of assistance founded upon mutual respect between equals. This more satisfactory relationship can become a factor inducing the Secretary of State to exercise the power conferred by section 426(11)(b) of the Insolvency Act so as to designate such a state as a 'relevant country or territory' for the purposes of that section of the Act, as discussed above.[141]

There is one further case of a special relationship with an independent legal system that deserves mention, namely that with the Republic of Ireland. During the period before Irish independence, when all of the island of Ireland formed part of the United Kingdom, bankruptcy legislation specially relating to Ireland was enacted at Westminster in the same manner as continues to occur for Scotland (and, indeed, for Northern Ireland).[142] Under the nineteenth century legislation, an English adjudication enjoyed immediate effect throughout Ireland in relation to both movable and immovable property of the bankrupt, and Irish courts were subject to the obligation to assist other 'British courts' in enforcing this regime as necessary.[143] With the granting of Irish independence in 1921, constitutional provision was made for the continuance in force of the then-existing laws relating to bankruptcy, so that for many years the same effects were produced under the law of the Republic of Ireland as had previously been directly imposed under the *vires* of the Westminster Parliament.[144] A new phase of relationship was commenced with the enactment in Ireland of the Bankruptcy Act 1988, in place of the antiquated legislation from the previous century. Passive fealty to the processes of English law is now a thing of the past, but a close cooperative tradition is sustained under section 142 of the 1988 Act, and the Companies (Amendment) Act 1990, section 36, which

[141] Commonwealth countries designated in this way are: Australia, Botswana, Canada, New Zealand, and Tuvalu (S.I. 1986 No. 2123); and Malaysia and South Africa: S.I. 1996, No. 253. For a survey of legal cooperation within the Commonwealth, relating to the pre-1986 phase, see the Report of a Meeting of Commonwealth Law Ministers at Basseterre, St. Kitts, in April 1978: *Recognition and Enforcement of Judgments and Orders and Service of Process within the Commonwealth* (Published by Commonwealth Secretariat, London, 1978). There is valuable information in Working Paper 12 (by J.D. McClean and K.W. Patchett), attached to the Report: see esp. chs. 5 and 6.

[142] See e.g. Irish Bankrupt and Insolvent Act 1857; Bankruptcy (Ireland) Amendment Act 1872. The legislation currently applicable in Scotland is the Bankruptcy (Scotland) Act 1985. In Northern Ireland the Acts of 1857 and 1872 have been replaced by the Insolvency (Northern Ireland) Order 1989 (S.I. 1989 No. 2045), bringing the law into alignment with that of England and Wales under the Insolvency Act 1986: see Fletcher [1991] 42 N.I.L.Q. 293.

[143] Irish Bankrupt and Insolvent Act 1857, ss.267, 268.

[144] Irish Constitution 1922, Art. 73; Constitution 1937, Art. 50; Bankruptcy (Ireland) Amendment Act 1872, s.71. See *Re Bolton* [1920] 2 I.R. 324; *Re Corballis* [1929] I.R. 266; *Re Bullen* [1930] I.R. 82; *Re Reilly* [1942] I.R. 416; *Re Gibbons* (1960) 26 Ir.Jur. 60; cf. *Re Jackson* [1973] N.Ir. 67.

give the Irish courts and their officers extensive powers to act in aid of their counterparts in the several parts of the United Kingdom, the Channel Islands and the Isle of Man. These powers are discretionary, however, and it must now be understood that the extent to which an English adjudication produces effects over property in the Irish Republic depends upon the operation of the Irish private international law in the context of the instant case. The close correspondence of the Irish and the English systems, including their shared jurisprudence, should ensure that their cooperation in insolvency matters remains particularly effective.[145]

The bankrupt's role in assisting overseas recovery of property

Although under modern conditions there are relatively few parts of the world where an English adjudication can command automatic effect, particularly as against immovable property, the task of the trustee in bankruptcy in establishing control over foreign assets may be rendered somewhat less arduous if the bankrupt can be made to render appropriate assistance. If, for example, the foreign law of the *situs* continues to regard the bankrupt as having full rights of ownership, a formal conveyance of that property by the bankrupt to the trustee for the benefit of his creditors, fully complying with the requirements of the *lex situs*, can accomplish the same goal. For this to be attainable, the bankrupt must remain personally amenable to the jurisdiction of the court of bankruptcy so that its directions can be enforced, if necessary, by appropriate sanctions.[146] Certain provisions in the Insolvency Act 1986 can usefully be brought to bear in this context. Both section 291 and section 312 impose duties upon the bankrupt to facilitate the work of the official receiver and the trustee in bankruptcy respectively by delivering up possession of the property, books, papers or other records to the office holder who for the time being has charge of the case. Section 291(2) further provides that in the case of any part of the bankrupt's estate which consists of things possession of which cannot be delivered, and in the case of any property that may be claimed for the bankrupt's estate by the trustee, it is the bankrupt's duty to do all things as may be reasonably required by the official receiver for the protection of those things or that property.[147] The coercive possibilities are reinforced by section 333(1), which imposes duties on the bankrupt to give the trustee such information as to his affairs, and to do all such other things, as the latter may reasonably require for the purposes of carrying

[145] For the views of Irish writers, see W. Binchy, *Irish Conflicts of Law* (1988), ch. 25, esp. at pp. 471–480; M. Forde, *The Law of Company Insolvency* (1993), pp. 96–97.

[146] *Royal Bank of Scotland v. Cuthbert* (1813) 1 Rose 462; *Re Harris* (1896) 74 L.T. 221; cf. *Re Maudslay, Sons & Field* [1900] 1 Ch. 602.

[147] For punishments to which a bankrupt is subject in the event of non-compliance without reasonable excuse, see the Insolvency Act 1986, ss.291(6),312(4).

out his functions under the Act. Using the powers to which this provision gives rise, the trustee can seek to extract information about the nature and whereabouts of any foreign assets, and then require the bankrupt to execute such legal instruments as may be needed to effect a transfer of the assets in question. Inevitably, it rests in the discretion of the courts of the *situs* to decide whether to recognise the validity of these enforced transactions, particularly where there are competing claims by local parties who have sought to enforce their rights over that same property.[148] Subject to such disturbances, turnover of the property to the trustee in bankruptcy may be attainable.

2.2.2 Selected comparisons

Each of the three systems has embraced the universality doctrine with respect to the effects claimed for its own adjudications. In each case, this is achieved by means of substantially identical provisions implanted into the statutory definition of 'property' for the purposes of the insolvency law in question, the consequence being that an extraterritorial operation is claimed for it. In **Australia**, section 5 of the Bankruptcy Act 1966 defines 'property' as denoting 'real or personal property of every description', and declares it to apply to property 'whether situate in Australia *or elsewhere*' (emphasis added). Likewise in **Canada**, section 67(1) of the Bankruptcy and Insolvency Act 1985 provides that the property of the bankrupt which vests in his trustee by virtue of section 71(2) comprises all present and after-acquired property *wherever situated*,[149] but excluding exempted property and property which had passed out of the ownership of the debtor before the earliest time at which the trustee's title can attach,[150] and also any property which is held in trust for a third party. The general definition of 'property' supplied in section 2 of the Act again includes the phrase 'or elsewhere', indicating that the universalist philosophy is consistently to be applied. The present **United States** Bankruptcy Code differs from the Anglocentric common law systems in that it has abandoned the former process under which there was an automatic vesting of the bankrupt's estate in his trustee. Under the current system, the consequence of adjudication is that all the debtor's property is constituted as the bankruptcy estate. It is then for the debtor to take active steps to claim any permitted exemptions, and for the trustee as representative of the estate to gather and administer it for the benefit of creditors. The vital definition of 'property', for the purpose of determining the contents of the bankruptcy estate, is supplied by section 541(a), and by the inclusion of the words

148 See e.g., *MacDonald v. Georgian Bay Lumber Co.* (1878) 2 S.C.R. 364.
149 Emphasis added.
150 *Broadhead v. Royal Bank of Canada* (1968) 70 D.L.R. (2d) 445 (Ont.).

'wherever located' the universalist ambitions of the Code are clearly affirmed.[151]

All three systems have to come to terms with the fact that the legislative language on which their claim of title to the bankrupt's foreign assets is founded can be but a point of departure as far as the courts of the *situs* are concerned. A trustee who ventures abroad in quest of such property must perforce take the law of the *situs* as he finds it, in terms of its willingness to accommodate the extraterritorial aspirations of the law under which the bankruptcy has been opened. The response can range from a full or partial acceptance of the universality principle, and of the logical consequences that follow from this, to a territorialist position under which no effect is conceded to foreign adjudications. Further barriers to turnover of assets by the foreign court may result from the application of the rules of law of the *situs* regarding the recognition of foreign proceedings, based upon the circumstances under which bankruptcy jurisdiction has been exercised, and the usual possibilities of there being competing proprietary claims to which the *lex situs* accords precedence over that of the trustee.[152]

2.2.3 Non-acceptance of trustee's claim

One problem resulting from the non-acceptance, by the law of the *situs* of movable property, of the title asserted by a trustee appointed in a jurisdiction claiming universal effect concerns the possible future removal of that property into the jurisdiction in which the bankruptcy proceedings were opened. Such an importation might be effected by the party in whose favour the court of the *situs* made its original award when finding against the claim made there by the trustee, or it may be effected by a third party who has subsequently acquired the property in good faith. This presents a dilemma for the courts of the forum of bankruptcy, who must decide whether to allow the trustee to reassert his title, based upon the principles followed by the law of the forum itself, or to uphold the rival principle under which the court of the *situs* is considered to be the competent authority to determine issues concerning title to property and its transmission to other parties. Although modern case authority is lacking in respect of this question, it may perhaps be appropriate to maintain a distinction between the two types of situation envisaged. Where a later disposition has taken place in circumstances where it is accepted that the law

[151] On the background to the insertion of the words 'wherever located' into the Code as enacted in 1978, see Nadelmann (1988), 29 Harv. Int'l Law Jnl. 27; Honsberger (1980), 30 Case Western Res. L. Rev. 631, at 659 *et seq*

[152] These approaches are examined in ch. 1 above. See also the discussion at 2.6 below. For a somewhat broader comparative survey of international recognition of insolvency proceedings, see Fletcher in I.F. Fletcher (ed.), *Cross-Border Insolvency: National and Comparative Studies* (1992), Part II, at pp. 284–289.

of the *situs* at the time in question is capable of overriding any previous claims to the property, it is submitted that this widely respected principle should be adhered to.[153] Where however the property remains in the hands of the party who succeeded in the foreign court in repelling the trustee's assertion of title, the requirements of public policy at the place of bankruptcy would seem to require the courts there to overreach the determination of the foreign court, and to re-assert that title which, according to the bankruptcy law of the forum to which the property has now travelled, either vested in the trustee, or was to be claimed by him on behalf of the creditors proving in the bankruptcy.[154]

2.3 CHOICE OF LAW

2.3.1 Generally

Procedural questions

For more than one hundred years, English courts have considered it to be axiomatic that English law, as *lex fori*, governs the process of administration and distribution of an insolvent debtor's estate under a bankruptcy adjudication pronounced in England.[155] While there are grounds for accepting the validity of the proposition as just stated, it is necessary to exercise a degree of caution when progressing from a contemplation of the distributional process, in the strict sense, to wider questions of the law to which reference should be made in the course of resolving numerous incidental matters that arise for determination during the course of collection and realisation of the bankrupt's property, and the investigation of all possible species of claims against and on behalf of the estate. It is certainly the case that the bankruptcy process embodies many rules that can properly be classified as procedural, and so fall within the orthodox principle of private international law that matters of procedure are governed by the *lex fori*.[156] These issues are encountered at all stages, from the taking of steps to commence bankruptcy proceedings by presentation of a petition, to the ensuing phases of hearings, meetings, processing of claims, and declaration and payment of dividends to creditors. The control exerted by the *lex fori* over the distributional process embraces such vital issues as the types of claim which qualify as provable debts, to the ranking of different types

[153] Cf. *Winkworth v. Christie, Manson & Woods Ltd.* [1980] Ch. 496; *Cammell v. Sewell* (1860) 5 H.& N.728; 157 E.R. 1381.

[154] So argued by Sykes and Pryles, *supra* n. 93, at p. 789.

[155] *Pardo v. Bingham* (1868) L.R. 6 Eq. 485; *Thurburn v. Steward* (1871) L.R. 3 P.C. 478 (PC); *Re Kloebe* (1884) 28 Ch.D. 175.

[156] *Thurburn v. Steward, supra* n.155, at p. 513 per Lord Cairns; *Re Doetsch* [1896] 2 Ch. 836.

of debt in terms of priority of payment. By parity of reasoning, English law regards any question of priority among creditors claiming in a foreign insolvency proceeding to be a matter for determination by the foreign *lex fori*. However, this rationale also enables an English court, in English proceedings, to disregard any purely procedural impediment, or different ranking in the hierarchy of priorities, to which a foreign creditor might be subject under the bankruptcy law of the country to which he or she belongs, or under whose law the claim originally arose. Once the validity of the substantive claim itself is confirmed, the different mode of treatment to which it would be subjected under the bankruptcy process of the foreign system are of no relevance when England is the forum of bankruptcy.[157]

Questions of substantive law

There are a number of situations in which the interests of parties whose debtor is undergoing bankruptcy proceedings can be materially affected by the outcome of a choice of law process which the law of the *forum concursus* will necessarily have to carry out. These include: the question of the avoidance law to be applied in relation to antecedent transactions entered into with the debtor; the effect of the insolvency proceedings upon current contracts to which the debtor is a party and the validity of any claims arising out of such contracts; the impact upon any type of security, or quasi-security, arrangement of which the creditor seeks to avail himself; and the availability of any right of set-off in the case of any creditor who is also a debtor to the bankrupt's estate. In addition to all procedural issues being governed by English law, many substantive issues are also dominated by the English bankruptcy law as *lex fori*. This is in large measure due to the fact that most of the relevant provisions of the English legislation are drafted in terms which make no mention of any territorial limitations in relation to their intended scope, so that they can be read as applying to all situations, and as against all parties involved, regardless of any ties to other jurisdictions and their laws.[158] A further, most important factor militating in favour of the sustained application of English law is the judicial conviction that insolvency law embodies a number of fundamental values which the courts have a solemn duty to defend, both in a purely internal context and also in a situation where the influx of international elements raises the possibility that a foreign substantive law may be considered to govern parties' rights and expectations. Under testing circumstances of this kind, a court sitting as the forum faces powerful temptation

[157] *Ex parte Melbourn* (1870) L.R. 6 Ch.App. 64, at 67–70 per Mellish L.J.

[158] Almost the only exception is found in the Insolvency Act 1986, s.426(5) (discussed at 2.2 above and 2.6 below), requiring the court to have regard to the rules of private international law.

to invoke public policy as a ground for preferring the rule belonging to its domestic system of law over any claim by a foreign system to regulate the outcome. This has proved to be true of English courts, with results that are not always readily defensible, although it must be conceded that on some occasions the courts have gone to considerable lengths to ensure that the law is applied in a non-discriminatory way as between domestic and foreign creditors. The foregoing themes will now be considered in more specific terms.

English courts seldom engage in open discussion of choice of law issues when giving judgment in cases falling within the ambit of the insolvency legislation. The awareness that they are administering what amounts to a statutory code has seemingly fuelled a judicial resolve to ensure that the wishes of Parliament are respected when issues are encountered in which a foreign law connection is present. Thus, fidelity to the *pari passu* principle, combined with a scrupulously even-handed approach to creditors irrespective of their nationality or domicile, is seen as one of the cornerstones of insolvency law. In *Re Wiskemann*,[159] the custodian of enemy property released a fund to which the bankrupt, a German national resident in England, was entitled. The terms of the release were expressly limited to allow the funds to be available only to creditors of British nationality. Although there were no German creditors, there were other foreign creditors who sought to prove in the bankruptcy, and P. O. Lawrence J. took the view that the distribution of funds under the provisions of the Bankruptcy Act 1914 was required to operate in favour of all creditors generally, without restriction. Accordingly, he directed the trustee to admit the foreign creditors to proof. Although the ruling undoubtedly involved a defiant refusal to implement the directive of a governmental agency, it can be noted that it was once again the procedural aspects of English law that were held to be applicable with mandatory and invariable effect. Moreover, there was no external system of law with which the English rules governing the distribution of property could be said to be in open conflict.

A less happy example of a case where public policy and Parliamentary resolve were invoked as the reason for superimposing the English law rule at the expense of a competing, and fundamentally different, foreign system of law was the more recent decision in *Re Bank of Credit and Commerce International SA (No. 10)*.[160] This was a case of company liquidation, in which the English proceedings were ancillary to main proceedings based in Luxembourg, which was the state of incorporation. A judicially sanctioned agreement had authorised the transmission to Luxembourg of funds collected elsewhere, for *pari passu* distribution on a worldwide basis

[159] (1923) 92 L.J.Ch. 349. [160] [1996] 4 All E.R. 796.

according to Luxembourg law. The question raised before Scott V.-C. was whether in so transmitting assets which had been collected in England the English liquidators were required to give mandatory effect to the English doctrine of set-off, whose effects would be far more favourable to creditors than would the more narrowly formulated doctrine of set-off under Luxembourg law. Basing his argument on the proposition that the doctrine of set-off constitutes one of the fundamentals of insolvency law, and that the terms of its application are a matter of public policy for the purposes of the English and Luxembourg systems respectively, the Vice-Chancellor concluded that an English court had no power to disapply the statutory scheme of insolvency enacted by Parliament, and consequently the impact of the English doctrine should be allowed for by the liquidators before transmitting funds to their Luxembourg counterparts.[161] With respect, it is deeply disappointing that the peremptory argument based on public policy was invoked, even in the still-evolving area of ancillary liquidations, instead of there being any attempt to develop a more internationalist approach to the problem, drawing on established choice of law techniques.

Choice of avoidance law

The drafting techniques favoured by those responsible for framing the English legislation affecting insolvency matters also contribute to the operational bias in favour of the application of the *lex fori*. Unqualified expressions such as 'any person' and 'any property' occur regularly throughout the 1986 Act, leaving the way open for a judicial ruling that the provision is in principle applicable to persons, to property, and to transactions entered into, regardless of the physical whereabouts of the persons or property at the relevant time, or of the legal context in which these were then placed.[162] Although it may be possible argue from expediency that such open-ended provisions can be invaluable when dealing with parties' attempts to exploit the possibilities offered by the ease and speed with which assets—particularly intangibles—can be moved between countries, the potential for the courts themselves to transgress the accepted canons of territorial application of laws is immediately obvious. It is therefore somewhat reassuring to note that the Court of Appeal showed themselves to be keenly aware of the need for courts to exercise self-restraint, when considering the question whether it was permissible to exercise jurisdiction over a non-resident person alleged to have been party to a transaction at an undervalue entered into by a company that was subsequently the

[161] *Ibid.*, at 811–813, and 821–822. For criticism of the decision, see Fletcher [1997] J.B.L. 471; Shandro [1998] 7 I.I.R. 63.

[162] See, e.g. Insolvency Act 1986, ss. 339(1) ('a transaction with any person at an undervalue'); 340(1) ('a preference [given] to any person'); 284(1) ('any disposition of property'). Note also the extraterritorial capabilities imparted by the words 'wherever situated' in the definition of 'property' in *ibid.*, s.436, discussed at 2.2 above.

subject of insolvency proceedings in England. In *Re Paramount Airways Ltd.*,[163] the phrase 'any person', as used in section 238(2) of the Insolvency Act in relation to transactions entered into by a company,[164] is not subject to any implied limitation as to its territorial effect and therefore applies to any person wherever resident. However, Nicholls V.-C. in delivering the judgment of the court went on to emphasise that it rests with the discretion of the court whether to exercise the jurisdiction thereby conferred, and that if a foreign element is involved the court will need to be satisfied that the defendant is sufficiently connected with England for it to be just and proper to make an order against him with a view to restoring the position for the benefit of the creditors.[165] Among the factors mentioned as relevant to the court's determination when exercising its discretion are 'the nature and purpose of the transaction being impugned, the nature and locality of the property involved, the circumstances in which the defendant became involved in the transaction . . . *and whether under any relevant foreign law the defendant acquired an unimpeachable title free from any claims even if the insolvent had been adjudged bankrupt or wound up locally*' (emphasis added).[166] Thus, although the Court of Appeal was not at that stage required to address the issue of choice of law in relation to the avoidance of the transaction itself, a clear indication was given that the effect of a relevant foreign law in conferring a protected title on the defendant may have to be recognised by English law.

The subject of what approach might be taken in selecting the avoidance rule to govern in a case with cross-border dimensions was left unexplored in the *Paramount* judgment, but will here be examined. In most instances, due to the sparsity of case authority, the English solution is presently a matter of some conjecture. The subject is not without practical importance, because in a case where a choice falls to be made between the application of the English avoidance rule and that of some other country with which the parties or the transaction were closely linked at the relevant time, the ultimate selection of the system whose rule will be applied can occasionally be vital to the final outcome, on account of the different formulations of the substantive rules.[167] There is no reported decision in which an

163 [1992] 3 All E.R. 1 (CA), revsg. [1992] Ch. 160.

164 Insolvency Act 1986, s.238(2) is for all essential purposes identical to *ibid.*, s.339(1), which applies to transactions previously entered into by a bankrupt individual.

165 [1992] 3 All E.R. 1, at 11–12.

166 *Ibid.*

167 For example, English law on avoidance of preferences requires that it be established that the debtor was influenced by the desire to prefer the creditor (Insolvency Act 1986, ss.239(5) (companies); 340(4) (bankrupts)); Australian law allows some transactions to be avoided where the actual effect is to prefer a creditor, without reference to the debtor's intention (Bankruptcy Act 1966, s.122; Corporations Law, s.588FA). For some comparisons of the avoidance rules of English, Canadian and American law, see chapters by Fletcher, Shanker and McLaren in J.S. Ziegel (ed.), *Current Developments in International and Comparative Corporate Insolvency Law* (1994), chs. 12, 13 and 14.

English court has laid down a choice of law rule for this purpose, although the assumption seems to have become prevalent that the English court will somehow contrive to apply the English avoidance rule whenever an attack is launched on an antecedent transaction during the course of English bankruptcy proceedings. Such seems to have been the expectation of the administrators of Maxwell Communication Corporation (M.C.C.), when they sought to utilise the courts of New York for the purpose of attacking certain payments to major creditors of the company made shortly before insolvency proceedings commenced. Although allowed by the English courts to pursue their application in New York, the administrators were unsuccessful in persuading the bankruptcy court there to accept jurisdiction.[168] The hypothesis that a court will ultimately apply the avoidance rule of the *lex fori* was therefore unconfirmed by the outcome of the proceedings, although the American courts did display a readiness to explore that issue as an important aspect of their assessment of whether to accept jurisdiction. Their preferred approach was to select the avoidance rule according to established choice of law principles evolved within the American conflict of laws tradition, and embodied in the 'significant contacts' approach of the Second Restatement. This entails taking into account a range of related factors including the place where the debtor's business is primarily conducted, where the debtor's 'nerve centre', assets and creditors are located, as well as the circumstances surrounding the transactions themselves. Although uncertainty of outcome is one of the principal disadvantages of this 'contact evaluation' rule, it has the merit of being capable of defeating parties' attempts to structure transactions in a way that may influence the outcome in terms of the avoidance law that may potentially be applied.[169]

Although it is submitted that an English court faced with a material question of which choice of law rule to apply might well aspire to emulate the approach foreshadowed by the American courts in the *M.C.C.* case, there is only limited scope for it to do so, in view of the way the existing

[168] See *Re Maxwell Communications Corporation plc (No. 2), Barclays Bank plc v. Homan* [1992] B.C.C. 757 (per Hoffmann J.) and 767 (CA); *Re Maxwell Communication Corporation plc* 170 BR 800, 801–807 (Bankr SDNY 1994), (Judge Brozman), aff'd 186 BR 807, 812–815 (SDNY 1995) (Scheindlin, USDJ), aff'd 593 F3d 1036 (2nd Cir 1996) (Cardamone, Circuit Judge).

[169] In favouring the traditional choice of law method, the American courts in the *Maxwell* case declined to adopt the special rule proposed by the court-appointed *amicus curiae*, Professor Westbrook, who recommended a choice of law rule in the avoidance area based upon the state of incorporation of the debtor company—the so-called 'home country' rule as offering simplicity and predictability of outcome, giving parties the opportunity to plan their business affairs with greater certainty: Amicus Brief at p. 16; Westbrook, 65 Am. Bankr. L.J. 475, 464–466 (1991); the same author, 17 Brook. J. Int. L. 499 (1991). Applied to the facts of the M.C.C. case itself, the 'home country' rule would have led to the application of the English avoidance rule. The solution preferred by the American courts would have reached the same conclusion, albeit for different reasons. Under other circumstances, of course, the two approaches could result in the selection of different countries' avoidance rules.

provisions of the Insolvency Act are drafted. Promisingly, both section 339(2) and section 340(2) empower the court to make 'such order as it thinks fit for restoring the position to what it would have been [if the transaction had not been entered into, or the preference had not been given]', which might suggest that the court could elect to exercise its discretion based upon the notional effects of applying the avoidance rule of the system with which the most significant contacts are found to exist. However, the logical difficulty arises that the court is inevitably subject to the further provisions within either section 339 or 340 (as the case may be), so that it is not easy to see how the substantive application of the avoidance rules within those sections can be disregarded. Realistically, the only reason why an office holder would wish to invoke a foreign avoidance rule before an English court would be that the foreign rule provides a stronger prospect of overturning the transaction than does the equivalent rule of English law. For an English court to purport to apply such a rule, under the pretext of disposing of an application brought under either section 339 or 340 (particularly the latter), would pose serious problems in terms of compliance with the surrounding provisions of the section under which the order of the court was made.[170] It would require a particularly bold act of judicial innovation to accede to a submission by a trustee in bankruptcy that, as a result of applying choice of law analysis to the circumstances surrounding a particular transaction, the avoidance rule of another country should be grafted on to the process of adjustment being conducted in the context of an English bankruptcy. Unless the value of the potential recovery for the benefit of creditors happens to be exceptionally large, it is unlikely that any office holder will see fit to incur the costs of pursuing such an argument beyond a court of first instance.

Contracts to which the bankrupt is party

The onset of bankruptcy has a variety of consequences with respect to any contracts to which the bankrupt is a party. These include the question whether bankruptcy can have the effect of releasing the parties from their contracts, and any further consequences that ensue from this. In principle, this is a matter to be referred to the governing law of the contract itself, together with any express provisions the parties happen to have included in their agreement. A further possibility may arise if it transpires that, under the foreign law by which the contract is governed, there are provi-

[170] For example, the forthright terms of s.340(4) of the 1986 Act (matched, in relation to company insolvency, by those of s.239(5)) appear to deprive the English court of the power to make an order in respect of a preference unless the requisite mental intention on the part of the debtor can be established. This would nullify the advantage sought by the office holder in invoking a foreign avoidance law which employs no such test of intention (see *supra* n.167).

sions capable of yielding some benefit for the creditors that might not be forthcoming under the rules of English law.[171] A further occasion for investigating the governing law of the contract is where it is necessary to determine the validity or amount of any claim, whether against or on behalf of the bankrupt's estate, and where the answer is at least partly dependent upon the system of law to be applied. For such purposes, an English court will determine the governing law by applying the Rome Convention on the Law Applicable to Contractual Obligations.[172] The special problem of the discharge of contractual obligations as a consequence of bankruptcy is separately considered at 2.5 and 2.7 below. For the present, we may note that in the event of any divergence between the effects generated by the governing law of the contract and those imposed by the law of bankruptcy itself, the latter will invariably prevail for the purpose of any proceedings over which the courts of the *forum concursus* have jurisdiction. Thus, the rights of a trustee in bankruptcy to disclaim onerous property (which expressly includes any onerous contract) under section 315 of the Insolvency Act, and the converse facility created by section 345 to enable a non-bankrupt party to a contract to apply to the court for an order discharging obligations thereunder in consequence of the other party's bankruptcy, can be invoked even though this may be at odds with the provisions of the governing law.[173]

Secured creditors' rights

The principal reason for effecting one of the recognised forms of security is that in the event of non-payment by the debtor—and particularly where the debtor is insolvent—the creditor is allowed to have recourse to the security in order to satisfy all or part of his claim against the debtor, instead of being restricted to lodging proof in the insolvency proceedings. In order to achieve this objective, the security must be recognised by the *lex concursus* as having the characteristic of retaining its enforceability in the event of the bankruptcy of the debtor. Where any creditor invokes some type of security in the context of an international insolvency case it may be necessary to refer to provisions of foreign law to establish the validity of the security, and also to determine some questions of priority. Security rights may be created in respect of both tangible and intangible

171 Cf. *Re Suse* (1887) 18 Q.B.D. 660 (CA), where it was held that the contract in question was not governed by the law of New York, whose statutory provisions appeared to confer an advantage from the creditors' point of view.

172 In force throughout the United Kingdom with effect from 1 April 1991, by virtue of the Contracts (Applicable Law) Act 1990. See *Dicey and Morris, The Conflict of Laws*, 12th edn. (1993), chs. 32, 33.

173 For a thorough and masterly examination of the treatment of executory contracts in bankruptcy, written from the perspective of American law, see Westbrook (1989) *74 Minn. L. Rev. 227*.

property, and can relate to both existing and future assets belonging to the debtor. Some species of real security, such as a lien or a pledge, involve the actual transfer of possession to the creditor, while others, such as the modern mortgage and various varieties of charge, allow the debtor to retain possession, control, and in some instances even the right to use and dispose of the asset in an unrestricted manner. To balance the extensive freedom and flexibility which are vital features of many types of security, special requirements of registration and notification may be prescribed by the controlling legislation.[174]

To determine the validity and effects of any transaction intended to give rise to some form of real security, English private international law takes as its starting point the law of the *situs* of the property at the time of the relevant events. Further reference may have to be made to the law governing any agreement between the parties to the creation of the security, where this is different from the *situs* of the property to be comprised in it. Once it can be confirmed that a valid and duly perfected security has been created according to the law of the place where the property was then located, it may be necessary (in the case of security over movables) to refer to the law of any country to which the property has subsequently been moved, to establish whether any events have occurred which have the effect of cancelling or overreaching the security interest, or of altering the relative priorities as between different parties claiming an interest in the same property, according to the law of the new *situs*.[175] Finally, the rules of English insolvency law, notably those concerned with the avoidance of prior transactions, may be brought into play. Although these appear capable of operating with an overarching effect, we have already noted that the Court of Appeal in the *Paramount* case foresaw the possibility that in some circumstances it could be inappropriate for an English court to seek to assert its power of avoidance.[176] This would be especially the case where the defendant had no personal links with this country, and could legitimately claim that the transaction was unimpeachable according to the law of the country where the interest was created.

Set-off

The current provision embodying the doctrine of set-off as applicable to bankruptcy is section 323 of the Insolvency Act 1986. Set-off in corporate insolvency is made the subject of a separate provision in Rule 4.90 of the

[174] The commercial aspects of different types of security device are discussed in R.M. Goode, *Legal Problems of Credit and Security*, 2nd edn. (1988), esp. in chs. 1,2 and 5. See also the same author's *Commercial Law*, 2nd edn. (1995), Parts 4 and 5.

[175] See e.g. *Cammell v. Sewell* (1860) 5 H. & N. 728; 157 E.R. 1371; *Winkworth v. Christie, Manson & Woods Ltd.* [1980] Ch. 496.

[176] *Re Paramount Airways Ltd.* [1992] 3 All E.R. 1 (CA), discussed *supra* n.163 *et seq.*

Insolvency Rules 1986. The two provisions are actually identical in terms of their substance, and it is therefore possible to refer to cases decided under either of them when assembling an overall view of the law and its working. As a matter of public policy the application of set-off in accordance with the enacted provisions is a mandatory requirement from which it is not possible for parties to exclude themselves by means of any contract or agreement.[177] As we have already seen, the High Court has gone so far as to assert that it is not open to the court itself to disapply the rules governing set-off, even in a case where the English insolvency proceedings are of an ancillary nature and are intended to function in collaboration with a foreign, main proceeding.[178] According to the terms in which the English doctrine is formulated, where before the commencement of the insolvency there have been mutual credits, mutual debts, or other mutual dealings between the insolvent debtor and any creditor proving or claiming to prove for a debt in the proceedings, an automatic, self-executing set-off takes place by operation of law. The consequence is that, as of the date of commencement of bankruptcy, or the date on which the company went into liquidation (as the case may be), only the net balance is owing to whichever of the parties had the larger claim. Under English law, mutuality results from the fact that parties have dealt with each other in identical capacities: it is not a requirement (as under some other systems of law) that the liabilities should actually arise from one and the same contract.

The English doctrine of set-off is highly advantageous from the standpoint of those creditors who are eligible to benefit from its operation. In effect, they are put into the position of secured creditors to the extent of the value of the debt which they owe to the insolvent estate, while remaining entitled to receive dividend on any balance of their claim *pari passu* with the other creditors whose claims rank alongside their own in terms of priority. Under these favourable circumstances, it is highly unlikely that any creditor would wish to urge an English court to disapply its own rule of set-off in favour of some alternative, foreign rule to be determined by means of a choice of law process of some kind. Indeed, it is possible to envisage some creditors seeking to enhance their prospects by taking any available steps to ensure that their debtor's bankruptcy is based in England, rather than in another possible forum where they would not enjoy the same rights of set-off. Since the net effect of set-off on the process of distribution is that some individuals experience an improved rate of recovery on their debts due from the bankrupt, at the inevitable expense

[177] *National Westminster Bank Ltd. v. Halesowen Presswork and Assemblies Ltd.* [1972] A.C. 785 (HL); *Stein v. Blake* [1996] A.C. 243 (HL).

[178] *Re Bank of Credit and Commerce International SA (No. 10)* [1996] 4 All E.R. 796, discussed *supra* n.160 *et seq.*

of a diminished return for all other, unsecured creditors, there is a case for introducing a more discriminating approach to the operation of the doctrine in cross-border insolvencies, where parties' mutual dealings may have taken place in the context of a very different set of assumptions as to the consequences of insolvency. It is submitted that, where the international nature of the parties' dealings with each other has resulted in their contracts being governed by different substantive laws, set-off should normally be available, in the event of the insolvency of either of the parties, only if a substantially similar doctrine of set-off operates within each of the systems concerned. Failing that, it would be incumbent upon the creditor to show cause why he should nonetheless be allowed to have the benefit of set-off, as having formed part of his legitimate expectations in the course of his dealings with the debtor. It must be conceded however that the prospects for such a development in English private international law seem negligible under current circumstances.[179]

2.3.2 Selected comparisons

Both Australian and Canadian law adopt the same stance as English law in affirming that all questions of the administration and distribution of the bankrupt's estate, including the question of priorities of debts, are for determination in accordance with the law of the *forum*.[180] With regard to matters of substantive law, the Canadian approach is particularly forceful in pressing the role of the *lex fori* in this area also, whereas the Australian writers incline to a more cautious view in the absence of any settled case law concerned with specific issues.[181] Under both systems however it is recognised that such matters as the validity of a debt may require reference to the proper law of the contract under which it has arisen, and that the role of the *lex situs* must likewise be respected in matters relating to property situated abroad.

In the USA the subject of applicable law in bankruptcy matters has long been a live and contentious one, due to the perpetual contest between the realms of State versus Federal law. Although the Bankruptcy Code is a Federal statute, and the bankruptcy courts are a nationwide network of the Federal judiciary, the interplay of State laws, with their inherent variability, is unavoidable in view of the need for the bankruptcy court to

[179] The modifications to the choice of law rules relating to set-off that would become applicable under Articles 4(2)(d) and 6 of the E.U. Convention on Insolvency Proceedings are discussed in Chapter 6 below.

[180] Both systems draw upon the basic authorities provided by the English decisions, cited at 2.3.1 above. See also *Re Sefel Geophysical Ltd.* (1989) 54 D.L.R. (4th) 117 (Alta).

[181] For Canada, see McLeod, *supra* n.101, at p. 440, citing *inter alia*, *Ross v. Necker* [1948] 4 D.L.R. 401; *Orient Leasing Ltd. v. The 'Kosei Maru'* (1978) 94 D.L.R. (3d) 658. For Australia, see Sykes and Pryles, *supra* n.93, at pp. 789–790.

determine civil matters related to the bankruptcy, such as contract or tort claims relating to the bankruptcy estate. The Supreme Court, while affirming the basic principle that State law prevails unless displaced by a Federal rule for reasons of Federal law or policy, has observed that the Bankruptcy Code constitutes precisely such a displacing enactment, and can be uniformly applied in all geographical locations in accordance with its own inbuilt provisions.[182] Even so, the terms of the Code itself may invite or require an onward reference to the provisions of some aspect of State law, for example with regard to exempted property retainable by the bankrupt.[183] In such matters as the avoidance of prior transactions, there can also be an inbuilt requirement that the bankruptcy court engage in a choice of law process. Thus, section 544(b) of the Code empowers the trustee to avoid 'any transfer of an interest of the debtor in property or any obligation incurred by the debtor that is *voidable under applicable law* by a creditor holding an unsecured claim' (emphasis added). This provision readily lends itself to the development of principled theories regarding the choice of the avoidance law that is applicable under given circumstances, a process which, as we have seen, is greatly impeded under English law due to the enclosed structure of the avoidance provisions in the insolvency legislation.[184]

2.4 CREDITORS AND CLAIMS IN AN ENGLISH BANKRUPTCY

We have seen that English insolvency law has a long-standing commitment to the principle of universality, and to the closely associated principle of collectivity as expressed in the maxim *par est condicio omnium creditorum*. The treatment of creditors and their claims is fully consistent with both of these principles. All creditors are allowed to lodge proof of claim, and a single process of classification and distribution takes place without any distinction as between domestic and foreign creditors, or as between debts governed by English law and those governed by some foreign law. The notion of equality of treatment of all creditors is pursued to its logical conclusion, namely that foreign creditors are entitled to receive dividends *pari passu* with English creditors whose debts qualify for inclusion within the same class, according to the rules of priority of distribution

[182] *Vanston Bondholders Protective Committee v. Green*, 329 U.S. 156, 91 L.Ed.162 (1946), reh.dnd. 329 U.S. 833, 91 L.Ed. 706 (1947).

[183] B.C., ss.522(b), 541(b). The homestead exemption laws are a striking example of the variability of State laws affecting the bankrupt's election between (local) State and Federal exemption lists. See Countryman (1972) 47 N.Y.U.L.Rev. 407, 631.

[184] See at 2.3 above, *Choice of avoidance law*.

maintained by English law.[185] It is important to observe that the classification of claims, and their allocation to a particular category of priority under the scheme of distribution, will be performed in accordance with the English approach. It does not follow therefore that a foreign claim will be accorded identical priority to that which it would enjoy under the insolvency law of the country to which the creditor belongs, or by whose law the claim itself happens to be governed.[186]

Foreign penal or revenue claims

An important exception to the above statement regarding the treatment of claims lodged by foreign creditors arises as a result of an established rule of English private international law relating to penal or revenue claims asserted by the public authorities of a foreign state. As a matter of public policy that is widely accepted by legal systems across the world, the courts of one country will refuse to enforce the penal or revenue laws of another, either directly or indirectly.[187] The principal basis for this exclusionary rule is that the imposition of criminal penalties, and the levying of taxation, are two of the principal manifestations of the sovereign authority vested in the state, and hence it is unacceptable (in the absence of some international treaty or agreement) that one sovereign state should serve as the agent for enforcement or collection of the impositions of another.[188] A potential modification of the operation of this rule in relation to the tax claims of the other Member States of the European Union could come about as a consequence of the implementation of the EU Convention on Insolvency Proceedings, discussed in Chapter 6.[189]

Restraining creditors' actions abroad

Although an English adjudication is of worldwide effect in the eyes of English law, the reality is, as we have seen, that the degree of recognition

[185] *Re Kloebe* (1884) 28 Ch. D. 175; *Re Wiskemann*(1923) 92 L.J.Ch. 349; *Re Azoff-Don Commercial Bank* [1954] 1 Ch. 315. For a survey of the ways in which the insolvency laws of some countries discriminate against foreign creditors, see Nadelmann (1946) 11 Law and Contemp. Prob. 696. For a detailed account of the past and current practice in Argentina, see Dobson in I.F. Fletcher (ed.), *Cross-Border Insolvency: Comparative Dimensions (The Aberystwyth Insolvency Papers)* (1990), ch. 7, at pp. 124–131.

[186] For an account of the English law's treatment of the process of distribution in bankruptcy, see I.F. Fletcher, *The Law of Insolvency*, 2nd edn. (1996), ch. 10.

[187] *Huntington v. Attrill* [1893] A.C. 150 (PC); *Government of India v. Taylor* [1955] A.C. 491 (HL); *Schemmer v. Property Resources Ltd.* [1974] 3 All E.R. 451; see also *Peter Buchanan Ltd. v. McVey* [1954] I.R. 89; *Re Gibbons* (1960) 26 Ir. Jur. 60. An Australian probate case, *Bath v. British and Malayan Trustees Ltd.* (1969) 90 W.N. (NSW) 44 offers a remarkable demonstration of the imaginative use of judicial discretion so as to deprive foreign tax authorities of the chance to 'capture' assets from those initially claiming them before the court.

[188] For a full account of the subject of exclusion of foreign law, see *Dicey and Morris, supra* n.9, ch. 6. The topic of non-enforcement of foreign penal or revenue laws is there dealt with in Rule 3, at p. 97 *et seq.*

[189] See Art. 39 of the EU Convention, considered below at p. 295.

and effectiveness enjoyed beyond the confines of the United Kingdom is in almost every instance dependent on the attitude of the foreign legal systems concerned. The possibility that some foreign systems may refuse to recognise or cooperate with the English trustee in bankruptcy, and the additional problems confronting the trustee in trying to locate and defend foreign assets, can give rise to opportunities for some creditors to take advantage of remedies which are more readily open to them under the law of the *situs* and thereby effect individual recovery of property in complete or partial satisfaction of their outstanding claims. Since such acts of individual diligence contravene the principle of collectivity, it is natural that English law should try to respond in whatever way it can with a view to preventing these actions from taking place, or at least nullifying the benefits gained thereby. However, it must be accepted that there are practical limits to the ability of the English court to enforce its own regime extraterritorially.

English courts have since the nineteenth century been prepared to employ the equitable remedy of injunction to restrain a creditor from taking proceedings abroad to enforce a debt which is owed by a debtor currently the subject of insolvency proceedings in this country.[190] This remedy, which in more recent times has become known as an 'anti-suit injunction', is made available only where the court in its absolute discretion deems it appropriate. Since its effectiveness is dependent on the court's ability to impose the sanction of punishment for contempt in the event of non-compliance by the party enjoined, no injunction will in practice be forthcoming where the defendant is not personally amenable to the *in personam* jurisdiction of the English court. This is a further instance of the application of the maxim that 'Equity does nothing in vain'. Jurisdiction sufficient for this purpose may be based on the fact that the defendant is resident or does business here, or is personally present under circumstances that can enable his subsequent physical movement to be made the subject of effective control. Alternatively, a creditor may voluntarily subject himself to the court's jurisdiction through the taking of action which places him within the ambit of the legal process, as where he lodges proof in the bankruptcy, or joins in the presentation of the petition or becomes party to an arrangement with creditors concluded by the debtor.[191] Where however the creditor lacks any residential or other sufficient ties with this country, the futility of the court issuing an injunction which it is powerless to enforce by sanction will result in a refusal of the

190 *Re Distin, ex parte Ormiston* (1871) 24 L.T. 197. Cf. the Scottish case of *Lindsay v. Paterson* (1840) 2 D. 1373.

191 *Re Tait & Co.* (1872) L.R. 13 Eq. 311; *Re Morton* (1875) L.R. 20 Eq. 733, esp at 738 per Bacon C.J.; see also *Ord v. Barton* (1847) 9 D. 541.

application.[192] So, too, if there are other factors relating to the foreign proceedings that call for the exercise of sensitive judgement based on wider considerations of international comity. For example, if it can be shown that the foreign court would have a legitimate reason to exercise jurisdiction if it elected to do so, and if furthermore there are good grounds for supposing that it can be relied upon to exercise that jurisdiction in a fair and balanced way that will not subvert the ultimate objective of an equitable distribution of the insolvent's estate, the English court will be reluctant to pre-empt by means of injunction the opportunity for the foreign court to arrive at its own view of how best to proceed.[193]

Reclaiming the fruits of creditors' actions against property abroad

Although prevention is usually better than cure, it may not be practicable for an English trustee to restrain one or more of the creditors from taking action abroad against assets belonging to the bankrupt's estate. It may be possible however for the trustee subsequently to employ countermeasures whose effect will be to redress the ensuing distortion of the process of *pari passu* distribution of the estate among all creditors on a collective basis. The first possibility arises if a creditor who has recovered property abroad by means of individual action—such as an execution or attachment, or by receiving dividend in a separate, foreign insolvency proceeding—takes the further step of lodging proof in the English bankruptcy because he has not succeeded in obtaining a full repayment of his debt. For more than two centuries, English courts have strenuously resisted any solution which would have the effect of rewarding those who have won such a 'race of diligence' at the expense of the other creditors. Consequently, the rule of hotchpot has been developed, whereby a creditor who seeks to claim the benefit of the English process of distribution must do so on the terms which supply the basis of that law's operation. He cannot therefore be permitted to lodge proof for dividend and at the same time insist on retaining any preferential advantages inconsistent with the principle of equality of distribution. Consequently, the creditor must account for what has been received through the use of legal process in a foreign country, or by other means, and will only be entitled to receive dividend after full credit has been given for what he has already received.[194] If that calculation reveals

[192] *Re Chapman* (1873) L.R. 15 Eq. 75.

[193] See *Re Maxwell Communications Corporation (No. 2), Barclays Bank plc v. Homan* [1992] B.C.C. 757 (Hoffmann J.), affd (CA) at 767; *British Airways Board v. Laker Airways Ltd.* [1985] A.C. 58 (HL). *Cf.* also *Moore v. Anglo-Italian Bank* (1879) 10 Ch.D. 681, where the English court refrained from interfering with foreign proceedings involving the realisation of security over immovable property pending before the courts of the *situs*.

[194] *Selkrig v. Davies* (1814) 2 Dow. 230, 3 E.R. 848 (HL) (a Scottish appeal); *Banco de Portugal v. Waddell* (1880) 5 App.Cas. 161 (HL); *Re Douglas, ex parte Wilson* (1872) L.R. 7 Ch.App. 490. For the identical approach under Scottish law, see *Stewart v. Auld* (1851) 13 D. 1337. Note the

that the rate of recovery already exceeds the rate of dividend available for distribution to the other creditors, the creditor in question will necessarily be excluded from participation.[195] An important qualification to the application of the hotchpot rule is that it presupposes that the creditor has taken action abroad that would be impermissible or invalid if taken in the domestic context. Since English insolvency law allows a secured creditor to enforce a valid, pre-existing security over the debtor's property, and also allows a creditor to retain the benefit of enforcement procedures that have been completed before the commencement of bankruptcy,[196] comparable actions taking place outside this country can be accorded parity of treatment, provided that they were also valid according to the law of the *situs*. Thus, while still required to give credit for the value of what has been received, the creditor will not be obliged to surrender the property itself into the general pool of the estate.[197]

The operation of the hotchpot rule is predicated upon the creditor attempting to participate in the further distributions of the bankrupt's property by the lodging of proof of debt. If however he declines to participate in the English process, the courts long ago acknowledged that there is no inherent power whereby the court can compel a creditor to lodge proof of debt.[198] This need not necessarily mark the defeat of the trustee's prospects for redressing the position in conformity with English notions of equity and fairness among the bankrupt's creditors as a whole. Authority exists in the form of a series of admittedly early cases in which it was held to be open to the trustee to pursue the alternative tactic of requesting the court to order the creditor to make restitution to the estate of the property recovered by foreign attachment or other process.[199] The action pursued by the trustee is for money had and received by the creditor to the trustee's

special facts operative in *Re Bowes* (1889) W.N. 53, where no deduction was required to be made in respect of foreign recovery affecting a separate debt which was not provable in England because it was time-barred in the eyes of English law. (The actual outcome of this case would be altered under present-day conditions, due to the effects of the Foreign Limitation Periods Act 1984, whereby limitation is to be classified as a matter of substance, and as such is governed by the *lex causae*).

195 For a comparative exploration of the concept of 'hotchpot', see Hanisch in I.F. Fletcher (ed.). *supra* n.185, ch. 11. See also K. Nadelmann (1946) 11 Law & Contemp. Prob. 696; (1952) 1 I.C.L.Q. 484.

196 See Insolvency Act 1986, ss.285(4), 346.

197 *Re Somes* (1896) 3 Mans. 131; *Re Sykes* (1932) 101 L.J.Ch. 298; *Re Bowes* (*supra* n.194). See also the earlier cases, *Neale v. Cottingham* (1764) 1 H.Bl. 132n, 126 E.R. 81, also in (1770) Finley's Digest & Index of the Irish Reports (1830) 36n, Wallis & Lyne, Ir.Ch.Rep. (1839), 54; *Brickwood v. Miller* (1817) 3 Mer. 279, 36 E.R. 108. Cf. *Cockerell v. Dickens* (1840) 3 Moo. P.C. 98, 13 E.R. 45, where the distinguishing point was taken that the immovable property attached by the creditor did not form part of the estate passing to the trustee in bankruptcy.

198 *Selkrig v. Davies* (*supra* n.194) per Lord Eldon L.C. at 2 Dow 249 *et seq.*,3 E.R. at 854–855.

199 *Neale v. Cottingham, supra n.197; Sill v. Worswick* (1791) 1 H.Bl. 665, 126 E.R. 379; *Hunter v. Potts* (1791) 4 Term Rep. 182, 100 E.R. 962; *Phillips v. Hunter* (1795) 2 H.Bl. 402, 126 E.R. 618; cf. *Brickwood v. Miller, supra* n.197.

use, and is based on the premiss that the trustee is the person in whom, according to English law, all the bankrupt's property has vested in consequence of the adjudication. The cases nowadays require to be read in the light of the modern alterations to the structure and content of the law of bankruptcy, but the underlying principles appear otherwise to remain sound, namely that a person who is amenable to the jurisdiction of the English court can be compelled to make restitution of benefits acquired through actions undertaken abroad in contravention of the proprietary interest vested in the trustee as plaintiff.

A distinctive aspect of the factual elements of the early cases in which the trustee successfully brought an action for money had and received was that the defendant creditor was either resident in England, or was involved in a business activity here, so as to be amenable to the *in personam* jurisdiction of the court, and it was also the case that the defendant had embarked on the foreign attachment with prior knowledge that the debtor had either become or was in imminent peril of becoming a bankrupt. The scope of application of the action under present-day conditions is regrettably unclear, given the dearth of reported authority. In one case the Court of Appeal made passing reference to the unsettled state of the law concerning jurisdiction to restrain creditors from taking proceedings abroad, or to compel them to refund property obtained abroad, but did not venture any opinion as to the appropriate solution.[200] It is submitted that both types of remedy are in actuality part of the general repertoire of English law, and are not inherently a part of the law of insolvency, albeit the trustee's purpose in invoking them is to fulfil his duties under insolvency law. Questions of the existence of a jurisdiction to grant these remedies should therefore be answered in a way that is consistent with their operation outside the special context of insolvency, while due regard is paid to the practical difficulties which confront an office holder who endeavours to uphold the principles of universality and collectivity in a world of independent states.[201]

[200] *Re Paramount Airways Ltd.* [1992] 3 All E.R. 1, at 10–11 per Nicholls V.-C. Any expression of opinion on the point would have been at best an *obiter dictum*.

[201] Cf. the divergent views on the appropriate test of jurisdiction suggested in *Dicey and Morris on the Conflict of Laws*, 12th edn. (1993), at pp. 1167–1168, and in *Cheshire and North's Private International Law*, 12th edn. (1992) at p. 910. Note also the approach of the Canadian courts in regarding a person domiciled in any part of Canada as being amenable to injunction ordering him to discontinue proceedings in respect of a debtor's movable property wherever situate: *Re Mount Royal Lumber & Flooring Co. Ltd., Morgan Lumber Co. v. Scott* [1927] 2 D.L.R. 866.

2.5 DISCHARGE OF OBLIGATIONS UNDER AN ENGLISH BANKRUPTCY

An English bankruptcy claims universality of effect over all the property of the bankrupt irrespective of its *situs*, and matches this by admitting to proof the claims of all creditors without any regard to their residence, domicile, nationality or place of business. As a logical consequence of these fundamental aspects of the English approach, section 281 of the Insolvency Act 1986 provides that the discharge obtained by a bankrupt who has undergone adjudication according to the Act shall have the effect of releasing him from 'all the bankruptcy debts'.[202] Accordingly, all debts which English law classifies as provable in bankruptcy are comprised in the discharge. Nowhere in the Act is there any provision whose effect is to refine or qualify the connotation of 'bankruptcy debt' so as to exclude debts which are owed to foreign creditors, or which are governed by foreign law or were originally payable abroad. The symmetry of the arrangements therefore appears to be complete: as far as English law is concerned, the discharge resulting from an English bankruptcy is a full and final barrier to any subsequent attempt to enforce any liability which counted as a provable debt in those proceedings, and should be so regarded by all courts in other foreign and independent jurisdictions.[203] Nevertheless, all is far from satisfactory with regard to the operation of the English doctrine of universal discharge.

In the first place, the sweeping proposition that the discharge applies to all debts and liabilities regardless of their governing law is inconsistent with the widely accepted principle of private international law whereby questions of the discharge or extinguishing of obligations are governed by the applicable law. This is a proposition to which English private international law also purports to subscribe, and to which it is committed by virtue of Article 10(1)(d) of the Rome Convention on the Law Applicable to Contractual Obligations. Indeed, as will be further and critically discussed at 2.7 below, there is an anomalous imbalance between the

[202] Insolvency Act 1986, s.281(1). The release is subject to certain exceptions that are defined in the further provisions of s.281. The expression 'bankruptcy debts' is defined in *ibid.*, s.382.

[203] *Royal Bank of Scotland v. Cuthbert* (1813) 1 Rose 462; *Odwin v. Forbes* (1817) Buck. 57 (PC) (discussed in Chapter 1 at 1.3 above); *Armani v. Castrique* (1844) 13 M.& W. 443, 153 E.R. 185, at 186 per Pollock C.B. in argument; *Gill v. Barron* (1868) L.R. 2 P.C. 157, at 175–176 per Kelly L.C.B.; *Ellis v. M'Henry* (1871) L.R. 6 C.P. 228; *Swiss Bank Corpn. v. Boehmische Industrial Bank* [1923] 1 K.B. 673 (CA), at 678 per Bankes L.J. and at 681 per Scrutton L.J. The same principle of universal discharge is applied in relation to sequestrations under Scottish bankruptcy law: *Sidaway v. Hay* (1824) 3 B.& C. 12, 107 E.R. 639; so too in the case of Irish bankruptcies in the period before Independence: *Ferguson v. Spencer* (1840) 1 M.& G. 987, 133 E.R. 632; *Simpson v. Mirabita* (1869) L.R. 4 Q.B. 257.

claims asserted by English law with respect to the international effects of an English discharge from bankruptcy, and the position taken by English law over the issue of recognition of the effects of discharge resulting from foreign proceedings. Under modern conditions, it is submitted, the English rule should be reformulated to include appropriate reference to the legitimate role of the applicable law in the process of determining the international effects of a discharge. It can be pointed out that the seminal authorities relating to the current formulation of the English rule are of considerable antiquity, and reflect an authoritarian, not to say imperialistic, view of the prowess of English law that is ill-suited to the more egalitarian ethos of the international legal community of the present day.

A further aspect of the operation of the traditional English approach that is difficult to justify is the insistence that the effects of the discharge are absolute, even in relation to a foreign-resident creditor who had no knowledge or notice of the bankruptcy proceedings, and accordingly took no part in the process of lodging proof of debt.[204] Admittedly, the harsh consequences of this approach for creditors in former times, when global communications were undeveloped, are less likely to be experienced nowadays by parties who maintain a reasonable level of diligence concerning their debtor's legal and financial situation. Nevertheless, every precaution needs to be taken by those who have conduct of insolvency proceedings where international elements appear to be present, to ensure that suitable efforts are made to discover the existence, and current whereabouts, of any overseas parties with a possible interest. Careful judgment then must be exercised as to the most effective means of bringing the proceedings to the notice of such parties, and allowing them a reasonable time in which to respond, having regard to any special difficulties caused by differences of language as well as the inevitable problems due to distance. These matters are further addressed in Part II in the discussion of international arrangements and conventions currently under development,[205] but much can be done at national level by regular monitoring of the way existing rules work with respect to participation by foreign creditors.

2.5.1 Voluntary arrangements

Under Part VIII of the Insolvency Act 1986 a procedure is established which enables a debtor to conclude a voluntary arrangement with creditors. Such an arrangement may take the form of a composition or scheme of arrangement and, if approved by the requisite majority of creditors at a formal meeting convened for the purpose, takes effect so as to bind every

[204] *Edwards v. Ronald* (1830) 1 Knapp P.C. 259, 12 E.R. 317; *Simpson v. Mirabita*, *supra* n.203.

[205] See, in particular, Chapters 6, 7 and 8 below for the rights of foreign creditors under the Istanbul and EU Conventions, and under the UNCITRAL Model Law, respectively.

person who in accordance with the rules had notice of, and was entitled to vote at, the meeting, whether or not he was present or represented at it, as if he were a party to the arrangement.[206] Thus, non-assenting creditors may be bound by the terms of an IVA even if unavoidably absent from the meeting at which it was adopted, provided that they had notice of the meeting and were eligible to vote.[207] The terms of the arrangement will typically involve the debtor obtaining a discharge from the debts comprised therein, in return for his making provision for the creditors to receive an agreed proportion of their debts. Unless the agreement expressly excludes debts owed to foreign creditors, or governed by foreign law, the same principle of universal effect appears to be applicable as in the case of a discharge through bankruptcy.[208] As was suggested above, the absence of any reference to the role of the applicable law of the obligation allegedly discharged by a process conducted under English insolvency law is an anomaly that should receive corrective attention.

2.5.2 Selected comparisons

Australian and Canadian law have once again been modelled closely on the English prototype, in regarding a discharge obtained through bankruptcy proceedings under their respective systems as releasing the debtor from all debts provable in the bankruptcy, irrespective of the governing law of the underlying obligation.[209] In the USA, the consolidation of the universalist position with respect to the effects of an adjudication, as noted at 2.2.2 above, has been balanced by the affirmation that all claims, whether domestic, foreign or mixed, are treated equally in all respects, and that accordingly all are released by the process of discharge. The need to uphold the requirements of due process can however be a factor, and it was accepted as long ago as under the Bankruptcy Act of 1898 that discharge does not have the effect of releasing any provable debts that were

[206] Insolvency Act 1986, s.260(2). The IVA procedure is described in detail in I.F. Fletcher, *The Law of Insolvency*, 2nd edn. (1996) ch. 4.

[207] The rules governing the summoning and conduct of the creditors' meeting, and eligibility to vote, are contained in the Insolvency Rules 1986 (S.I. 1986 No. 1925, as amended), rr.5.12–5.19. Also relevant is r.5.8 which specifies the particulars to be included in the debtor's statement of affairs. The requisite majority for approval of the debtor's proposal for a voluntary arrangement is a majority in excess of three-quarters in value of the creditors present in person or by proxy and voting on the resolution: r.5.18(1).

[208] Cf. *Ellis v. M'Henry, supra* n.203, decided under the English bankruptcy legislation in force in the nineteenth century. Note however the attitude of the Court of Appeal in *Re Nelson* [1918] 1 K.B. 459, in construing the effects of s.64 of the Irish Bankrupt and Insolvent Act 1857 in relation to an arrangement between the debtor and his creditors, and ruling that the effects did not extend to England so as to bar action by creditors who, despite having notice, had not participated in the Irish proceedings.

[209] ***Australia***: Bankruptcy Act 1966, s.153(1); **Canada**: Bankruptcy and Insolvency Act 1985, s.178(2). Both systems draw upon the English case law cited at 2.5 above.

not scheduled in time to enable proof and allowance to be properly completed, unless the creditor had actual knowledge of the bankruptcy proceedings.[210] Previously, during the nineteenth century the American courts displayed a division of opinion whether an American discharge served to bar a debt due to a foreign creditor where the debt was neither contracted nor payable in the USA. This was largely a reflection of the state of uncertainty at that period regarding the effects of an American adjudication upon the debtor's foreign assets, and also as to the scope of the concept of 'provable debts'.[211] Where a foreign creditor was afforded the opportunity to participate in the bankruptcy, but elected not to do so, the doctrine of estoppel might be invoked to prevent him from taking subsequent action inconsistent with the conclusion that his debt had been validly discharged.[212]

2.6 ENGLISH LAW'S RECOGNITION OF FOREIGN BANKRUPTCIES AND THEIR EFFECTS

2.6.1 Generally

The basis of recognition of foreign bankruptcies differs as between adjudications that take place in the other parts of the United Kingdom, and those which arise from any other part of the world. The former are the subject of a special statutory provision in section 426(1) of the Insolvency Act 1986, whereas nearly all other cases fall to be determined on the basis of common law authorities that provide a less than complete statement of the scope for recognition in the present day. We will first deal with the position at common law.

(a) General recognition

The recognition of bankruptcies which have been opened in countries outside the United Kingdom remains the province of English case law. As with many other aspects of the common law concerning international insolvency, the core authorities date from the formative period of English private international law, and there are many questions which await a proper determination under modern conditions. The early point of departure was the proposition that, since bankruptcy is a matter bearing upon personal status and capacity, and on the transmission of the debtor's property, the law of the debtor's domicile is the competent system to determine such fundamental matters, and hence the courts of the domicile are the

[210] US Bankruptcy Act 1898, s.35(3).
[211] See unsigned comment in (1930) 39 Yale L.J. 559–572, at 561 *et seq.*
[212] *Moore v. Horton*, 39 N.Y. Sup.Ct. 393 (1884).

competent jurisdiction in which such proceedings should take place. English law therefore chose the domicile of the debtor—in the special sense employed by English law itself—as its test for establishing the jurisdictional competence of the foreign court.[213] In keeping with the characteristic English approach to the recognition of foreign judgments, the actual grounds on which the foreign court itself had purported to exercise jurisdiction were not considered to be relevant: what mattered was that the court of bankruptcy should be based in the country in which, at the time, English law considered the debtor to be domiciled. Conversely, a foreign court's exercise of jurisdiction over a non-domiciliary would, of itself, command no recognition in the eyes of English law.[214] However, in a limited number of situations this objection to the foreign court's assumption of jurisdiction could be overcome. First, it is possible that English common law would maintain consistency with the practice followed in relation to other areas of law, such as the recognition of foreign decrees of divorce or nullity of marriage, where the primary rule is to accord recognition to the status-determining decrees of the domicile of the *propositus*. Therefore, if it can been shown that the foreign adjudication, though not pronounced by the court of the debtor's domicile, would be recognised as valid according to the law of that country, English law would normally be inclined to replicate that conclusion.[215] A separate, and direct, basis for accepting an adjudication by a non-domiciliary forum is where the debtor voluntarily participated in the foreign bankruptcy proceedings, either by presenting his own petition for adjudication,[216] or by appearing, either personally or through a legal representative,[217] and thus submitting to the court's jurisdiction.

(i) The need for a restatement of the rules for recognition. The English law position on recognition of foreign adjudications has been in a state of arrested development for most of the present century. It is plainly unsatisfactory that the acknowledged grounds for such recognition should be restricted to just two, namely domicile or submission, of which the former is further reduced in its scope because of the special features of the English

[213] *Re Blithman* (1866) L.R. 2 Eq. 23. The special features of the English doctrine of domicile are discussed at 2.1.1(b)(i) above.

[214] *Re Hayward* [1897] 1 Ch. 905.

[215] Cf. *Le Mesurier v. Le Mesurier* [1895] A.C. 517; *Armitage v. Attorney-General* [1906] P. 135; *Abate v. Abate* [1961] P. 29.

[216] *Re Davidson's Settlement Trusts* (1873) L.R. 15 Eq. 383; *Re Lawson's Trusts* [1896] 1 Ch. 175; *Re Burke, King v. Terry* (1919) 54 L.J.K.B. 430, 148 L.T.Jo. 175.

[217] *Houlditch v. Donegall* (1834) 2 Cl. 7 F. 470, 6 E.R. 1232; *Re Anderson* [1911] 1 K.B. 896; *Re Craig* (1916) 86 L.J.Ch. 62; *Bergerem v. Marsh* (1921) 125 L.T. 630. Cf. *Schemmer v. Property Resources Ltd.* [1975] Ch. 273, where absence of evidence of submission to the jurisdiction of the foreign court was a significant factor underlying the English court's refusal to recognise the appointment of a receiver against the defendant company.

common law concept of domicile. As the law is presently conceived, it would be perfectly possible for an individual to have been a resident of some foreign country for very many years without having a domicile there in the sense employed by English law. The courts of that country could very reasonably exercise bankruptcy jurisdiction over such a debtor and yet, in the absence of voluntary participation on his part, it would seem that English law has no settled rule under which the bankruptcy could be recognised here.

It is submitted that there are at least two further grounds on which the exercise of bankruptcy jurisdiction ought to qualify for recognition. These are, that the debtor was habitually resident in the country in question, or that he was carrying on business there. There is indeed Scottish authority which supports the second of these grounds, and it is submitted that an English court should be prepared to follow the same approach when a suitable opportunity arises.[218] To be commercially meaningful, a business-based rule of recognition would need to embrace the possibility, as does English law itself, that the carrying on of business for this purpose includes cases where it is carried on through membership of a firm or partnership, and also where it is carried on by an agent or manager for the individual, or for the firm or partnership, as the case may be.[219] It would also be necessary to specify some period of reference within which the business activity must have been conducted in order for an adjudication based on this criterion to qualify for recognition. To avoid giving rise to a need to accord recognition to assertions of jurisdiction under possibly exorbitant circumstances, it would seem preferable to confine the qualifying period under the recognition rule to the immediate vicinity of the commencement of the foreign proceedings. Hence, it would be necessary to show that the debtor was carrying on business in the foreign country at the time of opening of the insolvency proceedings in question. However, this restrictive rule could be ameliorated by applying the 'continuation' doctrine developed by the English courts in construing the equivalent provisions of English insolvency legislation, to the effect that a business is

[218] See *Obers v. Paton's Trustees* (1897) 24 R. 719; *Home's Trustee v. Home's Trustees*, 1926 S.L.T. 214. Cf. *Re Artola Hermanos* (1890) 24 Q.B.D. 640, where the Court of Appeal declined to recognise a French bankruptcy adjudication of a firm whose business headquarters were in Paris, where none of the partners was proved to be domiciled in France. The decision may be explained on the grounds that the issue before the English court was whether a foreign adjudication not made by the courts of the debtor's domicile should constitute a bar to bankruptcy proceedings being commenced in England, where the debtor was also amenable to English bankruptcy law. In this sense, the decision could be said to bear upon the *effects* accorded to a foreign bankruptcy, rather than on the pure question of its being recognised by English law.

[219] See Insolvency Act 1986, s.265(1)(c),(2), discussed at 2.1.1(iii)(B) above.

deemed to continue as long as debts and liabilities incurred in the course of that business remain unsatisfied.[220]

It is also submitted that the debtor's habitual residence in the foreign country should be added to the grounds for recognition accepted by English law. The concept of habitual residence has been specially developed in modern times to provide an acceptable alternative to the irreconcilably opposed connecting factors used for many private international law purposes by different groupings of countries. It has been included in a number of international conventions produced by the Hague Conference on Private International Law, particularly those concerned with international recognition of judicial decrees or judgments affecting fundamental questions of personal status.[221] The Conference has maintained a deliberate policy of refraining from any formal definition of the expression 'habitual residence' in any of its conventions to date, in the hope that this will allow scope for reasonable and flexible judgement to be exercised at national level in response to the circumstances encountered in actual cases. Legislation in the United Kingdom has made considerable use of the concept of habitual residence, both when implementing various Hague Conventions to which this country has become a party, and also in other contexts.[222] Although lacking any precise, statutory definition, the term has become an accepted part of modern legal vocabulary to convey the sense of a person's stable and settled abode in a particular country, voluntarily adopted as part of the regular order of that person's life for the time being. Such an association between an individual and a country or territory surely constitutes a sufficiently substantial basis for the exercise of bankruptcy jurisdiction by the courts of that place. If an English rule of recognition were formulated using this connecting factor, it would be for the English court to decide whether the debtor's personal circumstances and mode of life could be regarded as amounting to habitual residence in the country in question. This, it is submitted, would amount to a prudent reservation of the capacity to evaluate the conditions under which jurisdiction was exercised by the foreign court.

The above proposals are made in the light of the currently uncertain and undeveloped state of the English case authorities. Although attractive

[220] See at 2.1.1(iii)(B), above, and cases cited *supra*, n.57.

[221] e.g. Convention on the Conflicts of Laws Relating to Testamentary Dispositions (5 October 1961); Convention on Jurisdiction, Applicable Law and Recognition of Decrees Relating to Adoptions (15 November 1965); Convention, on the Recognition of Divorces and Legal Separations (1 June 1970); Convention Concerning the International Administration of the Estates of Deceased Persons (2 October 1973); Convention on the Law Applicable to Matrimonial Property Regimes (14 March 1978).

[222] See e.g. Wills Act 1963, s.1; Domicile and Matrimonial Proceedings Act 1973, s.5; Family Law Act 1986, ss.46, 57. See further the observations at 2.1.1(iii)(A) above on the uncertain correlation between 'ordinary' and 'habitual' residence.

arguments can be advanced for a re-interpretation of the old cases to produce doctrinal principles better in tune with modern needs,[223] a fresh approach, amounting to a restatement, would really be preferable. This could go some way towards redressing the lack of symmetry between the grounds on which English courts may themselves exercise jurisdiction in bankruptcy, and the extent to which they are currently willing to recognise the competence of foreign courts to do so. It is not here suggested that English law should resort to a recognition rule based on the principle of reciprocity, in the special sense of being disposed to recognise the acts of foreign courts which have taken jurisdiction under circumstances where, *mutatis mutandis*, an English court would be competent according to its own rules for this purpose.[224] Not only have the courts themselves shown a reluctance in more recent times to apply this doctrine of reciprocity, especially in a commercial context,[225] but there are also objections to the possibility of according international recognition to a foreign court's exorbitant jurisdiction merely because English law happens to have a domestic rule which is also capable of exorbitant application.[226] However, the received doctrine of international comity can certainly be invoked as a basis for reformulating English rules of recognition so that they enable our courts to respond in an appropriate manner when foreign courts have exercised jurisdiction in circumstances that comply with internationally accepted norms. A genuine and substantial connection between the debtor and the country in question, exemplified by either a stable residential connection or one based on the conduct of business, should be accepted—together with the possibility of the debtor's voluntary, and non-abusive, submission to the legal process of the foreign court—as a sound basis for recognition of the ensuing adjudication.

The foregoing proposals represent a first phase in the modernisation of this aspect of English law. It will be seen in Chapter 6 below that the need may arise in future to achieve a reconciliation of the rules of jurisdiction and recognition that are potentially applicable in England under the proposed regime of the European Union Convention on Insolvency Matters, with the separate system of rules already in force within the European Union for the conduct of civil and commercial litigation outside the sphere of insolvency.[227]

[223] See, notably, the vigorous analysis and rationalisation by P. Smart in *Cross-Border Insolvency* (1991), ch. 4, esp. at pp. 81–100.

[224] See at 2.1 above.

[225] See e.g. *Re Trepca Mines Ltd.* [1960] 1 W.L.R. 1273, at 1281–1282, per Hodson L.J.; *Schemmer v. Property Resources Ltd.* [1975] Ch. 273 at 285–286, per Goulding J.

[226] For example, the Insolvency Act 1986, s.265(1)(a) could enable English courts to make a bankruptcy order against a debtor based purely on temporary presence. Similarly, s.265(1)(a) could empower the court to take jurisdiction over a debtor whose English domicile is but a relic of past circumstances, while all other significant ties with this country have long since been severed.

[227] See Chapter 6, at 6.3.4 below, at p. 287 *et seq.*

(ii) Exception to recognition: tax bankruptcies. Mention has already been made of the exclusionary rule of English private international law regarding the enforcement in England of foreign claims classifiable as penal in nature, or which are revenue claims made by foreign state or public authorities.[228] This doctrine of exclusion also applies in cases where foreign insolvency proceedings, even though conducted in the country to whose jurisdiction the debtor is indubitably subject according to English rules of recognition, are categorised as a 'Tax bankruptcy' on account of the prevalence among the ranks of the unpaid creditors of claims for fiscal liabilities of various kinds. As a matter of public policy, recognition may be refused in such cases where there would otherwise be a possibility that the internal legal processes of this country might become the instruments of execution for the foreign state as the tax-levying power.[229] Although there are indications from other Commonwealth jurisdictions of a re-appraisal of the more extreme application of this exclusionary rule, given that it is highly likely under modern conditions of insolvency that fiscal claims will form a substantial component of the debts alongside those of ordinary private and commercial creditors, there has been no indication to date of a relaxation of the English rule which appears to regard even the presence of a foreign revenue claim as a fatal obstacle to recognition.[230]

(b) Recognition of foreign bankruptcy as an assignment of property

Once it is confirmed that a foreign bankruptcy meets the criteria for recognition that have been discussed above, the next question for consideration is what consequences follow from this. Foremost among the issues likely to confront an English court are the extent to which the bankruptcy is regarded as having effected a transfer of title to the bankrupt's property in this country, and the standing of the foreign trustee in bankruptcy to take proceedings here to protect and take control of that property, and repatriate the property or the proceeds of its realisation to the forum of bankruptcy for distribution according to the terms of that system. By virtue of a long-standing distinction made between succession to movable and immovable property respectively, English law operates two, separate rules to determine the immediate effects of a foreign bankruptcy on different parts of the bankrupt's estate.

[228] See at 2.4 above.

[229] See authorities cited at 2.4 above at n.187. For further aspects of the tax bankruptcy phenomenon see Graham in I.F. Fletcher (ed.), *Cross-Border Insolvency: Comparative Dimensions* (1990), ch. 12 (pp. 205–215).

[230] See *Ayres v. Evans* (1981) 39 A.L.R. 129; and *Priestley v. Clegg* (1985) (3) S.A. 955 for indications of a more liberal judicial approach to the relevance of a tax component in the debts comprised in the foreign administration.

(i) Movable property. In the middle years of the eighteenth century, a series of liberally conceived judgments of the English courts laid the foundation for a durable rule of recognition whereby a foreign bankruptcy (or equivalent) order which has the effect under the *lex concursus* of divesting the bankrupt of his property produces the selfsame effect as regards any movable property situate in England, and does so from the same moment as it is effective under the foreign law.[231] The rule applies to all types of movable property, both tangible and intangible. The process of automatic transmission of title is subject to an important qualification, however, which sustains the principle that a trustee in bankruptcy takes 'subject to equities' in becoming successor to the bankrupt's estate.[232] Consequently, in the case of a foreign adjudication the trustee's title to English property is subject to any rights of third parties which had been perfected, according to the requirements of the law of the *situs*, at a point in time prior to that at which the trustee's own title is considered by English law to have taken effect.[233] There is an unfortunate aspect to the operation of this supplementary rule, as English courts have chosen to construe it, in that the earliest point in time at which the trustee's title is treated as effective as against property in England is the actual moment at which, according to the process of the foreign law itself, the trustee became invested with that title. Any complementary rules of the foreign law whose effect is to cause the trustee's title to relate back to an earlier point in time, thereby defeating acts of diligence by creditors during the period immediately before the debtor's adjudication, are denied any extraterritorial effect over English assets.[234] This can appear anomalous under certain conditions, as where it transpires that there is an analogous rule of English domestic law which would have produced the same effect, in terms of relation back of the trustee's title, as is claimed for the foreign bankruptcy law. In this respect the trustee may fall between two stools, so to speak, although it may be possible to retrieve the situation—assuming action can be taken sufficiently promptly—by instigating a secondary, local bankruptcy in England for the deliberate purpose of procuring the appointment of a

[231] *Solomons v. Ross* (1764) 1 Hy.Bl. 131n, 126 E.R. 79, (also reported in Wallis v. Lyne, Irish Chancery Reports 59, note, (1839); *Richards v. Hudson* (1762) 4 T.R. 187n, 100 E.R. 962; *Jollet v. Deponthieu* (1769) 1 Hy.Bl. 132n, 126 E.R. 80; *Neale v. Cottingham* (1764) 1 H.Bl. 132n, 126 E.R. 81. See also *Alivon v. Furnival* (1834) 1 C.M.& R. 277, 149 E.R. 1084; *Araya v. Coghill* 1921 S.L.T. 321; *Macaulay v. Guaranty Trust Co. of New York* (1927) 44 T.L.R. 99. See also K. Nadelmann (1946) 9 M.L.R. 154. Cf. *Brand v. Green* (1900) 13 Man. R. 101.

[232] *Re Scheibler, ex parte Holthausen* (1874) L.R. 9 Ch.App. 722, at 726 per James L.J. See further at 2.2, above, for the 'subject to equities' doctrine.

[233] *Levasseur v. Mason & Barry* [1891] 2 Q.B. 73; *Galbraith v. Grimshaw* [1910] A.C. 508 (HL); *Singer v. Fry* (1915) 84 L.J.K.B. 2025; *Anantapadmanabhaswami v. Official Receiver of Secunderabad* [1933] A.C. 394 (PC).

[234] *Galbraith v. Grimshaw, supra* n.233. For cogent criticism of this decision see A.E. Anton, *Private International Law*, 2nd edn. (1990), p. 734.

trustee in bankruptcy enjoying the full status and powers conferred by English law, including the overreaching powers exercisable against prior transactions. As explained at 2.8 below, such parallel proceedings can be coordinated in the best interests of all creditors.[235] A further, more limited possibility of extending the temporal reach of the trustee's title may be by means of the provisions in section 426 of the Insolvency Act 1986, considered below.[236]

(ii) Immovable property. In contrast to the rule applicable to movable property, English law insists on upholding the principle that succession to immovable property is subject to the sovereign control of the *lex situs*, and that no foreign legal process such as the adjudication of the present owner of such property can of itself accomplish a transfer of title in favour of some other person.[237] Nevertheless, the foreign trustee may succeed in claiming the property on behalf of the creditors, whose interests he represents, by applying to the English court for assistance based upon recognition of his appointment according to the rules already discussed. The court's response may vary from exerting any direct control it may have over the bankrupt's person to compel him to execute a formal conveyance in favour of the trustee, to the court appointing the trustee to be receiver of the bankrupt's immoveables with authority to sell the property and to deal with the proceeds according to the requirements of the foreign *lex concursus*.[238] The court may impose conditions such as a requirement that the proceeds of sale be initially lodged in court to await directions, thus affording interested parties the opportunity to lodge any objection to the repatriation of the funds.[239] As in the case of movables, the 'subject to equities' principle will apply so that the trustee's claim may be subordinated to that of some other party whose interest in the property was perfected before that of the trustee. Moreover, the court may invoke its discretion to refuse to order the turnover of English assets where it concludes that, although the foreign adjudication was pronounced by a court whose jurisdiction is recognised under the English rules, the insolvency proceedings themselves suffer from some inherent flaw which warrants the withholding of assistance.

[235] See p. 111 below.

[236] Further aspects of the Insolvency Act 1986, s.426 are also discussed at 2.2 above at p. 59 *et seq.*, and in Chapter 4 below.

[237] *Waite v. Bingley* (1882) 21 Ch.D. 674; *Re Levy's Trusts* (1885) 30 Ch.D. 119. See also *Cockerell v. Dickens* (1840) 3 Moo.P.C. 98, 13 E.R. 45; *Phosphate Sewage Co.Ltd. v. Molleson* (1878) 5 R. 1125; *Araya v. Coghill*, 1921 S.L.T. 321. A foreign adjudication may however be effective to procure the operation of a forfeiture clause affecting an interest in real estate situate in England, and may therefore cause the interest to pass, in accordance with the default provision in the will or settlement, to the parties therein designated. *Re Aylwin's Trusts* (1873) L.R. 16 Eq. 585; *Re Levy's Trusts (supra).*

[238] *Re Kooperman* [1928] W.N. 101, 72 Sol.Jo. 400; *Re Levy's Trusts, supra* n.237, at 123 per Kay J.; *Re Osborne* (1931–32) 15 B. & C.R. 189.

[239] Cf. *Araya v. Coghill, supra* n.237.

Examples would be where the foreign proceedings amount to a 'tax bankruptcy', in that they are mainly or exclusively at the behest of the revenue authorities of that State,[240] or where there is a discriminatory aspect to the way the bankrupt's estate will be distributed under the foreign law which is unacceptably divergent from English notions of equal and fair treatment of creditors.[241]

(iii) Statute-based recognition and enforcement: Insolvency Act 1986, section 426. The provisions of section 426 of the Insolvency Act 1986 have already been noted at 2.2 above on account of their impact upon the international effects of an English bankruptcy order.[242] We must now observe that this section also has a special impact upon the recognition in England of certain types of foreign adjudication, and upon the effects they are to be accorded here. First, in the case of bankruptcy orders made in Scotland or Northern Ireland, section 426(1) of the 1986 Act imposes a requirement that they be accorded automatic recognition in England and Wales. As was seen at 2.2 above, that provision sets up a triangular network of mutual enforcement of each other's judicial orders between the courts of the constituent parts of the United Kingdom, by declaring that an order made by a court in any part in the exercise of jurisdiction in relation to insolvency law shall be enforced in any other part as if it were made there by a court exercising the corresponding jurisdiction. This appears to leave little or no scope for the enforcing court to question the circumstances in which the original proceedings were opened and the order made, the assumption being that any such grounds for objection can readily be pursued by means of an appeal in the jurisdiction of origin. However, there is a somewhat greater degree of discretion available to the English court (and likewise to the courts of other parts in comparable cases) by virtue of the reservation introduced by subsection (2) with respect to enforcement of an order made in one part of the United Kingdom in relation to property situated in another. Where, for example, it appears to the English court that the original proceedings in Scotland or in Northern Ireland were fatally flawed in some way, it would be possible for the court to withhold assistance with regard to any property located in England. To that extent, at least, the present position is somewhat more flexible than was the case under the insolvency statutes in force prior to 1986.[243] Subject to this, however, the effect of section 426(1) is to override the common law rules

[240] See p. 97 above.

[241] See the controversial decision in *Felixstowe Dock & Railway Co. v. U.S. Lines Inc.* [1989] Q.B. 360 (not a case of individual bankruptcy), discussed in Chapter 3, at 3.10 below.

[242] See p. 64 above.

[243] See, e.g. *Wilkie v. Cathcart* (1870) 9 M. 168; and *Salaman v. Tod* 1911 S.C. 1214, in which Scottish courts deferred to the imperative terms employed in the English Bankruptcy Acts of 1861 and 1883 respectively.

regarding the effects of foreign adjudications over property situate in England and Wales: whether the property is movable or immovable in nature, a bankruptcy order of a court in Scotland or in Northern Ireland causes the entirety of the estate to vest in the trustee, just as would be the case with a bankruptcy order made in England.

The provisions of section 426(4) and (5) have further implications for the enforcement in England of bankruptcy orders made in another part of the United Kingdom, and also have relevance in certain cases where proceedings are opened in one of the select group of countries which have been brought under the mantle of its operation.[244] A request pursuant to section 426(4) made to an English court by a court in any of the qualifying countries places the requested court under an obligation to assist, although this is subject to the exercise of its discretion as to how it should give that assistance.[245] By virtue of subsection (5), the requested court is empowered to apply, in relation to any matters specified in the request, the insolvency law which is applicable by either court in relation to comparable matters falling within its jurisdiction. It is submitted that one useful consequence of these provisions is that it can enable an English court, if it is so minded, to circumvent the effects of the House of Lords ruling in *Galbraith v. Grimshaw*,[246] whereby a foreign trustee was deprived of the advantage arising under his law of appointment (even if matched by an analogous rule of English law) whose effect was to cause the trustee's title to relate back to a time prior to his formal appointment. This would be of particular value in enabling the trustee to invoke rules for the avoidance of antecedent transactions to which the debtor was a party, or to claim for the estate any property acquired by the bankrupt after the commencement of bankruptcy, where the property concerned is currently situate in England. The rule applied by the English court in rendering its assistance might be that of English law, or that of the country from whose court the request had come: in selecting the system whose law is to be applied for this purpose, the court would observe the requirement imposed by the proviso to section 426(5) that it have regard to the rules of private international law.[247] In this way, a number of obstacles to the application of the

[244] See at 2.2 above at pp. 65–6 for the significance of the expression 'relevant country or territory' in the context of the Insolvency Act 1986, s.426. The full list of all countries currently so designated is: (by S.I. 1986 No. 2123)—Anguilla, Australia, the Bahamas, Bermuda, Botswana, Canada, Cayman Islands, Falkland Islands, Gibraltar, Hong Kong, the Republic of Ireland, Montserrat, New Zealand, St. Helena, Turks and Caicos Islands, Tuvalu, and the Virgin Islands; (by S.I. 1996 No. 253)—Malaysia and South Africa. In addition, s. 426(11)(a) of the 1986 Act provides that the expression 'relevant country or territory' includes any of the Channel Islands and the Isle of Man.

[245] See *Hughes v. Hannover Ruckversicherungs-AG* [1997] B.C.C. 921, at 938–939 per Morritt L.J. This case, and the wider aspects of the system of judicial cooperation under s.426 of the 1986 Act, are explored in Chapter 4 below.

[246] See *supra* n.233.

[247] See the observations at 2.2 above, at p. 65.

principle of collectivity, under the conditions that are characteristic of many cross-border insolvencies, may be overcome.

2.6.2 Selected comparisons

In **Australia** the underlying principles for recognising and giving effect to foreign bankruptcies are directly modelled on those of English law, and the English cases are frequently invoked as authority. There is a similar lack of certainty as to the grounds of jurisdiction used by the foreign court that will provide a basis for recognition in Australia. Beyond the established grounds of the debtor's domicile in the *forum concursus*, or submission to its jurisdiction, and possibly also where he has carried on business there, clear authority is lacking.[248] There is an obvious anomaly in the continued use of domicile as a connecting factor for establishing the jurisdiction of the foreign court, since this has ceased to be an available ground for the exercise of bankruptcy jurisdiction by the courts in Australia itself.[249] In the treatment of the effects of foreign bankruptcy on property in Australia, the law makes the familiar distinction between movables and immoveables, with the former being considered to vest automatically in the foreign trustee while the latter are not so affected, although judicial assistance can be sought by the trustee, either by way of a vesting order or appointment as receiver of the property.[250] The 'subject to equities' rule, and the legacy of the decision of the House of Lords in *Galbraith v. Grimshaw*,[251] are both operative in the treatment of the effectiveness of the foreign trustee's title in competition with that of other parties whose interest has been perfected, according to the domestic law of the *situs*, ahead of the moment when the trustee's title first becomes effective in Australia.[252] Assistance of the Australian courts may be obtained pursuant to section 29 of the Bankruptcy Act 1966, which empowers them to act in aid and be auxiliary to the counterpart courts of foreign countries.

In the case of requests for assistance made by the courts of so-called 'prescribed' countries, the obligation to assist is expressed in mandatory terms.[253] In the case of other countries, the giving of aid is left to the court's

[248] See Sykes and Pryles, *supra* n.93, at p. 790 *et seq*.

[249] See Bankruptcy Act 1966, s.43(1)(b), which lists the grounds currently available.

[250] See, in addition to English authorities mentioned *supra*, nn. 231–241, *Ex parte Bettle* (1895) 14 N.Z.L.R. 129; *Australian Mutual Provident Society v. Gregory* (1908) 5 C.L.R. 615; *Re Young* [1955] St.R.Qd. 254; *Radich v. Bank of New Zealand* (1993) 116 A.L.R. 676; *White v. Verkouille* [1990] 2 Qd.R. 191.

[251] See *supra*, n.233.

[252] See, in addition to the English authorities, *Union Bank v. Tuttle* (1889) 15 V.L.R. 258; *Hall v. Woolf* (1908) 7 C.L.R. 207 (the correctness of this decision was questioned in *Radich v. Bank of New Zealand*, *supra* n.250).

[253] Bankruptcy Act 1966 s.29(2)(a). By subsection (5), 'prescribed country' means: (a) the United Kingdom, Canada and New Zealand; (b) a country prescribed for the purposes of the subsection; and (c) a colony, overseas territory or protectorate of a country which qualifies

discretion.[254] By section 29(3) the powers exercisable by an Australian court in response to a request for aid are confined to such powers with respect to the matter as it could exercise if the matter had arisen within its own jurisdiction. There is thus no scope for application of any aspect of the law of the country from which the request has come, which contrasts with the power conferred on courts in the United Kingdom by section 426(5) of the Insolvency Act 1986, as stated above.

In **Canada**, the special position formerly accorded to adjudications pronounced in any part of the United Kingdom whereby all Canadian assets, both movable and immovable, became automatically vested in the trustee in bankruptcy, was discontinued from 1949 onwards under the terms of the Bankruptcy Act of that year.[255] No special status has subsequently been accorded to bankruptcies opened in the United Kingdom, which are therefore dealt with in the same manner as those of any other foreign jurisdiction. In the absence until 1997 of any express provisions in the Federal legislation relating to matters of conflict of laws provincial practice varied as between the common law Provinces and Quebec, with its civil law—and more territorialist—tradition.[256] While the latter Province was averse to recognising foreign bankruptcies under most circumstances, the common law Provinces absorbed the English approach in much the same way as did Australia. It became accepted that recognition was predicated on the debtor's domicile in, or submission to, the forum of bankruptcy, and that movable property in Canada would pass automatically to the trustee, subject to pre-existing equities and charges valid according to the *lex situs*.[257] Conversely, in the case of immoveables the familiar approach of non recognition of any direct disturbance to existing title was maintained.[258] However, foreign trustees wishing to attack prior transactions relating to property under the control of the Canadian courts have sometimes been met with a creative and internationally sensitive response. In

under either (a) or (b). Countries prescribed under (b) now include Singapore, Malaysia, Switzerland and the USA.

254 *Ibid.*, s.29(2)(b).

255 For the pre-1949 position, see *Re Eades Estate* (1917) 33 D.L.R. 335.

256 See Ziegel in I.F. Fletcher (ed.), *Cross-Border Insolvency: National and Comparative Studies (The Montreal Papers)* (1992), ch. 4, at pp. 89–91; Castel, *supra* n.101, at p. 530; McLeod, *supra* n.101, pp. 446–450.

257 See the English cases cited *supra*, n.124, and also *Douglas v. Atlantic Mutual Life Ins. Co. of Albany, New York* (1878) 25 O.R. Ch.Rep. 379; *Pickford v. Atlantic Transportation Co.* (1899) 40 N.S.R. 237; *Brand v. Green* (1900) 13 Man.R. 10; *Thorne, Ernst & Whinney Inc. v. Sulpetro Ltd.* (1987) 47 D.L.R. (4th) 315. For the competing claims of the trustee and local creditors seeking to complete attachment of assets, see *Re Universal Auto Bonders Ltd., Walton v. Skyline Motors Ltd.* (1958) 13 D.L.R. (2d) 459. See also Grace (1986) 35 I.C.L.Q. 664.

258 *Macdonald v. Georgian Bay Lumber Co.* (1878) 2 S.C.R. 364; *Re Stewart & Matthews Ltd.* (1916) 10 W.W.R. 154, 26 Man.R. 277; *Marine Trust Co. v. Weinig* [1935] O.W.N. 150, [1935] 3 D.L.R. 282.

Williams v. Rice and Rice Knitting Mills,[259] a Manitoba court applied American law to determine whether funds lodged in Canada could be recovered by a trustee under an American bankruptcy proceeding, on the basis that their transfer by the debtor had constituted a fraudulent transaction according to the law of the USA. In a subsequent case, the American law on voidable preferences was held to be applicable to test the validity of a payment made to a Canadian creditor by an American corporate debtor which was undergoing bankruptcy in its home country.[260]

The enactment of new provisions on international insolvency among legislative reforms made in April 1997 has provided a statutory basis and framework for the Canadian courts to cooperate with their foreign counterparts.[261] The courts are specifically authorised to continue to apply established principles of Canadian law, in addition to those introduced by the legislation, when dealing with cross-border cases of insolvency.[262]

In the **USA** questions of the recognition of foreign bankruptcy proceedings, and the mode of giving assistance to the foreign trustee have, since the enactment of the Bankruptcy Reform Act of 1978, been dominated by the innovative provisions of sections 303–306 inclusive of the Bankruptcy Code. In view of their inherent importance, and wide-reaching influence on modern legal developments at national and international level, these provisions are explored in Chapter 4, in section 4.2.

2.7 THE EFFECTS OF A DISCHARGE OBTAINED THROUGH A FOREIGN BANKRUPTCY

2.7.1 Generally

We have already seen that English law assumes the most extensive of effects for bankruptcy proceedings conducted under its own jurisdiction, and that this includes treating the effects of discharge as extending to all the bankruptcy debts, irrespective of their proper law.[263] When bankruptcy proceedings have taken place in a foreign country, culminating in the debtor receiving a formal discharge according to the *lex concursus*, questions may subsequently arise as to the extent to which English law recognises the effects of the foreign discharge. Typically, such issues arise

[259] [1926] 3 D.L.R. 225, (1926) 36 Man.R. 266.

[260] *Williams v. Meeker Cedar Products (1967) Ltd., Re Premium Plywood Products Inc.* (1973) 19 C.B.R. (N.S.) 76 (the claim of the foreign trustee was dismissed on the merits, for failure to establish the requisite elements essential for avoidance under American law).

[261] SC 1997, c.12.

[262] *Ibid.*, s. 268(5). For further discussion of the collaborative arrangements, see Chapter 4, at 4.4 below.

[263] See at 2.2 and 2.5 above.

when a creditor attempts to enforce the original debt or liability by means of a legally recognised process conducted in this country, having discovered the presence here of an asset of some kind belonging to the former bankrupt. Logically, if English law were to accord to the foreign discharge the same effects which it claims for a discharge resulting from English bankruptcy proceedings, the creditor ought to be refused any right of recovery in all circumstances, save perhaps where it can be shown that the foreign proceedings themselves were vitiated in some way amounting to a violation of the creditor's rights to due process of law. In reality, English law fails to maintain an even-handed approach to this matter, and it will be suggested that there is a need for the rules to be revised in line with more modern views of international comity.

The primary rule

The basic doctrine that has evolved through the cases decided over more than two and a half centuries seems sound enough. It is derived from the proposition that the extinction of obligations, just as much as their original creation, is a process whose validity is to be determined by reference to the governing law of the obligation itself.[264] Consequently, the primary rule established by English law is that a foreign discharge through bankruptcy will be recognised as valid and effective if it can be shown that the substantive obligation has been released according to the applicable law.[265] This effect can most readily be confirmed as taking place in those instances where the *forum* of bankruptcy happens to be the country whose law is the applicable—or 'proper'—law of the obligation whose discharge is later in issue: the self-contained nature of the reference to the foreign law ensures that the answer should be a foregone conclusion.[266] In other situations however, where the country of bankruptcy and the country of the applicable law are not one and the same, the outcome is less certain. It may be assumed (although the point seems not to have been resolved in any reported decision concerning bankruptcy) that English private international law would follow its traditional practice of referring to the recognition rules of the applicable law itself, to establish whether these have the effect of treating the substance of the obligation as fully discharged. If this is the case, English law would concur in that result.[267] This necessarily

[264] *Burrows v. Jemino* (1726) 2 Str. 733, 93 E.R. 815.

[265] *Potter v. Brown* (1804) 5 East 124, 102 E.R. 1016; *Quelin v. Moisson* (1828) 1 Knapp P.C. 265n, 12 E.R. 320, *Gardiner v. Houghton* (1862) 2 B.& S. 743, 121 E.R. 1247, at 748 per Cockburn C.J.; *Ellis v. M'Henry* (1871) L.R. 6 C.P. 228, at p. 234 *et seq.* per Bovill C.J.

[266] Unless the liability in question happens to belong to a category of debts which the local law of bankruptcy expressly excludes from being released by the bankrupt's discharge: cf. Insolvency Act 1986, s.281(3)–(6).

[267] Cf. *Armitage v. Attorney-General* [1906] P. 135; *Abate v. Abate* [1961] P. 29 (cases concerning the recognition at English common law of foreign decrees of divorce and nullity of

involves an investigation of the nature and contents of the rule of recognition—if any—that is contained in the conflicts law of that other system. Self-evidently, that rule must somehow be based on an assessment of the circumstances under which the court of the bankruptcy came to exercise jurisdiction. If the doctrinal position under the applicable law is to the same effect as that of English law, namely that all questions concerning discharge of obligations are to be determined by the applicable law, a *circulus inextricabilis* is created, for the path of inquiry leads back to the point where it began. Only by means of a subsidiary rule, whose purpose is to furnish the applicable law with a basis for regarding the obligation as having been discharged through a process conducted in some other jurisdiction, can the logical circularity be overcome.[268] Essentially, this entails a conceptual change of position from one which focuses exclusively on the contract and the law by which it is governed, to one whereby this is combined with a process of recognition of foreign proceedings and their effects upon parties' rights. At present, as will next be shown, English law itself does not allow for such an accommodation in the case of obligations where the applicable law is that of England itself.

The corollary to the rule

English law's concentration upon the role of the applicable law in deciding the effects of a foreign discharge gives rise to a secondary rule, to the effect that a discharge under bankruptcy proceedings in a foreign country does not operate as a discharge of an obligation whose applicable law was that of some other country than the *forum concursus*. The principal authorities involved contracts whose applicable law (to employ the terminology of today) was English,[269] and they resulted in plaintiff creditors being enabled to sue in the courts of this country in respect of debts which had been comprised in foreign insolvency proceedings.[270] The most widely cited instance of the application of this secondary rule actually involved a French, corporate debtor which had undergone an insolvency procedure

marriage respectively, where the decree was recognised as effective by the law of the matrimonial domicile although not originally obtained under the law of that country). The view expressed in the text receives support from the learned editors of *Dicey and Morris, The Conflict of Laws*, 12th edn. (1993) at pp. 1181–1182.

[268] For an example of a similar logical impasse arising under modern English legislation dealing with the recognition of foreign divorces, see North, *The Private International Law of Matrimonial Causes in the British Isles and the Republic of Ireland* (1977), at pp. 184–185 (with reference to the Recognition of Foreign Divorces and Legal Separations Act 1971, s.6. The same problem recurs under the Family Law Act 1986, s.46(2): see *Cheshire and North's Private International Law*, 12th edn. (1992), at p. 674).

[269] The nineteenth century judgments speak of contracts 'made and to be performed' in England, or of debts 'arising' there.

[270] *Smith v. Buchanan* (1800) 1 East 6, 102 E.R. 3; *Armani v. Castrique* (1844) 13 M.& W. 443, 153 E.R. 185, esp. at 447 per Pollock C.B.; *Bartley v. Hodges* (1861) 1 B.& S. 375, 121 E.R. 754; *Gibbs v. La Société Industrielle et Commerciale des Métaux* (1890) 25 Q.B.D. 399 (CA).

in its country of incorporation, concluding in a formal *concordat* whose effects were equivalent to a discharge in bankruptcy. The Court of Appeal in *Gibbs & Sons v. La Société Industrielle et Commerciale des Métaux*[271] held that this did not operate as a release from liability under a contract made and to be performed in England, even though the French proceedings had taken place in the country of the defendant's domicile, in the sense utilised by English law. In consequence, the English plaintiffs were allowed to maintain an action in England for damages for breach of contract, despite the fact of their having had timely notice of the French proceedings. Indeed, the unsatisfactory outcome of this case is compounded by the fact that the plaintiffs had lodged their claim for damages in the foreign liquidation, only to have part of their claim ruled inadmissible under French law. Lord Esher M.R., affirming the judgment of the lower court in the plaintiffs' favour inquired rhetorically:

> Why should the plaintiffs be bound by the law of a country to which they do not belong, and by which they have not contracted to be bound?

Indeed, the Master of the Rolls went further, and stated (albeit as an *obiter dictum*) that if the contract had been made in any foreign country other than France, the plaintiffs could sue upon it in England and their action would not be affected by the law of France.[272] With respect, this expansive *dictum* wholly overlooks the possibility that the third country's law may contain a rule which allows for discharge of the contract to take place, *inter alia*, as a consequence of any of the parties to it undergoing bankruptcy in a court of competent jurisdiction in the international sense

Criticism of the current law

For more than a hundred years the *Gibbs* case has been accepted as a definitive authority on English law's position concerning the effects of a foreign discharge. The decision has been consistently followed and applied, has been commended as correct by the House of Lords,[273] and has been accepted in Commonwealth countries, including Canada and Australia, as the basis for their own approach to this question. Nevertheless, the rule cannot escape criticism on a number of grounds, and it is submitted that it ought to be revised and restated.[274] The most glaring anomaly produced by the rule in its current form is the contrast between the narrow limits

[271] See *supra* n.270.

[272] (1890) 25 Q.B.D. at 406.

[273] *National Bank of Greece and Athens S.A. v. Metliss* [1958] A.C. 509, at 523 per Viscount Simonds; *Adams v. National Bank of Greece S.A.* [1961] A.C. 255, at 287 per Lord Denning.

[274] See the especially cogent critique of the *Gibbs* case and its consequences in F. Piggott, *Foreign Judgments and Jurisdiction*, 3rd edn. (1910), Part III, Book VI, at pp. 127–137. It is respectfully submitted that these still unanswered criticisms retain their validity today. See also the suggestions in Smart, *supra* n.75, in ch. 8, including the possible use of estoppel against parties who participated in the foreign insolvency.

within which a foreign bankruptcy is held to give rise to a discharge of liability, and the unconfined claims made by English law for the effects of a discharge under English bankruptcy proceedings. The latter type of discharge, as was seen at 2.5 above, is considered to release all liabilities which qualify as bankruptcy debts, irrespective of their applicable law. A related, and logically indefensible, aspect of the consequences of English law's treatment of foreign insolvency proceedings is that the generous, and mainly admirable, policy of recognition of the effects of a foreign adjudication in relation to the bankrupt's property wheresoever found, and the assistance available to the foreign trustee to reclaim English assets on behalf of the general body of creditors, results in the unjust situation that English law accepts that all the bankrupt's property has been lawfully taken away by virtue of the foreign insolvency process, while simultaneously holding him liable to be sued here in respect of liabilities comprised in those selfsame proceedings.

The law to be developed

It is submitted that what is required is a modern reformulation of the English rules so that they form a more coherent structure. In keeping with the universalist aspirations of English law towards its own insolvency proceedings, including the effects claimed for an English discharge, there needs to be a balanced approach over the question of the effects to be accorded to analogous, foreign proceedings. While it is doctrinally sound to make reference to the applicable law to determine questions of extinction or release of obligations, a rigid rule which in practice denies any possibility for discharge to come about by means of proceedings in any country other than that of the applicable law itself is an obstacle to the development of mature international relationships between legal systems, based on even-handedness and mutual respect.

The *Gibbs* doctrine belongs to an age of anglocentric reasoning which should be consigned to history. In its place, supplementary rules are required which take account of the circumstances under which the foreign proceedings were opened, and subsequently conducted, before reaching a conclusion about the international effects to be accorded to those proceedings and to any discharge or composition to which they give rise. Before any creditor can subsequently be permitted to take action in England to enforce an obligation which the defendant claims was comprised within the foreign discharge, but whose applicable law was not that of the country of bankruptcy, the court should have regard to whether the plaintiff had adequate notice of the foreign proceedings and a reasonable opportunity to participate in them in accordance with acceptable standards of fair and equal treatment. If this was the case, the remedies of English legal process should be withheld on the basis that the plaintiff is estopped from invoking them. In the case of a contractual obligation which happens to be governed by English law, a further rule should be developed whereby, if one of the parties to it is the subject of insolvency proceedings in a jurisdiction with which he has an established connection based on residence or ties of business, it should be recognised that the possibility of such proceedings must enter into the parties' reasonable expectations in entering their relationship, and as such may furnish a ground for the discharge to take effect under the applicable law. In seeking in this way to establish a more internationally enlightened mode of responding to the effects generated by foreign insolvency proceedings, English law would in fact be returning to the open-minded tradition of the formative period of this particular branch of our jurisprudence. It would be well to draw inspiration from the pioneering contribution of Jabez Henry himself, when presiding over the Anglo-Dutch colonial court of Demerara in the case of *Odwin v. Forbes*,[275] where suit was brought by creditors who had refrained from lodging proof in their debtor's bankruptcy in England, despite having had notice of those proceedings. After a most thorough review of English and comparative authorities, including doctrinal writings of many scholars, the court concluded that the requirements of comity and reciprocity of treatment, rather than any inherent power of English law to command extraterritorial effect, furnished a basis for finding the plaintiffs' action defeated by the English certificate of discharge.

Special cases under the current law

Two further matters require to be emphasised. First, in cases where the foreign discharge is the consequence of bankruptcy proceedings which have taken place in either Scotland or Northern Ireland, a special approach is substituted for the rules discussed above. Once again, under a succession of statutory provisions that reflect the constitutional affinities between the three parts of the United Kingdom, English law accords the same, comprehensive effects to a discharge gained in either jurisdiction as would be produced by a discharge in England itself.[276] Thus, all provable debts are held to be discharged, regardless of the applicable law of the obligation in question. Secondly, it should be noted that, as usual, English

[275] (1817) Buck. 57 (PC), discussed in Chapter 1, at 1.3 above, which also commemorates the contribution of Jabez Henry to the theoretical literature of international insolvency.

[276] For the current statutory provision, see the Insolvency Act 1986, s.426(1), discussed at 2.2 and 2.6 above. For illustrative cases decided under previous legislation, see: (for Scotland) *Sidaway v. Hay* (1824) 3 B.& C. 12, 107 E.R. 639; cf. *Phillips v. Allan* (1828) 8 B.& C. 477, 108 E.R. 1120, where the non-statutory procedure of *cessio bonorum* was ruled to fall outside the ambit of the system of mandatory recognition; (for Ireland) *Ferguson v. Spencer* (1840) 1 M.& G. 987, 133 E.R. 632; *Simpson v. Mirabita* (1869) L.R. 4 Q.B. 257. Contrast *Re Nelson* [1918] 1 K.B. 459 (CA), where the effects of the Irish legislation concerning arrangements with creditors were held to be confined to Ireland alone.

law refrains from according extraterritorial effects to foreign legal proceedings where no such effect is claimed for them by the law under which they have taken place.[277] So, too, where the effect of such discharge as is granted under the foreign law is to introduce a procedural bar to enforcement, as distinct from releasing the substance of the obligation itself.

2.7.2 Selected comparisons

The close correspondence between the laws of **Canada** and **Australia** with that of England, and in particular the influence of the *Gibbs* case, is again a conspicuous feature.[278] Therefore a foreign discharge from any debt or liability will only be recognised if it is a valid discharge by the proper law of the obligation. The Australian decision of *Glass v. Keogh*[279] provides a forceful example of the use of the doctrine of estoppel to prevent a creditor from taking proceedings against the former bankrupt in Australia where the plaintiff has previously taken advantage of the bankruptcy law of the foreign country by lodging proof and receiving dividend, even though the contract may be governed by the law of a different country. As for the **USA**, the impact on attitudes towards the cross-border effects of discharge in consequence of the historic shift from territoriality to universality was already referred to in section 2.5.1. above. This has cast doubt on the present-day authority of the early cases such as *Ogden v. Saunders*,[280] in which a foreign discharge was held to furnish no defence to an action by a creditor residing in the USA unless the creditor consented to the foreign court's exercise of jurisdiction over his claim. The progressive advance of the doctrine of comity as an influential force in American attitudes to transnational insolvency issues is also a relevant factor, although the rules of recognition themselves remain unsettled in a modern context.[281]

[277] Cf. *Ex parte Melbourn* (1870) L.R. 6 Ch.App. 64; *Philpotts v. Reed* (1819) 1 Brod. & B. 294, 129 E.R. 735, esp. at p. 297 per Dallas C.J.

[278] In addition to the English cases referred to at 2.7.1 above, see: *Smith v. Stewart* (1858) 3 N.S.R. 417 (CA); *Weatherbie v. Green* (1853) 1 P.I.E.R. 97; *Ohlemacher v. Brown* (1879), 44 U.C.Q.B. 366 (C.A.); *International Harvester Co. of Canada v. Zarbok* [1918] 3 W.W.R. 38, 11 Sask. L.R. 354. For recognition under Canadian law of foreign compositions and judicially supervised arrangements, see Honsberger in I.F. Fletcher (ed.), *Cross-Border Insolvency: Comparative Dimensions (The Aberystwyth Insolvency Papers)* (1990), ch. 9(a).

[279] (1867) 4 W.W.& A'B. (L) 189, at 191–192 per Stawell C.J., drawing inspiration from tentative *dicta* expressed in *Phillips v. Allan, supra* n.276, at 483–484 per Bayley J., and at 484–485 per Holroyd J.

[280] 25 U.S. (12 Wheat.) 213 (1827), also referred to in Chapter 1, at 1.3 above. See also *Moore v. Horton*, 39 N.Y. Sup. Ct. 393 (1884) (32 Hun), in which the New York Supreme Court ruled that a foreign discharge had no extraterritorial effect.

[281] For scholarly assessment, see Nadelmann (1948), 61 Harv. L.Rev. 804, 827; unsigned comment in (1930) *39 Yale L.J. 559*; Honsberger (1980) 30 Case Western Res.L. Rev. 631, at 663 *et seq*. See also Morales and Deutcsh, (1984) *39 Bus. Law. 1573.*

2.8 CONCURRENT BANKRUPTCIES

Given the considerable variety of grounds on which jurisdiction in bankruptcy may be based, it can readily be the case that a debtor whose private and business affairs are such as to create forensic links with more than one country may be simultaneously liable to undergo adjudication in two, or possibly more, places. Several different scenarios can be envisaged. It may be that all these proceedings take place outside the United Kingdom, so that the English court is largely concerned to resolve issues of competing claims to the assets by different, foreign office holders and others. Alternatively, one of the concurrent sets of proceedings may be in England itself (or in another part of the United Kingdom). The chronological sequence of the opening of the various bankruptcies may also be a relevant factor. We will here examine the rules and principles that provide the framework for dealing with concurrent, or successive, bankruptcies. Further aspects of the judicial approach to these increasingly complex issues are discussed in Chapter 4.

If all the bankruptcy proceedings are taking place in politically foreign countries, it may be necessary to decide, as between the respective office holders, which of them has the prior claim to any property situate in England. The English case law, employing the familiar line of reasoning that equates bankruptcy to a species of forcible assignment of the debtor's estate, accords priority to the trustee under the proceedings whose date of commencement is earliest.[282] Naturally, it must also be the case that the foreign proceedings meet the criteria for recognition that were explored at 2.6 above. The usual proviso will also be applicable, namely that the foreign trustee takes 'subject to equities'.[283] This rule whereby priority is accorded to the first in time is in contrast to the rule of domestic bankruptcy law for cases where a later bankruptcy is commenced while the bankrupt remains undischarged from an earlier one. In its treatment of such consecutive bankruptcies, English law causes the second bankruptcy to absorb the earlier one, while maintaining a necessary distinction between the two groups of creditors concerned in the earlier and the later bankruptcy, and between the pools of assets to which each group can legitimately be allowed to lay claim.[284] The rule concerning concurrent, foreign bankruptcies appears somewhat unsophisticated, in that there is no scope for carrying out an analysis of the relative claims of the overseas administrations to provide the principal seat of administering the bankrupt's

[282] *Re Anderson* [1911] 1 K.B. 896; *Re Temple* [1947] Ch. 345; *Re O'Reardon* (1873) L.R. 9 Ch.App. 74; *Geddes v. Mowat* (1824) 1 Gl.& J. 414 (HL).

[283] See at 2.2.1 and 2.6.1(b) above.

[284] See Insolvency Act 1986, ss. 335. The topic is discussed in I.F. Fletcher, *The Law of Insolvency*, 2nd edn. (1996), at pp. 229–301.

property. It may easily be supposed that proceedings could first be commenced in a country where there are comparatively few creditors, or few assets (or both), which may make it questionable whether the 'first past the post' rule of priority will necessarily ensure that the greatest benefit is shared among the greatest number of creditors. At the very least, it is submitted, the English court should scrutinise the general terms of distribution that will be applied to the assets it is being invited to turn over, in order to ascertain whether adequate rights of participation in the earlier proceedings will be afforded to the creditors who are concerned in those which opened later. If it transpires that the assets collected in the first proceedings will effectively be ring-fenced for the benefit of local creditors there, the English court should refuse turnover on the ground that public policy demands that creditors shall be afforded equality on a universal basis.

When it is the case that bankruptcy proceedings either have been, or in principle could be, opened in this country as well as in some foreign country, English courts are no longer in a position of neutrality, but must pay heed to the imperative requirements of English law itself. In purely abstract terms, the doctrine of universality would seem to preclude the possibility of a debtor being the subject of more than one set of bankruptcy proceedings at any one time. Logically, therefore, it might be supposed that English law would refuse to countenance a situation in which concurrent sets of proceedings are opened, one of them in England. In reality, a more pragmatic approach has been developed, which appears to recognise that there may well be sound, practical reasons for tolerating the subdivision of what is supposedly a singular case of insolvency into two or more concurrent administrations. This is especially true when there are sizeable groups of creditors, or substantial or complex claims, associated with a particular sphere of the debtor's international activities, or where there are significant assets in a particular jurisdiction which it may be difficult for an out-of-state trustee to administer efficiently. So it may be demonstrable that the additional costs of parallel administrations can be justified by the greater saving of value globally (including a reduction of the expense to be incurred by creditors in proving for their debts). Ideally, the principle of universality may be honoured in spirit, if not in fact, through a process of cooperation between the respective trustees. Just such a vision of constructive co-ordination of separate, parallel bankruptcies was expounded by Bigham J. in *Re P. MacFadyen & Co.*,[285] in which the English trustee and his foreign counterpart had reached agreement on a scheme for pooling all assets and all claims and administering them rateably as though forming a single entity. The fairness of this arrangement,

[285] [1908] 1 K.B. 675.

and the obvious advantages for all creditors of eliminating potential delay and expense resulting from litigation between the trustees, induced the learned judge to sanction the proposed scheme, despite the absence of any express provision in the bankruptcy legislation to authorise such initiatives.

Where the foreign bankruptcy is the first in time to commence, this poses certain conceptual problems for the English court to which a bankruptcy petition is presented. Assuming that the foreign proceedings meet the criteria for recognition under English private international law, this would result in a situation where all the debtor's property, apart from any English immoveables, has already vested in the foreign trustee.[286] Nevertheless, an overriding rule has been established, to the effect that the opening of a foreign bankruptcy does not deprive the English court of jurisdiction to adjudicate the same debtor bankrupt, although it can exercise its discretion in deciding whether a second adjudication will serve any useful purpose.[287] One factor to which the court pays close regard is whether there appear to be any assets in England which could be administered in bankruptcy proceedings here.[288] On the other hand, the extensive powers of investigation, and the powers of avoidance of prior transactions, that would be available to an English-appointed trustee may furnish reasons for not trusting to the mere appearance that there are no assets here, if there are reasonable grounds for suspecting otherwise. Under some circumstances however a technical obstacle may prevent the English court from making a bankruptcy order. For example, if the foreign bankruptcy has already progressed to an advanced stage, so that the bankrupt has obtained his discharge under those proceedings, this may produce the effect under English private international law that the debt on which the petitioning creditor in England has based his petition has thereby been released.[289] If so, the exacting requirements of section 267 of the Insolvency Act cannot be satisfied unless there is some alternative creditor willing to serve as substitute, whose debt happens not to have been comprised in the effects of the foreign discharge.[290]

[286] Under Scottish law this principle is accepted, with the consequence that a foreign bankruptcy renders a subsequent award of sequestration in Scotland incompetent: *Strother v. Read* (1803), Morrison, *Forum competens*, Appendix 4; *Goetze v. Aders* 1874, 2 R. 150; *Phosphate Sewage Co.Ltd v. Molleson* (1878) 5 R. 1125.

[287] *Re McCulloch* (1880) 14 Ch.D. 716 (CA);*Re Robinson* (1883) 22 Ch.D. 816 (CA); *Re Artola Hermanos* (1890) 24 Q.B.D.640 (CA); *Re a Debtor (No. 199 of 1922)* [1922] 2 Ch. 470 (CA); *Re a Debtor (No. 737 of 1928)* [1929] 1 Ch. 362 (CA).

[288] Cf. *Re Robinson, supra* n.287.

[289] Such a development was envisaged by James L.J. in *Ex parte Pascal* (1876) 1 Ch.D. 509 (CA). For recognition of the effects of foreign discharge, see at 2.7 above.

[290] Insolvency Act 1986, s.267 is discussed at 2.1.2 above, at p. 43.

Comparative aspects

The possibilities which are made available by modern legislation in Canada, Australia and the USA for international cooperation in cases of concurrent bankruptcies will be explored in Chapter 4 below.

3

Insolvency of Companies

PRELIMINARY

Although most of the fundamental principles of international insolvency law were originally conceived in the context of the insolvency of natural persons, it is undoubtedly the case that the area of greatest commercial significance—both in terms of the monetary amounts involved, and in terms of the complex issues encountered—concerns the insolvency of companies. Historically, corporate entities of various kinds have been endowed with legal personality under municipal law, ranging from ecclesiastical or public bodies to the merchant adventurers of medieval and later times. These forms of corporate status were usually conferred by means of a Royal charter.[1] However it was with the evolution, during the middle part of the nineteenth century, of the statute-based system for the formation of joint stock companies possessing corporate personality with limited liability, that the full possibilities were realised for legal persons, formed under the national law of one country, to become involved in international commercial ventures and legal relationships accompanied, inevitably, by the risk of financial failure. From these elements, the still-evolving fabric of international corporate insolvency law has been gradually assembled.[2]

Because of the inherent differences between legal and natural persons, it is only to be expected that numerous distinctions have arisen in the course of time with respect to the legal and procedural regimes that are applicable in the event of insolvency. Just as English domestic law of insolvency is notable for the extent to which such distinctions have evolved, and are maintained to the present day,[3] so too in relation to international insolvency the number of points of divergence is such as to necessitate a separate treatment in this chapter of the framework of rules and principles that operate in cases of corporate insolvency. It must be emphasised however that there are also many instances in which the two branches of law follow an identical path, so that each can freely borrow from the other in

[1] See *Gower's Principles of Modern Company Law*, 6th edn. (1997, by P.L.Davies), ch. 2.

[2] For a concise and illuminating account of the formative period of modern English company law, see Gower, *supra* n.1, ch. 3. See also *Palmer's Company Law*, 25th edn. (1992) (by G. Morse and others), Part 1.

[3] The historic reasons for these systemic differences are briefly surveyed in I.F.Fletcher, *The Law of Insolvency*, 2nd edn. (1996), ch. 1. See also the Cork Report, Cmnd. 8558 (1982), ch. 2.

terms of precedent and authority. Where this is the case, the reader will be referred to the appropriate section or passage in Chapter 2 above. As far as possible, the structure of the present chapter is modelled on that of Chapter 2, so that similar issues are considered at a matching position in the text. However, the fundamental nature of some of the differences renders a completely symmetrical treatment inappropriate.

3.1 CORPORATIONS: BASIC CONCEPTS AND SPECIAL PRINCIPLES

'Corporation' is the formal term used by English common law to designate an entity on which legal personality is conferred such as to be separate from the individuals comprising it. As a legal—or juristic—person a corporation is capable of enjoying and being subject to legal rights, duties and liabilities, and also enjoys the character of perpetuity, in the sense that its existence is maintained through the succession of new individuals as members in place of those who die or are removed. Unlike human beings, whose legal personality is inherent and not dependent on any special process of the law itself, a corporation can only exist as a legal person through having undergone a requisite process of formation whereby such grant of a legal *persona* took effect. English law distinguishes between two types of corporation, the 'corporation sole', consisting of one member only at any one time (such as the Crown), and the 'corporation aggregate', which may consist of several or many members contemporaneously whose individual identities can fluctuate over time. It is to the latter category that the type of entity which concerns us here—the joint stock company, formed through a process of registration under the Companies Acts—belongs.

We see therefore that the genesis of a company's legal personality is inescapably associated with the statutory framework in force to regulate such matters, as at the time of the alleged incorporation taking place.[4] The underlying logic of this appears to be straightforward: since legal personality can only arise through the operation of a recognised process of formation under a given, municipal law, it is to that system and its relevant rules that reference must be made for the purpose of confirming that an alleged incorporation has been validly accomplished. It is this argument from first principles which supplies the basis for the so-called 'state of incorporation' theory of international recognition of corporate personality that has been gained by formation under the laws of a particular State or

[4] For the current requirements for company formation under English law, see Gower, *supra* n.1, Part Two (chs. 5–7); Palmer, *supra* n.2, Part 2. The primary legislative provisions are contained in the Companies Act 1985, Part I.

country. According to this theory—to which English law subscribes along with the rest of the common law family of legal systems (together with some members of the civil law tradition)[5]—the formation, existence and dissolution of a corporation are determined by the system of law under which the corporation is alleged to have been formed.[6] By natural extension of this principle, it is to the law of the State of incorporation that reference is made to ascertain what are the incidents and other consequences of the process of formation, such as the powers and capacities with which the company is endowed, the rights and duties of the members *inter se*, and the extent to which the members' liability for the company's debts is limited.[7]

In the case of corporate formations taking place under English law, confirmation of the successful completion of the process and all attendant formalities can readily be gained by investigation of the records maintained by the Registrar of Companies, by whom the company's certificate of incorporation is issued and maintained in force. There are liberal aspects to the criteria for gaining registration which favour the use of the corporate form as a vehicle for international commercial activity. Thus, a company can be validly formed as an English company by complying with the prescribed requirements, which are mainly expressed in formal or quantitative terms, for example regarding the minimum number of persons who must subscribe to the memorandum of association, or the amount of its registered share capital.[8] No special, qualitative criteria are imposed to prevent the formation of a company where all of the members are foreign nationals resident overseas, or where most if not all of the company's business will be conducted outside this country.[9] Provided that the company's articles indicate that its registered office is located within England and Wales, the company may be registered even though there is no other

[5] For example, The Netherlands: Law of 25 July 1959, Official Gazette 1959, at p. 256.

[6] *Lazard Bros. v. Midland Bank Ltd.* [1933] A.C. 289 (HL), esp. at 297 per Lord Wright; *Dairen Kisen Kabushiki Kaisa v. Shiang Kee* [1941] A.C. 373 (PC); *Carl Zeiss Stiftung v. Rayner & Keeler Ltd.* [1967] A.C. 853 (HL); *National Bank of Greece and Athens S.A. v. Metliss* [1958] A.C. 509 (HL); *Adams v. National bank of Greece S.A.* [1961] A.C. 255 (HL). Also instructive are the earlier cases, e.g. *Henriques v. The General Privileged Dutch Company trading to the West Indies* (1727) 2 Ld. Raym. 1532, 92 E.R. 494; *Re Imperial Anglo-German Bank* (1872) 26 L.T. 228; *Russian Commercial and Industrial Bank v. Comptoir d'Escompte de Mulhouse* [1925] A.C.112 (HL); *Banque Internationale de Commerce de Petrograd v. Goukassow* [1925] A.C. 150 (HL); *Employers' Liability Assurance Corpn. Ltd. v. Sedgwick, Collins & Co. Ltd.* [1927] A.C. 95 (HL).

[7] *General Steam Navigation Co. v. Guillou* (1843) 11 M.& W. 877, 152 E.R. 1061; *Pickering v. Stephenson* (1872) L.R. 14 Eq. 322; *Baroness Wenlock v. River Dee Co.* (1883) 36 Ch.D. 674, esp. at 685 per Bowen L.J., affd. (HL) (1885) 10 App.Cas. 354; *Risdon Iron & Locomotive Works v. Furness* [1906] 1 K.B. 49 (CA); *Von Hellfield v. E. Rechnitzer* [1914] 1 Ch. 748 (CA).

[8] Companies Act 1985, ss.1, 2(5)(a). See also *ibid.*, ss.117, 118(1) for the requirement that a public company's alloted share capital must be not less than the authorised minimum amount of (currently) £50,000.

[9] *Reuss v. Bos* (1871) L.R. 5 H.L. 176.

address in this country at which any meaningful corporate activity takes place.[10] Accordingly, the functional connections between the company and its 'home' country may be, or may in the course of time become, minimal by virtue of the manner in which its operations are conducted. Hence there is an inbuilt potential, under the State of incorporation theory, for a divergence to occur between the location of the operational 'centre of gravity' of the company and the country on whose laws the company's legal personality depends for its very existence. Equally, there is the possibility that those responsible for the formation of a company may engineer its formation so that this takes place under the laws of a country whose regulatory regime for companies is especially indulgent towards those who control and manage it—the so-called 'Delaware syndrome'.

While vigorous commercial arguments can be marshalled in support of such a flexible legal doctrine, the scope offered for nefarious manipulation cannot be ignored. This helps to explain why some legal systems, especially from within the civil law tradition, continue in their adherence to the more exacting requirements of the 'real seat' theory of the acquisition and retention of legal personality. According to this theory, which owes much to French juristic reasoning, legal personality can only subsist on the basis of a genuine, and sustained, functional association between the company and the country whose laws supply its 'life force'. To achieve this, it must be demonstrable that the real centre of the company's financial and business operations (its *siège réel*, also termed *siège social effectif* by some writers), not merely its registered office (*siège social*) must lie within the frontiers of the country under whose laws it claims to enjoy its corporate identity.[11] This can result in a retrospective finding that a supposedly valid corporate formation was actually a nullity because of the view later taken by the court as to the whereabouts of the corporate 'seat'. When applied at the level of international recognition of corporate personality allegedly acquired under the law of a particular country, there is every possibility that courts in different countries may reach different conclusions, based on the same factual evidence, as to the correlation (or otherwise) between the real seat of the company and the country under whose laws it was purportedly formed.[12] *A fortiori*, if the validity of a particular

[10] Companies Act 1985, s.10(1)(a).

[11] On the doctrine of the real corporate seat in French law and in other civil law countries, see C. Livadas, *The Winding-up of Insolvent Companies in England and France* (1983), at pp. 5–8; M.Wolff, *Private International Law*, 2nd edn. (1955), ch. XXI; E. Rabel, *The Conflict of Laws, a Comparative Study*, 2nd edn. (1960), vol. 2, p. 27 *et seq.*, esp. at pp. 125–172.

[12] This possibility, and its implications for the proper functioning of the European Common Market as originally conceived, led to the inclusion in the EEC Treaty of 25 March 1957 of Art. 220(3), requiring the negotiation of a convention on mutual recognition of companies. The original six member states concluded such a convention on 29 February 1968, but it has remained dormant due to non-ratification by The Netherlands. See I.F.Fletcher, *Conflict of Laws and European Community Law* (1982), ch. 7.

company's formation is a material question in proceedings taking place in separate jurisdictions, of which one subscribes to the 'State of incorporation' theory while the other belongs to the 'real seat' school of thought, there is an even greater likelihood that divergent conclusions may be reached. This can give rise to genuine, and not merely theoretical, commercial problems when any question of the company's existence arises before a foreign court, including the basic question of the company's capacity to act and to conduct its business outside its state of formation.[13] The contrasting doctrinal positions of the two factions, as yet unreconciled, also manifest themselves with respect to the exercise of jurisdiction to wind up insolvent companies, and the recognition of foreign liquidations and other proceedings.[14]

3.1.1 Corporate domicile, residence and nationality

Once it had become established that a company which has undergone formation according to the requirements of the Companies Acts is accorded a legal personality in its own right,[15] English courts proceeded to explore the further attributes of such a *persona* against the background of the rules already developed for enforcing rights and remedies by and against natural persons. Given the traditional preference of English law to refer matters concerning the status of natural persons to the law of the domicile, and to rely on residence as an important connecting factor for many jurisdictional purposes, it not perhaps too surprising to discover that the same connecting factors have come to be applied to companies as well, albeit with certain modifications.[16] It is now accepted that a company is capable

[13] Cf. the Belgian case of *Lamot v. Société 'Lamot' Ltd.*, Cass. Nov. 12 1965; Pa. 1966 I.366; noted in (1967) Rev.Crit.D.I.P. 506 (Loussouarn), and in (1967) Clunet 140. See also A. Conard in C.M. Schmitthoff (ed.), *Harmonisation of European Company Law* (1973), p. 45 *et seq.* at p. 57.

[14] See Part II below on the various efforts aimed at achieving international *rapprochement* in these areas

[15] See, notably, *Salomon v. Salomon & Co.* [1897] A.C. 22 (HL), which may be interpreted as a triumph of formalism over substance, in that what was in essence a one-man company was finally held to enjoy the full attributes of a distinct legal personality because there had been compliance with the requirement, under the Companies Act 1862, that there must be a minimum of seven subscribers to the memorandum. Although S himself was the only one of the seven to acquire a shareholding of any substance (20,000 shares), while the other six, each of whom subscribed the bare minimum of one share each, were S's wife and their five children respectively, the validity of incorporation was upheld on the basis that the Act imposed no requirements that the subscribers must be independent of one another, or that they must take a substantial financial interest in the company at its formation. (For the current requirements under the Companies Act 1985, see *supra*, nn. 4 and 8 above. The essential principle as stated above has not been changed).

[16] The classic study on this subject is A. Farnsworth, *The Residence and Domicile of Corporations* (1939). Although this work was produced 60 years ago, it remains the essential point of first reference for the English law approach.

of having a domicile.[17] Using the argument that the formation of a company can be considered as analogous to the birth of a human being, the view has evolved that the domicile of a company is the country to whose laws it owes its being, namely its State of incorporation.[18] Since domicile is conceived as a forensic association between a person and a country (in the special sense meaning a 'law district') a corporate domicile must similarly be defined, if the State in question happens to be subdivided internally, by reference to the particular part with which the circumstances of its formation generate a recognised connection according to the domestic law of that State.[19] The analogy with the domicile of natural persons is seemingly not pursued to its logical limits, however, for whereas it is open to a natural person to effect a change of domicile during the course of a lifetime, the prevalent opinion is that a corporate domicile is immutable. This conclusion seems to be dictated by the realisation that, unlike a human being after birth, a company is logically unable to sever its umbilical connection to the legal system of which its very existence is a consequence.[20] A related, and thus far unresolved, question concerns the possibility for a company to possess more than one domicile, if the laws of its State of incorporation happen to allow it to re-incorporate in another State whilst retaining its original domicile in its 'home' State.[21] Although such a development is at present precluded for any company originally formed under United Kingdom companies legislation, the possibility of such processes taking place under foreign law would seemingly have to be recognised by English law as giving rise to such consequences as the respective laws of the States of incorporation, severally and jointly, can be shown to produce.[22] Apart from such hypothetical extensions, however, the English law position is that corporate domicile is unique and immutable. It will be suggested below that this is in need of revision and restatement. We may note at this point that, despite the apparent harmony between the principles underlying the State of incorporation theory and those applied by English law to determine the whereabouts of the corporate domicile, there are inherent tensions resulting from these doctrinal propositions when English courts encounter the need either to exercise jurisdiction to wind up a company not originally formed under English

[17] *Gasque v. Commissioners of Inland Revenue* [1940] 2 K.B. 80, vindicating the conclusions advanced by Farnsworth, *supra* n.16, ch. 6.

[18] Cf. Farnsworth, *supra* n.16, at p. 205. Perhaps the clearest articulation of the common law doctrine of the corporate domicile and its attribution is in the Canadian case of *National Trust Co. Ltd. v. Ebro Irrigation & Power Co. Ltd.* [1954] 3 D.L.R. 326.

[19] See Chapter 2, at 2.1.1(b)(i) above.

[20] *Gasque v. Commissioners of Inland Revenue, supra* n.17; *Carl Zeiss Stiftung v. Rayner & Keeler Ltd. (No. 3)* [1970] 1 Ch. 506, at 544 per Buckley J. See also Farnsworth, *supra* n.16, at p. 273.

[21] As is permitted, at least within the Federal system, under American corporations law.

[22] See, to the same effect, the suggestions of Smart in [1990] J.B.L. 126, and *Dicey and Morris, The Conflict of Laws*, 12th edn. (1993), at p. 1104.

law, and so not domiciled here, and likewise when the courts are considering whether to recognise foreign insolvency proceedings which have taken place in a country other than that in which the company is domiciled, in the English law sense of that term.[23]

English law has for some purposes made use of the concept of corporate residence as a connecting factor, for example to establish liability to United Kingdom taxation in the case of companies not originally formed and registered under our domestic law. Although residence has not hitherto been explicitly employed as a connecting factor in relation to international corporate insolvency law questions, it is worthwhile here to consider the way in which the concept of corporate residence has developed, partly because it has, at least implicitly, influenced the approach already taken towards some insolvency issues, and also because of its potential for meeting the need to devise new, internationally acceptable criteria for insolvency purposes. While it must be conceded that there is an element of artificiality about the attribution of a residence to an entity which has no bodily existence, practical necessity makes it essential that some way must be found of harnessing the law's established processes to the corporate *persona*, whose very reason for existence is to accomplish certain commercial objectives within a defined, legal framework. As with domicile, the technique of selective analogy has been deployed, resulting in a rule based on the notion that a company, like an individual trader, is to be regarded as residing in the place 'where its real business is carried on'. This expression has been further defined by the House of Lords as 'the place where the persons who control and direct the destinies of the corporation meet and exercise their functions, or, more simply, where "central control and management abides"'.[24] Unfortunately, as with any definition involving general or abstract terminology, difficulties can arise when applying notions such as 'real' or 'central' to the actual circumstances under which a given business operation is conducted. A degree of pragmatism is therefore required, as was demonstrated in *Swedish Central Railway Co. v. Thompson*,[25] where the functional migration to Sweden of an English-formed company was held to have given rise to a state of affairs where the company, at least for purposes of levying UK taxation, was resident both in this country and in Sweden. The concept of dual residence was therefore accepted, even at the cost of straining the linguistic sense of the term 'central', which might be

[23] See at 3.1, 3.2, 3.6, and 3.7 below.

[24] *De Beers Consolidated Mines Ltd. v. Howe* [1906] A.C. 455, 458 per Lord Loreburn, L.C.; *Egyptian Delta Land and Investment Co. Ltd. v. Todd* [1929] A.C. 1 (HL). See Farnsworth, *supra* n.16, chs. 4 and 5.

[25] [1925] A.C.495, distinguished and explained in *Egyptian Delta Land and Investment Co. Ltd. v. Todd*, *supra* n.24. See the useful comparative table presented by Farnsworth, *supra* n.16, at pp. 107–108, showing the material points of divergence between the facts of these two leading cases.

thought to denote a single locality. It is also established that English law bases its conclusion as to a company's place of residence upon an assessment of the actual manner in which its affairs are conducted, and is not content merely to inquire into the ostensible provisions under the company's own constitutional arrangements which purport to determine where its central management and control are to be exercised.[26] It is submitted that, having regard to the technological possibilities of the modern world, it must be assumed that systems of business organisation and management will become ever more sophisticated and complex, and will almost certainly defeat all attempts to apply precise definitions, expressed in concrete terms, for the purposes of regulating companies and subjecting them to legal proceedings. It is one of the positive attributes of the English common law, as will be further seen in the present chapter, that it has refused to allow considerations drawn from abstract logic alone to become an obstacle to the administration of practical legal remedies in response to commercial needs.[27]

With regard to the attribution of nationality to a company, English private international law, which seldom makes use of this connecting factor for its own purposes, has had comparatively little to say on the subject. However, since some other systems of law traditionally attach considerable importance to nationality as a connecting factor, and would normally refer to the law of the country of alleged nationality to verify the status of the *propositus* in this respect, we may note that the House of Lords have asserted that a corporation is considered to be a national or subject of the country in which it is incorporated.[28] Any supposed analogy with the attribution of nationality in the case of natural persons is once again diminished by the fact that a corporation is not regarded as having the capability of changing its nationality.[29]

3.1.2 Selected comparisons

Within the **USA**, the 'State of incorporation' doctrine is applied to determine questions as to the formation, existence and subsequent dissolution of a corporation.[30] The domicile of a corporation is also held to be in its

[26] *Unit Construction Co. Ltd. v. Bullock* [1960] A.C. 351 (HL).

[27] See at 3.2.2, 3.2.3 below.

[28] *Janson v. The Driefontein Consolidated Mines Ltd.* [1902] A.C. 484, esp. at 505 per Lord Lindley; *Kuenigl v. Donnersmarck* [1955] 1 Q.B. 515 at 535 per McNair J. See also Farnsworth, *supra* n.16, Appendix III.

[29] For comparative analysis written from a common law perspective, see Hilton-Young (1908) 22 Harv. L. Rev. 1; Schuster (1916) 2 Grot. Soc. 57; Vaughan Williams and Chrussachi (1933) 49 L.Q.R. 334.

[30] Restatement, Second, Conflict of Laws, ss.296, 299 (1971); *Chaplin v. Selznick*, 293 N.Y. 529, 58 N.E. 2d 719 (1944); *Bazan v. Kux Machine Co.*, 52 Wis. 2d 325, 190 N.W. 2d 521 (1971). For the pragmatic approach adopted in a case where the company's dissolution takes place

State of incorporation.[31] Because of the special problems raised under American law when proceedings involve diversity of citizenship, even as between different States of the Union, the citizenship of a corporation is a matter of live interest. To prevent the litigious advantages of diversity jurisdiction from being too freely exploited by corporations which have incorporated under the laws of one State, but which have mainly conducted their commercial affairs in some other State, a special provision of the Judicial Code declares that: 'a corporation shall be deemed a citizen of any State by which it has been incorporated and of the State where it has its principal place of business'.[32] Thus the possibility of dual citizenship is accepted.

Both **Australian** and **Canadian** law follow closely the approach of English law as depicted above. Thus, the status and powers conferred on a company or partnership by the law of the country where it was formed, will be recognised under the laws of the two countries, as will the effects of a process taking place under the law of the State of incorporation whereby the company is dissolved and its corporate personality extinguished.[33] Legislative provision has been made in Australia whereby, if it is necessary to determine whether a body or person has been validly incorporated under a law other than that of Australia itself, reference is to be made to the law applied in the place of incorporation.[34] There is also provision allowing a foreign corporation to apply to be registered as a domestic company under the Australian Corporations Law, provided that such re-incorporation is authorised under the law of the company's original incorporation.[35]

3.2 JURISDICTION

An account of the rules governing the exercise of jurisdiction by English courts in cases of international corporate insolvency may be thematically

in a foreign country under unstable political conditions, see *Sokoloff v. National City Bank of New York*, 145 N.E. 917 (1924) (N.Y.C.A.), at 918 *et seq.*, per Cardozo J.

[31] *Fourco Glass Co. v. Transmirra Products Corp.*, 353 U.S. 222, 226, 77 S.Ct. 787, 1 L.Ed. 2d 786 (1957); *Johnson & Johnson v. Picard*, 282 F. 2d 386 (6th Cir. 1960).

[32] 28 U.S.C.A., s. 1332(c).

[33] See, in addition to the English authorities cited above, (for **Australia**) *United Services Insurance Co. Ltd. (in liquidation) v. Lang* (1935) 35 S.R. (N.S.W.) 487; (for **Canada**) *National Trust Co. Ltd. v. Ebro Irrigation & Power Co. Ltd.*, *supra* n.18; *Brown, Gow, Wilson v. Beleggings-Societeit N.V.* (1961) 29 D.L.R. (2d) 673; *Skyline Associates v. Small* (1974) 50 D.L.R. (3d) 217.

[34] Foreign Corporations (Application of Laws) Act 1989, s.7. See also *ibid.*, s.8, which requires foreign proceedings purporting to affect a foreign corporation, its assets or dealings, to be denied recognition or effect in Australia if they were based on an assertion of sovereignty over the place where the foreign corporation was incorporated, unless recognition and effect would be accorded under the law of the place of incorporation.

[35] Corporations Law (Cth), s.133.

divided into two main categories. The first concerns those cases where an English-formed company happens to pursue most of its activities abroad. The second, more substantial category, concerns the possibilities for English courts to wind up a foreign-formed company having some kind of connection with England and its law. These will be considered in turn.

The Insolvency Act 1986, Part IV (sections 73–219 inclusive), deals in a comprehensive manner with the winding up of companies registered under the Companies Acts. The winding up of unregistered companies is dealt with in Part V of the Act, consisting of just ten sections (sections 220–229). This division is a reflection of English law's espousal of the 'state of incorporation' theory as its fundamental philosophical position, as explained above. One of the main planks of that doctrine is that it is the inherent right of the law under which a company has acquired its existence as a legal person to control the circumstances and the processes whereby that existence may be terminated through winding up and dissolution. Indeed, pushed to its logical limits the doctrine would establish a monopoly over such proceedings in favour of the State of incorporation, on the basis that it is the only jurisdiction whose law is competent to rule upon questions concerning the life and death of a corporate *persona* whose existence has come about as a product of that system. We shall see, however, that this degree of exclusivity is not maintained in practice, particularly in cases where it is sought to bring about the winding up in England of a foreign company.[36]

3.2.1 Winding up of English-formed companies doing business abroad

The jurisdiction of English courts to entertain winding-up proceedings under Part IV of the 1986 Act is expressed in direct and unequivocal terms by section 117(1), which states that the High Court has jurisdiction to wind up any company registered in England and Wales. This is augmented by section 117(2), which provides that where the amount of the company's share capital paid up or credited as paid up does not exceed £120,000, then the County Court of the district in which the company's registered office is situated has concurrent jurisdiction with the High Court to wind up the company.[37] The expression 'registered office' is defined by section 117(6) as meaning the place which has longest been the company's registered office during the six months immediately preceding the presentation of

[36] See at 3.2.2 below.

[37] By s.117(4) of the 1986 Act, the allocation of winding up jurisdiction to designated County Courts is placed under the control of the Lord Chancellor. See also at 2.1.2 above (text to nn. 68–72) concerning the parallel arrangements for allocation of bankruptcy jurisdiction at County Court level. The sum of £120,000 specified in s.117(2) is subject to variation by means of statutory instrument: s.117(3).

the petition for winding up. The terms of section 117(1) are cast in the form of an affirmation, effectively signifying that it is *by virtue* of the fact of registration that the English courts have jurisdiction. No other nexus with this country is mentioned in the section, and no further conditions are attached, so that the factor of registration is both necessary and sufficient for the purposes of founding jurisdiction under Part IV. Notably, the particular circumstances of the company's internal organisation and mode of conducting its business are of no relevance from the standpoint of jurisdiction. In an extreme case, therefore, a company might be formed and registered in England by persons from abroad, and it might also be the case that all shareholders and directors are foreign nationals resident and domiciled abroad, and that none of the company's business is done inside this country. Nevertheless, the company would qualify as a 'domestic' rather than as a 'foreign' company and would be at all times subject to the winding up jurisdiction of the English courts by virtue of section 117(1) and (2).[38]

Companies formed under the Companies Act 1985 are obliged to indicate in the memorandum of association whether the registered office of the company is to be situated in England and Wales, or in Scotland.[39] Where Scotland is specified for this purpose, this has the effect of precluding the English High Court from having jurisdiction to wind up the company. For such cases, the provisions of section 120 of the Insolvency Act are complementary to those of section 117 in declaring that the Court of Session has jurisdiction to wind up any company registered in Scotland.[40]

Two different modes of winding up are available under Part IV of the Insolvency Act, namely winding up by the court (also known as compulsory winding up), and voluntary winding up. Only the first of these is, as its name suggests, initiated by means of an order of the court in response to a petition presented by a party qualified to do so.[41] Hence, the issue of judicial jurisdiction only presents itself *in limine* in a case of winding up by the court. The voluntary winding up procedure in the case of a company not certifiable as solvent is known as a creditors' voluntary winding up, and is principally governed by Chapters IV and V of Part IV. Although the procedure can take place without any direct judicial involvement, the

[38] *Reuss v. Bos* (1871) L.R. 5 H.L. 176; *Re Tumacacori Mining Co.* (1874) L.R. 17 Eq. 534.

[39] Companies Act 1985, s.2(1)(b). This maintains the position under previous companies legislation, e.g. Companies Act 1948, s.2(1)(b). By s.2(2) of the 1985 Act the memorandum may contain a statement that the company's registered office is to be situated in Wales.

[40] Similarly, s.120(3) of the 1986 Act confers a concurrent jurisdiction, in the case of companies with not more than £120,000 share capital, on the sheriff court of the sheriffdom in which the company's registered office is situated. See also s.120(4) in the case where the company's registered office has been moved within the six months prior to the presentation of the winding up petition.

[41] See Insolvency Act 1986, s.124.

court may be invoked in case dispute arises at any stage, or if the need arises to seek directions on any matter.[42] What is certainly the case, however, is that a voluntary winding up can only take place under the Insolvency Act in the case of a company formed and registered under the Companies Acts, for only such an entity qualifies as a 'company' in the sense borne by that term throughout Part IV of the Insolvency Act.[43] It is therefore not possible for a company which has been formed under foreign law to purport to undergo a voluntary winding up in England, however substantial may be the company's functional ties with this country. This arises not merely as a consequence of the statutory meaning given to the term 'company', but is indeed the subject of an explicit provision in Part V of the Insolvency Act, where section 221(4) declares:'*No unregistered company shall be wound up under this Act voluntarily*'.

The position may be summed up as follows: a company registered in England and Wales may be wound up under Part IV of the 1986 Act, using either the compulsory or the voluntary mode of winding up, even though all or most of its functional operations, including its central control and management, are located abroad. Conversely, a company formed under foreign law, and so not meeting the criterion of being registered here, cannot be wound up under Part IV even though its central control and management, and all or most of its commercial activities, happen to be based in England. Such a company may however be eligible to be wound up here pursuant to the provisions of Part V of the Act, as will next be considered.[44]

3.2.2 Winding up of foreign companies in England

As explained above, the provisions of Part IV of the Insolvency Act 1986 are applicable exclusively to companies formed through the process of registration under the companies legislation currently or previously in force in relation to the United Kingdom.[45] Therefore, any corporate entity not so formed is classified as an 'unregistered company' for the purposes of the 1986 Act and other legislation relating to companies. Since the beginnings of the modern era of companies legislation in this country, provisions have been included in successive statutes to enable the winding up

[42] See Insolvency Act 1986, s.112. See also ss.100(3), 101(3), 104, 108, 114(2),116.

[43] See the definition of 'company' in the Companies Act 1985, s.735, which is applicable to the Insolvency Act 1986 by virtue of the rider to s.251 of that Act.

[44] See at 3.2.2 below. The further aspects of a winding up under Part IV are not here discussed. See, e.g. *Palmer's Company Law*, 25th edn. (1992, looseleaf), Part 15; I.F. Fletcher, *The Law of Insolvency*, 2nd edn. (1996), Part II, esp. chs. 18–21.

[45] The insolvency of companies in Northern Ireland is governed by separate, but closely similar, legislative provisions. See Insolvency (Northern Ireland) Order 1989 (S.I. 1989 No. 2045 (N.I.)).

to take place of any companies or associations which, for various reasons, had not utilised the procedure for registration. As the numbers and types of domestic companies still qualifying as unregistered have progressively dwindled, the provisions of what is now Part V of the 1986 Act have become applicable almost exclusively to cases where it is sought to wind up a foreign company in England. Such companies also come within the ambit of the provisions relating to unregistered companies, an expression which is defined by section 220(1) of the Act as including 'any association and any company, with [the exception of] a company registered in any part of the United Kingdom under the Joint Stock Companies Acts or under the legislation (past or present) relating to companies in Great Britain'. We will here consider the effects of the further provisions of Part V, as judicially interpreted, in relation to the winding up in England of foreign companies.

The key provision within Part V is section 221, which states that, subject to the further provisions of Part V itself, 'any unregistered company may be wound up under this Act'. The subsection further states that all the provisions of the Insolvency Act and the Companies Act about winding up apply to an unregistered company with the exceptions and additions mentioned in the other subsections of section 221. From the late nineteenth century onwards, the courts reached the conclusion that the statutory forerunners of what is now section 221 and its accompanying provisions were applicable to companies that had been incorporated under the law of a foreign country. The possibility that this might well have involved a process of registration in accordance with the laws of the State of incorporation did not prevent such foreign companies from being 'unregistered companies' for the purposes of English law.[46] Moreover, it may be noted that from a relatively early date the courts did not allow themselves to be deflected from making a winding up order by the fact that liquidation proceedings were known to be pending in the company's State of incorporation. Where it was perceived that some worthwhile objective could best be achieved by means of an English winding up, judicial creativity invariably proved equal to the challenge.[47]

Grounds for winding up

The grounds on which an unregistered company may be wound up by the court are listed in three separate paragraphs within section 221(5) of the Insolvency Act:

[46] *Re Commercial Bank of India* (1868) L.R. 6 Eq. 517; *Re Matheson Brothers Ltd.* (1884) 27 Ch.D. 225; *Re Mercantile Bank of Australia* [1892] 2 Ch. 204.

[47] *Re Matheson Brothers Ltd., supra* n.46; *Re Commercial Bank of South Australia* (1886) 33 Ch.D. 174; *Re Federal Bank of Australia* [1893] W.N. 77 (CA). See further, section 3.9. below regarding concurrent liquidations, and also Chapter 4 below.

(a) if the company is dissolved, or has ceased to carry on business, or is carrying on business only for the purpose of winding up its affairs;
(b) if the company is unable to pay its debts;
(c) if the court is of opinion that it is just and equitable that the company should be wound up.

Each of the above paragraphs furnishes an independent basis for winding up, and indeed paragraph (a) offers three separate grounds, any one of which will suffice.[48] The drafting of the subsection has remained virtually unchanged since its first enactment within the companies legislation of the mid-nineteenth century.[49] Some of the stylistic infelicities of the provision received judicial attention as long ago as 1870, when the use of the present tense in the opening phrase of paragraph (a) ('if the company *is* dissolved') was regarded as grammatically unsuitable in the context of the provisions which accompany it. The courts have subsequently followed the practice of transposing the tense as though it read 'if the company *has been* dissolved'.[50] Somewhat surprisingly, no steps have been taken to effect an alteration to the statutory drafting when the provision has been successively re-enacted down to and including the 1986 Act. It is also noteworthy that the possible grounds for winding up a company under Part V are considerably fewer than those listed in section 122 of the Act for the purposes of Part IV. Indeed, the grounds mentioned in section 221(5)(a) have no exact counterpart within section 122, although subsection (1)(d) allows the winding up of a registered company to take place if the company does not commence its business within a year from its incorporation or suspends its business for a whole year. On the other hand, the grounds specified in paragraphs (b) and (c) of s.221(5) correspond to those in paragraphs (f) and (g) of section 122(1).[51] It should be borne in mind that the primary purpose of the provisions of Part V as originally enacted was to provide a means for the winding up of various kinds of entity operating outside the newly-introduced system of incorporation by registration, but of domes-

[48] Cf. *Inland Revenue v. Highland Engineering Ltd.* 1975 S.L.T. 203.

[49] See Joint Stock Companies Act 1848, s.5(7); Companies Act 1862, s.199(3); Companies Act 1908, s.268(1)(iii); Companies Act 1929, s.338(1)(d); Companies Act 1948, s.399(5); Companies Act 1985, s.666(5) (all repealed).

[50] *Re Family Endowment Society* (1870) L.R. 5 Ch.App. 118, at 135–136 per Giffard L.J.; *Re Russian and English Bank* [1932] 1 Ch. 663; *Banque des Marchands de Moscou v. Kindersley* [1951] 1 Ch 112 (CA).

[51] There is one minor drafting discrepancy between s.221(5)(c) of the 1986 Act and s.122(1)(g), as currently enacted, namely the inclusion of the definite article before the word 'opinion' in paragraph (g) of s.122(1). Prior to 1985, the equivalent provision to what is now s.122(1)(g) commenced with the words 'if the court is of opinion'. The modified wording was first used in the Companies Act 1985, s.517(1)(g), and was retained when that provision was absorbed into the Insolvency Act 1986. No matching amendment was made in the case of s.666(5)(c) of the 1985 Act, re-enacted *verbatim* as s.221(5)(c) of the 1986 Act. It is not thought that the discrepancy of wording imports any difference in terms of the substance of the two provisions.

tic origin nonetheless. Judicial appreciation of the usefulness of applying this regime to the winding up of foreign-formed companies or associations, combined with the relative lack of detail in the enacted provisions themselves, have allowed the law to develop in a flexible manner, while generally (but not always exclusively) maintaining fidelity to the fundamental principles of insolvency.

The various grounds will now be considered in turn.

(a) Dissolution of the company, or cesser of its business

As was seen above, English law subscribes to the view that the extinction of the corporate personality by dissolution is a process which, just as with its first creation, is to be determined by the law of the company's State of incorporation.[52] To ascertain whether such dissolution has taken place, English law requires proof by the expert testimony of persons who are suitably qualified and experienced in the foreign legal system in question, and who can confirm that its effect in the circumstances of the instant case is that the company's legal existence and personality are dissolved.[53] Foreign law is thus treated as a question of fact, which the court must determine on the basis of the strength of the evidence adduced by the respective parties. The quality of the expert testimony is therefore of great importance.[54] Particular difficulties can arise when political or military events in a company's state of incorporation bring about a period of uncertainty regarding the identity of legitimate governmental authority in that place at any material time. The matter may be further complicated by the withholding by the governments of other States, including that of the

[52] See at 3.1 above, and authorities there referred to in nn. 6 and 7.

[53] *Lazard Bros. & Co. v. Midland Bank Ltd.* [1933] A.C. 289 (HL); *Re Russian Bank for Foreign Trade* [1933] 1 Ch. 745; *Banque des Marchands de Moscou v. Kindersley, supra* n.50; *Re Azoff-Don Commercial Bank* [1954] 1 Ch. 315. On the proof of foreign law as fact for the purposes of English civil proceedings, see Civil Evidence Act 1972, s.4, and see generally *Dicey and Morris, supra* n.22, ch. 9; *Cheshire and North's Private International Law*, 12th edn. (1992), ch. 7.

[54] Judicial comment upon the relative qualities of the expert witnesses giving evidence at trial may be found in a number of reported cases. See e.g. *Lazard Bros. & Co. v. Midland Bank Ltd.* [1933] A.C. 289 at 300–302 per Lord Wright; *Re Russian Bank for Foreign Trade* [1933] 1 Ch. 745 at 759–760 per Maugham J.; *Re Banque des Marchands de Moscou (Koupetschesky)* [1958] Ch. 182 at 193–202 per Roxburgh J. Cf. the contrary view of the effects of the same revolutionary events in Russia in and after 1918, reached on the basis of different testimony in *Russian Commercial and Industrial Bank v. Comptoir d'Escompte de Mulhouse* [1925] A.C. 112 at 125–128 per Lord Cave, followed in *Banque Internationale de Commerce de Petrograd v. Goukassow* [1925] A.C. 150, (decided by an identically composed committee of the House of Lords which gave judgment on the same day). Since the decision in 1933 of a differently constituted House in the *Lazards Bros.* case (*supra* n.53), it has been judicially accepted that the view arrived at in that later case concerning the legal consequences of the various Russian governmental decrees was the correct one, and that the private banks and insurance companies formerly incorporated under Imperial Russian law were thereby dissolved: *Russian and English Bank and Florence Montefiore Guedalla v. Baring Bros. & Co. Ltd.* [1936] A.C. 405 (HL); *Re Banque des Marchands de Moscou (Koupetschesky) (No. 2)* [1954] 1 W.L.R. 1108.

United Kingdom, of full international recognition of the new regime as the lawful government of that country. For there to be recognition under English law of the civil effects of the purported operation of the law prevailing at the place of the company's incorporation, it must be the case that Her Majesty's Government officially recognises that the foreign power constitutes at least the *de facto* government of the territory over which its acts are alleged to have operated. Once such recognition is accorded, it operates retrospectively to confer validity for the purposes of English law on acts which took place prior to the date of recognition. Although the practice of according formal recognition to foreign governments has been discontinued since 1980, the court may seek assistance from the Foreign and Commonwealth Office to certify the basis on which intergovernmental dealings have been conducted with the foreign power in question.[55]

Further, conceptual and doctrinal aspects of the winding up of dissolved foreign companies are considered at 3.2.3 below.

The two further grounds mentioned in section 221(5)(a) relate to the cesser of the company's business, either as an accomplished fact or as an impending prospect. These references to the carrying on of business by the company have at times prompted the suggestion that for a company to be capable of being wound up under Part V it must have, or have had, a place of business in England, or at the very least that it must have carried on business here. A closer examination of the actual terms of paragraph (a), and of section 221(5) as a whole, will show why this is not the case. Not only is there no mention of any need for the company to have such a thing as a place of business in this country, but indeed the references to the carrying on of the company's business contain no localising expression that would even make it a requirement that the company should at some time have carried on its business in England, either by direct or indirect means. While the fact of a company's having made use of this country as a place for conducting its business undoubtedly furnishes a reasonable basis for claiming jurisdiction over it, at least with respect to the English component of its operations, the non-specific form of wording used by the Parliamentary draughtsman leaves it open to the English court to order the winding up of a company whose contact with this country has taken some other form, amounting to a jurisdictional nexus on the basis of which

[55] See *Luther v. Sagor* [1921] 3 K.B. 532 at 557–559 per Scrutton L.J.; *Russian Commercial and Industrial Bank v. Comptoir d'Escompte de Mulhouse* [1925] A.C. 112 at 120 per Lord Cave; *Bank of Ethiopia v. National Bank of Egypt* [1937] 1 Ch. 513, at 519 per Clauson J.; *Banco de Bilbao v. Sancha* [1938] 2 K.B. 176 (CA). See also *Dicey and Morris, supra* n.22 at pp. 992–993. For a different approach devised by the New York Court of Appeals at a period when the American Government refused to recognise the Soviet Republic as the government of Russia, see *Sokoloff v. National City Bank of New York*, 145 N.E. 917 (1924).

the court is prepared to take action. This wider view of the court's jurisdictional remit is explored below.[56]

(b) Company unable to pay its debts

The provision in section 221(5)(b), which authorises the English court to wind up an unregistered company which is unable to pay its debts, matches the ground for winding up an English-registered company that is to be found in section 122(1)(f) of the 1986 Act. The latter is the most frequently utilised ground for bringing about the winding up of an insolvent company upon the petition of an unpaid creditor. As with domestic-formed companies, the expression 'unable to pay its debts' is of key importance, since the word 'insolvent' is not actually used as part of the statutory provisions dealing with the grounds for making a winding up order. The technical meaning of the expression, and the means of establishing a company's inability to pay its debts for the purposes of the Act, are the subject of the further provisions of sections 222 to 224 inclusive. These reveal that the alternative tests of insolvency known respectively as the 'cash-flow' and the 'balance sheet' basis are each available in relation to the winding up of unregistered companies, just as in the case of proceedings under Part IV of the Act.[57] This dual approach is especially important from the standpoint of an unpaid creditor from outside the company, who may have no realistic means of obtaining sufficient evidence about its financial status on a 'balance sheet' basis, where contingent and prospective liabilities have to be evaluated and brought into the calculation. Since the 'cash-flow' test is based upon the more readily verified proposition that the company is unable to pay its debts as they fall due, an unpaid creditor can use his own debt as a means of establishing that this test is satisfied. Indeed, these three sections of the Insolvency Act go further, by establishing a range of alternative procedures whereby the unpaid creditor can effectively coerce the debtor company into a public manifestation of its state of financial embarrassment, as follows.

(i) Statutory demand. First, section 222 enables the creditor of an unregistered company to utilise the procedure known as the service of a statutory demand. This is a written demand, in the form prescribed by the Insolvency Rules, requiring the company to pay the sum due, or to secure or compound for it to the creditor's satisfaction.[58] The creditor must serve the demand on the company by leaving it at its principal place of business, or by delivering it to the secretary or some director, manager or principal

[56] See p. 135 below, under the heading *Judicial development of the principles of jurisdiction.*

[57] See Insolvency Act 1986, s. 224(1)(d), (2), and cf. *ibid.*, s.123(1)(e), (2). For further analysis of the various tests of insolvency, with illustrative examples, see P. Totty and G. Moss (eds.), *Insolvency* (1986, looseleaf), s.A, paras A1.06—A1.09 inclusive.

[58] *Ibid.*, s.222(1)(a); Insolvency Rules 1986, rr.4.5, 4.6, and Form 4.1.

officer of the company, or by otherwise serving it in such manner as the court may approve or direct. If, for three weeks after the service of the demand, the company has neglected to pay the sum or to secure or compound for it to the creditor's satisfaction, the company is deemed (for the purposes of section 221) to be unable to pay its debts.[59] To be eligible to use a statutory demand in this way, the creditor must be one to whom the company is indebted in a sum exceeding £750 currently due.[60] It is permissible for the creditor's standing to have arisen through direct dealings with the company, or by assignment from a party to whom the company's debt was originally due.[61] Although there is a prescribed monetary threshold for use of the statutory demand, there is no requirement that the creditor must first have obtained judgment in any proceedings to recover the sum due. Where such judgment has been recovered however, the judgment creditor enjoys the option of using a statutory demand under section 222, or of resorting to execution or some other method of enforcement, in which case the provisions of section 224(1) become applicable (see below). Lastly, it may be noted that the Insolvency Rules 1986 make provision for service of documents, or of any process or order of the court, to take place out of England and Wales on any person required to be served for the purpose of insolvency proceedings. Such service out of the jurisdiction is subject to the discretionary control of the court, which may also impose conditions as to the place, mode and timing of such service, and as to the manner in which service is to be verified.[62]

(ii) Unsatisfied execution upon a judgment. Secondly, paragraphs (a), (b) and (c) of section 224(1) furnish means by which a creditor who has recovered judgment against the company can take further steps that will either yield payment or render the company liable to be made the subject of a petition for winding up. The steps to be taken differ according to whether the enforcement of the judgment is to take place in England and Wales, in Scotland, or in Northern Ireland. Enforcement in each of the three component parts of the United Kingdom is governed by the separate provisions of paragraphs (a), (b) and (c). In the case of enforcement in England and Wales, section 224(1)(a) provides that if execution or other process issued on a judgment, decree or order obtained in any court in favour of a creditor against the company, or any member of it as such, or any person autho-

[59] Insolvency Act 1986, s.221(1)(b).

[60] *Ibid.*, s.222(1). The amount of £750 can be varied by means of Ministerial regulations, but this cannot affect cases already commenced: *ibid.*, s.222(2).

[61] *Ibid.*, s.221(1). Such an assignment must be properly effective in order to confer on the assignee the full right to demand payment of the entire debt in his own name. An equitable assignee of part only of a larger indebtedness cannot utilise the statutory demand procedure: *Re Steel Wing Co.Ltd.* [1921] 1 Ch. 349.

[62] Insolvency Rules 1986, r.12.12(3).

rised to be sued as nominal defendant on behalf of the company, is returned unsatisfied, the company is deemed (for the purposes of section 221) to be unable to pay its debts.[63]

(iii) Debt remaining unsatisfied after action brought. Thirdly, section 223 contains a provision, unique to the winding up of unregistered companies, which is effectively a variant of the statutory demand procedure referred to above. The section states that an unregistered company is deemed to be unable to pay its debts (for the purposes of section 221) in the following circumstances, namely: if an action or other proceeding has been instituted against any member of the company for any debt or demand due, or claimed to be due, from the company, or from him in his character of member, and (a) notice in writing of the institution of the action or proceeding has been served on the company by leaving it at its principal place of business (or by delivering it to the secretary, or some director, manager or principal officer of the company, or by otherwise serving it in such manner as the court may approve or direct), and (b) the company has not within three weeks after service of the notice paid, secured or compounded for the debt or demand, or procured the action or proceeding to be stayed or sisted, or indemnified the defendant or defender to his reasonable satisfaction against the action or proceeding, and against all costs, damages and expenses to be incurred by him because of it. This provision can be particularly useful as a means of shortening the legal process in the case of a foreign company whose only human representative within the jurisdiction for the purposes of instigating proceedings may prove to be a man of straw, so that time and costs may be expended to no good purpose.

(iv) Proof of the company's commercial insolvency. Fourthly, there is the possibility of demonstrating the company's commercial insolvency to the satisfaction of the court, using the provision in section 224(1)(d). Mention has already been made of the significance of this paragraph of section 224(1), which confirms that the so called 'cash-flow' test of insolvency, also referred to as 'commercial insolvency', can be employed in establishing the company's inability to pay its debts. Paragraph (d) has a further

[63] The provisions of s.224(1)(b) and (c) of the 1986 Act make equivalent provision relating to the technical procedures for enforcement of judgments in Scotland and Northern Ireland respectively. The terms of paragraph (b), which relates to enforcement in Scotland, are identical to those of s.123(1)(c) within Part IV of the Act. The terms of s.224(1)(a) and (c) differ in several respects from their counterparts in s.123(1)(b) and (d), since the latter refer only to a judgment, decree or order of any court 'in favour of a creditor of the company', without reference to the taking of proceedings against any member of the company or against a person authorised to be sued on the company's behalf. Conversely, s.123(1)(b) embodies the phrase 'unsatisfied in whole or in part', thereby making it clear that nothing less than full satisfaction of the judgment debt (to which are added the costs of the execution) will suffice to avert the possibility of winding up.

significance, in that it enables an unpaid creditor to move speedily to cause the company to be put into liquidation, by persuading the court by means of any direct evidence available that the company is unable to pay its debts as they fall due. This can be of great practical importance where an insolvent company's assets are in danger of being dissipated, or may be removed from the jurisdiction, during the time that would be required to operate the statutory demand procedure (with its inbuilt waiting period of three weeks before a winding up petition can be presented), or to take steps to issue execution on a judgment (assuming that a final award has been obtained through previous legal proceedings). The possibilities for achieving 'direct entry' into winding up can thus be of great tactical value, provided they are properly used. In recent years, the equivalent provision under Part IV of the Act—section 123(1)(e)—has been developed into a tactical weapon providing a highly effective counter to the efforts of those in charge of ailing companies who seek to hold their creditors at bay by procrastination and evasion. In *Taylors Industrial Flooring Ltd. v. M. & H. Plant Hire (Manchester) Ltd.*[64] the Court of Appeal held that where a debt is owed by a company, and it is not disputed that it is due and payable, the failure by the company to pay the debt following a written request for payment from the creditor can be regarded by the court as conduct demonstrative of the company's inability to pay its debts as they fall due. It is therefore open to the creditor forthwith to present a petition for winding up, and for the court at its discretion to make a winding up order. There is no requirement that, as a matter of law, an unpaid creditor must first resort to the use of a statutory demand, or must seek to recover judgment against the debtor company, before being entitled to move for it to be wound up. Where, however, the company *bona fide* disputes its liability to pay the sum for which it is allegedly indebted, no inference of inability to pay can arise from the fact of non-payment, and the courts will be equally vigilant to protect a solvent company from being subjected by its creditor to the threat of presenting a 'direct entry' petition for winding up, as a means of putting it under pressure to pay a debt which is genuinely disputed. Such conduct will be dealt with as an abuse of the legal process, and the court can restrain the creditor's petition by means of an injunction, and may also penalise him in making its order for costs.[65]

(c) That it is just and equitable that the company should be wound up

The final ground for winding up an unregistered company is provided by section 221(5)(c) of the Insolvency Act, which enables an unregistered

[64] [1990] B.C.L.C. 216; (1990) B.C.C. 44. See also *Cornhill Insurance plc. v. Improvement Services Ltd.* [1986] 1 W.L.R. 114; [1986] B.C.L.C. 26 (Harman J.).

[65] See *Re a Company (No. 0010656 of 1990)* [1991] B.C.L.C. 464; *Re a Company (No. 0012209 of 1991)* [1992] 1 W.L.R. 351; [1992] 2 All E.R. 797.

company to be wound up if the court is of opinion that it is just and equitable that this should be done. This provision confers an extensive discretion upon the court, and appears to impose no formal limitations of any kind upon the exercise of this basis of jurisdiction, save for such as are generated by the court's own conscience and sense of propriety in the dispensing of justice. It is this ground which in recent times has proved the most fertile source of development of the jurisdiction to wind up foreign companies.

Judicial development of the principles of jurisdiction. In their quest to devise a principled basis for the exercise of their discretion to wind up a foreign company on the 'just and equitable' ground the courts have proceeded, case by case, to examine the nature and quality of the company's links to this country, to establish the existence of an appropriate nexus justifying the taking of jurisdiction by the court. In the earlier cases, such a nexus was perceived to be most readily supplied through it being demonstrable that the company had at some period been carrying on its business in England, so as to come within the grounds mentioned in what is now section 221(5)(a) of the 1986 Act. For a time this resulted in a rather restricted view of the possibility of winding up a company which had conducted its business here through agents, rather than by maintaining a branch in this country.[66] However, with the decision of the Court of Appeal in *Banque des Marchands de Moscou v. Kindersley*[67] a more liberal approach was embraced. The case concerned a Russian bank which had been dissolved by the Soviet Government in 1918, leaving undistributed assets in England. An English winding up order was sought as a means of bringing about an orderly distribution of the assets among persons claiming as creditors of the bank. While the court was prepared if necessary to find it proven that the foreign company had previously done business in England, it took the view that in the case of a foreign corporation which had been dissolved and extinguished in the country in which it was established it was not necessary as a statutory condition to the winding up jurisdiction of the English courts to prove that the company had previously established a branch or other place of business in England. It was sufficient that there were assets of the company in this country and persons here claiming as creditors of the company, or said to be indebted to it. These elements were sufficient in themselves to indicate that a business had 'in

[66] See *Re Lloyd Generale Italiano* (1885) 29 Ch.D. 219; *Re Tovarishestvo Manufactur Liudvig-Rabenek* [1944] Ch. 404. The reasoning in both these decisions was treated as unsound by the Court of Appeal in *Banque des Marchands de Moscou v. Kindersley* [1952] 1 Ch. 112, esp. at 127 per Evershed M.R. Contrast the decision in *Re Syria Ottoman Railway Co.* (1904) 20 T.L.R. 217. See also the judgment of Megarry J. in *Re Compania Merabello San Nicholas SA* [1973] 1 Ch. 75 at 91–92.

[67] See *supra* n.66.

some sense' formerly been conducted here, and a winding up was ordered to take place.[68]

The merit of conducting a winding up is that it imposes a method of distribution in which all creditors are enabled to participate on a basis of equality of treatment. This is considerably more fair and just than allowing the assets to be claimed by individuals relying on such remedies as might happen to be available to them. The *Kindersley* decision therefore represents a watershed, after which courts grew increasingly inventive in their willingness to find reasons for ordering an English winding up as a means of attaining distributive justice, measured in terms of the greatest good of the greatest number. In *Re Azoff-Don Commercial Bank*[69] another dissolved Russian bank had left behind substantial assets in England. The bank had never had an office or place of business here, but had carried out a number of mercantile transactions in this country. Wynn-Parry J. concluded that he had jurisdiction to make an order for winding up, and that its use would be justified. The alternative course, whereby the Crown would claim the assets of the dissolved company under the doctrine of *bona vacantia*, to be followed by a process of making *ex gratia* payments to creditors on an individual basis, was regarded by the judge as unmeritorious and contrary to the principle that assets should be distributed among the whole body of creditors.[70]

Full liberation from the constraints of former thinking about the winding up of foreign companies came with the judgment of Megarry J. in *Re Compania Merabello San Nicholas SA*.[71] On this occasion, the foreign company in question did not appear to have undergone dissolution, or otherwise ceased to exist, according to the law of its country of incorporation. On the other hand, the company was incorporated in Panama for the singular purpose of owning and operating a Panamanian-registered ship, and had apparently ceased to function actively for a long while prior to the English proceedings. There was no evidence to show that the company had ever carried on its business in England, much less that it had had a place of business here. However, the sole remaining asset of any value that was linked to the company consisted of its rights arising from membership of a mutual insurance club (a 'P. & I. Club') based in London, under which it was entitled to be indemnified against all liabilities in respect of the ship. In order to procure the payment from the underwriters of the sum arising under this right of indemnity, it became technically necessary that the company be made the subject of a winding up order.[72] Megarry J. ven-

[68] [1951] 1 Ch. at 126–128 per Lord Evershed M.R.

[69] [1954] 1 Ch. 315.

[70] [1954] 1 Ch. at 333, citing the pronouncement by Pearson J. in *Re Kloebe* (1884) 28 Ch.D. 175, 180.

[71] [1973] 1 Ch. 75.

[72] It is a curiosity of this case that the petitioning creditor, a Spanish company having a claim against the company arising from damage to its cargo when being carried by the

tured to summarise the essentials of the relevant law relating to the existence of jurisdiction to wind up a foreign company as follows:[73]

(1) There is no need to establish that the company ever had a place of business in England.
(2) There is no need to establish that the company ever carried on business here, unless perhaps the petition is based on the company carrying on or having carried on business.[74]
(3) A proper connection with the jurisdiction must be established by sufficient evidence to show (a) that the company has some asset or assets within the jurisdiction, and (b) that there are one or more persons concerned in the proper distribution of the assets over whom the jurisdiction is exercisable.
(4) It suffices if the assets of the company within the jurisdiction are of any nature; they need not be 'commercial' assets, or assets which indicate that the company formerly carried on business here.[75]
(5) The assets need not be assets which will be distributable to creditors by the liquidator in the winding-up: it suffices if by the making of the winding-up order they will be of benefit to a creditor or the creditor in some other way.
(6) If it is shown that there is no reasonable possibility of benefit accruing to creditors from making the winding-up order, the jurisdiction is excluded.

Having thus expounded a quite revolutionary framework of rules which even include the candid assertion that in some circumstances (as in the instant case) the making of a winding-up order would have an ulterior purpose placing it outside the orthodox concept of a collective administration of assets for the benefit of a numerous and diverse body of creditors, Megarry J. proceeded to reinforce his decision to make a winding-up order by reference to the terms of the statutory provisions themselves.[76] These provisions are reflected in the findings of the learned judge to the effect that the company was unable to pay its debts as they fell due, that if it ever carried on business within the jurisdiction it had ceased to do so, and that in all the circumstances of the case it was just and equitable that the company should be wound up.[77] However, it is the more radical passage of the judgment of Megarry J. consisting of a six-point manifesto, already quoted in full, that has been invoked in subsequent decisions as a precedent for similarly adventurous exercises in the winding up of foreign

company's vessel, would not ultimately need to lodge proof in the winding up, because the effect of the winding up order would be to cause the company's claim against the underwriters of the P. & I. Club to become vested in the petitioner under the Third Parties (Rights against Insurers) Act 1930, s.1, thus affording it a direct right to claim payment for itself. The winding up order was thus serving as a means to this end.

[73] [1973] 1 Ch. at 91–92. [74] See Insolvency Act 1986, s.221(5)(a), discussed above.

[75] This proposition is a strikingly bold advance beyond the reasoning adopted by the Court of Appeal in the *Kindersley* case (*supra* n.66).

[76] The relevant statutory provisions were at that date contained in the Companies Act 1948, s.399(5), whose wording is identical to the Insolvency Act 1986, s.221(5).

[77] [1973] 1 Ch. at 92.

companies, based upon the 'presence of assets' test formulated in propositions (3) and (4) as set out above.[78]

Judicial refinement and further extension of the jurisdiction to wind up foreign companies has continued in more recent years. In the case of *International Westminster Bank plc v. Okeanos Maritime Corporation*[79] Peter Gibson J. concluded that the English court has such jurisdiction even in respect of a foreign company which has no assets in the jurisdiction, if there is a sufficient connection with England and a reasonable possibility that benefit will accrue to the company's creditors from the winding up. The requisite quality of connection was held to exist, partly by virtue of the fact that the Liberian-formed company had obtained a loan of some $13.5 million from an English bank, the loan having been negotiated and executed in England where it was also to be performed. Further evidence also suggested that the company was effectively managed from England, either directly or through an intermediary, and that it carried on business in England. The significance of this decision therefore lies in that part of the ruling which holds that the presence of assets in England is not essential to confer jurisdiction to wind up a foreign company.[80] The learned judge also took the view that no other jurisdiction was more appropriate for the winding up of the company, since the connection with England was closer than its connection with its country of incorporation, or with any other country in which corporate activities had taken place. On the other hand, the courts remain alive to the need to ensure that, in a case where there are no assets within the jurisdiction, the alleged link between the company and this country is one of genuine substance. Thus the mere fact that there may be certain tangential contacts with this country would be unlikely to be regarded as a sufficiently strong nexus where, as in the case of *Re Real Estate Development Co.*,[81] the foreign company has never traded here, and has no assets here at the time the petition is presented, and where the petitioning creditor's debt, and the transaction from which it originated, also lack any substantial connection with this country.

The virtue of flexibility that is inherent in the 'just and equitable' ground for winding up can be especially valuable in cases where the activities in this country of a foreign-formed company are such as to constitute a menace to the public interest. The standing of the Secretary of State to petition

[78] See *Re Allobrogia Steamship Corporation* [1978] 3 All E.R. 423; *Re Eloc Electro-Optieck and Communicatie B.V.* [1982] Ch. 43; *Inland Revenue v. Highland Engineering Ltd.* 1975 S.L.T. 203.

[79] [1988] Ch. 210; [1987] 3 W.L.R. 339; [1987] 3 All E.R. 137; [1987] B.C.L.C. 450 (also reported *sub nom. Re a Company (No. 00359 of 1987)*). See Dine (1988) 9 Co. Law. 30. This decision was followed, in a case with somewhat similar factual elements, in *Re a Company (No. 003102 of 1991), ex parte Nyckeln Finance Co. Ltd.* [1991] B.C.L.C. 539 (Harman J.).

[80] The same proposition was also a basis of the earlier decision of Nourse J. in *Re Eloc Electro-Optieck and Communicatie B.V., supra* n.78.

[81] [1991] B.C.L.C. 210 (Knox J.).

for the winding up of such a foreign company under Part V of the Insolvency Act, in a similar way to the presenting of a public interest petition for the winding up of a domestic company under section 124A of the Act, was recognised in *Re Vanilla Accumulation Ltd.*[82]

3.2.3 Special problems encountered in the context of winding up companies which have been dissolved abroad

We have already seen that section 221(5)(a) of the Insolvency Act enables a winding up of an unregistered company to take place if the company has been dissolved.[83] This ground for winding up, when applied to the circumstances of a company formed under foreign law, gives rise to certain logical difficulties due to the interaction of seemingly incompatible legal principles. Considerable judicial ingenuity has been expended in overcoming these problems in the interest of ensuring that worthwhile practical objectives are not sacrificed on the altar of doctrinal purity. There are two main sources of difficulty.

First, the English law rule of recognition of the effects of foreign dissolutions, being based on the principle that the law of the company's state of incorporation controls all aspects of the company's existence as a legal person,[84] logically takes effect from the moment that the foreign law brings about the extinction of the company. Consequently, by the time that steps are begun in England to petition for the company to be wound up here, its legal identity has already been terminated so that, strictly speaking, there is no surviving entity in relation to which an English winding up can take place. In the face of this paradox, the courts have resorted to the technique of deeming the dissolved company to be reanimated, for the specific purpose of enabling it to be wound up and, this time finally, dissolved.[85] According to Lord Atkin, in a landmark decision of the House of Lords in 1936, the implication of the inclusion by the Legislature, in the provision corresponding to section 221(5) of the 1986 Act, of the power to wind up a dissolved company was to enable that company to be wound up as though it had not been dissolved, and had therefore continued in existence.[86] This ruling confirmed the correctness of the approach previously adopted by courts of first instance in giving literal effect to the statutory power in question.[87]

[82] *The Times*, 24 February 1998 (Rattee J.).

[83] See at 3.2.2(*a*) above, p. 129.

[84] See at 3.1 above.

[85] *Russian and English Bank and Florence Montefiore Guedalla v. Baring Bros. & Co. Ltd.* [1936] A.C. 405 (HL).

[86] *Ibid.*, at 425–428. See Lipstein (1952) 11 C.L.J. 198; F.A. Mann (1962) 11 I.C.L.Q. 471; M. Mann (1952) 15 M.L.R. 479, (1955) 18 M.L.R. 8.

[87] See, e.g., *Re Russian and English Bank* [1932] 1 Ch. 663; *Re Russian Bank for Foreign Trade* [1933] 1 Ch. 745.

The second source of difficulty arises as a further consequence of the recognition by English law of the effects of the foreign company's dissolution under the law of its incorporation. Under English domestic law, the extinction of the corporate *persona* unaccompanied by any process of distribution or transmission of the company's English assets results in their passing to the Crown under the ancient, feudal doctrine of *bona vacantia*.[88] If the effects of this internal process were pursued to their logical conclusion, the winding up would be deprived of any useful purpose because there would be no property available for the liquidator to administer. This outcome has been averted by a further judicial innovation whereby the title of the Crown is treated as defeasible under certain contingencies, as where municipal law expressly enables the effects of the foreign dissolution to be notionally overridden in the interests of accomplishing some further, worthwhile purpose.[89] Thus, the making of a winding-up order on the ground specified in (currently) section 221(5)(a) is treated in law as procuring the defeat of the title of the Crown to the company's English assets, while simultaneously effecting the revivification of the company itself. A similar element of pragmatism has been manifested by the courts in their response to objections raised in some instances to the eligibility of the petitioning creditor to seek a winding-up order, either because his debt is disputed or—more fundamentally—because the debt in question must be regarded as having been discharged or abrogated under the foreign law responsible for the company's dissolution. The preferred solution has been to allow the creditor to proceed with his petition, and to leave the issue of his status as a proving creditor to be decided subsequently on a more strict application of the law.[90]

The courts have also adopted a pragmatic approach to the technical requirement that a winding-up petition must be served on the company at

[88] Literally 'empty [i.e. ownerless] goods'. The doctrine operates internally in cases where property of deceased persons is not disposed of by will and there is no relation entitled on intestacy. It also applies, in the context of insolvency law, where onerous property is disclaimed by a liquidator or trustee in bankruptcy and no other party becomes successor by operation of law or by virtue of a vesting order: see Insolvency Act 1986, ss.178–182, 315–321. The application of the doctrine of *bona vacantia* following the dissolution of a company was explored in considerable depth in *Re Higginson and Dean* [1899] 1 Q.B. 325 (Wright J.), and in *Re Wells, Swinburne-Hanham v. Howard* [1933] 1 Ch. 29 (CA). For a celebrated example of the comparative doctrinal approaches of English and Continental legal systems to the concept of *bona vacantia*, see *Re Maldonado* [1954] P. 223 (CA). For the treatment of intangible movables as *bona vacantia*, see *Re Usines de Melle's Patent* (1954) 91 C.L.R. 42 (HCt Austr.).

[89] *Russian and English Bank, etc. v. Baring Bros & Co. Ltd., supra* n.85, at 426–427 per Lord Atkin; *Re Azoff-Don Commercial Bank* [1954] 1 Ch. 315 (referred to *supra*, nn. 69–70); *Re Banque Industrielle de Moscou* [1952] 1 Ch. 919; *Re Banque des Marchands de Moscou (Koupetschesky)* [1958] 1 Ch. 182 (with observations on the preceding case at pp. 192–193 per Roxburgh J.).

[90] See *Re Russian and English Bank* [1932] 1 Ch. 663; *Re Russian Bank for Foreign Trade* [1933] 1 Ch. 745; *Re Russo-Asiatic Bank* [1934] 1 Ch. 720; *Re Banque des Marchands de Moscou (Koupetschesky), Wilenkin v. the Liquidator* [1952] 1 All E.R. 1269; *Re Russian Commercial and Industrial Bank* (1963) 107 S.J. 415.

its registered office, after having been presented through the act of filing it in court.[91] In the case of a company which has been dissolved, or which has ceased to carry on its business, there may be no person on whom such service can be effected, and possibly no currently active address at which this can take place. In such cases it has long been the practice to regard the requirement of service as being fulfilled if a copy of the petition is left at the company's last known principal place of business within the jurisdiction.[92] Alternatively, service may be authorised to take place in some other manner as directed by the court, which may also exercise its discretion to order service to take place outside the jurisdiction in a manner to be specified.[93]

Some unresolved difficulties

Despite the judicial resourcefulness displayed in the cases referred to above, some elements of legal uncertainty or untidiness remain. Thus, although the doctrine of corporate reincarnation was originally expressed in terms which suggested that the foreign company was to be treated as though its dissolution had not taken place,[94] some judges at first instance were unwilling to give literal effect to that proposition when dealing with cases where persons who had purported to render services to, or to act on behalf of, the foreign company during the period between its dissolution and subsequent reanimation sought to claim in the liquidation in respect of the liabilities allegedly due to them. In two reported cases, the courts preferred to adhere to the orthodox principle of the law of agency that a person cannot act on behalf of a non-existent principal, or one who is for the time being not legally competent, in such a way as to generate an enforceable claim against the latter or its successors.[95] Conversely, in another decision also at first instance (founded upon the *dicta* uttered by Lord Atkin in the House of Lords, already referred to), Wynn-Parry J. accepted that the logical implications of the reanimation doctrine must be allowed to operate without exception for the purposes of distribution of

[91] Insolvency Rules 1986, rr. 4.7–4.9 inclusive.

[92] *Re Tea Trading Company, K. & C. Popoff Brothers* [1933] Ch. 647; *Re N.V.H. Wokar* [1946] Ch. 98. cf. the more exacting approach, in a case concerning a judgment obtained in default of appearance by the dissolved foreign company, in *Lazard Brothers & Co. v. Banque Industrielle de Moscou* [1932] 1 K.B. 617 (CA).

[93] Insolvency Rules 1986, rr. 4.8(6),(7); 12.12(3),(4).

[94] See the key passage in the speech of Lord Atkin in *Russian and English Bank, etc. v. Baring Bros. & Co. Ltd., supra* nn. 85, 86.

[95] *Re Banque des Marchands de Moscou (Koupetschesky), Wilenkin v. the Liquidator, supra* n.90 (Vaisey J.); *Re Russian Commercial and Industrial Bank* (1963) 107 S.J. 415 (Buckley J.). Cf. also the decisions taken by different judges at first instance during the earlier stages of the proceedings in *Russian and English Bank, etc. v. Baring Bros. & Co. Ltd., supra* n.85, prior to being overruled by a majority of the House of Lords: [1934] Ch. 276 (Bennett J.), and [1935] Ch. 120 at 123–124 (Clauson J.).

the assets among creditors in the English winding up, so that events were to be regarded hypothetically as though the dissolution had not taken place.[96] It is submitted that this latter view is to be preferred, given that the dominant consideration at this point should be the retrospective attainment of the fairest outcome for the various parties in interest.

One further curiosity of the law relating to dissolved foreign companies is the provision that is currently to be found in the Insolvency Act 1986 as section 225.[97] The provision was originally enacted as section 91 of the Companies Act 1928 for the deliberate purpose of overcoming uncertainty about the jurisdiction of the English courts to wind up companies which had been formed under the laws of Imperial Russia, and which had been dissolved during or after the Revolution of 1917, as already discussed. By the time the new provision entered into force, and came to be tested in litigation, it had been rendered largely superfluous thanks, as we have seen, to the innovative approach of the courts to the interpretation of what is now section 221(5)(a) of the 1986 Act. The ponderous terms of section 225, creating the dual requirement that the foreign company must have formerly carried on business in Great Britain and that it must have ceased to do so, are in any case a serious limitation to the usefulness of the provision. Moreover, any hopes that the section might at least deliver a clear signal as to the possibility of resolving the chaotic state of affairs inflicted on numerous banks and insurance companies, and their hapless customers and trading partners, by the events of 1917 received a severe reverse in consequence of the judgment of Bennett J. in *Re Russian and English Bank*.[98] That decision has been subsequently considered to have involved a ruling to the effect that the provision newly introduced by the 1928 Act, and later consolidated as section 338(2) of the Companies Act 1929, did not have retrospective effect, and so could not confer a jurisdiction on the English courts to wind up a foreign company which had ceased to do business here *before* the section first entered into force in 1928. The absurdity of this proposition is self-evident, for it robs the section of virtually all effect in relation to the very class of cases which prompted its enactment in the first place. The decision was subsequently criticised, in passages having the status of *obiter dicta*, by two members of the House of Lords in proceedings on appeal at a later stage in the course of the same liquidation.[99] However, since the main

[96] *Re Russian Commercial and Industrial Bank* [1955] Ch. 148.

[97] The Insolvency Act 1986, s.225 reads: 'Where a company incorporated outside Great Britain which has been carrying on business in Great Britain ceases to carry on business in Great Britain, it may be wound up as an unregistered company under this Act, notwithstanding that it has been dissolved or otherwise ceased to exist as a company under or by virtue of the laws of the country under which it was incorporated'.

[98] [1932] 1 Ch. 663, esp. at 668–669.

[99] *Russian and English Bank etc. v. Baring Bros. & Co. Ltd.* [1936] A.C. 405 at 415–416 per Lord Blanesburgh and at 424–425 per Lord Atkin.

effect of that same decision of their Lordships' House was to confirm the capability of what is presently section 221(5)(a) to provide a more flexible basis for an English winding up to be ordered, no occasion has arisen for the correctness of the decision of Bennett J. to be challenged in a material context, and therefore section 225 has remained a dead letter.

3.2.4 The limits of the English courts' jurisdiction

Wide though it may be, courtesy of a fertile and still evolving jurisprudence, the scope of the English courts' jurisdiction to wind up foreign companies does have certain limits. Some of these have been self-imposed by the judges themselves, who have ensured that their wide discretionary powers are exercised on a principled basis through the requirement that there must be a sufficient connection between the company and this country.[100] Other limitations arise from the meaning that has been ascribed to the term 'unregistered company' as used in section 220 of the Insolvency Act, for this is the very foundation upon which all such questions of jurisdiction finally depend. As was explained at the beginning of 3.2.2 above, the statutory meaning supplied by section 220 itself is somewhat imprecise, and has been rendered the more so over time due to the gradual elimination of most of the types of unregistered company that had previously existed in England. The unrepealed remnants of section 220 simply assert that, for the purposes of Part V of the Act, 'the expression' 'unregistered company' 'includes any association and any company', with the exception of a company registered in any part of the United Kingdom under what is termed 'the legislation (past or present) relating to companies in Great Britain'. This exclusionary provision in section 220(1)(b) has the effect of preventing a winding up from taking place in England under Part V in respect of a company formed under the Companies Acts (past or present) and registered in Scotland, and conversely precludes the winding up in Scotland of a company so formed and registered in England and Wales. In the case of a company registered in Northern Ireland however, the position is different. This is because the Province, while part of the United Kingdom, is not within Great Britain. In *Re Normandy Marketing Ltd.*,[101] it was held that a company incorporated in Northern Ireland may in principle be wound up in England as an unregistered company under Part V.

[100] See at 3.2.2 above.

[101] [1993] B.C.C. 879, also reported *sub nom. Re a Company (No. 007946 of 1993)* at [1994] 2 W.L.R. 438 (Morritt J.). In his judgment (at 882–883) the learned judge indicated his disagreement with statements made in the 11th edition of *Dicey and Morris on the Conflict of Laws*, at pp. 1144–1145, to the effect that a company incorporated in Northern Ireland cannot be wound up under s.221 of the 1986 Act, but only (if the conditions specified by that section are met) under s.225. The same statements are included in the 12th edition of the work at p. 1128, published in 1993 prior to the decision in the *Normandy Marketing* case.

However, section 221(2) imports a special limitation upon such proceedings, by providing that if an unregistered company has a principal place of business situated in Northern Ireland, it shall not be wound up under Part V unless it has a principal place of business situated in England and Wales or Scotland, or in both England and Wales and Scotland. Thus, if a company has been incorporated in Northern Ireland and also has a principal place of business there, winding up as an unregistered company in England or in Scotland can only take place if the requirements of section 221(2) are satisfied. However, no such restrictions would arise in the case of a company formed in Northern Ireland which has no principal place of business there.

A further source of limitation upon the jurisdiction of the courts under Part V results from the interpretation that has been applied to the term 'association' as used in section 220. It has been held to bear a restricted meaning so as to denote such associations as are formed for gain or profit, and hence it does not apply to organised bodies such as sporting or social clubs or societies not conducted in the form of partnerships nor in such a way as to render their members liable over and above the amount of their individual subscriptions.[102] In a decision of considerable international significance, the Court of Appeal held in *Re International Tin Council*[103] that an international organisation established by treaty, having its headquarters in London, was not liable to be wound up by the English court, nor to be made the subject of an order appointing a receiver of its property. This was in spite of the fact that the treaty whereby the organisation was established stated that the ITC 'shall have legal personality', and the further fact that implementing measures in the United Kingdom giving effect to the ITC agreement stated that the Council was to have 'the legal capacities of a body corporate'. The decisive factor was that both the international agreement and the implementing measure expressly conferred 'immunity from suit and legal process' upon the ITC, thereby rendering it exempt from all proceedings, including insolvency proceedings, to which its declared attributes would otherwise have given rise in consequence of the activities conducted from its centre of operations in this country.

Finally, it may be observed that the courts are increasingly attentive to the possibility that the ends of justice may best be served, in a given case,

[102] *Re St. James' Club* (1852) 2 De G.M. & G. 383, 42 E.R. 920; *Re International Tin Council* [1989] Ch. 309 (CA); *Re Witney Town Football and Social Club* [1993] B.C.C. 874.

[103] [1989] Ch. 309, affirming the decision of Millett J. reported at [1987] Ch. 419. Both reports are highly instructive in relation to many practical as well as theoretical aspects of international insolvency law. See also the final stage of those proceedings, in which the decision of the Court of Appeal was affirmed *sub nom. J.H. Rayner (Mincing Lane) Ltd. v. Department of Trade and Industry* [1990] 2 A.C. 418 (HL). Contrast the different outcome, based upon the status conferred on an organisation established by treaty, in *Arab Monetary Fund v. Hashim (No. 3)* [1991] 2 A.C. 114 (HL).

through the declining of jurisdiction by a court otherwise empowered to exercise it. The theme of jurisdictional abstention has already been considered in relation to the bankruptcy of individuals.[104] Some indication of judicial sensitivity to the question whether it is appropriate for an English court to exercise its winding up jurisdiction in an international case was given by Gibson J. in his judgment in *International Westminster Bank plc v. Okeanos Maritime Corporation*.[105] The reference by the learned judge in that case to the absence of any other more appropriate jurisdiction in which to conduct the winding up of the insolvent company does at least hint at the possibility that, if a more convenient forum were shown to exist, consideration would be given to adopting a solution allowing that jurisdiction to serve as the main centre for winding up purposes.[106] A more concrete example of the application of the modern doctrine of jurisdictional abstention in relation to the exercise of its winding-up jurisdiction (albeit in a case concerning a solvent company) was *Re Harrods (Buenos Aires) Ltd*.[107] The case involved a company incorporated in England, but whose business was carried on in Argentina where its central management and control was also based. The Court of Appeal concluded that on the facts Argentina was the appropriate forum for trial of the complex issues relating to the conduct of the company's affairs that would form a central part of the minority shareholder's action seeking an order for winding up as an alternative to other possible remedies. Although the material considerations would be considerably different in the case of an insolvent company, the spirit of openness and objectivity with which the question of appropriate venue was addressed could well serve as a basis for useful development in the future.

3.2.5 Selected comparisons

The basic principles followed in both **Australia** and **Canada** with regard to the winding up of foreign-formed companies are closely modelled on those of the English parent system. This affinity extends to the case law developments of more recent years, as described above. Under Part 5.7 of the Corporations Law of **Australia**, the court may wind up a foreign

[104] See Chapter 2, at 2.1.3 above.

[105] See *supra* n 79.

[106] See [1988] Ch. 210 at 226–227. The same line of reasoning was followed by Harman J. in *Re a Company (No. 003102 of 1991), ex parte Nyckeln Finance Co. Ltd.* [1991] B.C.L.C. 539, at 540–541. In the course of his judgment in *Re Wallace Smith & Co. Ltd.* [1992] B.C.L.C. 970 at 985, Edward Nugee Q.C. remarked that the question of appropriate forum, while not vital to the outcome of every case, was 'nevertheless an important one for the court to consider in deciding how to exercise its discretion'.

[107] [1992] Ch. 72 (CA) (proceedings were subsequently pursued on further appeal before the House of Lords, but the parties reached a settlement before final judgment could be delivered).

company as an unregistered company on grounds corresponding to those in Part V of the Insolvency Act 1986 (UK). This includes a jurisdiction to wind up a company which has been dissolved under the law of its country of incorporation (which can apply to the respective states of the Commonwealth of Australia itself).[108] The court has a discretion whether to order a winding up, but if there are local assets within Australia the court will be inclined to make the order if it will thereby prevent an individual creditor from obtaining an advantage over the general body of creditors, for example by completing execution against the assets in question.[109] The court will exercise its judgment independently of whether liquidation proceedings are already taking place abroad, but if such is the case the court may also elect not to exercise its jurisdiction, in the interests of sparing the duplication of costs, if it is satisfied that the foreign liquidator can adequately carry out all the necessary tasks involved in the case.[110] There is currently a lack of clear authority in Australia concerning the need for the existence of assets within the jurisdiction for the court to be prepared to make a winding-up order.[111] It remains to be seen whether the courts will follow the line taken by their English counterparts in recent years and reach the conclusion that the presence of assets within the jurisdiction, while perhaps desirable, is by no means an essential requirement for the court to be empowered to order a winding up. Alternative connecting factors might be held sufficient to establish the requisite connection with Australia, such as the carrying on of the company's business within the country. This is a test which is decided in the light of the factual evidence before the court, and it can sometimes be a delicate matter of judgement whether such activities as are attributable to the company amount to the carrying on of its business within the jurisdiction in question.[112]

In **Canada** the Winding Up Act[113] empowers the courts to wind up insolvent corporations that are doing business in Canada, or that are in liquidation or have been dissolved abroad.[114] The fact that winding-up proceedings are in progress in the company's state of incorporation does not prevent the Canadian courts from exercising jurisdiction, if they so

[108] Corporations Law (Cth), s.582(3). See *T.M. Burke Estates Pty. v. P.J. Constructions (Vic.) Pty. Ltd. (in liquidation)* [1991] 1 V.R. 610.

[109] *Mercantile Credits Ltd. v. Foster Clark (Australia) Ltd.* (1964) 11 C.L.R. 169.

[110] *Re New England Brewing Co. Ltd.* [1970] Q.W.N. 49.

[111] See B.H. McPherson,*The Law of Company Liquidation*, 3rd edn. (1987), ch. 16, at pp. 463–464. See also *Re Kailis Groote Eylandt Fisheries Pty. Ltd.* (1977) 2 A.C.L.R. 574, and cf. *Re Buildmat (Aust.) Pty. Ltd. and the Companies Act* (1981) 5 A.C.L.R. 689.

[112] See e.g. *Luckins v. Highway Motel (Carnarvon) Pty. Ltd.* (1975) 133 C.L.R. 164 (where the majority differed in their stated reasons for finding the company to have been carrying on its business in Western Australia). Cf. the Canadian case of *Linde Canadian Refrigerator Co. v. Saskatchewan Creamery Co.* (1915) 52 S.C.R. 400.

[113] R.S.C. 1985, c.W-11, as amended.

[114] *Ibid.*, ss. 6, 10.

choose.[115] Equally, the fact that no liquidation proceedings are taking place in the company's place of domicile does not prevent it from undergoing a winding up in Canada if it has done business there, and it is immaterial for this purpose that the company may have previously discontinued its Canadian activities if there are still unsatisfied obligations.[116] There must however be evidence to persuade the court that the company has at some time done business in Canada, and the court's discretion may also be influenced by its concern to be satisfied that a winding up will yield some benefit for interested parties.[117]

The **United States** Bankruptcy Code does not adopt the distinction between individual and corporate debtors that is characteristic of the other three common law systems. Aspects of the exercise of bankruptcy jurisdiction over foreign debtors were explored in Chapter 2 above.[118]

3.3 INTERNATIONAL EFFECTS OF AN ENGLISH WINDING UP

It is as well to begin this section by noting certain important distinctions. First, the extent and quality of the international recognition that can reasonably be expected for an English winding up will, for reasons already rehearsed at 3.1 above, differ according to whether it is an English-formed or a foreign company that is undergoing liquidation. Secondly, because of the fundamental difference between individual bankruptcy and company winding up with regard to the way in which the matter of title to the debtor's property is dealt with during the currency of the proceedings, the question of international recognition of the proprietary effects of an English winding up inevitably requires a different response from any foreign court before which such an issue may arise. Thirdly, it must be conceded that all questions of international recognition ultimately depend upon the rules and practice observed in the country before whose courts such questions arise for determination, and thus there is potential for results to vary due to the non-uniform state of private international law, compounded by differing attitudes as to the role and content of public policy, for example with regard to foreign penal or revenue claims when these form a part of the liabilities by which the insolvent debtor is encumbered.

[115] *Re Stewart River Gold Dredging Co. Ltd.*(1912) 7 D.L.R. 736; *Re Breakwater Co.* (1914) 33 O.L.R. 65; *Re Briton Medical and General Life Association Ltd.(No.2)* (1886) 12 O.R. 441; *Allen v. Hanson, Re Scottish Canadian Asbestos Co. Ltd.* (1890) 18 S.C.R. 667.

[116] *Scott v. Hyde* (1908) 18 Qu. K.B. 138.

[117] *Re Steel Realty Development Corp.* (1924) 27 O.W.N. 37; *Re Halifax Sugar Refinery Co. Ltd.* (1889) 22 N.S.R. 71 (CA). See also *Linde Canadian Refrigerator Co. v. Saskatchewan Creamery Co., supra* n.112.

[118] See at 2.1.4 above, pp. 56–8.

3.3.1 The general position on international effects

We have seen that English law's approach to international insolvency is based on the acceptance of the principle of universality.[119] Consequently, English law regards any proceedings which are commenced in this country pursuant to the provisions of the Insolvency Act 1986 that relate to company insolvency as being necessarily comprehensive in their effects, so as to embrace all the company's interests, all assets and all creditors and other related parties, wheresoever they may be. An English winding up is not confined to the company's English activities and business operations, but is intended to constitute a collective, global administration of its entire undertaking.[120] The statutory definition of 'property' supplied by section 436 of the Insolvency Act 1986, whose meaning and significance were examined at 2.2 above, applies to all Parts of the Act, including those dealing with company insolvency.[121] Therefore all references in the Act to 'the property of the company' must be taken to denote all forms of property, wherever situated. Thus the extraterritorial aspirations of an English winding up are deliberately implanted in the statutory provisions.

In those cases where the company was originally formed and registered under English law, international recognition is likely to be at its widest. If the company's central control and management has been exercised elsewhere than in England, however, this is likely to diminish the extent to which the proceedings will qualify for recognition under the laws of those countries which adhere to the 'real seat' theory for determining the governing law.[122]

A further attenuation of the extent of international recognition will take place where the English courts exercise their jurisdiction to wind up a company formed under foreign law, on any of the grounds examined at 3.2.2 above. Here, the issue of recognition may arise in several different ways, depending on the circumstances of the case. A major consideration is whether any parallel proceedings take place in the country of incorporation, since this is likely to be an important factor according to the recognition rules of third countries.[123] Alternatively, it may be the case that no winding-up proceedings take place in the state of incorporation, either

[119] See Chapter 1, esp. at 1.2 above, and also Chapter 2, at 2.2 above.

[120] *Re International Tin Council* [1987] Ch. 419 at 446 per Millett J. The learned judge, while acknowledging that a winding up in a country other than that of the company's incorporation might not be accorded international recognition in the way that would be normal where the company is wound up in its home country, added: 'But in theory the effect of the order is worldwide'. Cf. *Re Azoff-Don Commercial Bank* [1954] 1 Ch. 315, at 333 per Wynn-Parry J., invoking the general principle of international insolvency propounded by Pearson J. in *Re Kloebe* (1884) 28 Ch. D. 175.

[121] See Chapter 2 at pp. 59 *et seq.* above.

[122] See at 3.1 above.

[123] See further at 3.9 below, regarding concurrent liquidations.

because this is precluded on technical grounds, or because no qualified party chooses to initiate such proceedings, particularly where logistical or practical considerations militate against such a course being pursued.[124] Here, the pragmatic considerations that have been a prominent feature of the development of this aspect of the jurisdictional powers of the English courts in recent times may also commend themselves to the courts of third countries before which any question of recognition arises, for example if the liquidator seeks assistance in pursuing investigations into the company's affairs, or to recover assets actually found there. *A fortiori*, if the company has previously been dissolved under the law of its State of incorporation,[125] the probability of any continuing interest in the company's affairs on the part of that legal system is likely to be small. This may enable the courts in other jurisdictions to respond to the perception that the ends of justice will be best served by assisting the English liquidator to conduct a 'posthumous' liquidation of the company for the benefit of creditors whose claims are still unsatisfied, by administering all assets currently discoverable for their collective benefit. It is strongly urged that in such cases the liquidator's standing to act on behalf of all remaining creditors should be recognised internationally.

3.3.2 The effects of winding up on the company's property

The doctrinal and practical aspects of international recognition are likely to be encountered in their liveliest form when there is a contest between the English liquidator and some rival claimant to the company's property which happens to be situated in a foreign country. The rival may be an individual creditor (or several creditors) seeking to claim the asset under local enforcement processes as a means of obtaining satisfaction of any outstanding claims against the company. Just possibly, the rival claimant may be a liquidator appointed under parallel proceedings commenced in some third State. The principal issues to be resolved by the court of the *situs* are whether to recognise the status of the English liquidator, and if so with what effect so far as concerns any titular claims to the assets presently subject to its jurisdiction. In its evaluation of the liquidator's claim, the foreign court must first be satisfied that under the rule of recognition

[124] This may be a relevant factor where a company has been incorporated in a 'jurisdiction of convenience' which is geographically remote, and where there may be no known assets locally. Also relevant may be the known characteristics of the legal system of the State of incorporation, including the level of sophistication of its insolvency law. See, e.g., the indications of scope for delaying the progress of commercially urgent investigations, using the somewhat sedate and antiquated machinery of justice of the Channel Islands of Alderney and Guernsey, disclosed in *Re Seagull Manufacturing Co. Ltd.* [1991] 4 All E.R. 257.

[125] See at 3.2.2(a) and 3.2.3 above, with respect to the winding up of dissolved companies.

contained in its own system of private international law the English winding up can be recognised, as just considered.[126]

Assuming there is a positive finding on the general question of recognition, the matter of the liquidator's entitlement to the assets can be analysed. Here, it is essential to avoid any misunderstanding about the office holder's standing to lay claim to all property belonging to the company, despite the fact that under the English law of company insolvency itself there is no automatic alteration of the legal title to its assets as a consequence of the company going into liquidation. This is in marked contrast to the position in cases of individual insolvency, where there is clear and unequivocal provision in section 306 of the Insolvency Act 1986 to the effect that a bankrupt is divested of title to his available estate by operation of law, as a direct and immediate consequence of adjudication.[127] In the winding up of companies, on the other hand, the Act is curiously reticent about the proprietary effects of the making of a winding-up order (or of a company going into voluntary liquidation). Instead, there are detailed provisions in sections 143 to 170 inclusive, together with Schedule 4, setting out the liquidator's functions, powers and duties in a winding up. The missing information regarding the effect of a liquidation upon the matter of title to the company's assets has been supplied, since 1874, by means of case law, which has consistently maintained that the effect of the commencement of winding up is that the company is deprived of the beneficial title to its property, although the legal estate remains undisturbed during the course of the liquidation unless a specific order is made upon application to the court by the liquidator, vesting all or any part of the property in the liquidator in his official capacity.[128] The judicial rationalisation of this position is that the company is deprived of the right to use or dispose of the property for its own benefit, and that the property is cast into a position analogous to that of a trust fund, whose objectives it is the task of the liquidator to carry into effect in accordance with the provisions of the legislation, and by means of the powers thereby conferred on him. Therefore, for the purpose of assessing what effects to accord to the English liquidation, it is submitted that a foreign court should take account of the full course of the English procedure in its contextual setting. The salient features are that the process is intended to be a fully comprehensive liquidation and distribution of the company's entire undertaking among all creditors on a worldwide basis, and that the liquidator is delib-

[126] See at 3.3.1 above.

[127] See Chapter 2, at 2.2 above.

[128] *Re Oriental Inland Steam Co.* (1874) L.R. 9 Ch App. 557, at 559 per James L.J. and at 560 per Mellish L.J.; *New Zealand Loan and Mercantile Agency Co. Ltd. v. Morrison* [1898] A.C. 349 at 358 per Lord Davey (PC); *Ayerst v. C. & K. (Construction) Ltd.* [1976] A.C. 167 (HL), esp. at 179–180 per Lord Diplock. The court's power to make a vesting order upon application by the liquidator is conferred by the Insolvency Act 1986, s.145.

erately endowed with a full panoply of powers which, in the domestic arena, are in most cases perfectly sufficient to enable him to fulfil the statutory objectives of securing, realising and distributing the assets of the company among its creditors.[129] It is appropriate therefore to regard the liquidator as the legitimate representative of the collective interests of the general body of creditors, and hence to have the strongest claim to be accorded such recognition and assistance as is permitted under the rules of law applicable in the country of the *situs*, having regard in particular to the promptings of the doctrine of comity.

Thus, the international effects of an English winding up in relation to the company's foreign assets are subject to the control of the positive law of the *situs*. Even though the standing of the English liquidator may be recognised in principle, the local law may relegate his claim behind that of some other party, for example because the latter has succeeded in perfecting a security interest, or in completing a process of execution against the property, that is valid according to the law of the *situs*. Even though the transaction or execution in question might be capable of avoidance according to the provisions of English insolvency law, these provisions cannot command extraterritorial effect and it is therefore left to the law of the *situs* to control the outcome of this contest.[130] Similarly, if the law of the *situs* contains provisions designed to enhance the protection afforded to local creditors who have dealings with out-of-state companies which do business there (particularly in such fields as banking and insurance, and other financial services), the consequence may be that such assets as are situate within that country will be withheld from the liquidator unless and until the claims of the protected, local creditors have been satisfied.[131] Also potentially fatal to the liquidator's prospects of enlisting the aid of foreign courts in a concrete way is the abiding force of public policy, as conceived under the law of the *situs*. As has already been seen in relation to the parallel theme of international recognition of trustees in bankruptcy, the exclusionary rule of private international law which denies direct or indirect enforcement to foreign penal or revenue laws can mean that a liquidator in a winding up in which the fiscal authorities of the company's home State are major creditors may encounter the objection in many foreign jurisdictions that he is acting as a 'mere catspaw' of the Revenue Service, with the consequence that turnover of the assets will be refused.[132]

[129] See Insolvency Act 1986, s.143(1), and also ss.165–168 together with Schedule 4.

[130] Cf. the similar approach of English law towards the claims of a foreign trustee in bankruptcy, exemplified in *Galbraith v. Grimshaw* [1910] A.C. 508 (HL), discussed in Chapter 2 at 2.2 and 2.6 above.

[131] See *New Zealand Loan and Mercantile Agency Co. Ltd. v. Morrison* [1898] A.C. 349 (PC); *Re Standard Insurance Co. Ltd.* [1968] Qd. R. 118; *Re Air Express Foods Pty. Ltd.*[1977] Qd. R. 107.

[132] See authorities cited in Chapter 2, at 2.4—*Foreign penal or revenue claims*—and 2.6(a)—*Exception to recognition: Tax bankruptcies*—at pp. 84 and 97 respectively.

Lastly, it can be noted that the standing and titular claims of an English liquidator are likely to encounter the most severe resistance in any proceedings brought before the courts of the foreign country under whose laws the company was originally incorporated. If the English proceedings are considered to amount to an unwarranted incursion upon the prerogative of the State of incorporation to rule upon matters of the company's existence and ultimate dissolution, the courts of that country will have no compunction in repelling or disregarding any attempts by the liquidator appointed in such proceedings to seek their active assistance.[133] If however a more fraternal state of relations can be engendered between the English liquidator and his counterpart appointed under the law of the company's State of incorporation, more fruitful possibilities may result. This may give rise to a collaborative arrangement whereby the English liquidation will be ancillary to that which is taking place in the company's 'home' jurisdiction, with the English liquidator confining himself to collecting and administering the assets situate in England itself, or otherwise conveniently accessible, in accordance with a coordinated plan.[134] Such arrangements, involving a deliberate self-limitation with regard to the international effects claimed by each set of proceedings, will be considered at 3.9 below and in Chapter 4 below.[135]

3.4 CHOICE OF LAW IN AN ENGLISH WINDING UP

It has long been regarded as conclusively settled that in any winding up conducted pursuant to the English legislation relating to insolvent companies, English law will apply both as to matters of substance as well as to matters of procedure.[136] This matches the equally long established proposition regarding the governing law in the case of the bankruptcy of individuals that was examined at 2.3 above. Indeed, many of the matters there described are also applicable in the case of company winding up, and the observations already made concerning the need for a reconsideration of certain aspects of the law's operation are, it is submitted, equally applic-

[133] Cf. *National Trust Co. Ltd. v. Ebro Irrigation and Power Co. Ltd.* [1954] 3 D.L.R. 326.

[134] See *Re Matheson Brothers Ltd.* (1884) 27 Ch D. 225; *Re Commercial Bank of South Australia* (1886) 33 Ch.D. 174; *Re English, Scottish and Australian Chartered Bank* [1893] 3 Ch. 385; *Re Federal Bank of Australia* [1893] W.N. 77 (CA). These cases are further referred to at 3.9 below.

[135] In *Re Hibernian Merchants Ltd.* [1958] 1 Ch. 76, Roxburgh J. stated that it was not desirable to include an express provision in the winding-up order, limiting the liquidator's scope of action to getting in the foreign company's English assets. The liquidator could always seek further directions from the court at a subsequent stage.

[136] *Re English, Scottish and Australian Chartered Bank, supra* n.134, at 394 per Vaughan Williams J., affd. (CA) *ibid.*, at 394; *Re Suidair International Airways Ltd.* [1951] Ch. 165, at 173–174 per Wynn-Parry J. Cf. *North Australian Territory Co. Ltd. v. Goldsbrough, Mort & Co. Ltd.* (1889) 61 L.T. 716.

able, *mutatis mutandis*, to the insolvency of companies.[137] There are certain issues however which have no exact counterpart in cases of individual bankruptcy, and which require to be mentioned here.

First, in view of the seemingly paradoxical position whereby there can be a winding up in England of a company formed under the law of a foreign country—and, by English criteria of recognition, domiciled in that country and ultimately controlled by its law[138]—it is pertinent to consider what adjustment, if any, will be made to the rule that English law applies as *lex fori* to all aspects of the English proceedings. In truth, there are no indications that in such cases the courts have ever seriously considered the possibility of departing from the approach that is followed in relation to English-formed companies. The dominant consideration appears to be that, as a procedure that is entirely the product of statutory provisions in which the requirements of public policy are constantly to the fore, it would be unthinkable to attempt a fusion of legal cultures within the framework of an English liquidation. Even when the English proceedings are taking place contemporaneously with a winding up in the country of incorporation, so that the English proceedings are accorded ancillary status, the courts have over the years been at pains to insist that the integrity of the English process will not be compromised thereby. Thus, in a much-quoted *dictum* Vaughan Williams J. asserted, in *Re English, Scottish and Australian Chartered Bank*:

> the desire to act as ancillary to the court where the main liquidation is going on will not ever make the court give up the forensic rules which govern the conduct of its own liquidation.[139]

More recently, during the course of the notoriously complex series of judicial hearings arising out of the collapse of the Bank of Credit and Commerce International (B.C.C.I.), Scott V.-C. went so far as to rule that it was not within the inherent power of the English court, even in the context of an internationally agreed arrangement for pooling of claims, to disapply the provisions of the statutory insolvency scheme established under the English legislation.[140] The powerful grip of the *lex fori* upon the main structure of the insolvency process is seemingly unshakeable.

It must be remembered however that, during the course of administering the assets and claims, issues can be encountered which will involve the

[137] See, in particular, the passages at 2.3 above bearing the sub-headings *Questions of substantive law; Choice of avoidance law; Secured creditors' rights;* and *Set-off*, respectively.

[138] See at 3.1 above, and also at 3.2.2 above.

[139] [1893] 3 Ch. 385 at 394. See also the elucidation of this passage by Wynn-Parry J. in *Re Suidair International Airways Ltd.* [1951] Ch. 165 at 173–174.

[140] *Re Bank of Credit and Commerce International S.A. (No. 10)* [1996] 4 All E.R. 796, at 814–822. The inflexible sentiments disclosed in this passage were noted with regret in Chapter 2 above at pp. 74–5.

making of a reference to foreign law pursuant to the relevant English rule of conflict of laws. For example, claims of a contractual nature which are owed by or to the company may be subject to a dispute whose resolution will require reference to the governing law of the contract. All such matters, if arising in proceedings taking place under English jurisdiction, must be determined in accordance with the Rome Convention, even if the company which is being wound up in England has been incorporated in a country which is not a party to that Convention.[141] Reference to the governing law of the obligation will also be necessary if it is alleged to be unenforceable on account of some factor such as illegality, or the elapse of time under the applicable statute of limitations, or due to a discharge that is effective according to the governing law.[142] Where English law itself is the governing law of the obligation, a so-far uncorrected flaw in the structure of our legal rules prevents the recognition of a discharge resulting from insolvency proceedings conducted under foreign law, even though those same proceedings might independently qualify for recognition according to accepted principles. The unsatisfactory state of the law on this point was discussed in Chapter 2 above.[143] A further reason for referring to foreign law is where the status or capacity of any legal or natural person becomes material for some reason. This can include cases where it is alleged that a particular company or partnership was non-existent at a relevant point in time, either because it was never validly formed according to the applicable system of law, or because it had undergone dissolution by operation of that very law.[144] Likewise, if there is a need to ascertain the identity of the parties who are liable to make payment as contributories in the liquidation, or who are eligible to share in any surplus, under the English winding up of a foreign company, it may be necessary to consult the company law of the State of incorporation to discover the effects of its provisions in this respect.[145] So, too, where the matter for determination concerns the validity of the appointment of any of the

141 See references supplied in Chapter 2, at 2.3 above, in n.172.

142 *Gibbs and Sons v. La Société Industrielle et Commerciale des Métaux* (1890) 25 Q.B.D. 399 (CA); *Re Higginson and Dean* [1899] 1 Q.B. 325; *Re Banque des Marchands de Moscou (Koupetschesky), Royal Exchange v. The Liquidator* [1952] 1 All E.R. 1269; *Re Banque des Marchands de Moscou (Koupetschesky) (No. 2)* [1954] 1 W.L.R. 1108; *National Bank of Greece and Athens S.A. v. Metliss* [1958] A.C. 509 (HL); *Adams v. National Bank of Greece S.A.* [1961] A.C. 255 (HL).

143 See p. 107 above, referring to the *Gibbs* case cited *supra*, n.142.

144 *Maunder v. Lloyd* (1862) 2 J. & H. 718, 70 E.R. 1248; *Von Hellfield v. E. Rechnitzer & Mayer Frères & Co.*[1914] 1 Ch. 748 (CA). See also *Skyline Associates v. Small* (1974) 50 D.L.R. (3d) 217.

145 *General Steam Navigation Co. v. Guillou* (1843) 11 M. and W. 877, 152 E.R. 1061; *Re Banque des Marchands de Moscou (Koupetschesky)* [1958] Ch. 182. Cf. *Risdon Iron and Locomotive Works v. Furness* [1906] 1 K.B. 49 (CA). See also Insolvency Act 1986, ss. 74–82, 154 and 226(1), with regard to the position of contributories in a winding up.

company's officers or directors, or their capacity to bind the company by acts purportedly done on its behalf.[146]

Security rights created by companies

Choice of law matters associated with the enforcement of rights of secured creditors were considered at 2.3 above in relation to the bankruptcy of individuals.[147] The same principles also apply in cases where the debtor by whom the security has been granted is a company which subsequently undergoes insolvency proceedings. However, certain forms of security, and certain aspects relating to enforceability, are exclusively applicable to companies, and are therefore mentioned here.

First, it is necessary to observe that the type of security known as the floating charge is a unique feature of company law, and has no exact counterpart among the forms of security associated with individual debtors.[148] Various types of fixed security are in current use under English law, and may be created by individual or corporate debtors. Where a company is involved in granting security however, it may be necessary to determine whether it is fixed or floating in character, a task which can be sometimes difficult to perform in view of the increasingly elaborate and sophisticated forms of security instrument nowadays in use. The distinction between fixed and floating security is by no means a merely academic one, since the holder of a species of fixed security is in a far superior position in the event of the corporate debtor's insolvency.[149] The process of classification may therefore have to be undertaken as a first step in determining the validity and enforceability of the security in question. For this purpose, the *lex fori* is applicable to determine the character—as between fixed and floating—of any charge over its property allegedly created by an English-formed company, even in relation to property situate abroad. It has been held that an English company can grant a floating charge over foreign movable or immovable property which it owns, even where this happens to be situate

[146] *Banco de Bilbao v. Sancha* [1938] 2 K.B. 176 (CA).

[147] See p. 79 above

[148] The nature and characteristics of the floating charge are not explored in this book. For information about this form of security, see: R.M. Goode, *Commercial Law*, 2nd edn. (1995), ch. 25, and *Legal Problems of Credit and Security*, 2nd edn. (1988), chs. 3 and 4; W. Gough, *Company Charges*, 2nd edn., (1996), ch. 5; P.L. Davies (ed.), *Gower's Principles of Modern Company Law*, 6th edn., (1997), ch. 15.

[149] The holder of fixed security enjoys immediate rights of enforcement against the property comprised therein, and hence is able to stand outside the insolvency process to the extent of the value of the security. In contrast, the rights of a floating charge holder are relegated behind the entitlement of the preferential creditors to receive payment in full, with recourse as necessary to the property comprised in the floating charge. See Insolvency Act 1986, s. 175(2)(b), and also *ibid.*, ss. 251 (definition of 'floating charge'), and 386 together with Sch. 6 (categories of preferential debts). The principles of distribution of assets in a company liquidation are discussed in I.F. Fletcher, *The Law of Insolvency*, 2nd edn., (1996), ch. 24.

in a country whose laws do not recognise this species of security.[150] Although the proprietary aspects of this security may be ineffective according to the *lex situs*, English law will treat the agreement to create the charge as a valid equitable security, enforceable *in personam* against a chargor company that is subject to the equitable jurisdiction of the English court.[151] However, although such powers can extend to the punishment for contempt of any person who is interfering with the exercise of the chargee's rights concerning property abroad, English courts will respect any countervailing rights which have arisen under the foreign *lex situs*, for example by way of a completed execution under the local law.[152] In practice, therefore, the rights of the chargee are likely to be relatively weak unless it has been possible to effect some form of valid registration of the charge according to the law of the *situs*, so that rival claimants can be held at bay.

A further question of applicable law arises by virtue of the provisions contained in the English legislation itself which impose a requirement of registration with regard to a charge—whether of a fixed or floating type—created by a company by way of granting security on its property or undertaking. Part XII of the Companies Act 1985 establishes a regime for the registration of such charges, as listed in section 396, the consequence of non-registration being that the security conferred by the charge is void as against the liquidator or administrator and any creditor of the company.[153] Where a charge is created in the United Kingdom in relation to property situated within the Realm, the transaction calls for no special comment for the purposes of the present discussion. In an international context, on the other hand, several possible situations may be encountered. Thus, it may transpire that the company has created the charge by means of a transaction outside the United Kingdom, comprising property that is also situated overseas. Alternatively, the transaction may take place in the United Kingdom but comprise property situated elsewhere. In both situations, in addition to any compliance that may be necessary under the law of the *situs* to render the security interest valid and enforceable under that system of law, the transaction gives rise to a requirement of registration pursuant to the Companies Act in order to maintain the validity of the security for any purpose associated with the processes of English law, particularly in the event of the insolvency of the chargor. A further situation is governed by the provisions of section 409 of the 1985 Act, which extends the requirements of registration to charges on property in England and

[150] *British South Africa Company v. De Beers Consolidated Mines Ltd.* [1910] 1 Ch. 354, rvsd. on other grounds [1912] A.C. 52 (HL); *Re Anchor Line (Henderson Brothers) Ltd.* [1937] Ch. 483.

[151] *Penn v. Lord Baltimore* (1750) Ves. Sen 444; *British South Africa Company v. De Beers Consolidated Mines Ltd., supra* n.150; *Re Anchor Line (Henderson Brothers) Ltd., supra* n.150.

[152] *Re Maudslay, Sons & Field* [1900] 1 Ch. 602, esp. at 611–612 per Cozens-Hardy J.

Wales which are created, and to charges on such property which is acquired, by a company incorporated outside Great Britain which has an established place of business in England and Wales. Therefore, foreign companies which fulfil this criterion are subject to the same regime as domestic companies when creating charges over their property in England and Wales, whether the transaction itself takes place inside or outside the United Kingdom. In this respect, the regime contained in Part XII of the Companies Act 1985 has overreaching force by virtue of the fact that the chargor is a company subject to that Act and to the Insolvency Act 1986, and in any winding up conducted in this country the consequences of non-registration are potentially serious from the secured party's point of view (albeit that the invalidation of the security will release the asset in question so that it becomes available either to another creditor who holds a junior security, or for the benefit of the creditors generally).

The impact of the above rules, and their capability of affecting the position of parties in other jurisdictions having dealings with companies that are subject to the English law's regime, may be seen in the case of *Re Weldtech Equipment Ltd.*[154] In that case, an English company had contracted with a German seller of welding equipment, under a contract whose terms included a reservation of title clause which purported to extend the seller's rights so as to include the proceeds of any resale of the goods by the buyer. Although section 396 of the Companies Act, as currently drafted, does not have the effect that a 'simple' reservation of title clause is a registrable charge for the purposes of Part XII of the Act, this exemption can be lost through the introduction of any provision which, as in the instant case, seeks to enhance the seller's protection by encumbering property to which other parties, including the buyer, have title.[155] In this context, the property in question may consist of money that is the product of an onward sale, or it may be an intangible such as an uncollected book debt arising from that transaction. Hoffmann J. concluded that the clause in question amounted to a charge upon its book debts created by the buyer company, and so was registrable under section 396(1)(e) of the 1985 Act. This was the case even though the contract provided that its construction and effect were to be governed by German law, and despite the fact that under German law a clause of that kind would be valid and enforceable without registration. The learned judge held that the provisions of section 395 apply to all charges created by companies registered

[153] Companies Act 1985, s. 395(1).

[154] [1991] B.C.C. 16; [1991] B.C.L.C. 393 (Hoffmann J.).

[155] For the main principles, see *Clough Mill Ltd. v. Martin* [1984] 3 All E.R. 982, [1985] 1 W.L.R. 111 (CA); *Re Bond Worth Ltd.* [1980] Ch. 228; *Borden (U.K.) Ltd. v. Scottish Timber Products Ltd.* [1981] Ch. 25 (CA); *Armour v. Thyssen Edelstahlwerke AG* [1991] 2 A.C. 339 (HL). See also G. McCormack, *Reservation of Title*, 2nd edn. (1995).

in England whatever may be the proper law of the instrument which creates the charge. Since the charge was over the book debts of the English company, the actual whereabouts of the goods themselves at any material time—including at the time of any resale—was not relevant.

3.5 CREDITORS AND CLAIMS IN AN ENGLISH WINDING UP

Although English law maintains a distinctive separation between company and individual insolvency, with separate procedures for each of these two broad categories of debtor, the two branches of insolvency are essentially governed according to a single framework of fundamental principles. This is especially true of the process of distribution of the insolvent debtor's property, and the treatment of creditors and their claims in accordance with the principle of collectivity, as understood and applied within English tradition. Accordingly, what was said at 2.4 above concerning the treatment of creditors and claims in an English bankruptcy may be taken to apply equally to the situation where the insolvency proceedings consist of the winding up of a company which has either been formed under English law or, having been formed under foreign law, is amenable to the jurisdiction of the English court for this particular purpose.[156] Reference should therefore be made to the discussion at 2.4 above, noting that many of the cases there referred to were in fact concerned with companies. The following observations are intended to supplement the contents of that section.

Enforcement of the automatic stay of actions and executions

The making of a winding-up order has the consequence that an automatic stay is imposed upon actions or proceedings against the company or its property, such that these can neither be commenced nor proceeded with except by leave of the court, and subject to such terms as the court may impose.[157] Moreover section 128 of the Insolvency Act 1986 provides that where a company registered in England and Wales is being wound up by the court any attachment, sequestration, distress or execution put in force against the estate or effects of the company after the commencement of the winding up is void. Further provisions in the Insolvency Act have the

[156] See at 3.2.2 above.

[157] Insolvency Act 1986, s.130(2). See also *ibid.*, s.126 which empowers the court to impose a stay on actions or proceedings during the period between the presentation of a winding-up petition and the making of a winding-up order. On the exercise of the court's discretion to lift the stay imposed by s.130(2), see I.F. Fletcher, *The Law of Insolvency*, 2nd edn. (1996), at pp. 555–557.

effect of depriving any creditor of the benefits of an execution against the goods or land of the company, or an attachment of any debt due to it, unless the execution or attachment were completed before the commencement of the winding up.[158] The purpose of these provisions is to ensure that the *pari passu* principle of distribution is applied to all the creditors collectively, and that no individual is allowed to exploit some chance opportunity to seize an undue share of the assets, at the expense of the others.[159] The effects of these provisions with respect to winding-up proceedings taking place in England are extended to the other parts of the United Kingdom as one of the consequences of the system of mutual enforcement and cooperation maintained by section 426 of the Insolvency Act.[160] The current provision is, for this purpose, a continuation of arrangements that have been continuously in force since the era of the Companies Act 1862.[161]

Although the mantle of legislation covers all parts of the United Kingdom, it can claim no such authority over courts belonging to politically foreign countries. The automatic stay resulting from an English winding-up order does not apply to proceedings pending in such courts.[162] However, the English courts are not entirely powerless to prevent individual creditors from pursuing unilateral initiatives in foreign jurisdictions. We have seen that the court's equitable jurisdiction *in personam* may be used to restrain such actions on the part of creditors who are subject to its control, using its power to punish any act of defiance as a contempt of court, and that further remedies may be invoked to claw back the fruits of foreign diligence by such means as the 'hotchpot' rule.[163] While these powers are of no avail against creditors having no personal amenability to the processes of English law, they can become applicable if such persons seek to prove in the liquidation for any unsatisfied balance

[158] *Ibid.*, s.183. See also *ibid.*, s.127, which makes void any disposition of the company's property made after the commencement of the winding up, unless the court makes a validation order to override the effect of that section. For the effects of these and related provisions of the Act, see Fletcher, *supra* n.157, at pp. 628–633, together with pp. 240–244. The expression 'commencement of winding-up' is defined in ss. 86 and 129, for the purposes of voluntary and compulsory winding up respectively.

[159] *Re Thurso New Gas Co. Ltd.* (1889) 42 Ch. D. 486.

[160] See s.426(1)–(6) of the 1986 Act, and comments relating thereto made at 2.2 above (*Effects within the United Kingdom*).

[161] See, e.g. *Re International Pulp and Paper Co.* (1876) 3 Ch.D. 594; *Re Hermann Loog Ltd* (1887) 36 Ch. D. 502; *Re Thurso New Gas Co., supra* n.159; *Martin v. Port of Manchester Insurance Co. Ltd.* 1934 S.C. 143; *Boyd v. Lee Guinness Ltd.* [1963] N. Ir. 49; *Re Dynamics Corporation of America* [1972] 3 All E.R. 1046, [1973] 1 W.L.R. 63.

[162] *Re Vocalion (Foreign) Ltd.* [1932] 2 Ch. 196.

[163] See at 2.4 above, at pp. 84–8 (*Restraining creditors' actions abroad; Reclaiming the fruits of creditors' actions against property abroad*).See also section 2.1.3. (*Jurisdictional abstention; forum non conveniens)* for discussion of the modern approach to the exercise of jurisdiction.

of debt, thereby submitting to the court's full jurisdiction.[164] Conversely, a creditor who is personally amenable to the jurisdiction can be restrained by means of injunction from taking action abroad, regardless of whether he has chosen to participate in the English winding up through submitting a proof of debt.[165]

Where overseas proceedings are instituted by a creditor who is not personally amenable to the jurisdiction of the English court, an alternative strategy must be pursued. The English liquidator may seek to enlist the cooperation of the courts of the foreign country in question, presenting himself as the legitimate representative of the collective interests of all creditors wheresoever they happen to reside. On the premise that the English proceedings qualify for recognition under the law of the *situs* of the property whose destiny is in contention, the liquidator may be able to avail himself of remedies under the local law, including any which may be designed to assist a foreign representative to accomplish his mission as office holder in a foreign insolvency proceeding.[166] A further possibility may be to bring about the opening of insolvency proceedings in the country of the *situs*, to ensure that a process of collective distribution will take place locally, with the potential for this to be coordinated with the English liquidation. A further advantage of such a manoeuvre is that the local law may then be used to overturn the effects of local acts of diligence, and to impeach antecedent transactions from which certain individuals have benefitted.

Secured creditors' exemption from the automatic stay

A creditor who holds a duly perfected, real security over property of the company is entitled to enforce that security without being impeded by the effects of the automatic stay. It is one of the integral purposes of such security that it will enable the creditor to stand outside the insolvency process in which his debtor is involved. Accordingly, a secured creditor will not be restrained by injunction from taking appropriate steps to realise his security. This is so whether the property comprised in the security is situate in England or elsewhere.[167]

[164] See the authorities cited at 2.4 above at nn. 188–190 inclusive, and also *Re Maudslay, Sons & Field* [1900] 1 Ch. 602 at 611–612 per Cozens-Hardy J.; *Re Oriental Inland Steam Co.* (1874) L.R. 9 Ch. App. 557, at 559 per James L.J.; *Re North Carolina Estate Co. Ltd.* (1889) 5 T.L.R. 328; *Re Vocalion (Foreign) Ltd., supra* n.162.

[165] *Re Central Sugar Factories of Brazil (Flack's Case)* [1894] 1 Ch. 369.

[166] Examples of such provisions for international cooperation are discussed in Chapter 4 below.

[167] *Moore v. Anglo-Italian Bank* (1879) 10 Ch.D. 681; *Re West Cumberland Iron and Steel Co.* [1893] 1 Ch. 713; *Minna Craig Steamship Co. v. Chartered Mercantile Bank of India, London and China* [1897] 1 Q.B. 460 (CA); *Re Derwent Rolling Mills Co.* (1904) 21 T.L.R. 81, affd. (CA) *ibid.* 701.

3.6 DISCHARGE AND DISSOLUTION UNDER AN ENGLISH WINDING UP

Company winding up results in the dissolution of the company, which comes about at the conclusion of the process of administration and distribution of its property.[168] Therefore, in contrast to the outcome in the case of the bankruptcy of an individual, whose life continues and whose civil and commercial capacities can be fully restored through the granting of discharge from bankruptcy, the legal existence of a company is terminated at the conclusion of the winding up. Moreover,the concept of limited liability means that with the dissolution of the company there is no surviving person against whom the company's original liabilities can be enforced. In the case of creditors whose debts were provable in the liquidation, their rights were automatically transformed via the insolvency process into a right to participate in the process of distribution, according to the amount of their claim admitted to proof by the liquidator and then according to the ranking of their claim within the hierarchy of priority as prescribed by law. The process of *pari passu* distribution is carried out sequentially, class by class, according to that prescription.[169] Once the pool of available assets is exhausted, the outstanding balances of debts are inevitably destined to remain unsatisfied. Even more unenviable is the predicament of any creditor whose debt is classified as non-provable under the provisions of insolvency law, for such persons face the prospect that not only are they excluded from participating in the process of distribution, but also there will be no continuing *persona* against which their claims may be maintained at some later date.[170]

As we have seen, a winding up under English law is considered to have universal effect, and to embrace all property, and all creditors and their claims, throughout the world. Where the company in question was formed under English law, the central tenets of the 'State of incorporation' theory supply the basis for recognition of the company's dissolution by the laws of those countries which subscribe to that doctrine.[171]

[168] See Insolvency Act 1986, ss. 201–205.

[169] For an account of the rules governing the process of distribution, see the references supplied *supra* n.149.

[170] Prior to 1986, unliquidated claims of a tortious nature were non-provable as debts in a bankruptcy or an insolvent liquidation. Although a bankrupt tortfeasor might later be pursued by the victim after gaining discharge from bankruptcy, there was no such possibility if the tortfeasor was an insolvent company. See e.g. *Re Great Orme Tramways* (1934) 50 T.L.R. 450, and see the absurdity posited by Vinelott J. in *Re Berkeley Securities (Property) Ltd.* [1980] 3 All E.R. 513 at 525–530. Unliquidated tort claims are now included within the category of provable debts: Insolvency Act 1986, ss. 322(3), 382(3); Insolvency Rules 1986, rr.4.86, 12.3. The types of debt which are non-provable or postponed under the current law are set out in r.12.3(2),(2A).

[171] See at 3.1 above.

Recognition may not be so readily forthcoming from those legal systems which adhere to the 'real seat' theory, at least in those cases where the English-formed company demonstrably did not have its real centre of financial and business operations somewhere within England (or, at least, within the United Kingdom).[172] Where there has been an English winding up of a company whose formation took place under foreign law, the position is rather less straightforward. In the first place, the main doctrinal position accepted by English law itself proclaims it to be the function of the law of the company's State of incorporation to govern the fundamental matters concerning the beginning and end of the company's legal existence. Thus, while a separate set of arguments has resulted in the development of a jurisdictional capability to *wind up* foreign companies in England, the logical conundrum concerning the competence of the English proceedings to accomplish the *dissolution* of such companies has remained a matter of considerable obscurity. On the face of it, international recognition of this aspect of the winding up process would be least likely to be forthcoming among the members of the 'State of incorporation' school of belief whereas, paradoxically, countries which follow the 'real seat' philosophy might be more inclined to accept the possibility of such a dissolution, at least if the company's central control and management was based in England at the time of the winding up.

Little assistance towards the resolution of the foregoing uncertainties is to be derived from an examination of the provisions within Part V of the Insolvency Act, under which the winding up of foreign companies in England is enabled to take place.[173] Section 221(1) contains the promising statement that:

> Subject to the provisions of this Part, any unregistered company may be wound up under this Act; and all the provisions of this Act and the Companies Act about winding up apply to an unregistered company with the exceptions and additions mentioned in the following subsections.

Unfortunately, the 'following subsections' of section 221 itself, and the other provisions in Part V, do not address the question of the dissolution of any foreign company when it is wound up here as unregistered. On the other hand, section 221(3) provides that *for the purpose of determining a court's winding up jurisdiction* an unregistered company is deemed to be registered in England and Wales, or in Scotland, according as its principal place of business is situated in one or other of those countries (or in both of them). The express limitation of the effects of this provision appears to preclude any suggestion that a foreign company could be deemed to be registered in England for the purpose of claiming international effects for its purported dissolution after having been wound up here. On the other

[172] See at 3.1 above. [173] See at 3.2.2 above.

hand, it is perhaps unlikely that this confused doctrinal position will be allowed to give rise to insoluble practical difficulties, should the situation arise in which the company's continued existence becomes a material issue either in its own country of incorporation or elsewhere.[174] This is particularly true for those cases where concurrent insolvency proceedings take place in the company's country of incorporation, whose law can then conveniently assume responsibility for effecting the definitive act of dissolution. A further category of cases for which it seems possible to achieve a reconciliation between apparently contradictory principles is where an English winding up takes place of a foreign company which has previously been dissolved under the law of its incorporation.[175] Here, the chief conceptual dilemma consists of the seeming illogicality of conducting a legal process in relation to an entity which is already non-existent. Since, as we saw, the chosen solution under English law has been to deem the company to be reanimated for the purpose of enabling it to be wound up, it could readily be deduced that the concluding phase of this process consists of the dissolution of such notional existence as the revived company temporarily had, by virtue of English law, during the course of those proceedings. This would appear to pose no serious challenge to the primary authority of the law of the country of incorporation.

With regard to the effects of English insolvency proceedings upon the debts and other liabilities owed by a corporate debtor, this is again a matter for the private international law of any country whose courts encounter the question whether an obligation subsists or has been discharged or otherwise ceased to be enforceable in its original character. In principle, the universal character of an English winding up should give rise to international recognition of the outcome in terms of the extinction of obligations in their original form, with creditors' claims being transformed into the right to receive dividend in the liquidation to the extent that the realised assets allow. Once the process of distribution is completed, and the liquidator has been released from office and the company dissolved, the possibility that creditors might retain the right to pursue remedies based upon the unsatisfied balance of their debts might appear somewhat academic. The issue may become a live one however if assets later come to light in some other jurisdiction. Among the possibilities ensuing from such a discovery, individual creditors may aspire to claim the property for

[174] It might come about that, despite the English winding up, the company continues to pursue its business in its home country, or in some third country, and that unpaid creditors there seek to argue that those responsible for managing the company have been deprived of the protection of limited liability, due to the company having been previously dissolved through the English liquidation. The outcome of such an attempt to impose direct, personal liability upon those concerned will depend on the result of applying the relevant recognition rule under the private international law of the country in question.

[175] See at 3.2.2 and 3.2.3 above.

themselves, or alternatively a local winding-up may be instigated, along lines analogous to the winding up in England of companies dissolved abroad. In the former situation, it is submitted, the original claims of the creditors ought to be regarded as having been discharged through the English liquidation, thereby putting an end to their rights to seek individual satisfaction. Conversely, in a local winding up, the collective rights previously enjoyed by all creditors entitled to prove in the English proceedings should be capable of revival under the new process of distribution. Indeed, such an analysis could be helpful in that, through lapse of time, the original obligations themselves may have become barred by limitation, whereas the theory that the commencement of insolvency proceedings stops the running of time for limitation purposes could be regarded as having left the creditors' rights to receive dividend 'frozen' until such time as funds become available to enable further payments to be made to them.[176]

There remains at least one problem that is seemingly intractable under present circumstances. This concerns the possibility that the laws of other countries may operate in a way comparable to the previously criticised refusal by English courts to accept the effectiveness of any discharge resulting from foreign insolvency proceedings with respect to an obligation whose proper law is English.[177] What may be envisaged is that a winding-up has taken place in England, and that a creditor ('C') from country X, whose debt was also governed by the law of X, has failed to receive payment in full out of the funds at the liquidator's disposal. Later, assets may come to light in X to which C lays claim for the purpose of satisfying the balance of his debt. C's action may take place in competition with those of other creditors whose debts were not governed by the law of X, or possibly in competition with the English liquidator, if still in office. In such circumstances, there is a distinct possibility that the courts of X could pronounce in favour of C, on the ground that C's debt is not considered to have been affected or discharged by proceedings taking place in a foreign country whose law did not govern the contract in question.[178] Even though the separate rules of the law of X concerning the recognition of foreign insolvency proceedings, and of the position of a liquidator appointed in such proceedings, may otherwise indicate that the English winding up can be recognised in X, the liquidator may well deem it inex-

[176] By way of analogy, the creditors to whom dividends were belatedly paid out of English assets in many of the 'Russian Bank' cases referred to at 3.2 above were sometimes in the position of receiving their payments more than 30 years after the original events which deprived them of access to their funds deposited with the dissolved banks.

[177] See the discussion, *inter alia*, of *Gibbs & Sons v. La Société Industrielle et Commerciale des Métaux* (1890) 25 Q.B.D. 399 (CA) at 2.7 above.

[178] Cf. the rhetorical exclamation of Lord Esher M.R. in the *Gibbs* case (*supra* n.177) at 406, quoted at 2.7 above at p. 107.

pedient to commit resources to contesting C's claim before the foreign court. The irony of such a challenge might become forcefully apparent, were it to be pointed out to the court of X that, in a converse situation, the English courts, according to long-established authority, would currently refrain from giving effect to a foreign discharge.[179]

3.7 ENGLISH LAW'S RECOGNITION OF FOREIGN LIQUIDATIONS AND THEIR EFFECTS

3.7.1 Generally

(a) General recognition

As with recognition of foreign bankruptcies,[180] there are separate bases of recognition of foreign liquidations as between those which are commenced in another part of the United Kingdom, and those commenced elsewhere in the world. The former are accorded automatic recognition in England and Wales by virtue of section 426(1) of the Insolvency Act 1986, whose provisions have already been explained at 2.6 above, to which reference should be made making the necessary adjustments for the terminology appropriate to company winding up.[181] An intermediate category of statute-based recognition and assistance towards foreign liquidation proceedings can also be noted at this point. This consists of the discrete group of countries and territories which have been designated for the purposes of section 426, as has been previously explained.[182] When company insolvency proceedings are opened in any of the countries belonging to that group, the court with jurisdiction over the case can avail itself of the assistance of the English court according to the provisions of section 426(4) and (5), as described at 2.6 above. However, the express stipulation in subsection (5) to the effect that the English court is required to have regard in particular to the rules of private international law ensures that the following account of the general approach to recognition that is derived from the case law will be influential in determining the extent to which assistance will be forthcoming. Further aspects of the arrangements for judicial cooperation under section 426 are examined in Chapter 4 below.

The case law concerning the recognition in England of foreign liquidations has been strongly influenced by the principles applied in the parallel situation of bankruptcy. However, due to the different structures of bankruptcy and winding-up procedures under our domestic law, English

[179] See the discussion of the *Gibbs* doctrine at 2.7 above, esp. at pp. 107–109, where it was urged that the law should be changed.

[180] See at 2.6 above.

[181] See Chapter 2 above, at pp. 100–101.

[182] See at 2.2 above at p. 66, and at 2.6 above at p. 101.

courts have adopted a modified position towards certain important matters. The most significant modification is with regard to the effect of a foreign liquidation upon the company's English assets, as discussed below. In the first place, however, we may note the strong parallel with bankruptcy in the approach to according recognition to foreign insolvency proceedings relating to companies. Just as the country of an individual's domicile has been traditionally regarded by our law as the 'natural' forum for proceedings having a bearing upon that person's civil status and capacity, including bankruptcy proceedings,[183] so in the case of companies the importance attached to the law of the country of incorporation in determining the essential qualities concerning the company's birth, life and also its demise ensures that the English recognition rule looks primarily to the courts of that country to supply the forum for winding up.[184] This approach also reflects the view of English law that the domicile of a corporation is located, possibly immutably, in its country of formation.[185]

It follows therefore that winding-up proceedings that have commenced in the country under whose laws the company was originally incorporated will be recognised in England. This would appear to hold true even in cases where the company's central management and control are shown to be located in some other jurisdiction: the analogy with the statutory precept whereby the English court retains the competence to wind up any company registered in England and Wales is likely to provide a powerful argument for accepting the competence of the foreign court in a like situation, although the point appears never to have arisen in a reported case.[186] It also follows that, as an aspect of the recognition accorded to proceedings conducted under the law of the company's country of incorporation—also constituting the corporate domicile—the office holder appointed under those proceedings will be accepted in England as the person with standing to represent the collective interests of creditors and to invoke the assistance of the courts here.[187] The office holder's eligibility to

[183] See at 2.6 above.

[184] The 'State of incorporation' doctrine is discussed at 3.1 above. On the role of the law of that State in effecting the dissolution of the company's legal *persona*, see cases cited at 3.1 above at n.6, together with *Bank of Ethiopia v. National Bank of Egypt* [1937] 1 Ch. 513 at 524 per Clauson J.; *Banco de Bilbao v. Sancha* [1938] 2 K.B. 176 at 193–195 per Clauson L.J.

[185] See at 3.1 above at p. 120 (*Corporate domicile, residence and nationality*), and cases and writings there referred to in nn. 16–23 inclusive.

[186] See Insolvency Act 1986, s. 117(1), discussed at 3.2.1 above.

[187] For cases illustrative of this principle, and the converse approach where the party before the English court cannot claim to be clothed with legitimate authority according to the company's domiciliary law, see e.g. *Sea Insurance Co. v. Rossia Insurance Co. of Petrograd* (1924) 20 Ll. L. Rep. 308 (CA); *Bank of Ethiopia v. National Bank of Egypt, supra* n.184; *Banco de Bilbao v. Sancha, supra* n.184; *Burr v. Anglo-French Banking Corpn. Ltd.* (1933) 49 T.L.R. 405; *Onassis v. Drewry* (1949) 83 Ll. L. Rep. 249 (CA); *Baden and others v. Société Générale pour Favoriser le Développement du Commerce et de l'Industrie, S.A.* [1992] 4 All E.R. 161, esp. at 229–230. Cf. the Canadian cases in which the same principles were followed: *National Trust Co. Ltd. v. Ebro*

maintain any claim to the company's English assets is subject, however, to there being confirmation that he is clothed with the requisite rights and powers over the company's property by the law under which his appointment has originated, and that his powers are by that law intended to be exercisable over property situated beyond the frontiers of that country.[188]

Where the foreign liquidation has been commenced in a country other than that in which the company's incorporation occurred, there is considerable uncertainty with regard to the prospects of such proceedings being recognised in England, and on what principles this might take place. The lack of explicit authority on this matter in the reported cases is to be regretted. Clearly, the possible circumstances in which such foreign liquidations may take place can vary considerably, so that it is important that a flexible approach should be adopted. One situation in which the English position seems to be reasonably predictable is where the foreign liquidation concerns a company actually formed and registered in England. The primacy of the law of the country of incorporation is likely to form the basis of the English court's reaction to such a case. If winding-up proceedings are already in progress in this country, it might possibly be conceded that the foreign proceedings should be recognised as ancillary to these, particularly if it happens to be the case that the bulk of the company's business has been conducted in the other country.[189] If the company's connection with the foreign jurisdiction has been of a less substantial nature, English recognition may be less readily forthcoming. However, if no winding-up proceedings are taking place in England, despite the company having been formed here (as may be the case if there are no assets in this country, and perhaps no English creditors with interests to defend), it may be that the foreign proceedings can be considered to be the most appropriate way in which to wind up the company, although it is possible that the final process of effecting the dissolution might be reserved by English law to itself, using the power of the Registrar of Companies to strike it off the register as a defunct company.[190]

A further range of possibilities arises where the foreign liquidation proceedings are in relation to a company formed in some third country. Again, it may be supposed that where concurrent proceedings are taking

Irrigation & Power Co. Ltd. [1954] 3 D.L.R. 326; *Re I.I.T.* (1975) 58 D.L.R. (3d) 55, 19 C.B.R. (N.S.) 263.

[188] *Macaulay v. Guaranty Trust of New York* (1927) 44 T.L.R. 99, [1927] W.N. 308; *Onassis v. Drewry, supra* n.187. Cf. the Canadian cases of *National Trust Co. Ltd. v. Ebro Irrigation & Power Co. Ltd.*, and *Re I.I.T.*, both *supra* n.187. The effects of a foreign liquidation over English assets are considered below at p. 169.

[189] See *North Australian Territory Co. Ltd. v. Goldsbrough, Mort & Co. Ltd.* (1889) 61 L.T 716 (where the English proceedings were in the form of a voluntary liquidation, which Kay J. nevertheless concluded would be the principal liquidation in relation to the compulsory winding up in Australia).

[190] Companies Act 1985, ss.652, 652A.

place in the country of incorporation, English law will regard the latter as having primary status, and that any other liquidation will be purely ancillary, and hence territorial, in nature. In the absence of such 'home state' proceedings however, the degree of uncertainty over English recognition rises to its maximum. Typically, English law might incline towards recognition where it could be shown that the law of the company's domicile—i.e. of its State of incorporation—recognises the proceedings. In reality, such evidence is unlikely to be forthcoming in a sufficiently clear form, for the very reason that, as with English law itself, there is a lack of authoritative indication of the attitude and policy of legal systems across the world towards foreign liquidation proceedings relating to companies that were originally formed under their law.[191] Failing any resolution of the issue of recognition by reference to the law of the company's 'home' state, English law must perforce supply a rule which would take into account the circumstances under which the foreign court came to exercise jurisdiction to wind up a company not originally formed in that country. Here, there is an initial temptation to suggest that English law should recognise foreign proceedings which have been commenced using a rule of jurisdiction analogous to one which could be employed by an English court to wind up a foreign company in this country.[192] English private international law has certainly made use, albeit for rather special purposes, of this type of 'reciprocal' recognition of foreign judgments or orders.[193] In commercial matters however the balance of judicial opinion seems to be against making use of this basis for recognition.[194] This is not quite as perverse as may at first sight appear, for it can sometimes be a justifiable course, as we have seen, for the English courts to wind up a foreign company which has some assets in England, even if other contact between the company and this country is perhaps negligible.[195] The practical utility of such an initiative can be such as to outweigh the possible objection that the exercise of jurisdiction is exorbitant under the circumstances, and that international

[191] A similar omission on the part of the legal systems of the world to provide a clear statement of position was noted at 2.7 above with regard to the possible recognition by the law of the country whose law governs a particular contract, of the effects of foreign bankruptcy proceedings whereby the obligations of one of the parties to the contract is allegedly discharged. See p. 105.

[192] See at 3.2.2 above.

[193] For example, in relation to the recognition of foreign decrees of divorce or nullity of marriage during the years immediately prior to the major statutory reforms of this subject effected by the Recognition of Divorces and Legal Separations Act 1971. See *Travers v. Holley* [1953] P. 246; *Merker v. Merker* [1963] P. 283. This form of 'reciprocal recognition' was abrogated by s.6 of the 1971 Act.

[194] See *Re Trepca Mines Ltd.* [1960] 1 W.L.R. 1273 at 1281 per Hodson L.J.; *Société Coopérative Sidmetal v. Titan International Ltd.* [1966] 1 Q.B. 828 at 838–841 per Widgery J.; *Schemmer v. Property Resources Ltd.* [1975] Ch. 273, 287 per Goulding J. Cf. *Re Dulles' Settlement (No. 2)* [1951] Ch. 842, 851 per Denning L.J.

[195] See at 3.2.2 above.

recognition is unlikely to be forthcoming. It would be detrimental to the cause of bringing about an efficient and equitable distribution of assets, if the consequence was to compromise the position of English courts concerning the recognition of foreign liquidations. The better approach, it is submitted, is for the English courts to retain an element of discretion whether to recognise liquidations which take place outside the country of incorporation, and that the basis for recognition should be expressed with reference to whether there is a sufficiently substantial connection between the company and the jurisdiction in question for it to be appropriate for the proceedings to be commenced there. In the interest of promoting some certainty about the likely attitude of the English court, it should be accepted that (unless there are strong reasons to the contrary) recognition should normally be forthcoming where the company has had a place of business, or has carried on business, in the country in question, or where its central management and control has been, or is, based there.[196]

(h) Effects in relation to assets in England

Even though a foreign liquidation is accorded recognition in the general sense, English law has consistently maintained that this entails no direct or automatic consequences in relation to any property of the company that happens to be situated in England. This is in contrast to the position in the case of individual bankrupts where, as we have seen, movable property in England is able to become vested in the foreign trustee in bankruptcy, in emulation of the effects produced under the foreign *lex concursus*.[197] The reason for not applying the same treatment to the property of insolvent companies would appear to be the assumption that the insolvency laws of other countries follow the English approach in differentiating between the treatment of individuals and corporations, in that only the former are automatically divested of their assets in consequence of the commencement of the bankruptcy or liquidation process. Although this amounts to an oversimplification of the true position worldwide,[198] the relatively liberal policy of English courts in giving assistance to foreign liquidators has largely, though not entirely, overcome the practical consequences of this somewhat distorted view of the world. The foreign liquidator can

[196] Cf. the proposals made by P. Smart, *Cross-Border Insolvency* (1991), ch. 5, at pp.104–112.

[197] See at 2.6(b) above, p. 97. See *New Zealand Loan and Mercantile Agency Co. Ltd. v. Morrison* [1898] A.C. 349 (PC) at 357 per Lord Davey, where the distinction between bankruptcy and winding up is made.

[198] For example, under the United States Bankruptcy Code the liquidation process of Chapter 7 applies to individual and corporate debtors alike. On the other hand, the actual mechanics of the Chapter 7 process do not depend on automatic divesting of the debtor, but on a removal of the powers of management, control and disposal of the assets comprised in the estate in bankruptcy. This, if anything, makes it rather more questionable whether English law should regard the movable property of an individual debtor as being automatically vested in his trustee in bankruptcy when the proceedings have commenced in the USA.

make direct application to the English court, based upon his having been appointed in circumstances which qualify for recognition under the principles discussed above, and seek an order investing him as liquidator with title to any property, movable or immovable, belonging to the company which is within the court's jurisdiction. The position is thus identical to that which obtains with respect to the English immoveables belonging to an individual who is adjudicated bankrupt in foreign proceedings.[199] As in the case of a foreign bankruptcy, the court at its discretion may appoint the foreign liquidator to be receiver of the company's property, with powers to sell it and to deal with the proceeds in accordance with the provisions of the law under which he was appointed.[200]

The chief disadvantage of the absence of any rule of automatic vesting of the company's assets in the foreign liquidator, judged from the standpoint of the liquidator himself and of those creditors on whose behalf he is acting, is that an interval of time will inevitably elapse between the commencement of the liquidation under the law of the foreign country and the moment at which the English court makes its order recognising his claim to the company's assets and enabling him to take control of them. During that period, other parties may succeed in completing individual acts of execution or attachment against some of these assets, thereby exacerbating the adverse effects of the 'subject to equities' rule upon quality of the liquidator's net return.[201] As has already been explained in Chapter 2 above, the present, unhappy state of the law deprives the foreign office holder of the possibility of reversing the effects of such actions by creditors by means of remedies contained in either the English or the foreign insolvency law which are aimed at imposing a collective regime from the moment of commencement of insolvency, or indeed even earlier.[202] The severity of the losses inflicted by individual creditors' acts of private diligence upon the value of the funds eventually recovered by the liquidator for the benefit of the general body of creditors will inevitably vary according to circumstances, but in some instances the liquidator's efforts may be completely frustrated, with consequential loss to the estate in terms of costs and disbursements. The very fact that such an outcome is foreseeable can suffice to deter the liquidator from mounting a vigorous challenge to such acts of diligence, unless the values involved happen to be particularly large.[203] The irony and inequity of such a state of affairs is especially acute

[199] See at 2.6(b) above, at p. 99 (*Immovable property*).

[200] See cases referred to at 2.6(b) above in nn. 234–236.

[201] For the 'subject to equities' rule, see at 2.2 above, at p. 61.

[202] See at 2.6(b) above at p. 98, with reference to the effects of *Galbraith v. Grimshaw* [1910] A.C. 508 (HL).

[203] In a number of large-value cases in recent years, the sums at stake sometimes totalled many millions of pounds sterling, and office holders were able to justify the high costs of multi-jurisdictional litigation in view of the potential gains to creditors. The cases of *B.C.C.I.*

where it proves to be the case that the avoidance provisions of both systems of law, where they can be applied, are practically at one in treating the creditors' acts as impeachable at the instance of the liquidator. The need for English law to rethink its position on this matter has already been argued.[204] It is submitted that the principles of insolvency law should be maintained through a twofold approach. First, the time at which the foreign liquidator's entitlement to the English assets is deemed to become effective should be backdated so as to coincide with the commencement of his appointment under the foreign law. Secondly, the powers of avoidance of antecedent transactions, and of cancellation of the benefits of incomplete executions, should be made available to a foreign liquidator whose general standing, and entitlement to claim property here, is recognised by English law.

3.7.2 Selected comparisons

Australian law closely follows English law in its approach to recognition of foreign liquidations. This includes making the same distinction between bankruptcy and winding up in the fundamental matter of the divesting of title to the debtor's property, which only occurs automatically in the case of bankruptcy. A liquidator who has been appointed in the country where the company is domiciled is considered to have the power of collecting in a foreign country the assets of the company that happen to be situated there, but this is achieved not on the basis that any title to the assets has vested in him directly, but because under the law of the company's domicile the liquidator has been endowed with the sole right of using the company's name in litigation, and of managing and disposing of its property.[205] Doctrinal writers on the subject of recognition of the status and capacity of foreign office holders have suggested that the technical distinctions between bankruptcy and liquidation should be overridden if necessary, where this will best ensure the efficient and comprehensive administration of an insolvent debtor's property so as to accord equality of treatment among all creditors.[206] The possibility has also been advanced that Australian law should follow the enlightened example of their

and *Maxwell Communications Corporation*, referred to elsewhere in this book, are foremost examples of this type of case.

[204] See at 2.2 above at p. 63, and at 2.6 above at p. 93.

[205] *Primary Producers Bank of Australia v. Hughes* (1931) 32 S.R. (N.S.W.) 14, disapproving (at 17–19 per Harvey C.J.) the reasoning of Griffiths C.J. in *Re Alfred Shaw & Co. Ltd.* (1897) 8 Q.L.J. 93, in which a foreign liquidator was treated as though standing in an equal position to a trustee in bankruptcy with regard to the title conferred on him.

[206] So argued by Dr. Bray, Q.C. (later Chief Justice of South Australia) in an unpublished, but frequently cited, LLD thesis, *Bankruptcy and the Winding-up of Companies in Private International Law* (University of Adelaide, 1937), whose work is endorsed by B.H. McPherson, *The Law of Company Liquidation*, 3rd edn. (1987), ch. 16 (*passim*).

Canadian counterparts in being prepared to recognise foreign insolvency proceedings commenced in a country with which the debtor corporation has a real and substantial connection, and also in cases where the foreign winding-up order was based on a jurisdictional ground similar to any of those on which Australian courts will currently take jurisdiction in respect of a foreign company.[207]

3.8 THE EFFECTS OF DISSOLUTIONS AND DISCHARGES OF OBLIGATIONS RESULTING FROM FOREIGN LIQUIDATIONS

Most of the issues concerning the recognition at English law of the dissolution of a company as a result of foreign liquidation proceedings—or other legal processes whose purpose is to terminate the company's legal existence—have been explored in the context of the preceding sections of this chapter.[208] We have seen that the guiding principle is one of respect for the conclusions bearing upon this matter which are arrived at under the law of the country of incorporation, and that a number of consequential rules and doctrines have also been evolved.[209] Mention is here made of certain further aspects of the operation of the established principles.

English branch of a dissolved foreign company

Where a foreign company has conducted its business in England by means of a branch, rather than through the medium of a locally-formed subsidiary company, English law regards the branch as legally indistinct from the foreign parent. Consequently, if the parent undergoes a process of dissolution according to the law of its country of incorporation, this has the effect of simultaneously extinguishing the legal personality and competence of the English branch, and of those who there purport to carry on its business.[210] Thereafter, acts performed in the company's name, and

[207] E.I. Sykes and M.C. Pryles, *Australian Private International Law*, 3rd edn. (1991), at pp. 399–400. For the Canadian approach to recognition, see at 2.6.1. above, and for the Australian and Canadian practice on jurisdiction over foreign companies, see at 3.2.4 above. Cross-border judicial cooperation is discussed in Chapter 4 below.

[208] See especially at 3.1 and 3.7 above.

[209] As to the former, see the authorities referred to above, at 3.1 above at nn. 6 and 7, and at 3.7.1(a) at n.187. For the consequential and supplementary doctrines, see at 3.2.2(a) and 3.2.3 above.

[210] This proposition reflects the principles underlying the courts' decisions in several of the 'Russian bank' cases, although in some of them the result turned upon the court's finding that the parent company had not been dissolved at the time of the relevant events. See, e.g. *Russian Commercial & Industrial Bank v. Comptoir d'Escompte de Mulhouse* [1925] A.C. 112 (HL); *Banque Internationale de Commerce de Petrograd v. Goukassow* [1925] A.C. 150 (HL); *Employers' Liability Assurance Corpn. Ltd. v. Sedgwick, Collins & Co. Ltd.* [1927] A.C. 95 (HL); *Russian and English Bank, etc. v. Baring Brothers & Co. Ltd.* [1936] A.C. 405 (HL); *Re Banque*

legal proceedings purporting to be undertaken by or against the company itself, are a nullity and so are devoid of legal effect.[211] However, despite the termination of the legal personality of both the parent and its dependency, the branch, it is possible that the branch may continue to function, and so to exist on a *de facto* basis, for some time afterwards. This is particularly likely to be the case where the dissolution of the parent company is associated with a protracted period of political upheaval, or even civil conflict, in the foreign country in question, so that overseas commercial activities are conducted under conditions of uncertainty pending the resolution of the crisis.[212] If the activities of the English branch involve the deployment of a substantial quantity of financial or material resources, the operation may be functionally self-sufficient for an almost indefinite period, a state of affairs that is reinforced in this respect by English law's rule that a foreign liquidation has no direct or automatic effect upon title to the company's English assets. The personal financial risks incurred by those who continue to conduct such an enterprise after the demise of the corporate *persona*, with consequent termination of the protection of limited liability, clearly demand that the operations of the English branch should be brought to an orderly conclusion as soon as is practicable.[213] This can be a reason for utilising the jurisdiction of the English court to wind up an already-dissolved foreign company, in the way already described.[214]

Discharge of debts

As was seen in Chapter 2 above in relation to the recognition of discharge resulting from a foreign bankruptcy, English law appears to suffer from a form of schizophrenia when contemplating the effects of foreign insolvency proceedings on obligations to which the debtor was a party.[215] Thus, while prepared to recognise that the foreign proceedings are

Industrielle de Moscou [1952] 1 Ch. 919. See also *Bank of Ethiopia v. National Bank of Egypt* [1937] 1 Ch. 513; *Onassis v. Drewry* (1949) 83 Ll. L. Rep. 249 (CA).

[211] See cases cited *supra*, n.210, and also: *Lazard Brothers & Co. v. Banque Industrielle de Moscou* [1932] 1 K.B. 617 (CA); *Lazard Brothers & Co. v. Midland Bank Ltd.* [1933] A.C. 289 (HL); *Burr v. Anglo-French Banking Corpn. Ltd.* (1933) 49 T.L.R. 405; *Re Russo-Asiatic Bank* [1934] 1 Ch. 720 (also holding that the dissolution of the foreign company suspends the running of time for the purposes of the Statute of Limitations, since one consequence is that there is no debtor who can be sued).

[212] This was true on a massive scale in the case of the Russian Revolution of 1917, and has been a periodic phenomenon throughout the modern era.

[213] See the state of affairs disclosed in *Sea Insurance Co. v. Rossia Insurance Co. of Petrograd* (1924) 20 Ll. L. Rep. 308 (CA), where the refugee directors carrying on business at the dissolved company's Paris branch were in law 'merely individuals trading under the name and style of the Rossia Insurance Company'.

[214] See Insolvency Act 1986, ss. 221(5)(a) and 225 at 3.2.2(a) and 3.2.3 above.

[215] See at 2.7 above, where criticisms are made of the decision in *Gibbs & Sons v. La Société Industrielle et Commerciale des Métaux* (1890) 25 Q.B.D. 406 (CA), and associated cases there cited. For the present, however, the *Gibbs* case remains good law.

capable of bringing about the discharge of all obligations whose governing law is that of the country where the proceedings themselves take place, a debt whose governing law is that of some other country, and *a fortiori* one which is governed by English law, is not considered to be so extinguished. This position is maintained despite the fact that English law claims universality of effect for a discharge resulting from its own insolvency proceedings, irrespective of their governing law.[216] The same approach is employed in the case of a foreign liquidation, or other insolvency proceedings relating to companies. This can lend additional significance to the process of determining the governing law of an obligation, since the conclusion about its possible discharge may depend on whether its governing law is that of the *forum concursus*, or of some other country including, of course, England itself. For this purpose, it is to the rules of English private international law that reference must be made to establish the governing law of the obligation in question. If the application of the relevant rule leads to the conclusion that the obligation is governed by the law of a third country, it is in theory possible that the discharge of the obligation can be recognised in England if it can be shown that this effect is recognised under the law of the third country. However, as already explained, English law is by no means unique in having thus far refrained from developing a rule under which a foreign discharge can be treated as effective with regard to an obligation governed by English law itself.[217]

Therefore, the paradox is sustained whereby English law, acting in one mode, can recognise the foreign liquidation in the general sense and also recognise the standing of the foreign liquidator, while conducting those proceedings, to claim English assets; in a contrary mode, however, once the foreign proceedings have concluded with the supposed discharge of all provable claims, any that happen to be governed by a law other than the *lex concursus* are not considered to be discharged in the eyes of English law, but could be re-asserted if, for example, further assets come to light in this country.[218]

[216] See the cases and writings referred to at 2.7 above, in nn. 264–275 inclusive.

[217] See at 2.7 above, esp. at p. 107.

[218] The most equitable solution in such cases is for there to be an English liquidation of the dissolved foreign company, for the purpose of administering the assets among all creditors whose claims are still unsatisfied. On the other hand, a discharge may also come about under the terms of a composition or arrangement whereby the company is enabled to exit from the process of liquidation that would lead to its dissolution,and to continue in business. Those who draw up the terms of such a composition need to be mindful of the possibility that creditors with claims governed by English law (or by the laws of other countries which adopt the same approach) may later try to exploit the legal opportunities described above in the text.

3.9 CONCURRENT LIQUIDATIONS

From the account given above of the possibilities for English winding-up proceedings to take place in a variety of circumstances, sometimes involving debtor companies whose main legal or functional links (and sometimes both) lie outside this country,[219] it may readily be envisaged that circumstances will arise in which the same company is simultaneously amenable to be wound up in two or more jurisdictions, of which England may be one. Although the basic English approach carries an inbuilt bias in favour of universality, and is favourably disposed towards the country of corporate formation as the appropriate forum for insolvency proceedings to take place, these twin ideals have not been allowed to become the basis of an unduly dogmatic policy, where justice and convenience may best be achieved through some alternative solution. If anything, English law places a higher priority on ensuring that the goal of equality of treatment of all creditors is achieved as the *net result* of the insolvency process. Where necessary, a pragmatic view can be adopted of the most suitable and cost-effective means by which to bring this about. While duplication of proceedings can be wasteful under some circumstances, at other times it may offer significant advantages in terms of efficiency and speed, at the same time preserving or enhancing the value made available to creditors. This usually presupposes some arrangement or understanding to ensure the coordination of concurrent liquidations. There is no absolute requirement that such arrangements should be in place, or be agreed in principle, for an English court to be prepared to allow a winding up to take place in parallel with foreign proceedings involving the same debtor: even if there is no prospect of collaboration it may be demonstrable that the fairest way in which to administer such assets as are subject to the control of the English court is to enable them to be distributed through a liquidation.[220]

Despite the absence of any directive provisions in the past or current Companies Acts, or in the Insolvency Act itself, to indicate what approach is to be pursued, or what judicial powers are exercisable, when concurrent liquidations are in prospect, the courts have long been prepared to respond to the promptings of good sense, and to act upon the maxim that 'what is not expressly forbidden may, if reasonable, be done'.[221]

[219] See at 3.2 above.

[220] This may be the case, for example, if the foreign proceedings are destined to be conducted in a manner which unfairly discriminates against foreign creditors, or if they are so substantially dominated by claims of the local revenue authorities that a pooling of assets between the two administrations would risk violating the rule of English public policy that forbids the direct or indirect enforcement of foreign penal or revenue claims (see at 2.4 above, p. 84 *et seq.*).

[221] Cf. the enlightened response of Bigham J. in *Re P. MacFadyen & Co.* [1908] 1 K.B. 675 (a bankruptcy case referred to at 2.8 above), in which counsel had submitted that a scheme for

Instinctively, a sense of structure and order has been introduced in a way that also respects the special claims of the country of incorporation to serve as the primary forum for proceedings which take place on a multi-jurisdictional basis. The principle that has been regularly applied is that the proceedings in the country of the company's domicile—its State of incorporation—are regarded as the principal liquidation, and any other courts are to act as ancillary, as far as they can, to the principal liquidation.[222] So, in the comparatively early case of *Re Matheson Brothers Ltd.*,[223] Kay J. was prepared to make a winding-up order in respect of a New Zealand company which had an English branch, although liquidation proceedings were already pending in New Zealand. An English winding up was held to be the best way of securing the assets for the time being, without prejudice to the possibility that the New Zealand liquidators might subsequently enter into an arrangement to enable a *pari passu* distribution to take place, in which all creditors could participate. A similar approach was adopted by North J. in *Re Commercial Bank of South Australia*[224] when making an order for the winding up of an Australian banking company with a branch office in London. The English assets had been initially safeguarded by the appointment of a provisional liquidator, and by the time of hearing the winding-up petition it had transpired that a petition was pending in Australia, and that a provisional liquidator had also been appointed there. North J. concluded that the developments in Australia did not deprive him of jurisdiction to make a winding-up order, but he stated that if an order was made in that country the English winding up would be ancillary to that in Australia. The learned judge further declared that it would be his policy, while in control of the English proceedings, to take care that there should be no conflict between the two courts, and to have regard to the interests of all the creditors and all the contributories, while endeavouring to keep down the expenses of the winding up as far as possible.[225] With respect, it is submitted that this exemplary display of praetorian jurisprudence by a greatly respected Chancery judge has rightly stood for over a hundred years as embodying the spirit of internationalism at its best. The precedent has been consistently endorsed and

collaboration between the English and Indian trustees in bankruptcy, though nowhere expressly authorised by the Bankruptcy Act 1883, was 'manifestly for the benefit of all creditors, and would tend to avoid delay and expensive litigation between the trustees'. Similar considerations, albeit on a vastly greater scale, lay behind the pooling arrangements negotiated, and judicially sanctioned, in the *B.C.C.I.* case: see *Re Bank of Credit and Commerce International S.A. (No. 3)* [1993] B.C.L.C. 106, esp. at 111 (Nicholls V.-C.); *(the same) (No. 10)* [1996] 4 All E.R. 796 (Scott V.-C.).

[222] So stated by Vaughan Williams J. in *Re English, Scottish and Australian Chartered Bank* [1893] 3 Ch. 385 at 394.

[223] (1884) 27 Ch. D. 225.

[224] (1886) 33 Ch. D. 174.

[225] *Ibid.*, at 178.

followed by later courts, including the Court of Appeal, and continues to express the essential English position on concurrent liquidations.[226]

The need for a modern restatement of the law

The English law concept of principal and ancillary liquidations (and the analogous treatment of concurrent bankruptcies)[227] has provided a useful means to the entirely laudable end of attaining the most fair and reasonable outcome under certain situations of international insolvency. In one sense, the lack of any formal statutory provisions down to the present time has left the courts free to improvise, which they have done in a mostly constructive manner. However, the judicial pronouncements have at times been somewhat imprecise, and perhaps even deliberately obscure, with regard to the detailed implications of what was being authorised by the court in question. Although the English approach has been emulated in other common law jurisdictions, including Australia and Canada,[228] the full possibilities that exist under English law are less widely known than they deserve to be. This is possibly on account of the relative inaccessibility of case law, as opposed to legislation, when viewed from the standpoint of those operating outside the common law tradition. In the interests of clothing this increasingly important aspect of the law with a greater element of certainty, it is submitted that the time is now ripe for the essential principles of the treatment of concurrent liquidations to be restated in statutory form. This should be done in such a way as to allow flexibility, through the retention of judicial discretion with regard to the final disposition of particular cases. Nevertheless, the broad framework of the court's powers in such matters should be laid down within the governing legislation, so that its full potential may be more widely appreciated. This theme will be further developed in Chapter 4, when discussing the more restricted availability of judicial assistance under section 426 of the Insolvency Act.[229]

[226] See *Re English, Scottish and Australian Chartered Bank* [1893] 3 Ch. 385 (Vaughan Williams J., affd. CA); *Re Federal Bank of Australia* [1893] W.N. 46 and 77 (Vaughan Williams J, affd. CA); *Sedgwick Collins & Co. v. Rossia Insurance Co. of Petrograd* [1926] 1 K.B. 1 (CA), esp. at 13 per Scrutton L.J. (diss.), *Re Vocalion (Foreign) Ltd.* [1932] 2 Ch. 196 (Maugham J.); *Re Hibernian Merchants Ltd.*[1958] 1 Ch. 76 (Roxburgh J.); *Re Bank of Credit and Commerce International S.A. (No. 10)* [1996] 4 All E.R. 796 at 814–822 (where the case law on ancillary liquidations is reviewed by Scott V.-C.). Note also the position in *North Australian Territory Co. Ltd. v. Goldsbrough, Mort & Co. Ltd* (1889) 61 L.T. 716, where the English voluntary winding up constituted the principal liquidation, to which the Australian compulsory liquidation was regarded as being ancillary.

[227] See at 2.8 above.

[228] See e.g. *Re Alfred Shaw & Co. Ltd.* (1897) 8 Q.L.J. 93; *Re Standard Insurance Co. Ltd.* [1968] Qd. R. 118; *Re Air Express Foods Pty. Ltd.* [1977] Qd. R. 107; *Re National Benefit Assurance Co.* [1927] 3 D.L.R. 289 (Man. CA).

[229] See also Chapter 8 below, with reference to the potential adoption of the UNCITRAL Model Law.

3.10 RECOGNITION OF FOREIGN RECEIVERSHIPS AND NON-LIQUIDATION PROCEDURES

In addition to the two modes of liquidation—voluntary and compulsory—with which this chapter has been thus far concerned, other types of procedure have been developed by English law to meet a variety of needs of insolvent companies and their creditors. The primary purpose of such proceedings is not the liquidation of the company (although this may take place at a later stage if the company cannot be restored to solvency). Rather, different solutions may be explored ranging from a composition or scheme of arrangement to a wholesale restructuring of the company or the sale and transfer of its business as a going concern. These options may be pursued through the various procedures in Parts I, II and III of the Insolvency Act 1986,[230] and in Part XIII of the Companies Act 1985.[231] The insolvency laws of other countries likewise contain a number of non-liquidation procedures, some of them analogous to those available under English law while others have no exact counterpart here. From time to time the issue of recognition of such proceedings arises before the English courts, usually when the overseas representative of the debtor company who has official conduct of the proceedings has occasion to claim the company's English assets, or to defend them against attachment by individual creditors. This aspect of private international law has hitherto been relatively undeveloped, but is nowadays increasingly important due to the burgeoning interest in corporate rescue procedures whose ultimate success may depend on securing international collaboration by the courts in those jurisdictions where the company's assets, and principal activities, are located.

Receiverships

The appointment of a receiver of a company's property at the instance of a secured creditor may take place either as a private act by the creditor in exercise of rights conferred by the instrument granting the security, or it may come about through the exercise by the court of its power to make such an appointment where it appears just and equitable to do so.[232] Court-appointed receiverships are somewhat uncommon in England, where private appointments by creditors holding floating-charge security,

[230] Part I deals with Company Voluntary Arrangements; Part II with Administration Orders; and Part III with Receivership, including Administrative Receivership. For accounts of these, see e.g. I.F. Fletcher, *The Law of Insolvency*, 2nd edn. (1996), chs. 14, 15 and 16.

[231] Part XIII deals with Arrangements and Reconstructions, and includes provision under s.425 for a company to conclude a compromise or arrangement with its creditors, or any class of them. See *Palmer's Company Law*, 25th edn. (1992, looseleaf), Part 12A.

[232] Supreme Court Act 1981, s.37(1).

or under the terms of section 101(1)(iii) of the Law of Property Act 1925, provide a far readier and less costly means for the creditor to initiate a receivership in a domestic context. Internationally, however, such out-of-court appointments suffer the disadvantage that there is a considerable reluctance by the courts in countries outside the common law tradition to recognise the receiver's standing to claim assets comprised in the security. The distinction between private appointments, and those made by the court, is also relevant when consideration is given to the potential recognition of a foreign receivership at English law.[233]

In the case of foreign, court-appointed receiverships the English courts are willing both to recognise, and to give assistance to, a receiver appointed by a court whose competence is recognised by English law on the basis of there being a sufficient connection between the company and the foreign court. Such competence arises either by virtue of the debtor company's incorporation under the law of the foreign country in question,[234] or through its having submitted to the jurisdiction of the courts of that country in the proceedings from which the receivership has resulted.[235] It is possible that English law would recognise an appointment which, though not made by the court of the company's country of incorporation, can be shown to enjoy recognition under the law of that country.[236] Also plausible, though the point awaits judicial determination, is the suggestion that there could be recognition of an appointment by the court of the place where the company's central management and control are established.[237] In addition to scrutinising the jurisdictional competence of the foreign court, English law requires that in the case of a receivership arising from some charge or other security given by the company the charge must be valid and enforceable under the law of the company's domicile and (if different) the law under which it was created. It is not sufficient to show that, had the charge been created in England by a company subject to English law, it would have been valid and enforceable.[238] Lastly, there must have been compliance with any formal requirements, such as registration, imposed by the law of the *situs*.[239] Where

[233] See H. Picarda, *The Law Relating to Receivers, Managers and Administrators*, 2nd edn. (1990), ch. 40.

[234] *Macaulay v. Guaranty Trust of New York* (1927) 44 T.L.R. 99. An appointment by way of equitable execution may be denied recognition, where the defendant was not subject to the *in personam* jurisdiction of the foreign court: *Perry v. Zissis* [1977] 1 Lloyd's Rep. 607, 615 (CA), dist. in *White v. Verkouille* [1990] 2 Qd. R. 191 (McPherson J.). See also the Canadian cases, *Re Sorrel Resources Ltd.* (1987) 63 C.B.R. 187; *Thorne, Ernst & Whinney Inc. v. Sulpetro Ltd.* (1987) 47 D.L.R. (4th) 315; *Canadian Imperial Bank of Commerce v. Idanell Korner Ranch Ltd.* [1990] 6 W.W.R. 610 (Sask.).

[235] *Schemmer v. Property Resources Ltd.* [1975] Ch. 273.

[236] *Ibid.*, at 287 per Goulding J.

[237] *Ibid.*, at 287–288.

[238] *Carse v. Coppen* 1951 S.C. 233. See Collins (1978) 27 I.C.L.Q. 691.

[239] See at 3.4 above at p. 155, *Security rights created by companies*.

recognition is accorded, the English court's assistance can take various forms. The receiver may be allowed to sue directly in his own name to recover assets over which his appointment extends, or alternatively an auxiliary receivership may be constituted in England, under which the foreign receiver may be appointed, subject to any impediment which may arise due to the requirements elsewhere under English insolvency law that an office holder must be an authorised insolvency practitioner.[240] Where the objectives of the foreign receivership are being thwarted, in relation to assets located in a third country, through the actions of persons who are subject to the jurisdiction of the English court, the receiver may request that the persons concerned be ordered to desist from such interference, and do all in their power to ensure that his mission can be fulfilled.[241]

There is sparse authority directly relating to the recognition of foreign receiverships where the appointment is made out of court. It has been indirectly suggested by the Court of Appeal,[242] and more directly held by the High Court of Ontario,[243] that the appointment of a receiver by a competent authority—such as a debenture-holder—in a foreign jurisdiction can be recognised abroad provided that the powers which the receiver seeks to exercise are recognised by the law of the company's country of incorporation. On this basis, full effect can be accorded to the proprietary consequences flowing from the exercise by the secured creditor of his right of appointment, including the crystallisation of the floating charge accompanied by the automatic, equitable assignment in favour of the debenture-holder of all the assets of the company wheresoever situate. This can be of vital significance in enabling the receiver to establish priority of entitlement to assets in this country, over which other creditors may have sought to assert various kinds of rights through proceedings of an *in rem* or an *in personam* character.[244] Other forms of assistance may be given as appro-

[240] See *Macaulay v. Guaranty Trust Co. of New York*, *supra* n.234; *Schemmer v. Property Resources Ltd.*, *supra* n.235, at 287 per Goulding J.; *Re Young* [1955] St. R. Qd. 254. For the requirement that certain kinds of office holder must be authorised to act as such, see Insolvency Act 1986, Part XIII, esp. ss.388, 389.

[241] Cf. *Re Huinac Copper Mines Ltd.* [1910] W.N. 218.

[242] *Cretanor Maritime Co. Ltd. v. Irish Marine Ltd.* [1978] 3 All E.R. 164, 173, [1978] 1 W.L.R. 966, 975, per Buckley L.J.

[243] *Re C.A. Kennedy & Co. Ltd. and Stibbe-Monk Ltd.* (1977) 74 D.L.R. (3d) 87, citing in support several English decisions on the recognition of the status of foreign-appointed receivers, including *Macaulay v. Guaranty Trust Co. of New York*, *supra* n.234, and *Dulaney v. Merry & Son* [1901] 1 K.B. 536.

[244] In the *Kennedy* case (*supra* n.243), a local creditor in Ontario had obtained judgment against the company and subsequently sought to garnish a debt due to it from another Ontario company. The receiver's claim prevailed. In the *Cretanor* case (*supra* n.242), a *Mareva* injunction, being an *in personam* remedy, was held not to prevail as against the proprietary rights of the debenture-holder albeit these had not crystallised until after the injunction had been granted.

priate, using the range of remedies mentioned in relation to court-appointed receivers.

In the case of a receiver appointed in Scotland, the provisions of section 72 of the Insolvency Act 1986 may give rise to a direct right to exercise his powers in England, so far as their exercise is not inconsistent with the law applicable there. The qualifying requirements are that the receiver must be appointed in respect of the whole or any part of any property or undertaking of a company and in consequence of the company having created a charge which, as created, was a floating charge. Section 72 is restricted to cases where a receiver appointed in either England or Scotland wishes to act in the other part of Great Britain. It consequently has no application to Northern Ireland. Court-appointed receivers appointed in any part of the United Kingdom may however avail themselves of the provisions in section 426(1) of the Act, which requires court orders to be enforced throughout the United Kingdom if made by a court in any part of the Realm.[245] Under normal circumstances, administrative receivers, and other receivers appointed out of court, do not come within the ambit of section 426 for the very obvious reason that their appointment is not brought about by a court order. It may perhaps be possible for such a receiver to generate the requisite standing to invoke section 426 in other parts of the United Kingdom by first making application to the court under section 35 of the Act for directions in connection with the performance of his functions. Any order made by the court on such an application might provide a platform for further assistance to be sought under section 426, but the point is apparently untested.

Foreign corporate rescue procedures

In many countries, including the United Kingdom, a number of types of insolvency procedure have been developed in recent times for the purpose of facilitating the rescue and rehabilitation of financially ailing companies.[246] Although not involving the liquidation of the company, such procedures frequently impose a comprehensive moratorium—sometimes known as an 'automatic stay'—on all species of action or execution against

[245] Insolvency Act 1986, s.426(1) and related provisions are discussed at 2.2 above at p. 64 *et seq*.

[246] For example, the Administration Order procedure under Part II of the Insolvency Act 1986; the 'Chapter 11 Bankruptcy' procedure under the United States Bankruptcy Code. For critical and comparative accounts of these, together with the reorganisation procedures of several other countries, see the papers collected in Section II of J.S. Ziegel (ed.), *Current Developments in International and Comparative Corporate Insolvency Law* (1994), chs. 5–11 inclusive. See also: A. Sorensen and P.J. Omar, *Corporate Rescue Procedures in France* (1996); P. Crutchfield, *Corporate Voluntary Administration Law*, 2nd edn. (1997); A. Keay, *Insolvency*, 2nd edn. (1994), ch. 5; D. Tay, *Canadian Bankruptcy Reform: the Move from Liquidation to Rehabilitation* (1993) 2 I.I.R. 44; E.B. Leonard and C.W. Besant (eds.), *Current Issues in Cross-Border Insolvency and Reorganisations* (1994).

the company and its property, in the interests of preserving the status quo so as to maximise the prospects for the rescue to succeed. This also entails a freezing of the usual rights of secured creditors to enforce their security. When the company's assets are dispersed across several jurisdictions, the viability of the rescue procedure will be partly dependent upon the extent to which the moratorium is recognised by the courts of the *situs*, and also upon the extent to which those courts are prepared, if so requested, to allow assets to be administered or repatriated pursuant to the terms of any rescue plan or scheme of arrangement that is concluded under the auspices of the foreign proceedings.

On this subject, the law of international recognition is still in an inchoate state, as many courts are only gradually becoming acquainted with the different types of corporate rescue procedures that have been evolved, and whose structures tend to reflect the varying national attitudes towards the concept of a 'rescue culture' and its realisation in practice.[247] As a non-liquidation procedure, whose aim is the very opposite of a winding up and dissolution of the company, there is every prospect that inappropriate criteria may be applied by courts more accustomed to evaluating the merits of foreign liquidation proceedings. The time-honoured principles which may be indispensable to the maintenance of just treatment of creditors in a liquidation may, perversely, be detrimental to the attainment of the altered goals in a case of attempted rescue. When confronted by the unfamiliar, judges generally tend to err of the side of caution, and may be reluctant to respond to overseas requests for turnover of assets so that they can be repatriated in furtherance of the rescue plan. To the judge at the *situs*, such a request may present the dilemma that the removal of the assets from that jurisdiction almost certainly puts an end to any prospects for local creditors to recoup their losses through recourse against them. At the same time, the uncertainty surrounding the eventual success of the rescue may cause the court to question the prudence of releasing its judicial hold on the 'bird in the hand'. Such appear to have among the concerns uppermost in the mind of Hirst J. in reaching his decision in *Felixstowe Dock and Railway Co. v. U.S. Lines Inc.*[248] A Delaware-registered company, which operated a global shipping business, went into a Chapter 11 proceeding in the USA. In England, English and Dutch creditors with substantial claims against the company obtained *Mareva* injunctions to prevent the removal from the jurisdiction of assets from which they might hope to satisfy their claims. When application was made by the

[247] For graphic depictions of the range of legal and commercial cultures across the world, as reflected in the underlying bias (from pro-creditor to pro-debtor) exhibited by their financial and insolvency laws, see P.R. Wood, *Maps of World Financial Law (Allen & Overy Global Law Maps)*, 3rd edn. (1997).

[248] [1989] Q.B. 360, [1988] 2 All E.R. 77.

company for the injunctions to be set aside so as to enable the assets to be remitted to the USA for administration under the terms of the scheme of reorganisation, Hirst J. concluded that, despite the promptings of the principle of comity to which he would otherwise have wished to defer, the apparently prejudicial terms of the Chapter 11 scheme as far as the European creditors of the company were concerned furnished a powerful reason for the court not to relinquish its control over the assets. In the absence of a genuine *quid pro quo*, viewed from the admittedly parochial standpoint of the local—including Continental European—creditors, the judge opted to refrain from authorising the release of the English assets.[249]

Future prospects for recognition

It is submitted that the *Felixstowe Dock* case, while providing a useful illustration of the complex issues and conflicting interests to be encountered in a case of international corporate rescue, should not be regarded as a signal of negative intentions towards the recognition of such proceedings. If viewed in the context of its own special facts, it may be rationalised as a case where the English court could not be convinced that the substance and intended effects of the foreign reorganisation plan were such as to offer a proportionately fair compensation to the English and European creditors of the debtor company, as compared to their material prospects if the alternative of a liquidation were to be pursued. A more sensitively designed plan might not have encountered the same, defensive judicial response. In the quest to formulate suitable criteria for according recognition and assistance to foreign proceedings of this nature, it is especially important to avoid dogmatic, or over-generalised, declarations of policy. Indeed, so widely do the various national regimes for corporate rescue differ from one another in ways that are truly fundamental, that it would be totally unrealistic to treat all of them as though they comprised a single, discrete group. A more discriminating analysis is necessary, dealing with each foreign procedure on its own terms, and on merit, at the point of first encounter. On principle, one might expect English law to require that the foreign system, and the particular instance of its operation that is presented in any given case, should satisfy certain minimum standards of integrity and due process, including adequate protection for individual creditors, or for groups or classes among them, to safeguard them against unfairly prejudicial treatment in the context of the attempted rescue. Factors such as the adequacy of notice periods in the case of distant creditors resident in foreign countries, and the extent to which genuine efforts are made to afford such parties an opportunity to participate effectively in

[249] [1989] Q.B. at 376 and 389, [1988] 2 All E.R. at 91 and 96. See the observations of Westbrook in A. Clarke (ed.), *Current Issues in Insolvency Law* (1991), p. 27.

the proceedings in which their interests are also at stake, should also be taken into account.[250]

As a basic rule of recognition, it is suggested that proceedings which have been commenced under the law of the company's formation (or within a sister jurisdiction in the case of a federal system such as that of the USA) should be eligible for recognition. Serious consideration should also be given to recognising proceedings which take place in the country where the company's central management and control have been established, where this is not also the country of incorporation. Provided that the company's association with the forum of the proceedings is bona fide and has been in existence for a reasonable time, it should be accepted that a rescue can be embarked upon under the law of the country with which the company is functionally connected in this way.[251] However, in view of the way in which such procedures can radically alter the balance of the debtor-creditor relationship with retrospective effect, special attention would have to be paid to the matter of the reasonable assumptions underlying parties' dealings with the company prior to its entry into the rescue process. If the company's international *modus operandi* was such that parties might legitimately suppose that its fundamental connections continue to be with its country of registration (so that they would naturally look to the provisions of the laws of that country when trying to calculate any legal or economic hazard to which their dealings might expose them) there should be an extra onus upon those seeking to have the proceedings recognised in England, to satisfy the court that no material prejudice will be experienced by such creditors in consequence of the rescue being governed by a different country's law.

To conclude with a more positive example of cross-border recognition of corporate rescue proceedings between the United Kingdom and the USA, the case of *Maxwell Communication Corporation* (*MCC*),[252] although in many ways unique, may serve as an instructive paradigm for the future. The case concerned an English-formed company with extensive activities in North America, involving numerous subsidiary companies with a

[250] *Cf.* the criteria prescribed by s.304 of the United States Bankruptcy Code for the courts of the USA to refer to when asked to provide ancillary assistance to a foreign representative. See Chapter 4 below.

[251] In this context, attention is drawn to a striking feature of the EMLICO insurance company liquidation, in which a Massachusetts-formed insurance company redomesticated itself to Bermuda in 1995 as part of a strategic plan designed to sever the profitable sectors of its business from its environmental liability sector. Within four months of transferring its domicile to Bermuda, the company presented its own petition for winding up on the ground of insolvency. The saga is described in the judgment of Morritt L.J. in *Hughes v. Hannover Ruckversicherungs-Aktiengesellschaft* [1997] 1 B.C.L.C. 497 at 500–502.

[252] For a more complete account of the facts of this case, as bearing upon the subject of cross-border cooperation, see the judgments delivered in *Re Maxwell Communication Corporation plc, Barclays Bank v. Homan* [1992] B.C.C. 757 (Hoffmann J.), affd (CA) at 767.

substantial asset value. Although the subsidiaries were mostly profitable and viable, the parent company was massively insolvent. In order to achieve an orderly disposal through sale of the subsidiaries as going concerns, the protective mantle of an internationally-effective moratorium was imperative. MCC's substantial business involvement in the USA made it eligible to seek Chapter 11 protection by filing there, and its board of directors duly did so. Shortly thereafter, concerned lest the effects of the Chapter 11 stay might not be fully recognised in England,[253] the board arranged for the company to present a petition for an administration order under Part II of the Insolvency Act 1986. Although this initially created the potential for a damaging conflict between rival procedures simultaneously in force with respect to the same company, a structured, Anglo-American 'cohabitation agreement' was gradually evolved, whereby each procedure was recognised by the courts of the other country, and the administrators appointed by the order of the English High Court were acknowledged to be the corporate governance of MCC for the purposes of the American proceedings, with consequent standing to function as the debtor-in-possession under the framework of Chapter 11.[254] Progressively, the corporate assets of MCC have been disposed of, and creditors' claims dealt with, in accordance with an internationally-agreed Protocol judicially approved in both jurisdictions. Although the objective throughout has been the orderly disposal of the assets of MCC, rather than its rescue, the method devised by the courts and practitioners in charge of the proceedings undoubtedly ensured the preservation of value for interested parties, by maintaining the viable businesses as going concerns, and enabling them to be sold as such.

[253] This concern was to some extent a product of the uncertainty engendered by the *Felixstowe Dock* case, described above.

[254] For further details of the resolution of the complex legal and practical issues by practitioners closely involved in the conduct of the *MCC* case, see the papers by Grierson, and by Flaschen and Silverman, in J.S. Ziegel (ed.), *supra* n.246, chs. 24 and 25 respectively

4

Judicial Assistance in Cross-Border Insolvencies: Current Provisions under National Law

PRELIMINARY

In the preceding two chapters, we have considered the approaches to recognition of foreign insolvency proceedings, and of the consequences flowing from them, that have been evolved under English common law.[1] We saw that these approaches embody principles mainly developed by the courts over a considerable span of time, and that in some respects there are significant imbalances between the international effects claimed by English law for insolvency proceedings which take place in this country, and the effects which will be accorded in England to proceedings opened in other countries. Nevertheless, the overall position, with respect to both individual and company insolvencies, may be summed up as one which is imbued with a spirit of positive intent to facilitate international cooperation between the different jurisdictions which happen to be in some way concerned in any particular case. One of the leading virtues of the English approach to giving recognition and assistance to foreign insolvency proceedings, and to the office holders conducting them, is its essentially non-discriminatory policy in terms of the foreign countries with which such cooperation and assistance may in principle be shared. Although the English court has a residual discretion over such matters, and could elect to refrain from giving assistance where the foreign proceedings are considered to violate principles of fairness and due process that are here regarded as fundamental, there is no predisposition on the part of the English courts to confine themselves to assisting foreign representatives from certain, favoured countries only: the potential scope of assistance is genuinely worldwide. However, certain factors appear to militate against this facility being more frequently invoked, even against a background of steady growth in the numbers of insolvencies with cross-border aspects. One reason is the relatively under-publicised state of the law, much of which is contained in reports of cases originally decided many years ago. Uncertainty about the existing possibilities may be compounded by a con-

[1] See at 2.6, 2.8, 3.7, 3.9 and 3.10 above.

cern on the part of some office holders to refrain from making any direct inquiry or application to the English courts, lest this result in their being held to have submitted to the jurisdiction of the court and thereby rendered themselves, and the estate they are administering, amenable to process in respect of further liabilities arising within this country.[2]

In conceding that the common law, for all its remarkable qualities, does not appear to provide a fully balanced and readily accessible framework for cross-border assistance, it is important to acknowledge the great difficulties—both technical and also political—that confront any attempts to transform the arrangements for international cooperation so that they can be more widely known and understood, and also operate under conditions of greater certainty, speed and effectiveness. Many of the attendant difficulties can only be satisfactorily resolved by means of international agreements embracing a significant proportion of the countries potentially concerned, and in Part II of this book a number of such regional and global initiatives will be examined. The present chapter will show how legislative provisions enacted in the United Kingdom, the USA, Australia and Canada have in their different ways demonstrated the further possibilities for national laws to be reshaped, or selectively enhanced, to the consequent benefit of office holders and creditors in many types of foreign proceeding. However, as will also become apparent, nationally-based solutions to the problems of multi-jurisdictional insolvencies are by their very nature a source of fresh complexities, since they differ from one another in an almost infinite number of ways, both in substance and in terms of the style and manner of their application by the courts and officials of the countries by which they are enacted. They do, nevertheless, enjoy the priceless virtue of being already in force and available for use, whereas the ideal of a more uniform and comprehensive regime, to be supplied by means of a pan-global treaty, remains a distant prospect for the time being.

4.1 INTERNATIONAL COOPERATION BY UNITED KINGDOM COURTS UNDER SECTION 426 OF THE INSOLVENCY ACT 1986

4.1.1 Generally

Although it is partly based upon the provision, formerly contained in section 122 of the Bankruptcy Act 1914, requiring mutual aid and assistance

[2] An example of such apprehensions affecting the procedural strategy of a foreign liquidator is the *Herstatt* case, during 1974–75, in which the German liquidator refrained from participating in proceedings in New York, to avoid any risk of submission to that forum. See K. Nadelmann (1977) 52 N.Y.U.L. Rev. 1, at 7–8 (esp. n.37); Becker (1976) 62 A.B.A.J. 1290.

to be given between themselves by 'every British court' in 'all matters of bankruptcy', section 426 of the Insolvency Act 1986 is in many respects a new element in the English law of international insolvency. It embodies the substance of the recommendation in Chapter 49 of the Cork Report,[3] that a suitably modernised version of section 122 should be enacted, applicable to corporate as well as to individual insolvency, to provide for reciprocal enlargement of the power to give international assistance, particularly within the Commonwealth.

Some aspects of section 426 have already been considered in view of their impact upon the internal enforcement of court orders in insolvency proceedings as between different parts of the United Kingdom, and also within the Commonwealth.[4] However, the section itself is elaborately constructed, and deals with a number of different matters which are grouped together beneath the somewhat misleading heading: *'Co-operation between courts exercising jurisdiction in relation to insolvency'*. This might suggest that the section's aim is that courts in the United Kingdom should enjoy a general authorisation to deliver assistance to their counterparts in other countries throughout the world. On closer inspection, the section makes provision for such cooperation to take place on a selective basis, and does not confer anything like so broad and unqualified a mandate for courts in the United Kingdom to give assistance based upon this section.[5] Therefore the common law rules that were discussed in Chapters 2 and 3 continue to supply the basis for recognition and enforcement of foreign insolvency orders in all cases apart from those which are about to be described. For proceedings opened in all countries of the world except for those expressly brought within the ambit of section 426, the extent to which assistance can be obtained from the English courts will depend upon the law and practice derived from the case precedents.

Restricted availability of section 426 assistance

While the first three subsections of section 426 are exclusively concerned with matters that are internal to the United Kingdom, genuinely international cases are assimilated into the scope of subsection (4). This is so drafted as to embrace both the giving of mutual assistance between courts

[3] Cmnd. 8558 (1982), esp. at paras. 1908–1913. For further comment and analysis of the significance of s.426, see Woloniecki (1986) 35 I.C.L.Q. 644; Polonsky (1996) 113 S.A.L.J. 109; P. Smart, *Cross-Border Insolvency* (1991), ch. 14 at p. 259 *et seq.*

[4] See at 2.2 above at pp. 64–9.

[5] Compare the absence of any country-specific barriers to access under the United States Bankruptcy Code, s.304 (at 4.2 below), and under Part XIII of the Canadian Bankruptcy and Insolvency Act (at 4.4 below) and also the stratified approach adopted in Australian law, whereby no foreign country is potentially excluded from access to the aid and assistance which the courts of that country may provide under s.581 of the Corporations Law, and s.29 of the Bankruptcy Act: see s.581(2)(b) and s.29(2)(b) respectively (at 4.3 below).

in different parts of the United Kingdom, and the giving of assistance by courts in any part of the United Kingdom to certain types of court in a carefully defined category of external countries and territories. The drafting device employed for this purpose identifies the qualifying countries by referring to them as 'relevant' countries or territories, whose meaning for this purpose is defined in subsection (11). Section 426(4) provides:

> The courts having jurisdiction in relation to insolvency law in any part of the United Kingdom shall assist the courts having the corresponding jurisdiction in any other part of the United Kingdom or any relevant country or territory.

Section 426(11) then provides that the expression 'relevant country or territory' means:

> (a) any of the Channel Islands or the Isle of Man, or
> (b) any country or territory designated for the purposes of this section by order made by statutory instrument.

Thus do the terms of section 426 establish a barrier to entry which can only be surmounted through the taking of positive action, on a country-specific basis, by the Government itself. The power conferred by subsection (11)(b) has been used sparingly, and selectively. Since 1986, only two orders have been made pursuant to this provision. The first of these, made in 1986, designated seventeen countries and dependent territories, all but one of which were then members of the Commonwealth, for the purposes of section 426.[6] Subsequently, in 1996, two further Commonwealth members, South Africa and Malaysia, were added to the list of designated countries.[7] At the time of its inclusion among the designated territories in the 1986 Order, Hong Kong was still a British colony. With the restoration of Chinese sovereignty over Hong Kong from 1 July 1997, that territory became only the second non-member of the Commonwealth—the other being the Republic of Ireland—to be designated for the purposes of section 426. It is therefore apparent that, for the time being, assistance under this section is available on a very restricted basis, and that many states with which the United Kingdom enjoys close relationships, notably in the economic and commercial spheres, are presently omitted from the list of 'relevant' countries.[8]

[6] Co-operation of Insolvency Courts (Designation of Relevant Countries and Territories) Order 1986 (S.I. 1986 No. 2123), operative from 29 December 1986. The countries and territories scheduled to the Order are: Anguilla, Australia, the Bahamas, Bermuda, Botswana, Canada, Cayman Islands, Falkland Islands, Gibraltar, Hong Kong, Republic of Ireland, Montserrat, New Zealand, St.Helena, Turks and Caicos Islands, Tuvalu, and the Virgin Islands.

[7] Co-operation of Insolvency Courts (Designation of Relevant Countries) Order 1996 (S.I.1996 No. 253), operative from 1 March 1996.

[8] The USA is a conspicuous example of such omission, as are all the current members of the European Union apart from the Republic of Ireland. Many sovereign members of the

Which courts may seek, and give, assistance?

It should be noted that the international assistance for which provision is made by section 426(4) is limited not only in terms of the foreign countries from which requests for such assistance can be entertained, but also in terms of the authorities by which it may be requested and provided. The only form of assistance that can be obtained is on a 'court-to-court' basis: it is not open to an office holder appointed in foreign insolvency proceedings to make a direct, personal request for assistance to an English court, nor to any other person or authority, under the auspices of this statutory provision.[9] Moreover, the ambit of the power to give assistance is narrowed still further, since it is expressed to be exercisable by 'the courts having jurisdiction in relation to insolvency law in any part of the United Kingdom', in response to requests for assistance submitted by 'the courts having the corresponding jurisdiction' in a country or territory which has been designated for this specific purpose, as seen above. It is therefore necessary to determine which courts are qualified to participate in the process, a question whose resolution is partly dependent on the arrangements in force, in the United Kingdom and in the other country concerned, for the allocation of jurisdiction in relation to insolvency law. More fundamentally, however, it is necessary to establish the meaning of the expression 'insolvency law' in this context. Here, the answer is supplied by section 426(10), which provides:

In this section 'insolvency law' means—

(a) in relation to England and Wales, provision made by or under this Act or sections 6 to 10, 12, 15, 19(c) and 20 (with Schedule 1) of the Company Directors Disqualification Act 1986 and extending to England and Wales;
(b) in relation to Scotland, provision extending to Scotland and made by or under this Act, sections 6 to 10, 12, 15, 19(c) and 20 (with Schedule 1) of the Company Directors Disqualification Act 1986, Part XVIII of the Companies Act or the Bankruptcy (Scotland) Act 1985;
(c) in relation to Northern Ireland, provision made by or under the Insolvency (Northern Ireland) Order 1989 or Part II of the Companies (Northern Ireland) Order 1989;
(d) in relation to any relevant country or territory, so much of the law of that country or territory as corresponds to provisions falling within any of the foregoing paragraphs;

Commonwealth—indeed, the majority of them—are also omitted from the list of designated countries.

[9] Cf. the more direct access afforded in the USA under s.304 B.C. to allow a 'foreign representative' to seek assistance from the bankruptcy court: see at 4.2 below.

and references in this subsection to any enactment include, in relation to any time before the coming into force of that enactment the corresponding enactment in force at that time.

The concept of 'insolvency law' is thus formulated with reference to specific legislative enactments in force in the various parts of the United Kingdom. The use of the phrase 'by or under' allows for the defining provisions to be contained in primary or secondary legislation, but otherwise the drafting of paragraphs (a), (b) and (c) appears to ignore those aspects of insolvency law which are purely the product of case decisions, and which have never been the subject of any statutory enactment.[10] However, in the case of paragraph (d), where the less specific term 'law' is used, allowance is apparently made for the possibility that elements of the law of certain 'relevant' countries or territories which correspond to the 'touchstone' provisions of United Kingdom insolvency law may not exist in statutory form in every instance. By combining the elements of subsection (10) with the rules for allocating jurisdiction, it is potentially possible for either the High Court or a County Court having an insolvency jurisdiction to be concerned in the giving of assistance under section 426. In most cases it is likely that a request for assistance will be addressed to the High Court, as the court endowed with a comprehensive jurisdiction covering both individual and corporate insolvency.[11] However, it should be noted that where the debtor has a residential address, or carries on business, within a County Court insolvency district outside the London Insolvency District or (in the case of a company) has its registered office in such a district outside London, the County Court in question has a jurisdiction concurrent, and also co-extensive, with that of the High Court.[12] In terms of speed, and also cost, there may sometimes be advantages in addressing a request for assistance to the appropriate County Court.

[10] For example, the 'subject to equities' rule described in Chapter 2 above at p. 61 *et seq.* is purely the product of past case decisions. So, too, the doctrine known as the Rule in *Ex Parte James* (1874) 9 Ch. App. 609, which applies to office holders in bankruptcy, compulsory winding up, and company administration (but not in cases of voluntary winding up or administrative receivership), has never been the subject of any legislative provision. However, to the extent that these, and other rules and doctrines belonging to the 'common law of insolvency' are the products of the courts' exercise of their general jurisdiction and powers, they may—should the need arise—be capable of being considered to fall within the overall scope of the s.426 regime, as elucidated by Morritt L.J. in *Hughes v. Hannover* [1997] 1 B.C.L.C. 497 at 517; [1997] B.C.C. 921 at 938 (discussed below).

[11] Insolvency Act 1986, ss.117(1), 373(1).

[12] *Ibid.*, ss. 117(2),(5), 373(1)–(3) inclusive. Note however that the County Court only has such jurisdiction, in the case of a company, where the company's paid up share capital does not exceed £120,000: *ibid.*, s.117(2).

4.1.2 The nature and extent of the assistance available under section 426(4)

Section 426(4)—which is reproduced in full above[13]—consists of a single sentence, and is expressed in the manner of a command. The sense of an obligation, cast upon the court to which a request for assistance is addressed, is conveyed by the use of the words 'shall assist', unaccompanied by any qualifying or limiting proviso such as 'to the best of its ability' or 'so far as is reasonably practicable'. A literal reading of subsection (4), taken in isolation, might therefore yield the conclusion that the English court has an unconditional duty to provide assistance to courts which meet the stated criteria rendering them eligible to request it. Such a conclusion would be premature however, because subsection (4) itself supplies no indication as to the nature of the assistance which the courts are required to provide. For this, it is necessary to refer to subsection (5), whose full provisions are as follows:

> For the purposes of subsection (4) a request made to a court in any part of the United Kingdom by a court in any other part of the United Kingdom or a relevant country or territory is authority for the court to which the request is made to apply, in relation to any matters specified in the request, the insolvency law which is applicable by either court in relation to comparable matters falling within its jurisdiction.
>
> In exercising its discretion under this subsection, a court shall have regard in particular to the rules of private international law.

Subsection (5) is expressed in terms of empowerment, and in so doing it openly refers to the court having a discretion with regard to the use of the powers conferred upon it. The concluding proviso also imposes a requirement upon the court to have regard 'in particular' to the rules of private international law. Several further questions arise in consequence of the terms in which subsection (5) is drafted, including that of the interrelationship between it and subsection (4). These must be addressed in turn before it is possible to arrive at any conclusion about the nature and extent of the obligation to give assistance imposed by subsection (4).[14]

First, it is pertinent to observe the remarkable quality of the powers which the court is authorised to apply: the reference to 'the insolvency law which is applicable by *either court*' (emphasis added) means that the court, in responding to the request for assistance, may draw upon the provisions of two distinct legal systems, to the extent that their respective provisions are applicable to broadly identical situations which are to be determined,

[13] See p. 189.

[14] Cf. *Hughes v. Hannover*, *supra* n.10, in the judgment of Morritt L.J. at [1997] 1 B.C.L.C., 506 *et seq.*, [1997] B.C.C. 929 *et seq.*

for the purpose in hand, by reference to such matters as are 'specified in the request'. The search agenda is thus established by the terms of the foreign court's request for assistance, and by the 'matters' specified therein. This necessarily requires the court entertaining the request—which we will here assume to be a court in England and Wales—[15] to undertake a process of characterisation, to determine what the terms of the request signify—and in particular what substantive issues are raised by them—from the standpoint of a court operating within the English legal system. Having thus 'interpreted' the request, the court must then establish what provisions and remedies of its domestic 'insolvency law' (as defined by section 426(10)[16]) are applicable in relation to the matters so specified. The court may next proceed to consider what substantive provisions of insolvency law are applicable by the court which made the request in relation to comparable matters falling within its own jurisdiction.[17] Having assembled the necessary information, the English court must decide in what way it is to exercise its powers of 'ambidextrous' application of the laws of two separate systems. Various possibilities may suggest themselves, according to what is discovered about the way in which each system would deal with the matters under consideration. It may transpire that the approaches of the two systems are essentially identical to each other for the purpose in hand; alternatively, they may differ from each other in significant, and even in fundamental, ways. In the former situation, the court is spared any need to search its conscience before applying a solution that is common to both concerned systems, whereas the latter situation poses major questions of policy and principle, which apparently are left to the court to resolve through the exercise of its 'discretion'. It may also be the case that one system has no counterpart of provisions made by the other for dealing with some matter specified by the request for assistance.[18] Although this does not confront the court with so obvious a dilemma of conscience, it may at least be suggested that some caution is appropriate, in case there is an underlying element of opportunism which suggests that those responsible for instigating the foreign court's request for assistance may be motivated by a desire to exploit some

[15] As explained above, this is likely to be the High Court, but could in some circumstances be a County Court exercising jurisdiction in insolvency.

[16] See above.

[17] It should be noted that the English court does not investigate matters of foreign law of its own motion, but only does so if one of the parties before it seeks to persuade the court to apply it, in which case it will also be incumbent upon that party, in the usual way, to prove the meaning and content of the relevant parts of the foreign law in question. See *Dicey and Morris on the Conflict of Laws*, 12th edn. (1993), ch. 9.

[18] As in *Re Bank of Credit and Commerce International S.A. (No. 9)* [1994] 3 All E.R. 764, [1994] 2 B.C.L.C. 636 (Rattee J.).

feature within the English insolvency law that is lacking under the system by which the proceedings are principally governed.[19]

It is apparent that, according to the circumstances of the case and the respective contents of the two systems of law concerned, the English court may face the need to exercise a degree of choice regarding the exercise of its powers under the authority conferred by section 426(5). Neither the subsection itself, nor any other provision in the Act or the Rules, offers any guidance or further direction as to the manner in which this task is to be performed, nor as to the policy objectives by which the court should be guided in exercising its discretion.[20] The only internal indication of what is required of the court is contained in the proviso to subsection (5) itself, which specifies that in exercising its discretion '*under this subsection*' a court '*shall have regard in particular*' to 'the rules of private international law' (emphasis added). It may be observed that, whether by accident or design, the drafting of this provision is vague and oblique. The reference to 'the rules of private international law' is non-specific, and could merely be a reminder that the court must observe established conventions such as that the forum always applies its own rules of procedure, and never applies a procedural rule belonging to any foreign system. On the other hand, the direction could have more far-reaching connotations, and effectively amount to a requirement that the court must bring to bear the full repertoire of choice of law rules, and conflict of laws technique, to discover which substantive rule to apply, as between the alternatives to be found within the insolvency laws of the two systems.

Some insight into the intended effects of subsection (5) when first enacted as part of the Insolvency Act 1985 (later consolidated without amendment into the 1986 Act), may be discerned from the Hansard report of the Ministerial arguments urged in support of the clause when introduced by means of a government amendment moved at the Commons Committee stage of proceedings.[21] In addition to meeting the recommendation that the existing arrangements for reciprocal assistance in matters of personal bankruptcy should be extended to all types of corporate insol-

[19] See, e.g., *Hughes v. Hannover*, *supra* n.10, where the Court of Appeal declined to provide the foreign liquidators with the potent tactical advantages they were seeking in the form of a worldwide *Mareva* injunction against a party which was not subject to the jurisdiction of the court of Bermuda,where the liquidation was taking place. Cf. also the persistent endeavours of the administrators in the *Maxwell Communications Corporation* case to be allowed to bring action for avoidance of preferential transactions in the USA, rather than in England, in view of the differences in the laws of the two systems (see Chapter 2, at 2.3. above, at pp. 75–8).

[20] Contrast the explicit policy guidelines specified in s.304(c) of the US Bankruptcy Code (discussed at 4.2 below).

[21] Hansard, HC Standing Committee E, 18 June 1985, col. 423, statement of David Trippier moving the clauses which eventually became s.213(3) and (4) of the Insolvency Act 1985. See also the further statements made at the Report Stage on 18 July 1985, Hansard H.C. vol. 83, at cols. 550 and 551.

vencies, it was explained that the new clause would give courts sufficient flexibility to solve complicated matters involving plural jurisdictions in the manner best suited to the facts of the case before them. A concrete example was put in which an English-registered company had entered into an under-value transaction with a person in Scotland prior to going into liquidation, so that the liquidator might be uncertain whether to bring avoidance proceedings in England or Scotland, and whether English or Scottish law would apply to determine whether the transaction should be set aside. The solution envisaged would involve the liquidator going in the first instance to the English court, which might consider that the matter would more appropriately be dealt with under the law of Scotland. The English court would issue a request to its Scottish counterpart to assist the liquidator, and the requested court would deal with the matter by applying its rules of private international law to determine the law applicable to the transaction in question.[22] The intention, very clearly, was that the judicial 'discretion', under what is now section 426(5), should it appropriate be exercised on the basis of a full choice-of-law process conducted by the court responding to the request. Unfortunately the Ministerial example omitted to indicate what course should be followed in a less simple case, where the conclusion reached by applying the rules of private international law to the facts is that the transaction in question was properly governed by the law of some third country. Subsection (5) itself only authorises the court to apply the insolvency law of its own domestic system, or the corresponding law of the country from which the request was made. In view of this limitation, perhaps the most that could be expected is that the English court would 'have regard' to the effects produced by application of the rules of private international law, and so fashion its assistance as to match as closely as possible the result that would be arrived at under the law of the third country.

A further matter for comment arising from the drafting of the proviso to section 426(5) is that the insertion of the words 'in particular' makes the provision open to more than one interpretation. One possibility is that it may be designed as an emphatic reminder to the court to ensure that the appropriate choice-of-law process is integrated into its method of responding to the request for assistance. An alternative way of reading the concluding clause of the proviso is that it is alluding to the existence of a range of possible factors to which the court may have regard in the course of exercising its discretion, of which the rules of private international law are singled out for special mention. Irrespective of the preferred interpretation, it is at least clear that the use of the word 'shall' means that the court is placed under an obligation to have regard to the rules of private

[22] *Ibid.*

international law, whereas other matters may be taken into consideration as necessary or appropriate. One such factor, to which an English court would invariably have regard when exercising an otherwise unqualified discretion, is the omnipresent concern to uphold the requirements of public policy pertaining to the general law of this country, and not merely as applicable within the more circumscribed ambit of 'insolvency law' alone. A further, general factor inseparable from the court's exercise of its discretion is the aspiration to further the ends of justice in whatever way may prove to be appropriate in the context of the proceedings with which it is concerned. Thus, it may be expected that in exercising its discretion under subsection (5) a court will ultimately have regard to what will be most conducive to bringing about a fair, just and convenient outcome in the light of all the circumstances of which it is aware, and which it can properly take into consideration. It can therefore be appreciated that the judicial processes which are destined to take place whenever this provision of the Insolvency Act is invoked are both delicate and complex, and cannot readily be reduced to a standardised series of precepts.

The scope of the court's discretion

Although section 426 was conceived as an instrument to further the cause of international cooperation, its bemusing and elliptical drafting has proved an obstacle to ready understanding and application. The first reported decisions by courts of first instance, while displaying a judicial concern to respect the spirit of the provisions of subsections (4) and (5), revealed some basic confusion with regard to the correct meaning to be ascribed to the letter of the enacted law.[23] In their decision in *Hughes v. Hannover*,[24] in which Morritt L.J. delivered the single judgment of the court, the Court of Appeal endeavoured to transcend the confusing signals emitted by these early efforts at interpreting the new provisions. In seeking to deduce the correct approach, Morritt L.J. observed that section 426 was built upon the foundations of the previous provisions for mutual cooperation in bankruptcy matters, which had also embodied a drafting formula imparting an authorisation to give 'ambidextrous' assistance to the foreign court.[25] Thus, without actually mentioning the word 'discre-

[23] See *Re Dallhold Estates (UK) Pty. Ltd.*[1992] B.C.C. 394, [1992] B.C.L.C. 621; *Re Bank of Credit and Commerce International S.A. (No .9)* (*supra* n.18); *Re Focus Insurance Co. Ltd.* [1997] 1 B.C.L.C. 219, [1996] B.C.C. 659.

[24] [1997] 1 B.C.L.C. 497, [1997] B.C.C. 921. The full name of the case is *Hughes v. Hannover Ruckversicherungs-Aktiengesellschaft*. It is sometimes referred to as the '*Hannover Re.*' case, after the convenient abbreviation adopted in the judgment of Morritt L.J. to refer to the defendant reinsurer. The litigation is also referred to as the 'EMLICO' case, based on the initials of the name of the insolvent insurance company, Electric Mutual Liability Insurance Co. Ltd., whose liquidation formed the background to the proceedings.

[25] See the successive provisions of: Bankruptcy Act 1869, s.74; Bankruptcy Act 1883, s.118; Bankruptcy Act 1914, s.122.

tion' the statutory predecessors of section 426(4) and (5) had also rendered it necessary for the English court to exercise a choice with regard to the appropriate way in which to furnish assistance. Quite logically, when construing those former statutory provisions, the courts had perceived themselves to be called upon to exercise a discretion as to what assistance they ought to give under the circumstances of the instant case.[26] At the same time, they had recognised the existence of an element of internal contradiction between the purported exercise of a discretion and the statutory obligation whereby the court was bound to give its assistance. Previously, the judges had sought to resolve this tension by deeming themselves to be bound to give all possible assistance compatible with their broader, permanent duties of upholding the principles of justice and public policy.[27] Morritt L.J. recognised that the recasting of the statutory provisions in the 1986 Act, with many new features, necessitated a reappraisal of the judicial approach.[28] The learned Lord Justice considered that in enacting section 426(4) and (5) Parliament had not intended to restrict the jurisdiction or ability of the English courts to afford assistance, but indeed had sought to enhance them in certain carefully controlled ways. Consequently, when performing their functions under those provisions, the courts retain their usual jurisdiction and powers, in addition to those specially conferred for the purpose in hand.

The above line of reasoning led Morritt L.J. to conclude—correctly, it is submitted—that in responding to a request for assistance submitted by a competent court under section 426, the English court has available to it:

(a) its own general jurisdiction and powers vested in it under the laws of England and Wales; and either
(b) the insolvency law of England and Wales as defined by section 426(10)(a);[29] or
(c) so much or the law of the relevant country as corresponds to that comprised in (b).[30]

Turning to the vital matter of the nature of the discretion which the court can exercise when drawing upon the powers available to it, Morritt

[26] *Re Osborne* [1931–32] 15 B. & C.R. 189, at 194 per Farwell J.; *Re Jackson* [1973] N.I. 67 at 72 per Lord Lowry; *Re a Debtor, ex parte Viscount of the Royal Court of Jersey* [1981] Ch. 384 at 402 per Goulding J. The pre-1986 cases are reviewed by Morritt L.J. at [1997] 1 B.C.L.C. 506–510, [1997] B.C.C. 929–932.

[27] *Ibid.*

[28] [1997] 1 B.C.L.C. at 510–517, [1997] B.C.C. at 932–938.

[29] See at p. 190 above.

[30] [1997] 1 B.C.L.C. 517, [1997] B.C.C. 938. The one reported instance to date where the English court has applied the insolvency law of the requesting court as the basis for its decision is *Re Business City Express Ltd.* [1997] B.C.C. 826, where Rattee J., with some reluctance, made an order whereby a scheme of composition already approved by the Irish court should be made binding upon the UK creditors of the company.(This judgment was delivered eight days before the decision of the Court of Appeal in *Hughes v. Hannover, supra* n.24).

L.J. emphasised that the court is obligated to respond in a genuine way to the request for assistance: the force of the words 'shall assist' in subsection (4) makes it incumbent upon the court to give such assistance as can properly be granted in accordance with the law to be applied. While these considerations might influence the shape of the assistance finally given, the essential spirit of the required approach to the exercise of the court's discretion may be summed up in a single sentence thus: 'The particular assistance requested should be given unless there is some good reason for not doing so'.[31] The English court is not relegated to the status of a mere automaton, whose predictable responses can be triggered by the act of presenting it with a request for assistance under section 426. The court's assistance is individually fashioned in response to the elements present within the instant case, and its discretion can be employed to enable it to perform its normal function of seeking to do justice in accordance with the law.[32]

Examples of assistance provided under section 426

Although there have been only a small number of reported decisions involving questions of interpretation of section 426, it is already apparent that it can provide a useful vehicle for the delivery of effective assistance by the English courts. An early example of such creative use of the powers conferred by these provisions was *Re Dallhold Estates (UK) Pty. Ltd.*[33] where liquidation proceedings were pending in Australia in respect of an Australian-formed company which had assets in England. The company was the tenant of land in England under a lease terminable on bankruptcy or winding up, and it was therefore vital to find some way of preserving the value represented by this asset without causing the forfeiture to operate. An appropriate procedure for this purpose was identified, namely the Administration Order procedure under Part II of the Insolvency Act 1986. Two significant obstacles appeared to preclude the taking of this preferred course, however. First, at the time of the proceedings (during the concluding months of 1991) Australian law of company insolvency offered no procedure comparable to Administration, which had been introduced as one

[31] The words in parentheses are adapted from the judgment of Rattee J. in *Re Bank of Credit and Commerce International S.A. (No. 9)* [1994] 3 All E.R. 764 at 785, quoted by Morritt LJ in his judgment in *Hughes v. Hannover* at [1997] 1 B.C.L.C. 513–514, [1997] B.C.C. 935. Cf. however the different nuance in the form of words used by some other judges in expressing the same proposition: 'unless there is some compelling reason why that should not be done': *Re Dallhold Estates (UK) Pty. Ltd.* [1992] B.C.L.C. at 627 (Chadwick J); *Re J.N. Taylor Finance Pty. Ltd., England v. Purves* [1998] B.P.I.R. 347 (Evans-Lombe J).

[32] See, e.g. the views of Rattee J. in the passage referred to in the previous footnote, and those of Scott V.-C. in *Re Focus Insurance Co. Ltd.* [1997] 1 B.C.L.C. 219 at 227 and at 230. See also the robust endorsement of this approach by Morritt L.J. in *Hughes v. Hannover*, *supra* n.24, at [1997] 1 B.C.L.C. 517–518, [1997] B.C.C. 938–939.

[33] See *supra* n.23.

of the innovations in the United Kingdom insolvency law reforms of 1985–1986. There were prospects for the introduction of an analogous procedure in Australia, but at that date the reforms had not been enacted into law.[34] Secondly, the prevailing view of the operation of Part II of the 1986 Act was that it was only possible for an English court to make an administration order in relation to a company formed and registered under United Kingdom companies legislation.[35] Chadwick J. concluded that it was nevertheless possible for him to give an affirmative response to the request by the Federal Court in Australia for assistance in the form of an administration order against the company. This was because the purpose of section 426(5), in the estimation of the learned judge, was to give the requested court a jurisdiction it might not otherwise have under domestic insolvency law in order that it can give assistance to the requesting court. This is achieved by authorising the court to exercise powers on a hypothetical basis so that it is able, in spite of the foreign element in the case, to make an order which it would be competent to make in a comparable matter falling within its jurisdiction.[36]

A further demonstration of flexible use by the English court of the 'ambidextrous' powers enjoyed under section 426 was the decision of Rattee J. in *Re Bank of Credit and Commerce International S.A. (No. 9)*[37] where a company forming part of the BCCI banking conglomerate was being wound up by the Grand Court of the Cayman Islands. That particular company had been incorporated in the Cayman Islands, whose companies legislation is based upon that of the United Kingdom but has not yet assimilated the fruits of the reforms of more recent times, notably in the field of insolvency law. Of particular relevance to the instant case, where enormous losses had been caused to creditors and depositors by mismanagement and fraud on the part of some directors and managers of the bank, was the absence from the statutory provisions in force in the Cayman Islands of any counterparts to sections 212, 213, 214 and 238 of the Insolvency Act 1986. It was therefore not possible for the liquidators to

[34] For an account of the UK Administration Order procedure, see I.F. Fletcher, *The Law of Insolvency*, 2nd edn. (1996), ch. 16. For the Australian Corporate Voluntary Administration, see P. Crutchfield, *Corporate Voluntary Administration Law*, 2nd edn. (1997); A.R. Keay, *Insolvency*, 2nd edn. (1994), ch. 5.

[35] Cf. the subsequent decision in *Re Devon and Somerset Farmers Ltd.* [1993] B.C.C. 410, distinguishing *Re International Bulk Commodities Ltd.* [1993] Ch. 77 (both cases were concerned with aspects of the law of receivership but involved the same essential point, namely the possibility of interpreting the word 'company' as used in the Insolvency Act so that it can refer to a company not formed under UK companies legislation). See Moss (1993) 6 *Insolvency Intelligence* 19.

[36] [1992] B.C.L.C. 626. Cf. the extra-judicial observation made by Millett L.J. in (1997) 6 I.I.R. 99 at 104: 'by virtue of the request the court can exercise a jurisdiction which neither court would possess alone'.

[37] See *supra* n.18.

use local law to bring proceedings against a former director and employee of BCCI for misfeasance or for wrongful or fraudulent trading, nor to apply for orders to procure the avoidance of transactions the company had been caused to enter into at an undervalue. In considering the request from the Grand Court to assist in overcoming these *lacunae* in the Cayman Islands law, Rattee J. took into account the fact that the affairs of the BCCI companies were all hopelessly intertwined in such a way as to render traditional international boundaries irrelevant. The only sensible solution lay through the giving of whatever mutual assistance lay in the power of the various national courts to provide. Moreover, the operational links of BCCI with London and with England had been substantial, so that it was not inappropriate for proceedings against directors and others, and for the impeachment of prior transactions, to be conducted by the liquidators before the English court, and the requisite orders were made to enable them to do so.[38]

However, in the subsequent case of *Re Focus Insurance Co. Ltd.*[39] Scott V.-C. resisted the attempt by the liquidators of a Bermudan insurance company, which was being wound up in Bermuda, to persuade him to make an order against a former director with a view to securing the latter's examination in England so that details of his assets could be obtained. The decisive factor which persuaded the court to exercise its discretion, on this occasion, not to provide the requested assistance was that the Bermudan liquidators had pursued a parallel strategy against the director by commencing bankruptcy proceedings against him in England on the basis of a default judgment obtained in Bermuda. It would therefore be for the trustee in bankruptcy to investigate the bankrupt's affairs and seek to recover assets for the benefit of the creditors proving under the bankruptcy. Scott V.-C. was concerned by the potential for such a twin-track approach to give rise to oppressive consequences for the individual concerned, and he concluded that the liquidators, having decided to invoke English bankruptcy as the means of getting in the asset claimed on behalf of the company's creditors, could not thereafter turn around and pursue remedies which were inconsistent with the bankruptcy which they themselves had commenced.[40] So, too, in the case of *Hughes v. Hannover*[41] the Court of Appeal concluded that the joint liquidators in the EMLICO liquidation, again based in Bermuda, were resorting to tactical use of the section 426 facility for the purpose of seeking a worldwide *Mareva* injunction against a party not amenable to the jurisdiction of the Bermudan courts.

[38] [1994] 3 All E.R. 785.

[39] See *supra* n.23.

[40] [1997] 1 B.C.L.C. 232, [1996] B.C.C. 670. See also *Re J.N. Taylor Finance Pty. Ltd., England v. Purves* [1998] B.P.I.R. 347, where a request for examination of certain parties in England was also refused.

[41] See *supra* n.10 *et seq.*

The court, having first satisfied itself that the powers exercisable when acting under the provisions of section 426 include the jurisdiction to grant a *Mareva* injunction where it is just and equitable to do so, decided that the circumstances of the case before it were such that it would be inappropriate to grant an injunction of that kind, and discretion was accordingly exercised to refuse the assistance requested.[42] As already explained above, the English courts in discharging the duties cast upon them by section 426 insist upon the ultimate freedom to decide for themselves whether the ends of justice will be properly served by an affirmative response to the foreign court's request.

4.2 ANCILLARY PROCEEDINGS PURSUANT TO SECTION 304 OF THE UNITED STATES BANKRUPTCY CODE

Alongside the numerous innovations to the domestic bankruptcy law of the USA that were made by the Bankruptcy Reform Act of 1978, the provisions contained in section 304 of the Act can be credited with having brought about a transformation of the American approach in the field of international insolvency that was little short of revolutionary.[43] Indeed, the section still represents a benchmark in terms of the liberal, universalist approach to the problems posed by multi-jurisdictional insolvencies. Although its provisions, and the manner in which they have sometimes been judicially interpreted and applied, have not entirely escaped critical censure, there is a broad consensus of scholarly acclaim for their inspired originality of vision.

Prior to the reforms of 1978, there were no specific legislative provisions in force within the USA to enable the courts to deal with international cases in an effective way. Moreover, the legacy of past case law together with much of the doctrinal writings from the previous century showed a strong preference for a territorial approach and a resistance to the idea that the bankruptcy laws of foreign countries might produce effects within the USA, especially in terms of transfer of property or the discharge of

[42] [1997] 1 B.C.L.C. 519–524, [1997] B.C.C. 939–944, per Morritt L.J. Note that is now possible for interim relief—such as a *Mareva* injunction—to be sought by a representative in foreign insolvency proceedings by application to the English court pursuant to the Civil Jurisdiction and Judgments Act 1982 (Interim Relief) Order 1997 (S.I. 1997 No. 302). The Order, made under the Civil Jurisdiction and Judgments Act 1982, s.25(3), is so worded that its provisions are applicable in relation to foreign proceedings from any jurisdiction of the world, and irrespective of whether the subject matter of those proceedings falls within the scope of the Brussels or Lugano Conventions. See Smart (1998) 11 *Insolvency Intelligence* 9–11.

[43] 11 U.S.C. s.304 is reproduced in full, together with ss.303, 305 and 306 and relevant definitions from s.101, in Appendix I below.

obligations.[44] By the latter half of the twentieth century however the tide of informed opinion had begun to flow ever more strongly in the direction of reform, reflecting the unsatisfactory experiences meted out to foreign creditors and their representatives in multinational bankruptcy proceedings.[45] Sometimes, American judges were prepared to invoke the doctrine of comity and exercise discretion to award turnover of local assets to a foreign representative bold enough to pursue an application before them.[46] Nevertheless, the lack of consistency and predictability made it almost impossible for foreign representatives to assess whether it would be worthwhile to commit resources to the pursuit or defence of proceedings in an American court. A new, essentially receptive, climate of cooperation was ushered into being with the enactment of section 304.

The concept of ancillary proceedings

The principal conceptual innovation achieved by section 304 is that it makes available a broad range of types of assistance of which a foreign representative can take advantage without the need for formal bankruptcy proceedings to be commenced in the USA. The name 'ancillary proceeding' is a convenient shorthand for the full term employed by section 304: 'a case ancillary to a foreign proceeding'. It is used to denote a formal

[44] *Harrison v. Sterry*, 9 U.S. (5 Cranch) 289 (1809) (Marshall C.J.); *Ogden v. Saunders*, 25 U.S. (12 Wheat.) 213 (1827). See also J. Story, *Commentaries on the Conflict of Laws*, 4th edn. (1852), paras. 403–405, 410–417. For further information about the historic background to the 1978 reforms, see Riesenfeld (1976) 24 A.J.C.L. 288, and (1947) 31 Minn. L. Rev. 401, and in Musielak and Schurig (eds.), *Festschrift fur Gerhard Kegel* (1977), p. 483; Honsberger (1980) 30 Case Western Res. L. Rev.631; Nadelmann (1988) 29 Harv. Int'l Law Jnl. 27, and (1963) 12 I.C.L.Q. 684; Given and Vilaplana (1983) Arizona State L.J. 325; Morales and Deutcsh (1984) 39 Bus. Law 1573; Booth (1991) 9 Boston Univ. Intn'l. L. J. 1 and further references there supplied at n.3.

[45] The most celebrated—or, rather, notorious—such case was that of the *Herstatt Bank*, in which proceedings related to the main, German liquidation were pending in the Southern District of New York during 1974–1975. The limitations and uncertainties of the American law were major reasons why the interested parties opted for a settlement before the court could adjudicate upon the legal issues. See Nadelmann (1977) 52 N.Y.U.L.Rev. 1; Becker (1976) 62 A.B.A.J. 1290, and in (1983) 11 Intn'l Bus. L. 239; Gitlin and Flaschen (1987) 42 Bus. Law. 307. Much of the prevailing uncertainty regarding the treatment of foreign representatives was attributable to the Supreme Court decision in *Disconto Gesellschaft v. Umbreit*, 208 U.S. 570 (1908), which held that each State of the Union was free to decide what cooperation, if any, to accord such representatives. See Boshkoff (1987) 36 I.C.L.Q. 729 at 730–732.

[46] See e.g. *Canada Southern Railway Co. v. Gebhard*, 109 U.S. 527 (1883); *Clarkson Co. v. Shaheen*, 544 F.2d. 624 (2nd. Cir. 1976); *Waxman v. Kealoha*, 296 F.Supp. 1190 (D. Hawaii 1969); *Israel-British Bank (London) Ltd. v. Federal Deposit Insurance Corp.*, 536 F.2d. 509 (2nd. Cir. 1976), cert. denied, 429 U.S. 978 (1976); *Banque de Financement, S.A. v. First National Bank of Boston*, 568 F.2d. 911 (2nd. Cir. 1977). The principal source of authority for the application of the doctrine of comity in relation to foreign insolvency proceedings was (and remains) *Hilton v. Guyot* 159 U.S. 113 (1895), a case in which the Supreme Court by a majority of 5 to 4 ultimately held that, for want of reciprocity, no comity existed between French and American courts for the purpose in hand. The many unclear or ambiguous features of this decision resulted in uncertainty and unevenness in later cases.

process of obtaining assistance from the American court that avoids the complications, and duplication of costs, that are the usual consequences of generating two, full-scale bankruptcies even if one is somehow cast in the role of a secondary proceeding.[47] If it should prove necessary to resort to full-scale bankruptcy proceedings under American law, this can be accomplished by using the specially designed provision in section 303(b)(4) which enables an involuntary case under Chapter 7 or 11 to be commenced against a person by the filing of a petition with the bankruptcy court by a foreign representative of the estate in a foreign proceeding concerning the person in question.[48] This could be a worthwhile tactic to employ if it is deemed essential to obtain the comprehensive protections of the automatic stay under section 362 of the Code.[49] However, judicial injunction to halt any action against the debtor or its property is one of the remedies that can be sought via an ancillary proceeding under section 304. To commence such a case, the foreign representative has merely to take the step of filing a petition with the bankruptcy court under section 304 itself.[50]

The court's powers exercisable under section 304

Section 304(b) specifies the range of powers which the court is permitted to exercise in a case ancillary to a foreign proceeding. These are:

(1) enjoin the commencement or continuation of—
  (A) any action against—
    (i) a debtor with respect to property involved in such foreign proceeding; or
    (ii) such property; or
  (B) the enforcement of any judgment against the debtor with respect to such property, or any act or the commencement or continuation of any judicial proceeding to create or enforce a lien against the property of such estate;
(2) order turnover of the property of such estate, or the proceeds of such property, to such foreign representative; or

47 There is an unfortunate terminological confusion over the use of the term 'ancillary' in differing senses under the insolvency law systems of different countries. The expression 'ancillary proceeding' as used in the context of American law has a very different connotation from that which it would bear under the law of the United Kingdom (where it has come to be used as a virtual synonym for 'secondary' proceedings that are linked to a principal liquidation or bankruptcy taking place in another jurisdiction. See Chapters 2 and 3 above, at 2.8 and 3.9 respectively).

48 A further option is for the foreign representative to commence a voluntary proceeding under Chapter 7 or Chapter 11 pursuant to 11 U.S.C. s.301.

49 11 U.S.C. s.362(a) does not mention s.304 among the proceedings to which the automatic stay 'applicable to all entities' operates as a consequence of the filing of a petition under any of the specified sections. The sections mentioned are ss.301, 302 and 303, so the omission of s.304 can scarcely have been accidental.

50 11 U.S.C. s.304(a).

(3) order other appropriate relief.

The particularised powers conferred by paragraphs (1) and (2) are extensive in themselves, and it is to be observed that the further authorisation in paragraph (3) amounts to a wide discretion allowing the court to draw upon its full repertoire of powers to attain whatever objective it considers to be 'appropriate' under the circumstances. However, the opening words of subsection (b) are also important. These indicate that the powers conferred are exercisable subject to the provisions of subsection (c) (discussed next below), and they further state that the court's authorisation to exercise its powers is subject to the proviso that 'a party in interest does not timely controvert the petition, or after trial'. There are thus opportunities for challenge to be mounted from various possible quarters, aimed at dissuading the court from granting the cooperation sought by the foreign representative. These may range from a fundamental questioning of the latter's standing as 'foreign representative' in the eyes of American law,[51] or of the conformity of the foreign proceeding with the definition in section 101(23),[52] to arguments as to the merits of the foreign representative's claim to particular assets. It is also possible that one or more of the criteria listed in subsection (c) may be invoked in an attempt to persuade the court to withold its cooperation by reason of the consequences that will or may ensue.

Factors influencing the court's discretion: section 304(c)

In exercising its widely-drawn powers under section 304(b) the court is required to observe the guidelines listed in subsection (c). These attempt to give legislative force to a number of factors which have received the endorsement of American courts at various times when addressing questions of international cooperation in bankruptcy matters.[53]

[51] 11 U.S.C. s.101(24) defines 'foreign representative' as 'a duly selected trustee, administrator, or other representative of an estate in a foreign proceeding'.

[52] Section 101(23) states: ' "foreign proceeding" means proceeding, whether judicial or administrative and whether or not under bankruptcy law, in a foreign country in which the debtor's domicile, residence, principal place of business, or principal assets were located at the commencment of such proceeding, for the purpose of liquidating an estate, adjusting debts by composition, extension or discharge, or effecting a reorganisation'. Cf. *Re Goerg*, 844 F.2d. 1562 (11th Cir. 1988), cert. denied, 109 S. Ct. 850 (1989) (German proceedings to administer the estate of a deceased insolvent treated as a 'foreign proceeding' for s.304 purposes, although under American domestic law such proceedings cannot be the subject of bankruptcy proceedings because a decedent's estate is not 'a person'); *Re Taylor*, 176 B.R. 903, 26 Bankr. Ct. Dec. (CRR) 716 (Bankr. S.D. Cal. 1995) (Receivership of an Australian company held 'clearly within the definition of "foreign proceeding" ' in s.101(23)). The latter case goes a considerable way towards answering earlier doubts whether an administrative receivership under English insolvency law would be accepted as meeting the definition of 'foreign proceeding', although it is capable of being used to effect a reorganisation. See Boshkoff (1987) 36 I.C.L.Q. 729 at 742 (citing, but dissenting from, Collier *Bankruptcy Practice Guide* (1986), vol. 2, para. 19.04[1]).

[53] See *Re Culmer*, 25 Bankr. 621, 629 (Bankr. S.D.N.Y. 1982).

The provisions of section 304(c) are as follows:

(c) In determining whether to grant relief under subsection (b) of this section, the court shall be guided by what will best assure an economical and expeditious administration of such estate, consistent with:

(1) just treatment of all holders of claims against or interests in such estate;
(2) protection of claim holders in the United States against prejudice and inconvenience in the processing of claims in such foreign proceeding;
(3) prevention of preferential or fraudulent dispositions of property of such estate;
(4) distribution of proceeds of such estate substantially in accordance with the order prescribed by this title;
(5) comity; and
(6) if appropriate, the provision of an opportunity for a fresh start for the individual that such foreign proceeding concerns.

As aspirational guidelines to the exercise of judicial discretion in the area of international insolvency the directives contained in subsection (c) are, both individually and collectively, almost entirely commendable.[54] Inevitably, with so extensive a catalogue of precepts, the complaint may be advanced that the task of the court is rendered excessively intricate, as it contrives to test any proposed form of assistance against all the criteria mentioned within the six paragraphs, together with the introductory rubric. Moreover, it may be observed that the court is furnished with no assistance in the event of a need to prioritise as between different factors, to the extent that it may not prove possible to fulfil all the criteria simultaneously in the context of a given case. The drafting of the subsection also gives rise to some difficulty in this respect, because the use of the single linking word 'and' after the penultimate paragraph (5), may be interpreted as imposing a requirement in every instance that all the first five criteria must be fully met (and also the sixth criterion, where this is 'appropriate'). Such a task may well prove impossible to accomplish under the circumstances of some cases, and in the light of the current diversity between the various national insolvency laws. Ultimately, the successful application of the ambitious terms of section 304 as a whole is dependent upon the good sense of the court in charting a path that amounts to a reasonable and defensible exercise of discretion under conditions so infinitely variable as to defy the possibility of comprehensive legislative prescription.

[54] Some reservation must be voiced regarding para. (2), in that it may lend itself to an over-indulgent attention towards the interests and convenience of American claim-holders and in this way operate in contradiction to the principle proclaimed in para. (1). Likewise, the requirements of para.(4) may give rise to tensions, due to differences between American and foreign systems of distribution, that may disturb the process of cooperation and detract from the principle of universality. See *Re Toga Manufacturing Co.*, 28 B.R. 165 (Bankr. E.D. Mich. 1983); *Re Lineas Areas de Nicaragua*, 10 B.R. 709 (Bankr. S.D. Fla.1981).

The exercise of discretion under section 304

The universalist spirit which permeates section 304 is one to which, in most instances, bankruptcy courts in the USA have responded in a positive and constructive manner.[55] Admittedly, there is ample scope for judges to differ from one another in their subjective understanding of the meaning of such an abstract and imprecise concept as 'comity', or as to the appropriate degree of protection of American claim holders that is required by subsection (c)(2), or the margins of divergence between principles of distribution that are permitted under the test of 'substantial' similarity imported by subsection (c)(4). An early demonstration of judicial willingness to meet the challenge of accepting on their own terms the myriad variations to be encountered under the laws of other countries, even when possessing a common legal heritage within the Anglo-American tradition, was provided in *Re Culmer*,[56] where the court granted injunctions at the request of the liquidators of a banking company being wound up in the Bahamas, to restrain American creditors from perfecting any liens over local assets of the bank, or engaging in any forms of attachment. For good measure, and despite the vigorous protests of the American creditors, the court exercised its power under section 304(b)(2) to order turnover to the liquidators of the bank's local assets, to be administered in the Bahamas in accordance with the principles of distribution of Bahamian law. Although those principles differed from the United States Bankruptcy Code in a number of respects, the divergence was not such as to disturb the conclusion that there was 'substantial similarity' between the two systems. On the basis of comity, the court concluded that foreign-based rights should be enforced unless to do so 'would be the approval of a transaction which is inherently vicious, wicked or immoral, and shocking to the prevailing moral sense'.[57] Essentially, this approach has been maintained in subsequent cases, with each foreign system—and each type of foreign proceeding—having to be appraised in order to establish whether it meets

[55] For assessments of the results achieved under s.304, see Given and Vilaplana (1983) Arizona State L.J. 325; Morales and Deutcsh (1984) 39 Bus. Law. 1573; Becker (1981) 29 A.J.C.L. 706; Nielsen (1984) 22 Col. J. Transnatn'l L. 541; Honsberger (1980) 30 Case Western Res. L. Rev. 631 at 655 *et seq.*; Unger (1985) 19 Int. L. 1153; Wolff (1983) 100 Banking L.J. 4; Boshkoff (1987) 36 I.C.L.Q. 729; Gitlin and Flaschen 42 Bus. Law 307 (1987). See also the annual assessments of case law in *Annual Survey of Bankruptcy Law* (Editor-in-Chief, W.L. Norton Jr.).

[56] 25 B.R. 624 (Bankr. S.D.N.Y. 1982).

[57] *Ibid.*, at 629. For a similar appraisal of the compatibility of Bahamian liquidations with American standards, see *Re Hackett*, 184 B.R. 656, 27 Bankr. Ct. Dec. (CRR) 631 (Bankr. S.D.N.Y. 1995). See also *Cunard Steamship Co. v. Salen Reefer Services AB*, 773 F.2d. 452 (2nd Cir. 1985); *Cornfield v. Investors Overseas Services Ltd.*, 471 F. Supp. 1255 (S.D.N.Y. 1979), aff'd 614 F.2d. 1286 (2nd Cir. 1979); *Re Axona International Credit and Commerce Ltd.*, 88 B.R. 597 (Bankr. S.D.N.Y. 1988).

American notions of justice, and provides 'a reasonable degree of certainty that the consideration of all parties' rights will be fair and impartial'.[58]

One matter which is of major importance to any foreign representative wishing to launch an ancillary proceeding under section 304 is that of venue. If the assets and interests of the debtor are located in several American judicial districts, the operation could be rendered more costly and complex if it were necessary to file multiple applications, treating each district as a separate entity. In *Evans v. Hancock, Rothert & Bunshoft (In re Evans)*[59] the Bankruptcy Court of the Southern District of New York held that to oblige a foreign representative to file separate ancillary proceedings in each district where property is located, or where an injunction is sought, would defeat the objective of section 304 of the Bankruptcy Code to facilitate the economical and expeditious administration of the estate, and would result in a 'procedural nightmare'. The court concluded that it is sufficient for the foreign representative to commence ancillary proceedings in the district where the debtor's principal place of business or principal assets are located, and that turnover and injunctive orders may thereafter be sought from the court of that district, regardless of the location of the assets in question. The good sense of granting such nationwide injunctions, to avoid piecemeal litigation over the foreign debtor's assets dispersed across the USA, is readily apparent. In granting such relief, the court is likely to require verification that all parties in interest in any pending actions anywhere within the USA have received adequate notice of the proceedings.[60]

4.2.1 Jurisdictional immunity of the foreign representative

One of the most troublesome aspects of international insolvency is the ever-present risk that a liquidator or trustee, in attempting to conduct his mission to collect and administer the assets in foreign jurisdictions, will suffer a double penalty in that, not only may the foreign court decline to provide cooperation, but it may treat any application or appearance by the foreign representative, even if unsuccessful, as amounting to submission

[58] *Re Hourani*, 180 B.R. 58 at 64 (Bankr. S.D.N.Y. 1995) (concluding that Jordanian liquidation proceedings did not meet American standards for the purposes of s.304); *Re Tam*, 170 B.R. 838, 25 Bankr. Ct. Dec. (CRR) 1635 (Bankr. S.D.N.Y. 1994) (holding that voluntary liquidation of a Cayman Islands corporation did not qualify as a 'foreign proceeding' under s.304); *Re Kojima*, 177 B.R. 696, 26 Bankr. Ct. Dec. (CRR) 881 (Bankr. D. Colo. 1995) (holding that Japanese bankruptcy law comports with American standards of fairness); *Re Brierly*, 145 B.R. 151, 23 Bankr. Ct. Dec. (CRR) 429 (Bankr. S.D.N.Y. 1992) (holding that UK administration order proceedings are substantially similar to American insolvency proceedings and are not repugnant to the public policy of the USA).

[59] 177 B.R. 193, 26 Bankr. Ct. Dec. (CRR) 637 (Bankr. S.D.N.Y. 1995).

[60] *Re Kingscroft Insurance Co. Ltd.*, 150 B.R. 77 (Bankr. S.D. Fla. 1992) (see also the earlier stage of this case, reported at 138 B.R. 121).

to the jurisdiction in a more general sense. As observed at the beginning of this chapter, this leads to the possibility that other proceedings may then be commenced by parties having claims against the insolvent estate, seeking to recover judgment against the foreign representative.[61] The foreign representative may conclude that the perils occasioned by this procedural 'pole-trap' are such as to outweigh the potential benefit to creditors of pursuing assets in a particular jurisdiction.[62] However, the dilemma of the foreign representative may be intensified by local creditors resorting to the tactic of filing an involuntary case against the debtor in the USA. This enables them to prepare an ambush for the foreign representative if he appears in order to oppose such a proceeding, while at the same time they threaten to wage international 'warfare' through the maintenance of a rival bankruptcy proceeding if he elects not to register a challenge. This unpleasant contingency is anticipated and overcome by section 306 of the Code, which allows the representative to undertake certain types of proceeding in the USA on a 'limited appearance' basis, thereby preserving his jurisdictional immunity for any purposes falling outside the scope of the proceeding in question. The protection of section 306 applies to an appearance in a bankruptcy court by a foreign representative in connection with a petition or request under section 303, 304 or 305 of the Code. It is expressly stated that such an appearance does not submit the foreign representative to the jurisdiction of any court in the USA for any other purpose. A proviso is appended to the effect that the bankruptcy court may condition any order under section 303, 304 or 305 on the foreign representative's compliance with the orders of the bankruptcy court itself.

The protective mantle of section 306 makes a vital contribution to the effective delivery of cross-border cooperation. Without the reassurance conveyed by this statutory provision, the undoubted merits of the assistance on offer under section 304 would in many cases be of purely theoretical value. It is noteworthy that the Canadian legislative reforms of 1997 governing international insolvencies include a provision, clearly inspired by section 306, which confers jurisdictional immunity on a foreign representative for any purpose falling outside the application for assistance under that Part of the Canadian legislation.[63] It is submitted that these examples are worthy of emulation in other jurisdictions, including the United Kingdom.

[61] See *supra* n.2 for an example of the impact of such possibilities upon the conduct of the American stage of proceedings in the *Herstatt* case.

[62] For notorious examples of such procedural entrapment, not involving bankruptcy proceedings, see *Harris v. Taylor* [1915] 2 K.B. 580 (CA); *Henry v. Geoprosco International* [1976] Q.B. 726 (CA). These decisions were subsequently reversed by the Civil Jurisdiction and Judgments Act 1982, s.33.

[63] Bankruptcy and Insolvency Act, Part XIII (amendment made April 1997) (SC 1997, c.12), s.272. See at 4.4 below.

4.2.2 Jurisdictional abstention

Section 305(a) of the Bankruptcy Code contains authorisation for the bankruptcy court to dismiss a case under Title 11 United States Code, or to suspend all proceedings in a case, at any time. The conditions under which the court enjoys a discretion to exercise such powers of abstention are stated in subsection (a) in the following terms:

> if—(1) the interests of creditors and the debtor would be better served by such dismissal or suspension;
>
> (2) (A) there is pending a foreign proceeding; and (B) the factors specified in section 304(c) of this title warrant such dismissal or suspension.

Various possible scenarios can arise under which section 305 may be invoked. Thus, local creditors who are of the opinion that the foreign proceedings do not constitute a justifiable basis for cooperation by the American court may urge dismissal of a section 304 case by using section 305(a)(2)(B) to call the court's attention to any alleged incompatibility between the granting of assistance and the criteria listed in section 304(c).[64] Alternatively, a foreign representative may seek the dismissal of an involuntary case initiated by local creditors seeking to have the debtor's American assets administered according to the principles of American bankruptcy law.[65] Section 305(b) expressly provides that a foreign representative may seek dismissal or suspension under section 305(a)(2), and in such circumstances it would appear to be incumbent upon the foreign representative to make out a positive case, based on the criteria in section 304(c), to show why the American bankruptcy case should be dismissed in favour of giving assistance under section 304 itself.

Finally, it may be noted that section 305(c) declares that an order under subsection (a) dismissing a case or suspending all proceedings in a case, or a decision declining to do either of these things, is not reviewable ... appeal or otherwise by the court of appeals under sections 158(d), 12... 1292 of Title 28 of the United States Code, or by the Supreme Cou... section 1254 of Title 28. This places a very high level of responsi... the trial court when exercising its powers under section 30... time, the bar on appellate review ensures that it is not o... parties who happen to have deep pockets to resort ... whose ulterior purpose is to exhaust the resour... through the launching of successive rounds of a...

[64] See p. 205 above.

[65] *Re Gee* 53 B.R. 891 (Bankr. S.D.N.Y. 1985). Se... *Commerce Ltd.*, 88 B.R. 597 (Bankr. S.D.N.Y. 1988... Bankr. Ct. Dec. (CRR) 1611 (Bankr. S.D. Fla. 1993)... B.R. 9 (S.D.N.Y. 1992).

order or decision. The provision in section 305 applies in the case of a decision by the bankruptcy court to abstain from an entire case brought under Title 11 of the Code. Where the court pursues a more restricted course of abstaining from a particular proceeding within the case, the relevant power is that contained in Title 28, section 1334(c)(1).

4.2.3. Concluding observations

As stated above, section 304 in conjunction with sections 305 and 306 amount to a breakthrough in terms of empowering national courts to give international assistance in a spirit that is positively inclined towards the furtherance of the principle of universality. Although widely and publicly admired since their introduction, these provisions have only slowly begun to attract the sincerest, and more concrete, form of flattery on the part of national legislatures.[66] It must be suspected that among the reasons for the apparent reluctance among other sovereign countries to join this new trend towards open embodiment of principles of cross-border assistance in their enacted laws is an apprehension on the part of those with knowledge and influence in such matters that the relaxation of barriers to entry by foreign representatives is not likely to be matched, for the foreseeable future, by comparable generosity in terms of the letter of the law, or the spirit of its application, on the part of many of the other foreign systems (America apart) from which such representatives may come. Fears that the actuality of international cooperation will prove to be one-sided, or at least uneven, furnish a powerful incentive to maintain the status quo until such time as it becomes clear that conditions elsewhere have also changed, or are in the process of changing, in a genuinely substantial way. Hence, it may be suspected that the surest method by which to accelerate the much-needed revolution in international insolvency practice is by way of initiatives taken at international level among a significant number of States, as will be discussed in Part II of this book.

One final matter to be noted is that there are no provisions within sections 304, 305 or 306 to give guidance on any questions of choice of law which may have to be considered by American courts when exercising their powers under any of those sections. It has therefore been left to the courts themselves to draw upon established and familiar principles when performing their functions under these provisions of the Code.[67]

6 See the Canadian reforms introduced in 1997, discussed at 4.4 below.

See Trautman (1988) 29 Harv. Int'l L.J. 49; Nadelmann (1988) 29 Harv. Int'l L.J. 27; man, Westbrook and Gaillard (1993) 41 A.J.C.L. 573 at 609–622; Westbrook (1991) 65 cy.L.J. 457; Westbrook (1991) 17 Brooklyn Jnl. Intnl. L. 499.

4.3 INTERNATIONAL JUDICIAL ASSISTANCE UNDER AUSTRALIAN INSOLVENCY LAW

Australian law draws upon its English common law heritage in enabling its judges to give appropriate assistance to foreign representatives holding appointment under proceedings recognised in Australia according to the principles already reviewed in Chapters 2 and 3 above. The principles of cooperation originating from the case law have been given statutory embodiment, first under section 29 of the Bankruptcy Act 1966 and more recently by matching amendments introduced into the Corporations Law in 1992 as sections 580 and 581.[68] The distinctive feature of the statutory regime for assistance is that it has a two-tiered structure, whereby the courts are subject to a mandatory duty to give assistance to sister courts in a prescribed group of countries, while any request for assistance from a court in any other country may be dealt with on a discretionary basis.

Mandatory assistance to courts of prescribed countries

Section 29(2)(a) of the Bankruptcy Act (to which the corresponding provision, in the case of companies, is section 581(2)(a) of the Corporations Law) declares that in all matters of bankruptcy, the court in Australia:

(a) shall act in aid of and be auxiliary to the courts of the external Territories, and of prescribed countries, that have jurisdiction in bankruptcy;[69]

The mandatory obligation to assist a foreign court which is within the ambit of section 29(2)(a) is imported by the word 'shall' in that part of the subsection. Section 29(5) defines 'prescribed country' in this context as meaning: (a) the United Kingdom, Canada and New Zealand; (b) a country prescribed for the purposes of this subsection (i.e. subsection (5)); and (c) a colony, overseas territory or protectorate of a country specified in paragraph (a) or of a country so prescribed. The list of prescribed countries, for the purposes of the provision in section 29(5)(b), is contained in Schedule 5 to the Act, and currently comprises: Jersey, Malaysia, Papua New Guinea, Singapore, Switzerland, and the United States of America.[70]

[68] Bankruptcy Act 1966, s.29, and Corporations Law (Cth), ss.580, 581, are reproduced in Appendix I below.

[69] The wording of the Corporations Law, s.581(2)(a) uses modified terminology, but otherwise embodies the same substantive requirement to give assistance: '(2) In all external administration matters, the court: (a) shall act in aid of, and be auxiliary to, the courts of the excluded Territories, and of prescribed countries, that have jurisdiction in external administration matters'.

[70] The same countries as those which qualify as prescribed countries under the Bankruptcy Act, s.29 are also 'prescribed countries' for the purposes of the Corporations Law, s.581.

Discretionary assistance to courts of other countries

Section 29(2)(b) of the Bankruptcy Act (and in the case of companies, section 581(2)(b) of the Corporations Law) confers a discretion upon the Australian courts to act in aid of and be auxiliary to the courts of other countries that have jurisdiction in bankruptcy, or in company insolvency matters, as the case may be. The scope for exercise of this discretionary power of assistance is not restricted in terms of the countries from which requests for assistance may be entertained. This is in contrast to the position under section 426 of the Insolvency Act of the United Kingdom,[71] which is restrictively designed so that only the courts of such countries as are expressly designated for the purposes of section 426 can obtain any assistance under that section from the courts of any part of the United Kingdom. The Australian approach is a more accommodating one, at least at the outset, and it is left to the court to exercise its judgment as to the appropriateness of the giving of any assistance, and if so in what form to do so, consistently with the terms of section 29(3) or 581(3), as the case may be. No guidelines are prescribed for the Australian court to follow, but it is open to the court to have regard both to the nature and substance of the insolvency law system of the particular foreign country from which the request has emanated, and to the circumstances in which the instant proceedings have come about (including any question as to the grounds on which jurisdiction was exercised by the other court).

The nature of the assistance available

The scope of the Australian court to give aid to sister courts in foreign countries is prescribed by section 29(3) of the Bankruptcy Act and (in terms which are again identical as to substance) section 581(3) of the Corporations Law. These provisions both state that where a letter of request is filed in the court by a court of a country outside Australia, requesting aid in a matter of bankruptcy or company insolvency, the Australian court may exercise such powers with respect to the matter as it could exercise if the matter had arisen within its own jurisdiction. Thus, in contrast this time to the more liberal scope of the jurisdiction conferred on the courts of the United Kingdom under section 426 of the Insolvency Act 1986,[72] Australian courts can only provide aid to foreign courts to the extent that they could do so in a domestic case of analogous facts. However, this can still provide ample opportunity for judicial creativity to be exercised in the furtherance of the most rational and efficient administration of an insolvent estate. For example, if the court concludes that an Australian winding up or bankruptcy would be unnecessary, and would

[71] See at 4.1 above. [72] See at 4.1 above.

merely result in duplication of costs, it may decline to make an order for a parallel procedure to be commenced in Australia, thereby leaving the foreign office holder in sole charge of the case.[73] It has also been held that the statutory directive in section 29(2)(a) of the Bankruptcy Act imposing a mandatory obligation to give aid to foreign courts of the prescribed countries is sufficiently cogent as to override the force of the traditional rule of public policy that precludes the direct or indirect enforcement of tax obligations owed to the authorities of foreign states.[74]

4.4 INTERNATIONAL JUDICIAL ASSISTANCE IN CANADA UNDER PART XIII OF THE BANKRUPTCY AND INSOLVENCY ACT

In recent times Canadian courts have been in the forefront of developments aimed at enhancing the climate of international understanding and cooperation in insolvency matters. In several instances, successful resolutions have been reached in major cross-border cases through an activist judicial approach, drawing upon discretionary common law and statutory powers, in the interests of preserving the maximum possible value for creditors' benefit.[75] These initiatives have been consolidated through the enactment in 1997 of Part XIII of the Bankruptcy and Insolvency Act, comprising sections 267 to 275 inclusive, which confer a range of discretionary powers and provisions applicable to international insolvencies.[76]

Scope of Part XIII: meaning of 'debtor', etc.

Section 267 contains definitions of three key terms for the purposes of Part XIII. The definition of 'debtor' is of special importance. It means:

> an insolvent person who has property in Canada, a bankrupt who has property in Canada or a person who has the status of a bankrupt under foreign law in a foreign proceeding and has property in Canada.

Thus, the need for there to be property in Canada is made a precondition for the purposes of Part XIII and its provisions. This concept of an

[73] Cf. *Re New England Brewing Co. Ltd.* [1970] Q.W.N. 49.

[74] *Re Ayres* (1981) 51 F.L.R. 395; 34 A.L.R. 582, aff'd by the full bench of the Federal Court *sub nom. Ayres v. Evans* (1981) 56 F.L.R. 235; 39 A.L.R. 129. (It seems probable that the same position would now be adopted in cases involving company insolvency, in the light of the enactment of the Corporations Law, s.581(2)(a), in terms essentially identical to those of the Bankruptcy Act s.29(2)(a)). For the traditional treatment of tax bankruptcies, see at 2.6 above at p. 97.

[75] See Leonard (1997) 6 I.I.R. 127, esp. at 131–134; Hon. Mr. Justice Farley in (1997) 6 I.I.R. 139–144, 237–241.

[76] The amendments were made by SC 1997, c.12, in force for cases commenced after 30 September 1997. Part XIII is reproduced in Appendix I below.

assets-based approach is carried through into the definitions of 'foreign proceeding' and 'foreign representative', each of which interlock with the concept of 'debtor'. Significantly however no restrictions are imposed in terms of the countries from outside Canada to which the provisions of Part XIII are in principle applicable. No foreign countries are mentioned by name as enjoying any specially advantaged position in the eyes of Canadian law in this respect, and correspondingly no countries are excluded by name or by implication from the scope of these provisions.

With regard to the types of proceedings, and the types of foreign representative, which come within the ambit of Part XIII, the definitions in section 267 indicate that it is court-based proceedings of a collective nature that are to enjoy the advantages available under the succeeding sections: 'foreign proceeding' means 'a judicial or administrative proceeding commenced outside Canada in respect of a debtor, under a law relating to bankruptcy or insolvency and dealing with the collective interests of creditors generally'. The expression 'foreign representative' is defined as meaning: 'a person, other than a debtor, holding office under the law of a jurisdiction outside Canada who, irrespective of the person's designation, is assigned, under the laws of the jurisdiction outside Canada, functions in connection with a foreign proceeding that are similar to those performed by a trustee, liquidator, administrator or receiver appointed by the court'. The deliberate exclusion of the debtor from the range of persons who may be a foreign representative means that foreign proceedings which utilise the 'debtor in possession' concept—as in the case of Chapter 11 proceedings under the United States Bankruptcy Code—do not come within the ambit of Part XIII. However, if a case of this kind arises in which there are Canadian assets, and it is desirable to obtain assistance from the Canadian courts, it may be possible to superimpose a court-appointed office holder, such as an examiner, for this purpose.[77] The reference to 'collective interests of creditors generally' in the definition of 'foreign proceeding', together with the emphasis on 'receiver appointed by the court' in the list of analogous office holders recognised as eligible to be regarded as a 'foreign representative', together make it impossible for an administrative receiver appointed out of court by the holder of a floating charge, and similar kinds of receiver and manager, to be regarded as a foreign representative under these legislative provisions.[78]

[77] The appointment of an examiner was resorted to in the Anglo-American case of *Re Maxwell Communication Corporation plc*. See the trial stage of the American proceedings concerned with the English administrators' attempt to attack certain transactions under American law as voidable preferences, reported at 170 B.R. 800, 801–807 (Bankr. S.D.N.Y. 1994) (Judge Brozman).

[78] See also at 3.10 above.

Nature of the assistance available

Section 268(1) contains the helpful provision that allows the fact of making an insolvency order in respect of a debtor in a foreign proceeding to constitute *prima facie* proof of the debtor's insolvency for the purposes of proceedings in Canada. The production of a certified copy of the foreign order not only serves as proof of insolvency (which it is then incumbent on any opposing party to disprove by suitable evidence), but also constitutes proof of the appointment of the foreign representative himself. It is also provided that a foreign representative is not prevented from making application to the Canadian court by reason only that proceedings by way of appeal or review have been taken in the foreign proceeding.[79] This ensures that the taking of timely and effective action in respect of Canadian assets or interests of the debtor cannot be impeded by the expedient of an appellate proceeding in the foreign country in question. Even more important is the express provision of section 272 proclaiming that an application to the Canadian court by a foreign representative under Part XIII does not submit the applicant to the jurisdiction of the court for any other purpose except with regard to the costs of the proceedings.[80] Thus the jurisdictional immunity of the foreign representative need not be compromised through the very act of seeking assistance from the Canadian court.

Section 268(3) specifies the powers the court may exercise in respect of a debtor. A broad discretion is conferred whereby the court may make such orders and grant such relief as it considers appropriate to facilitate, approve or implement arrangements that will result in a coordination of proceedings under the Canadian Act with any foreign proceedings.[81] Section 270 enables the foreign representative to commence and continue proceedings under Canadian insolvency legislation in respect of the debtor as if the foreign representative were a creditor, trustee, liquidator or receiver of property of the debtor, or even as if he were the debtor himself. This is important in itself, but has added significance in view of the provision in section 269 to the effect that a stay of proceedings that operates against creditors of the debtor in a foreign proceeding does not apply in respect of creditors who reside or carry on business in Canada with respect to property in Canada unless the stay of proceedings is the result

[79] Bankruptcy and Insolvency Act, s.273.

[80] Cf. the almost identically worded provision of s.306 of the U.S. Bankruptcy Code, noted at 4.2 above. Both provisions include a proviso allowing the court to make any order arising from the application conditional on the compliance by the foreign representative with any other order of the court.

[81] See also Bankruptcy and Insolvency Act, s.268(4) enabling the court at its discretion to attach terms and conditions to any order it may make.

of proceedings taken in that jurisdiction.[82] Further powers are conferred on the court under section 271(3), whereby on an application by a foreign representative the court may, where it is satisfied that it is necessary for the protection of the debtor's estate or the interests of one or more creditors, take appropriate measures to conserve property, including appointing an interim receiver of Canadian property of the debtor, or conversely to dispose of property that is perishable or likely to depreciate rapidly in value.

Lest it might be supposed that the new statutory provisions in Part XIII are intended to replace pre-existing rules based on case decisions, section 268(5) states that the court remains free to apply, on the application of the foreign representative or any other interested person, such legal or equitable rules governing the recognition of foreign insolvency orders and assistance to foreign representatives as are not inconsistent with the provisions of the Act.[83] Canadian courts are also expressly empowered by section 271 to seek aid and assistance of a court, tribunal or other authority in a foreign proceeding by order or written request or otherwise as the court considers appropriate. The concluding phrase of this provision gives statutory authorisation to the evolving practice, of which Canadian courts have been in the vanguard, whereby judges may utilise modern telecommunications facilities to establish direct contact with their counterparts in other jurisdictions concerned in a case, in order to achieve the most expeditious resolution of any matters as and when they arise, and to secure the most fruitful outcome overall.[84] Notably, the Canadian legislation refrains from introducing any new form of proceeding that is to be employed for the purpose of obtaining assistance from the Canadian courts. Instead, access is granted to the foreign representative to make use of the existing range of proceedings under Canadian insolvency law, while the court is empowered to use its wide discretionary powers to fashion its assistance in a way that will best serve the needs arising within the particular case. The onus is thus cast upon the judges to exercise these powers with skill and imagination, within the prevailing spirit of international cooperation which has self-evidently fuelled the legislative approach to the enactment of Part XIII.

[82] See also *ibid.*, s.271(2) with respect to grant of stay of proceedings in Canada pending the conclusion of foreign proceedings for effecting a composition, an extension of time or a scheme of arrangement, or in respect of the bankruptcy of the debtor.

[83] Note also the safeguard provision in *ibid.*, s.268(6) to the effect that the court is not required by anything in Part XIII to make any order that is not in compliance with the laws of Canada or to enforce any order made by a foreign court.

[84] See remarks of Farley J. at a judicial colloquium in New Orleans in March 1997, reproduced in (1997) 6 I.I.R. 237 at 238–241.

Distributional fairness: the hotchpot rule

In enacting Part XIII of the Bankruptcy and Insolvency Act the Canadian Legislature took the opportunity to give statutory form to the so-called 'hotchpot rule' that has long been an important doctrine within common law systems which have taken their inspiration from English law. Indeed, the doctrine enjoys a wide acceptance in the field of international insolvency, and is recognised within the civil law tradition as well.[85] Section 274 of the Canadian statute provides:

Where any receiving order, proposal or assignment is made in respect of a debtor under this Act,

(a) the amount that a creditor receives or is entitled to receive outside Canada by way of a dividend in a foreign proceeding in respect of the debtor, and
(b) the value of any property of the debtor that the creditor acquires outside Canada on account of a provable claim of the creditor or that the creditor acquires outside Canada by way of a transfer that, if it were subject to this Act, would be set aside or reviewed under sections 91 to 101.2,

shall be taken into acccount in the distribution of dividends to creditors of the debtor in Canada as if they were part of that distribution, and the creditor is not entitled to receive a dividend from the distribution in Canada until every other creditor who has a claim of equal rank in the order of priority established under this Act has received a dividend, the amount of which is the same percentage of that other creditor's claim as the aggregate of the amount referred to in paragraph (a) and the value referred to in paragraph (b) is of that creditor's claim.

Although the above provision is necessarily complex in its drafting, it is submitted that it succeeds in establishing the basis for application of this important principle of international insolvency law as an obligatory part of the process of distribution of an estate in a multi-jurisdictional context. As such, it deserves to receive serious consideration as a model for inclusion in the legislation of other countries.[86]

[85] See Hanisch in I.F. Fletcher (ed.), *Cross-Border Insolvency: Comparative Dimensions* (1990), ch. 11. See also at 2.4 and 3.5 above.

[86] Provisions embodying the hotchpot rule have been included in recent years in international conventions and model legislation applicable to international insolvency: see the (unenacted) European Union Convention on Insolvency Proceedings, Art. 20 (discussed in Chapter 6 below); the Council of Europe's Istanbul Convention of 5 June 1990, Art. 24 (discussed in Chapter 7 below; and the UNCITRAL Model Law on Cross-Border Insolvency, adopted in 1997, Art. 32 (discussed in Chapter 8 below).

Part II

INTERNATIONAL REGULATION OF INTERNATIONAL INSOLVENCY

5

Latin America and Scandinavia

PRELIMINARY

Historically, the first examples of international treaties which attempted in some way to make provision for the better regulation of cross-border insolvencies were bilateral treaties, concluded between States which were either close neighbours geographically, or which had particularly close relationships involving commerce and trade between their citizens. There were numerous examples of such treaties in the period between the eighteenth and the mid-twentieth century.[1] In the context of their period, they were able to offer useful solutions to the most basic, and still the most common, of the factual situations that can be experienced in cross-border insolvency, namely where the significant assets and liabilities are dispersed between only two jurisdictions. Such bilateral arrangements between States continue to have their practical value in the present day. With the great advances in international mobility, industrial mass production and distribution, and the globalisation of commercial and financial activities that have been an increasingly dominant characteristic of life since the middle of the nineteenth century, the inherent limitations of bilateral arrangements have become a growing source of frustration for those charged with the task of trying to effect the rescue of a financially distressed business, or to conduct a fair and efficient administration of an insolvent debtor's property for the benefit of creditors generally. The arguments in favour of a wider, multilateral arrangement concluded by international negotiation have long been, and remain, compelling; the practical and technical difficulties of achieving a satisfactory regulation on terms acceptable to all parties have been, and continue to be, daunting. To date, very few examples of such multilateral instruments have been successfully concluded and brought into force among the States which participated in the negotiations. In this Part, the handful of conventions and international arrangements that either have entered into effect, or which presently appear to have some prospect of doing so, will be examined.

Logically, the most promising basis on which to attempt to conclude a multilateral insolvency treaty is to enlist the participation of States which

[1] For an account of the treaties during this period in which some provision was made for bankruptcy matters, with source references, see K. Lipstein in I.F.Fletcher (ed.) *Cross-Border Insolvency: Comparative Dimensions (The Aberystwyth Insolvency Papers)* (1990), ch. 14.

have a strong common interest in the venture, coupled with a close affinity in as many relevant matters as possible, including legal and cultural traditions, social and economic value systems, and international outlook. Although many points of resemblance may be present between States which are geographically a great distance apart—as where a former colony, now possessing independent statehood, retains many of the traditions and institutions of the Mother country—the more coherent case for putting such arrangements into place is likely to arise among states which are regionally grouped in such a way that functional interaction takes place constantly, and at many levels. In this chapter we examine regional conventions concluded between groups of States possessing such characteristics to a particularly high degree. The results, nevertheless, will be seen to be less than uniformly successful.

5.1 THE MONTEVIDEO TREATIES OF 1889 AND 1940

South America appears to possess many of the characteristics referred to above as conducive to the development of regional treaties dealing with international insolvency. During the period of European colonisation, the dominant colonial power throughout most of the South American continent, and also in much of Central America and the Caribbean, was Spain. This factor resulted in a remarkable homogeneity in terms of the initial structure and content of the legal systems which evolved in the states of Latin America which gained independence during the nineteenth century. In the case of the most conspicuous exception to this general statement—namely Brazil, which was a colony of Portugal—the close historic affinities between the Spanish and Portuguese legal traditions (both ultimately traceable to roots in Roman law) yielded a broad similarity between the Brazilian legal system and those of its Spanish-speaking neighbours. Nevertheless, during the course of the nineteenth century the newly autonomous States took full advantage of their sovereign capabilities to develop their laws along individual lines, with the consequence that divergence and disharmony began to pose serious obstacles to intra-regional trade.

Given that there were minimal prospects of bringing about a unification of national substantive laws, the more realistic course was pursued of seeking to harmonise principles of private international law among the states of South America. Among the first of these initiatives was the Lima Treaty, concluded in 1856 between Peru, Chile and Ecuador and covering such topics as the recognition and enforcement of foreign judgments.[2] A

[2] See J. Irizarry y Puente (1943) 37 A.J.I.L.(Supplement) 111 *et seq.*

more ambitious attempt was pursued by the Peruvian government between 1875 and 1878, convening a Lima Congress in conjunction with seven other Latin American States for the purpose of establishing uniform rules for many aspects of private international law. Only Peru ratified the Lima Treaty of 9 November 1878, which therefore failed to enter into force. Although recognition and enforcement of judgments was included in Title VI, bankruptcy was not covered. It was only with the convening at Montevideo of the first South American Congress of Private International Law, during the years 1888–89, that the subject of bankruptcy came to be addressed on a regional basis. A total of eight conventions were concluded, of which the Treaty on International Commercial Law, dated 12 March 1889, deals with bankruptcy in a specific Title X, comprising Articles 35 to 48 inclusive.[3] This treaty was ratified by Argentina, Bolivia, Paraguay, Peru and Uruguay between 1889 and 1903; Colombia acceded to the treaty in 1933.

Second Montevideo Congress

A second South American Congress of Private International Law was convened at Montevideo between 1939 and 1940 for the purpose of revising and updating the treaties concluded in 1889. Among this second collection two, both dated March 19 1940, have relevance to matters of insolvency. The Treaty on International Commercial Terrestrial Law contains Title VIII, dealing with Bankruptcy (Articles 40 to 53 inclusive). These provisions build upon those of Title X of the 1889 Treaty, and are designed to replace them for those States which become ratifying parties.[4] In addition, the Treaty on International Procedural Law contains, in Title IV (Articles 16 to 25 inclusive) provisions concerning Civil Meetings of Creditors.[5] In combination, the provisions of 1940 deal with a wider range of issues and types of proceedings than the 1889 Treaty. Unfortunately, only Argentina, Paraguay and Uruguay became ratifying parties to the treaties produced by the Second Congress, with the consequence that cases involving any of those three States, singly or in combination, in conjunction with any of the three States which are parties only to the 1889 Treaty have to be governed by the earlier text. It will thus be appreciated that the results of this

[3] For the text see: E. Restelli (ed.), *Actas y Tratados del Congreso Sud-americano de Derecho Internacional Privado, Montevideo 1888–1889* (Buenos Aires, 1928); Clunet 1897, 895. An unofficial English translation of Title X of the 1889 Convention is printed in Appendix V(A) below.

[4] For the text see: *Segundo Congreso Sudamericano de Derecho Internacional Privado, Acta Final, Segunda Edicion* (Montevideo 1940) at 61–72; for English translation (by J. Irizarry y Puente and G.L. Williams), see 37 (1943) A.J.I.L. (Supplement) at 132–141. The translation of Title VIII is reproduced in Appendix V(B) below.

[5] For the text, see *Segundo Congreso Sudamerican, supra* n.4, at 41–48. For English translation (details as supplied in n.4), see (1943) 37 A.J.I.L. (Supplement), at 116–122. The translation of Title IV is reprinted in Appendix V(C), *post*, at pp. 445–6.

regional initiative have been somewhat limited, with just six States participating in the 1889 Treaty and only three in the more recent Treaty of 1940. Moreover, there is considerable potential for confusion due to the fact that three States are simultaneously subject to both treaties, so that the question of which text is applicable is determined by reference to the other States with which a given case happens to be connected.

5.1.1 Scope and effects: the 1889 Treaty

In a way that has since become typical of the conceptual dilemma confronting those who try to design insolvency treaties, the 1889 text aspires to establish a clear rule that will result in unity of proceedings, based in a jurisdiction that is readily and unambiguously identifiable. This is declared by Article 35 to be fixed by reference to the place of the debtor's commercial domicile, both for natural persons and for corporations. The court of that place is stated to retain jurisdiction even when the insolvent debtor occasionally carries out commercial activity in another State, or maintains agencies or branches there which operate on behalf of the principal establishment. However, Article 36 concedes that unity cannot be preserved when the debtor has two or more independent commercial establishments in different territories: the courts of each respective domicile are competent to entertain bankruptcy proceedings in respect of each one of them. Thereby, concurrent proceedings may take place under some circumstances. The lack of any formal definition of the concept of 'commercial domicile' in the 1889 Treaty (in contrast to the text of 1940)[6] provides further scope for divergent findings to be arrived at by the courts of different States.

Where a case falls within Article 36, giving rise to the possibility of plural proceedings, Article 37 declares that with the opening of bankruptcy in one State the protective measures prescribed in those proceedings shall also be enforceable in respect of the property of the bankrupt located in other States, but without prejudice to the rights accorded to the local creditors by the subsequent articles of Title X. These rights commence with the requirement in Article 38 to the effect that the court of the State in which such protective measures have been complied with by means of the appropriate letters rogatory must within sixty days order the publication of notices announcing both the adjudication of bankruptcy and the protective measures which have been prescribed. Local creditors are permitted, within the sixty-day period fixed by Article 38 (but counting from the day after publication of the notices), to petition for a fresh adjudication against the bankrupt in their country, or to bring a civil action

[6] Montevideo Treaty on International Commercial Terrestrial Law, 1940, Art. 3 (see below).

against him if a bankruptcy adjudication is unobtainable. In that event, completely separate bankruptcy proceedings will take place, each respectively conducted according to the law of the country where it has been opened.[7] The expression 'local creditors', in relation to a bankruptcy opened in a given State, is declared by Article 40 to include those whose claims ought to be discharged in that place. Hence, the creditor's nationality, domicile or place of residence is not necessarily determinative of who are to be treated as 'local' creditors for this purpose.

Although the 1889 Treaty contemplates that plural proceedings may take place entirely separately, each conducted according to the local law, Article 41 makes a belated attempt to introduce an element of unity by providing that any surplus remaining after completion of the process of distribution in one State shall, instead of being restored to the bankrupt, be at the disposition of the creditors in the other State or States. It is firmly stipulated, without any further guidance being provided, that the respective judges should reach agreement with that end in view. Where it transpires that there is only a single bankruptcy proceeding, either because the case falls within Article 35 or because the local creditors have not made use of the rights accorded to them under Article 39, a universal process of administration and distribution can take place. Article 42 decrees that all the creditors of the bankrupt shall present their claims and exercise their rights before the judge or tribunal which pronounced the adjudication of bankruptcy. Express provision is made by Article 43 to enable mortgagees and pledgees whose rights predate the opening of bankruptcy to exercise their rights before the courts of the country of the *situs* of the property to which their security is attached.

A special rule is provided by Article 44 to preserve the priority rights of any creditor in relation to specific property (such as a charge or lien), created in the country of the bankruptcy and acquired prior to the commencement of the proceeding. Even if the property is taken to another country where bankruptcy or civil proceedings are in progress concerning the same bankrupt, the creditor's special right of priority must be respected, provided that the transfer of the property took place during the so-called 'suspect period', within which any transactions or dispositions of property are void. This extraterritorial assertion of acquired rights of priority, even overriding any contrary conclusions to be derived from the law of the country into which property has been brought, is one of the few genuinely 'universal' principles contained in the Treaty. A similarly forthright declaration in Article 45 requires that the authority of the trustee in bankruptcy or other legal representative of the bankruptcy proceeding must be recognised in all the contracting States, provided that it is

[7] Montevideo Treaty on International Commercial Law, 1889, Art. 39.

recognised by the law of the country in whose territory the proceeding originates. Office holders must be allowed in all cases to exercise the functions entrusted to them under the law of that country and under the Treaty itself.

The final three articles in Title X of the 1889 Treaty provide, in the case of Article 46 that where plural bankruptcies take place it is the court within whose jurisdiction the bankrupt resides which is exclusively competent to determine what personal disqualifications and civil disabilities shall be imposed upon him, while Article 47 states that the debtor shall only gain an effective discharge from bankruptcy when this has been granted in all the proceedings in which he is involved. Finally, Article 48 states that the provisions in the Treaty which make reference to bankruptcy shall be applicable to limited companies, whatever may be the form of liquidation for which provision is made by the laws of the Contracting States in cases where they commit a suspension of payment.

5.1.2 Scope and effects: the 1940 Treaties

Although the Montevideo Treaties of 1940 were intended to revise and replace the earlier texts concluded in 1889, we have seen that this objective was only partially achieved due to the failure of a number of States parties to the earlier treaties to ratify those of 1940. It is therefore necessary to give a separate account of the effects of the treaties on International Commercial Terrestrial Law and on International Procedural Law, both dated 19 March 1940, which currently are only in force between Argentina, Paraguay and Uruguay. Certain points of divergence between the more recent treaties and the 1889 original will be noted in passing.

Title VIII of the Commercial Law Treaty, comprising Articles 40 to 53 inclusive, provides the main body of rules for cases of bankruptcy. These are reinforced by the provisions in Title IV of the Procedural Law Treaty, which deals with civil meetings of creditors. As in the case of the 1889 Treaty, that of 1940 confers jurisdiction to pronounce adjudication of bankruptcy upon the courts of the domicile of the merchant or commercial partnership involved (Article 40). This jurisdiction is not displaced in cases where the debtor may incidentally be engaged in acts of commerce within another State or States, or may have, in one or more of these, agencies or branches which operate on behalf of, and on the responsibility of, the principal establishment. Article 3 of the Treaty declares the commercial domicile to be the place where the principal seat of business of the merchant or commercial partnership is located. No special guidance is given as to the test to be applied for determining which is to count as the 'principal' seat, in a situation where business activities are dispersed between different States, nor does the Treaty contain any inbuilt device, such as a rule of presumption, to assist in carrying out this task. Article 3 does however include a proviso to the effect that if merchants or partnerships set up establishments, branches or agencies in other States, they shall be considered as domiciled in the place where they operate, and as subject to the jurisdiction of the local authorities, in respect of their transactions in that place. This provision is complemented by that of Article 42, which requires that an adjudication of bankruptcy, and other acts that are related to this, and whose publication is required by the law of the State in which bankruptcy has commenced, must also be publicly announced (in accordance with the formalities prescribed under the local law) in the States where the bankrupt has agencies, branches or establishments.

The concept of unity of bankruptcy proceedings is abandoned in cases where the bankrupt has two or more independent commercial establishments in different states. Article 41 supplies a rule whose substance corresponds to that of Article 36 of the 1889 Treaty, enabling the courts of each respective domicile to exercise bankruptcy jurisdiction. However, the 1940 Treaties provide a more detailed series of provisions relating to such plural bankruptcies.[8] There are broadly similar provisions in Articles 43 and 44 to those in Articles 37 and 38 of the 1889 Treaty (see above), whereby protective measures taken pursuant to the law of the state of bankruptcy are also made enforceable in respect of the bankrupt's property located in other States, such enforcement to be in conformity with the local law of the *situs*. Article 44 requires the judge to whom letters rogatory are addressed for the purpose of obtaining local enforcement of such protective measures to order publication during a thirty-day period of advertisements announcing both the adjudication of bankruptcy and the measures which have been prescribed.[9] Article 45 then allows local creditors[10] to institute new proceedings against the bankrupt in their respective States, within a period of sixty days following from the last publication of advertisement effected under the terms of Article 44. If a bankruptcy adjudication is not obtainable, other civil proceedings may be brought against the debtor notwithstanding his bankruptcy having been pronounced in one or more other States. The scenario to be envisaged is thus one of parallel, independent proceedings, each of which is conducted according to its own local law, with the open possibility that the proceedings in some

[8] 1940 Treaty on International Commercial Terrestrial Law, Arts. 45, 46; 1940 Treaty on International Procedural Law, Arts. 16–25.

[9] Cf. Art. 38 of the 1889 Treaty (above), which specifies a 60-day period for such advertisements. See also Art. 19 of the 1940 Procedural Law Treaty, which imposes additional requirements concerning the information to be included in the local advertisements, namely the insolvency hearing, the appointment of the receiver and his domicile, the time limit for submitting the evidence of claims, and the preventive measures which have been taken.

[10] Article 46 defines the expression 'local creditors' in terms whose substance is identical to those of Art. 40 of the 1889 Treaty, described above.

jurisdictions may not even be conducted under the local bankruptcy law. However, the provisions of Article 43 apply freshly to each instance of making an adjudication of bankruptcy, so that a further series of advertisements, and orders enforcing any protective measures, must take place in the other States in which property of the bankrupt is located. The duplication of such formalities, and the absence of any directions requiring coordination between the parallel proceedings during their active stages, seem with respect to be highly regrettable, and to belie the notion that a genuinely regional philosophy was operative in the framing of these provisions. Further incentive for local creditors to avail themselves of the right to bring about local proceedings is provided by Article 20 of the Procedural Law Treaty, which emphasises that in the case of such proceedings, just as in cases involving a single insolvency conducted at the place of the debtor's domicile, the local creditors shall have preferential rights in regard to property located in the territory where their claims should be met. Although the classification of 'local creditors' includes those whose claims are dischargeable in the jurisdiction in question,[11] the net effect of this provision is to institutionalise the 'ring-fencing' of assets for the benefit of creditors who can claim membership of this privileged category.

Even in cases where only one bankruptcy proceeding takes place, the proclamation of unity made by Article 48 is openly flawed by a discriminatory rule favouring local creditors. Despite the initially promising statement to the effect that 'all of the creditors of the bankrupt shall present their claims and exercise their rights in conformity with the law, and before the judge or tribunal, of the State which has pronounced the adjudication of bankruptcy', Article 48 concludes with the adamantly non-unitary assertion that: 'In such cases, the local claims existing in a particular State enjoy preference over those existing in other States, with respect to the sum total of the assets in the State where the former are located'. The reference to the exercise of rights in conformity with the local law thus becomes the basis for a perpetuation of the notorious tradition, under the laws of many Latin American States, of blatant discrimination against foreign creditors.[12] The elevation of the rights of local creditors is only curtailed in the case of mortgagees and pledgees whose security rights were constituted before the date of definitive stoppage of payment by the debtor, which marks the point after which transactions are deprived of

[11] See *supra* n.10.

[12] For an account of the treatment of foreign debts under the law of Argentina, see J.M. Dobson in I.F. Fletcher (ed.), *Cross-Border Insolvency: Comparative Dimensions (The Aberystwyth Insolvency Papers)* (1990), ch. 7, at pp. 124–131. For further discussion of the discriminatory policies encountered within the laws of various Latin American States, see K.H. Nadelmann (1944) 93 U. Pa. L. Rev. 58; (1946) 11 Law and Contemp. Prob. 696.

validity under the rules of bankruptcy law. Article 50 provides that such holders of properly and timely constituted security may exercise their rights before the judges of the State where the property mortgaged or pledged is located.[13]

Further scope for extending the advantages which are potentially afforded to local creditors under the 1940 Treaty is provided by the terms of Article 51. In cases involving more than one proceeding in bankruptcy, property belonging to the debtor and located in the territory of another State where no proceeding in bankruptcy, civil action of insolvency, or other, analogous proceeding has been instituted, is to form part of the bankruptcy assets in the particular proceeding whose judge has been the first to act. This provision raises several issues of principle, since it creates an incentive for creditors to move pre-emptively to bring about the commencement of bankruptcy in the awareness that their local proceeding, if first in time of opening, will become the receptor for any foreign assets in countries where insolvency proceedings happen not to take place. There appears to be no rational reason why such assets should belong to one bankruptcy estate alone, in a case where there are plural proceedings involving the same debtor. As with the 1889 Treaty, no provision is made to encourage, much less to require, coordination of the parallel bankruptcies or cooperation between those responsible for conducting them. Only in the event that a surplus remains after the proceedings in one State are concluded does Article 47 stipulate that the surplus is to be placed at the disposal of the judge who has cognizance of the bankruptcy proceedings in another State, as was also required by Article 41 of the 1889 Treaty.[14]

The provision in Article 49 of the Treaty of 1940, concerning recognition in all of the contracting States of the authority of the trustee in bankruptcy, exhibits several differences from the equivalent provision—namely Article 45—of the Treaty of 1889.[15] Article 49 is expressed to apply only in the case of a single bankruptcy proceeding, thereby avoiding the potential confusion that might result from the requirement to accord equal recognition to the exercise of conflicting functions and rights maintained by the respective office holders in rival, parallel proceedings. From this more circumspect basis, Article 49 proceeds to delineate the rights of such office holders to take actions outside the jurisdiction in which they are

[13] Note also that Art. 22 of the 1940 Procedural Law Treaty supplies special rules for the treatment of liens. Basically, these are determined exclusively by the law of the State where each proceeding is opened, but subject to exceptions which allow the law of the *situs* to govern cases of special liens on immovables and real rights of mortgage, and also in the case of special liens on movables, albeit the latter are subject to the rights of the State in regard to taxes due. For a description of the rules of priority, and the various types of security rights, recognised under Argentine law (as an example of Latin American systems more generally) see Dobson, *supra* n.12, at pp. 131–132 and 135–137.

[14] See at 5.1.1 above.

[15] See at 5.1.1 above.

appointed. They may undertake measures of conservation or administration, appear in lawsuits, and exercise the functions and rights accorded them by the laws of the State where the adjudication of bankruptcy was pronounced.[16] This amounts to a significant concession to the extraterritorial exercise of powers conferred under the law of the office holder's appointment, although it is immediately qualified by a proviso which states that execution in regard to assets located outside the jurisdiction in which the proceedings are based must conform to the law of the *situs*. When, conversely, more than one bankruptcy proceeding takes place, Article 52 supplies a matching rule, in terms of substance, to that of Article 46 of the 1889 Treaty, whereby it is made the prerogative of the court of the debtor's domicile to determine the civil disabilities and disqualifications to which he will be subject.[17] There is no equivalent provision in the 1940 Treaty to that of Article 47 of the 1889 text, concerning the procedure for granting discharge where there are plural bankruptcies. However, Article 24 of the 1940 Treaty on International Procedural Law merely states that the rehabilitation (i.e. discharge) of the insolvent party and the effects thereof shall be governed by the same rules as those which control the imposition of civil incapacities upon the bankrupt. Accordingly, the granting of discharge and reinstatement of full civil capacity is for the judge of the debtor's domicile, applying the law of that jurisdiction for this purpose. Finally, both the Treaties of 1940 contain identical provisions whose effect is to extend the application of the Treaty rules relating to bankruptcy proceedings so as to be equally applicable to judicial liquidations, compositions with creditors, suspensions of payments and other analogous measures which are provided for in the laws of the Contracting States.[18]

5.1.3 General observations

It could be argued that the overall approach adopted in each of the Montevideo Treaties in their treatment of international insolvencies is essentially a pragmatic acceptance of the regional realities, in which the

[16] See also Art. 23 of the Procedural Law Treaty, which states: 'The authority of the receivers, or of the legal representatives of the creditors, shall be recognised in all of the States; and these shall permit in their territory the exercise of the functions allowed the said receivers and representatives by the insolvency law and by the present treaty'.

[17] See also Art. 24 of the Procedural Law Treaty, which additionally provides that 'Incapacity relative to property located in other countries may be declared by the local tribunals in accordance with their own laws'. For explanation of the meaning to be ascribed to the term 'domicile' as used in Art. 52 of the 1940 Treaty, see Dobson in I.F. Fletcher, *supra* n.12, ch. 15 at p. 242, together with n.46 printed at p. 248 (where it is submitted that the term must mean the actual 'residence' of the debtor, in order to assign exclusive jurisdiction to one court in a case of plural proceedings).

[18] Treaty on International Commercial Terrestrial Law, Art. 53; Treaty on International Procedural Law, Art. 25.

maintenance of national and local interests is of paramount importance. How else to explain the unquestioning acceptance of the preferential treatment of local creditors with respect to the process of distribution, even in the case of a unitary bankruptcy in which all creditors, whatever their affiliation or domicile, are obliged to participate? The treaties certainly take a realistic approach to the possibility of plurality of proceedings where the debtor has maintained one or more independent commercial establishments outside his—or its—State of domicile. On the other hand, the absence of any attempt to introduce a procedural framework for the purpose of facilitating cooperation between parallel administrations, with a view to securing some kind of parity of treatment among all creditors of the one debtor, suggests that such concerns were not uppermost in the negotiators' minds, even at the time of the 1940 revision. Given the abundance of common legal heritage among the members of this regional grouping of States, it is initially somewhat surprising to discover that the Montevideo Treaties make only a modest attempt to impose a unified, regional approach to the process of administration and distribution of a multi-jurisdictional estate. Numerous concessions are made to the special rights of local creditors in relation to property located in that country, with the consequence that the outcome of some international cases is likely to be rendered somewhat arbitrary by reason of the chance—or predetermined—dispersal of assets at the moment of bankruptcy.

Finally, as has already been observed, the Treaties have had a somewhat restricted appeal even within the region for which they were created. Essentially, the participating States belong to the 'River Plate' sub set of Latin American States, leaving many notable—and economically significant—absentees, the majority of which have opted instead to become parties to the Bustamante Code of Havana (see below). There is a curious lack of conclusive data regarding the actual working and effects of the Montevideo Treaties. One searches in vain for any documented instances of the treaties' provisions having been instrumental in enabling a cross-border case to be administered with greater ease or efficiency than might otherwise have been possible. Admittedly, the States concerned are all civil law jurisdictions in which reported case law tends not to feature prominently in the doctrinal literature. On the other hand, there are some indications—mainly of an anecdotal nature—to suggest that non-local creditors in the region may be disposed to accept it as their fate that they will receive no return in the form of dividend at the conclusion of their debtor's bankruptcy.

5.2 THE BUSTAMANTE CODE OF THE HAVANA CONFERENCE (1928)

A comprehensive Convention on Private International Law was concluded and signed on 20 February 1928 at the Sixth Panamerican Conference, held at Havana, Cuba.[19] The Havana Convention is customarily known as the 'Bustamante Code' in recognition of the profound influence upon its structure and contents exerted by the Cuban jurist, Antonio Sanchez de Bustamante y Sirven. Title IX of the Convention, comprising Articles 414 to 422 inclusive, deals with the subject of Bankruptcy or Insolvency.

As the title 'Panamerican Conference' implies, the Havana Conference was attended by representatives of States in both hemispheres. In all, twenty-one states were represented, including the USA. Ultimately, fifteen states ratified the Convention, which first entered into force on 25 November 1928 when it had attracted the requisite five ratifications. Neither the USA nor Mexico became parties to the Convention. Of the South American States which were parties to the Montevideo Treaty of 1889,[20] four—Argentina, Colombia, Paraguay and Uruguay—declined to become signatories to the Havana Convention, while the remaining two—Bolivia and Peru—became parties to both.[21]

5.2.1 Scope and effects

Although Article 1 of the Convention proclaims that its application is restricted to nationals of the contracting parties—reflecting the traditional emphasis among many members of the civil law 'family' upon the dominant role of the factor of nationality in the processes of private international law—Title IX introduces a further connecting factor, namely the debtor's civil or commercial domicile, as the special criterion to regulate the operation of the rules relating to insolvency. On the basis of this double-filter approach to determining the scope of application of those provisions, the Convention provides for the twin principles of unity and universality of bankruptcy to be respected and applied among the

[19] For the full text of the Havana Convention see (1929) 86 L.N.T.S. No. 1950, at 112–244 (Spanish and French texts), and 246–381 (English and Portuguese). See also Hudson, *International Legislation* IV (1928–1929) 2279 at 2340. The English text of Title IX (Bankruptcy or Insolvency) is reproduced in Appendix V (D) below.

[20] See at 5.1 above.

[21] The 15 parties to the Havana Convention are: Bolivia, Brazil, Costa Rica, Cuba, Chile, Ecuador, El Salvador, Guatemala, Haiti, Honduras, Nicaragua, Panama, Peru, Dominican Republic, and Venezuela. Bolivia and Peru have declared that the Montevideo Treaties are to prevail in their relations with each other.

Contracting States, subject to the fulfilment of the criterion stated at the outset of Article 414. That Article declares that:

If the insolvent or bankrupt debtor has only one civil or commercial domicile, there can be only one preventive proceeding in insolvency or bankruptcy, or one suspension of payments, or a composition (*quita y espera*) in respect of all his assets and his liabilities in the contracting States.

Conversely, if the debtor's circumstances, and mode of conducting commercial activities, do not permit a finding that the unitary criterion is fulfilled, plural proceedings are authorised to take place concurrently. Article 415 provides:

If one and the same person or partnership should have in more than one contracting State various commercial establishments entirely separate economically, there may be as many suits for preventive proceeding in bankruptcy as there are commercial establishments.

It may be noted that the toleration of plurality of proceedings is strictly confined by reference to the maintenance of economically independent commercial establishments in other contracting States. The mere presence of assets belonging to the debtor, or the engagement in economic activities on an occasional basis or by means of non-independent branches or agencies, does not enable the principle of unity to be displaced by the bringing of insolvency proceedings in the other States where such connections happen to exist. In this respect, the Convention follows the same approach as the Montevideo Treaties in maintaining unity of proceedings in cases where the debtor has a single commercial domicile.[22] On the other hand, where plural proceedings are permissible on the basis of Article 415, the Havana Convention is completely silent about the consequences, and provides no guidance as to the course to be followed, even in the event that a surplus results from the proceedings held in one of the States concerned.[23]

The second chapter of Title IX bears the heading: 'Universality of Bankruptcy or Insolvency, and their effects'. The provisions contained within Articles 416 to 420 are succinctly expressed, but their consequences are far-reaching. Essentially, they commit each Contracting State to accepting the extraterritorial effect of insolvency proceedings commenced in any other State Party, and to enforcing such decrees as are rendered by the other's courts with effect as from the date of first pronouncement, subject only to the need for compliance with any local rules for registration or publicity.[24] Article 416 declares that a decree establishing the incapacity of

[22] See the provisions of the Montevideo Treaties, Arts. 35 and 36 (1889) and Arts. 40 and 41 (1940), discussed at 5.1.1 and 5.1.2 above.

[23] Cf. the Montevideo Treaties, Arts. 41 (1889) and 47 (1940), discussed at 5.1.1 and 5.1.2 above.

[24] Havana Convention, 1928, Arts. 416, 417, 419.

an insolvent or bankrupt debtor has extraterritorial effect in each of the contracting States, while Article 417 provides that a decree of bankruptcy or insolvency, rendered in one of the contracting States, shall be executed in others in the same manner as with other types of judicial determination to which the Convention applies. The Article further specifies that the decree shall have the force of *res judicata* from the moment it is made final, with respect to the persons whom it is to affect. This latter provision is especially important, in that it ensures that there is no 'hiatus' between the activation of legal effects—such as the moratorium on creditors' individual acts of enforcement or diligence—under the laws of the respective States. In the absence of such a provision, a window of opportunity would be made available to creditors not personally subject to the jurisdiction of the court by which the original decree is made, to take various steps against property located in other Contracting States during the time necessary to complete the local formalities for registration and publicity.

The potent extraterritorial provisions of Articles 416 and 417 are reinforced, and significantly extended, by those of Articles 418 and 419. The former provides that the powers and functions of the trustee in bankruptcy appointed in one of the Contracting States in accordance with the provisions of the Convention shall have extraterritorial effect in the others, without the necessity of any local proceeding. Thus, the trustee's powers of action in the other States are co-extensive with those conferred under the law of his appointment, and are exercisable as of right, without need to obtain a local order for this purpose. This should in theory enable the taking of prompt and decisive action to protect and administer the bankrupt's foreign property, and it is somewhat remarkable that no proviso is inserted to the effect that the trustee's actions must be carried out in conformity with the requirements of the local law concerning the sale or disposition of property. In this respect, the Havana Convention appears to be less attentive than are the Montevideo Treaties to the tradition of deference to the role of the law of the *situs* of property in matters concerning its transfer by a foreign trustee or liquidator.[25] An equally striking manifestation of the unqualified universalism espoused by the Havana Convention is the provision in Article 419, whereby the retroactive effect of a bankruptcy adjudication, and the annulment of transactions in consequence of the debtor's adjudication, are declared to be governed by the law of the State where bankruptcy is pronounced, and to be applicable in the territory of the other contracting States. While such extensive effects are for the most part defensible in the context of a unified insolvency proceeding embracing property and parties dispersed through multiple jurisdictions, it may be questioned whether sufficient consideration has been

[25] Cf. Montevideo Treaties, Arts. 45 (1889) and 49 (1940), discussed at 5.1.1 and 5.1.2 above.

given to the predicament of parties who may have dealt in good faith, and in circumstances where their transaction would be unimpeachable under the local law (and under the law by which it was governed at the time in question), but who find that it is capable of avoidance under the insolvency law of the State in which the debtor is subsequently made bankrupt. The onus seems to be upon parties who have dealings which otherwise are in full conformity with their local law, to be aware of the personal circumstances of the other party to the extent that these may render the latter subject to the insolvency laws of another State (and, furthermore, to be aware of any provision in the foreign insolvency law which would render the transaction impeachable). Much may depend upon the breadth of interpretation given to Article 420, which states:

> Real actions and rights of the same nature shall continue to be subject, notwithstanding the declaration of bankruptcy or insolvency, to the law of the situation of the things affected thereby and to the competence of the judges of the place where they are found.

This provision appears to go beyond the scope of the usual provisions whose purpose is to preserve the rights of secured creditors to enforce rights duly created over property of the debtor, and could be invoked by those who have acquired a proprietary interest in property either through direct dealings with the debtor, or indirectly through dealings with third parties.

Extraterritorial effects are also conferred upon a decree of discharge, or rehabilitation, pronounced by the competent court or tribunal. Article 422 specifies that this shall take effect in the other Contracting States as soon as the judicial determination by which it is ordered becomes final. Further extension of the scope of the Havana Convention comes about by Article 421, which accords extraterritorial effect to compositions and judicial settlements concluded between creditors and their insolvent debtor, albeit there is a proviso reserving the rights of dissenting creditors to enforce any rights *in rem* to which they may be entitled.

5.2.2 General observations

In its forceful combination of the principles of unity and universality, the Havana Convention demonstrates the capability of States which are regional neighbours, and which share a broadly similar legal culture, to create a framework of rules for cross-border insolvency based upon acceptance of extraterritoriality, and the consequent overriding of locally-based rights and remedies. The provisions themselves are notable for their broad and general terms, leaving many important questions of detail unresolved. For example, in cases where only one set of proceedings takes place, the Convention provides no indication of how the rights of all creditors, especially those who are non-local with respect to the place where the proceedings are constituted, shall be marshalled and respected. Such questions are apparently left for determination by the law of the State of bankruptcy. However, as we have seen, it is quite characteristic of many national insolvency laws within this region to discriminate in favour of local creditors, thus negating the principle of equality among creditors as a general body. To perpetuate such practices, while at the same time conferring upon the trustee in bankruptcy the exceptional extraterritorial powers for which Title IX of the Convention makes provision, appears to the outside observer to compound the disadvantages of those who happen not to belong to the same State as their insolvent debtor. Such a state of affairs would furnish a powerful disincentive to intra-regional economic activities involving credit in any form, unless effective security arrangements and collateral guarantees can be obtained.

It may also be noted that the series of provisions in Chapter II which impose the regime of universality make no reference to any distinction between cases of unitary proceedings, as determined by the rule in Article 414, and cases where there may be plural proceedings according to Article 415. In the latter situation, it would be unrealistic to attempt to apply the provisions of Articles 416 to 422 in a literal way, without any modification or accommodation of the overlapping claims of two or more concurrent sets of proceedings. The most likely outcome in such cases would be that the courts of each jurisdiction in which proceedings are opened would resist all claims by foreign trustees to any assets located in that State, and in practice it is most unlikely that such claims would even be seriously pressed. However, in contracting States in which no proceedings happen to take place, the absence of any rule to provide a principled means of resolving which of the concurrent, foreign proceedings should be accorded primacy of entitlement to any locally-found assets is an unfortunate *lacuna*, since it leaves the way open for various, possibly arbitrary, solutions to be devised in a spontaneous manner. The probable result is that there is a further erosion of the principle of equality of treatment of creditors.[26]

[26] For a more positive assessment of the Bustamante Code, in conjunction with the provisions of the Montevideo Treaties, as a potential basis for a Pan-American Insolvency Law, see Dobson in I.F. Fletcher (ed.), *Cross-Border Insolvency: Comparative Dimensions (The Aberystwyth Insolvency Papers)* (1990), ch. 15(II), pp. 249–255.

5.3 THE NORDIC BANKRUPTCY CONVENTION OF 7 NOVEMBER 1933

Among the States of the European continent, political and legal history has produced a present-day situation of considerable diversity in the area of bankruptcy law, both domestic and international.[27] However, within the region of Scandinavia the same historic processes have brought about a close alignment of philosophy and approach towards the administration of law in general, and towards insolvency law and practice in particular, between five neighbouring States, namely Denmark, Finland, Iceland, Norway and Sweden. Linguistic affinities between four of the nations comprised within this group, and the presence of a Swedish-speaking population within Finland, further facilitate a sense of common identity among these five, independent nations. This has resulted in an established pattern of close collaboration in international legal matters, including in the area of insolvency.[28] A Convention Regarding Bankruptcy, generally known as the Nordic Bankruptcy Convention, was concluded at Copenhagen on 7 November 1933 and continues in force to the present day.[29]

5.3.1 Scope and effects

The Nordic Convention is a deceptively brief instrument—consisting of just seventeen Articles in all. Its provisions are notable for the extent of the technical detail included in the text, and for the range of matters actually covered. Not only are the subjects of jurisdiction, and international effects and recognition, dealt with, but also rules of choice of law are included. In addition to bankruptcy and liquidation proceedings, judicially-approved compositions, the liquidation of banks, and the administration of estates of deceased insolvents are also dealt with by means of specific provisions.

[27] For some indications of the general divisions, in Europe and elsewhere, to be found in national approaches to insolvency, see Fletcher, 'General Report and Comparative Study', in I.F. Fletcher (Ed.), *Cross-Border Insolvency: National and Comparative Studies (Reports delivered at the XIII International Congress of Comparative Law, Montreal 1990)* (1992), at p. 267 *et seq.*, esp. at 270–274. See also Philip R. Wood, *Maps of World Financial Law*, 3rd. edn. (1997), pp. 12–23.

[28] See Bogdan, 'International Bankruptcy Law in Scandinavia', (1985) 34 I.C.L.Q. 49. See also Philip (1959–I) 96 Hague Rec. 245 *et seq.*

[29] No. 3574, (1935) 155 L.N.T.S. at 115 (Danish and Finnish texts), 123 (Icelandic, Norwegian and Swedish), and 133–139 (French and English). The English text is reproduced in Appendix VI below. Amendments to certain points of detail in the Nordic Convention were made in 1977 and 1982, and have entered into force between Denmark, Finland, Norway and Sweden; the original version of the Convention remains applicable in Iceland. For comment and assessment of the Convention's provisions, see M. Bogdan in J.S. Ziegel (ed.), *Current Developments in International and Comparative Corporate Insolvency Law* (1994), ch. 31 (pp. 701–708); Philip, *supra* n.28, at pp. 316–324.

The central idea within the framework of the Convention's provisions is based upon the common position, to which all five systems strongly subscribe, that the optimum forum for bankruptcy purposes is that with which the debtor has the closest economic connection. Although uncertainty can sometimes arise in individual cases due to their exceptional, or marginal, circumstances, the preferred point of departure is the debtor's domiciliary forum. This is assessed by reference to place of residence in the case of individuals not engaged in commerce, and by reference to the principal place from which business activity is administered and carried on in the case of companies or of persons engaged in some business or profession.[30] The concept of the domiciliary bankruptcy is thus placed at the core of the Convention's provisions, although alternative possibilities are also envisaged and, to a certain extent, tolerated as exceptions to the norm.

Jurisdiction

The primary rule of jurisdiction is not actually stated in explicit terms, but has to be deduced from the Convention's direct and indirect indications.[31] The somewhat oblique reference in Article 13 to the exercise of bankruptcy jurisdiction based upon 'a fact unconnected with the residence of a bankrupt individual or with the registered offices of a company, association or foundation which has been declared bankrupt' reveals that the Convention makes the tacit assumption that the courts of the five contracting States will normally exercise jurisdiction over debtors domiciled in their territory. Since it is nowhere forbidden for courts to take jurisdiction on grounds other than domicile, however, the Convention must be classified as being of the 'simple' or 'indirect' type,[32] which merely establishes jurisdictional criteria which, if met in any given case, will render the proceedings eligible to benefit from the convention's further provisions. Such a convention leaves national courts free to continue to apply other rules of jurisdiction, albeit the proceedings in those cases will for most purposes be deprived of the advantages furnished under the convention.

As it happens, Article 13 of the Nordic Convention takes care to provide that, although a non-domiciliary proceeding will fall outside its sphere of application, that proceeding may be continued irrespective of any subsequent bankruptcy proceedings in any of the other States. Thus, the usual extraterritorial effects that would apply throughout all five States by

[30] See Bogdan (1985) 34 I.C.L.Q. 49, at 52–54; Philip, *supra* n.28, at pp. 265–271.

[31] See Nordic Convention, *supra* n.29, Arts. 10, para.1, and 13, together with the Nordic Convention on the Recognition and Enforcement of Judgments, 16 March 1932, (1935) 139 L.N.T.S. 186, Art. 3(1).

[32] As distinct from the 'double' or 'direct' type of convention, best exemplified by the EC Convention of 27 September 1968 on Jurisdiction and the Enforcement of Judgments in Civil and Commercial Matters (the Brussels Convention), and the Draft EU Convention on Insolvency Proceedings, as to which see Chapter 6 below.

virtue of Article 1 in the event of opening domiciliary proceedings admit of exception in the case where a non-domiciliary proceeding has previously commenced in one of the other States. Concurrent proceedings are therefore in prospect, although the fact that Article 13 is worded in permissive terms leaves open the possibility that the non-domiciliary proceeding could be stayed in the interests of allowing consolidation of the insolvency process within the domiciliary forum, if it should transpire that the debtor is domiciled in another Nordic State. Where, on the other hand, the debtor's domicile is in some third State, the terms of Article 13 readily allow as many local proceedings to be opened as may be appropriate. However, as the words quoted above serve to indicate, the Article imposes a requirement, which must be observed on every occasion when a court is proposing to open a non-domiciliary proceeding, to state the fact on which jurisdiction has been exercised in the judgment by which bankruptcy is declared. This has the effect of requiring the court first seized of insolvency proceedings concerning a particular debtor to make a careful determination as to that person's domicile. This task needs to be performed with some sensitivity, since there is no further guidance in the Convention concerning the means of resolving any confusion potentially resulting from a conflicting decision by a court of another State as to the location of the debtor's domicile.[33]

International effects

Given that a domiciliary proceeding constitutes the normal case under the Nordic Convention, the qualities of unity and universality are secured by means of the various provisions within the text. Thus, paragraph 1 of Article 1 states:

> A declaration of bankruptcy in any of the contracting States shall also apply to the bankrupt's property in the territory of the other States.

This extraterritorial effect as regards property is automatic and instantaneous, and requires no further formality such as registration or the obtaining of an order of *exequatur* in the other States in which property is located. Paragraph 2 of Article 1 provides that, unless otherwise provided, the law of the country in which bankruptcy takes place shall determine its effects in the following matters:

—divesting the bankrupt of administration of his property;
—the extent of the assets forming the bankrupt's estate, and the property comprised therein;
—the property capable of being reincorporated in the estate in consequence of annulment proceedings;
—the bankrupt's rights and obligations during bankruptcy;

[33] See Bogdan in J.S. Ziegel (ed.), *supra* n.29, at p. 702.

—the administration of the bankrupt's property and transactions in respect thereof;
—the rights of creditors in respect of the payment of their claims;
—the allocation of the assets;
—any composition with creditors or other mode of settlement.

The above list of matters to which the *lex concursus* is applicable by virtue of the choice of law provision in Article 1, paragraph 2 is affected by the exception created by paragraph 3, which requires the question whether any particular item of property is exempt from seizure in satisfaction of claims in bankruptcy to be determined by the law of the country in which the property is situate. This rule is unqualified by any reference to the circumstances under which the property came to be located in a jurisdiction under whose law it enjoys exempt status. It is therefore a question for the law of the *situs* to determine whether illicit removal of property—for example if this is done virtually on the eve of bankruptcy, and with a view to gaining the benefit of the exemption in question—shall disentitle the bankrupt to retain the property.

Further choice of law provisions bearing upon the ultimate destination of assets affected by an insolvency are contained in Articles 4, 5 and 6. Article 4, paragraph 1 concerns the validity of transactions entered into prior to bankruptcy whereby the debtor created rights in respect of immovable property and its accessories. Questions as to the need for registration of such acts, as a necessary condition to their validity as against the bankrupt estate, and also questions as to the invalidation of the acts themselves, are to be determined according to the law of the *situs*. Similar questions regarding registered ships or aircraft are to be settled in accordance with the law of the country to which the ships or aircraft belong. In the case of movable property, any questions of the need for registration or publicity as a necessary condition to the validity of alienation or hypothecation of such property, together with questions of the validity of such acts themselves, are to be determined by the law of the Contracting State in which the property is situate at the beginning of the bankruptcy proceedings.[34]

In the case where measures of execution have been carried out by creditors prior to or contemporaneously with the commencement of bankruptcy proceedings, the effect of bankruptcy upon the rights of the executing creditors are to be determined by the law of the place where execution has taken place.[35] Article 5 imports additional rules in favour of the application of the *lex situs*, in relation to the rights of creditors whose claims are secured by mortgage or pledge to enforce their security irrespective of the bankruptcy, or to exercise rights of retention (liens). To

[34] Nordic Convention, Art.4, para.2. [35] *Ibid.*, Art. 4, para. 3.

cover all cases, including both movable as well as immovable property, the *situs* of the property at the time when bankruptcy takes place is the decisive factor. Similarly, the effect of bankruptcy upon creditors' rights to pursue measures of execution against property shall be determined by the law of the State in which execution takes place.[36] Since these matters are susceptible of subtle variation as between the laws of different States, depending on the precise drafting employed and its bearing upon the circumstances of the particular case, these choice of law rules are of considerable importance. A further, and quite standard, rule is contained in Article 6 requiring the sale of property forming part of the bankrupt estate to be conducted in accordance with the procedure prescribed by the law of the *situs*.

Advertisement and inventory

In view of the fact that the Convention produces immediate and automatic effects throughout all five Nordic countries from the moment a declaration of bankruptcy takes place, it is essential that proper procedures are followed in order to give prompt and thorough publicity to this event. Article 2 provides that if there is property in any of the other States which is affected by a declaration of bankruptcy, the bankruptcy officers[37] must forthwith give notice by means of an announcement in the Official Journal of the State or States in question, and must take steps in accordance with the local law of the *situs* to bring about the requisite entry in the Land or Shipping Registers, and in other public registers. Furthermore, notification must be sent as soon as possible to all known creditors in the other States, regardless of whether there happen to be assets in those countries.[38] Such creditors must also be notified if there are any objections against their claims. However, no consequences or sanctions are prescribed in the event of failure to comply with any of these requirements. Parties who suffer loss or prejudice as a consequence of not having received timely notification of the bankruptcy or its progress are restricted to such redress as may be provided for under the law where the proceedings are centred.

To assist the bankruptcy officers responsible for a case governed by the Convention, Article 3 requires the courts of other Contracting States, if so requested, to make an inventory of the property situate in their territory and take the necessary steps for its provisional conservation, or for its sale if this is not practicable. In respect of property situate in another State from

36 *Ibid.*, Art. 5, para. 2.

37 The expression 'bankruptcy officers' is not precisely defined in the Convention, but *ibid.*, Art. 14 provides that the term 'shall be deemed to include any legal authority competent in bankruptcy matters'.

38 *Ibid.* Art. 2, para. 2. An exception is provided in the case of creditors whose claims have been entered in the debtor's statement of assets and liabilities without specific application on their part.

that in which proceedings have opened, the bankruptcy officers have the same rights to request assistance from the authorities at the *situs* as would bankruptcy officers of that country.[39] Thus, the rights of bankruptcy officers to act in relation to property situate in other contracting States are variable, according to the place where such assistance is to be sought, rather than being co-extensive with the rights they would enjoy under the law of the State in which they are appointed. The costs of such assistance are recoverable from the officers who request it, as expenses of their administration.

Preferential claims

The treatment of preferential claims in cross-border insolvencies is a notoriously controversial subject. Articles 7 and 8 of the Nordic Convention contain detailed provisions for this purpose, including several choice of law rules for specific situations. These constitute exceptions to the general rule embodied in Article 1 whereby the process of distribution, and the rights of creditors in respect of payment of their claims, are governed by the *lex concursus*. Article 7, paragraph 1 establishes a rule to the effect that the *lex situs* (as at the date of bankruptcy) shall govern preferential claims against particular assets and the question of priority as between such preferential claims, mortgages, pledges or other rights *in rem* attaching to such assets. It is further stated that such specific preferential rights shall have priority over all general preferential rights. This represents an interesting synthesis of potentially conflicting principles. As far as general preferential claims are concerned, Article 1 (see above) causes the assets collected from any part of the Nordic States' territory to be available as a general fund for distribution among all preferential creditors, whose status as such is however a matter for the *lex concursus* to determine. This approach respects the principle of equality of treatment of creditors of the same class, but under some circumstances this could take place at the expense of a defeat of pre-existing expectations, if it transpires that a particular creditor's preferential status is not recognised under the insolvency law of the debtor's State of domicile. Such cases are likely to be rare, however, given the close similarity of approach followed under the insolvency laws of the five States in question. The special rule of Article 7, however, ensures that the enjoyment of specific claims over particular assets is in each instance linked to the location of the asset in question, and that such assets are removed from the general pool of the debtor's available estate.

Paragraph 2 of Article 7 contains a further, special provision covering the preferential treatment of fiscal claims and other public dues. These constitute a further sub-set of claims whose treatment in cross-border

[39] Nordic Convention, Art. 3, para. 2.

cases is the very stuff of controversy, on account of the deep-rooted aversion to the enforcement of taxes claimed by a foreign sovereign.[40] Typically, those holding such claims will be treated as ineligible to participate in the process of distribution by reason of the public policy requirements of the *lex concursus*. Alternatively, they may be admitted to dividend among the ranks of ordinary creditors, thereby losing the preferential status accorded them under the law of the State where the taxes are payable. The Nordic Convention effects a special compromise by providing that the extent of the preferential treatment of any claims for taxes or other public dues levied by a Contracting State other than that in which bankruptcy has been declared shall be governed by the law of the State to which such taxes and dues are payable. Thus, the preferential status of foreign fiscal claims is preserved, but its practical effect is carefully limited by the further provision in paragraph 2 which causes such preferential rights to apply only to the property of the bankrupt in the State by which the relevant taxes and dues are levied. Thus, a series of 'sub-estates' is specially created for the purpose of satisfying the respective fiscal claims of the other Contracting States. When each pool of available assets has been exhausted with respect to the fiscal claims which enjoy preferential status according to the local law, the authorities of that State are eligible to be treated as ordinary, non-preferential creditors in the central process of distribution in respect of any unsatisfied balance.[41]

The drafting of Article 7 is rendered still more tortuous by reason of the insinuation of a further provision dealing with the preferential rights of a lessor of premises located in the territory of one of the Contracting States, other than that in which the bankruptcy is centred. The extent of any preferential entitlement of such a lessor-proprietor is to be determined by the law of the *situs* of the premises, and any questions of relative priority as between different preferential rights are the subject of an elaborate choice of law rule, also applicable to fiscal claims. Since the provisions of Article 7 make it necessary to determine the situation of property at the time when bankruptcy takes place, Article 8 provides some assistance by declaring that any claim possessed by the bankrupt shall be regarded as situate in the State in which bankruptcy is declared. On the other hand, if the claim is attested by a promissory note or other document the production of which is necessary in order to obtain payment, the claim is considered as

[40] The long-established position of English law regarding such matters is discussed in Chapter 2, at 2.4 above.

[41] The amendments to the Nordic Convention made in 1982 introduced a further refinement in the treatment of general preferential claims of tax authorities, so that a proportion of each local asset pool is deducted and made available to meet non-fiscal claims of a preferential nature. The modification (which is not yet in force for Iceland) is discussed, with a worked example, by Bogdan, *supra* n.29, at pp. 704–705. See also Philip, *supra* n.28, at pp. 322–323.

situate in the same State as the document in question. Moreover, registered ships or aircraft are deemed to be situated in the State to which they belong, except as regards the application of the provision in Article 6 concerning the procedure to be followed in the case of sale of such property.[42]

Compositions

The Nordic Convention also makes provision for the recognition and enforcement of compositions with creditors. Article 10, paragraph 2 declares that judicial decisions given in any of the States for the purpose of confirming a composition with creditors shall also apply in the other States, and that this shall be the case irrespective of whether the bankrupt possesses property in the territory of only one of them. Thus, compositions concluded as a means of resolving bankruptcy proceedings effective under the Convention on account of their domiciliary character will likewise carry full effects throughout all five States.

It is also possible for composition procedures to be initiated as an alternative to bankruptcy. If these take place in the debtor's domiciliary State, they are accorded the same universal effects as in the case of a domiciliary bankruptcy.[43] Article 15 provides that the opening of such a compulsory composition in one of the Contracting States shall preclude both a declaration of bankruptcy and an opening of compulsory composition proceedings in the other States, and that any moratorium over executions shall be universally effective to the same extent as in the country of composition itself. If the procedure results in a confirmed composition, this will likewise be binding in the other Contracting States.

5.3.2 General observations

For some sixty-five years, the Nordic Convention has provided a quietly effective example of the possibilities that can be embraced among regional partners who have a high level of mutual confidence in the integrity of each other's institutions and legal processes.[44] The according of automatic, extraterritorial effects to domiciliary bankruptcies and compositions reflects a basic unity of approach to the actual administration of these procedures, including an essential absence of discrimination against non-local creditors. Care has also been taken to ensure that vital interests intimately

[42] Nordic Convention, Art. 8, para. 2. Art. 6 is mentioned at p. 241 above.

[43] *Ibid.*, Art. 15, para. 3, which cross-refers to Art. 13, discussed above. Conversely, non-domiciliary composition procedures are outside the scope of the Convention, and the court by which such proceedings are administered is required to give clear indication of the ground on which jurisdiction has been taken, so that this fact can be readily appreciated.

[44] According to one distinguished commentator upon the Convention and its working, the absence of case law relating to the Convention should be interpreted as an indication that it is working well, and without major difficulties: see Bogdan, *supra* n. 29, at p. 706.

associated with the location of property are generally respected by means of special choice of law rules in favour of the *lex situs*. Even the fiscal authorities have been allowed to share in the 'group philosophy' which is characteristic of the Nordic approach, to an extent which is so far unmatched by any other international treaty on insolvency matters.[45]

What must be borne in mind however is the quite exceptional regional homogeneity within these five Nordic countries. Among a more diverse grouping of sovereign States, both technical and political difficulties quickly surface, resulting in an eventual dilution of such agreement as can be concluded, as will be seen in the two chapters next following. It is also to be observed that the Nordic Convention does not aspire to build bridges with the wider world, and offers no guidance on how to deal with cases where proceedings are taking place in third States, or significant assets are located outside Scandinavia. Although there are no provisions trenching upon such currently topical matters as the according of recognition and access to external proceedings and those conducting them, the Nordic Convention offers important opportunities for creditors to display tactical adroitness, by taking advantage of the effects which follow upon the commencement of proceedings at their debtor's domiciliary forum.

[45] For the potential treatment of fiscal claims under Art. 39 of the EU Convention on Insolvency Proceedings, see Chapter 6 below at p. 295.

6

The European Union Convention on Insolvency Proceedings

PRELIMINARY

This chapter is concerned with the protracted—and so far unsuccessful—attempt to conclude a convention among the Member States of the European Union, to regulate the conduct of insolvency proceedings as between themselves. Although the need for such arrangements was foreseen at the time of drafting the Foundation Treaty of the European Economic Community, and was indeed covered by the terms of a specific provision of that Treaty,[1] successive initiatives have failed to realise this goal, although at various times it has seemed possible that agreement could be achieved among the States then participating. In the most recent disappointment to have befallen this project, in May 1996, a finalised Convention that had been signed by fourteen of the fifteen current members of what had by this time become the European Union, failed to come into effect due to the withholding of the signature of the United Kingdom. This had the unfortunate consequence of causing the text, negotiated by and apparently acceptable to all fifteen States, to lapse.

No public initiative has subsequently been taken under the auspices of the European Union to revive the Insolvency Convention project, and its future prospects remain uncertain. However, it is submitted that both the practical need for such a convention—and indeed the legal requirement under European Union law that effective cross-border arrangements be put in place—are inescapable realities.[2] Whatever solution is finally adopted, it is likely that most if not all of the provisions of the Draft tabled for signature during 1995–1996 will be retained in something like their published form. Therefore, the structure and contents of that text will be examined here.

[1] Treaty Establishing the European Economic Community, signed in Rome on 25 March 1957, commonly known as the (first) Treaty of Rome. Article 220(4) of the Treaty commits the Member States to negotiating a series of conventions for the benefit of their nationals, including one to secure 'the simplification of formalities governing the reciprocal recognition and enforcement of judgments of courts or tribunals and of arbitral awards'.

[2] The logical and legal bases for standardising the intra-Community treatment of insolvency matters are more fully explored in I.F. Fletcher, *Conflict of Laws and European Community Law* (1982), chs. 1,2 and 6, esp. at pp.187–190.

6.1 OUTLINE HISTORY OF THE CONVENTION PROJECT; EVOLUTION OF THE TEXT

Over the period from 1960 to 1996 the Insolvency Convention project was an item on the agenda of the institutions of the European Community/European Union, particularly the Commission and the Council. During those years, work advanced in various stages interspersed by periods of almost total quiescence. The most intense periods of activity may be broadly divided into two principal phases, of which the first can be subdivided into two parts. The first part of Phase I occurred in the years prior to February 1970, when a group of experts drawn from the original six Member States,[3] convened by the European Commission, produced a text published as the Preliminary Draft Convention.[4] Following the accession of the first three additional Member States from 1 January 1973, work was resumed on the basis of the 1970 text, with a view to its being adopted by all nine Members. During this second part of Phase I, numerous modifications were made to the original text, partly as a reflection of the general thrust of critical comments published after 1970, and partly in response to particular concerns of the new participants in the negotiations. The essential features of the Preliminary Draft were nevertheless largely carried through into the Draft Convention submitted to the Council in April 1980 for further study and potential adoption.[5] However, sustained resistance on the part of several Member States resulted in the discreet abandonment of further attempts to promote the adoption of the 1980 Draft, although no formal announcement was made of this. Several years of inactivity and uncertainty ensued.

[3] The original six Members of the European Communities (including the Coal and Steel and Atomic Energy Communities, as well as the Economic Community), were Belgium, France, (West) Germany, Italy, Luxembourg and The Netherlands.

[4] E. Comm. Doc. 3.327/1/XIV/70 F, dated 16 February 1970. An Explanatory Report, known as the *Noël-Lemontey Report*, was published as E. Comm. Doc. 16.775/XIV/70–F. English versions of both texts were later published under the same documentary reference numbers, but substituting the suffix-letter 'E' in place of 'F'. The English version of the text of the Preliminary Draft Convention was published as Appendix 10 to the Report of the Bankruptcy Convention Advisory Committee, published in August 1976, Cmnd. 6602. The chairman of the Advisory Committee was Mr. Kenneth Cork who subsequently, as Sir Kenneth Cork, was chairman of the Insolvency Law Review Committee whose report, generally known as The Cork Report, was published in June 1982, Cmnd. 8558. To avoid confusion, the Report of the Advisory Committee is sometimes referred to as the 'Cork Report No. 1'.

[5] E. Comm. Doc. III/D/72/80. The text of the Draft EEC Convention on Bankruptcy, Winding-up, Arrangements, Compositions and Similar Proceedings was published in E.C. Bull. Supp. 2/82, together with a Report by J. Lemontey. The text was also published by the Department of Trade in April 1980 and is reproduced as Appendix C in I.F. Fletcher, *supra* n.2. See also O.J. 1981, L391/23, for the Commission Opinion on its suitability for adoption.

The initiative which resulted in a relaunching of the project was taken by the Council of Ministers which, in May 1989 with the Community's membership already enlarged to twelve and soon destined to grow to fifteen,[6] established a new working party on the Bankruptcy Convention under the chairmanship of Dr Manfred Balz. Phase II was pursued with much vigour, and was also characterised by a greater openness in that the emerging versions of the text were given a considerable measure of publicity and exposure to informed comment, in marked contrast to the prevailing taste for secrecy which had attended most of the developments during Phase I. One source of inspiration for those engaged upon the task of shaping the Phase II text was the recently concluded Istanbul Convention produced under the auspices of the Council of Europe, and opened for signature on 5 June 1990.[7] In addition to adapting some innovations of the Istanbul text, the working party resurrected certain features of the Phase I concept, while expunging or modifying others in the interests of achieving a more workable, and politically acceptable convention in terms of the existing realities among a community of fifteen States whose domestic laws exhibit numerous differences in matters concerning credit, security and insolvency.

During the course of the working party's cycle of activity, the European Community officially transformed itself into the European Union following the ratification of the Treaty of Maastricht, and a further impetus was imparted to such unifying projects as the Convention on Insolvency Proceedings. At a meeting of the EU Council of Ministers on 25 September 1995, the finalised text of the Convention was tabled for approval and, if possible, immediate adoption. The more cautious—and in a European Union context somewhat novel—course was taken of an 'initialling' of the text by all fifteen Member States, thereby precluding any further negotiation, or textual amendment. It was agreed that after a brief interval to allow governments to study this final version, the Convention would be opened for signature for a limited period of six months, within which it would have to be signed by all the fifteen States, as required by Article 220 of the Treaty of Rome, or otherwise lapse.[8] This was carried into effect at

[6] Greece became the tenth member of the EC in January 1981; Spain and Portugal joined in January 1986. A further three accessions took place in January 1993, when Austria, Finland and Sweden became members of what had by that time become known as the European Union, in consequence of the coming into force of the Treaty on European Union (the Maastricht Treaty) of 7 February 1992: O.J. 1992, C224/1.

[7] European Convention on Certain International Aspects of Bankruptcy, E.T.S., No. 136. The text is reproduced in Appendix III below. See Chapter 7 below.

[8] Insolvency Convention, Art. 49(2),(3) (see section 6.3. below). Community Conventions under Art. 220 E.C.T. are negotiated by all existing Members of the Community (now the EU), as at the time of their adoption, and require the ratification of all Members in order to enter into force. Indeed, the Convention of 29 February 1968 on the Mutual Recognition of Companies has never entered into force, for want of the necessary complement of

a further meeting in Madrid on 23 November 1995, on which date twelve States signed the Convention.[9] Within the following months, two of the remaining three Members—Ireland and The Netherlands—added their signatures. During that period, an approved and revised version of the Explanatory Report to the Convention was put into circulation, thereby overcoming one of the technical obstacles to acceptance of the text of the Convention that had been raised by some members of the Council at the session in September.[10] The state of uncertainty whether the United Kingdom would become a signatory before the expiry of the six-month time limit on 23 May 1996 was maintained by the terms of a Report of the House of Lords Select Committee on the European Communities dated 26 March 1996.[11] The Committee's concluding opinion and recommendation, while acknowledging the generally favourable views of many of those whose evidence it had received, nevertheless advocated a cautious approach, and the need for further study and consideration, before a final decision should be taken by the Government.[12] This proved to be ominous, and when the deadline for completion of signatures passed on 23 May that of the United Kingdom remained outstanding for reasons which have only subsequently become apparent and which will be considered at the conclusion of this chapter.[13] For the time being however the EU Insolvency Convention languishes in an uncertain limbo. Despite this, the contents of its intended provisions merit careful study, since not only do they retain some prospect of entering into force in their current form, or something closely akin to it, but they also represent a significant advance

ratifications. Once a convention is in force, a requirement is imposed upon States which subsequently join the Community/Union to negotiate their accession to it as soon as practicable, as one of the terms of Membership. Article 50 of the finalised Insolvency Convention confirms this requirement.

[9] The 12 States which signed the EU Convention on the day it was opened for signature (23 November 1995) were: Austria, Belgium, Denmark, Finland, France, Germany, Greece, Italy, Luxembourg, Portugal, Spain, and Sweden. The text of the Convention in its finalised state for signature is reproduced in Appendix II below. See also (1996) 35 I.L.M. 1223.

[10] The Report on the Convention on Insolvency Proceedings, prepared by Professor M. Virgos and M. E. Schmit (hereafter referred to as 'Virgos-Schmit Report'), was circulated as EU Council document 6500/96, DRS 8 (CFC), bearing the date 3 May 1996. It has not yet been officially published, and remains unapproved by the Council, with the consequence that it is technically open to further modification. An earlier, English version of the Virgos-Schmit Report, bearing the reference coding 11900/1/95 REV 1, was published as Annex B to a Consultative Document, *EC Convention on Insolvency Proceedings*, published in February 1996 by the Insolvency Service of the Department of Trade and Industry. The latter version should be regarded as having been superseded by the revised text of 3 May. Many invaluable insights into the Convention's intended effects can be found in Balz (1996) 70 Am. Bankr. L. J. 485.

[11] Session 1995–96, 7th Report: *Convention on Insolvency Proceedings* (HL Paper 59). The Chairman of the Select Committee was Lord Hoffmann.

[12] *Ibid.*, paras. 35–42. The minutes of oral and written evidence supplied to the Select Committee are annexed to the Report, separately paginated (pp. 1–52).

[13] See at 6.4 below.

in the concept of what can be accomplished at regional level among a community of States with a sense of common purpose.

6.2 THE PHASE I DRAFT CONVENTION (1960–1980): PRINCIPAL FEATURES

Although the Draft Convention that evolved over the years from 1960 to 1980 is primarily of historic interest, it is as well that its principal features, and also the reasons for its ultimate failure, should be commemorated here in the hope that the same errors will not be repeated in the course of some future project of this kind. A detailed analysis of the text will not be undertaken, however.[14]

The destiny of this first phase was effectively shaped by the circumstances under which the project began its life, during the early years of existence of the EEC itself. This was a period of rapid advance along the path towards European integration, with a Community of manageable size (consisting of the six founding Members) being guided by a Commission whose zeal for the task entrusted to it was, for the first and perhaps only time in its history, matched by a generally favourable political climate across the Community.

The Committee of experts originally formed in July 1960 to undertake the task of fulfilling the obligations imposed by Article 220 of the Treaty of Rome,[15] took an early decision to regard insolvency and related matters as a special subject requiring separate treatment. Thereafter, work continued towards the preparation of what was to become the Brussels Convention of 27 September 1968 on Jurisdiction and the Enforcement of Judgments in Civil and Commercial Matters, Article 1(2) of which expressly declares

[14] For detailed discussion of the Preliminary Draft Convention of 1970, see: Noel and Lemontey (1968) 4 Rev. Trim. Dr. Eur. 703; Hirsch, C.D.E. 1970, 50; Ganshof, C.D.E. 1971, 146; Hunter (1972) 21 I.C.L.Q. 682 and (1976) 25 I.C.L.Q. 310; K. Nadelmann, *Conflict of Laws, International and Interstate* (1972), p. 340, and in (1970) Riv. Dir. Int. Priv. e Proc. 501; the same author, (1977) 52 N.Y.U.L.R. 1, at pp. 27–32; Jahr (1972) 36 Rabels Z. 620; K. Lipstein, *The Law of the European Economic Community* (1974), p. 284; Coppens, in *Idées Nouvelles dans le droit de la Faillite (4ème Journée d'études juridiques Jean Dabin, 17 Mai 1968)* (Bruxelles, 1968), Part III; Hillman (1974) 48 Am. Bankr. L.J. 369; Lemontey (1975) Rev. Trim. Dr. Eur. 172; Noel (1976) Rev. Trim. Dr. Eur. 159; Farrar [1977] J.B.L. 320; Fletcher, in K. Lipstein (ed.), *Harmonisation of Private International Law by the EEC* (1978), p. 119 (also published in (1977) E.L.R. 15). From the United Kingdom perspective, the Report of the Bankruptcy Convention Advisory Committee (*supra* n.4) is of enduring value: see esp. the 'Note of Reservations' by Mr. A.E. Anton, at pp. 105–128.

For critical assessments of the 1980 version of the Draft Convention, see Thieme (1981) 45 Rabels Z. 459; Nadelmann (1982) 27 McGill L.J. 541; the same author, (1982) 56 Am. Bankr. L.J. 65; I.F. Fletcher, *Conflict of Laws and European Community Law* (1982), ch. 6, pp. 187–249; D. Lasok and P. Stone, *Conflict of Laws in the European Community* (1987), ch. 10, pp. 397–413.

[15] See *supra* n.1.

that the Convention shall not apply to: 'bankruptcy, proceedings relating to the winding-up of insolvent companies or other legal persons, judicial arrangements, compositions and analogous proceedings'. A parallel group of experts drawn from the six Member States was therefore convened by the Commission to develop a Bankruptcy Convention which, it was envisaged, would complement the Brussels Convention and thereby accomplish the task of 'simplification of formalities governing the reciprocal recognition and enforcement of judgments' mentioned in the fourth indent of Article 220. Although it was accepted that the ultimate shape and content of the Bankruptcy Convention would be determined by the special characteristics of its subject matter, the fundamental approach followed by the expert negotiators clearly mirrored that of the main, and faster-moving, project relating to civil and commercial judgments. In particular, the innovative approach embodied in the Brussels Convention of superimposing rules of direct jurisdiction in place of individual rules previously applied by the Member States in relation to matters governed by the Convention, was emulated in the terms of both the Phase I versions of the Bankruptcy Draft as published in 1970 and in 1980 respectively.[16] Thus, the EEC Convention was conceived as a 'double', or 'direct' convention, a radical advance upon anything previously attempted in the history of multilateral treaties in the field of bankruptcy.

Advocates of the use of a 'direct' type of convention could legitimately emphasise its suitability for use within a Community of States pursuing an integrationist programme whose aims included the creation of an internal market based upon the so-called 'four freedoms', namely the free circulation of persons, services, goods and capital. To attain this goal, it was necessary to address the problem of distortion caused to the commercial and economic environment of the Community by differences in the Member States' legislative and administrative provisions. In this context, both the Brussels Convention and the proposed Bankruptcy Convention could be viewed as having an important role to play in terms of providing for the free circulation of judgments in a way that complements the freedoms expressly established by the Treaty of Rome. By imposing a uniform code of rules for the exercise of jurisdiction in international cases, the conventions would enable the recognition and enforcement of judgments and orders to become virtually automatic processes, with minimal scope allowed for parties to challenge or resist at the enforcement stage. The Member States, and the courts and officials operating within them, would be obliged to give 'full faith and credit' to the legal determinations of equivalent institutions belonging to sister States.[17]

[16] See 1970 Draft, *supra* n.4, Title II (Arts. 3–17); 1980 Draft, *supra* n.5, Title II (Arts. 3–16).

[17] The rationale behind the programme of legal harmonisation of the EEC/EU, including the 'full faith and credit' concept in relation to civil and commercial judgments, is explored

By opting for the more audacious, and dirigiste, model for the Bankruptcy Convention the negotiators simultaneously assumed a more exacting responsibility in the matter of the technical quality of the convention's design. Under a 'direct' convention, all interested parties are compelled to rely almost totally on the integrity of the legal process at the point where jurisdiction is first exercised: there is only a limited possibility to rectify any misapplication or misuse of the convention's provisions, and the expense of doing so can be considerable. Not only must the rules for allocation of jurisdiction be intrinsically sound and sensible, but also they must be well drafted so that their meaning and effects are as clear and unambiguous as possible, in the interests of enabling parties to understand their legal position and arrange their affairs with adequate certainty.

Unfortunately, the jurisdictional provisions of both of the principal Phase I texts failed to match these exacting, but vital, requirements. What was proposed was a three-tier hierarchy of jurisdictional criteria linking the debtor to the territory of the State in which proceedings could be opened. The first rank was accorded to the Contracting State in which the debtor's 'centre of administration' (*centre des affaires*) is situated, the courts of that State being declared to have 'exclusive jurisdiction to declare the debtor bankrupt'.[18] The second rank was intended to apply to situations where the debtor's centre of administration is not located in any of the Contracting States. In that event, the courts of any Contracting State in which the debtor has an establishment are awarded jurisdiction to declare the debtor bankrupt.[19] Thirdly, where neither the centre of administration nor any establishment is situated in a Contracting State, an 'open season' is effectively declared by authorising the courts of any Contracting State whose law so permits to declare the debtor bankrupt. However, whereas the 1970 Draft would have allowed such bankruptcies to enjoy the full advantages of recognition and enforcement throughout the Community, the 1980 text was modified so as to exclude such bankruptcies from falling within the scope of the Convention.[20] Even in this modified form, how-

in I.F. Fletcher, *supra* n.2, in chs. 1, 2 and 4. The application of these arguments to the area of bankruptcy is addressed in *ibid.*, ch. 6 at pp. 187–194.

[18] See Art. 3(1) of both the 1970 and 1980 versions of the Draft (the wording is identical).

[19] See Art. 4(1) of both the 1970 and 1980 versions (the wording is again identical).

[20] See Art. 5 in the respective versions of 1970 and 1980. It may be observed that the earlier text was apparently intended to duplicate the effect of Art. 4 of the Brussels Convention of 27 September 1968 (in force from 1 February 1973) which, controversially, allows the courts of Contracting States to deploy their full repertoire of domestic rules of jurisdiction—including those of an exorbitant nature—against defendants in civil or commercial proceedings who happen not to be domiciled in any of the Contracting States. Judgments in such cases are nevertheless accorded the benefit of full faith and credit throughout the EC/EU territorial area. For trenchant criticism of this aspect of the Brussels Convention see, e.g. Nadelmann in (1967) 67 Colum. L. Rev. 995; in (1967–68) 5 C.M.L.Rev. 409; and in (1968) 82 Harv. L. Rev. 1282; Hay (1968) 16 A.J.C.L. 149, esp. at 160–162.

ever, the proposed jurisdictional scheme was fraught with perils and uncertainties. Thus, as regards the primary criterion based upon the location of the debtor's 'centre of administration', there was scope for divergent approaches to be adopted when applying the concept to the facts of actual cases. Although each version of the Draft supplied a definition of the expression as meaning 'the place where the debtor usually administers his main interests', this appears only to raise a whole series of further questions.[21] Similarly, with the secondary tier of jurisdictional competence, based upon the presence of an establishment, the Draft failed to match the need that it should embody certain and sensible principles. The 1970 Draft did not contain any definition of 'establishment', while the 1980 text merely offered the inadequate pronouncement that 'an establishment exists in a place where an activity of the debtor comprising a series of transactions is carried on by him or on his behalf'.[22] Given that this could result in the courts of several Contracting States having concurrent jurisdiction, the sensitive issue of priority demands a carefully designed rule to promote the fairest and most efficient solution, rather than one which rewards pre-emptive tactics on a 'winner takes all' basis. Sadly, the Phase I Drafts promised no such outcome. Instead of a qualitative test to determine the most appropriate forum, purely mechanical rules were proposed which would have awarded Community-wide supremacy to the proceedings which were chronologically the first to open.[23] Worse yet—and surely the height of absurdity as a proposed rule for adoption by a sophisticated Community of States—was the 'tie-breaking' provision, intended for cases where proceedings were commenced on the same day in different courts having coordinate jurisdiction: it was solemnly proposed that precedence should be determined by the alphabetical order of the place-names of the courts concerned![24]

The shortcomings of the jurisdictional rules of the Phase I Drafts were compounded by the unsuccessful attempt to simulate the embodiment of the twin principles of unity and universality of bankruptcy, and to misrepresent the degree to which they had genuinely been absorbed into the substance of the provisions to which the Contracting States would be

[21] See Art. 3(2) of the 1970 Draft; cf. Art. 3(2) and (3) of the 1980 Draft. Although both versions embody a rebuttable presumption, in the case of firms, companies and legal persons, that the registered office is the place where the debtor's main interests are usually administered, the manner of rebutting this presumption, and the degree of proof needed, are left uncertain. Given the scope for different views regarding what amount to a debtor's 'main' interests, the potential instability of this basis of jurisdiction was disturbing. See also the various approaches offered by Arts. 6 and 7 of the 1970 and 1980 Draft, respectively, for cases where there has been a transfer of the centre of administration.

[22] See Art. 4(2) of the 1980 Draft.

[23] See Arts. 15(2) and 52(1) of the 1970 Draft; Arts. 13(2) and 58(1) of the 1980 Draft.

[24] See Art. 52(2) of the 1970 Draft; Art. 58(2) of the 1980 Draft.

committing themselves.[25] If the proclamations within the texts themselves were taken at face value, proceedings opened according to the primary or secondary rules of jurisdiction would constitute the sole proceedings permitted to take place throughout the Contracting States, and would have automatic effect in relation to the debtor's property anywhere within those States. By virtue of the choice of law rules within the Draft Convention, whose effect is generally to require the application of the l aw of the State in which proceedings are opened (the *lex concursus*) for most purposes associated with the proceedings and the administration and distribution of the estate,[26] it ought to follow that the rights of all creditors—secured or unsecured; preferential or non-preferential—would be determined by the provisions of the *lex concursus*. In reality, the negotiators arranged matters somewhat differently, so that the rights of secured and preferential creditors belonging to any of the Contracting States could continue to be governed by the law of the *situs* of any secured property, and by the local law of the State under which a creditor's preferential status, and its relative ranking, was generated.[27] The negotiators had discovered at an early stage of their deliberations that the existing domestic laws of the original six Member States of the EEC differed from one another so fundamentally in such matters as their treatment of security, and the rights of preferential creditors, that it was impractical to attempt an alignment and harmonisation of substantive laws for the foreseeable future.[28] However, the very same reasons which made it politically unacceptable for the Member States to abandon deeply-embedded national traditions towards the treatment of these issues made it equally unthinkable for them to accept the subordination of the rights and expectations of local creditors to the regime of the *lex concursus*, where this happened to be that of some other State.

The theoretically elegant precepts of the scheme based upon unity and universality therefore yielded to the political imperatives of the shared desire on the part of the participating States to defend local practices in matters of the preferential treatment of certain types of claim in the process of distribution on an insolvency. This was achieved by means of an inelegant, and cumbersome, arrangement whereby the existence and ranking of preferential rights would be determined by the law of each

[25] See Art.2 (both Drafts), which bears the heading: *Unity of the Bankruptcy*, and Art. 33 of the 1970 Draft and Art. 34 of the 1980 Draft, both headed *Universality of the Bankruptcy*. For discussion of the two principles of unity and universality, see Chapter 1 above.

[26] See Arts. 17, 18, 19, 20–22, 28, 30 and 32 of the 1970 Draft; Arts. 15, 17, 18, 20–22, 29, 31 and 33 of the 1980 Draft.

[27] See Section VI of the two Drafts: Arts. 40–46 of the 1970 Draft; Arts. 43–52 of the 1980 Draft.

[28] See a comparative survey by Professor M. Sauveplanne, published in October 1963 as EEC Commission Doc. 8838/IV/63–E.

Contracting state under which a creditor was eligible to invoke such personal advantage, but only with respect to such assets as were actually situated in that State on the day when the bankruptcy opened.[29] This would have entailed the creation of a series of sub-estates, for accounting purposes, formed from each pool of assets realised in each of the States concerned. The sheer complexity of the exercise was truly horrifying, and would have resulted in much wasteful expenditure of administrative resources. Even less palatable, however, was the cynical proposal for the manner of dealing with any assets recovered in non-Contracting States, and with the claims of creditors from outside the frontiers of the European Community. Here, and here alone, the full rigours of the principles of unity and universality were to be applied, so that assets recovered from third States were to be amalgamated with those located in the *forum concursus* itself, and were likewise to be distributed in accordance with the rules contained in the *lex concursus*. It is surely distasteful, and also embarrassing, to have to acknowledge that such blatantly discriminatory treatment was considered by the authors of the successive versions of the Phase I Draft Convention to be an acceptable approach to the regulation of international insolvency, and was intended to be collectively embraced by an alliance of powerful, but not omnipotent, economically advanced States. Yet such was indeed the case, as the documentary evidence reveals. Fortunately, in the years after 1980, the tide of opposition to this fatally flawed, meretricious and unworkable Draft gradually grew stronger, and it was consigned to oblivion.

6.3 PHASE II: THE CONVENTION ON INSOLVENCY PROCEEDINGS (1995)[30]

As mentioned above, the Committee of Experts convened by the Council in 1989 to relaunch the project for a Bankruptcy Convention adopted an eclectic approach in going about their task. Drawing together the more satisfactory elements from the two models closest to hand—the Phase I Draft EC Convention and the Istanbul Convention which was opened for signature on 5 June 1990—the committee sought to combine these with fresh elements of its own devising. It also appears to have been guided by a strong instinct to provide a workable set of rules that respond to issues

[29] See Arts. 40–46 of the 1970 Draft; Arts. 42–52 of the 1980 Draft.

[30] Throughout this section the expression 'the Convention' denotes the European Union Convention on Insolvency Proceedings, opened for signature in Madrid on 23 November 1995 and signed by 14 of the 15 Member States (the exception being the United Kingdom) between that date and 23 May 1996, when the period permitted for signature expired. (See the Preliminary section of this chapter and at 6.1 above, and 6.4 below).

actually encountered in practice, rather than to pursue some impossible and almost abstract theory about the way in which to legislate for the problems of international insolvency. The finished text produced by the Balz Committee is one which, while by no means devoid of imperfections, has many positive virtues which under normal circumstances would have ensured its implementation by all Members of the European Union. These features will now be examined.

6.3.1 Structure and main features of the Convention

The Convention consists of a total of fifty-five Articles, arranged into six chapters of varying length, together with three Annexes. It is evidently the product of a realistic appraisal of the limited prospects for achieving any fundamental harmonisation of the domestic laws of the fifteen EU Member States in relation to credit, security or insolvency matters. That being the case, the most important requirement in the context of the EU internal market is to establish clear rules to determine in which State insolvency proceedings are capable of being commenced, and what choice of law rules are to be applied in those proceedings in relation to the crucial issues typically to be encountered in a cross-border case. In that way, parties can arrange their affairs, and structure their business transactions, on the basis of reasonably dependable predictions concerning the substantive law by which their rights will be governed. The Convention therefore adopts the same strategic approach as the Phase I models, in that it is a 'direct' or 'double' convention whose effect is to impose a uniform set of jurisdictional rules which must be applied in all the Contracting States in cases which fall within the ambit of its provisions.[31] Having laid the ground rules for jurisdiction and choice of law,[32] the Convention addresses the practical concerns of the office holder who is responsible for administering the insolvency proceedings (referred to throughout as 'the liquidator'),[33] by provisions for recognition of the proceedings and the exercise of the liquidator's powers in other Contracting States.[34] The concerns of creditors involved in a multi-jurisdictional insolvency are also taken into account in various ways, including simplification of the procedure for proving their claims.[35] The special facility available under Chapter III to enable secondary proceedings to be opened, with effects restricted to the territory of a single Contracting State, also carries important advantages for certain

[31] See Art. 3 of the Convention, further discussed below. This contrasts with the Istanbul Convention (*supra* n.7), which is an 'indirect' convention containing rules for recognition and enforcement only. See Chapter 7 below.

[32] Choice of law rules are contained in Arts. 4–15 inclusive, and are discussed below.

[33] Art. 2(b) of the Convention.

[34] See Chapter II of the Convention (Arts. 16–26 inclusive) below.

[35] Chapter IV of the Convention (Arts. 39–42 inclusive) below.

types of creditor.[36] Lastly, to ensure that the Convention receives a unified interpretation from the outset, provision is made in Chapter V for the European Court of Justice to have jurisdiction to deliver interpretative rulings concerning the Convention and its various Annexes.[37]

Scope of the Convention

Article 1(1) defines the scope of the Convention in positive terms, by declaring that it 'shall apply to collective insolvency proceedings which entail the partial or total divestment of a debtor and the appointment of a liquidator'. The Convention provides no definition of 'insolvency', and it is therefore left to each Contracting State to administer its own procedures according to the test of insolvency laid down by its national law and practice. Article 2, which supplies the definitions of a number of the expressions used in the Convention, states that 'insolvency proceedings' means the collective proceedings referred to in Article 1(1) as listed in Annex A, which is to form an integral part of the Convention. Annex A contains a list of those insolvency proceedings, as contained in the laws of each Contracting State, which are thereby brought within the ambit of the Convention. Consequently, the opening of such proceedings in the State in question must take place in conformity with the relevant provisions of the Convention, and is no longer a matter of unrestricted jurisdictional competence for the courts of that State. In the case of the United Kingdom, for example, the following are declared to be 'insolvency proceedings' for the purposes of the Convention:

(a) Winding up by the court (compulsory winding up)
(b) Bankruptcy (England and Wales, Northern Ireland)
(c) Administration of the insolvent estate of a deceased person (England and Wales, Northern Ireland)
(d) Administration by a judicial factor of the insolvent estate of a deceased person (Scotland)
(e) Sequestration (Scotland)
(f) Creditors' voluntary winding up (with confirmation by the court)
(g) Administration
(h) Voluntary arrangements under the Insolvency Act 1986 or the Insolvent Partnerships Order 1994.

With respect to the above list, it can be noted that the none of the types of receivership available under the laws of the various parts of the United Kingdom are included within the ambit of the Convention.[38] This is

[36] See Arts. 27–38 inclusive, discussed below.
[37] See Arts. 43–46 inclusive, discussed below.
[38] This exclusion applies to Administrative Receiverships and other types of Receiverships under Part III of the Insolvency Act 1986, and also to Receiverships under the Law of Property Act 1925, s.101.

explicable in view of the fact that such procedures are properly to be considered as remedies invoked by individual creditors and also because, in most instances, the court is not directly involved in the receivership process. The exclusion of Administrative Receivership from the ambit of the Convention is a factor to be borne in mind for the future when planning the rescue of a financially ailing business with a cross-border dimension: it may be more effective to resort to Administration, to which the Convention's provisions will be fully applicable, rather than the hitherto more favoured option of Administrative Receivership. Also noteworthy is the inclusion within the scope of the Convention of creditors' voluntary liquidations, which are of a collective nature but which do not normally require the active participation of the court. This has been effected subject to the proviso that there must be a judicial confirmation of the voluntary proceedings if they are to enjoy the benefits of extraterritorial recognition and effectiveness by virtue of this Convention.[39]

It may also be observed that Article 1(1) carefully restricts the application of the Convention to proceedings which 'entail the partial or total divestment of a debtor and the appointment of a liquidator', thereby excluding any types of insolvency proceeding which, though of a collective nature, leave the debtor in full control of his estate and business under some form of 'debtor in possession' principle. Although partial divestment suffices, there must be some degree of loss of the debtor's powers of administration and control over his affairs, whatever form this may take.[40] The expression 'liquidator' is defined in Article 2(b) to mean: 'any person or body whose function is to administer or liquidate the assets of which the debtor has been divested or to supervise the administration of his affairs'. Annex C lists, for each Contracting State respectively, the persons or bodies which qualify to be regarded as 'liquidator' in proceedings commenced under the laws of that State. As is also the case with Annexes A and B, this device has the advantage of eliminating any uncertainty regarding the types of proceeding, and the types of office holder, to which the Convention applies. The technique of listing all included subject matter by name has been adapted from the Istanbul Convention.[41] Article 54 of the EU Convention provides a relatively simple procedure for amendment of the Annexes at any time: any Contracting State wishing to do so is

[39] Although no provision is currently made by the Insolvency Act 1986 for the court to 'confirm' a creditors' voluntary winding up, it would be possible for the voluntary liquidator to apply to the court under the broadly-drawn provisions of s.112 of the Act, seeking directions and authorisation to undertake necessary action in other jurisdictions in furtherance of the liquidation. Alternatively, a specific provision might be enacted at a future date to meet the requirements of this proviso of the Convention.

[40] See Virgos-Schmit Report, *supra* n.10, para. 49(c).

[41] See *supra* n.7, and Art. 1(1) and (3)(a) together with Appendixes A and B of the Istanbul Convention (Appendix III below).

required to address a declaration of its proposed amendment to the Secretariat of the Council, which in turn must notify all signatory and Contracting States of its content. Unless any State raises objections within three months, the amendment is deemed to be accepted and will subsequently enter into force.

Article 1(2) sharpens the boundaries of the Convention's sphere of application, by providing that it shall not apply to insolvency proceedings concerning insurance undertakings, credit institutions, investment undertakings which provide services involving the holdings of funds or securities for third parties, or to collective investment undertakings. Entities of the kinds expressly excluded from the ambit of the Convention are usually subjected to special regulatory regimes under national laws, including special procedures in the event of insolvency. It is also the case that specific measures are being developed by the European Union to subject such entities to harmonised standards of regulation by means of Directives. Hence, a separate framework will eventually be put in place to deal with the insolvencies of these undertakings in the context of the European Union.[42]

6.3.2 International jurisdiction

Article 3 of the Convention is intended as the vehicle by means of which a uniform set of jurisdictional rules becomes applicable by all the Contracting States. It is therefore central to the negotiators' aspiration to design a 'direct' type of convention. With respect, the drafting of this provision is somewhat reticent about its intended effect, which is not immediately apparent from a reading of the text.[43] The Article contemplates only two categories of proceedings for the purposes of the Convention's wider scheme of operation, namely main proceedings (determined by reference to the location of the centre of the debtor's main interests), and secondary proceedings (based upon the presence of an establishment of the debtor within the Contracting State in question). Proceedings which qualify as main proceedings according to the terms of Article 3(1) are accorded the fullest benefits under the Convention and enjoy extraterritorial effects throughout all the Contracting States; the effects of proceedings which qualify as secondary proceedings under Article 3(2) are restricted to the territory of the State in which they are commenced, but are important

[42] See Virgos-Schmit Report, *supra* n.10, paras. 54–60.

[43] The drafting of Art. 3 may be contrasted with that of Arts. 2 and 3 of the Brussels Convention on Jurisdiction and the Enforcement of Judgments in Civil and Commercial Matters, Art. 2 of which, for example, proclaims: 'Subject to the provisions of this Convention, persons domiciled in a Contracting state shall, whatever their nationality, be sued in the courts of that State'.

inasmuch as they amount to a localised derogation from the universal effects otherwise enjoyed by main proceedings involving the same debtor. Any insolvency proceedings which fail to qualify as either main or secondary proceedings within the terms of Article 3 are altogether outside the scope of the Convention, and can derive no benefit from its provisions regarding international effects and recognition. Accordingly, they remain subject to national law for purposes of jurisdiction, and are dependent upon the ordinary rules of private international law for such recognition as they may receive from foreign States, including those which are Members of the European Union.[44] The precise criteria for the opening of main or secondary proceedings therefore require careful consideration.

Main proceedings (Article 3(1))

Article 3(1) enables the courts of the Contracting State within whose territory the centre of the debtor's main interests is situated to open insolvency proceedings having the character of main proceedings. Such proceedings have universal scope and are intended to encompass the debtor's assets on a worldwide basis and to affect all creditors, wherever located.[45] The principle of unity is also applicable to main proceedings, in that only one set of such proceedings may be opened in the territory covered by the Convention. Conversely, should the debtor's centre of main interests be located outside the territory of the Contracting States, no Contracting State has jurisdiction to open any insolvency proceedings within the scope of the Convention, and no attempt is made to regulate the taking of jurisdiction in such circumstances, nor to exert any influence on their international effect.[46] In other words, the Convention only has application in cases where the debtor's centre of main interests ('COMI') lies within the territory of one of the Contracting States. It is therefore of vital importance to be able to determine the whereabouts of the debtor's COMI. The Convention itself supplies no definition of the expression, nor any hint as to its intended meaning. Article 3(1) does however state that:

In the case of a company or legal person, the place of the registered office shall be presumed to be the centre of its main interests in the absence of proof to the contrary.

Thus, in a manner that is reminiscent of the terms of the Phase I Draft Convention,[47] a rebuttable presumption as to the location of the COMI is

[44] Consequently, the various grounds on which insolvency proceedings can be commenced in England against foreign debtors—including foreign companies—would remain operative even when the Convention is in force, save in those cases where the debtor's centre of main interests is in the territory of another Contracting State. See Chapters 2 and 3 above, esp. sections 2.1. and 3.2.2.

[45] Virgos-Schmit Report, *supra* n.10, para. 73.

[46] *Ibid.*, para. 82.

[47] See *supra* n.21, referring to the presumption offered by Art. 3(2) of the successive versions of that Draft. The counterpart of 'centre of main interests' in the earlier texts was the

to operate with respect to corporate debtors. Since no further guidance is given as to the mode of disproving the presumption this will be a matter for the court before which the issue presents itself to determine in accordance with its own practice and standards. It may be supposed that the burden of proof will fall upon those who seek to persuade the court of the State where the registered office is situated that the debtor's COMI is actually elsewhere, and that it accordingly lacks jurisdiction. It is not impossible however that, under some circumstances, the courts of two different Contracting States could reach the conclusion that the debtor's COMI is located within their territory, thereby giving rise to a positive conflict of jurisdiction for whose resolution the Convention provides no obvious solution short of a costly and time-consuming reference to the Court of Justice.[48] Also possible, if somewhat unlikely, is a negative conflict in which each court concludes that the COMI is *not* located in its territory, and that in consequence it cannot exercise jurisdiction.

In the absence of clear guidance in the text of the Convention itself regarding the meaning to be ascribed to the expression 'centre of main interests', reference has to be made to the Virgos-Schmit Report. Paragraph 75 declares that the concept 'must be interpreted as the place where the debtor conducts the administration of his interests on a regular basis and is therefore ascertainable by third parties'. The Report adds that the rationale for this is that insolvency is a foreseeable risk and that it is important that international jurisdiction be based on a place known to the debtor's potential creditors, in order that the legal risks assumed through dealing with that party in the event of its insolvency can be calculated. It is also explained that the term 'interests' was selected as being apt to encompass not only commercial, industrial or professional activities, but also general activities of private individuals, such as consumers and non-traders. The Report asserts that:

> In principle, the centre of main interests will in the case of professionals be the place of their professional domicile and for natural persons in general, the place of their habitual residence.[49]

debtor's 'centre of administration': it is perhaps significant that the same presumptive formula is used in both the Phase I and Phase II models for identifying the whereabouts of the key jurisdictional factor for cases of companies and legal persons.

[48] See Chapter V of the Convention, discussed at 6.3.7 below. According to Art. 44, such references can only be submitted by the court of final resort of the State in question. An example of the way in which such conflicts could arise is provided by the case of *Bank of Credit and Commerce International S.A.*, whose state of incorporation was Luxembourg but whose operational base was at most material times in England. See Fletcher (1997) 23 Brook. J. Int'l L. 25 at 37; Segal, *ibid.* at 66–67. (Aspects of the *B.C.C.I.* case are discussed in Chapters 3 and 4 above). See also Balz, *supra* n.10, at 504–505.

[49] Virgos-Schmit Report, *supra* n.10, para. 75, which also states, in relation to the presumption established by Art. 3(1) in the case of a company or legal person that the COMI is the place of the registered office: 'This place normally corresponds to the debtor's head

Secondary (territorial) proceedings (Article 3(2)–(4))

The provisions relating to secondary proceedings exhibit the most radical realignment of approach to insolvency jurisdiction, as compared to that of the Phase I Draft.[50] Despite the superficial resemblance, in that the criterion for secondary jurisdiction is in both instances the presence of an establishment of the debtor within the territory of the State in question, the concept of secondary proceedings in the finished Convention is completely different. Under the terms of Article 3(2), secondary proceedings can only be opened in circumstances where the centre of the debtor's main interests is situated within the territory of one of the Contracting States.[51] Where this condition is fulfilled, the courts of another Contracting State have jurisdiction to open insolvency proceedings against that debtor only if he possesses an establishment within the territory of that other Contracting State. Moreover, it is expressly stated that the effects of those proceedings under Article 3(2) shall be restricted to the assets of the debtor situated in the territory of the State in which they are opened. Thus, such proceedings are of purely local effect, and it is appropriate to refer to them as 'territorial'. However, it should be noted that they are not permitted to take place in complete isolation, and that the provisions of Chapter III of the Convention are designed to ensure that secondary proceedings are integrated into the overall process of administering the insolvent debtor's estate for the benefit of creditors generally.

In practice, for reasons that will become apparent, proceedings will generally take place under the provisions of Article 3(2) concurrently with main proceedings opened under Article 3(1). Usually, it should be the case that the main proceedings are the first in time to open. Paragraph (3) of Article 3 stipulates that when main proceedings have been opened, any proceedings opened subsequently under paragraph (2) shall be secondary proceedings, thereby making them subject to the provisions of Chapter III. It is additionally specified that these latter proceedings must be winding-up proceedings. This has the effect of considerably narrowing the range of options available, in terms of the types of proceedings which can be resorted to. This is because the definition of 'winding-up proceedings'

office'. Paragraph 76 concedes that the Convention provides no rule for cases of groups of affiliated companies, and states that to open or consolidate insolvency proceedings against related companies jurisdiction must exist according to the Convention for each of the concerned debtors with a separate legal identity. In practice, this would leave internationally-constituted groups beyond the reach of the present Convention, and it would require a specific European Directive to provide a proper solution for such cases.

[50] See section 6.2. above, with reference to Art. 4(1) of the 1970 and 1980 versions of the Phase I Draft.

[51] By contrast, Art. 4(1) of the Phase I Draft only permitted second-tier jurisdiction, based on presence of an establishment, to be exercised where the debtor's centre of administration was *not* situated in a Contracting State.

supplied by Article 2(c) is limited to 'insolvency proceedings (within the meaning of paragraph (a)) involving realising the assets of the debtor', with the procedures which qualify for this purpose being listed in Annex B to the Convention. The procedures listed, State by State, in Annex B are considerably fewer than are included in Annex A.[52] The consequence appears to be that in cases where the main proceedings consist of an attempt to bring about the rescue of a business which maintains one or more foreign establishments, the prospects of success could be seriously undermined by any creditors who avail themselves of the opportunity to commence secondary proceedings in the States where the establishments are located.[53] In certain situations however parties may wish to open territorial insolvency proceedings under Article 3(2) where no main proceedings have been commenced. This may be because, under the law of the State within whose territory the debtor's COMI is situated, the law does not allow such proceedings to be commenced.[54] Alternatively, the opening of main proceedings may be delayed for some technical reason, or simply because those who are eligible to petition for such proceedings delay, or altogether refrain, from doing so. Article 3(4) makes special provision for both these contingencies, by allowing territorial proceedings to be opened prior to any main proceedings being commenced. In the absence of evidence to the effect that main proceedings cannot be opened because of the conditions laid down by the law of the Contracting State where the debtor's COMI is located, the opening of territorial proceedings can only be requested by a creditor who has his domicile, habitual residence or registered office within the Contracting State in whose territory the establishment is situated, or whose claim arises from the operation of that establishment.[55] These restrictions upon the right to request the opening of independent territorial proceedings are clearly aimed at preventing disruptive tactics on the part of creditors who do not have a close personal nexus with the jurisdiction in which the debtor's establishment is located.

[52] In the case of the United Kingdom, Annex B lists only the following as constituting 'winding-up proceedings': winding up by the court (compulsory winding up), bankruptcy (England and Wales, Northern Ireland); administration of the insolvent estate of a deceased person (England and Wales, Northern Ireland); administration by a judicial factor of the insolvent estate of a deceased person (Scotland); and sequestration (Scotland). It will be noted that Creditors' voluntary liquidations, though included in Annex A, are omitted from Annex B, as are company administrations and all types of voluntary arrangements.

[53] See the further discussion of this problem, in relation to the provisions of Chapter III of the Convention, at 6.3.5 below.

[54] The laws of a number of the Contracting States follow the tradition whereby insolvency proceedings cannot take place against non-traders (*non-commerçants*). This is the case, e.g. in Belgium, France, Greece, Italy, Luxembourg, Portugal and Spain. Indeed, in the case of Italy, even small-scale traders (*piccoli imprenditori*) are excluded from the operation of the bankruptcy law by Art. 2083 of the Civil Code.

[55] See Art. 3(4)(b).

The key concept in relation to the opening of secondary (territorial) insolvency proceedings is therefore the existence of an 'establishment' belonging to the debtor. Article 2(h) defines the term as meaning:

any place of operations where the debtor carries out a non-transitory economic activity with human means and goods.

The significance of the above definition is somewhat clarified by paragraphs 70 and 71 of the Virgos-Schmit Report, which disclose that this provision was the cause of much debate during the negotiations. The exclusion of any possibility for proceedings to be opened on the basis of the mere presence of assets of debtor, in the absence of any establishment, represents a deliberate decision to restrict the number of opportunities for creditors to avail themselves of the personal and tactical advantages to be gained by means of secondary proceedings. A contrast may be drawn between the 'passive' quality of assets (even if of very substantial value), and the 'active' quality of the concept of an establishment. Also to be emphasised are the requirement that the economic activity be of a 'non-transitory' nature, and that it be carried out with 'human means *and* goods'.[56] Thus a purely occasional place of operations could not be classified as an establishment, although neither the Convention nor the Report ventures any suggestion as to the minimum length of time after which an activity ceases to be considered as 'transitory': it will be a matter of judgment for the court, taken in the light of all relevant circumstances. Effectively, the court will be seeking to ascertain whether the debtor maintains a 'place of business' within its jurisdiction.[57] In their approach, courts should bear in mind that the Convention's intended purpose is to serve as an integral component in the legal infrastructure sustaining the European Union's internal market. The underlying rationale for allowing insolvency proceedings to be opened on the basis of an establishment is that foreign participants in the economic activities conducted within a given Member State should be subject to equal rules and conditions as compared to national operators with whom they are competing. In this way, potential creditors do not have to concern themselves unduly whether the debtor is ultimately 'foreign' in orientation, provided that the external appearances suggest a locally-established business operation. The external impression

[56] Emphasis added: the test is thus a compound one. cf. the definition of 'establishment' contained in Art. 2(f) of the UNCITRAL Model Law on Cross-Border Insolvency, described in Chapter 8 below at p. 336, where the concluding phrase of the definition refers to 'human means and goods or services'. The Istanbul Convention, conversely, permits the opening of secondary bankruptcy on the basis of presence of assets: see Art. 17, discussed in Chapter 7, section 7.4.

[57] Cf. the approach of English courts to determining whether a debtor satisfies jurisdictional criteria concerned with the carrying on of business, discussed above in Chapter 2, section 2.1.1.*(b)(iii)(B)*, and in Chapter 3, section 3.2.2.*(a)*. See also Balz, *supra* n.10, at 505.

is therefore the decisive factor, rather than the subjective intentions of the debtor.[58]

6.3.3 Choice of law rules

Articles 4–15 inclusive establish a miniature code of uniform conflicts rules which are to form an integral aspect of the Convention's operation. All insolvency proceedings that are opened in accordance with the provisions of the Convention will thus be subject to the same, standardised choice of law rules regarding matters falling for determination in the context of those proceedings. The uniform rules indicate, as between various Contracting States whose laws may be applicable in a given situation, which State's law shall govern. In the absence of any prospect that the substantive insolvency laws of the EU Member States can be harmonised in the foreseeable future, the adoption of uniform conflicts rules is the only practical means of supplying the essential requirement of predictability for parties who need to calculate the legal consequences of their actions within an intra-Union context. Variability of outcome will remain a possibility for cases where the potentially applicable law is that of some third State, since the Convention's provisions are so drafted as to restrict their effects to situations where the competing laws are those of different Contracting States. Where the circumstances are such as to give rise to a conflict between the laws of a Contracting State and those of some third party, the Convention's provisions do not purport to regulate the outcome, which thus falls to be determined by any parallel rule belonging to the conflicts law of the State concerned.[59] As is emphasised in paragraph 44 of the Virgos-Schmit Report, the Convention is deliberately limited to regulating the 'intra-Community effects' of insolvency proceedings: where non-Member States are concerned it is the responsibility of each Member State to define the appropriate conflict rules. This is, unfortunately, a recipe for instability and uncertainty, particularly where the assets to which the alternating conflicts rules are to apply are mobile, and therefore capable of being subject to different rules according to their whereabouts at the relevant time.

Renvoi

An important general point about the choice of law provisions in the Convention is that wherever they make reference to 'the law', this denotes the substantive, domestic law of the Contracting State concerned. The

[58] Virgos-Schmit Report, *supra* n.10, para. 71.

[59] See Virgos-Schmit Report, *supra* n.10, paras. 44,93; Balz, *supra* n.10, at 507. On the problems caused by parallel rules of conflict of laws, see I.F. Fletcher, *Conflict of Laws and European Community Law* (1982), ch. 3.

complexities—not to say inconsistencies—of the doctrine of *renvoi* are not intended to form part of the approach to be followed under the Convention. In modern treaties which embody uniform conflicts rules, it is quite often the case that a specific provision is included to the effect that references to the law of a State or country are not to be interpreted as including a reference to the choice of law rules which are in force there.[60] Indeed, to allow recourse to *renvoi* would defeat the very objective of seeking to harmonise choice of law rules by means of such an international agreement. The EU Insolvency Convention is intended to follow this approach, although no express provision to that effect was incorporated into the actual text.[61]

The basic rule (Article 4): Lex concursus

Article 4 expresses the basic principle that the law of the Contracting State in which proceedings are opened according to the Convention (referred to as 'the State of opening') is to be applied to those proceedings, and shall determine their effects, except in so far as the Convention expressly provides to the contrary. The matters which are to be governed by the law of the State of opening (the *lex concursus*) are mentioned in a non-exhaustive list in Article 4(2), while the particular exceptions to the regime of the *lex concursus* are contained in Articles 5 to 15. The opening words of Article 4(2) supply a broad proposition to the effect that the *lex concursus* shall determine the conditions for the opening of the proceedings, their conduct and their closure. Under this formula, many matters of substance are determined by the law of the State of opening, as well as all matters of a procedural nature which, in conformity with accepted principles of conflict of laws, are governed by the *lex fori*. Thirteen matters are singled out for special mention in Article 4(2) as being for determination by the *lex concursus*. These are:

(a) against which debtors insolvency proceedings may be brought on account of their capacity;
(b) the assets which form part of the estate and the treatment of assets acquired by or devolving on the debtor after the opening of the insolvency proceedings;
(c) the respective powers of the debtor and the liquidator;
(d) the conditions under which set-offs may be invoked;[62]

[60] See, e.g. EC Convention on the Law Applicable to Contractual Obligations (the Rome Convention), of 19 June 1980, Art. 15 (which has the heading:'Exclusion of *renvoi*'): 'The application of the law of any country specified by this Convention means the application of the rules of law in force in that country *other than its rules of private international law*' (emphasis added).

[61] See Virgos-Schmit Report, *supra* n.10, para. 87.

[62] See Art. 6 below *(Exception II)*.

(e) the effects of insolvency proceedings on current contracts to which the debtor is party;[63]
(f) the effects of the insolvency proceedings on proceedings brought by individual creditors, with the exception of lawsuits pending;[64]
(g) the claims which are to be lodged against the debtor's estate and the treatment of claims arising after the opening of insolvency proceedings;
(h) the rules governing the lodging, verification and admission of claims;
(i) the rules governing the distribution of proceeds from the realisation of assets, the ranking of claims and the rights of creditors who have obtained partial satisfaction after the opening of insolvency proceedings by virtue of a right in rem or through a set-off;[65]
(j) the conditions for and the effects of closure of insolvency proceedings, in particular by composition;
(k) creditors' rights after the closure of insolvency proceedings;
(l) who is to bear the costs and expenses incurred in the insolvency proceedings;
(m) the rules relating to the voidness, voidability or unenforceability of legal acts detrimental to all the creditors.[66]

Although many of the matters referred to in paragraphs (a) to (m) above are largely self-explanatory, some comments are appropriate here. Paragraph (a) is particularly significant in view of the wide diversity between the insolvency laws of the fifteen EU Member States concerning the types of debtor to which the different kinds of insolvency proceedings are applicable.[67] Variations also occur with regard to the treatment of after-acquired property, the composition of the estate available for distribution among creditors, and the extent to which certain assets are exempt from forming part of it. These are among the issues which paragraph (b) brings under the control of the *lex concursus*. The importance of paragraphs (g), (h) and (i) should also be noted, since they ensure that the law of the State of opening is determinative of each stage of the process of distribution of the estate, including the matter of what debts are, and are not, provable; the treatment of post-commencement claims against the estate; all aspects bearing upon proof and admission of claims; and the vital question of the ranking of claims for purposes of dividend, and also the treatment of partly-secured creditors who wish to lodge proof for the balance of any claim which has been partly recouped through the enforcement of *in rem* security or the operation of set-off. The basic approach to be followed in relation to set-off is also that of the State of opening by virtue

[63] See Art. 8 below *(Exception IV)*.
[64] See Art. 15 below *(Exception X)*.
[65] See Arts. 5 and 6 below *(Exceptions I and II)*.
[66] The provision in Art. 4(2)(m) is given precedence over the special rules in favour of application of some law other than the *lex concursus*, in Arts. 5, 6 and 7: see Arts. 5(4), 6(2) and 7(3). However, paragraph (m) is expressly prevented from applying in cases governed by Art. 13 (below).
[67] For example, the restriction under the laws of certain States whereby only traders can be the subject of insolvency proceedings: see *supra* n.54 above.

of paragraph (d), so that parties' expectations of how the doctrine of set-off will affect their position in the event of their debtor's insolvency are primarily determined by reference to the law of the State where insolvency proceedings can be opened.[68]

The potential for impeachment of an insolvent debtor's pre-bankruptcy transactions, and likewise of any acts or dispositions of property carried out after the opening of proceedings, is one of the key aspects of the insolvency process. Moreover, the relevant rules are subject to crucial variations as between different jurisdictions. Hence the importance of Article 4(2)(m), which establishes the basic rule that the *lex concursus* shall be applied to determine the validity or otherwise of the debtor's legal acts detrimental to the general body of creditors. This provision is particularly far-reaching in its effect, because it is intended not merely to determine what procedural steps must be taken to bring about the invalidation or avoidance of such transactions, but also to displace any law which might otherwise have been applicable to govern the transaction, had bankruptcy not supervened.[69] However, Article 13 superimposes a rule whose effect is to disapply Article 4(2)(m) in certain circumstances, with the consequence that the avoidance rule of the *lex concursus* is displaced in favour of the rule of some other State. This is to occur where the person who benefited from a legal act detrimental to all the creditors provides proof that: (i) the act in question is subject to the law of a Contracting State other than that of the State of opening of proceedings; and (ii) that law does not allow any means of challenging that act in the relevant case. Protection is thereby given to parties who have reasonably relied upon the validity of a transaction whose governing law happens to be that of a Contracting State, and which is unimpeachable under the concrete circumstances of the case according to both the insolvency law and the general law of that State.[70]

A further notable effect of Article 4(2)(m) is that it has been designed to surmount one of the controversial aspects of the application of transaction avoidance rules in cases of conflict of laws, namely the possibility of cumulative application of the rules of more than one system in order to decide whether the transaction is valid. Under most circumstances, only a single avoidance rule—that of the *lex concursus*—is applicable. This greatly simplifies the task of the liquidator in seeking to bring about the avoidance of such transactions. However, in the special situation covered by Article 13 the other party to the transaction with the debtor is effectively allowed to interpose, by way of defence to any attack based upon the avoidance

[68] However, these expectations may be supplemented in certain cases by the impact of Art. 6, as to which see below.

[69] Virgos-Schmit Report, *supra* n.10, para. 90. See also Balz, *supra* n.10, at pp. 511–512.

[70] Virgos-Schmit Report, *supra* n.10, paras. 135–139.

rule of the *lex concursus*, the fact that it is valid and unimpeachable according to the law by which it is properly governed.

The above account of the dominant role accorded to the *lex concursus* serves to emphasise the substantial benefits which accrue from the opening of proceedings within the scope of application of the EU Convention. The basic choice of law rule established by Article 4 applies both to main proceedings within Article 3(1) and to territorial proceedings (whether secondary or independent in character) within paragraphs (2) to (4) of that Article.[71] This supplies one of the main reasons for parties to avail themselves of any opportunity to bring about the commencement of secondary insolvency proceedings under the Convention, since this will result in the application of the law of that Contracting State, instead of the law of the State in which the main proceedings have been opened, to the process of administering and distributing the assets located within the State in which the secondary proceedings take place.[72]

Exceptions to the basic rule (Articles 5–15)

Exception I: third parties' rights in rem *(Article 5)*

The first major exception to the *lex concursus* rule of Article 4 is provided by Article 5, whose purpose is to confirm the rights of parties to enter into transactions under which proprietary interests are created in favour of a creditor by way of security for the debt or obligation due from the debtor. In practice, the essential purpose of such forms of security is that it enables the secured party to have direct recourse to the collateral in the event that the debtor does not pay or perform—and especially where this occurs by reason of the debtor's insolvency. For this purpose to be achieved, it is vital that the laws of every concerned jurisdiction should fully accept that the right *in rem* is valid and enforceable even in the event of the debtor's insolvency. The possibility which has to be confronted in a cross-border case is that the location of the collateral, either at the time of opening of proceedings or at some other material time, may be in a different State to that in which insolvency proceedings are opened. In that event, given the variations between national laws concerning real security and the impact of insolvency upon such arrangements, there is a very real prospect of different conclusions as to the secured creditor's rights being reached under the *lex concursus* and the *lex situs*. Such uncertainty is a commercial anathema, and has serious repercussions for the stability and cost of transactions concluded in a transnational context. Also of concern to a secured creditor is the extent to which, even if the right *in rem* is recognised, its enforcement or realisation may be inhibited in some way which may erode its economic value, for example through the application of a

[71] See at 6.3.2 above. [72] Secondary proceedings are discussed below at 6.3.5.

comprehensive stay and moratorium during the course of a reorganisation procedure.

Article 5 supplies a rule which significantly reinforces the position of the secured creditor whose collateral is situated, at the time of opening of proceedings, in a different Contracting State to that in which insolvency proceedings take place. To the extent that the *lex situs* upholds the rights of the secured creditor, and allows him to enforce those rights over the collateral, for example through sale or foreclosure, in spite of the debtor's insolvency, such rights are to be respected even if this is contrary to the effects that would be produced according to the *lex concursus*. Article 5(1) states:

> The opening of insolvency proceedings shall not affect the rights in rem of creditors or third parties in respect of tangible or intangible, movable or immovable assets belonging to the debtor which are situated within the territory of another Contracting State at the time of the opening of proceedings.

It should be noted how widely the terms of this provision are drawn in relation to the types of asset to which it can have application. All types of property are capable of being affected, including such commercially important items as book debts and other receivables, and assets that are of a future character at the time the security interest is created but which have come into existence by the time that insolvency proceedings are opened. However, an asset is only within the ambit of this Article if it is located within the territory of one of the Contracting States at the time of opening: where the *situs* of the asset at the relevant time is in some third State, Article 5 is not applicable and it is left to the *lex concursus* alone to determine to what extent, if at all, rights which are dependent on the law of the *situs* can be respected or in some way taken into account.

The situs *of property.* There is an obvious need for certainty with regard to the method of identifying the location of an asset for the purposes of applying the rule in Article 5. Some assistance is provided by Article 2(g), which defines the expression 'the Contracting State in which assets are situated' in the case of three particular kinds of property, namely tangible property, registrable property, and 'claims'. In the case of tangible property, the physical location of the property is, somewhat prosaically, identified as the *situs*. In the case of property and rights to which there attaches a requirement of public registration, the *situs* is in the Contracting State under whose authority the register is kept. In the case of 'claims' (in the sense of liabilities that are enforceable *by* the insolvent debtor against some other party), these are declared to be situated in the Contracting State in which the obligated party has his centre of main interests, to be determined according to the test employed under Article 3(1).[73] Consequently,

[73] On the centre of main interests, see at 6.3.2 above.

the place at which a debt is expressed to be payable, or at which the debtor expressly agreed to be sued in the event of non-payment, does not constitute the *situs* of the debt for the purposes of Article 5.

The time factor. The relevant time at which the situation of an asset is to be determined is the opening of insolvency proceedings. This could give rise to difficulties, and be a cause of injustice, if the asset is of a movable nature and its location has changed between the time at which the right *in rem* was created and the time when proceedings are opened. This would be especially suspicious if the consequence of relocation is that the asset in question has been removed from the territory over which the *lex concursus* is applicable, with the possibility that the rights of the secured creditor are less susceptible to impeachment than they would otherwise have been. This contingency is countered by the provision in Article 5(4), which preserves the applicability of the actions for avoidance of antecedent transactions of the *lex concursus*, as laid down in Article 4(2)(m). Conversely, a creditor who takes security over movable property on the basis that the law of its current *situs* confers satisfactory protection in the event of the debtor's insolvency, must consider the possibility that the asset may be moved to another Contracting State, or to some third State, and thereby become subject to a different legal regime at the relevant time. If possible, the terms of the transaction should be so designed as to minimise the consequent risks of such relocation.

Meaning of 'rights in rem*'.* The Convention does not supply an exhaustive definition of the expression 'rights *in rem*'. However, Article 5(2) and (3) furnish some indication of the meaning to be attributed to the expression, while supplementary guidance can be found in the Virgos-Schmit Report.[74] Article 5(2) is essentially concerned to describe the nature and content of rights which qualify as rights *in rem* within paragraph (1). It states that they shall, in particular, mean:

(a) the right to dispose of assets or have them disposed of and to obtain satisfaction from the proceeds of or income from those assets, in particular by virtue of a lien or a mortgage;

(b) the exclusive right to have a claim met, in particular a right guaranteed by a lien in respect of the claim or by assignment of the claim by way of a guarantee;

(c) the right to demand the assets from, and/or to require restitution by, anyone having possession or use of them contrary to the wishes of the party so entitled;

(d) a right in rem to the beneficial use of assets.

The above list of attributes that are associated with various kinds of right *in rem* is intended as a guide to the task of characterisation, which

[74] Virgos-Schmit Report, *supra* n.10, paras. 94–106 inclusive. For critical discussion of the treatment of secured creditors under the Convention, see Garrido [1998] 7 I.I.R. 79.

however remains a matter for the State where the assets are located. The Convention has deliberately refrained from imposing its own definition of a right *in rem* which could result in assets having to be classified in a way which is in conflict with the approach followed by the law of the *situs*.[75] Nevertheless, a more *dirigiste* approach is taken by Article 5(3) in respect of rights which are recorded in a public register and enforceable against third parties, whereby a right *in rem* may be obtained. Such a right is to be considered a right *in rem* throughout all Contracting States, irrespective of any contrary conclusions to be derived from the provisions of national law.[76] The Virgos-Schmit Report emphasises that the provisions of Article 5 only protect pre-existing rights which were created before the insolvency proceedings were opened.[77] Therefore, creditors who have not succeeded in perfecting their right to be treated as secured under the law of the *lex situs* before the time of opening of insolvency proceedings in another Contracting State, are subject to the effects of the *lex concursus*, in accordance with the basic principle of Article 4. This would be the case, for example, with creditors who have commenced such processes as distress or execution which are incomplete at the time of opening of insolvency.[78]

Floating charge security, etc. In the absence of an exhaustive definition of 'rights *in rem*' for the purposes of Article 5, or more generally, particular interest will arise in relation to the status of certain types of security, such as the floating charge, in the context of this important exception to the regime of the *lex concursus*. Since this form of security is recognised under the laws of only a minority of the Contracting States—notably the United Kingdom and Ireland—the possibility of conflicting classifications by courts in States belonging to the civil and common law traditions respectively is an issue of no little practical importance. Similar conflicts of characterisation may occur in relation to other kinds of security device developed in recent times, such as the currently accepted practice of creating a fixed charge over future book debts, which can be analysed as having the effect of purporting to give rise to a present right *in rem* without either surrender of possession or even an existing subject matter to which the right can attach. Paragraph 104 of the Virgos-Schmit Report attempts to clarify the position as follows:

> A right *in rem* may not only be established with regard to specific assets but also with regard to assets as a whole. Security rights such as the 'floating charge' recognised in United Kingdom and Irish law can, therefore, be characterised as a right *in rem* for the purposes of the Convention. Likewise, rights characterised under national law as rights *in rem* over intangible assets or over rights are also included.

75 Virgos-Schmit Report, *supra* n.10, para. 100.
76 *Ibid.*, para. 101.
77 *Ibid.*, paras. 96, 103.
78 See, e.g., Insolvency Act 1986, ss.130(2), 183, 184, 346, 347.

One final observation may be made with respect to Article 5 and its effects. Although it can provide protection for the secured creditor against the direct disturbance of expectations founded upon the provisions of the *lex situs*, it does not immunise the creditor against the invocation of processes which may be available under that very law in the event of the debtor's insolvency. In order to bring such remedies into operation however it would be necessary for the liquidator in the main proceedings, or some other qualified party, to procure the opening of secondary bankruptcy proceedings under the *lex situs*, and in this way provoke such consequences for the holder of the right *in rem* as may be available under the insolvency law of that State. Naturally, such secondary proceedings can only be commenced if the debtor has an establishment in that Contracting State.[79]

Exception II: set-off (Article 6)

The laws of the Contracting States diverge sharply over the operation of set-off in the event of a debtor's insolvency. In the United Kingdom, set-off is treated as a mandatory process which must be applied, as a matter of public policy, in both individual and corporate insolvencies in which the necessary requirement of mutuality is present.[80] In most civil law systems, on the other hand, the prevailing view is that set-off constitutes a violation of the principle of *pari passu* distribution, and that as a matter of public policy it must be confined to the most carefully limited circumstances, as where the cross-liabilities arise out of one and the same contract or obligation. Therefore, in a cross-border insolvency, the outcome for any creditor who is also a debtor to the estate can be drastically affected by the way in which the issue of applicable law is resolved, if the competing laws happen to represent the different schools of opinion with regard to set-off.[81] Particularly in major commercial operations where large sums of money are involved, the ability to predict the applicable law and to take its provisions on set-off fully into account is vitally important in the assessment of risk. Clear, and uniformly applicable, choice of law rules are therefore essential.

We have seen above that Article 4(2)(d) establishes a basic rule to the effect that it is for the *lex concursus* to determine the conditions under

[79] Virgos-Schmit Report, *supra* n.10, para.98.

[80] For an account of the English approach to insolvency set-off, see I.F. Fletcher, *The Law of Insolvency*, 2nd edn. (1996), pp. 272–276, 599–600. There are two substantial works dealing with the subject: P.R. Wood, *English and International Set-Off* (1989); R. Derham, *Set-Off*, 2nd edn. (1996). The law was reviewed and restated by the House of Lords in *Stein v. Blake* [1996] A.C. 243.

[81] The most vivid illustration of this problem in recent times was seen in the case of *Re Bank of Credit and Commerce S.A. (No. 10)* [1996] 4 All E.R. 796. For comment and criticism of this case see Fletcher [1997] J.B.L. 471–476; Shandro [1998] 7 I.I.R.63.

which set-offs may be invoked. Accordingly, any party who wishes to calculate the consequences of the insolvency of a debtor with whom international transactions take place which generate debts or liabilities in both directions must first determine which Contracting State is destined to become the forum for main bankruptcy proceedings, or for any secondary proceedings, involving the other party as the insolvent debtor. It is of course perfectly possible that the mutual dealings between the parties may have as their respective governing laws either the same country's law, or the laws of different countries, and that these may or may not happen to be Contracting Parties to the EU Convention. The possible variations are therefore very numerous. Under the rule of Article 4(2)(d), however, it is entirely a matter for the *lex concursus* to determine whether, in the course of applying its doctrine of set-off, any account will be taken of the fact (if such is the case) that either of the cross-obligations is governed by a foreign law under which a different approach is followed. Clearly, there are latent perils for the unwary, whose assumptions may be founded upon familiar rules of the law of the State in which their own business has been conducted, and of the law or laws by which their contractual relationships are designed to be governed.

Although the fate of any creditor who is simultaneously a debtor to the insolvent estate is primarily controlled by the set-off rule of the *lex concursus*, Article 6 establishes one, carefully limited, exception to this. If the effect of the *lex concursus* is that set-off is not applicable to the circumstances of the cross-claims in question, the creditor may be able to derive assistance from the provision in Article 6(1) which states that the creditor shall not be deprived of the right to demand the set-off of his claims against the claims of the debtor 'where such a set-off is permitted by the law applicable to the insolvent debtor's claim'. This somewhat ponderous phrase is intended to denote 'the law applicable to the claim where the insolvent debtor is the creditor in relation to the other party'.[82] To establish the law by which the relevant claim is governed (assuming it to be contractual), a common set of choice of law rules is supplied by the Rome Convention on the Law Applicable to Contractual Obligations, to which all Member states of the European Union are, or are destined to become, Contracting Parties. The Rome Convention is based upon the principle that the governing law may be that of some third State, rather than being limited to the laws of the Contracting States themselves. Significantly, Article 6 of the Insolvency Convention omits any reference to 'the Contracting States', or their respective laws, in creating the exception in favour of the rule of set-off that is operated by 'the law applicable to the insolvent debtor's claim'. It therefore

[82] Virgos-Schmit Report, *supra* n.10, para. 108. Some writers employ the expression 'passive claim' to denote this aspect of the set-off relationship, to be contrasted with the 'active' claim owed to the estate by the creditor.

appears to be the case that in this instance the law of some third State could furnish the basis for allowing the creditor to have the benefit of set-off which would otherwise be excluded under the regime of the *lex concursus*. Where parties are in a position to exercise choice regarding the law by which their transactions are governed, they may well deem it expedient to ensure that a clear, express choice is made in favour of the law of a country whose rule concerning set-off is most suited to their requirements. Article 3 of the Rome Convention gives effect to such an act of choice, which can be made with respect to the whole or to a particular part of the contract.[83] One notable feature of Article 6 is that it can only operate, if at all, in such a way as to allow a set-off to be invoked in circumstances where otherwise it would be excluded: it does not allow a creditor to be denied the benefit of a set-off which is available under the *lex concursus* in accordance with the rule in Article 4(2)(d).

Once again, it is to be observed that Article 6(2) preserves the application of Article 4(2)(m) in relation to cases benefiting from the exception created under paragraph (1). Consequently, the avoidance rules of the *lex concursus* continue to be applicable to any challenge to the validity or enforceability of any claim to which the doctrine of set-off may otherwise be applicable by virtue of Article 6(1).

Exception III: Reservation of title (Article 7)

The practice of including a reservation of title clause within a contract of sale, as a means of affording protection to an unpaid seller in the event of the buyer's insolvency, is treated in different ways under the laws of the Member States of the European Union.[84] To minimise the uncertainty associated with cross-border cases, special rules are needed. Article 7 provides two such rules, which introduce exceptions to the application of the *lex concursus* in relation to contracts to which the insolvent debtor is a party. The rules deal, respectively, with the insolvency of the buyer or of the seller, and in each instance the relevant factor is the *situs* of the subject matter of the contract of sale at the time of opening of insolvency proceedings. Where this is in a Contracting State other than the State of opening, the provisions of the *lex concursus* are displaced by the rules contained in Article 7(1) or (2), as the case may be.

[83] Rome Convention of 19 June 1980, Art. 3(1). Note also that Art. 3(2) allows the parties to agree at any time to subject their contract to a law other than that which previously governed it, whether as a result of earlier choice or by reason of absence of choice as to governing law. There is a proviso to para.(2) whose effect is to prevent such subsequent changes from adversely affecting third parties (such as creditors generally), and it is also the case that any change of this nature would have to be effected prior to the opening of insolvency proceedings.

[84] On the inability of the EU States to harmonise their treatment of reservation of title clauses, see G. McCormack, *Reservation of Title* (1990), pp. 210–220.

Article 7(1) applies in a case where insolvency proceedings are opened against the purchaser of an asset for which the price has not been paid in full. It provides that the seller's rights based on a reservation of title ('ROT') clause shall not be affected by the opening of proceedings where the asset in question is at that time situated within the territory of a Contracting State other than the State of opening. Therefore, any provisions within the *lex concursus* whereby the ROT clause is rendered ineffective as against the claims of the liquidator—for example due to lack of formal registration, or on other grounds—would not affect the seller's right to retake the asset provided that such a right is conferred by the *lex situs* under the circumstances existing at the relevant time. The terms of Article 7(1) are such as to make it irrelevant, apparently, whether the asset in question is moved to the territory of some other Contracting State subsequently to the opening of proceedings.[85] However, the exact way in which this provision will operate in practice is far from clear. It is to be noted that there is no positive provision to the effect that the *lex situs* is to apply: all that is stated is that the opening of proceedings 'shall not affect the seller's rights based on a reservation of title'. This phrase implies that the determinative factors are the provisions of the contract itself and—of necessity—the law by which it is governed. It seems to be envisaged that these factors will be assimilated into the process of determination under the law of the Contracting State in which the asset happens to be situated, although the details are not explained.

Article 7(2) is concerned with the position where it is the seller of an asset who, following its delivery, is the subject of insolvency proceedings. Where, due to the effects of a ROT clause, the seller retains ownership of the asset even after delivery, the consequence might be that the asset is regarded as part of the insolvent estate and thus liable to repossession by the liquidator, leaving the buyer to lodge proof for any damages occasioned through the loss of bargain.[86] The provision in paragraph (2) alleviates the buyer's predicament by declaring that the opening of insolvency proceedings shall not constitute grounds for rescinding or terminating the sale, and shall not prevent the buyer from acquiring title, where at the time of opening the asset sold is situated within the territory of a Contracting State other than the *forum concursus*. This provision is not a choice of law rule, but is a uniform rule of substantive law whose application is confined to specially defined circumstances.

Finally, Article 7(3) preserves the application of the avoidance rules of the *lex concursus* in cases falling within the ambit of either paragraph (1) or (2). The fact that in each of those paragraphs reference is made to the *situs* of the asset as being within the territory of a Contracting State necessarily

[85] So stated by the Virgos-Schmit Report, *supra* n.10, para. 113.
[86] Such a claim would of course be subject to deduction of the price due from the buyer.

means that Article 7 has no application to cases where the asset is situated in some third State at the relevant time.

Exception IV: contracts relating to immovable property (Article 8)

It is usually the case that a liquidator is empowered to elect whether to confirm or to terminate any executory contract to which the debtor is a party at the time of commencement of insolvency proceedings.[87] Article 4(2)(e) asserts the basic principle that the *lex concursus* determines the effects of insolvency upon current contracts to which the debtor is a party. However, Article 8 creates an exception to this rule for cases of contracts conferring the right to acquire or make use of immovable property which is situated within the territory of a Contracting State other than the State of opening. The Article provides that the effect of insolvency upon such contracts will be governed solely by the *lex situs*. The Virgos-Schmit Report explains at paragraph 118 that the reference to the exclusive application of the law of the *situs* includes the insolvency law of that State, so that parties to an international contract for the sale of land or the leasing of immovable property need to inform themselves about the relevant provisions of the insolvency law of the State in question, in order to discover the consequences of the insolvency of the other party. This provision is not applicable to cases where the property is situated in some third State, and it is therefore left to the *lex concursus*, including the conflicts rules of that system, to resolve the issue. However, it is generally the case that questions concerning rights over, and succession to, immovable property are referred to the *lex situs*.

Exception V: payment systems and financial markets (Article 9)

An especially sensitive area, in view of its commercial importance, is the effect of insolvency upon executory contracts between parties operating within an organised payment or settlement system, or a particular financial market. In the interest of sustaining confidence in the integrity of the arrangements to which the participants have originally assented upon joining the system or market in question, Article 9(1) imposes a special choice of law rule whereby the effects of insolvency proceedings on the rights and obligations of parties to a payment or settlement system or to a financial market will be governed solely by the law of the Contracting State applicable to that system or market.[88] This rule in favour of the

[87] This important subject has received less attention in the English legal literature than it deserves. A systematic treatment is long overdue. For a valuable analysis of the problems of executory contracts from the standpoint of American law, see Westbrook (1989) 74 Minn. L. Rev. 227; Countryman (1973) 57 Minn. L. Rev. 439 and (1974) 58 Minn. L. Rev. 479.

[88] Examples of such special markets, whose rules contain provisions for closing out contracts and netting in the event of the insolvency of a member, are the London International Financial Futures Exchange, the International Stock Exchange of the United Kingdom and

exclusive application of the systemic law is reinforced by the provision in Article 9(2) whereby any action for voidness, voidability or unenforceability of payments or transactions carried out under the system or market in question, and which may be detrimental to creditors generally, are nevertheless declared to be subject to the law applicable to the relevant payment system or financial market. The usual practice followed elsewhere in the Convention, of reserving the application of the avoidance rule of the *lex concursus*, is here relinquished in favour of the total prevalence of the law which is applicable to the payment system or market, thereby enabling parties to base their expectations purely upon a single set of rules without having to take into account the various national laws to which counterparties may be personally subject, and by which the insolvency of any of them may happen to be governed.

It is necessary to observe that the rules of Article 9 are only applicable in a situation where the system or market is operating under the law of one of the Contracting States. Moreover, there is a special proviso in Article 9(1) to the effect that it is without prejudice to the effect of Article 5, which subjects the protection of rights *in rem* over assets belonging to the debtor to the law of the *situs*.[89]

Exception VI: contracts of employment (Article 10)

A further category of executory contracts for which special considerations arise is the employment relationship. Indeed, special rules are already operative under the Brussels Convention and the Rome Convention to regulate jurisdictional and choice of law aspects of contracts of employment.[90] Article 10 of the Insolvency Convention stipulates that the effects of insolvency proceedings on employment contracts and relationships shall be governed solely by the law of the Contracting State applicable to the contract of employment. To ascertain the applicable law, the courts of all Contracting States will apply the provisions of the Rome Convention, notably Articles 3, 6 and 7 thereof. If this produces the conclusion that the contract is governed by the law of one of the Contracting States, the rule of Article 10 of the Insolvency Convention will apply. If the law of some third State is indicated however, the effects of insolvency will be determined by the *lex concursus*, with reference as appropriate to any provisions of the private international law of that system. It should also be emphasised that Article 10 is confined to the question of the effect of insolvency upon the

the Republic of Ireland, the London Metal Exchange, and the London Commodity Exchange Limited. See Companies Act 1989, Part VII, together with S.I. 1991 No. 880.

[89] See above, *Exception I*.

[90] See Convention on Jurisdiction and the Enforcement of Judgments in Civil and Commercial Matters, 27 September 1968, Art. 5(1) (as amended by the San Sebastian Convention of 1989, O.J. 1989 L.285); and the Convention on the Law Applicable to Contractual Obligations, 19 June 1980, Art. 6.

contract of employment as such, including the issue whether the contract is automatically terminated by the insolvency of either party to it, or whether the liquidator has the option to affirm or rescind the contract, subject to specified terms. Article 10 does not purport to regulate other issues such as the ranking of employees' claims for unpaid wages or salary, and the mode of treatment to be accorded to these claims. Such questions remain subject to the *lex concursus*, in accordance with Article 4(2)(h).[91] It is also the case that in many States nowadays there is a statutory scheme under which, in the event of their employer's insolvency, employees are guaranteed a measure of payment out of a national fund, with the State then becoming subrogated to the employee in respect of that portion of the latter's claim against the employer. Paragraph 128 of the Virgos-Schmit Report asserts that such guaranteed payments, since they are maintained under provisions of the national law of the Contracting State concerned, are subject to the law of that State.

Exception VII: rights subject to registration (Article 11)

National laws usually operate a system of public registration for many kinds of right or interest over immovable property. Such registration forms an essential aspect of the safeguards for other parties who may have or acquire interests in the same property. Certain kinds of movable property, including ships and aircraft, are likewise subject to public registration in the State in which they are principally kept, or from which they are operated. Such registers play important roles in the protection of trade and certainty, and in the maintenance of health and safety regulations affecting the assets in question. The casual location of such assets, which may be of very large value, should not be the decisive criterion with regard to the effects of insolvency proceedings upon the rights of the debtor in relation to them. Both with immovable property and with movables of this kind, there is the possibility of a conflict between the provisions of the law of the State under whose authority the register is maintained and the provisions of the *lex concursus*. Article 11 provides that, where the register is kept under the authority of a Contracting State, it is the law of that State, and not the *lex concursus*, which shall determine the effects of insolvency proceedings on the rights of the debtor in immovable property, a ship or an aircraft subject to public registration. However, it should be noted that this choice of law provision does not include the word 'solely', and that this omission is intended to enable the *lex concursus* to continue to play a part in the process of determining the net effect of insolvency upon the rights which are the subject of registration. In the words of paragraph 130 of the Virgos-Schmit Report, 'a sort of cumulative application of both laws is

[91] Virgos-Schmit Report, *supra* n.10, para. 128.

necessary'. What appears to be envisaged is that there should be an interaction between the liquidator and the official by whom the relevant register is maintained, to arrange for appropriate entries to be made in the register that will reflect the fact that insolvency proceedings are taking place in a different Contracting State. It will remain a matter for the law of the State of registration to determine what effects this process shall have upon the rights of the debtor in the property concerned.

Exception VIII: community patents and trade marks (Article 12)

In view of the fact that arrangements are already in force within the European Union to regulate patents, trade marks and the rights of plant breeders throughout the whole territory of the Union,[92] it is appropriate that the Convention should endeavour to complement the provisions already operative with regard to the treatment of such forms of intellectual property in cases of insolvency of those who own or have interests in the rights concerned. Each of the existing arrangements under E.U. law contains a rule to the effect that a Community right arising thereunder may be included only in the first proceedings that are opened in a Contracting State.[93] Under the provisions of the Insolvency Convention however, it can sometimes happen that the first proceedings to be opened are not main proceedings under Article 3(1), but are territorial proceedings within the meaning of Article 3(2) and (4).[94] This has necessitated a special rule, contained in Article 12, whereby a Community Patent, a Community Trademark or any similar right established by Community Law may be included only in main insolvency proceedings which are opened under Article 3(1). This provision is operative only when the debtor has his centre of main interests in a Contracting State, for this is an essential condition to the opening of proceedings under Article 3(1). Where the debtor's centre of main interests is located outside the E.U., the rules of the individual enactments relating to intellectual property are applicable without modification, with the consequence that the right in question is included in the insolvent estate of the first proceedings to be opened in a Contracting State.[95]

Exception IX: protection of third-party purchasers (Article 14)

It is usually the case that under the provisions of national law the opening of insolvency proceedings causes the debtor to be deprived of the capac-

[92] Community Patent Convention of December 15, 1975 (O.J. 1975 L17/1), as modified by the Luxembourg Agreement of December 30, 1989 (O.J. 1989 L401/10); Directive 89/104 of December 21, 1988 and Council Regulation (EC) 40/94 of December 20, 1993 on the Community Trademark; Council Regulation (EC) 2100/94 of July 27, 1994 on Community Plant Variety Rights.

[93] Luxembourg Agreement, Art.41; Trademark Regulation, Art.21; Regulation on Plant Variety Rights, Art.25 (see previous n.).

[94] See section 6.3.2. above.

[95] See Virgos-Schmit Report, paras.133, 134.

ity to deal with or dispose of property to the detriment of the general body of creditors. Such transactions may be declared to be void under all circumstances, or may only be validated by the court upon certain conditions.[96] However, where the property which is the subject of an improper act of disposal by the debtor is subject to some form of public registration, a policy dilemma is caused by the possibility that the transaction with the third party may take place before the fact of the insolvency is placed upon the record. Such parties, consulting the record in its unamended state, may be prejudiced by their reliance upon the information thereby obtained. Consequently, in the interest of maintaining confidence in the integrity of the public register, the national law of the State in which the register is maintained may contain a rule to protect a party who has dealt in good faith and for valuable consideration, and in reliance upon the information carried on the face of the register at the time in question. In cases of international insolvency, where the State of opening of proceedings and the State where the register is maintained are separate from each other the interval before the register can be amended may be even longer, thus allowing more time in which such transactions may take place. If the protection to be accorded to the third party is made to depend upon the *lex concursus*, that party may suffer injustice due to reliance that was originally and reasonably placed upon the rule contained in the *lex situs* (in the case of immovable property), or in the law of the State in which the register is maintained (in the case of ships or aircraft, or of securities whose existence is dependent upon registration). Article 14 of the Convention accordingly creates a rule to protect third party purchasers to whom the debtor, other than gratuitously, has disposed of any of these kinds of asset by an act concluded after the opening of insolvency proceedings. The validity of the act of disposal is governed by the *lex situs* in the case of an immovable asset, and in the case of registrable assets by the law of the State under whose authority the register is kept.

The drafting of Article 14 omits any reference to 'Contracting State' in its provision regarding the law to govern the validity of the acts to which it is applicable, and it would therefore appear that the provision can be applied to cases where the *situs* of the immovable, or the place where the register is maintained, is located in some third State. However, the Virgos-Schmit Report appears to contradict the indications conveyed by the terms of the Article itself, by consistently referring to 'Contracting State' in relation to the scope of its application.[97] Conversely, the scope of the Article is widened in another respect by a further statement in the Report that: 'An act of disposal must be understood to include not only transfers of ownership but also the constitution of a right *in rem* relating to such property'.[98]

[96] See e.g. Insolvency Act 1986, s.127.
[97] Virgos-Schmit Report, *supra* n.10, paras. 140, 141.
[98] *Ibid.*, para. 141.

Exception X: effects on pending lawsuits (Article 15)

The laws of the Member States of the European Union differ from one another with regard to the effect of insolvency proceedings on a pending lawsuit to which the debtor is a party. These differences concern not only the forcible interruption of proceedings by virtue of an automatic stay, but also the possible removal of litigation from the civil or commercial court which would normally have jurisdiction, into the exclusive control of the bankruptcy court, under the principle known as *vis attractiva concursus*. This principle is by no means universally, or even uniformly, applied, and there are likewise variations of approach to such matters as the possible lifting of the stay upon proceedings at the discretion of the bankruptcy court. Potentially, much confusion and uncertainty could result in a given case due to the presence of conflicting rules under the *lex concursus* and under the law of the State in which the litigation is pending.

Article 15 imposes a uniform choice of law rule in favour of the sole application of the law of the forum in which the lawsuit is pending. The scope of this rule is likely to be of considerable practical importance, and hence the terms of the Article should be noted with some care. First, a distinction is to be made between the effects of insolvency on individual enforcement actions (such as distress, execution, attachment, sequestration), as opposed to pending lawsuits. The former are governed by the law of the State of opening, as provided by Article 4(2)(f), whereas only the latter are affected by Article 15. The Article refers expressly to 'a lawsuit pending concerning an asset or a right of which the debtor has been divested'. Accordingly, if the asset happens to be excluded from the effects of insolvency according to the *lex concursus*, it would be unaffected by Article 15.[99] It is also essential to the application of Article 15 that the lawsuit in question be pending in another Contracting State: litigation in third States is not within the ambit of this provision. Where the rule applies, it is for the law of the State where litigation is pending (including the procedural law of that State) to determine whether or not the proceedings are to be suspended or whether they may continue subject to terms or conditions, including any procedural modifications which may be necessary in view of the fact that the debtor has been deprived of the powers of administration and disposal of his property, with the liquidator having been substituted in his place.

[99] For an account of the position under English law concerning property in the ownership of the bankrupt which does not vest in the trustee in bankruptcy, see I.F. Fletcher, *The Law of Insolvency*, 2nd edn. (1996), pp. 209–220.

6.3.4 Recognition of insolvency proceedings

Chapter II, comprising Articles 16 to 26 inclusive, contains important provisions concerning the recognition of insolvency proceedings opened under the Convention, and the effects of recognition including the powers exercisable by the liquidator in other Contracting States. From the practical aspect of enabling the liquidator to administer a cross-border insolvency in an efficient and cost-effective manner, these provisions represent a significant advance upon the existing, piecemeal arrangements available under the laws of individual EU Member States.

Basic Principle: automatic recognition

The opening paragraph of Article 16(1) establishes the basic principle of recognition for cases where insolvency proceedings are opened under the Convention, as follows:

> Any judgment opening insolvency proceedings handed down by a court of a Contracting State which has jurisdiction pursuant to Article 3 shall be recognised in all the other Contracting States *from the time that it becomes effective in the State of the opening of proceedings.*[100]

The principle of immediate, automatic recognition is one whose importance it would be difficult to over-emphasise. The elimination of any lapse of time between the proceedings becoming legally effective in the State of opening and their being recognised throughout the other Contracting States—and hence having the same authority in all of them as they enjoy in their State of origin—removes one of the principal opportunities for foreign creditors to engage in a 'race of diligence' during the hiatus between the commencement of insolvency proceedings in the debtor's 'home' country and the moment when the liquidator can succeed, country by country, in obtaining a judicial order granting powers of enforcement over such assets as are located within each jurisdiction. The temporal immediacy of this provision is sharpened by the definition supplied in Article 2(f), whereby 'the time of the opening of proceedings' is declared to mean 'the time at which the judgment opening proceedings becomes effective, whether it is a final judgment or not.' Thus, a judgment opening insolvency proceedings can have extraterritorial effects even if it is not a final judgment, provided that its effects have not been stayed by the court which granted it. This might lead one to suppose that an appointment of a provisional liquidator by a court in the United Kingdom could be considered to carry such consequences.[101] However, it must be borne in mind that recognition under Article 16 is only accorded to insolvency

[100] Emphasis added. [101] See Insolvency Act 1986, s.135.

proceedings within the scope of the Convention, and expressly listed in the Annexes thereto. Since a provisional liquidator is not included among the types of office holder listed in Annex C, the automatic recognition of such an appointment is precluded.[102] It may be noted however that, in the case of creditors' voluntary liquidation, the 'time of opening of proceedings' for the purposes of recognition under Article 16 is the date of passing of the resolution for winding up, rather than the date of subsequent confirmation by the court.[103]

The second paragraph of Article 16(1) confirms that the rule of recognition will also apply where, on account of the debtor's capacity, insolvency proceedings cannot be brought against the debtor in other Contracting States. Therefore, the fact that a debtor is not considered to be insolvent according to the relevant test under the law of another Contracting State, or that he is there regarded as belonging to a category of debtor who is excluded from the operation of insolvency law, cannot be a reason for refusal of recognition to insolvency proceedings opened in the first State. Article 16(2) supplies a crucial proviso to the basic principle of recognition, to the effect that the recognition of main proceedings opened under Article 3(1) shall not preclude the opening of secondary proceedings under Article 3(2) by a court in another Contracting State in which the debtor has an establishment.[104] It should also be noted that where such secondary proceedings are opened, or where independent, territorial proceedings are opened under the circumstances specified in Article 3(4), these too are within the ambit of the basic principle of automatic recognition established by Article 16(1), which makes no distinction between main and secondary—or independent—proceedings for this purpose. Of course, the effects of secondary or independent proceedings are restricted to assets of the debtor situated in the territory of the State of opening, but it may well be necessary for the liquidator to undertake some actions in other Contracting States during the course of his administration, notably where assets which properly form a part of the secondary estate are found to have been repositioned elsewhere.[105]

[102] For the scope of the Convention, and the significance of Annexes A, B and C, see at 6.3.1 above. It may be possible for a provisional liquidator to invoke the provisions of Article 38, which enable a 'provisional administrator' appointed by a court which has jurisdiction under Art. 3(1) to request any measures to secure and preserve any of the debtor's assets situated in another Contracting State. This is a less effective process, however, because of the inevitable delay in obtaining the judicial order in the State where an asset is situated.

[103] Virgos-Schmit Report, *supra* n.10, para. 68, which goes on to state that the liquidator will not be empowered to exercise his powers on the territory of another Contracting State until the date of the court confirmation of the liquidation and of his appointment. See at 6.3.1 above, esp. at n.39 and text thereto.

[104] Article 3(2) is discussed at 6.3.2 above. Secondary insolvency proceedings are further considered at 6.3.5 below.

[105] See Art. 18(2). The secondary liquidator may also take action to bring about the

International effects

The basic principle of recognition under Article 16 is reinforced by the further provisions in Articles 17 and 18. The former provides that the opening of main proceedings under Article 3(1) will, *with no further formalities*, produce the same effects in any other Contracting State as under the law of the State of opening. This ensures that the effects of such proceedings are genuinely universal in character, and will not be subject to variation according to the domestic laws of the individual States. Article 17(1) concedes two grounds of exception to this principle, namely where the Convention itself provides otherwise (for example, through the effect of the choice of law rules contained in Chapter I), or where secondary proceedings are opened in another Contracting State. In order to respect the integrity of such secondary proceedings, an accommodation must be reached between the effects enjoyed by the main proceedings—which relate to the bulk of the debtor's estate—and those enjoyed by the secondary proceedings, which are by definition territorial in scope. Article 18(1) complements the preceding Article by providing that the liquidator in main proceedings opened under Article 3(1):

> may exercise *all the powers conferred on him by the law of the State of the opening of proceedings in another Contracting State*, as long as no other insolvency proceedings have been opened there nor any preservation measure to the contrary has been taken there further to a request for the opening of insolvency proceedings in that State. He may in particular remove the debtor's assets from the territory of the Contracting State in which they are situated, subject to Articles 5 and 7.[106]

Thus, the powers of the liquidator in main proceedings are essentially uniform throughout all the Contracting States, and do not suffer from abatement (or even enhancement) to bring them into line with the powers which a local counterpart would have in equivalent proceedings opened under the law of the State where the powers are exercised. The power to remove assets from one Contracting State to another, and to do so as of right and without requiring the formality of an order of the court of the *situs*, constitutes a substantial improvement of the liquidator's capability to act incisively, and should avoid costly and cumbersome delays. Article 18(3) obliges the liquidator, in exercising his powers, to comply with the general law of the State in which he intends to take action, in particular with regard to procedures for the realisation of assets. Direct recourse to the use of force or coercive action is expressly excluded, even though such

avoidance of transactions which took place at the expense of the secondary estate and those who are its creditors.

[106] Emphasis added. The exceptions based upon the effects of Articles 5 and 7 refer to the position of secured creditors, and of parties having the benefit of a reservation of title clause, respectively. See at 6.3.3, *Exception I* and *Exception III*, above.

powers might be exercisable under the law of the liquidator's appointment.

Although the liquidator is enabled to exercise his powers in other Contracting States without the need to obtain formal authorisation, it will be necessary in practice for the liquidator to be able to establish his credentials for the purpose of invoking his rights under the Convention. Article 19 facilitates this by providing a standard formulation of the nature of the evidential material necessary to support the liquidator's assertion of his authority. All that is required is a certified copy of the original decision appointing him, or any other certificate issued by the court which has jurisdiction under the Convention. It is expressly stated that 'No legalisation or other similar formality shall be required', thereby excluding the need to obtain an *exequatur* from the local court, or to procure the preparation of an '*Apostille*' in conformity with the provisions of the Hague Convention Abolishing the Requirement of Legalisation for Foreign Public Documents.[107] However, Article 19 does permit a Contracting State in which the liquidator intends to act to require that the certificate of appointment be translated into its official language (or one of them). Although the Convention is silent upon the point, the Virgos-Schmit Report declares that in the case of doubt concerning the scope of the liquidator's powers under the law of his appointment, the onus of proof rests with the liquidator who must, if necessary, obtain a further certificate of confirmation from the court under whose authority his appointment originates. The cost of securing such clarification, and also the cost of providing any translation that may be required, will also fall upon the liquidator as an expense to be borne by the estate.

Publicity and registration of proceedings

The Convention imposes no requirement that there must be advertisement in other Contracting States of the opening of insolvency proceedings, or of the liquidator's appointment, as a precondition to the recognition of the proceedings, or the exercise of the liquidator's powers. Nevertheless, it may be advisable that such advertisement be effected upon the liquidator's initiative, particularly in States where the debtor has had extensive dealings or where substantial assets are known to be located. The advantages of such publicity are twofold. First, it serves the ends of justice and certainty by informing interested parties of a development having major significance for their relationship with the debtor and any property belonging to his estate. Secondly, it can ensure that the legal position of the liquidator is strengthened in relation to third parties who may subsequently have dealings involving the debtor's estate: to the extent that their

[107] Convention of 5 October 1961. See esp. Art. 4 and the Annexed *Model of Certificate*.

transactions might benefit from any protective rule under the *lex situs* in favour of a party who has dealt in good faith, for value and without knowledge of the debtor's insolvency, the effecting of formal advertisement or registration in accordance with the provisions of the local law may have the effect of depriving the third party of any protection even if there was actual lack of knowledge of the debtor's insolvency, or it may affect the burden of proof of such lack of knowledge by making it incumbent on the third party to prove that he was unaware of the debtor's insolvency at the relevant time. Article 21 authorises the liquidator to request that advertisement of the judgment opening insolvency proceedings, and of his own appointment, be published in any other Contracting State in accordance with its local procedure for this purpose.[108] Article 22 similarly authorises the liquidator to request that the judgment opening main proceedings under Article 3(1) be registered in the land register, the trade register and any other public register kept in the other Contracting States. The costs of advertisement or registration will be borne by the estate.[109]

Article 24 supplies a rule to deal with cases where a third party has fulfilled an obligation—typically, by making a payment—to the debtor against whom insolvency proceedings had already opened in another Contracting State. The principle of automatic recognition would have the consequence that the payment in question should have been made to the liquidator, thereby giving rise to the possibility that the paying party may be obliged to pay twice. Article 24 absolves the paying party from that predicament if he was unaware of the opening of proceedings at the time of making the payment or other performance. If at that time the local advertisement provided for in Article 21 had not taken place, there is a rebuttable presumption that the paying party was unaware of the opening of proceedings; whereas, if such local advertisement had already been effected, the presumption is reversed.[110]

Relationship to the Brussels Convention: refusal of recognition

As explained at 6.1 above, the Insolvency Convention was since its inception intended to complement the provisions of the Brussels Convention of 27 September 1968, which deals with recognition and enforcement of civil and commercial judgments. Article 1(2) of that Convention was inserted for the purpose of excluding bankruptcy and related proceedings from coming within its scope. Although the Brussels Convention has been in

[108] Article 21(1) indicates that the advertisement must also specify whether jurisdiction was taken under Article 3(1) or (2). Article 21(2) provides that any Contracting State where the debtor has an establishment may require mandatory publication, and that in such cases the liquidator or the duly empowered authority in the State of opening must take all necessary measures to ensure such publication.

[109] See Art. 23.

[110] See Art. 24(2).

force since 1973, initially among the Community of Six and subsequently among all fifteen current Members of the European Union,[111] the 'circle' has remained incomplete due to the delay in finalising and adopting the Insolvency Convention. Article 25 is designed to complete the scheme for recognition and enforcement of judgments and orders made during the course of proceedings opened under the Insolvency Convention, by the court whose judgment opening those proceedings is recognised in accordance with Article 16, or by another court of that State exercising jurisdiction in a case deriving directly from the insolvency proceedings and closely linked with them. Examples of such related judgments are those concerning the further conduct of the proceedings; judicial approval of compositions; the adjustment or avoidance of antecedent transactions; the imposition of civil liability upon directors and others held responsible for mismanagement; and the formal closure of the insolvency proceedings. Article 25(1) provides that such judgments shall be recognised with no further formalities, but that their enforcement shall take place in accordance with Articles 31 to 51 of the Brussels Convention, with the exception of Article 34(2) of that Convention.[112] The latter exception is important because it has the effect of eliminating Articles 27 and 28 of the Brussels Convention, which provide a number of grounds on which an application for enforcement of a foreign judgment may be refused. In place of these provisions, Article 26 of the Insolvency Convention supplies a general rule to the effect that:

> Any Contracting State may refuse to recognise insolvency proceedings opened in another Contracting State or to enforce a judgment handed down in the context of such proceedings, where to do so would be manifestly contrary to that State's public policy, in particular its fundamental principles or the constitutional rights and liberties of the individual.

The intention underlying this provision is that is shall not be open to the courts of Contracting States to review the bankruptcy judgments of sister States as regards their substance (also known as *révision au fond*), nor to review the jurisdiction of the court of the State of origin. It is for the judicial authorities of the State from which the judgment originated (F1) to verify and regulate the exercise of international jurisdiction under the Convention: the role of the courts of the requested State (F2) is limited to verifying that the judgment emanates from a court of a Contracting State which claims jurisdiction under Article 3 of the Convention.[113] Any chal-

[111] See *supra* n.90.

[112] For an account of the recognition and enforcement of judgments under Arts. 31–51 of the Brussels Convention, see e.g. Dicey and Morris, *The Conflict of Laws*, 12th edn. (1993, with Supplements, General Editor, Lawrence Collins), ch. 14, at pp. 530–544; Cheshire and North's *Private International Law*, 12th edn. (1992, by P.M. North and J.J. Fawcett), ch. 16.

[113] Virgos-Schmit Report, *supra* n.10, para. 202. See also *ibid.*, paras. 189–201 on the rationale behind the recognition and enforcement rules in Art. 25.

lenge to the jurisdiction of the F1 court must therefore be pursued via the appellate courts of that State.[114] Also relevant in the context of enforcement of insolvency judgments is the provision in Article 25(3) to the effect that the Contracting States shall not be obliged to recognise or enforce a judgment referred to in Article 25(1) which might result in a limitation of personal freedom or postal secrecy.[115]

Equality between creditors: the hotchpot rule

It is a notorious fact that there are numerous ways in which, in a cross-border case, some creditors may be able to avail themselves of the opportunity to receive a payment, or seize an asset, before the liquidator can intercept the process or establish a superior entitlement under the applicable law. To counteract the arbitrary unfairness, relative to the general body of creditors, of such windfall advantages obtained by individual creditors, various remedies have been developed under national insolvency laws, including the celebrated *'hotchpot'* rule devised by English law, and adopted throughout the common law legal family.[116] This equalisation device has been incorporated into the Convention by Article 20, which bears the somewhat beguiling title 'Return and imputation'. The substance of the Article applies to a creditor who, after the opening of main proceedings under Article 3(1), obtains by any means (in particular through enforcement) total or partial satisfaction of his claim on the assets of the debtor situated in another Contracting State. In the first instance, it is provided that the creditor shall return what he has obtained to the liquidator, although this does not apply in the case of a secured creditor enforcing security over collateral, or against a seller exercising rights under a reservation of title clause.[117] Secondly, in the case of a creditor who has obtained a dividend in the course of other insolvency proceedings in respect of the same claim as that for which proof is lodged in proceedings governed by the Convention, Article 20(2) declares that he shall share in distributions made in the further proceedings only where creditors of the same ranking or category have obtained an equivalent dividend. The essential principles are the maintenance of equality between creditors, and the need to ensure that no creditor shall obtain more than

[114] Virgos-Schmit Report, *supra* n.10, para. 202. If necessary, a reference for interpretation by the European Court of Justice could be made under Chapter V of the Convention: see at 6.3.7 below.

[115] Cf. Insolvency Act 1986, ss.364–366, 371. For discussion of the civil liberties aspects of the power under s.371 to order the redirection of a bankrupt's mail, see Jaconelli (1995) 8 *Insolvency Intelligence* 1.

[116] See Chapter 2, at 2.4 above (for the English law position), and Chapter 4, at 4.4 above (with reference to Canada).

[117] See Arts. 5 and 7, discussed at 6.3.3 above. On the requirement to return assets to the liquidator, see Virgos-Schmit Report, *supra* n.10, paras. 171–173.

100 per cent of his claim by means of composite acts of individual diligence together with the lodging of proof in as many proceedings as are available for this purpose.[118]

6.3.5 Secondary insolvency proceedings

Chapter III of the Convention, comprising Articles 27 to 38 inclusive, governs the opening and mode of administration of secondary insolvency proceedings. Such proceedings can only be opened, in accordance with Article 3(2), following the opening of main proceedings, and then only in a Contracting State in which the debtor possesses an establishment.[119] On the other hand, by virtue of the fact that the main proceedings are required to be recognised in all Contracting States, including any in which such an establishment exists, secondary proceedings can be opened without any need for the debtor's insolvency to be established according to the law of the State in which they are to take place.[120] However, the only kinds of proceedings which can be opened are those which the Convention refers to as 'winding-up proceedings', and which are listed in Annex B with regard to the State in question.[121] The concept of 'secondary proceedings' is one of several innovations contained in the Istanbul Convention which, as already observed, have been incorporated into the EU Convention.[122]

The purpose of bringing about the opening of secondary proceedings in the European Union context will usually be to enable local creditors in the State of opening to retain any special advantages which they enjoy under the terms of the local law, particularly the provisions of its insolvency law, and which would possibly not be maintained under the regime of the main proceedings. All of the rules of the Convention concerning choice of law are equally applicable to secondary proceedings, although the effects of such proceedings are confined to property of the debtor situated in the territory of the State in which they are opened.[123] Nevertheless, to the extent that those assets happen to have sufficient value, the expectations of local creditors—especially those such as employees, or the revenue authorities, whose debts are classified as preferential by the local law—are likely to fare better than would be the case under the distributional process of the main proceedings. Also relevant may be the relative cost to creditors of lodging their claims in a local proceeding, as opposed to one being con-

[118] See Virgos-Schmit Report, *supra* n.10, paras. 174–176.

[119] See at 6.3.2 above.

[120] See Art. 27.

[121] See Arts. 3(3), 27. Annex B is considered at 6.3.2 above. For an assessment of the Convention's implications for corporate rescue strategies, see Johnson [1996] 5 I.I.R. 80.

[122] The Istanbul Convention is discussed in Chapter 7 below. On the background to the adoption of secondary proceedings in the EU Convention, see Balz (1996) 70 Am. Bankr. L.J. 485 at 520–522.

[123] See Arts. 3(2),28. For the choice of law rules of the Convention, see at 6.3.3 above.

ducted in another State, and possibly through the medium of a different language. A further reason why creditors may utilise the facility to open secondary proceedings may be tactical, particularly if the main proceedings are aimed at rescue and reorganisation of the debtor's business. Since secondary proceedings can only be winding-up proceedings, their continuation could be detrimental to the rescue plan. Accordingly, some accommodation of the interests of the creditors responsible for the secondary proceedings will be necessary, in order to bring about their conclusion through some form of composition or arrangement. Under some circumstances, the bargaining power thereby enjoyed by those in a position to initiate secondary proceedings may be substantial, and may enable even those creditors who do not have preferential status to secure a worthwhile advantage through negotiation with the liquidator in the main proceedings. Eligibility to request the opening of secondary proceedings is determined in the first instance by reference to the provisions of the law of the Contracting State within whose territory the proceedings are to open: such persons or authorities as are empowered by the local law to request the opening of proceedings of the kind listed in Annex B, may do so.[124]

It may also be expedient under some conditions for the liquidator in the main proceedings to initiate the opening of secondary proceedings. Article 29(b) enables this to be done. Among the reasons for such a proceeding may be the size and complexity of the local estate and the local claims, thus making it cost-effective to engage a local expert practitioner to administer this portion of the debtor's total estate. It may also transpire that the local law confers superior powers or remedies upon the liquidator, by comparison to those enjoyed under the law of the main proceedings. The opening of secondary proceedings will result in the application of the local rule for avoidance of prior transactions, and the local law imposing a stay upon creditors' individual acts of enforcement of security, or execution of other rights.[125] This may enable the main liquidator to defend the interests of the general body of creditors to optimum effect. It is permissible for the court to which a request for opening of secondary proceedings is presented to require that the applicant makes advance payment, or lodges security, to cover the costs and expenses of the proceedings to the extent prescribed under the local law.[126] This is an essential safeguard against the possibility that parties might seek to exploit the nuisance value of such applications, and inflict further costs upon the main estate.

Interrelationship between proceedings

Although the motivation behind the recourse to secondary proceedings may be the gaining of some specific advantage for certain creditors, the

124 See Art. 29(a). 125 See Art. 28. 126 See Art. 30.

Convention does not allow a total severance—also known as 'ring-fencing'—of the secondary proceedings and the assets comprised in them. The concept of universality is allowed to become fragmented, but is not altogether renounced. This is achieved by a series of provisions which establish a relationship between the main proceedings and any secondary proceedings that may open. First, Article 31 asserts that the liquidator in the main proceedings and the liquidators in the secondary proceedings 'shall be duty bound to communicate information to each other' and that they are similarly 'duty bound to cooperate with each other'.[127] Article 31(3) also imposes an obligation upon the secondary liquidator to give the main liquidator an early opportunity of submitting proposals on the liquidation or use of the assets in the secondary proceedings. However, there is no requirement that the secondary liquidator must accede to such proposals, nor is any mechanism provided for resolving any disagreement between the two office holders regarding the approach to be adopted. Secondly, Article 32(1) establishes the principle that: 'Any creditor may lodge his claim in the main proceedings and in any secondary proceedings'. This provision establishes that the respective administrations being conducted by the main and secondary liquidators ultimately form part of a single, greater whole. To the extent that the law of the State of the secondary proceedings is prepared to accord preferential status to claims of creditors from outside that jurisdiction, they are eligible to participate alongside local creditors in the distribution of the assets located in that State. Even if treated non-preferentially, foreign creditors may participate in the process of distribution, to the extent the assets are sufficient to enable dividends to be paid to them alongside the local creditors of the same rank. The actual process of multiple cross-filing by creditors on an individual basis could be both complex and costly. In practice the more efficient approach may lie through the provision in Article 32(2) which requires the liquidators in the main and any secondary proceedings to lodge in other proceedings claims which have already been lodged in the proceedings for which they were appointed, provided that this is in the interests of creditors in the latter proceedings. If operated in conjunction with the duties of mutual communication and cooperation imposed under Article 31, the practice of collective filing by liquidators on behalf of all creditors who are participating in each respective set of proceedings would seem to be the best approach.[128] By coordinating all information about the creditors participating in the process of distribution, the main and secondary liquidators will also equip themselves with the means of ensuring that the requirements of the 'hotchpot' provisions of Article 20

[127] See Art. 31(1),(2).

[128] See Art. 32(2) preserves the right of any creditor to withdraw the lodging of his claim where the law applicable so provides.

are properly respected, so that no creditor obtains a relative advantage, by comparison to others of the same rank in terms of priority, through participation in the concurrent proceedings. It is also to be observed that Article 32(3) authorises the main and secondary liquidators to participate in the other proceedings on the same basis as a creditor, and in particular to attend creditors' meetings. A final indication of the ultimate unity of the process of administering the debtor's estate is provided by Article 35, to the effect that if there is a surplus remaining after the liquidation of the assets comprised in the secondary proceedings, after all claims allowed under those proceedings have been met, the secondary liquidator must transfer the remaining assets to the main liquidator. Although it is difficult to conceive of circumstances under which this rule would need to be applied in practice, it reinforces the principle of combination between the main and secondary estates.

Stay of secondary proceedings

Further provisions to coordinate the concurrent proceedings are contained in Article 33, which enables the liquidator in the main proceedings to apply to the court which opened secondary proceedings, seeking a stay of the latter. Such a request may only be rejected if it is manifestly of no interest to the creditors in the main proceedings. The stay may be ordered for up to three months, and may be continued or renewed for similar periods.[129] The court which imposed the stay can terminate it either at the request of the main liquidator, or of its own motion, or at the request of a creditor or of the secondary liquidator if the stay no longer appears justified, particularly in terms of the interests of the creditors in either of the sets of proceedings.[130] What may be envisaged is a situation where the secondary proceedings, which of necessity must be winding-up proceedings, pose a threat to the successful outcome of main proceedings aimed at the rescue, or sale as a going concern, of a business which has one or more foreign branches. The main liquidator may attempt to convince the parties to the secondary proceedings that they should adopt a supportive approach, which might be accomplished via provisions in the law applicable to the secondary proceedings allowing them to be closed without liquidation by a rescue plan, a composition or some similar measure. Failing a sudden, mass conversion to altruism, creditors who have already gained for themselves such a vital tactical advantage are likely to insist upon terms of settlement that offer them some material advantage over the alternative of continuing the liquidation. Article 34 expressly empowers the main

[129] See Art. 33(1). No limit is specified on the number of renewals of the stay, nor on the maximum duration for which such a cumulative stay of secondary proceedings may be imposed.

[130] See Art. 33(2).

liquidator to propose such a measure, and also clothes him with a limited power of veto over the closure of secondary proceedings by this means, in the light of the consequences for the creditors in the main proceedings. Thus, an unduly favourable settlement independently agreed to by the creditors in the secondary proceedings, which has adverse consequences for the general body of creditors, could be blocked by the main liquidator.[131] During the period when a stay is in force under the provisions of Article 33, only the main liquidator or the debtor (with the consent of the main liquidator) may propose the closure of the secondary proceedings by a rescue plan or composition: no other proposal of this nature can be put to the vote or approved.

Finally, the provisions of Articles 36 and 37 should be noticed. These anticipate the case where independent, territorial proceedings have been commenced in a Contracting State by virtue of Article 3(2) at some time before the opening of main proceedings in another Contracting State under Article 3(1).[132] This event has the consequence that the territorial proceedings ought to be reclassified as secondary proceedings, although there is no provision that this shall occur automatically. However, the provisions of Articles 31 to 35 are retrospectively applied to the secondary proceedings, in so far as this is possible in view of their progress prior to the time of transformation.[133] If it is the case that the territorial proceedings were originally of a kind not classified as winding-up proceedings under the Convention, their subsequently altered status as quasi-secondary proceedings means that logically they should undergo a formal conversion under the law of the State in which they were opened. Article 37 enables the main liquidator, at his discretion, to request such conversion into one of the proceedings listed in Annex B if this proves to be in the interests of the creditors in the main proceedings. The court with jurisdiction under Article 3(2) must order such conversion into one of the proceedings listed in Annex B, if an application is made. However, if the main proceedings are also not intended to effect the winding up of the debtor, the main liquidator may wish to explore the alternative course of coordinating the existing proceedings for the purpose of effecting a cross-border rescue plan.

6.3.6 Creditors' right to lodge claims and to receive information

One of the principal benefits which ought to accrue from the conclusion of an E.U. Convention in fulfilment of Article 220(4) of the EC Treaty is a

[131] See Art. 34(1),(2). See Virgos-Schmit Report, *supra* n.10, paras. 248–251.

[132] The circumstances under which this can occur are specified in Art. 3(4), discussed at 6.3.2 above.

[133] See Art. 36.

significant enhancement of the position of creditors confronted by the need to pursue their claims in a foreign insolvency proceeding. Chapter IV, consisting of Articles 39 to 42, establishes a somewhat limited, but nevertheless useful, series of rights in favour of creditors embroiled in a cross-border case. As a guiding principle, the Convention is committed to upholding the general rule forbidding any discrimination on grounds of nationality within the sphere of application of the Treaties establishing the EEC and the European Union.[134] In the context of the insolvency Convention, the concept of nationality is ignored, and other criteria have been preferred. Article 39, concerning the right to lodge claims, declares as follows:

> Any creditor who has his habitual residence, domicile or registered office in a Contracting State other than the State of the opening of proceedings, including the tax authorities and social security authorities of Contracting States, shall have the right to lodge claims in the insolvency proceedings in writing.

Thus, even non-nationals of EU States may have the benefit of this provision if they satisfy at least one of the specified criteria. Also significant is the express confirmation that the tax and social security authorities of the Contracting States have the right to lodge claims in insolvency proceedings opened in sister States. This represents a reversal of the established policy under private international law of refusal to enforce foreign revenue, or analogous, claims either directly or indirectly. In the case of the United Kingdom, it would involve the partial overruling of the rule confirmed in *Government of India v. Taylor*[135] with respect to the admissibility to proof of fiscal or social security claims of other EU Member States. While it may be true that on a literal reading of its terms Article 39 appears only to speak of the right to *lodge* proof, and makes no mention of any right to *receive* dividend, it would undoubtedly violate the spirit of the provision, and simultaneously the principle of nondiscrimination, if any State were to base its conduct on a sophistry of this kind. On the other hand, it may be considered acceptable for foreign tax and social claims to be treated as non-preferential debts, even though the equivalent claims of the authorities of the State where the proceedings are conducted are accorded preferential status under the law of that State. Such a 'compromise' nevertheless involves discriminatory treatment of claims which are otherwise similar or even identical in character, and it may be that the European Court of Justice will be required to rule on the matter, since Article 4(2)(i) of the Convention places the process of

[134] See EC Treaty, Art. 7, renumbered as Art. 6 by the Treaty of European Union, as of 1 July 1992.

[135] [1955] A.C. 491 (HL), considered in Chapter 2, at 2.4 and 2.6 (pp. 84 and 87) above.

distribution, including the ranking of claims, under the governance of the *lex concursus*.[136]

Among the practical disadvantages experienced by creditors in cross-border insolvencies is the delay in receiving notification of the proceedings, and the possible loss of the opportunity to lodge their claims within the time allowed. Article 40 imposes a duty upon the court having jurisdiction, or the liquidator appointed by it, to inform known creditors who have their habitual residences, domiciles or registered offices in the other Contracting States. The notification must take place immediately upon the opening of insolvency proceedings, and must be effected by means of an individual notice specifying, *inter alia*, time limits, the body or authority empowered to accept the lodgement of their claims, and other material information. Although individual notification is required, it need only be expressed in the official language (or one of the official languages) of the State of opening of proceedings. The only multi-lingual information prescribed by the Convention is that the form of notification must bear the heading: 'Invitation to lodge a claim. Time limits to be observed' in all the official languages of the European Union.[137] However, a creditor is permitted by Article 42(2) to lodge his claim in an official language of the Contracting State in which he has his habitual residence, domicile or registered office. The claim must bear a heading to the effect that it is a 'Lodgement of claim', using an official language of the State of opening of proceedings. In addition, at the liquidator's discretion a creditor may be required to provide a translation, into that official language, of the full text of the statement of claim.[138] Thus the burdens faced by many creditors of communicating with the liquidator through the medium of a foreign language remains inescapable, and the additional cost will continue to fall upon the creditors concerned. The required contents of the creditor's proof of claim are specified in Article 41.

6.3.7 Interpretation by the Court of Justice

Chapter V confers jurisdiction on the European Court of Justice to give rulings on the interpretation of the Convention, including its three Annexes, and any later instruments of accession to the Convention by States which become Members of the European Union at a later date. By integrating this chapter into the body of the Convention, rather than dealing with the jurisdiction of the Court of Justice in a separate protocol, the draftsmen have attempted to overcome the inconvenience caused in the past due to the

[136] See at 6.3.3 above. The Virgos-Schmit Report (*supra*, n.10), at paras. 265–270, also concedes that under Art. 4(2)(h) the national law of the state of opening will govern such questions as 'the admissibility and well-foundedness' of the lodgement of claims.

[137] See Art. 42(1).

[138] See Art. 42(2).

coming into force of Community Conventions some years before the Court of Justice became empowered to rule upon their meaning and application.[139] Under Article 44 the right to request a preliminary ruling on a question raised in national proceedings is restricted to appellate courts and the courts of final resort of the respective Contracting States. A court of first instance is denied the right to request a preliminary ruling. Thus, for the United Kingdom the courts competent to request a ruling are the House of Lords and other courts from which no further appeal is possible in the circumstances of the case concerned, and any court which is acting as an appeal court against the judgment of a lower court.[140] The decision whether to request a ruling is in all cases a matter for discretion for the national court, even if it is a court of final resort. Moreover, the court must consider that a decision on the question of interpretation is 'necessary to enable it to give judgment'.[141] As is now well established in relation to the jurisdiction of the Court of Justice to give preliminary ruling on matters of community law, the final determination of the case remains under the control of the national court, following its receipt of the ruling of the Court of Justice. Since this can considerably prolong the process of determining proceedings whose urgency is particularly acute in the context of insolvency, it is reasonable to assume that national courts will be cautious in their resort to the preliminary ruling facility. The Virgos-Schmit Report appears to appreciate, and even to emphasise, the need for speed and flexibility in this context, while exhorting national courts to be mindful of their international responsibilities. It is also appropriate to allude here to the principle of 'Community trust' by which all national courts and authorities are expected to abide in their dealings with one another within the scope of the Convention.[142]

Lastly an alternative basis on which the Court of Justice can be requested to deliver interpretative rulings is supplied by Article 45. This allows 'the competent authority of a Contracting State' to request such a ruling if judgments by courts of that State conflict with the interpretation given by either the Court of Justice itself or in a judgment of one of the

[139] The Brussels Convention of 27 September 1968 first entered into force among the six original EC Member States on 1 February 1973, the Protocol on the Interpretation of the Convention by the Court of Justice did not enter into force until 1 September 1975. The Rome Convention of 19 June 1980 entered into force on 1 April 1991; two Protocols signed in 1988 to confer jurisdiction on the Court of Justice to interpret the Rome Convention have yet to enter into force.

[140] In cases of appeals from orders in bankruptcy or in company winding up made by a County Court, or by a High Court registrar, appeal lies to a single judge of the High Court, with further appeal, by leave only, to the Court of Appeal: Insolvency Act 1986, s.375(2); Insolvency Rules 1986, r.7.47(2). It is submitted that either the single judge, or the Court of Appeal, could request a preliminary ruling under Art. 44.

[141] See Art. 44, opening paragraph.

[142] Virgos-Schmit Report, *supra* n.10, paras. 284–292, esp. para. 289. The 'principle of trust' is referred to in para. 220, commenting on Art. 27.

courts of another Contracting State. This procedure is in the interests of curing divergence between the national courts in their application of the Convention, and has the merit that it can be invoked in a more circumspect manner, without the pressure associated with a case that is pending. It is expressly declared that the Court of Justice ruling under this procedure does not affect the judgments which gave rise to the request for interpretation.[143]

6.4 CURRENT SITUATION AND PROSPECTS FOR THE EU CONVENTION

As already described, the eventual fate of the EU Convention remains a matter of much uncertainty.[144] Since 23 May 1996 the refusal of the United Kingdom government to become the fifteenth, and last, signatory of the text by that date at the latest has given rise to a situation where the Convention is technically defunct, but is arguably capable of revival by unanimous assent of all fifteen States. What has subsequently been lacking is any clear indication that the necessary political will exists on the part of all the Member States collectively. At the time when the prearranged, six-month deadline for signature was due to expire, relations between the United Kingdom and the other Member States and institutions of the Union were severely distorted in consequence of the crisis in the British beef and dairy industry occasioned by the BSE epidemic.[145] During the very week in May 1996 when signature of the Insolvency Convention was required in order to prevent it from lapsing, the United Kingdom Government chose to embark upon a policy of non-cooperation with its European partners, as a gesture of dissatisfaction over the 'beef crisis'. This political imbroglio was thus assumed, on the basis of external evidence at the time, to have been the cause of the Convention's unfortunate demise. Subsequent developments have made it apparent however that this is by no means the root cause of the United Kingdom's aversion to becoming a Contracting Party to the Convention in its existing form. A more durable impediment appears to exist in the form of the centuries-old controversy between the United Kingdom and Spain regarding sovereignty over the small territory of Gibraltar.

The Gibraltar syndrome

Under the terms of the Treaty of Utrecht, signed on 11 April 1713, at the conclusion of the war of Spanish Succession, England was granted sover-

[143] See Art. 45(2). [144] See at 6.1 above.

[145] The initials 'BSE' signify the disease termed 'bovine spongiform encephalopathy', popularly named as 'mad cow disease'.

eignty over Gibraltar in perpetuity. Although successive Spanish governments down to the present day have sought the restoration of Spanish sovereignty, Gibraltar remains an autonomous European possession for whose international relations the United Kingdom is responsible. The delicacy of the situation has been enhanced since the accession of Spain to full membership of the European Union in 1989. The United Kingdom has sought to avoid any circumstances resulting from the implementation of EU law and policy whereby the status of Gibraltar as a British possession might be compromised, directly or indirectly. A potential source of such embarrassment was the Brussels Convention on Jurisdiction and the Enforcement of Judgments in Civil and Commercial Matters, to which the United Kingdom was already a Contracting Party at the time of Spanish accession, and to which Spain duly became a party under the San Sebastian Convention of 26 May 1989.[146] Foreseeably, if the Brussels-San Sebastian Convention were to be applicable to Gibraltar, an apparent erosion of British sovereignty would occur, due to the obligation to recognise and enforce Spanish civil or commercial judgments under the terms of the Convention. This contingency has been averted by means of the provision in Article 60, which prevents the Convention from applying to:

> any European territory situated outside the United Kingdom for the international relations of which the United Kingdom is responsible, unless the United Kingdom makes a declaration to the contrary in respect of any such territory.[147]

The United Kingdom has not lodged any declaration in respect of Gibraltar, with the consequence that the Brussels-San Sebastian Convention is not applicable there.

With hindsight, it may be deemed to have been unfortunate that the Insolvency Convention was not constructed along similar lines to the Brussels Convention with regard to its application to the external territories belonging to the intended Contracting States. Somewhat surprisingly, the text of the Convention makes no reference to its territorial scope. The Virgos-Schmit Report endeavours to account for this omission, and retrospectively to atone for it, by explaining that the textual silence on this point has the consequence that Article 29 of the 1969 Vienna Convention on the Law of Treaties is applicable together with the general rules of public international law. On this basis, the Report asserts that the Insolvency Convention applies to the whole territory of the Contracting States, including any non-European territories which are an integral part of those

[146] O.J. 1989, L285, implemented in the UK by S.I. 1990 No. 2591; in force for the UK from 1 December 1991.

[147] This provision has the effect of excluding the Brussels Convention from applying to the Isle of Man, the Channel Islands and the British Sovereign Bases in Cyprus, in addition to Gibraltar.

States, but conversely that it does not apply to those territories whose international relations are undertaken by any of the Contracting States but which, being a separate entity, do not form an integral part of their territory.[148] This interpretation of the territorial application of the Convention implies, but does not expressly state, that the Convention would not apply to Gibraltar unless the United Kingdom, as the State with responsibility, wished it to do so and encountered no objection from any other Contracting State. With respect, it may be observed that this *ex post* rationalisation of the territorial scope of the Insolvency Convention in the concluding pages of the Explanatory Report appears far less secure, as a basis for resolving the vital question of the territorial scope of an international convention, by comparison to the express terms incorporated into the body of the Brussels Convention by its Article 60. What is undoubtedly true is that the onus lay with the United Kingdom to anticipate this problem at a stage in the negotiations when appropriate steps might have been taken to rectify it. It is a matter of national embarrassment that this did not occur, and has certainly caused much distress and offence to the United Kingdom's European partners.

The way forward

It may prove to be the case that the 'Gibraltar syndrome' will prevent the EU Insolvency Convention from being adopted in its current form by all fifteen Member States. While it might theoretically be possible to cure this problem by means of a textual amendment, or a special declaration appended to the Convention, such a course is probably precluded by reason of the text having to be regarded as 'frozen' in the form in which it was initialled by all fifteen States on 25 September 1995. In principle, it rests within the power of those same States to allow an exception to their previous resolution, as a means of enabling their Herculean efforts to be crowned with success. Politically, however, it might be impossible to concede only a single exception to accommodate the special concerns of one Member State: other States might wish to reopen other provisions that were previously thought to have been finalised, and so the process of negotiation might resume almost indefinitely.

An unlikely alternative might be for the fourteen States which signed the Convention before 23 May 1996 to agree that the text will enter into force among themselves. This would necessarily have to take place outside the scope of the European Union, and the provisions conferring jurisdiction on the Court of Justice would have to be excised on that account. Not only would this leave the underlying requirements of EU law, and of

148 Virgos-Schmit Report, *supra* n.10, ch. VI, paras. 300–302. The information printed on the title page of the Report indicates that the comments on territorial application were contributed by Professor Virgos, of the Universidad Autonoma of Madrid.

the Internal Market, unresolved, but it would be commercially far from satisfactory for the United Kingdom to remain outside the arrangements for regulating cross-border insolvencies among its fellow Member States. Therefore, the alternatives appear to be that a vigorous attempt should be made among the fifteen to achieve a politically acceptable compromise that will allow the existing text to be adopted with minimum adjustment, or that an entirely new initiative should be embarked upon to bring about the necessary harmonisation of insolvency law by means of one or more Directives which, in the last resort, can be enacted on the basis of a majority vote of the EU Council of Ministers. Although the Convention might serve as a model for some of the provisions of a harmonising Directive, the course of evolution of such a programme would be unpredictable. Several years would certainly elapse before such harmonised provisions could enter into force in the national laws of all Member States.

In conclusion therefore, it is urged that a further attempt should be made to secure the implementation of the Convention as finalised in 1996.[149] It represents the fruits of many years of intensive activity and progressive technical refinement, and holds the prospect of significant practical benefits for those involved in insolvency proceedings, whether as debtors, as creditors or as practitioners. Despite the failure of one State to append its formal signature (for reasons which, as has been seen, are politically tangential to the technical purposes of the Convention itself), it should be remembered that all fifteen Member States were actively involved in the negotiations which produced the finished text, and that fourteen of them actually signed it. That is a significant accomplishment which ought not to be allowed to become a mere footnote of legal history without having been tested in practice. It is to be hoped that an occasion will present itself in the near future to return to this item of unfinished business, when a favourable tide flows once again in the affairs of the European Union.

[149] See, to the same effect, Balz, *supra* n.10, at 529, Bogdan (1997) 6 I.I.R. 114 at 126.

7

Council of Europe Convention of Istanbul, 5 June 1990

PRELIMINARY

The European Convention on Certain International Aspects of Bankruptcy, concluded under the auspices of the Council of Europe, was opened for signature in Istanbul on 5 June 1990.[1] For ease of reference and identification, the Convention is usually known as the Istanbul Convention. Under Article 34 of the Convention, it will enter into force after a minimum of three ratifications have been lodged in accordance with Article 33. To date, eight of the Member States of the Council of Europe have signed the Istanbul Convention, and one—Cyprus—has ratified it.[2] Although there is some reason to doubt whether the Convention will succeed in attracting many more ratifications, it is nevertheless a significant landmark on the road towards the development of regional—and in due course, global—arrangements to provide better coordination of international insolvencies. In particular, it provided a symbolic demonstration that a multilateral convention could be concluded among a grouping of European States having divergent legal traditions, and with wide differences of approach to matters of insolvency. The timing of this development was especially significant, since it took place during a period when it appeared improbable that the Member States of the European Community (subsequently to become the European Union) would succeed in concluding a Bankruptcy Convention for themselves. Not only can the Istanbul Convention be seen to have served as a catalyst for the concluding phase of the work on the European Union Insolvency Convention, as described in Chapter 6, but indeed several of its innovative concepts were adapted into the final version of the EU Convention.[3] The present chapter will therefore examine the principal features of the Istanbul Convention, with appropriate references to their influence upon the EU Convention.

[1] (1990) E.T.S., No. 136. The text of the Convention is reproduced in Appendix III below.

[2] The States which have signed the Convention to date are: Belgium, Cyprus, France, Germany, Greece, Italy, Luxembourg, and Turkey. The sole ratification, that of Cyprus, was lodged on 17 March 1994.

[3] See at 6.1 and 6.3 above.

7.1 AIMS AND SCOPE OF THE ISTANBUL CONVENTION

The Council of Europe was among the first of the international organisations to have been formed in Europe after the Second World War, in the movement to promote resurgence and unification in place of historic enmities and ruinous strife.[4] Although committed by its Statute to achieving 'a greater unity between its members', the Council of Europe is based on a relatively loose commitment to cooperation in comparison with the European Union. Consequently, many more States have become members of the Council of Europe, whose programmes—including more than 150 conventions—allow members the option whether to become Parties or not. Conventions can therefore enter into force even though many of the members elect not to sign or ratify them, although they may have participated fully in the process of negotiation.

The above realities help to explain the approach adopted by the representatives of the Member States, meeting between 1981 and 1990 within the European Committee on Legal Cooperation, who developed the text of what would become the Istanbul Convention. In keeping with the general spirit of flexibility, the Convention was designed so as to avoid intrusive interference with the existing law and policy of those who might become signatories to it. Paradoxically, the numerous concessions to allow freedom of choice may have deprived the Convention of any practical value, because its effects may differ from State to State according to the particular mixture of options that are selected. The original intention was to devise an international instrument of modest aims, limited to enabling the office holder in insolvency proceedings to act in other jurisdictions as the representative of the creditors' collective interests, and to take protective measures and participate in legal proceedings outside the State of his appointment. Additionally, it was proposed that the position of foreign creditors should be ameliorated by provisions to clarify their rights of participation in insolvency proceedings, and to improve their rights to receive relevant information. Gradually, these modest but worthwhile ambitions were expanded, until the Convention was in peril of encountering similar objections to those which had defeated the EC Draft Convention of 1980, namely the unwillingness of many States to accept the total 'package',

[4] For an historical account of the formation of the Council of Europe, and of other European institutions established in the latter half of the twentieth century, see A.H. Robertson, *European Institutions*, 3rd edn. (1973), esp. ch. 2. The Statute of the Council of Europe was opened for signature on 5 May 1949. The current membership of 40 States includes all 15 States which are currently Members of the European Union, as well as all prospective members of the EU. The two organisations are completely distinct from each other, although they cooperate as and when appropriate.

even if certain aspects seemed useful in themselves.[5] This seems to have influenced the final form of the Convention, whereby it was left open to the States Parties to opt out of applying either Chapter II or Chapter III.[6] A very confused, and complicated, situation is in prospect if these opt-out facilities are utilised.

As befits the non-intrusive traditions of the Council of Europe, the Istanbul Convention is of the 'simple' or 'indirect' type, which merely lays down rules of indirect international jurisdiction to identify the circumstances under which proceedings opened in one Party will be recognised in the others, and will produce certain further effects under the Con vention.[7] This contrasts with the 'direct' approach under the EU Insolvency Convention, which imposes uniform rules of international jurisdiction for all cases falling within its scope.[8] The Istanbul Convention leaves the Parties free to continue to apply their existing national rules of jurisdiction, even against debtors resident or domiciled in another Party. The only consequence of any exercise of jurisdiction under circumstances which do not conform to the criteria for indirect international competence is that the proceedings which are opened on that occasion do not benefit from any of the other provisions of the Convention. The Convention consists of forty-four Articles, plus two Appendices, which are declared to be integral to the Convention. It is not, strictly speaking, a 'recognition and enforcement' convention, but limits itself to providing for certain consequences to follow from the opening of proceedings by a competent court or authority, as determined under Article 4. The principal consequences are that the liquidator may exercise his powers in other Parties, within prescribed limits (Chapter II); that secondary bankruptcies may be opened in other Parties (Chapter III); and that foreign creditors resident in other Parties have the right to receive information, and to lodge proof of their claims in the proceedings (Chapter IV).[9]

Language and interpretation

The official languages of the Council of Europe are English and French. The Istanbul Convention was concluded in bilingual, parallel texts, which are declared to be equally authentic. An Explanatory Report to the Convention, approved by the Committee of Ministers of the Council of Europe, is intended to assist courts in their task of interpreting the

[5] See Chapter 6 at 6.2 above.

[6] See at 7.3 and 7.4 below. The opt-out facility under Art. 40 has given rise to the unflattering description of the Convention as 'the *à la carte* Convention'.

[7] The provisions concerned with jurisdiction are contained in Art. 4, discussed in at 7.2 below.

[8] The jurisdictional rules of the EU Convention are discussed in Chapter 6 at 6.3.2 above.

[9] See Art. 1(2).

Convention, when it is in force.[10] Unlike the European Union, the institutions of the Council of Europe do not include a Court of Justice, since the organisation does not generate an autonomous legal order that would make it necessary to establish a body of this kind. With the exception of the European Convention on Human Rights, for whose interpretation specific judicial and administrative machinery is in place,[11] the task of applying the conventions of the Council of Europe is left to the national courts, who must resolve any questions of construction or interpretation on the basis of the English and French texts, with such assistance as can be derived from the Explanatory Report. There is an element of risk, in the case of a technical area of law such as insolvency, that divergent interpretations will be placed on key terms in the text, leading to further uncertainty and unevenness. If this were to give rise to serious practical difficulties, the matter might be referred to the *ad hoc* group of experts for which provision is made by Article 42. The terms of reference of this group are to assess the implementation of the Convention and to make any relevant suggestions.

Scope of application

Article 1(1) declares that the Convention 'shall apply to collective insolvency proceedings which entail the disinvestment of the debtor and the appointment of a liquidator and which may entail the liquidation of the assets'. Such proceedings are referred to throughout the Convention as 'bankruptcy'. The use of the unfamiliar, and unidiomatic, word 'disinvestment' appears to be a transposition of the French term '*dessaisissement*', where the word 'divestment' might well have been employed.[12] The expression 'disinvestment of the debtor' is defined by Article 1(3)(b) as meaning: '*placing the power to manage, control and dispose of the assets in the hands of a liquidator*'. The meaning of the term 'liquidator', according to Article 1(3)(a), is: '*any person or body whose function is to administer or liquidate the assets of the bankrupt or to supervise the activities of the debtor*'.[13] The persons and bodies who, for each State Party, are to be regarded as within

[10] Explanatory Report to the Istanbul Convention, adopted by the Committee of Ministers at its 434th meeting, 19–23 February 1990.

[11] European Convention on Human Rights, adopted 4 November 1950 ((1970) E.T.S., No. 5; (1965) U.K.T.S. 38, Cmnd. 2643), Art. 19, establishing the European Commission and Court of Human Rights, respectively, in their original form. The 11th Protocol to the Convention, opened for signature on 11 May 1994, replaces this two-tier structure with a single Court. The Protocol took effect into 1998.

[12] EU Insolvency Convention, Art. 1(1) (see Chapter 6, at 6.3.1 above), which resembles Art. 1(1) of the Istanbul Convention in several respects, uses the term 'divestment'. In early drafts of the English version of the EU Convention, until as late as 1993, the term 'disinvestment' was used.

[13] This definition closely resembles the definition of 'liquidator' furnished by Art. 2(b) of the EU Convention. See Chapter 6, at 6.3.1 above.

the definition of 'liquidator' for the purposes of the Convention are listed in Appendix B. This technique, which has the advantage of supplying a precise answer to the question of the scope of application of the Convention, is also employed for the purpose of identifying which proceedings, under the laws of each State, qualify as 'bankruptcy' wherever that term is used throughout the Convention, the listings being assembled in Appendix A.[14] It is expressly stated that the Convention does not apply to proceedings relating to insurance companies or credit institutions.[15]

The scope of territorial application of the Convention is ultimately a matter for each ratifying State to determine, as regards territories over which it exercises sovereignty, or for whose international affairs it is responsible. Article 37(1) allows each State at the time of ratification to specify the territory or territories to which the Convention shall apply.[16]

7.2 RULES OF INTERNATIONAL JURISDICTION: THE OPENING OF A BANKRUPTCY

Articles 3 and 4 contain rules governing the opening of bankruptcy, and the competence of courts or other authorities to do so for the purposes of bringing the Convention's further provisions into play. Article 3 specifies three basic conditions which must be satisfied in order that the decision to open a bankruptcy shall bring those consequences about. First, the decision must emanate from a court or other authority having competence under Article 4; secondly, it must be effective in the territory where the bankruptcy is opened; and thirdly, it must not be manifestly contrary to the public policy of the Party in which further acts under the terms of either Chapter II or Chapter III are to take place.[17] The second of these conditions stops short of requiring that the decision to open the bankruptcy must be final and unappealable. However, it does render it necessary that the decision shall be valid and enforceable in its current form, even if constitutes only a provisional order. This should suffice, for example, to enable a provisional liquidator appointed by an English court to exercise

[14] See Art. 1(1) together with Appendix A. The listings in the Appendix are arranged into sub-categories (a, b and c) to indicate which proceedings are referred to for the purposes of Chapters II, III and IV of the Convention, respectively. The same technique of listing national proceedings, etc. in an integral Annex is employed in the EU Convention: see Annexes A, B and C (Chapter 6, at 6.3.1 above).

[15] Cf. the similar, but more extensive, exclusion made by Art. 1(2) of the EU Convention.

[16] From a UK point of view, the absence of a comparable provision in the EU Convention has previously been noted, in view of the resulting uncertainty regarding the application of that Convention to such external territories as Gibraltar, the Channel Islands or the Isle of Man. See Chapter 6, at 6.4 above.

[17] Art. 3 a, b and c. The provisions of Chapters II and III respectively are considered at 7.3 and 7.4 below.

his powers in other Parties to the Convention. The reference to public policy, even though qualified by the term 'manifestly', leaves the way open to a variable approach on the part of the States concerned. It would allow States such as the United Kingdom to maintain their traditional policy of refusal to enforce foreign fiscal or other public laws, which could result in a foreign trustee or liquidator being prevented from exercising his powers in the United Kingdom when the foreign insolvency proceedings have been instigated, largely or wholly, by the revenue authorities of the Party in question.[18]

Article 4, which bears the heading 'Indirect international competence', establishes a two-tier structure of jurisdictional competence, based upon the strength of the connection between the debtor and the State of opening of bankruptcy. The primary category of jurisdictional competence is allocated to 'the courts or other authorities of the Party in which the debtor has the centre of his main interests'.[19] The Convention does not define the concept of 'centre of main interests', although Article 4(1) contains the supplementary stipulation that: 'For companies and legal persons, unless the contrary is proved, the place of the registered office shall be presumed to be the centre of their main interests'. No further guidance is provided with regard to the nature or degree of proof required to rebut this presumption, although the Explanatory Report offers the suggestion that such refutation might take place 'if it is proved that the entity's management decisions are taken elsewhere'.[20] It would be reasonable to expect that the onus of proving that the centre of main interests is in a different State to the place of the registered office will fall upon the party who seeks to allege that this is the case. No mechanism is provided for resolving any positive or negative conflicts that may result if it should happen that courts in two different Parties form different conclusions as to the location of the centre of main interests of a particular debtor company. In the absence of any court having overarching jurisdiction to resolve matters of interpretation arising under a Council of Europe convention of this kind, it is left to the national courts to try to resolve the difficulty on an *ad hoc* basis.[21]

[18] On the treatment of so-called 'tax bankruptcies' under English private international law, see Chapter 2, at 2.4 and 2.6 (pp. 84 and 87) above.

[19] See Art. 4(1). The concept of the 'centre of main interests' was also adopted as the primary criterion of competence for the EU Insolvency Convention: see *ibid.*, Art. 3(1), discussed in Chapter 6, at 6.3.2 above, and also for the UNCITRAL Model Law on Cross-Border Insolvency: see *ibid.I*, Arts.2(b), 17(2)(a), discussed in Chapter 8, at 8.2 below.

[20] Explanatory Report, para. 27. The Report is otherwise unable to shed any light upon the intended meaning of the expression 'centre of main interests'. EU Convention, Art. 3(1), contains a presumption, identical in substance to that in Art. 4(1) of the Istanbul Convention. See Chapter 6, at 6.3.2 above.

[21] Cf. Trautman, Westbrook and Gaillard (1993) 41 A.J.C.L. 573, at 589, where it is suggested that the task of resolving such disputes might be assigned to the court where the first petition was filed.

The second tier of indirect, international competence is allocated by Article 4(2) to 'the courts or other authorities of the Party in whose territory the debtor has an establishment'. Two separate contingencies are provided for: first, where the centre of the debtor's main interest is not located in the territory of any Party, and secondly where bankruptcy cannot be opened within the Party competent under Article 4(1) because of the provisions of its national law and of the capacity of the debtor.[22] No definition of the term 'establishment' is provided by the Convention. This is doubly unfortunate, because the same ground of jurisdiction is used in Chapter II as one of the bases for opening secondary bankruptcies in cases where a main bankruptcy has been opened under Article 4(1).[23] Divergent views and approaches may well emerge from different national courts with regard to the necessary attributes of an 'establishment' (as distinct from the merely 'passive' presence of assets belonging to the debtor). Again, it must be noted that there is no mechanism under this Convention for resolving such conflicts of conceptualisation in cases where they arise. The Convention does anticipate the possibility that a debtor may have two or even more establishments, located in more than one Party. In that event, the proviso to Article 4(2) declares that the court or authority which first gave judgment shall alone be considered competent. The point has already been made in Chapter 6, when commenting on the defects in the Phase I Drafts of the EU Convention, that it is an unsound approach in cases of international insolvency to provide an incentive to creditors to initiate insolvency proceedings as early as possible, in order to gain tactical advantages over creditors in other jurisdictions.[24] It is regrettable that a crude, 'winner-takes-all' rule has been adopted by the Instanbul Convention: the relative merits of the competing jurisdictions receive no consideration in the process of deciding which Party's court will enjoy sole competence. This will also jeopardise attempts to avert bankruptcy or liquidation through a coordinated 'workout' or arrangement: a pre-emptive strike by creditors in one country could destabilise the debtor's business, leaving liquidation as the only feasible alternative.

[22] See Art. 4(2), a and b. In the second case, the Party where the centre of main interests is located is not obliged to apply the Convention. On the provision in Art. 3(4)(a) of the EU Convention for cases where national law excludes the debtor from bankruptcy on account of status (e.g. non-traders, small businesses, farmers, and others), see Chapter 6, at 6.3.2 above, esp. at n.53.

[23] See Art. 17, discussed in at 7.4 below. By contrast, Art. 2(h) of the EU Convention supplies a definition of 'establishment', as discussed in Chapter 6, at 6.3.2 above. That definition has been incorporated, in slightly embellished form, in Art. 2(f) of the UNCITRAL Model Law: see Chapter 8, at 8.2 below, at p. 336.

[24] See Chapter 6, at 6.2 above.

Proof of the liquidator's appointment

When bankruptcy has opened in accordance with the jurisdictional rules contained in Article 4, the office holder (who is referred to in the Convention as 'the liquidator') will wish to avail himself of the further facilities extended under Chapters II and III.[25] The first requirement is that there should be a simple and rapid means of establishing the liquidator's credentials that will be accepted in each Party in which he wishes to act, and that costly formalities can be minimised. Article 2 provides that the appointment of the liquidator shall be evidenced by a certified copy of the original decision appointing him or by an official certificate of appointment issued by the court or any other competent authority which has opened the bankruptcy.[26] Although the liquidator can be required to furnish a translation into one of the official languages of the Party where he exercises his powers, it is expressly stated that no legalisation or other similar formality will be required.[27]

7.3 EXTRATERRITORIAL EXERCISE OF THE LIQUIDATOR'S POWERS

The Istanbul Convention operates within rather modest limits. Although rules of indirect international jurisdiction are contained among the general provisions in Chapter I, the fact that a bankruptcy has been opened in conformity with one of those rules gives rise to comparatively unspectacular consequences. There are no provisions to impose any requirement on the other Parties to recognise or enforce the bankruptcy in question; still less is there anything to the effect that direct, extraterritorial effects are to ensue in relation to property situated outside the territory of the Party in which the bankruptcy is opened.[28] The principal advantage of the Convention's jurisdictional criteria being met is that the liquidator is eligible to exercise certain of his powers in the territory of another Party, pursuant to the provisions contained in Chapter II. To the extent that such provisions furnish the liquidator with the means to take effective and timely action to protect and preserve assets, and in due course administer

[25] See at 7.3 and 7.4 below.

[26] See Art. 7, which requires the liquidator to present the documentary proof of his appointment as one of the conditions of exercise of his powers under Chapter II (see at 7.3 below).

[27] See Art. 2. This provision is reproduced, almost *verbatim*, in Art. 19 of the EU Convention (see Chapter 6, at 6.3.4 above, where the concept of 'legalisation' is also considered).

[28] Contrast the effects produced under Chapter II of the EU Convention, discussed in Chapter 6, at 6.3.4 above, or under the Nordic Convention discussed in Chapter 5, at 5.3 above.

them for the benefit of creditors generally, this can be seen as a worthwhile advance in the prolonged struggle to overcome the classic obstacles to efficient management of international cases. However, the substantive provisions of Chapter II are likely to be of limited value in practice. It should also be noted that, as already stated, Article 40 allows any ratifying State to declare that it will not apply Chapter II.

Protection and preservation of the assets: provisional measures

Article 6 indicates that Chapter II applies not only to the actual bankruptcy proceedings as defined by Article 1(1), but also to provisional proceedings commenced on the order of a court or other authority for the purpose of providing protection of the assets of the debtor following a request for the opening of such a collective procedure. This allows an office holder whose terms of appointment do not correspond to the definition of 'liquidator' in Article 1(3)(a), to exercise powers for the purpose of protecting the debtor's foreign assets (for example, a provisional liquidator). The qualifying condition for this is that the appointment is coupled to a pending application for the opening of insolvency proceedings which constitute 'bankruptcy' within the meaning of the Convention. The actual extent of the liquidator's scope for taking measures to protect or preserve the assets located in other Parties is indicated by Article 8. This states that from the date of his appointment, the liquidator may take or cause to be taken any necessary steps to protect or preserve the value of the assets, including the seeking of assistance from competent authorities in the Party in which he wishes to act. Although the liquidator is clothed with the right to act from the date of his appointment, two significant provisos are included in the terms of Article 8. These are, that the liquidator must act 'in accordance with the law of the Party in which he intends to act', and that when acting under this Article he may not remove any assets from the territory of the Party where they are situated.[29] The Explanatory Report confirms that the protective measures which it is open to the liquidator to take in this context are those which are provided under the local law of the place of acting: there is no importation of powers which may be available under the law of the Party where bankruptcy proceedings are opened, but which possibly may not be replicated under the *lex situs*.[30]

Advertisement of the liquidator's appointment; suspension of exercise of powers

Article 9 imposes a requirement that a summary of the decision appointing the liquidator, as provided by Article 2, must be advertised pursuant to the method of publication determined by the Party in which the liquidator intends to act. Such advertisement is to take place after any neces-

[29] See Art. 10, below, for the possibility of repatriation of assets.
[30] Explanatory Report, paras. 41–43.

sary authorisation has been obtained from the authorities of the State of acting. Thus the local authorities are in full control of the form and mode of advertisement, and can specify the information to be contained in it. The purpose of this provision is to ensure that local creditors are aware of the appointment of the liquidator, and of any powers he may be capable of exercising. It also serves to inform creditors of their rights, including the lodging of their claims. The date of publication of the advertisement has an additional significance in that it marks the commencement of a two-month period, as specified in Article 11, during which the liquidator's powers of administration, management and disposal are placed in suspension in relation to assets located in the Party where the advertisement has been published. Local creditors are thus enabled to take further steps which may effectively neutralise the liquidator's powers with respect to the assets in question, for example by requesting the opening of a local bankruptcy, or of proceedings to prevent bankruptcy, or by mounting a specific challenge to the liquidator's right to exercise his powers over particular assets.[31] Article 11(1) further provides that if during the two-month moratorium period, or at any later stage, any request for bankruptcy or for proceedings to prevent bankruptcy has been made against the debtor in the Party where the assets are located, the powers of the liquidator shall be further suspended until any such requests have been heard and determined.

The tactical implications of the provision enabling local creditors to bring about a moratorium against the liquidator's exercise of his powers are considerable. Unless he has previously taken effective steps to assert some degree of control over the assets, using Article 8, there is an appreciable risk that some creditors may succeed in completing actions under local law which will allow them to defeat any eventual claim by the liquidator to the asset in question. This prospect is only slightly diminished by the provision in Article 11(2) which restricts the categories of creditor who are allowed to commence or pursue individual legal action against the assets of the debtor during the moratorium period. Freedom of action is accorded to creditors whose claims are classified as preferential under the law of *situs*, or who would have enjoyed such status if the bankruptcy had been opened in that Party. Also free to pursue actions are creditors who have a claim arising from the public law of the Party in question, and any creditors who have a claim arising from the operation of an establishment of the debtor or from employment in that Party. Therefore, local preferential creditors, and also some non-preferential claimants, may consolidate their hold over local assets while the liquidator's hands are

[31] See Art. 12, which places the onus upon the liquidator, whose exercise of powers is challenged, to establish the extent of his powers and his right to exercise them under the Convention.

effectively tied. A possible means by which the liquidator can try to limit the potential damage resulting from such developments is to take the initiative, as permitted by Article 11(1), of himself lodging an application for a local bankruptcy to be opened. For this purpose, it is necessary that the conditions for opening such a proceeding under the local law of that Party are met. In practice, it is probable that the delay caused by the liquidator's need to advertise his appointment locally, and the two-month period of suspension thereafter, will enable many local creditors to consolidate their position, at the expense of the main estate.

Further limitations to the liquidator's exercise of his powers can be brought about under the provisions of Article 14. First, Article 14(1) becomes applicable if bankruptcy proceedings or proceedings which prevent bankruptcy are opened, in the manner envisaged by Article 11, in the Party in which the liquidator intends to exercise his powers. The opening or recognition of such proceedings in the Party in question prevents the liquidator from exercising his powers in that State.[32] Thereby, the temporary suspension of the liquidator's powers under the moratorium generated by Article 11 can be rendered permanent under the terms of Article 14(1). This is one of the consequences of the opening of a secondary bankruptcy under Chapter III.[33] Specific restrictions on the liquidator's exercise of his powers are imposed by Article 14(2), which prohibits the performance of an act which is: (a) contrary to any security held by the debtor over land or other property established or recognised by the law of the Party in which the power is invoked; or (b) manifestly contrary to the public policy of that Party. Both individually and cumulatively, the limitations upon the liquidator's scope to take effective action in the territory of the other Parties are substantial, and combine to convey a decidedly negative impression of the Convention's commitment to securing worthwhile gains in the administration of cross-border insolvencies. Only a modicum of consolation is likely to be forthcoming in practice from the provision in Article 15 whereby any Party may permit the foreign liquidator to exercise on its territory wider powers than those laid down in Chapter II. It may be suspected that the minimum standards for which the Chapter makes provision will in most cases be regarded as the norm.

Exercise of the liquidator's powers (Article 10)

In those cases where he is allowed to do so, given the foregoing limitations and suspensions, the liquidator's exercise of powers under Chapter II is

[32] The reference to the recognition of proceedings allows for the possibility that proceedings opened in a third State may be recognised by virtue of some other convention, even with a non-Party to the Istanbul Convention. The prevalence of such conventions over the terms of the Istanbul Convention is facilitated by Art. 38(1).

[33] See at 7.4 below.

governed by Article 10. The first paragraph of this Article states that the liquidator may act within the powers conferred on him under the law of the Party in which the bankruptcy was opened, and on that basis take or cause to be taken any acts to administer, manage or dispose of the debtor's assets, including removing them from the territory of the Party where they are situated. Ostensibly, this appears to afford the prospect of the liquidator exercising in an extraterritorial manner the powers conferred under the law of his appointment. However, Article 10(1) includes the proviso that such exercise of powers is subject to the conditions set out in the further provisions of Chapter II which, as has been seen, combine to impose substantial restrictions on the liquidator's true scope for action. Moreover, Article 10(2) declares that the implementation of the measures which the liquidator is able to take shall be subject to the law of the Party in whose territory the assets are situated.[34] Since the individual national laws remain unharmonised, there are likely to be cases in which the law of the State of bankruptcy and the law of the State in which assets are to be administered are at variance with each other in ways which are material, for example over the procedure and method of disposing of assets by means of a sale. Somehow, a composite process will have to be devised on an *ad hoc* basis to enable the requirements of the two systems of law to be applied in the way that Chapter II requires. It may also transpire that persons have dealings with the liquidator, only to have the validity of that transaction called into question by some other party. Article 13 provides protection for those who have made a payment or delivery of assets to the liquidator in good faith, in the supposed performance of their obligations towards him in his capacity as representative of the debtor's estate. Such payment or delivery will constitute a valid discharge for the party in question if made in good faith, which will be presumed to be the case if made after the advertisement of the liquidator's appointment has taken place according to the requirements of Article 9, or if the certificate mentioned in Article 2 was produced.

7.4 SECONDARY BANKRUPTCIES

Chapter III, comprising Articles 16 to 28 inclusive, establishes rules to enable secondary bankruptcies to be opened in any other Party, following the opening of a main bankruptcy under the terms of Article 4(1).[35] This is the principal innovation of the Istanbul Convention, and has been adapted—with significant modifications—into the structure of the EU

[34] The Explanatory Report, at paras. 47–54, further reinforces the impression that the liquidator's true scope for acting is heavily restricted.

[35] See Art. 4(1), discussed at 7.2 above.

Insolvency Convention, as described in Chapter 6.[36] The rationale behind the concept of secondary bankruptcies as embodied in the Istanbul Convention appears to represent a compromise between the out-and-out 'territorialist' approach, whereby locally-collected assets are essentially reserved for the payment of local claims (particularly those having preferential status under local law), and the advocates of a more 'internationalist' approach, whereby all creditors are treated on an equal basis, and the assets are similarly administered as a unified fund. As embodied in the present Convention, secondary bankruptcy operates primarily in favour of the first school of approach, with only a somewhat belated gesture in the direction of the latter. The 'compromise' is decidedly less than even-handed.

Jurisdiction: entitlement to request the opening of secondary bankruptcy (Articles 16–18)

Article 16 declares that upon the opening of a main bankruptcy in the Party where the centre of the debtor's main interests is located (Article 4(1)), the debtor may, by virtue of this fact alone, be declared bankrupt in any other Party, whether or not he is insolvent in that Party. Therefore, it matters not whether the debtor's operations within the State of secondary bankruptcy, viewed in isolation, are solvent or indeed profitable, or that the other prerequisites under the local law to allow the opening of bankruptcy proceedings are not met. All that is required is that the decision opening the main proceeding was made in accordance with paragraphs a and b of Article 3 (namely that it is valid and effective where made, and that it is not manifestly contrary to the public policy of the Party where secondary bankruptcy is requested), and that no bankruptcy or proceedings to prevent bankruptcy have already been opened in that Party.[37] Article 17 supplements the unharmonised national rules for exercise of bankruptcy jurisdiction, by supplying a harmonised rule of direct international competence that is based upon the presence of either an establishment or assets of the debtor. This rule, which is expressed to be without prejudice to the other grounds of competence provided for by national law, is intended to overcome any inhibition regarding the exercise of bankruptcy jurisdiction in those States where competence is considered to be exclusively vested in the courts of the debtor's domicile,

[36] See at 6.3.5 above. For an assessment of the practical advantages of the system of secondary bankruptcies, see Hanisch [1993] 2 I.I.R. 151; Trautman, Westbrook and Gaillard, *supra* n.21, at 595–601.

[37] Local proceedings may have opened before the main proceedings were commenced under Art. 4(1), or may have opened subsequently, for example during the moratorium imposed under Art. 11(1) over the liquidator's exercise of powers in the Party in question. See at 7.3 above.

habitual residence or principal place of business.[38] It has already been observed at 7.2 above that the lack of standardised definition of 'establishment' may give rise to uneven interpretations by national courts in their application of Article 4(2). In the case of secondary bankruptcies under Article 17, the consequences of such divergent national approaches will be less serious in view of the fact that competence may also be based upon the simple presence of assets, irrespective of value. When these grounds are combined with any rules of jurisdiction that are contained in existing national laws, it can be appreciated that the scope for opening of secondary bankruptcies will be extensive.

Article 18 indicates which parties are entitled to request the opening of a secondary bankruptcy upon production of the decision opening the main proceeding. They are:

(a) the liquidator in the main proceeding; or

(b) any other person or body granted the right to request the opening of a bankruptcy by the law of the Party where the opening of the secondary bankruptcy is requested.

The number of parties possessing the capability to request the opening of secondary proceedings is potentially quite large. The option accorded to the liquidator in the main proceedings is to be commended, since it enables him to assess the relative merits of trying to administer the debtor's assets and interests in the State concerned as part of the main bankruptcy, or as a separate exercise. The latter course may be advisable if there are complicated issues requiring considerable attention to aspects of local law, for example if there is a local establishment of the debtor which operates in a fairly substantial way. In the majority of cases however the request for secondary proceedings is likely to be made by local creditors intent upon preserving their advantages as preferential or secured creditors under the provisions of the local insolvency law, and at the same time decoupling the pool of local assets so that they can be available to satisfy their claims in this respect. The full significance of this tactical use of secondary bankruptcy becomes apparent when the further provisions of Chapter II are fully appraised.

Applicable law: lodgement and payment of claims

Article 19 states that, except as otherwise provided by the Convention, the applicable law in a secondary bankruptcy shall be the law of the Party

[38] For example, in Belgium, and also in The Netherlands, jurisdictional competence is traditionally confined to debtors who are locally domiciled. See Fletcher in I.F. Fletcher, *Cross-Border Insolvency: National and Comparative Studies (Reports delivered at the Montreal Congress of Comparative Law, 1990)* (1992), Part II, at pp. 275–280; Colle and t'Kint, *ibid.*, Part I, ch. 3 at pp. 52–58; Dalhuisen, *ibid.*, ch. 10 at pp. 191–193. See also Torremans (1994) 3 I.I.R. 102 at 106–112.

where that bankruptcy is opened. Although the Convention contains no provision which expresses a rule about the law which is to govern main proceedings opened under Article 4, the assumption would be that the *lex concursus* applies. Therefore, Article 19 provides a means by which parties whose interests are better served under the regime of their local law may procure its substitution in place of that of the Party in which the main proceedings are conducted. The principles of distribution which are to be followed in the secondary bankruptcy are therefore predominantly those of the local law, applied against the background of the rule as to payment of claims that is contained in Article 21. This restricts the process of payment to those claims which are classified as preferential, or as public law claims, or which are claims arising from the operation of an establishment of the debtor or from employment in the Party where the secondary bankruptcy is opened. Also payable are claims enjoying a security over land or other property. All such claims, when verified, are to be paid from the proceeds of the liquidation of the assets of the secondary bankruptcy. The broad catchment of the terms of eligibility to receive payment under Article 21, while principally of advantage to preferential creditors, are also capable of benefitting certain kinds of non-preferential creditor, such as those whose debts have arisen from dealings with an establishment, or employees with claims for salary or other entitlements, to the extent that these may exceed the limits within which such claims have preferential status.[39]

When the process of payment of claims under Article 21 is completed, any surplus is declared to form part of the assets in the main bankruptcy, and the secondary liquidator must forthwith perform the requisite transfer to his counterpart who holds office in the main proceedings.[40] In a somewhat belated fashion therefore, the Convention acknowledges, even if only symbolically, the essential unity of the insolvent debtor's estate. Realistically, perhaps, the cases in which such a surplus survives the process of distribution among those permitted to participate in the secondary bankruptcy will be somewhat rare. This makes it all the more curious that Article 20(1) should contain the forthright declaration that: 'Any claim may be lodged in a secondary bankruptcy'.

In practice, it is hard to envisage that many non-preferential creditors from outside of the State where the secondary bankruptcy is opened will avail themselves of the right to lodge their proof in this indirect way, when there is no prospect of participating in the distributions over which the secondary liquidator will preside. Although Article 20(2) requires the secondary liquidator to notify the main liquidator of all claims lodged with him, and further declares that all claims so notified shall be regarded as

[39] See, e.g. Insolvency Act 1986, Sch. 6, Category 5.

[40] See Art. 22. See also Art. 28(2), which enables the main liquidator to request the transfer of the surplus assets from the secondary bankruptcy.

validly lodged in the main bankruptcy, there appears to be no provision to cure any bureaucratic lapses which may occur after a claim has been lodged in the secondary bankruptcy, and which result in a failure of notification of the creditor's claim. The more prudent course, save where there are very clear advantages for the creditor in terms of the working language in which the secondary proceedings are being conducted, or the relative accessibility of their administrative location, is to lodge proof of claim in the main bankruptcy and to establish direct communications with the liquidator responsible. Although Article 25 imposes upon the liquidators in the main and secondary proceedings a duty to communicate promptly with each other any information which might be relevant to the other proceedings, it is as well to bear in mind that the mutual exchange of information may be impeded in practice, due to linguistic barriers or the pressing burden of other work for the practitioner concerned. Creditors would be well advised to minimise the risks of interruption of communications, or of the loss of vital documentation, where this could retard the processing of their claims.

A further provision whose apparent purpose is to reunite the creditors whose ranks were previously sundered by the opening of a secondary proceeding is Article 25. This bears the heading 'Equality of creditors', and states that creditors in the main proceedings who are entitled to receive a dividend from assets coming from the secondary bankruptcy shall be treated equally, regardless of any privileges or other exceptions to the principle of equality between creditors provided by the law of the main bankruptcy. The precise effect of this provision, which purports to override the provisions of the law of the main bankruptcy, is far from clear, but it appears to create a 'sub-estate' out of the transferred surplus, and to require it to be treated in a different manner from the pool of assets originally belonging to the main bankruptcy.[41]

Claims arising after the opening of the main bankruptcy

The possibility that secondary proceedings may be opened at some time after the commencement of main bankruptcy poses special problems for any party who has had dealings with the debtor in the interval between the opening of the two bankruptcies. For the purposes of the main proceedings, the transaction has taken place after commencement of bankruptcy, and will in consequence not be regarded as a provable claim (although under some circumstances it may qualify for reimbursement on some other basis, for example as an expense of the bankruptcy). On the other hand, since the transaction took place prior to the opening of the secondary proceedings, it may be admissible in the secondary bankruptcy,

[41] The Explanatory Report, paras. 118–134, offers a number of hypothetical examples of the intended application of Arts. 21–24.

if allowable under Article 21. If the dealings between debtor and creditor took place in the Party where the secondary proceedings are opened, the possibility of the creditor's claim being lodged in the main proceedings may be somewhat enhanced by virtue of Article 23(1). This provides that such claims cannot be rejected in the main bankruptcy solely on the ground that they arose after the opening of the latter bankruptcy. On the other hand, Article 23(2) has the effect of restricting the creditor's scope of recovering payment in the form of dividend in the main proceedings to a right of participation in the distribution of any surplus assets transferred from the secondary bankruptcy pursuant to Article 22. If there is no such surplus, the creditor's prospect of receiving dividend from the secondary proceedings depends on the circumstances in which the claim arose: if it arose in dealings with an establishment of the debtor in that State, the claim is admissible under Article 21; otherwise, it may fall outside the categories of claims allowed to participate in the secondary distribution.

Conclusion of secondary bankruptcy

Articles 26 and 27 are concerned with the ending of secondary bankruptcy in various ways, either by reaching their natural point of conclusion through the completion of the procedure that was embarked upon (Article 26), or by the conclusion of a composition where such is allowed under the law of the bankruptcy (Article 27). In each case it is provided that the secondary proceedings cannot be terminated, nor the composition take place, without the liquidator in the main proceeding having an opportunity to voice an opinion. In the case of a composition, the main liquidator's powers are more extensive, in that he can impose a veto upon the composition where it will be detrimental to the interests of the creditors in the main bankruptcy.

Application of the principle of 'hotchpot' under the Istanbul Convention

The creation of a facility for the opening of secondary bankruptcies—of which there could potentially be several, in any given case—logically requires that some consideration should be given to the consequences of such plural proceedings, from the standpoint of the distribution process and the principle of equality between creditors. Article 5, which is placed among the General Provisions in Chapter I, expresses the basic approach that is to be followed. While respecting the special position of secured creditors, who are allowed to enforce and realise their rights over land or other property, Article 5 states that a creditor who has received part payment in respect of his claim in a bankruptcy opened in one Party may not participate in a dividend for the same claim in a bankruptcy opened with regard to the same debtor in another Party, so long as the dividend received by other creditors in the bankruptcy opened in that other Party is less than the dividend he has already received. This provision embodies the essential concept of 'hotchpot', as developed within the common law legal tradition, and widely accepted as a pragmatic rule to impose a somewhat rough and approximate kind of equality among creditors, if circumstances so permit. A closely similar rule is included as Article 20(2) of the European Union Convention on Insolvency Proceedings, discussed in Chapter 6.[42]

7.5 CREDITORS' RIGHTS TO RECEIVE INFORMATION AND TO LODGE CLAIMS

Within just four Articles (29 to 32 inclusive), Chapter IV of the Convention addresses some of the familiar problems which confront those creditors who become involved in a foreign insolvency proceeding. Although of somewhat modest aspiration, the provisions contained in this chapter are sensible and worthwhile. The scope of Chapter IV is actually broader than is the case with the first three chapters of the Convention: Article 29 states that it shall also apply to proceedings which do not entail the 'disinvestment' of the debtor or which cannot entail the liquidation of assets, as well as to secondary bankruptcy proceedings.[43] The consequences of this expanded application can be readily appreciated upon examining the contents of Appendix A, which forms an integral part of the Convention.[44] The proceedings to which Chapter IV applies are listed, for each Contracting Party, as sub-category 'c', which mentions at least twice as many proceedings as are contained in combined lists 'a' and 'b'.[45]

Article 30 is concerned with the problems caused due to lack of timely information to creditors concerning the foreign proceedings. It is made a requirement that as soon as proceedings mentioned in Appendix A or secondary proceedings are opened in a Party, the competent authority of that State, or the liquidator appointed in it, shall inform the known creditors promptly and individually. The notification must contain what are termed 'the appropriate details', whose content is largely left to the initiative of the notifying party, and to such provision as may be made in the local law. However, Article 30(2) states that the notice must, in particular, supply details as to time limits and measures to be taken, and must also indicate

[42] See at 6.3.4 above, esp. at n.115 for references to other parts of this work. See also Hanisch in I.F. Fletcher (ed.), *Cross-Border Insolvency: Comparative Dimensions (The Aberystwyth Insolvency Papers)* (1990), ch. 11.

[43] On the meaning of the term 'disinvestment', and the scope of the Convention generally, see at 7.1 above.

[44] See Art. 1(1).

[45] In the case of the United Kingdom, list a + b specifies six proceedings; list c specifies twelve. (See Appendix III below for the full text).

whether creditors whose claims are preferential or secured need lodge their claims. The Article only stipulates that notice must be given to known creditors residing in other Contracting Parties. It is to be observed, not without regret, that there is no requirement that notice be given to known creditors residing in other States—which would be in furtherance of the principle of maintaining genuine equality of treatment of creditors—nor is there any requirement that appropriate means should be employed to bring the proceedings to the notice of other creditors whose exact addresses may not be known. It is also unfortunate that, if the terms of Article 30 are applied literally, the obligation to notify foreign creditors is limited to the first occasion upon the opening of the proceedings: it would seem logical and just that any subsequent notices issued to creditors generally should be sent to foreign as well as domestic creditors, but the Convention does not actually impose such a requirement.

Problems of language differences are a notorious feature of international insolvencies. Article 32(1) affords some useful assistance to those creditors who are unfamiliar with the language in which the insolvency proceedings are being conducted. While it is permissible for the notice under Article 30 to be drawn up in the official language of the authority which has opened the procedure, it is further required that if that language is not one of the official languages of the Council of Europe nor that of the creditor nor that of the Party where he resides, a translation into one of these languages must be attached to the notice. However, this helpful provision is subject to the facility afforded by Article 39(1) whereby States may declare at the time of ratifying the Convention that the notice under Article 30 shall be drawn up exclusively in its official language. Clearly, if advantage is taken of this facility the benefits of Article 30 will be severely reduced.

The procedure whereby foreign creditors may lodge their claims is prescribed in Articles 31 and 32(2). The former enables any creditor residing in a Party other than that in which the proceedings have opened to lodge his claim in writing to the competent authority or liquidator referred to in Article 30. The creditor is required to send copies of supporting documents, if any, and to indicate the nature of the claim, the date on which it arose, its amount, and also whether or not it is preferential and, if applicable, the assets affected by the preference. The principal advantage for the creditor is that no particular form is prescribed for the lodging of proof, which should obviate the need to try to obtain, and then to complete and return, any officially prescribed form issued under the law of the State in which the proceedings are opened, and in the working language of those proceedings. The Explanatory Report confirms that any kind of written communication will suffice for the purposes of this Article.[46] Article 32(2)

[46] Explanatory Report, paras. 158–163.

reinforces to a certain extent the concessions in favour of foreign creditors by allowing the written claim to be drawn up in the language of the creditor. However, if this language is not that of the authority which has opened the procedure, a translation in that language or one of the official languages of the Council of Europe must be attached to it. This is further subject to the provision in Article 39(2), allowing a ratifying State to declare that the written lodgement of claims mentioned in Article 31 may be drawn up in any language other than those mentioned in Article 32(2). Therefore, a Party may relax the more exacting linguistic requirements to which a foreign creditor would otherwise be subject.

7.6 ENTRY INTO FORCE OF THE CONVENTION: ACCESSION BY NON-MEMBERS OF THE COUNCIL OF EUROPE

The Istanbul Convention remains open to signature by the Member States of the Council of Europe, and is subject to ratification, acceptance or approval.[47] Article 34 provides that the Convention will enter into force following the deposit of the third instrument of ratification by a Member State. As mentioned at the outset of this chapter, to date only one such ratification has been lodged, and only eight States in total have signed the Convention.[48] The initial surge of interest which greeted the Convention when it was first opened for signature in 1990 appears to have receded. Among the Member States of the European Union, six of whom signed the Istanbul Convention during 1990 or 1991, enthusiasm for the Convention seems to have abated in favour of the revived (but again dormant) EU Convention project discussed in Chapter 6, or possibly the UNCITRAL Model Law, to be discussed in Chapter 8. Therefore, the current prospects for the Istanbul Convention are somewhat less than promising, and there is a distinct possibility that it may never enter into force.

Even if the more pessimistic forecast of the Convention's prospects proves to be correct, one further provision of the Convention deserves final mention, since it may serve as a model for inclusion in other conventions in due course. This is the facility created by Article 35, which enables non-member States of the Council of Europe to accede to the Convention if they so wish, and if their accession is acceptable to the Member States. What is first required is that the Convention shall have entered into force. Thereafter, a non Member may request to be invited to accede to the Convention, at the same time submitting a list of the proceedings to be included in Appendix A, and the persons or bodies to be included in

[47] See Art. 33. [48] See *supra* n.2.

Appendix B.[49] The Member States, meeting within the Committee of Ministers, may then resolve by a majority to invite the applicant State to accede to the Convention. The virtues of this procedure are, first, that it enables a convention initially concluded among a discrete grouping of States which share certain values and interests, to be extended in scope so as to become applicable to other States which are willing to subscribe to the same set of provisions, thereby broadening the international reach of the arrangements which have been put in place. Secondly, although the initiative may rest with the non-member to indicate a willingness to accede, the final decision on whether to extend an invitation to do so remains exclusively with the Member States themselves, (or a specified majority of them). This control mechanism may be increasingly necessary in the future, for it may be the case that requests to accede may be submitted by States whose standards of judicial efficiency and integrity do not equate with those of the established members of such international organisations.[50]

[49] See Art. 35(2).

[50] Cf. the situation which arises under the UNCITRAL Model Law on Cross-Border Insolvency, discussed in Chapter 8 below.

8

A Global Initiative: UNCITRAL Model Law on Cross-Border Insolvency

PRELIMINARY

The record thus far of the various regional initiatives examined in Chapters 5, 6 and 7 suggests that, despite their undoubted potential to serve as vehicles for effective international cooperation, the effort involved in negotiating and bringing into effect a regionally-based treaty of a commercially sophisticated nature is likely to be substantial. Indeed, the greater the degree of practical utility that is pursued by means of a treaty, the greater the difficulty in bringing it to fruition, and hence the greater the risk of ultimate failure.[1] A further, inescapable feature of any treaty whose effects are confined within the boundaries of a discrete, regional grouping of contracting States is that, self-evidently, the pattern and spread of the international elements in many real-life insolvencies will extend into non-participating jurisdictions. Indeed, for some debtors and their legal advisers certain non-contracting States may gain an added attraction for the purposes of structuring transactions, or of situating assets, by virtue of their imperviousness to the inter-State arrangements created by the regional insolvency treaty to whose regime the debtor's assets and affairs would normally be subject. Such shortcomings by no means invalidate the entire purpose of regional treaties, because there will be numerous cases in which the outcome is appreciably improved by comparison to the former, unregulated state of affairs. Nevertheless, the logical limitations placed upon these benefits have to be acknowledged.

The goal of an ever-wider, and ultimately global, regime for regulating international insolvency must therefore be addressed. In principle the task is daunting, not least because the complexities which pose near-intractable impediments to the conclusion of regional treaties are greatly magnified at the global level. This is not merely a question of the logistical problems of conducting detailed, technical negotiations among a much larger number of participants, but is also a consequence of the wider disparities that exist

[1] The EU Convention project, discussed in Chapter 6, is the most striking example of this proposition. It is also noteworthy that the Istanbul Convention, though less ambitious in its material scope and substance than that of the EU, has not yet entered into force (see Chapter 7 above).

between them, in terms of legal culture and tradition, and especially in their policy and approach towards insolvency itself. Under these circumstances, the very notion of producing a single instrument to which all participating States will commit themselves under terms requiring reciprocity, and also uniformity of application, already seems fanciful in the extreme. To suppose that the substantive provisions of such an instrument might actually provide a practical framework for dealing with the problems encountered in real cases—as distinct from some idealised, theoretical model—could well be regarded as hopelessly unrealistic.[2]

Although the prospects of concluding a full-scale treaty for global implementation are currently so remote as to render it unlikely that today's world community would regard it as justifiable to allocate resources to such a quest it is arguably the case that other, less ambitious, projects are capable of yielding substantial benefits at greatly reduced cost.

An alternative pathway to the ultimate goal of global harmonisation has begun to be explored in recent years. This consists of a progressive examination of those problems which are widely acknowledged among insolvency practitioners to represent key obstacles to the efficient administration of cross-border cases, accompanied by the formulation of solutions which, in the estimation of those destined to make use of them, are likely to offer worthwhile results without the participating States being required to commit themselves to the kinds of intrusive obligations which apparently make international insolvency treaties so difficult for them to accept. The preferred vehicle for dissemination of these solutions is in the form of a set of model legislative provisions which States are then at liberty to incorporate into their domestic laws to the extent that they themselves consider acceptable, and in whatever form best accords with the traditions and processes of that particular system. This approach relies heavily on the persuasive power of example, whereby those States which demonstrate their willingness to make voluntary changes to their laws in the interests of improving the workings of international insolvency can generate a steady momentum of support which, given time and experience, should induce more States to overcome their initial reluctance to participate.

Inevitably, the broad margins of self-determination conceded to any State which elects to adopt the model law carry their own species of risks, including that of possible non-uniformity between the internal application

[2] As an example of the Utopian schemes of former times, a Model Treaty on Bankruptcy was adopted by the 5th Conference on Private International Law at The Hague in 1925, but progressed no farther and was never ratified by any State. For an account of this episode, and an English translation of the text of the 1925 Draft Treaty, see Nadelmann (1944) 93 U. Pa. L. Rev. 58.

of the different versions of the model law as enacted by various States. However, this danger is also present to some extent in the case of an international treaty, which may be imperfectly transposed into domestic law or incorrectly applied by national courts. Of greater concern is the possibility that interested parties from non-participating States may exploit the opportunities available in States which have enacted 'open door' provisions based upon the model law, whereas no reciprocal facilities are available to outsiders under the laws of the States in question. A partial answer to this problem lies in the discerning use of discretionary powers by judges when invited to recognise and give assistance to foreign representatives appointed under the insolvency laws of any State which has not already implemented the model law's provisions. Ultimately, however, it must be hoped that the authorities of that State will feel impelled to address the moral dilemma presented by a state of affairs which they alone are capable of rectifying.

In this chapter, we will examine the most promising initiative of this kind to have emerged in recent times, namely the Draft Model Legislative Provisions on Cross-Border Insolvency, adopted on 30 May 1997 by the United Nations Commission on International Trade Law (UNCITRAL). For convenience of reference, this instrument has become known as 'the UNCITRAL Model Law on Cross-Border Insolvency', and will be so referred to hereafter.

8.1 HISTORY AND EVOLUTION OF THE UNCITRAL MODEL LAW

The first modern example of a 'Model law' approach to receive wide attention was the so-called 'Model International Insolvency Co-operation Act (MIICA)', developed under the auspices of the International Bar Association during the 1980s.[3] Although the MIICA was much debated in and even beyond the international community of insolvency practitioners, its potential for winning the active support of governments and legislators seemed to suffer from a serious disadvantage in that, due to the dominant role played by lawyers from the USA in the process of developing its provisions, it was perceived as something of a 'Trojan horse' in terms of aspiring to gain international recognition and effects for the type of 'debtor in possession' procedure best exemplified by Chapter 11 bankruptcy proceedings under the United States Code. This engendered a climate of caution bordering on hostility among States traditionally averse

[3] For the text of MIICA, and discussion of its provisions, see I. F. Fletcher (ed.), *Cross-Border Insolvency: Comparative Dimensions (The Aberystwyth Insolvency Papers)* (1990), App. I, pp. 287–296.

to allowing an insolvent debtor to retain control of its estate and affairs.[4] Nevertheless, the enduring significance of the MIICA is that the concept of a model law came to be perceived as a viable way of resolving the *impasse* caused by persistent international failures to conclude a global treaty in the realm of insolvency.

By 1993, recent experiences involving large-value international insolvencies had reinforced the widely shared conviction that a renewed effort should be made to improve the framework for cross-border cooperation. A timely convergence of resolve to work to this end emerged from two different organisations, UNCITRAL and INSOL International (the International Association of Insolvency Practitioners), which together formed a coalition of forces and constituencies which complemented each other in an ideal way. On the one hand, UNCITRAL is an organ of the United Nations whose special mission, since its foundation in 1966, has been 'the promotion of the progressive harmonisation and unification of the law of international trade'.[5] As a respected and effective forum for inter-governmental collaboration in matters bearing upon trade and commerce, it was in many ways perfectly suited to the task in hand. Lacking its own in-house team of insolvency specialists, however, UNCITRAL would be dependent upon the expertise of those representing the participating governments, together with other invited participants.[6] Among the non-governmental organisations invited by the Commission to join in the process of developing the Model Law was INSOL, whose own cycle of activities had in fact served as a catalyst for the initiative being undertaken.[7]

[4] The conventional wisdom among perhaps the majority of English insolvency practitioners prior to the transatlantic saga of *Maxwell Communications Corporation plc* (discussed in Chapter 3 above at pp. 184–5) was that American Chapter 11 proceedings were culturally and technically incompatible with English law procedures, such as company administrations and receiverships. At the very least, that case demonstrated that a mode of cohabitation, even if not amounting to a true marriage, was possible given the right circumstances.

[5] For the official record of the foundation of UNCITRAL by the General Assembly of the United Nations on 17 December 1966, with related documentation, see UNCITRAL Yearbook, vol. 1, 1968–1970, Part I, pp. 5–67.

[6] The current membership of the Commission comprises 36 states. Other Member States of the United Nations may be represented at the sessions of UNCITRAL by observers. For details of the States and organisations attending the 30th Session, at which the Model Law was adopted, see United Nations General Assembly Official Records, 52nd Session, Supplement No. 17 (A/52/17), 12–30 May 1997, at paras. 4–8 inclusive.

[7] Founded in 1982, INSOL International currently consists of an international alliance of 26 nationally-based organisations formed by insolvency practitioners (chiefly accountants and lawyers). Individual members may join INSOL directly, and thus become involved in its work even if they do not belong to any national organisation affiliated to INSOL. By 1998 global membership of INSOL was in excess of 6,800, from more than 60 different countries, and the organisation had attracted the participation of significant groups of bankers, lenders, insurers, regulators and academics, in addition to those describing themselves as insolvency practitioners.

In July 1993 UNCITRAL adopted a resolution to investigate 'the desirability and feasibility of harmonised rules of cross-border insolvencies'.[8] In furtherance of this investigation, UNCITRAL and INSOL held a joint Colloquium on Cross-Border Insolvency in Vienna in April 1994.[9] This proved to be an historic watershed, as a consensus emerged that not only was international action imperative, but that it could be greatly facilitated through the direct involvement of INSOL, with its unique pool of resources in terms of human expertise and experience. There ensued a period of vigorous activity, during which a Report on Cross-Border Insolvency Access and Recognition was compiled by an Expert Committee consisting of seven members of INSOL, working together with a representative of the UNCITRAL Secretariat.[10] Prominent among the numerous insights which had emerged during the Vienna Colloquium was the recognition that the judiciary are destined to play a key role in the operation of any international arrangements that are put into effect. Accordingly, in preparation for the active phase of work upon the text of the prospective model law, a further joint conference was organised in Toronto in March 1995 with the special purpose of enabling members of the judiciary from a wide range of countries to engage in a candid debate structured around the contents of the Report of the Expert Committee.[11] A judicial consensus also emerged endorsing the recommendation of the Report that this first venture should be restricted to modest goals, in the interests of ensuring concrete progress. It was agreed that the soundest way forward lay through a progressive, pragmatic approach, rather than reaching too far too quickly.

Fortified by the increasingly positive sentiment towards the model law project on the part of those attending the Toronto Colloquium, the

[8] Official Records of the General Assembly, 48th Session, Supplement No. 17, (A/48/17), paras. 302–306. See also *Uniform Commercial Law in the Twenty-first Century: Proceedings of the Congress of the United Nations Commission on International Trade Law, New York, 18–22 May 1992* (UN publication, Sales No. E.94.V.14), esp. at pp. 155, 158, 251 and 274.

[9] The proceedings of the Colloquium, based on the recorded transcript of the working sessions, are published in [1995] 4 *International Insolvency Review, Special Conference Issue*. For the official report on the Colloquium, see doc.A/CN.9/398, UNCITRAL Yearbook, vol. XXV:1994, Part Two, V, B. See further doc.A/49/17, paras. 215–222; UNCITRAL Yearbook, vol. XXV:1994, Part One, A.

[10] The Expert Committee's Report, as presented for consideration by the Judicial Colloquium at Toronto in March 1995 (see below) was published in [1996] 5 I.I.R. 139. The Joint Reporters were Evan Flaschen and Ron Harmer. A related study was undertaken of the insolvency law and practice of some 40 jurisdictions representing different regions and legal traditions of the world. This study was later published as: N. Cooper and R. Jarvis, *Recognition and Enforcement of Cross-Border Insolvency* (1996).

[11] The UNCITRAL-INSOL Judicial Colloquium on Cross-Border Insolvency, Toronto, 22–23 March 1995: reported in doc.A/CN.9/413, UNCITRAL Yearbook, vol. XXVI:1995, Part Two, IV, A. For subsequent considerations of the Commission, see doc.A/50/17, paras. 382–393, UNCITRAL Yearbook, vol. XXVI:1995, Part One, A. A transcript of those parts of the proceedings which were regarded as 'on the record' was published in [1996] 5 I.I.R. 162.

Commission in May 1995 formally approved the preparation of uniform legislative provisions on judicial cooperation in cross-border insolvencies, on court access for foreign insolvency administrators and on recognition of foreign insolvency proceedings.[12] For this purpose, in line with the established practice of UNCITRAL, an inter-governmental working group was constituted as the Working Group on Insolvency Law. In addition to the experts representing the Member States of UNCITRAL, the Working Group's sessions were attended by invited representatives of non-governmental organisations, including both INSOL and the International Bar Association. Conveniently, many of those who had taken a prominent part in the earlier phases of this process were also involved in the deliberations of the Working Party, whether as members of their country's national delegation, or on behalf of the non-governmental invitees. Thus, continuity and momentum were maintained, with beneficial consequences.

Responding to the Commission's indication that it would welcome the opportunity to consider a draft instrument for adoption at its thirtieth session in 1997, the Working Group applied itself to its allotted task with exceptional tenacity and made unusually rapid progress, relative to the standard pace of international negotiations at this level. In March 1997 a provisional version of the Draft Model Law was tabled for scrutiny and debate by those attending a Second UNCITRAL-INSOL Multinational Judicial Colloquium on Cross-Border Insolvency, held in New Orleans.[13] Once again the overall sense of the meeting was strongly affirmative. At the thirtieth session of the Commission in Vienna in May 1997, the Draft Model Law submitted by the Working Party was considered and further amended, and was adopted by decision upon a formal resolution moved at the 630th meeting of the Commission on 30 May.[14] The full text of the decision reads as follows:

The United Nations Commission on International Trade Law,

Recalling its mandate under General Assembly resolution 2205 (XXI) of 17 December 1966 to further the progressive harmonization and unification of the law of international trade, and in that respect to bear in mind the interests of all

[12] Twenty-eighth Session of UNCITRAL, May 1995: Official Records of the General Assembly, 50th Session, Supplement No. 17 (A/50/17), paras. 387 and 391.

[13] 22–23 March 1997. A transcript of the concluding evaluation by a panel of five judges is reproduced at [1997] 6 I.I.R. 236–251. See also *ibid.* at p. 139 for the text of the Report upon the Colloquium delivered by a member of that panel, Mr. Justice Farley, to the plenary session of the 5th World Congress of INSOL International, meeting in New Orleans from 23 to 26 March.

[14] Report on the work of the 30th Session of UNCITRAL, 12–30 May 1997: Official Records of the General Assembly, Fifty-second Session, Supplement No. 17 (A/52/17) Part Two, B, at paras. 221–222. The text of the Model Law as adopted after amendment by the Commission at its Thirtieth Session is included as Annex I to the Report, at pp. 68–78. That text is reproduced in Appendix IV below.

peoples, and in particular those of developing countries, in the extensive development of international trade,

Noting that increased cross-border trade and investment leads to greater incidence of cases where enterprises and individuals have assets in more than one State,

Noting also that when a debtor with assets in more than one State becomes subject to an insolvency proceeding, there often exists an urgent need for cross-border cooperation and coordination in the supervision and administration of the insolvent debtor's assets and affairs,

Considering that inadequate coordination and cooperation in cases of cross-border insolvency reduce the possibility of rescuing financially troubled but viable businesses, impede a fair and efficient administration of cross-border insolvencies, make it more likely that the debtor's assets would be concealed or dissipated, and hinder reorganizations or liquidations of debtors' assets and affairs that would be the most advantageous for the creditors and other interested persons, including the debtors and the debtors' employees,

Noting further that many States lack a legislative framework that would make possible or facilitate effective cross-border coordination and cooperation,

Being convinced that fair and internationally harmonized legislation on cross-border insolvency that respects the national procedural and judicial systems and is acceptable to States with different legal, social and economic systems, would contribute to the development of international trade and investment,

Considering that a set of internationally harmonized model legislative provisions on cross-border insolvency is needed to assist States in modernizing their legislation governing cross-border insolvency,

1. *Adopts* the UNCITRAL Model Law on Cross-Border Insolvency;

2. *Requests* the Secretary-General to transmit the text of the UNCITRAL Model Law on Cross-Border Insolvency, together with the Guide to Enactment of the Model Law prepared by the Secretariat, to governments and other interested bodies;

3. *Recommends* that all States review their legislation on cross-border aspects of insolvency to determine whether the legislation meets the objectives of a modern and efficient insolvency system and that, in that review, give favourable consideration to the UNCITRAL Model Law on Cross-Border Insolvency, bearing in mind the need for an internationally harmonized legislation governing instances of cross-border insolvency.

The entire text of the decision is, with respect, a remarkable and succinct statement of the compelling reasons why the Model Law is a timely and historic document. As such, the decision should be included among the materials to which reference is made in future by national legislatures which are in the process of enacting measures to implement the Model Law (or which are debating whether to do so), as well as by courts before which any matter arises in which the effects of the Model Law are in point. As an indicator of the fundamental purposes which underlie the Model Law initiative, and as an aid to interpretation of the provisions as transposed into national law, it deserves to be given prominence.

At the time of adopting the Model Law, the Commission had before it the draft version of the Guide to Enactment that is referred to in paragraph 2. of the active part of the decision reproduced above.[15] Following the finalisation of the text of the Model Law, the Commission requested the Secretariat to prepare a final version of the Guide to Enactment, incorporating the adjustments made at the concluding Session. This work was duly carried out by December 1997.[16] The Guide is primarily intended to provide a resource for those charged with the task of preparing national legislation for their country, to enable it to signal its adoption of the Model Law. However, in presenting an article-by-article explanation of the Model Law's provisions, the Guide is also suitable to function as a point of reference for those who later need to interpret the Law as enacted, and it should therefore be considered as belonging to the domaine of *travaux préparatoires*.[17]

8.2 SUMMARY AND SUBSTANCE OF THE UNCITRAL MODEL LAW

The essential purpose of the Model Law is to create a better environment for dealing with international insolvency, supported by appropriate provisions of the enacting States' domestic legislation, thereby giving rise to uniformity of approach in a range of key matters pertaining to cross-border cases. To facilitate this process, the Model Law is so drafted as to enable each enacting State to insert into the text of the enacted Article such specific references as are necessary to enable the provision to function as an integral part of the insolvency law of that State. This is achieved by means of instructions, printed within square brackets, which indicate

[15] The draft Guide to Enactment of the UNCITRAL Model Provisions on Cross-Border Insolvency, prepared by the Secretariat, is published as document A/CN.9/436.

[16] General Assembly, document A/CN.9/442, dated 19 December 1997, bearing the title: *Guide to Enactment of the UNCITRAL Model Law on Cross-Border Insolvency*. For convenience, this document is referred to hereafter as 'Guide to Enactment'.

[17] Also eligible for inclusion among the *travaux preparatoires* to the Model Law is the published Report of the 30th Session of the Commission (A/52/17), referred to *supra* at n.14. Chapter II, B of the Report (paras. 25–225) records the discussion about the various Articles of the Model Law that were amended or approved at that Session. Although the Guide to Enactment draws upon that record, it does not reproduce the contents in their entirety. Hence it may sometimes be useful to refer to the more complete record of the 30th Session in relation to certain questions of interpretation.

Further insight into the process of development of the text can be gained from the Reports of the Work of the Working Group on Insolvency Law, published after each of the four sessions devoted to the Model Law project between 1995 and 1997. See: 18th Session, 30 October to 10 November 1995 (A/CN.9/419 and Corr.1); 19th Session, 1 to 12 April 1996 (A/CN.9/422); 20th Session, 7 to 18 October 1996 (A/CN.9/433); and 21st session, 20 to 31 January 1997 (A/CN.9/435).

what terms, or cross-references to the enacting State's existing legislation, should be inserted into the text of the Article at that point.[18] Naturally, in every instance these details will be unique to the circumstances of the enacting State in question. Cumulatively, however, the States which do so will develop a *corpus* of mutually compatible legislative provisions. Once a critical mass of enacting States has been achieved, the practical benefits will become substantial, and the sense of moral obligation incumbent upon other States to accept these standardised provisions should intensify.

Among the many differences between a Model Law and a treaty or convention, as vehicles for bringing about international harmonisation of laws and procedures, is that States enjoy a much greater degree of freedom as to which parts of the Model Law they will enact at any particular time. States are also free from any obligation to lodge notice—either with UNCITRAL itself or with other enacting States—of their decision to 'opt in' to the Model Law. As already mentioned, the Law's provisions are not predicated upon any condition of reciprocity, which was explicitly suggested, debated and rejected by the Working Group. Hence each State which opts in must do so out of a conviction that this is an appropriate way of advancing the cause of greater fairness and efficiency in cross-border insolvency, and that it will make a positive contribution to economic and commercial stability and certainty.[19]

The selected aims

The strategy underlying the Model Law aims to achieve effectiveness through selectivity. By identifying those matters which, in the light of practical experience, are perceived as functionally of the greatest importance in the successful management of a cross-border case, this initiative represents an exercise in realism and in 'the art of the possible'. The principal themes addressed by the Model Law are:

(a) to establish the principle that a foreign representative, holding office under an insolvency proceeding opened under the law of one State, has a right of direct access to the courts of other States where it may be expedient to take action of some kind;
(b) to establish basic principles and procedures for the recognition of foreign insolvency proceedings and for the provision of relief and assistance in cross-border cases;

[18] See the full text of the Model Law, as reproduced in Appendix IV below.

[19] Cf. the objectives stated in paras. (a) to (e) inclusive of the Preamble to the Model Law, and also the Recitals to the UNCITRAL decision of 30 May 1997 whereby the Law was adopted, reproduced at 8.1 above. On the issue of reciprocity, see the Report of the 18th Session of the Working Group (*supra* n.17), at paras. 42–45.

(c) to establish a positive legal framework sanctioning cooperation between courts in different jurisdictions, and between courts and foreign representatives;
(d) to establish a framework of basic rules to be applied in cases where concurrent insolvency proceedings take place, so that coordination can be optimised in the interests of attaining the fairest possible outcome for all creditors and other parties concerned (including the debtor).

The four cornerstones of the Model Law can be represented by four primary concepts: Access; Recognition; Relief; and Cooperation. These have emerged through a sustained process of analytical debate among the experts participating in the various phases of the Law's gestation, as described above.[20] Even as early as the Vienna Colloquium in April 1994, a certain unity of vision began to be discernible, as speakers from various backgrounds and perspectives delivered their observations regarding the essential *desiderata* of any worthwhile international arrangements.[21] During the following three years, a process of distillation occurred in which the truly fundamental requirements were identified, and the text embodying them was progressively developed and refined. In this context, the Expert Committee's Report, issued in 1995, made a significant contribution by transforming the previously fluid lines of debate into a more structured and coherent statement of issues and principles.[22] Among the principles of application of the Model Law's provisions, it was agreed that special emphasis should be placed upon speed and nondiscrimination.

Scope of application of the Model Law

In keeping with the guiding intention to refrain from any attempt at a comprehensive regulation of cross-border matters, the Model Law is carefully limited in scope, both as to the situations and also as to the types of proceedings to which it can apply. In consequence, only the following issues are addressed:

(a) recognition in the enacting State of foreign insolvency proceedings, and the effects thereof (Article 1(1)(a); Chapter III);
(b) direct rights of access to the courts and legal processes within the enacting State for foreign representatives and creditors (Article 1(1)(a),(d); Chapter II);

[20] See at 8.1 above.
[21] See the various published records of the proceedings of the Vienna Colloquium of April 1994, referred to *supra* n.9.
[22] See the references given *supra* n.10.

(c) the correlative rights of courts and office-holders within the enacting State to make outward-bound requests to courts in foreign jurisdictions for recognition of proceedings commenced in the enacting State and to apply for assistance and relief, and for office holders to commence or participate in proceedings under the insolvency laws of the other State (Articles 1(1)(b), 5; Chapter IV);
(d) cooperation between courts and office holders from different jurisdictions (Article 1(1); Chapter IV); and
(e) coordination of concurrent proceedings taking place in two or more different jurisdictions (Article 1(1)(c); Chapter V).

Almost equally important are the issues to which the Model Law does not have any application. Thus, there is no interference with the rules of jurisdiction in insolvency matters that are in force in the enacting States: while criteria are laid down to limit the benefits of access and recognition to those cases where jurisdiction has been exercised according to defined principles, these in no way oblige an enacting State to desist from deploying rules of 'extended' jurisdiction—such as jurisdiction based upon the presence of assets belonging to the debtor,[23] or upon a concept of personal domicile not linked to any requirement of factual residence.[24] No exception to this *laissez-faire* approach arises even in cases where the debtor happens to have the centre of its main interests within the territory of another enacting State. This contrasts with the regime designed to come into force under the EU Convention which imposes mandatory rules of jurisdiction to which all the Contracting States would be bound.[25] The Model Law deliberately refrains from introducing any choice of law rules for adoption by the enacting States. This leaves States free to continue to deal with matters of conflict of laws according to their established rules and practices, and is once again in marked contrast to the approach under the EU Convention, where the Contracting States would be required to apply uniform rules of choice of law in cases falling within the ambit of that convention.[26]

The Model Law embodies further, self-imposed limitations upon its scope of application by carefully defining the types of foreign proceeding which are covered by its provisions on access, recognition, relief and cooperation. According to Article 2(a), which defines the expression 'foreign proceeding' wherever it is used throughout the Model Law, it must be a collective proceeding, whether judicial or administrative in nature, pursuant to a law relating to insolvency in the foreign State in which the

[23] For example, the English law doctrine permitting the winding up of foreign companies with assets in England, as discussed in Chapter 3, at 3.2.2(c) above.
[24] This alludes to the provision in the Insolvency Act 1986, s.265(1)(a), discussed in Chapter 2, at 2.1.1(a) above.
[25] See Chapter 6 above, at p. 259.
[26] See Chapter 6 above, at p. 265.

proceeding originates, and it must be a proceeding in which the assets and affairs of the debtor are subject to control or supervision by a foreign court, for the purpose of reorganisation or liquidation. This configuration of criteria has the consequence that an English law administrative receivership, in its present form, could not be classified as a 'foreign proceeding' in view of its essentially non-collective character, and also possibly because the notion of 'control or supervision of the court' is a somewhat latent one in this type of proceeding. On the other hand, both the English administration order procedure under Part II of the Insolvency Act 1986 and the Chapter 11 reorganisation procedure under the United States Bankruptcy Code would qualify as'foreign proceedings', since both are collective in nature and each involves the court in prominent, if different, ways. There is nothing within the Model Law to suggest that an insolvency proceeding which embodies the 'debtor in possession' concept is *per se* debarred from qualifying as a foreign proceeding, although certain technical adjustments may be necessary in order to enable a designated individual to claim official standing as the 'foreign representative' capable of acting on behalf of the debtor in foreign jurisdictions.[27] Also arguably within the definition of 'foreign proceeding' is the procedure for creditors' voluntary liquidation under Part IV of the Insolvency Act 1986. Although not initiated by means of a court order, the procedure is undoubtedly collective in character, and express statutory provision is made for matters to be referred to the court at any stage.[28] A provisional liquidator undoubtedly qualifies as a 'foreign representative', because Article 2(a) expressly includes interim proceedings for this purpose, and the definition of 'foreign representative' in paragraph (d) contains an echoing phrase to the same effect.

A further, optional facility is available to allow enacting States to exclude insolvency proceedings concerning certain categories of debtor from the ambit of the Model Law as applicable in that jurisdiction. This marks a prudent concession to the widely observed practice of treating certain types of entities, such as banks and insurance companies, as requiring special attention in the event of their insolvency, so that it is usual for them to be excluded from the general regime of the domestic insolvency legislation. Article 1(2) enables States which subject such entities to a special insolvency regime to exclude those types of debtor from the scope of

[27] 'Foreign representative' is defined in Article 2(d) in terms which cross-relate to the concept of 'foreign proceeding'. See further below.

[28] Insolvency Act 1986, ss. 110(3), 101(3), 104, 108, 112, 113, 114(2), 116. Contrast the EU Convention (Chapter 6 above), where careful provision was made for creditors' voluntary liquidation to be included within the procedures covered by the convention, provided 'confirmation by the court' has been obtained (see Annex A to the Convention, reproduced in Appendix II below). If intending to act abroad on the basis of the provisions of the Model Law, it may be prudent policy for a voluntary liquidator to take the precaution of obtaining such judicial sanction in advance by application to the English court.

the Model Law in their country. A further range of possible matters for exclusion under the laws of some enacting States consists of the various categories of debtor which are traditionally left completely outside the operation of the insolvency law of that country, such as non-traders, or debtors whose total liabilities do not exceed a prescribed monetary amount.[29]

The five types of issue listed above as falling within the scope of the Model Law will next be considered in sequence.

8.2.1 Recognition of foreign proceedings

The key to all the procedural benefits which are available under the Model Law is the recognition of foreign proceedings by the courts of the enacting States. This is the central premise, around which all else revolves. The criteria for recognition are specified in Articles 15–17 inclusive, which must be read in conjunction with the definitions supplied in Article 2. The essential concept of a 'foreign proceeding', as supplied by Article 2(a), has already been explained. The associated sub-categories of 'foreign main proceeding' and 'foreign non-main proceeding', defined in paragraphs (b) and (c) respectively, are important because they introduce further conditions upon eligibility to receive recognition under the Model Law. To qualify as a 'foreign main proceeding', it is necessary that the proceeding should be taking place in the State where the debtor has the centre of its main interests. This latter expression is not defined in the Model Law, but has been directly assimilated from the European Union Convention on Insolvency Proceedings,[30] in the interest of promoting a consistent approach to international recognition. However, the EU Convention likewise abstains from offering any formal definition of 'centre of main interests', apparently on the basis that it is better to leave some scope for judicial discretion and common sense to be exercised in the light of circumstances encountered in each case. Instead, the approach employed by both the Model Law and the EU Convention is to introduce rebuttable presumptions concerning the whereabouts of the centre of main interests. Article 16(3) of the Model Law declares that in the absence of proof to the contrary, the debtor's registered office, or habitual residence in the case of

[29] See the Guide to Enactment, *supra* n.16, at paras. 60–66. The facility to exclude so-called 'consumer debtors' (whose debts have been mainly incurred for personal or domestic purposes, rather than in the course of a trade or business), mentioned *ibid.* at para. 66, may be utilised by the USA when enacting the Model Law: see at 8.3 below. (I am grateful to Professor J.L. Westbrook for alerting me to this possibility at an early stage of the American legislative process).

[30] See Chapter 6 above. See esp. Art. 3 of the EU Convention, discussed at p. 259 above, where potential problems regarding the application of this connecting factor are considered.

an individual, is presumed to be the centre of the debtor's main interests.[31] The concept of a 'foreign non-main proceeding' is defined in Article 2(c) as one, other than a foreign main proceeding, taking place in a State where the debtor has an establishment. The latter term is further defined in paragraph (f) and means: 'any place of operations where the debtor carries out a non-transitory economic activity with human means and goods or services'. This definition has also been borrowed from the EU Convention, but with the addition of the last two words—'or services'—which provide a useful extension to the original version.[32]

Foreign proceedings which have been commenced in a jurisdiction where the debtor has neither the centre of its main interests nor an establishment do not qualify for recognition in an enacting State. This is of particular relevance in cases where national law allows jurisdiction to be based upon the presence of assets belonging to the debtor. It is important to note that the Model Law does not set its face totally against the use of 'asset-based' jurisdiction in cases of international insolvency—indeed, Article 28 specifically sanctions the commencement of proceedings based on the presence of assets there, following recognition of a foreign main proceeding. However, this is subject to the proviso that such a proceeding is limited to assets situate within the enacting State in question, and to assets which according to its law ought to be administered there. Hence there is no obligation making it incumbent upon other States to recognise such asset-based proceedings (with all the consequences that flow from such recognition), but it is left as a matter for resolution under the provisions of Chapter IV of the Model Law, relating to international cooperation.

The chain of interlocking concepts formed by the five definitional paragraphs of Article 2 is completed by paragraphs (d) and (e), which define 'foreign representative' and 'foreign court' respectively. Again it may be noted that the root term 'foreign proceeding' appears in both definitions. 'Foreign representative' is defined as:

> [A] person or body, including one appointed on an interim basis, authorised in a foreign proceeding to administer the reorganisation or the liquidation of the debtor's assets or affairs or to act as a representative of the foreign proceeding.

The expression 'foreign court' is given an extended meaning in paragraph (e) to accommodate the fact that under the laws of some countries insolvency proceedings are administered by non-judicial authorities which nevertheless assume an equivalent role to that of courts elsewhere,

[31] Cf. EU Convention, Art. 3(1), which does not supply any presumption for the case of a non-corporate debtor. See further, Chapter 6 above, at p. 260.

[32] Cf. EU Convention on Insolvency Proceedings, Art. 2(h), discussed in Chapter 6 above, at p. 264.

in terms of supervising the operation of the law governing insolvency matters. Paragraph (e) states: ' "foreign court" means a judicial or other authority competent to control or supervise a foreign proceeding'. This definition has to be borne in mind whenever the expression 'foreign court' is encountered anywhere in the text of the Model Law, including Article 2(a), because the repeated use of the word 'court' may generate a misconception. It is really a conveniently compressed term of reference denoting a variety of institutions and authorities capable of being a legitimate source from which a foreign proceeding, and the appointment of a foreign representative, may originate.

Application for recognition

Article 15(1) enables a foreign representative to apply to the court of the enacting State for recognition of the foreign proceeding in which he has been appointed. Under Article 4, the enacting State is required to designate the courts, or other authorities, which are to perform the relevant functions the Model Law assigns to 'the court'. By the use of the words 'shall recognise', Article 17(1) makes it obligatory for the court to recognise a foreign proceeding if each of four stated criteria are met. These are: (a) that the foreign proceeding satisfies the definition supplied by Article 2(a); (b) that the foreign representative applying for recognition fulfils the definition in Article 2(d); (c) that the application satisfies the formal requirements contained in Article 15(2) regarding the documentation required to accompany it;[33] and (d) that the court to which the application has been submitted is the court designated for this purpose by the enacting State, pursuant to Article 4.

The prospects of a successful outcome for the application are enhanced by the various presumptions contained in Article 16. These provide that if the documentation submitted for the purposes of Article 15(2) indicate that the foreign proceeding complies with the definition in Article 2(a), and that the foreign representative fulfils the definition in Article 2(d), 'the court is entitled to so presume'.[34] This authorises the court to proceed on

[33] Article 15(2) requires the application to be accompanied by either a certified copy of the decision whereby the foreign proceeding was commenced and the representative appointed, or a certificate from the foreign court affirming the existence of the foreign proceeding and of the appointment of the foreign representative. In the absence of either of these, the court is authorised to proceed on the basis of such alternative evidence as it considers acceptable. In theory, this could enable a creditors' voluntary liquidation commenced in England to be recognised on the basis of the documentation generated by the resolution for winding up passed by the company meeting, together with the records of the members' and creditors' meetings through which the liquidator's appointment took effect (see Insolvency Act 1986, ss. 84, 98 and 100). However, the entire matter rests in the discretion of the recognising court, and it is therefore advisable to seek a confirmatory order from the English court, using s.112 of the 1986 Act, prior to any application for recognition by foreign courts.

[34] See Art. 16(1) of the Model Law.

the basis of *prima facie* evidence, but does not oblige it to do so. On the other hand, it should serve a useful purpose in States where courts are somewhat hesitant to take a decision recognising the validity of foreign legal proceedings unless the documentary evidence is in some way corroborated by further and independent evidence. The same purpose underlies the provision in Article 16(2) which authorises the court to presume that documents submitted in support of the application for recognition are authentic, 'whether or not they have been legalized'. The final phrase refers to a formality, particularly common in jurisdictions belonging to the civil law tradition, whereby formal authentication of a document for use in court proceedings has to be obtained from a diplomatic or consular representative of the State in which the document is to be used, who is serving in the country from which the document originates. This procedure is not only cumbersome and time-consuming, but also adds to the costs of any recognition proceedings in which it is required to be performed. Once again, it must be noted that the Model Law does not oblige enacting States to discontinue their traditional practice in such matters, but merely seeks to encourage its relaxation in cases where, for example, there are no obvious reasons why the court should mistrust the authenticity of the documentation submitted in support of the application for recognition.[35]

Two additional burdens are imposed upon the applicant for recognition, under the further provisions of Article 15. First, the application must also be accompanied by a statement identifying all foreign proceedings in respect of the debtor that are known to the foreign representative.[36] This requirement is imposed not only in the interests of promoting full disclosure to the court of the current state of affairs relating to the case with which it is asked to deal, but also to equip it to take appropriate action if, either before or after it has taken its decision on the granting of recognition, it is asked to provide relief and assistance in the case.[37] This requirement to make disclosure to the court is reinforced by the provisions of Article 18, which make it incumbent upon the foreign representative, from the time of filing the application for recognition of the foreign proceeding, to inform the court promptly of any substantial changes in the status of the recognised foreign proceeding or in his own status, and also to inform the court of any other foreign proceeding regarding the same debtor which becomes known to him. Secondly, Article 15(4) allows the court to require a translation of documents supplied in support of the application into an

[35] There has been international progress in recent times towards the progressive removal or relaxation of traditional requirements of legalisation of documents for use in legal proceedings in foreign jurisdictions. Thus, the Hague Convention Abolishing the Requirement of Legalisation for Foreign Public Documents, of 5 October 1961, provides for simplified procedures to be applicable between its signatory States.

[36] See Art. 15(3) of the Model Law.

[37] See Arts. 19–23 inclusive, which are discussed below.

official language of the enacting State. Again, it should be emphasised that this provision merely authorises such a requirement to be imposed, and does not make it a formal obligation that the court must do so. This may be helpful where the linguistic abilities of the judges or officials hearing the case enable them to dispose of the matter without adding to the costs and delays that would be caused thereby.

In its approach to the task of determining an application for recognition, as with all matters involving the Model Law's implementation, the court of the enacting State should be mindful of the general admonition embodied in Article 8, to the effect that in the interpretation of the Law regard is to be had to its international origin and to the need to promote uniformity in its application and the observance of good faith. This proposition tactfully invokes the formal statements of purpose set out in the Preamble to the Model Law, and leads back further to the motivational themes identified during the Law's formative process, as already described. Furthermore, in the interests of expedition, which is such a crucial factor in nearly every case of cross-border insolvency, Article 17(3) declares that an application for recognition shall be decided upon at the earliest possible time. However, the significance of the opening words of Article 17(1) must not be overlooked. These indicate that the requirement to recognise a foreign proceeding is subject to the provision in Article 6, which contains the exception—virtually standard for international agreements and conventions in this field—whereby enacting States retain the right to refuse to take an action governed by the Model Law if the action would be manifestly contrary to the public policy of the State in question.[38] The use of the adverb 'manifestly' indicates that the public policy exception should be interpreted restrictively and that national courts should invoke it only where a case involves matters considered to be of fundamental importance.[39] As a final safety device to avert the perils caused by altered circumstances, or imperfect information, which may upset the calculations upon which a decision to recognise a foreign proceeding was originally based, Article 17(4) allows the recognition to be modified or even terminated if it is shown that the grounds for granting it were fully or partially lacking or have ceased to exist.

Interim relief

As noted above, in cross-border insolvency speed and timing are of the essence. Even in a straightforward case, and with a court that is disposed to reach its decision on recognition at the earliest possible time, some delay is inevitable between the formal commencement of insolvency

[38] Cf. EU Convention on Insolvency Proceedings, Art. 26; Istanbul Convention, Arts. 3(c), 14(2)(b).

[39] See Guide to Enactment, *supra* n.16, at paras. 86–89.

proceedings in the foreign State, and the pronouncement of the decision of the recognising court. During that time, parties not directly subject to the jurisdiction and control of the foreign court may take various kinds of action within the State where recognition is being sought. To minimise the potential damage to the collective interests involved, Article 19 provides for discretionary relief to be available under the law of the enacting State from the time of filing of an application for recognition until the application is decided upon. Provisional relief is available at the discretion of the court upon request by the foreign representative, who must show that relief is urgently needed to protect the assets of the debtor or the interests of the creditors. The forms of such relief are listed in non-exhaustive terms in Article 19(1) as including: (a) the staying of execution against the debtor's assets; (b) entrusting the administration or realisation of all or part of the debtor's local assets to the foreign representative or another person designated by the court, to protect and preserve the value of assets of a perishable or wasting nature, or which are otherwise in jeopardy; and (c) to grant any of the forms of relief mentioned in Article 21(1)(c), (d) and (g), which are otherwise available only after recognition has been granted.[40] There may be provision for challenge to the provisional relief by the parties affected, and it is also provided that the court may refuse to grant provisional relief where this would interfere with the administration of a foreign main proceeding.[41] This is a reminder of the need to promote coordination of proceedings as far as is practicable, and also indicates that it is to the foreign main proceeding that the maximum consideration should be accorded when concurrent proceedings are taking place in different foreign States. Finally, Article 22(3) empowers the court, either at the request of the foreign representative or a person affected by the relief granted under Article 19, or at its own motion, to modify or terminate the relief so granted.

The decision to recognise

As previously stated, the terms of Article 17(1) impose a mandatory requirement that, subject to Article 6, a foreign proceeding must be recognised if it meets the formal criteria which have already been described. According to Article 17(2), recognition must be ascribed to one of two possible categories: either as a foreign main proceeding if it is taking place in the State where the debtor has the centre of its main interests, or as a foreign non-main proceeding if the debtor has an establishment (as defined in Article 2(f)) in the foreign State.[42] The distinction between the two cat-

[40] These three forms of relief are considered below.

[41] See Art. 19(4) of the Model Law. See also Art. 22(2), whereby the court is given the discretion to attach conditions to any provisional relief it grants under Art. 19.

[42] See Art. 17(2)(a),(b) of the Model Law. See above for discussion of the definitions of key terms, as supplied by Art. 2.

egories is important, both because it readily suggests a hierarchy between foreign proceedings based on different degrees of contact between the debtor and the State in which foreign proceedings have commenced, and because the Model Law itself provides that different consequences, and different types of relief, follow upon the respective categories of recognition.[43] In reaching its decision on recognition, the court is not authorised to embark upon a review of the merits of the decision of the foreign court, whereby the proceeding was commenced. Provided that the jurisdictional competence of the other court is established for the purpose of its serving as the forum of a main, or non-main, proceeding (as the case may be), the enacting State is expected to trust the integrity of the foreign legal process, and should only take the exceptional course of refusing recognition on the basis of Article 6 if the foreign proceeding amounts to a flagrant and unacceptable violation of the standards of justice which the enacting State and its institutions are committed to uphold. Nevertheless, in the subsequent exercise of its discretionary powers to grant relief, notably under Articles 21 and 22, and in considering in what way to cooperate with the foreign court and the foreign representative, the court will inevitably be influenced by its view of the compatibility between the standards and processes of the foreign law and those of its own, domestic law.

Effects of recognition: (i) foreign main proceedings only

Article 20 applies only to cases where a foreign proceeding is recognised as a main proceeding. Significantly, the provisions of this Article apply automatically as a consequence of recognition, and do not depend on the exercise of any discretion or the making of any further order by the recognising court.[44] Three effects are specified in Article 20(1) as coming into operation upon the recognition of a foreign proceeding. These are as follows:

(a) A stay over the commencement or continuation of individual actions or individual proceedings concerning the debtor's assets, rights, obligations or liabilities. The sweeping terms of the stay are designed to cover measures initiated both in and out of court by creditors seeking to enforce their claims. However, the automatic stay does not preclude the commencement of individual actions or proceedings to the extent necessary to preserve a claim against the debtor.[45] This limited exception is necessary to prevent a creditor's claim from becoming time-barred, whether under the provisions of the law of the enacting

[43] See Arts. 20–24 of the Model Law (discussed below): Art. 20 is applicable exclusively to foreign proceedings recognised as 'main'.

[44] This contrasts with the granting of relief under Art. 19 (see above) or Arts. 21 and 22 (see below).

[45] See Art. 20(3) of the Model Law.

State itself or under the law of some other State by which it happens to be governed according to the conflicts rules of the former. Not all systems of law treat the formal opening of insolvency proceedings, or the formal service by the creditor of a demand for payment or performance, as bringing about the cessation of the running of time for purposes of limitation. However, once the preservation of the creditor's procedural rights has been achieved, actions or proceedings to enforce the claim remain subject to the stay.

(b) A stay over any type of execution against the debtor's assets. This additional provision is especially useful in the light of the distinction made within some jurisdictions between 'execution' (of various kinds) and 'actions or proceedings'.[46] Such terminological niceties do not give rise to a *lacuna* in the automatic stay.

(c) The debtor's right to transfer, encumber or otherwise dispose of any assets is suspended.

It is conceivable that under some circumstances the provisions of Article 20(1) will give rise to the paradoxical situation that the effects of the automatic stay within the enacting State are more extensive than those which are imposed under the insolvency law of the State in which the foreign main proceeding is taking place. This is because the Model Law establishes standardised effects of recognition, to be put into force under the law of the enacting State. In contrast, the EU Convention allows the effects generated under the law of the State in which proceedings have been opened to be imported into the other Contracting States for the purposes of administering the assets comprised in that case.[47]

The further provisions of Article 20 establish two significant provisos to the seemingly sweeping terms of the automatic stay under paragraph (1). First, the enacting State is permitted to superimpose any exceptions or limitations in respect of the automatic stay which are to be found within the provisions of its domestic insolvency law, so that they are replicated in relation to the stay or suspension resulting from recognition of a foreign main proceeding.[48] Thus, such standard provisions as those which authorise the enforcement of security rights by creditors in whose favour they have been unimpeachably constituted, or which allow for the validation of payments or dispositions made by the debtor after commencement of insolvency proceedings (subject in each of those cases to certain conditions which have to be satisfied) may be made equally applicable under circumstances where the stay or suspension is as a result of a foreign, rather

[46] This is the case under English law: see Insolvency Act 1986, ss.126, 128, 130(2), 183, 285, 346 and 347. Cf. *Re Memco Engineering Ltd.* [1986] Ch. 86.

[47] See EU Convention, Arts. 17 and 18, discussed in Chapter 6 above, at pp. 285–6.

[48] See Art. 20(2) of the Model Law.

than a domestic, proceeding. Secondly, Article 20(4) makes it clear that the operation of the automatic stay under paragraph (1) does not affect the right of a qualified party to request the commencement of an insolvency proceeding under the domestic law of the enacting State, and also to file claims in such a proceeding.[49] Where such a parallel proceeding takes place under the local law, Article 29 together with Articles 25–27 inclusive have the effect of imposing the requirement to bring about coordination of proceedings through international cooperation, as discussed below.[50]

Any question concerning the consequences of contravention of the automatic stay imposed under Article 20(1), including possible penalties or punishments to be imposed on those responsible, is a matter for the local law of the enacting State. The Model Law makes no attempt to introduce a uniform set of provisions regarding these matters.[51]

Lastly, it should be noted that Article 31, located in Chapter V dealing with Concurrent Proceedings, has relevance to the situation where a foreign main proceeding has obtained recognition in an enacting State. Article 31 provides that, in the absence of evidence to the contrary, such recognition is, for the purpose of commencing an insolvency proceeding under the local law of that State, proof that the debtor is insolvent. This creates a rebuttable presumption whose purpose is to satisfy any requirement under the local law whereby the debtor's insolvency must be established as a precondition to the opening of a proceeding. It is even possible that, viewed in isolation, the debtor's financial situation and conduct within the frontiers of the enacting State may not satisfy the tests of insolvency specified by the local law.[52] This could result in additional delay and expense for any party wishing to bring about the commencement of a local proceeding. The terms of Article 31 are deliberately designed to confine its application to cases of foreign main proceedings: non-main proceedings do not benefit from the presumption of insolvency.

Effects of recognition: (ii) both types of foreign proceeding

Article 21 of the Model Law specifies the forms of relief that may be granted by the court of the enacting State upon recognition of a foreign proceeding, whether as a main or as a non- main proceeding.[53] The

[49] The rights of a foreign representative, or of foreign creditors, to initiate or participate in local proceedings in the enacting State are dealt with in Arts. 11–13 inclusive, together with Art. 28, as discussed below.

[50] See below, at pp. 355 and 357.

[51] See Guide to Enactment, *supra* n.16, at para. 147.

[52] e.g. the debtor's 'balance sheet' of assets against liabilities may be in surplus locally, and it may also be the case that the debtor has sufficient local liquidity to continue to pay debts there as they fall due.

[53] For the distinction between 'main' and 'non-main' proceedings, see Art. 2(a),(b) and (c) of the Model Law, considered above at p. 335 above.

opening statement in paragraph (1) of the Article indicates that relief may be granted 'where necessary to protect the assets of the debtor or the interests of the creditors'. The court is empowered to grant 'any appropriate relief' at the request of the foreign representative. The broad nature of the discretion conferred on the court is indicated by the expressions 'may . . . grant' and 'any appropriate relief'. The court is left to determine the extent to which it will exercise its jurisdiction to grant relief, and indeed whether to do so at all. A non-exhaustive list of seven types of relief which the court may grant is set out in paragraphs (a) to (g) of Article 21(1), but the court is left at liberty to draw upon the full repertoire of remedies and powers available to it under its domestic law.[54] The court's powers are further augmented by Article 22(2), which authorises it to attach any conditions it considers appropriate to relief granted under Article 21.

The illustrative list of examples of the relief the court may grant is as follows:

(a) staying the commencement or continuation of individual actions or individual proceedings concerning the debtor's assets, rights, obligations or liabilities, to the extent they have not been stayed under Article 20(1)(a) (which applies only in the case of a foreign main proceeding);
(b) staying execution against the debtor's assets to the extent it has not been stayed under Article 20(1)(b);
(c) suspending the right to transfer, encumber or otherwise dispose of any assets of the debtor to the extent this right has not been suspended under Article 20(1)(c);
(d) providing for the examination of witnesses, the taking of evidence or the delivery of information concerning the debtor's assets, affairs, rights, obligations or liabilities;
(e) entrusting the administration or realisation of all or part of the debtor's assets located in the enacting State to the foreign representative or another person designated by the court;
(f) extending any provisional relief granted under Article 19(1);
(g) granting any additional relief that may be available to an office holder appointed under the insolvency law of the enacting State.

The forms of relief described in paragraphs (a) to (c) inclusive of Article 21(1) correspond to those which take effect under the automatic stay imposed by Article 20(1) in the case of a foreign main proceeding.[55] In the

[54] This would include the exercise of powers that are locally considered to form part of the inherent jurisdiction of the court. Cf. *Hughes v. Hannover Ruckversicherungs-Aktiengesellschaft* [1997] 1 B.C.L.C. 497, [1997] B.C.C. 921 (CA), discussed in Chapter 4, at 4.1.1 above, at pp. 196–8.

[55] See the discussion above of the automatic stay imposed by Art. 20(1), and of the significance of certain technical terms employed.

case of a non-main proceeding, the foreign representative will need to make application to the court in order to obtain the same quality of relief, and will be dependent upon the court exercising its discretion in his favour. The remaining types of relief, described in paragraphs (d) to (g) inclusive, must be sought by way of specific application to the court in all cases. The prospect of utilising the powers contained in the law of the enacting State to examine witnesses and to obtain information, while welcome in itself, will also result in the kind of paradox already noted in relation to other provisions of the Model Law, namely that the foreign representative may sometimes discover that the powers of examination available under the law of the recognising State are more extensive than those found in the law of the State in which he was appointed. Of course, the converse situation is equally possible.

The making of application along the lines suggested in paragraph (e), for the court to entrust the task of administration or realisation of local assets to the foreign representative (or to some other person) is likely to be a routine procedure in cross border cases, as a necessary step towards achieving a coordinated administration of assets dispersed across two or more jurisdictions. An order of this kind should not be confused with an order for turnover of assets in the sense generally employed in this context. For the court to authorise the foreign representative to undertake the distribution of the assets collected in its jurisdiction a further range of factors has to be taken into account, since the logical consequence of such turnover, unless accompanied by specific conditions and undertakings to be honoured by the foreign representative, would be that the assets would be assimilated into the general pool of the insolvent estate and would be distributed according to the principles of the law of the State from which his appointment is derived. The provision to enable such turnover to be requested is to be found in Article 21(2), thereby emphasising the distinctive character of such an application. Turnover may be requested in both main and non-main proceedings, although it would seem likely that the court will require to hear especially cogent reasons in support of turnover in the case of a foreign non-main proceeding.[56] Notably, the court's discretion to authorise turnover is subject to the proviso that it must be satisfied that the interests of local creditors in that State are adequately protected. Moreover, the court may elect to use the power conferred under Article 22(2) whereby it can subject the relief granted to conditions it

[56] For example, it may be the case that the only jurisdiction in which it is practicable to conduct the insolvency proceeding is in a State where the debtor happens to have an establishment. This may be because the law of the State where the centre of the debtor's main interests is located does not permit insolvency proceedings to be opened, or because that place is geographically remote from the locations where the principal assets, and the majority of creditors, are to be found. Note also the effect of Art. 21(3) (mentioned below).

considers appropriate. These could, for example, include obtaining an undertaking from the foreign representative to the effect that creditors from the enacting State whose claims would have preferential status under the local insolvency law shall not be deprived of that advantage in the process of distribution taking place under foreign law.

A further, necessary safeguard is provided by Article 21(3), which applies to all cases where relief is granted to a representative of a foreign non-main proceeding. The court is required to be satisfied that the relief relates to assets that, under the law of the enacting State, should be administered in the foreign non-main proceeding or concerns information required in that proceeding. The drafting of this provision clearly envisages that it may sometimes be necessary for the court to decide which of two or more foreign proceedings has the better claim to assets located within its jurisdiction, where each of the foreign laws purports to affect the debtor's property 'wherever situate'.[57] It will normally be the case that the claim on behalf of a main proceeding will prevail over that of a non-main. Where both foreign proceedings are non-main, however, the matter is apt to be less clear-cut, although it may be possible to establish that the local assets, or some of them, are more closely associated with the operations of a particular foreign establishment of the debtor, in which case the proceeding in the country of that establishment may have the stronger claim. A further possibility may be that property has been wrongfully transferred from one jurisdiction to another, thereby depleting the pool of assets available for distribution in the former. In tailoring its relief under Article 21, the court may be in a position to redress the consequences of such impropriety.

Finally, in relation to relief available at the discretion of the court under Article 21 (and also under Article 19), Article 22(3) enables the court at any time to modify or terminate any relief that has been granted. This may be done upon application made by the foreign representative or by a person affected by the relief granted, or at the court's own motion. By this means, a creditor who is able to show good cause—such as disproportionate hardship or unfair prejudice to himself as a consequence of the relief as granted—may request that it be modified or lifted with respect to himself. In all instances, when granting or denying relief or when modifying or terminating it, the court must bear in mind the general admonition in Article 22(1) requiring that it be satisfied that the interests of the creditors and other interested persons, including the debtor, are adequately protected.[58]

[57] See the discussions of the issue of extraterritorial effects of insolvency in Chapters 2 and 3 above at pp. 59 and 147 respectively.

[58] Cf. the wording of a proposed alternative to the provision now embodied in Art. 22(1) (previously numbered as Art. 19), which was rejected at the final working session of the Commission in May 1997: see Doc. A/52/17 (*supra* n.12) at paras. 82–85. The rejected

Action by the foreign representative in the recognising State

The most effective way of protecting the assets of the debtor that are located in a State in which the foreign proceeding is recognised will very often be through the direct use of procedures within the local law for the avoidance of acts detrimental to creditors, or by intervention in any proceedings to which the debtor may already be a party. Articles 23 and 24 enable either or both of these courses to be pursued.

Under Article 23 the enacting State would make explicit provision in its domestic law to the effect that upon recognition of a foreign proceeding the foreign representative has standing to initiate the types of actions which are available under the local law to the office holder in insolvency proceedings, for the purpose of avoiding or rendering ineffective acts which are detrimental to the collective interests of the creditors. The nature and function of such remedies differs from State to State. Sometimes it is contained within the local insolvency law, and its use is expressly restricted to the office holder in specific types of insolvency proceeding.[59] In other cases, avoidance provisions are contained within the general law and are not necessarily restricted to cases where insolvency proceedings are taking place, and may be invoked by other parties such as individual creditors.[60] The drafting of Article 23 is carefully designed to confine the right to invoke such local remedies to the foreign representative, and to accord him standing to invoke such remedies on terms that are exactly analogous to those applicable to an office holder in insolvency proceedings under the local law. Individual creditors from outside the enacting State do not gain any procedural standing under the terms of Article 23. It must also be acknowledged that the resolution of the substantive complaint brought by the foreign representative, including any conflict of laws questions that may arise, is left under the full control of the court of the enacting State. The chief advantage of Article 23 is that it overcomes the barrier to access which typically confronts a foreign representative, and establishes a positive rule in favour of his being able to initiate an avoidance action under the local law.[61]

proposal would have reversed the sentiment of the provision, by strengthening the autonomy of the recognising court in its approach to the granting of relief. Contrast the comments to Art. 22 in the Guide to Enactment, *supra* n.16, at paras. 161–164.

[59] e.g. the provisions for avoidance of antecedent transactions that are contained in the Insolvency Act 1986, ss. 238–241, are available for use by a liquidator or administrator, but not by an administrative receiver. See also ss. 339(1) and 340(1), with respect to the equivalent powers of a trustee in bankruptcy.

[60] e.g. the remedy in the Insolvency Act 1986, ss. 423–425, regarding transactions in fraud of creditors. The best known example of such a general avoidance action in civil law countries is the Paulian Action derived from Roman law, as found in the civil codes of many countries. As an example, see the French *Code Civil*, Art. 1167.

[61] Cf. the unsatisfactory outcome of the case of *Galbraith v. Grimshaw* [1910] A.C. 508 (HL), criticised in Chapter 2, at 2.6.1(b) above, at p. 98.

The sensitivity of the distinction between foreign representatives appointed under main, as opposed to non-main, proceedings is emphasised by the provision in Article 23(2). This declares that in the case of a foreign non-main proceeding the court must be satisfied that the avoidance action relates to assets that, under the law of the enacting State, should be administered in the foreign non-main proceeding in which the representative was appointed.

A second provision to assist the foreign representative to take effective action on behalf of creditors' interests is contained in Article 24, under which the law of the enacting State would embody a clear rule to the effect that the foreign representative may intervene in any proceedings in which the debtor is a party. Once again, this overcomes any question of lack of standing under the procedural law of the recognising State. A proviso is inserted to the effect that all other requirements of the local law must be met, thereby ensuring that the foreign representative's procedural position is exactly equated to that of any internal party who seeks to intervene. The type of proceeding covered by the right of intervention under this Article is where an individual action is brought by or against the debtor. In the case of collective insolvency proceedings the foreign representative enjoys the more substantial rights of 'participation', pursuant to Article 12.[62] Moreover, it must be supposed that the proceedings in which intervention is to take place have for some reason escaped from the effects of any stay resulting from Articles 20(1)(a) or 21(1)(a). The unrestricted terms of Article 24 result in its provisions being applicable to both main and non-main proceedings.[63]

8.2.2 Direct rights of access to courts and legal processes in the enacting State

Chapter II of the Model Law, comprising Articles 9 to 14 inclusive, contains provisions whose purpose is to enable foreign representatives and creditors to have rights of access to the courts of the enacting State, and to participate in and even initiate legal processes under the insolvency law of that jurisdiction. The importance of such rights cannot be over-emphasised. Access to justice is an indispensable prerequisite to the attainment of justice itself. Therefore, the opportunity for the foreign representative to exercise the right of making direct and timely application to the court of the enacting State is potentially the most significant advance, in terms of practical improvement of the international insolvency process, that may emerge as a consequence of widespread implementation of the Model Law.

[62] See at p. 350 below, concerning rights of access under Chapter II of the Model Law.

[63] See the Guide to Enactment, *supra* n.16, paras. 168–172. For background debate regarding the intended scope of this provision, see U.N. doc. A/52/17 (*supra* n.14) at paras. 117–122.

(a) Access of foreign representatives

Articles 9 to 12 are concerned with foreign representatives' rights of access to courts and proceedings. The foremost, and most succinct, proposition is contained in Article 9, which states: 'A foreign representative is entitled to apply directly to a court in this State'. The absence of any express precondition to the vesting of the right of direct access is especially striking. Thus, there is no requirement that the foreign proceeding must first have been recognised by the court of the enacting State before the representative can exercise the right of access. Indeed, if it were otherwise there would be a logical impediment to the foreign representative's ability to make application for recognition of the foreign proceeding from which his appointment is derived. In the interests of avoiding such 'chicken and egg' circularities, a forthright declaration of the principle of direct access is essential.

Nevertheless, the matter of definition cannot be evaded: to qualify to invoke the right of access, the person doing so must necessarily be a 'foreign representative' within the meaning established by the various component definitions in Article 2, previously explored.[64] Moreover, it is reasonable to assume that the purpose of an application to the court is to secure the procedural and other advantages, and in particular relief and assistance, which are the subject of further provisions of the Model Law. Since the right to make application for these is for the most part limited to cases where the foreign proceeding has been recognised by decision taken by the local court, it would be a largely futile and wasteful exercise for a foreign representative to aspire to exercise the right of access under Article 9 without having assessed the probability that the circumstances of his appointment would in principle bring him within the four corners of the Model Law and its definitional framework. Hence, the criteria for recognition of a foreign proceeding, which were examined in the previous sub-section above,[65] should be scrutinised in advance of any formal application in order to confirm that there is a *prima facie* case for recognition to be granted by the court of the enacting State. Otherwise, the applicant risks all the usual consequences of an unfavourable ruling by the court, including possible claims for damages if other parties' interests have been adversely affected due to his ill-judged foray into that jurisdiction.

Where a foreign representative is properly qualified, in the eyes of the Model Law, to invoke its provisions outside the State of his appointment, there is a further question of 'procedural safe conduct' that needs to be taken into account. This is the possibility that, under the procedural rules of some jurisdictions, any voluntary appearance in legal proceedings renders the party in question vulnerable to process on any other matter, even if unrelated to the cause on which the appearance was entered. To protect

[64] See above (*Scope of application*) at p. 333.

[65] See pp. 335–9 above.

foreign representatives against such unwelcome prospects, Article 10 imports the concept of limited jurisdiction, already familiar under the international insolvency legislation of such countries as the USA and Canada.[66] The Article provides that the *sole* fact[67] that an application pursuant to the Model Law is made to a court of the enacting State by a foreign representative does not subject the applicant or the foreign assets and affairs of the debtor to the jurisdiction of the courts of that State for any purpose other than the application. The terms of the immunity should be carefully noted, however, because they do not amount to a blanket exemption from responsibility for conduct or actions of the foreign representative which contravene local law, or which have the effect of throwing away his 'shield' of immunity according to recognised principles of private international law. Moreover, in its response to an application for relief under the provisions in Chapter III of the Model Law, the court may utilise its power conferred by Article 22(2) to attach conditions to the relief to be granted, which may include the giving of an undertaking by the representative to comply with any further order of the court.

Commencement of local insolvency proceedings. The provisions of Articles 11 and 12 confer further procedural rights upon the foreign representative which are of the utmost practical importance. When insolvency proceedings have commenced in the State in which the debtor's centre of main interests is located, or where an establishment is maintained, a tactical race usually ensues in any other jurisdiction where assets are to be found. Creditors will hasten to complete some form of seizure or attachment of such assets before the foreign representative can trace their whereabouts and obtain orders from the courts of that State granting recognition and relief. The debtor may also attempt to deal with or dispose of assets while they remain inaccessible to the foreign representative. Although interim relief may be applied for under Article 19, any order staying execution will lack retrospective effect, and may come too late to achieve any useful purpose. Hence, the most potent weapon with which to counteract the dissipation of the assets is to bring about the opening of local insolvency proceedings in that jurisdiction. Not only will this give rise to an automatic, and comprehensive, stay upon all further executions and dispositions, but also it will usually be the case that the local insolvency law contains provisions capable of nullifying such transactions retrospectively, thus allowing assets to be clawed back.

Article 11 stipulates that a foreign representative is entitled to apply to commence a proceeding under the insolvency laws of the enacting State if

[66] See Chapter 4 above at pp. 207 and 215, with reference to the US Bankruptcy Code, s.306 and the Canadian Bankruptcy and Insolvency Act, s.272.

[67] Emphasis added.

the conditions for commencing such a proceeding are otherwise met. This removes any uncertainty as to the standing of the representative to make such application, but does not create any special exception to the need to satisfy the requirements of the local law to enable an involuntary proceeding to be commenced. However, it is again significant that the right of application under this Article does not depend upon prior recognition of the foreign proceeding, and that the provision is applicable both to a main and a non-main proceeding.

The provision in Article 12 (which logically should have been located in Chapter II of the Model Law along with other Articles dealing with recognition and its consequences) states that upon recognition of a foreign proceeding the foreign representative is entitled to participate in a proceeding regarding the debtor under the insolvency laws of the enacting State. Both main and non-main foreign proceedings are within the ambit of this provision. However, the concept of 'participation' is a somewhat restricted one, and merely gives the representative procedural standing to make petitions, requests or submissions concerning the manner in which the insolvency should progress under the control of the person appointed to administer it.[68] It might seem arguable that the right of 'participation' could be interpreted to mean that the foreign representative is entitled to lodge proof in the local proceeding on behalf of all creditors claiming in the foreign proceeding. However, this does not appear to have been the intended effect of the language used. Any coordination between concurrent administrations must be brought about under the provisions in Chapter V of the Model Law.[69]

(b) Access of foreign creditors

Although the insolvency laws of many States make no overt distinction between the rights and status of domestic and foreign creditors, it is seldom the case that an express provision is included to confirm that foreign creditors enjoy full rights of participation in local proceedings on equal terms with their domestic counterparts. Even where the law does not embody a policy of deliberate discrimination, the lack of clear information available to foreign creditors may have the effect of discouraging them from expending resources in a quest to ascertain their true legal position. Hence, a *de facto* disadvantage is likely to result. Article 13 of the Model Law supplies the means to overcome this problem by generating a provision in the law of the enacting State that foreign creditors have the same rights as local creditors regarding the commencement of, and participation in, an insolvency proceeding.

[68] See Guide to Enactment, *supra* n.16, at paras. 100–102. [69] See below.

While establishing the principle of equality of treatment between foreign and local creditors, Article 13 carries a proviso, in paragraph (2), to affirm that this does not affect the ranking of claims in an insolvency proceeding under the local law. This leaves open the possibility that enacting States may keep in place any provisions in their distributional rules which allocate a special ranking to claims of foreign creditors. Although this may suggest that the second paragraph of Article 13 takes away much of the benefit which paragraph (1) purports to bestow, a certain degree of comfort is provided by the subordinate proviso which states that foreign creditors shall not be ranked lower than the class of general, non-preferential claims according to the local law.[70] If enacted in these terms, Article 13 would have the potential effect of eliminating the practice, widely followed by many States, of refusing to regard foreign fiscal claims as provable debts in insolvency proceedings.[71] At the very least, it would be obligatory for such claims to be admitted among the ordinary, non-preferential debts for purposes of *pari passu* distribution. It is possible that in States in which the exclusion of foreign fiscal claims is regarded as a matter of public policy, the exception under Article 6 might be invoked as a basis for refusal to accept such claims. The situation would remain confused however, and it might require costly litigation to test the matter conclusively. Therefore, for those States which wish to preserve their traditional policy of excluding such claims from the process of distribution, the Model Law offers an alternative version of Article 13(2) whose effect is to maintain such exclusion in force.[72] It may well be the case that most if not all of the States which currently apply this policy will avail themselves of the opportunity to continue to do so.[73]

A necessary counterpart to the creation of rights of foreign creditors to participate in local proceedings is the putting in place of a framework of provisions to ensure that such rights can be exercised in a timely and

[70] This 'sub-proviso' admits of yet a further exception, however, in the case where the foreign claim is of a type which, in the case of similar claims arising under local law, is ranked below the general, non-preferential claims. Examples of such debts carrying deferred status under English insolvency law are: loans to a bankrupt's spouse (Insolvency Act 1986, s.329); debts affected by the terms of ss. 2 and 3 of the Partnership Act 1890 (loans to a company in consideration for a share in its profits); and debts due from a company to a person found guilty of wrongful or fraudulent trading (Insolvency Act 1986, s.215(4)).

[71] See Chapter 2, at 2.4 above, for the English law position on the exclusion of foreign revenue claims.

[72] See Guide to Enactment, *supra* n.16, at paras. 103–105. The variant to Art. 13(2) is reproduced in Appendix IV below.

[73] Member States of the European Union would be required to admit each others' fiscal claims as provable debts under the terms of the EU Insolvency Convention, Art. 39. As between those States the provisions of Art. 3 of the Model Law enable their obligations under the EU Convention to prevail over any provision of the Model Law with which there is a conflict. Fiscal claims of States not party to the EU Convention would continue to be excluded from insolvency proceedings, to the same extent as heretofore.

effective manner. Failing this, the factors of distance, linguistic problems, and above all the lack of adequate notice of proceedings and of the requisite dates within which formalities must be completed will combine to negate the advantages conferred. Article 14 addresses these matters by means of a series of requirements which are to be put into force in the laws of enacting States. First, in every instance where the local law requires that notification is to be given to creditors, such notification must also be given to known creditors that do not have addresses in the enacting State.[74] Once again, the principle of equality of treatment is to apply, which means that foreign creditors' experiences of the effects of this provision will vary according to the requirements of the local laws of different enacting States. Secondly, the stipulation is made that notification must be made to foreign creditors individually, unless the court considers that, under the circumstances, some other form of notification would be more appropriate.[75] The purpose of this provision is to counter the possibility that under some States' laws notification is routinely effected by means of advertisement, either in newspapers or in an official gazette. In such cases, the principle of equality of treatment would fail to ensure that foreign creditors have reasonable opportunity to become aware of the notice. Hence, it is made mandatory that any digression from the requirement of notifying foreign creditors on an individual basis shall take place as the result of a conscious decision of the court in the light of the prevailing circumstances.

Article 14 contains a third series of requirements concerning notification to be given to foreign creditors of the commencement of a proceeding. In order to compensate for the logistical disadvantages to which the recipients of such notice may be subject, paragraph (3) specifies that the notification must indicate a reasonable time period for filing claims and specify the place for their filing, and must also indicate whether secured creditors need to file their secured claims. This latter provision is included because national rules differ as to the need for such notice to be filed, and also as to the consequences for the secured creditor if the local requirement is not fulfilled.[76] Finally, the notification must contain any other information required to be included in notification to creditors generally, pursuant to the local law and the orders of the court. It should be observed that there is no requirement that notification to foreign creditors should carry any special information in a language other than that in which the proceedings are being conducted. Nor is there any concession under the Model Law to

[74] See Art. 14(1). The court may order appropriate steps to be taken with a view to notifying any creditor whose address is not known at the time in question.

[75] See Art. 14(2). In the interest of eliminating costly formalities it is also stated that no letters rogatory or other, similar formality is required. See Guide to Enactment, *supra* n.16, paras. 108–110.

[76] See Guide to Enactment, *supra* n.16, para.111, which suggests (with good reason) that it would be appropriate for the enacting State to include a requirement that the notification should provide information of the effects of filing, or failing to file, secured claims.

allow foreign creditors to lodge proof of claim in their own, or any other, language if different from the procedural language of the case. It will continue to be the responsibility of the foreign creditor to bear any extra costs of participating in proceedings conducted in a language with which he or she is not personally conversant.[77]

8.2.3 Rights of courts and office holders to request recognition, information and assistance in a foreign State

Article 1(1)(b) of the Model Law indicates that its scope includes cases where assistance is sought in a foreign State in connection with an insolvency proceeding under the law of the enacting State. Such outward-bound requests may be made by the court or by the office holder in the proceedings in question. In the case of the latter, Article 5 specifically authorises the person or body administering a reorganisation or liquidation under the law of the enacting State to act in a foreign State on behalf of the proceeding in question. Thereby, a clear provision is implanted in the enacting State's law conferring positive authority for an office holder to act abroad in the role of foreign representative, and to apply for recognition and assistance according to the terms of the Model Law as enacted by other States, or under such alternative provisions as are to be found in their existing laws and jurisprudence.[78] The concluding words of Article 5 indicate that the office holder's scope of action in a foreign State is circumscribed by the provisions of the applicable foreign law. Further authorisation to take international action in furtherance of the administration of a case is to be found within Chapter IV (see next section below). Article 26(2) asserts that an office holder is entitled, subject to the supervision of the court, to communicate directly with foreign courts or foreign representatives.

Although the Model Law places primary emphasis on the exercise of rights of direct access by foreign representatives, the special value of court-to-court cooperation is both appreciated and facilitated. Chapter IV, consisting of Articles 25 to 27, addresses this theme, and is discussed below. For present purposes, it should be noted that Article 25 is designed to confer unequivocal authorisation for a court of an enacting State to cooperate and communicate directly with foreign courts or foreign representatives, or to request information or assistance directly from them. This is particularly important in the case of States where the prevailing tradi-

[77] Contrast the more accommodating terms of Art. 42 of the EU Convention on Insolvency Proceedings, discussed in Chapter 6 above, at p. 296.

[78] See for example the possibilities currently offered by virtue of English common law for giving assistance to foreign representatives: Chapter 2, esp. at 2.6 and 2.8 above, and Chapter 3, esp. at 3.7 and 3.9 above.

tion precludes the taking of any such initiative by the courts of that jurisdiction in the absence of clear statutory authority to that effect.[79] A first, and very necessary, step towards the development of a general judicial disposition to adopt a positive approach in such matters is to provide a precise legal basis within the State's own legislation. Once this is accomplished, there are also enhanced opportunities for office holders appointed in that jurisdiction to take effective action abroad, by obtaining the support of their local court in submitting a formal request for recognition and assistance to a court of another State.

8.2.4 Cooperation between courts and office holders from different jurisdictions

For numerous reasons, including those rehearsed immediately above, it is a leading aim of the Model Law to function as a catalyst in the process of building up an international framework of cooperation in insolvency matters. The three Articles which comprise Chapter IV together establish the foundation for such a framework to develop in an empirical manner in relation to any matters specified in Article 1 as falling within the scope of the Law's application.[80]

Article 25(1) imposes a mandatory duty that the court of the enacting State shall cooperate '*to the maximum extent possible*' with foreign courts or foreign representatives.[81] Such cooperation is to take place either directly or through any person or body serving as office holder in a proceeding under the insolvency law of the enacting State. The importance of such a provision when enacted is not merely the command which is conveyed to that country's courts, but also the signal which is transmitted to courts and office holders in foreign States regarding the receptive ethos prevalent within that jurisdiction. Nevertheless, although the use of the words 'shall cooperate' have the effect of placing the court under an obligation to do so, it remains a matter for the court's discretion to determine what mode of cooperation is appropriate in a given case, and also what degree of cooperation constitutes 'the maximum extent possible'. Under certain conditions, it may be reasonable and even appropriate for the court to conclude that no cooperation is possible.

[79] See comments placed on record at various stages of the debates conducted during the Judicial Colloquia jointly organised by UNCITRAL and INSOL (referred to *supra* nn. 11 and 13). The main conclusions and suggestions are summarised in the Guide to Enactment, para. 179.

[80] See at p. 332 *supra*, for consideration of the scope of application of the Model Law. The opening words of Arts. 25(1) and 26(1) respectively confine their effects to 'matters referred to in Article 1'.

[81] Emphasis added.

Similarly, Article 26(1) makes it a matter of mandatory duty for an office holder in a reorganisation or liquidation under the law of the enacting State to cooperate to the maximum extent possible with foreign courts or foreign representatives. This is required to take place in the context of the exercise of the office holder's functions, and subject to the supervision of the court. Hence, it is a matter for the local law to set the terms and conditions under which the court's supervisory role is to be performed. Subject to this, it is for the office holder to assess what potential for cooperation exists, and how to maximise it. The authorising provisions in Articles 25(2) and 26(2) with respect to direct communications with foreign courts and representatives, already referred to,[82] establish opportunities for international dialogue and negotiation, which may result in the conclusion of some formal 'Protocol' or 'Concordat' by analogy with the solutions pioneered in various *causes célèbres* of recent times.

While recognising that it is important to refrain from being over-prescriptive in matters of international cooperation under the infinitely variable circumstances of cross-border insolvency, the practical utility of an illustrative list of examples was also appreciated by those responsible for shaping the text of the Model Law. Therefore Article 27, while stating that cooperation under Articles 25 and 26 may be implemented 'by any appropriate means', provides some typical examples of forms which such cooperation may take.[83] Such illustrative guidance may prove especially helpful in States with little or no developed tradition of engagement in cross-border cooperation. It may also serve as a more general aid to the imagination of those charged with the task of applying the Model Law irrespective of their background and experience. It should be observed that the duty of cooperation under Articles 25 and 26 is not dependent upon the prior taking of a formal decision to recognise the foreign proceeding in question. Therefore, even at the earliest point of encounter the requirements of that duty should be respected, although there must necessarily be an exercise of judgment as to the degree of such cooperation that is either prudent or possible during the early stages. A further matter of general relevance to the duty of cooperation is that it is applicable irrespective of whether any formal insolvency proceeding takes place in the enacting State in question. On the other hand, if such a proceeding does take place, this raises the further issue of coordination of concurrent proceedings, which are considered next below.

[82] See at p. 354 above.

[83] See Art. 27(a)–(e) of the Model Law, reproduced in Appendix IV below. Note that the 'blank' Art. 27(f) provides the opportunity for enacting States to include additional forms or examples of cooperation. See also the summary of points extracted from the discussions at the 1997 Judicial Colloquium (*supra* n.13) set out in the Guide to Enactment, *supra* n.16, para. 179.

8.2.5 Coordination of concurrent proceedings

Chapter V of the Model Law contains provisions relating to situations where concurrent insolvency proceedings take place in different jurisdictions with respect to the same debtor. This is a logical continuation of the theme of international cooperation, but requires special attention in view of the more profound level of engagement of the legal systems in which the parallel proceedings happen to be taking place. Fundamental differences concerning the policies and approaches of the respective systems, including their treatment of different classes of claim under their distributional regimes for insolvency, can give rise to what is in effect a power struggle for control over assets and the mode of distribution to which they will be subjected.[84] While such contests are unedifying, they are almost inevitable under currently prevailing conditions. Realistically, Chapter V does not attempt to superimpose a preconceived solution to such difficulties, but rather to create an environment in which there are opportunities for the representatives, and for the courts of the concerned jurisdictions, to try to reach an accommodation through the process of cooperation and dialogue.

The two general scenarios that are envisaged are, first, where one of the concurrent proceedings takes place in the enacting State, and secondly where such proceedings take place in more than one foreign State. In the former situation, self-evidently, the policy and interests of the local insolvency law are more actively engaged, whereas in the second the court may be in a position to adopt a more neutral and objective stance, unless local proceedings also take place. The first of these alternatives is addressed by Articles 28 and 29. Where a foreign main proceeding has opened, and has been recognised as such in the enacting State in accordance with the provisions in Chapter III,[85] the terms of Article 28 impose restrictions upon the possibility for an insolvency proceeding subsequently to be opened in that State. The Article stipulates that a proceeding may be commenced only if the debtor has assets in the jurisdiction, and that the effects of the proceeding will be restricted to those assets. Other assets of the debtor may also be brought within the scope of the proceeding provided that the local law regards them as properly within the scope of an administration conducted under its jurisdiction, but this is subject to the further proviso that such an extension over foreign assets shall only occur to the extent necessary to implement cooperation and coordination under Articles

[84] For a vivid example of such a struggle for mastery between the diametrically opposed approaches of the concerned systems (those of Luxembourg and England), relating to the treatment of set-off in insolvency, see *Re Bank of Credit and Commerce International S.A. (No. 10)* [1996] 4 All E.R. 796, discussed above in Chapter 2, at 2.3 above, at pp. 74 and 81.

[85] See at p. 335 above.

25–27 inclusive.[86] These restrictions are intended to curb the potential for conflict between the local and the foreign main proceeding where both would otherwise purport to have universal effect over all the debtor's property. At the same time, there is allowance for the possibility that it may be justifiable for the local administration to claw back assets that were improperly exported abroad and which ought to form part of that estate. Additionally, there may be assets in third countries which can more conveniently be administered from the jurisdiction where the local proceeding is taking place, than from the State of the main proceeding. This is exactly the kind of situation in which the office holders in the two proceedings should cooperate with each other to make whatever arrangement will yield maximum value for creditors, and minimise administrative costs.

Article 29 contains further provisions to regulate the position where one of the concurrent proceedings takes place in the enacting State itself. A general reaffirmation is issued of the obligatory duty for the local court to seek cooperation and coordination under Articles 25–27, and further, particularised rules are laid down for the alternative possibilities that the first proceeding to commence is the local proceeding, or the foreign proceeding, as the case may be. When the local proceeding is already taking place at the time when the application for recognition of the foreign proceeding is filed, the court is directed that any relief granted under Article 19 or 21 must be consistent with the local proceeding, and that if the foreign proceeding is recognised in the enacting State as a main proceeding, Article 20 does not apply.[87] The vital, if unstated, principle to be discerned from these provisions is that the fact that local proceedings have already commenced does not preclude the recognition of a foreign proceeding, either as a main or as a non-main proceeding. This should perhaps have been expressly stated at this point in the text of the Model Law, in the interests of overcoming any preconceptions about whether such recognition is logically possible if, as is frequently the case, the insolvency law of the enacting State claims universal effect for a proceeding that has commenced in that jurisdiction.[88] What is also foreseen however is that the local court, when taking its decision on recognition, may take a position different to that of the foreign court on a key matter such as the whereabouts of the centre of the debtor's main interests, based upon the evidence presented

[86] See at p. 355 above.

[87] See Art. 29(a)(i), (ii). See at pp. 339 and 341 above for Interim (Art. 19) and Post-recognition (Art. 21) relief, and for the provisions of Art. 20 concerning the effects of recognition of a foreign main proceeding in cases not governed by Art. 29(a)(ii).

[88] The assertion that recognition of a foreign proceeding is not in principle incompatible with the commencement of a local one is made in the Guide to Enactment, *supra* n.16, at para. 189. See the discussion of the claims made by English law for universal effect of its insolvency proceedings in Chapter 2, at 2.2 above, and in Chapter 3, at 3.3 above.

and on the court's view of the conclusions to be derived from it. The local court is left in no doubt that it is to act in such a way as to maintain internal consistency within the system in which it is constituted, and that such relief as it may grant to the foreign representative must be a reflection of that requirement. Furthermore, the potential for incompatibility between the domestic effects of the local proceeding and the effects within that system which would ordinarily follow if the foreign proceeding is recognised as a main proceeding are averted through the express exclusion of Article 20 from having application in those circumstances.

The converse situation, where the proceeding in the enacting State commences after recognition, or after the filing of application for the recognition, of the foreign proceeding is dealt with in Article 29(b). This requires the court to review any relief in effect under Article 19 or 21 and to modify or terminate it if it is inconsistent with the local proceeding. Also, if the foreign proceeding is a main proceeding the automatic stay and suspension which takes effect in the enacting State by virtue of Article 20(1) is to be reviewed, and modified or terminated pursuant to paragraph (2) of that Article, if inconsistent with the local proceeding. Thus the policy of non-intrusion into the autonomy of the enacting State is fully respected in the provisions relating to concurrent proceedings, one of which takes place in the enacting State.[89]

The coordination of concurrent proceedings taking place in more than one foreign jurisdiction is dealt with in Article 30. The provision is applicable irrespective of whether an insolvency proceeding is also pending within the enacting State itself, but in the latter event the court must base its actions on the combined provisions of Articles 28, 29 and 30, according to the circumstances of the case. The provisions of Article 30 are essentially a command to the court to follow the dictates of common sense. Thus, the court is instructed that it must maintain consistency in its granting, or modification, of relief under Article 19 or 21 after recognition of one foreign proceeding if, subsequently, another foreign proceeding also gains recognition, resulting in there being one main, and one non-main, proceeding. The overall position must be reviewed and any necessary adjustments made in the light of the relative standing of the two proceedings, viewed from the standpoint of the court of the enacting State.[90] If both foreign proceedings gain coordinate recognition as non-main proceedings, the court is simply directed to grant, modify or terminate relief for the

[89] This is also true of the provision in Art. 29(c) concerning the granting of relief to a representative of a foreign non-main proceeding: it is a matter for the local court, applying the local law, to determine whether the assets to which the relief relates should be administered in the foreign proceeding. This provision largely repeats that contained in Art. 21(3) Post-recognition relief (see p. 346 above).

[90] Article 30(a),(b).

purpose of coordination of proceedings.[91] It will be apparent that, apart from the reiteration of the command that the court must seek cooperation and coordination under Articles 25 to 27 inclusive, there is no attempt under Article 30 to issue prescriptive instructions as to the manner in which the court is to deal with the issues which it will encounter in the course of its involvement in multi-jurisdictional proceedings. In truth, dogmatic approaches are seldom if ever of value in such situations, for perfect justice is by definition unattainable in a case of genuine insolvency. In cases where reorganisation is being attempted, an open and flexible approach on the part of the judiciary under whose jurisdiction the issues are determined greatly enhances the prospects for a commercially satisfactory outcome.

Hotchpot

The final Article of the Model Law, Article 32, embodies one of the central principles which are widely recognised as supplying the most satisfactory basis on which to administer multi-jurisdictional insolvencies in a manner that is both realistic and fair. This is the so-called 'hotchpot' rule, whereby a creditor who seeks to participate in a process of distribution taking place under the law of a given jurisdiction must furnish a full account of any payment that has already been received in respect of the same claim in any foreign proceeding.[92] On the basis of this disclosure, the creditor is not allowed to receive a payment of dividend after lodging proof of claim as long as the payment received by the other creditors of the same class is proportionately less than the payment the creditor has already received. By this means, *de facto* equality of treatment of creditors is maintained according to the rules of distribution followed in the jurisdiction where the Hotchpot rule is applied. The doctrine does not purport to affect the system for ranking of different categories of claims under the law of the State in question. Hence, the comparator for the purposes of applying the hotchpot rule is the ranking which that creditor's claim has under the system in which proof is currently lodged, rather than the class to which it was assigned under the law of any State in which payment was previously obtained.

Article 32 opens with a statement to the effect that it operates without prejudice to secured claims or rights *in rem*. This is to preserve the rights of a creditor who holds a security over particular assets of the debtor, or who has rights relating to a particular property that are enforceable

[91] Article 30(c).

[92] See the discussion of the hotchpot rule in English law in Chapter 2, at 2.4 above. A simple example is given in para. 198 of the Guide to Enactment, *supra* n.16, to illustrate the working of the rule. See also Art. 20 of the EU Convention (Chapter 6, at 6.3.4 above) and Art. 5 of the Istanbul Convention (Chapter 7, at 7.4 above).

against third parties even in the event of the insolvency of the grantor. Depending on the value of the rights in question, that party may not need to participate in the process of *pari passu* distribution, or may only need to lodge proof for the unsecured balance of claim. In that event, the proportion of the original claim that was covered by the realised value of the security is ignored for the purpose of dealing with the unsecured balance of the debt. By the same token, it cannot be made a basis of objection to the secured creditor enforcing his security that he will thereby obtain a greater proportion in payment of his gross claim than is destined to be received by unsecured creditors of the same class whose only return comes by way of dividend.

Article 32 does not provide a model legislative provision that might be used for the purpose of transposing the hotchpot rule into the law of the enacting State. As with all other Articles of the Model Law from which positive legislative provisions are intended to emerge, it is left to the enacting State to resolve for itself the technical drafting problems that may arise by virtue of the specific conditions that are found within the legal system in question.[93]

8.3 THE NEXT PHASE: STATE ENACTMENT OF THE MODEL LAW

The proof of the Model Law will be in the enactment. The crucial question is not only the number of States which take a conscious decision to enact the Law, but the extent to which they do so, both individually and collectively. The fact that it is open to a State to enact as much, or as little, of the Model Law as it pleases is likely to be viewed by some as an Achilles' heel of this form of international harmonisation. It is true that there is no guarantee of uniformity of acceptance, whether measured in terms of the quantity of the Law's provisions that are adopted, or in terms of the technical quality of the implementation provisions as an accurate embodiment of their intended substance. These limitations have to be accepted as an inherent aspect of the Model Law concept. What is being attempted is simply a first-base advance along the arduous path of the journey towards a really worthwhile and effective model of international regulation of cross-border insolvency. Seen in these terms, the hope must be that a sufficiently large number of commercially significant States demonstrate a commitment to implementing the Law more or less in its entirety within

[93] For an example of a statutory provision embodying the hotchpot rule in the Canadian legislation concerning international insolvency, see the Bankruptcy and Insolvency Act, s.274, discussed in Chapter 4, at 4.4 above, at p. 217.

their domestic legislation. In this way, other States may be influenced into overcoming their scepticism about the Law's value.[94]

It is understandable that some States may be reluctant to enact legislation which carries the prospect that their courts may become committed to recognising foreign judgments and orders, and giving access and assistance to courts and representatives, from literally any jurisdiction in the world, without the prior condition of reciprocity, or mutual negotiation and agreement, having taken place. The more extreme possibilities to which such international openness may give rise can perhaps be attenuated by means of the facility enshrined in Article 6 enabling the court to refuse to take any action pursuant to the Law's provisions if this would be manifestly contrary to the public policy of the State in which it sits. Further reassurance that the Law does not carry the potential to cause a State to violate any international agreements or treaties to which it is a party is provided by Article 3, which provides that to the extent that such a conflict arises, the requirements of the treaty or agreement are to prevail. This is of particular relevance to those States which are potential parties to the European Union Convention on Insolvency Proceedings,[95] or to the Istanbul Convention.[96] Participation in either or both of these conventions, or in other regional conventions such as those in force in Scandinavia or Latin America,[97] need not therefore be an impediment to a State taking the decision to enact the UNCITRAL Model Law.

The mode of enactment is also a matter requiring careful consideration on the part of States which decide to take this course. To the extent that existing provisions within a State's legislation or even the fruits of its case law appear to meet, or possibly exceed, the requirements of the Model Law, there may be a strong inclination to make little or no alteration to the fabric and content of the existing provisions. In the interests of providing a clear and coherent indication of the State's alignment with this international initiative, however, the option of creating a specific chapter within the relevant statute or code, expressly dedicated to international insolvency matters, deserves serious consideration. Although the Law is deliberately drafted in such a way as to enable States to introduce their own technical terminology into the enacted text, it is very desirable that it should be clearly apparent to an external party, who may be unfamiliar with the style and nuances of that legal system, that the Model Law has in fact been enacted. It is suggested that such transparency is best achieved

[94] UNCITRAL conducts a programme of monitoring the rate of progress in implementation of its conventions and model legislative provisions by States, and their application by courts throughout the world. The collected information is published under the title *Case Law on UNCITRAL Texts* (CLOUT). This database is accessible electronically at the following Website: <http://www.un.or.at/UNCITRAL>

[95] See Chapter 6 above. [96] See Chapter 7 above. [97] See Chapter 5 above.

by means of an identifiable chapter within domestic insolvency legislation, amongst whose provisions the material contents of the Model Law should be readily discernible.[98] Such a development would, it is submitted, be both timely and appropriate in the case of the United Kingdom, where the complex provisions of section 426 of the Insolvency Act 1986 should be reorganised as part of a more comprehensive overhaul of law and policy towards international cases.[99] If the lessons taught by international experience during the past decade have been properly absorbed, the advantages of having in place a series of internationally standardised provisions designed to answer the needs of those most directly involved in the administration of cross-border cases ought to be widely appreciated. Even if the only motivation were to be that furnished by enlightened self interest, the active promotion of the Model Law should be regarded as a sound policy for the United Kingdom to embrace. As an opportunity to display leadership by example in matters of international insolvency, this is also an occasion to demonstrate the qualities of idealism balanced by pragmatism that can rightly be claimed to belong to the English legal tradition.

[98] An early example of such an approach could be provided in the USA. In April 1998 Bill S.1914 was introduced into the US Senate. One part of the Bill would have amended the Bankruptcy Code by adding a new Chapter 6, bearing the title: 'Ancillary and other Cross-Border Cases'. The proposed contents of the new chapter would have implemented the majority of the provisions of the Model Law in terms strikingly close to the original. Certain matters were excluded, namely proceedings concerning those categories of debtor already excluded from the ambit of the Bankruptcy Code under its s.109(b), and 'consumer debtors' as defined by s.109(e), who are citizens or permanent residents of the USA. Although the Bankruptcy Reform Bill of 1998 failed to complete its legislative stages before the conclusion of the 105th Congress, and accordingly lapsed, it appears possible that fresh initiatives aimed at enacting the Model Law will take place during the course of the 106th Congress, commencing in January 1999. At the time of writing, the prospects for early enactment of this measure in its proposed form are uncertain. (I am grateful to Professor J.L. Westbrook for alerting me to the contents of this proposal).

[99] See Chapter 2, at 2.2 above and Chapter 4, at 4.1 above for discussion of the various aspects of s.426 of the 1986 Act in relation to both intra-UK and genuinely international situations.

9

Conclusion: Achievements, Trends and Prospects

9.1 NATIONAL APPROACHES TO INTERNATIONAL INSOLVENCY

In Part I of this book, the problems of international insolvency were examined from the standpoint of the rules and procedures developed at national level, and administered by the courts and agencies established within individual legal systems. The primary focus was upon English law, supplemented by references to the laws of other leading representatives of the common law tradition, namely Australia, Canada, and the USA. While each system now has its own distinctive characteristics, it is possible to discern a number of shared, fundamental principles. These are partly a reflection of the common heritage from which the four systems have evolved. But in their current tendencies they also reflect the growing perception among those whose vocation it is to address the issues of cross-border insolvency in some way, that a genuinely internationalist spirit must be an essential part of the approach. In an age of globalisation, it is neither prudent nor realistic to adopt an insular philosophy when confronted by such challenges. This trend of thought is most clearly demonstrated by the legislative innovations which have been introduced during the past twenty years in each of the four jurisdictions referred to, and which were explored in Chapter 4. In their different ways, each system has sought to address the problems raised in a multi-jurisdictional insolvency by entrusting its courts with enhanced powers of assistance and cooperation with their foreign counterparts, or with foreign representatives conducting insolvency proceedings commenced abroad.

An important feature of the provisions empowering courts to provide international cooperation and assistance is that they include a substantial element of discretion and selectivity of response. This is essential in order to allow each case to be dealt with on its individual merits, and in response to its particular requirements, while respecting the overall standards and principles of the system from which that assistance is provided. When such enabling provisions in national legislation are combined with a positive spirit of judicial activism, impressive results can be achieved in alleviating the inevitable economic discomfort of those caught up in an insolvency with international dimensions.[1] Amid the more ambitious debate about treaty-based arrangements for international cooperation, it should be remembered that it lies within the capacity of every independent State to remodel its national law so as to create the necessary conditions under which prudent and measured collaboration can take place. Despite certain shortcomings that were noted in the course of discussion in Chapter 4, the great virtue of these provisions is that they are already in force and available to be used: it is of little consolation to parties involved in a current case to be told that their predicament might have been alleviated under the terms of an international convention which, for various reasons, has not yet entered into effect.

While recognising the virtue of immediacy with regard to the resources offered under existing national law, it must also be acknowledged that the consequent diversity, when the laws of different States are set alongside each other, is calculated to confuse and perplex. Of particular concern, from the standpoint of United Kingdom law, are the relatively narrow terms of availability of assistance under section 426 of the Insolvency Act 1986, when compared to the essentially open-minded policy built into the provisions of section 304 of the United States Bankruptcy Code, and into the Australian and Canadian legislation, respectively.[2] In most instances, unfortunately, those contemplating an approach to the English courts in their quest for assistance must somehow inform themselves of the current law and practice, to the extent that these may be deduced from the reported precedents, some of which were decided more than two centuries ago. In the account of the law given in Chapters 2 and 3 above, the positive virtues of many of these case decisions—including some of the earliest in terms of their chronological date—are frequently acclaimed. In their manifest desire to deal with all creditors in an even-handed way, without discrimination between domestic and foreign creditors, the English courts have generally shown themselves to be committed to an internationalist approach which is happily in keeping with the concepts of best practice that are prevalent today.[3] On the other hand, the record is not

[1] See, e.g. the creative use of the powers conferred by the Insolvency Act 1986, s.426, in *Re Dallhold Estates (UK) Pty. Ltd.*[1992] B.C.C. 394, [1992] B.C.L.C. 621 (Chadwick J.); and in various episodes of the prolix proceedings in the *B.C.C.I.* case, including *Re Bank of Credit and Commerce International S.A. (No. 9)* [1994] 3 All E.R. 764, [1994] 2 B.C.L.C. 636 (Rattee J.). Both cases are discussed in Chapter 4, at 4.1 above

[2] See Chapter 4, at 4.1 above (*Restricted availability of s.426 assistance*), and cf. the comments at 4.2 above with respect to the access afforded to a foreign representative under s.304 of the US Bankruptcy Code; at 4.3 above with respect to Australian courts' powers to provide international assistance under s.29(2) of the Bankruptcy Act 1966 and under s.581(2) of the Corporations Law; and at 4.4 above with respect to Canadian courts' powers in international insolvency cases under Part XIII of the Bankruptcy and Insolvency Act, as amended in 1997.

[3] For examples of the internationalist approach as exhibited through the English case law, see the discussions in Chapters 2 and 3 of the treatment of creditors and claims in English

entirely an unblemished one, and attention has already been drawn to some instances in which English law continues to embody unsatisfactory rules, based on precedents which have not been overturned and which are simply inconsistent with the creed of internationalism, as nowadays understood.[4]

The need for a modern review and restatement of the English law

As the foregoing comments are intended to suggest, the current state of English law concerning international insolvency is in need of a revision and restatement, so as to rectify the anomalies and inconsistencies which have arisen over the course of time. An authoritative statement of the relevant principles, matched to the conditions and requirements of the present day, would be of much value to those, both at home and abroad, who need an accurate and accessible account of the law in its current state. Such an exercise might be carried out by an expert committee specially constituted for the purpose, or it might be undertaken by the Law Commission as part of their mission to keep under review 'all the law, with a view to its systematic development and reform'.[5] Although the Cork Report of 1982 did allocate a chapter to the Extra-Territorial Aspects of Insolvency Law[6] and a further chapter to the subject of United Kingdom Insolvency Law and the EEC,[7] both were brief (especially the latter) and somewhat general in content, although one positive outcome of the advice

proceedings (at 2.4 and 3.5 above); the recognition of foreign proceedings and their effects on property in England (at 2.6, 3.7 and 3.10 above); and the judicial approach to international cooperation in cases of concurrent proceedings (at 2.8 and 3.9 above).

[4] Among the most conspicuous lapses noted in Chapters 2 and 3 above are: the one-sided treatment by English law of the effects of discharge of obligations through insolvency proceedings, based on the decision in *Gibbs v. La Société Industrielle et Commerciale des Métaux* (1890) 25 Q.B.D. 399 (CA), criticised at 2.7 above; and the technical wrong-footing of a foreign trustee or liquidator seeking to impeach transactions which took place prior to the date of his formal appointment, in consequence of the decision in *Galbraith v. Grimshaw* [1910] A.C. 508 (HL), criticised at 2.6.1(b) above. The unhappy breakdown of international comity over the matter of set-off was also acknowledged at 2.3 above, in the light of the decision in *Re Bank of Credit and Commerce International SA (No. 10)* [1996] 4 All E.R. 796.

[5] Law Commissions Act 1965, s.3(1). Unfortunately, there is no counterpart within the United Kingdom of the American Law Institute, which has served since 1923 as an authoritative vehicle for the promotion of reform and improvement of the law in the USA, and which unites within its membership a distinguished alliance of judges, practising lawyers and legal scholars. The A.L.I. Restatements of the law represent the fruits of a rigorous process of research and analysis of the law and its principles, expressed in coherent and systematic terms with supporting commentary. They are a model worth emulating in other jurisdictions where the law's development is taken seriously.

[6] Cmnd. 8558, ch. 49 (containing paras. 1902–1913 of the Report). See also the Australian Law Reform Commission, Report No. 45, General Insolvency Inquiry (2 vols., 1988), ch. 19 ('Cross-frontier insolvency'), esp. the recommendations listed at para. 975. (Chapter 19 is reproduced in full as ch. 16 of I.F. Fletcher (ed.), *Cross-Border Insolvency: Comparative Dimensions (The Aberystwyth Insolvency Papers)* (1990)).

[7] *Ibid.*, ch. 50 (containing paras. 1914–1921).

of the Committee was the enactment of section 426 of the 1986 Act. A more detailed investigation of the problems of international insolvency was conducted by the precursor to the Cork Committee of 1976–82, namely the Advisory Committee established in 1973 to consider the terms of the Draft EEC Bankruptcy Convention. This Committee, also convened under the chairmanship of Mr. Kenneth Cork, delivered its report in August 1976.[8] Although mainly concerned with the terms of the Draft Convention and its implications from the standpoint of the United Kingdom, the Advisory Committee's Report includes numerous insights into the state of English law at that period. The Committee's concluding observations included an indication that, if the EEC Convention in its then-current form were to be adopted, it might necessitate an entire review of domestic insolvency laws.[9] Although, as was seen in Chapter 6 above, the EU Convention is still not adopted, the time is surely ripe for a review of the international aspects of English and Scottish insolvency law, particularly in view of the fact that substantial reforms have been carried out of the domestic laws of both countries in the meantime.[10] The international aspects of insolvency law still await the overhaul and modernisation anticipated by the Advisory Committee more than twenty years ago.

9.2 INTERNATIONAL APPROACHES TO INTERNATIONAL INSOLVENCY

Vital though they are to the attainment of fair and just results in the benighted circumstances of a cross-border insolvency, national laws also have their inescapable limitations. Since the writ of an individual legal system cannot run beyond the boundaries of its territorial jurisdiction, save by the *fiat* and licence of those other sovereign authorities within whose domain the completed effects of a transnational legal process are to take place, some form of international cooperation is ultimately indispensable. It is one of the purposes of private international law to attempt to produce orderly solutions out of the chaos caused by the diversity of domestic laws and policies that are potentially applicable to a particular situation, relationship or transaction. Left to their own devices, however,

[8] Cmnd. 6602. See also the account in Chapter 6, at 6.1 above, of the evolution of the EEC Bankruptcy Convention during the period at which the Advisory Committee was conducting its evaluation.

[9] *Ibid.*, para. 421.

[10] Scottish law concerning the insolvency of individuals was separately reviewed by the Scottish Law Commission in a report, published in 1982, (H.C. Paper 176, Scot. Law Comm. No. 68) which resulted in the enactment of the Bankruptcy (Scotland) Act 1985. Reform of company insolvency in Scotland and England was effected on a joint basis, via the provisions of the Insolvency Acts of 1985 and 1986, some of whose provisions apply exclusively to Scotland.

the individual national systems of private international law have the propensity to generate fresh levels of diversity and, potentially, harmful chaos. To avert these unwelcome consequences, successive international efforts have been embarked upon with a view to establishing some kind of framework of rules and procedures for resolving the problems which typically arise in this context. In Part II of this work, the fruits of a number of such multilateral ventures were examined, and their respective merits and deficiencies appraised.

On the whole, the lessons to be drawn from a review of the regional, and global, conventions and agreements are chastening. Even between States which ostensibly have much in common, as in the case of the Member States of the European Union, the fact that insolvency has such profound effects upon a range of nationally sensitive matters, including property, security interests, personal status, and the management of the commercial economy and the credit system, has so far proved to be an insurmountable barrier to the conclusion of a worthwhile and effective European Insolvency Convention.[11] To date, the most successful of the regionally-based agreements is the Nordic Bankruptcy Convention, as described in Chapter 5 above.[12] This only serves to accentuate the great difficulties of establishing such international arrangements between less closely affiliated groupings of States, because the level of homogeneity among the five Nordic countries is almost certainly unique. Without such similarity of purpose and philosophical approach, there are minimal prospects for concluding a multilateral convention that embodies strong principles governing the exercise of jurisdiction and the extraterritorial effects of proceedings. For the foreseeable future, therefore, the Nordic Convention of 1933 may remain the solitary example of effective cooperation among European States in this field.

'The art of the possible'

Given the difficulties of attaining effective international agreement even at a regional level, it can readily be appreciated how much greater are the obstacles to the creation of a framework of rules for adoption on a global basis. Far more realistic, it is submitted, is the strategy underlying the recently concluded UNCITRAL Model Law on Cross-Border Insolvency, described in Chapter 8 above. This initiative has drawn much inspiration from the active contributions of those with first-hand experience of the problems of cross-border insolvency, namely insolvency practitioners and judges from many different jurisdictions and legal traditions throughout the world. By concentrating on the creation of minimum conditions to

[11] See Chapter 6 above. The equally uncertain destiny of the Istanbul Convention of the Council of Europe is examined in Chapter 7 above.

[12] See at 5.3 above.

facilitate the development of workable solutions under the circumstances of the instant case, rather than seeking to impose a comprehensive regime of rules of jurisdiction, choice of law, recognition and enforcement, the authors of the Model Law have engaged in the practice of the 'Art of the Possible', viewing this as a first (but vital) step along a gradual course of development. By opting for the form of a model law, rather than a convention, the authors have accepted the risk that initially only a small number of States may wholeheartedly embrace this concept, and implement its provisions fully in their national legislation. What is important, however, is that an early example should be set by a critical mass of commercially important States, who thereby display moral leadership in setting global standards in the provision of cross-border access and assistance in matters of insolvency.

It was suggested in the concluding section of Chapter 8 above, and is again submitted here, that the UNCITRAL Model Law currently offers the best prospects of generating an *ad hoc* network of complementary provisions within the laws of a widening circle of States across the world, that will enable cases to be administered more rapidly, and in a more cost-effective way, thereby preserving value for the benefit of all interested parties. While the stimulus to this global initiative may well have been the widely publicised series of large-value, multi-jurisdictional insolvencies which have occurred during the past decade, the potential benefits of effective international arrangements for those concerned with smaller-value cases should not be overlooked. These are, after all, by far the most common sort of case to be encountered in practice. And yet they are precisely the cases in which, under present conditions, the resources needed to overcome the difficulties in reclaiming or administering overseas assets are least likely to be available. In the larger cases, the substantial costs of the professional services required to cope with the factors of geographical distance and legal diversity may assume a less daunting character, when viewed in relation to the overall value of the assets whose destiny is at stake. The economies of scale tend to operate in a contrary manner when total asset values are small. Therefore, to the extent that international developments such as the Model Law succeed in simplifying the process of administering foreign assets, this will in many instances improve the prospects of return for those involved in the smaller-value cases.

As was urged at the conclusion of Chapter 8 above, it is very much hoped that the United Kingdom will take active steps to ensure that it is among the first States to embody the principles of the UNCITRAL Model Law in its national legislation.[13] It could well be the case that the familiar process will be followed of establishing a committee to examine the case

[13] See at 8.3 above.

for enactment of the Model Law, as has previously occurred with regard to the EU Convention.[14] The deliberations of such a committee might well be undertaken in conjunction with the task of conducting a review of the existing law and practice concerning international insolvency, as advocated at 9.1 above. In any event, it is essential that a properly coordinated approach be followed in preparing for a recasting of English (and Scottish) law in a way that is fully consistent with the emerging trend of international cooperation. It should also be emphasised that the Model Law does not represent a complete alternative to the adoption of the EU Convention, for those States which are members of the European Union. Indeed, the two instruments are designed to serve separate, but compatible, objectives: the acceptance of a closely-controlled regime for the conduct of insolvency proceedings within the European Union in no way obviates the need for all the Member States to implement further legal provisions to facilitate an accommodation with the world outside the frontiers of the Union. Although neither is ultimately dependent upon the other, it would certainly be possible for both the EU Convention and the UNCITRAL Model Law to be endorsed as part of a 'twin-track' approach which would have the additional merit of helping to dispel the impression of the European Union as a largely inward-looking and self-absorbed alliance.[15]

9.3 THE FUTURE

International insolvency law has arrived at the threshold of an exciting period of development. Recent experiences have demonstrated the limitations of the separate national approaches, based on outmoded perceptions of the appropriate relationship between internal and external interests, and between domestic and foreign legal processes. The imperative need to build bridges between the individual national systems, and to create adaptable structures that will enable communication and cooperation to take place in response to the particular elements present within each case, requires a new vision, and new modes of thought, from all participants. In giving the name 'internationalism' to the spirit which underlies the current trend of thought, this author detects important affinities with the historic roots of the English approach to international insolvency, as

[14] See the 1976 Report of the Advisory Committee, referred to *supra* n.8, and the 1996 Report of the House of Lords Select Committee on the European Communities, 7th Report (H.L. Paper 59, Session 1995–96), referred to in Chapter 8 above at n.11.

[15] See the criticisms in Chapter 6, at 6.2 above, of the unpalatable features of the Phase I Drafts of the EEC Bankruptcy Convention, in which xenophobic tendencies were much in evidence. Happily, these qualities have been purged from the finalised version of the Insolvency Convention, as described at 6.3 above.

depicted throughout this book.[16] In calling for a modern revision and restatement of the English law, it is submitted that this presents the opportunity to reaffirm many positive virtues of our past tradition, while enabling the less satisfactory and errant features to be corrected. The law needs to be restated in terms which give a clear indication of systemic commitment to the cause of collectivity, accompanied by a readiness to provide international cooperation and assistance in support of that principle. The courts should retain a controlling discretion over the form and mode of collaboration to be undertaken in a given case: over-prescriptive and over-detailed legislative directions should be avoided, in the interests of allowing solutions to be devised which are both workable and fair. Although (as should be apparent from many passages within this book), the author fervently disclaims any intention to hint at a doctrine of judicial infallibility, he is thoroughly convinced that enormously beneficial consequences have ensued in recent times from the prudent application of the principle of judicial activism. In affirming a non-dogmatic, constructive approach to the resolution of problems experienced in a case of cross-border insolvency, the substance and quality of the result should be the dominant concern, rather than the imposition of any preconceived notion about the form in which the solution should be embodied:

Whate'er is best administer'd, is best'.[17]

[16] See Chapter 1, at 1.2, 1.3 above.

[17] Pope, *An Essay on Man* (1733), III.304.

APPENDICES

Appendix I

Selected National Legislation

(A) UNITED KINGDOM: INSOLVENCY ACT 1986, SECTION 426

426 Co-operation between courts exercising jurisdiction in relation to insolvency

(1) An order made by a court in any part of the United Kingdom in the exercise of jurisdiction in relation to insolvency law shall be enforced in any other part of the United Kingdom as if it were made by a court exercising the corresponding jurisdiction in that other part.

(2) However, without prejudice to the following provisions of this section, nothing in subsection (1) requires a court in any part of the United Kingdom to enforce, in relation to property situated in that part, any order made by a court in any other part of the United Kingdom.

(3) The Secretary of State, with the concurrence in relation to property situated in England and Wales of the Lord Chancellor, may by order make provision for securing that a trustee or assignee under the insolvency law of any part of the United Kingdom has, with such modifications as may be specified in the order, the same rights in relation to any property situated in another part of the United Kingdom as he would have in the corresponding circumstances if he were a trustee or assignee under the insolvency law of that other part.

(4) The courts having jurisdiction in relation to insolvency law in any part of the United Kingdom shall assist the courts having the corresponding jurisdiction in any other part of the United Kingdom or any relevant country or territory.

(5) For the purposes of subsection (4) a request made to a court in any part of the United Kingdom by a court in any other part of the United Kingdom or in a relevant country or territory is authority for the court to which the request is made to apply, in relation to any matters specified in the request, the insolvency law which is applicable by either court in relation to comparable matters falling within its jurisdiction.

In exercising its discretion under this subsection, a court shall have regard in particular to the rules of private international law.

(6) Where a person who is a trustee or assignee under the insolvency law of any part of the United Kingdom claims property situated in any other part of the United Kingdom (whether by virtue of an order under subsection (3) or otherwise), the submission of that claim to the court exercising jurisdiction in relation to insolvency law in that other part shall be treated in the same manner as a request made by a court for the purpose of subsection (4).

(7) Section 38 of the Criminal Law Act 1977 (execution of warrant of arrest throughout the United Kingdom) applies to a warrant which, in exercise of any

jurisdiction in relation to insolvency law, is issued in any part of the United Kingdom for the arrest of a person as it applies to a warrant issued in that part of the United Kingdom for the arrest of a person charged with an offence.

(8) Without prejudice to any power to make rules of court, any power to make provision by subordinate legislation for the purpose of giving effect in relation to companies or individuals to the insolvency law of any part of the United Kingdom includes power to make provision for the purpose of giving effect in that part to any provision made by or under the preceding provisions of this section.

(9) An order under subsection (3) shall be made by statutory instrument subject to annulment in pursuance of a resolution of either House of Parliament.

(10) In this section 'insolvency law' means—

(a) in relation to England and Wales, provision made by or under this Act or sections 6 to 10, 12, 15, 19(c) and 20 (with Schedule 1) of the Company Directors Disqualification Act 1986 and extending to England and Wales;

(b) in relation to Scotland, provision extending to Scotland and made by or under this Act, sections 6 to 10, 12, 15, 19(c) and 20 (with Schedule 1) of the Company Directors Disqualification Act 1986, Part XVIII of the Companies Act or the Bankruptcy (Scotland) Act 1985;

(c) in relation to Northern Ireland, provision made by or under the Insolvency (Northern Ireland) Order 1989 or Pt. II of the Companies (Northern Ireland) Order 1989;

(d) in relation to any relevant country or territory, so much of the law of that country or territory as corresponds to provisions falling within any of the foregoing paragraphs;

and references in this subsection to any enactment include, in relation to any time before the coming into force of that enactment the corresponding enactment in force at that time.

(11) In this section 'relevant country or territory' means—

(a) any of the Channel Islands or the Isle of Man, or

(b) any country or territory designated for the purposes of this section by the Secretary of State by order made by statutory instrument.

(12) In the application of this section to Northern Ireland—

(a) for any reference to the Secretary of State there is substituted a reference to the Department of Economic Development in Northern Ireland;

(b) in subsection (3) for the words 'another part of the United Kingdom' and the words 'that other part' there is substituted the words 'Northern Ireland';

(c) for subsection (9) there is substituted the following subsection—

'(9) An order made under subsection (3) by the Department of Economic Development in Northern Ireland shall be a statutory rule for the purposes of the Statutory Rules (Northern Ireland) Order 1979 and shall be subject to negative resolution within the meaning of section 41(6) of the Interpretation Act (Northern Ireland) 1954'.

(B) USA: BANKRUPTCY CODE (11 U.S.C.), §§ 101(23), (24); 304–306

§ 101 Definitions

(23) 'foreign proceeding' means proceeding, whether judicial or administrative and whether or not under bankruptcy law, in a foreign country in which the debtor's domicile, residence, principal place of business, or principal assets were located at the commencement of such proceeding, for the purpose of liquidating an estate, adjusting debts by composition, extension, or discharge, or effecting a reorganization.

(24) 'foreign representative' means duly selected trustee, administrator, or other representative of an estate in a foreign proceeding.

§ 304 Cases ancillary to foreign proceedings

(a) A case ancillary to a foreign proceeding is commenced by the filing with the bankruptcy court of a petition under this section by a foreign representative.

(b) Subject to the provisions of subsection (c) of this section, if a party in interest does not timely controvert the petition, or after trial, the court may—

(1) enjoin the commencement or continuation of—

(A) any action against—

(i) a debtor with respect to property involved in such foreign proceeding;

or

(ii) such property; or

(B) the enforcement of any judgment against the debtor with respect to such property, or any act or the commencement or continuation of any judicial proceeding to create or enforce a lien against the property of such estate;

(2) order turnover of the property of such estate, or the proceeds of such property, to such foreign representative; or

(3) order other appropriate relief.

(c) In determining whether to grant relief under subsection (b) of this section, the court shall be guided by what will best assure an economical and expeditious administration of such estate, consistent with—

(1) just treatment of all holders of claims against or interests in such estate;

(2) protection of claim holders in the United States against prejudice and inconvenience in the processing of claims in such foreign proceeding;

(3) prevention of preferential or fraudulent dispositions of property of such estate;

(4) distribution of proceeds of such estate substantially in accordance with the order prescribed by this title;

(5) comity, and

(6) if appropriate, the provision of an opportunity for a fresh start for the individual that such foreign proceeding concerns.

§ 305 Abstention

(a) The court, after notice and a hearing, may dismiss a case under this title, or may suspend all proceedings in a case under this title, at any time if—

(1) the interests of creditors and the debtor would be better served by such dismissal or suspension; or

(2) (A) there is pending a foreign proceeding; and

(B) the factors specified in section 304(c) of this title warrant such dismissal or suspension.

(b) A foreign representative may seek dismissal or suspension under subsection (a)(2) of this section.

(c) An order under subsection (a) of this section dismissing a case or suspending all proceedings in a case, or a decision not so to dismiss or suspend, is not reviewable by appeal or otherwise by the court of appeals under section 158(d), 1291, or 1292 of title 28 or by the Supreme Court of the United States under section 1254 of title 28.

§306 Limited appearance

An appearance in a bankruptcy court by a foreign representative in connection with a petition or request under section 303, 304, or 305 of this title does not submit such foreign representative to the jurisdiction of any court in the United States for any other purpose, but the bankruptcy court may condition any order under section 303, 304, or 305 of this title on compliance by such foreign representative with the orders of such bankruptcy court.

(C) AUSTRALIA: CORPORATIONS LAW, SECTIONS 580, 581; BANKRUPTCY ACT 1966, SECTION 29; SCHEDULE 5

Division 9 [of the Corporations Law]: Co-operation between Australian and Foreign courts in external administration matters

Interpretation

580 In this Division:

'external administration matter' means a matter relating to:
- (a) winding up, under this Chapter, a company or a Part 5.7 body;
- (b) winding up, outside Australia, a body corporate or a Part 5.7 body; or
- (c) the insolvency of a body corporate or of a Part 5.7 body;

'prescribed country' means:
- (a) a country prescribed for the purposes of this definition; or
- (b) a colony, overseas territory or protectorate of a country so prescribed.

Courts to act in aid of each other

581 (1) [Courts having jurisdiction under local Corporations Law] All courts having jurisdiction in matters arising under the Corporations Law of this jurisdiction, the Judges of those courts and the officers of, or under the control of, those courts must severally act in aid of, and to be auxiliary to,
- (a) each other; and
- (b) all courts having jurisdiction in matters arising under corresponding laws, the Judges of those courts and the officers of, or under the control of, those courts; in all external administration matters.

(2) [Where excluded Territories and prescribed and other countries] In all external administration matters, the Court:
- (a) shall act in aid of, and be auxiliary to, the courts of the excluded Territories, and of prescribed countries, that have jurisdiction in external administration matters; and
- (b) may act in aid of, and be auxiliary to, the courts of other countries that have jurisdiction in external administration matters.

(3) [Powers upon court's request for aid] Where a letter of request from a court of an excluded Territory, or of a country other than Australia, requesting aid in an external administration matter is filed in the Court, the Court may exercise such powers with respect to the matter as it could exercise if the matter had arisen within its own jurisdiction.

(4) [Power to request a court's aid] The Court may request a court of an excluded Territory, or of a country other than Australia, that has jurisdiction in external administration matters to act in aid of, and be auxiliary to, it in an external administration matter.

Section 29 [of the Bankruptcy Act]: Courts to act in aid of each other

29(1) [All Courts with jurisdiction] All Courts having jurisdiction under this Act, the Judges of those Courts and the officers of or under the control of those Courts shall severally act in aid of and be auxiliary to each other in all matters of bankruptcy.

(2) [Aid to external Territories, other countries] In all matters of bankruptcy, the Court

(a) shall act in aid of and be auxiliary to the courts of the external Territories, and of prescribed countries, that have jurisdiction in bankruptcy; and
(b) may act in aid of and be auxiliary to the courts of other countries that have jurisdiction in bankruptcy.

(3) [Request for aid] Where a letter of request from a court of an external Territory, or of a country other than Australia, requesting aid in a matter of bankruptcy is filed in the Court, the Court may exercise such powers with respect to the matter as it could exercise if the matter had arisen within its own jurisdiction.

(4) [Court may request aid] The Court may request a court of an external Territory, or of a country other than Australia, that has jurisdiction in bankruptcy to act in aid of and be auxiliary to it in any matter of bankruptcy.

(5) ['Prescribed Country'] In this section, 'prescribed country' means—

(a) the United Kingdom, Canada and New Zealand;
(b) a country prescribed for the purposes of this subsection; and
(c) a colony, overseas territory or protectorate of a country specified in paragraph (a) or of a country so prescribed.

Schedule 5 [of the Bankruptcy Act]: Prescribed countries: paragraph 29(5)(b) of the Act

Jersey, Bailiwick of
Malaysia
Papua New Guinea
Singapore
Switzerland
United States of America

(D) CANADA: BANKRUPTCY AND INSOLVENCY ACT, PART XIII (SECTIONS 267–275)

Part XIII: International Insolvencies

Interpretation

267 In this Part,

'debtor' means an insolvent person who has property in Canada, a bankrupt who has property in Canada or a person who has the status of a bankrupt under foreign law in a foreign proceeding and has property in Canada;

'foreign proceeding' means a judicial or administrative proceeding commenced outside Canada in respect of a debtor, under a law relating to bankruptcy or insolvency and dealing with the collective interests of creditors generally;

'foreign representative' means a person, other than a debtor, holding office under the law of a jurisdiction outside Canada who, irrespective of the person's designation, is assigned, under the laws of the jurisdiction outside Canada, functions in connection with a foreign proceeding that are similar to those performed by a trustee, liquidator, administrator or receiver appointed by the court.

General

268 (1) For the purposes of this Part, where a bankruptcy, insolvency or reorganization or like order has been made in respect of a debtor in a foreign proceeding, a certified or exemplified copy of the order is, in the absence of evidence to the contrary, proof that the debtor is insolvent and proof of the appointment of the foreign representative made by the order.

Partie XIII: Insolvabilité en Contexte International

Définitions

267 Les définitions qui suivent s'appliquent à la présente partie,

'débiteur' La personne insolvable ou le failli qui a des biens au Canada ainsi que la personne qui se trouve, par application du droit étranger, en situation de failli au titre de procédures intentées à l'étranger et a des biens au Canada.

'procédures intentées à l'étranger' Les procédures judiciaires ou administratives engagées à l'étranger contre un débiteur au titre du droit relatif à la faillite ou à l'insolvabilité et touchant les droits de l'ensemble des créanciers.

'représentant étranger' Sauf le débiteur, la personne qui, au titre du droit étranger applicable, exerce, dans le cadre de procédures intentées à l'étranger, des fonctions semblables à celles d'un syndic, liquidateur, administrateur ou séquestre nommé par le tribunal, quel que soit son tire.

Dispositions générales

268 (1) Pour l'application de la présente partie, une copie certifiée conforme ou une ampliation de l'ordonnance de faillite, d'insolvabilité ou de réorganisation ou de toute ordonnance semblable, rendue contre un débiteur dans des procédures intentées à l'étranger, fait foi, sauf preuve contraire, de l'insolvabilité de celui-ci et de la nomination du représentant étranger au titre de l'ordonance.

(2) Where a foreign proceeding has been commenced and a receiving order or assignment is made under this Act in respect of a debtor, the court may, on application and on such terms as it considers appropriate, limit the property to which the authority of the trustee extends to the property of the debtor situated in Canada and to such property of the debtor outside Canada as the court considers can be effectively administered by the trustee.

(3) The court may, in respect of a debtor, make such orders and grant such relief as it considers appropriate to facilitate, approve or implement arrangements that will result in a co-ordination of proceedings under this Act with any foreign proceeding.

(4) An order of the court under this Part may be made on such terms and conditions as the court considers appropriate in the circumstances.

(5) Nothing in this part prevents the court, on the application of a foreign representative or any other interested person, from applying such legal or equitable rules governing the recognition of foreign insolvency orders and assistance to foreign representatives as are not inconsistent with the provisions of this Act.

(6) Nothing in this Part requires the court to make any order that is not in compliance with the laws of Canada or to enforce any order made by a foreign court.

(2) Lorsque des procédures ont été intentées à l'étranger et qu'une ordonnance de séquestre a été rendue ou qu'une cession a été déposée au titre de la présente loi contre un débiteur, le tribunal peut, sur demande et aux conditions qu'il estime indiquées, limiter les pouvoirs du syndic aux biens du débiteur situés au Canada et aux biens situés à l'étranger que le syndic est apte, de l'avis du tribunal, à bien administrer.

(3) En vue de faciliter, d'approuver ou de mettre en oeuvre les arrangements permettant de coordonner les procédures intentées à l'étranger, le tribunal peut, à l'égard du débiteur, rendre les ordonnances et accorder les redressements qu'il estime indiqués.

(4) Le tribunal peut assortir ses ordonnances des conditions qu'il estime indiquées dans les circonstances.

(5) La présente partie n'a pas pour effet d'empêcher le tribunal d'appliquer, sur demande faite par le représentant étranger ou tout autre intéressé, des règles de droit ou d'équité relatives à la reconnaissance des ordonnances étrangères en matière d'insolvabilité et à l'assistance au représentant étranger, qui ne sont pas incompatibles avec les dispositions de la présente loi.

(6) La présente partie n'a pas pour effet d'exiger du tribunal qu'il rende des ordonnances qui sont contraires au droit canadien ou qu'il donne effet aux ordonnances rendues par un tribunal étranger.

269 A stay of proceedings that operates against creditors of a debtor in a foreign proceeding does not apply in respect of creditors who reside or carry on business in Canada with respect to property in Canada unless the stay of proceedings is the result of proceedings taken in Canada.

269 Dans le cas où des procédures sont suspendues à l'égard d'un débiteur dans le cadre de procédures intentées à l'étranger, la suspension n'est opposable aux créanciers qui résident ou font affaires au Canada en ce qui touche les biens du débiteur situés au Canada que si elle résulte de procédures intentées au Canada.

270 A foreign representative may commence and continue proceedings pursuant to sections 43 and 46 to 47.2 and subsections 50(1) and 50.4(1) in respect of a debtor as if the foreign representative were a creditor, trustee, liquidator or receiver of property of the debtor, or the debtor, as the case may be.

270 Les procédures visées aux articles 43 et 46 à 47.2 et aux paragraphes 50(1) et 50.4(1) peuvent être intentées ou continuées par un représantant étranger comme si celui-ci était créancier, syndic, liquidateur ou séquestre aux biens du débiteur, ou le débiteur, selon le cas.

271 (1) The court may seek the aid and assistance of a court, tribunal or other authority in a foreign proceeding by order or written request or otherwise as the court considers appropriate.

(2) On application by a foreign representative in respect of a foreign proceeding commenced for the purpose of effecting a composition, an extension of time or a scheme of arrangement in respect of a debtor or in respect of the bankruptcy of a debtor, the court may grant a stay of proceedings against the debtor or the debtor's property in Canada on such terms and for such period as is consistent with the relief provided for under sections 69 to 69.5 in respect of a debtor in Canada who files a notice of intention or a proposal or who becomes bankrupt in Canada, as the case may be.

271 (1) Dans le cadre de procédures intentées à l'étranger, le tribunal peut, par ordonnance, demander le concours d'une cour, d'un tribunal ou d'une autre autorité à l'étranger. Il peut également présenter sa demande par écrit ou de la manière qu'il estime indiquée.

(2) Sur demande présentée par le représentant étranger relativement à des procédures intentées à l'étranger en vue d'un concordat, d'un atermoiement ou d'un accommodement visant un débiteur ou concernant la faillite d'un débiteur, le tribunal peut suspendre les procédures visant le débiteur ou ses biens situés au Canada, aux conditions et pour une période qui sont compatibles avec les redressements prévus aux articles 69 à 69.5 relativement à un débiteur au Canada qui a déposé un avis d'intention ou une proposition ou qui a fait faillite au Canada, selon le cas.

(3) On application by a foreign representative in respect of a debtor, the court may, where it is satisfied that it is necessary for the protection of the debtor's estate or the interests of a creditor or creditors,

(a) appoint an interim receiver of all or any part of the debtor's property in Canada, for such term as the court considers appropriate; and
(b) direct the interim receiver to do all or any of the following:
  (i) take conservatory measures and summarily dispose of property that is perishable or likely to depreciate rapidly in value,
  (ii) take possession of all or part of the debtor's property mentioned in the appointment and exercise such control over the property and over the debtor's business as the court considers appropriate, and
  (iii) take such other action as the court considers appropriate.

(4) Section 47.2 applies, with such modifications as the circumstances require, in respect of an interim receiver appointed under subsection (3).

(5) On application of a foreign representative in respect of a debtor, the court may authorize the examination under oath by the foreign representative of the debtor or of any person in relation to the debtor who, if the debtor were a bankrupt referred to in subsection 163(1), would be a person who could be examined under that subsection.

(3) Sur demande présentée par le représentant étranger à l'égard d'un débiteur, le tribunal peut, s'il est convaincu que la mesure est nécessaire pour protéger l'actif du débiteur ou les intérêts d'un ou de plusieurs créanciers:

(a) nommer, pour la période qu'il estime indiquée, un séquestre intérimaire à tout ou partie des biens du débiteur situés au Canada;
(b) ordonner au séquestre intérimaire:
  (i) de prendre des mesures conservatoires et de disposer sommairement des biens sujets à s'avarier ou susceptibles de dépréciation rapide,
  (ii) de prendre possession de tout ou partie des biens du débiteur mentionnés dans la nomination et d'exercer sur ces biens ainsi que sur les affaires du débiteur le degré de contrôle que le tribunal estime indiqué,
  (iii) de prendre toute autre mesure que le tribunal estime indiquée.

(4) L'article 47.2 s'applique, avec les adaptations nécessaires, au séquestre intérimaire nommé en application du paragraphe (3).

(5) Sur demande présentée par le représentant étranger à l'égard du débiteur, le tribunal peut l'autoriser à interroger sous serment le débiteur ou toute autre personne qui, si le débiteur était le failli mentionné au paragraphe 163(1), pourrait être interrogé au titre de ce paragraphe.

272 An application to the court by a foreign representative under this Part does not submit the foreign representative to the jurisdiction of the court for any other purpose except with regard to the costs of the proceedings, but the court may make any order under this Part conditional on the compliance by the foreign representative with any other order of the court.

272 Le représentant étranger n'est pas soumis à la jurisdiction du tribunal pour le motif qu'il a présenté une demande au titre de la présente partie, sauf en ce qui touche les frais des procédures; le tribunal peut toutefois subordonner l'ordonnance visée à la présente partie à l'observation par le représentant étranger de toute autre ordonnance rendue par lui.

273 A foreign representative is not prevented from making an application to the court under this Part by reason only that proceedings by way of appeal or review have been taken in a foreign proceeding, and the court may, on an application where such proceedings have been taken, grant relief as if the proceedings had not been taken.

273 Le fait que les procédures intentées à l'étranger font l'objet d'un appel ou d'une révision n'a pas pour effet d'empêcher le représentant étranger de présenter la demande visée à la présente partie; malgré ce fait, le tribunal peut, sur demande, accorder des redressements.

274 Where any receiving order, proposal or assignment is made in respect of a debtor under this Act,

(a) the amount that a creditor receives or is entitled to receive outside Canada by way of a dividend in a foreign proceeding in respect of the debtor, and

(b) the value of any property of the debtor that the creditor acquires outside Canada on account of a provable claim of the creditor or that the creditor acquires outside Canada by way of a transfer that, if it were subject to this Act, would be set aside or reviewed under sections 91 to 101.2,

274 Lorsqu'une ordonnance de séquestre est rendue ou qu'une proposition ou une cession est faite au titre de la présente loi à l'égard d'un débiteur, les éléments énumérés ci-après doivent être pris en considération dans la distribution des dividendes aux créanciers d'un débiteur au Canada comme si ces éléments faisaient partie de la distribution:

(a) les sommes qu'un créancier a reçues à l'étranger, à titre de dividende, dans le cadre des procédures intentées à l'étranger contre le débiteur, ou auxquelles il a droit;

(b) la valeur de tout bien du débiteur que le créancier à acquis à l'étranger au titre d'une créance prouvable ou par suite d'un transfert qui, si la présente loi lui était applicable, serait écarté ou révisé en vertu des articles 91 à 101.2.

shall be taken into account in the distribution of dividends to creditors of the debtor in Canada as if they were a part of that distribution, and the creditor is not entitled to receive a dividend from the distribution in Canada until every other creditor who has a claim of equal rank in the order of priority established under this Act has received a dividend, the amount of which is the same percentage of that other creditor's claim as the aggregate of the amount referred to in paragraph (*a*) and the value referred to in paragraph (*b*) is of that creditor's claim.

Un créancier n'a toutefois pas le droit de recevoir un dividende de la distribution faite au Canada tant que les titulaires des créances venant au même rang que la sienne dans l'ordre de collocation prévu par la présente loi n'ont pas reçu un dividende dont le pourcentage d'acquitement est égal au pourcentage d'acquittement des éléments visés aux alinéas *a*) et *b*).

275 A claim for a debt that is payable in a currency other than Canadian currency shall be converted to Canadian currency.

(a) in the case of a proposal in respect of an insolvent person and unless otherwise provided in the proposal, where a notice of intention was filed under subsection 50.4(1), as of the day the notice was filed or, if no notice was filed, as of the day the proposal was filed with the official receiver under subsection 62(1);

(b) in the case of a proposal in respect of a bankrupt and unless otherwise provided in the proposal, as of the date of the bankruptcy; or

(c) in the case of a bankruptcy, as of the date of the bankruptcy.

275 La réclamation visant une créance en devises étrangères doit être convertie en monnaie canadienne au taux en vigueur:

(a) dans le cas d'une proposition visant une personne insolvable et sauf disposition contraire de la proposition, à la date de dépôt de l'avis d'intention au titre du paragraphe 50.4(1) ou, en l'absence d'avis, à la date de dépôt de la proposition auprès du séquestre officiel au titre du paragraphe 62(1);

(b) dans le cas d'une proposition visant un failli et sauf disposition contraire de la proposition, à la date de la faillite;

(c) dans le cas d'une faillite, à la date de la faillite.

Appendix II

European Union Convention on Insolvency Proceedings[1]

Preamble

THE HIGH CONTRACTING PARTIES TO THIS CONVENTION, MEMBER STATES OF THE EUROPEAN UNION,

DESIRING to implement Article 220 of the Treaty establishing the European Community, by virtue of which they undertook to secure the simplification of formalities governing the reciprocal recognition and enforcement of the judgments of courts or tribunals,

ANXIOUS to strengthen in the Community the legal protection of persons therein established,

CONSIDERING that it is necessary for that purpose to determine the jurisdiction of their courts or authorities with regard to the intra-Community effects of insolvency proceedings, to create certain uniform conflict-of-laws rules for such proceedings, to ensure the recognition and enforcement of judgments given in such matters, to make provision for the possibility of opening secondary insolvency proceedings and to guarantee information for creditors and their right to lodge claims,

AWARE that this convention does not affect the application of the provisions of Community law which, in relation to particular matters, lay down rules relating to insolvency proceedings or of national law harmonized in implementation of such Community law,

MEETING WITHIN THE COUNCIL,

HAVE DECIDED AS FOLLOWS:

Chapter I: General Provisions

Article 1 Scope

1. This Convention shall apply to collective insolvency proceedings which entail the partial or total divestment of a debtor and the appointment of a liquidator.

2. This Convention shall not apply to insolvency proceedings concerning insurance undertakings, credit institutions, investment undertakings which provide services involving the holding of funds or securities for third parties, or to collective investment undertakings.

[1] Text as open for signature between 23 November 1995 and 23 May 1996. See Chapter 6, at 6.1 and 6.4 above.

Article 2 Definitions

For the purposes of this Convention:

(a) 'insolvency proceedings' shall mean the collective proceedings referred to in Article 1(1). These proceedings are listed in Annex A, which shall form an integral part of this Convention.

(b) 'liquidator' shall mean any person or body whose function is to administer or liquidate assets of which the debtor has been divested or to supervise the administration of his affairs. Those persons and bodies are listed in Annex C, which shall form an integral part of this Convention.

(c) 'winding-up proceedings' shall mean insolvency proceedings within the meaning of point (a) involving realizing the assets of the debtor, including where the proceedings have been closed by a composition or other measure terminating the insolvency, or closed by reason of the insufficiency of the assets. Those procedures are listed in Annex B, which shall form an integral part of this Convention.

(d) 'court' shall, with the exception of Articles 44 and 45, mean the judicial body or any other competent body of a Contracting State empowered to open insolvency proceedings or to take decisions in the course of such proceedings.

(e) 'judgment' in relation to the opening of insolvency proceedings or the appointment of a liquidator shall include the decision of any court empowered to open such proceedings or to appoint a liquidator.

(f) 'the time of the opening of proceedings' shall mean the time at which the judgment opening proceedings becomes effective, whether it is a final judgment or not.

(g) 'the Contracting State in which assets are situated' shall mean, in the case of:

— tangible property, the Contracting State within the territory of which the property is situated;

— property and rights ownership of or entitlement to which must be entered in a public register, the Contracting State under the authority of which the register is kept;

— claims, the Contracting State within the territory of which the third party required to meet them has the centre of his main interests, as determined in Article 3(1).

(h) 'establishment' shall mean any place of operations where the debtor carries out a non-transitory economic activity with human means and goods.

Article 3 International jurisdiction

1. The courts of the Contracting State within the territory of which the centre of a debtor's main interests is situated shall have jurisdiction to open insolvency proceedings. In the case of a company or legal person, the place of the registered office shall be presumed to be the centre of its main interests in the absence of proof to the contrary.

2. Where the centre of a debtor's main interests is situated within the territory of a Contracting State, the courts of another Contracting State shall have jurisdiction to open insolvency proceedings against that debtor only if he possesses an estab-

lishment within the territory of that other Contracting State. The effects of those proceedings shall be restricted to the assets of the debtor situated in the territory of the latter Contracting State.

3. Where insolvency proceedings have been opened under paragraph 1, any proceedings opened subsequently under paragraph 2 shall be secondary proceedings. These latter proceedings must be winding-up proceedings.

4. Territorial insolvency proceedings referred to in paragraph 2 may be opened prior to the opening of main insolvency proceedings in accordance with paragraph 1 only:

(a) where insolvency proceedings under paragraph 1 cannot be opened because of the conditions laid down by the law of the Contracting State within the territory of which the centre of the debtor's main interests is situated, or

(b) where the opening of territorial insolvency proceedings is requested by a creditor who has his domicile, habitual residence or registered office in the Contracting State within the territory of which the establishment is situated, or whose claim arises from the operation of that establishment.

Article 4 Law applicable

1. Save as otherwise provided in this Convention, the law applicable to insolvency proceedings and their effects shall be that of the Contracting State within the territory of which such proceedings are opened, hereafter referred to as the 'State of the opening of proceedings'.

2. The law of the State of the opening of proceedings shall determine the conditions for the opening of those proceedings, their conduct and their closure. It shall determine in particular:

(a) against which debtors insolvency proceedings may be brought on account of their capacity;

(b) the assets which form part of the estate and the treatment of assets acquired by or devolving on the debtor after the opening of the insolvency proceedings;

(c) the respective powers of the debtor and the liquidator;

(d) the conditions under which set-offs may be invoked;

(e) the effects of insolvency proceedings on current contracts to which the debtor is party;

(f) the effects of the insolvency proceedings on proceedings brought by individual creditors, with the exception of lawsuits pending;

(g) the claims which are to be lodged against the debtor's estate and the treatment of claims arising after the opening of insolvency proceedings;

(h) the rules governing the lodging, verification and admission of claims;

(i) the rules governing the distribution of proceeds from the realization of assets, the ranking of claims and the rights of creditors who have obtained partial satisfaction after the opening of insolvency proceedings by virtue of a right in rem or through a set-off;

(j) the conditions for and the effects of closure of insolvency proceedings, in particular by composition;

(k) creditors' rights after the closure of insolvency proceedings;

(l) who is to bear the costs and expenses incurred in the insolvency proceedings;
(m) the rules relating to the voidness, voidability or unenforceability of legal acts detrimental to all the creditors.

Article 5 Third parties' rights in rem

1. The opening of insolvency proceedings shall not affect the rights in rem of creditors or third parties in respect of tangible or intangible, movable or immovable assets belonging to the debtor which are situated within the territory of another Contracting State at the time of the opening of proceedings.

2. The rights referred to in paragraph 1 shall in particular mean:
(a) the right to dispose of assets or have them disposed of and to obtain satisfaction from the proceeds of or income from those assets, in particular by virtue of a lien or a mortgage;
(b) the exclusive right to have a claim met, in particular a right guaranteed by a lien in respect of the claim or by assignment of the claim by way of a guarantee;
(c) the right to demand the assets from, and/or to require restitution by, anyone having possession or use of them contrary to the wishes of the party so entitled;
(d) a right in rem to the beneficial use of assets.

3. The right, recorded in a public register and enforceable against third parties, under which a right in rem within the meaning of paragraph 1 may be obtained, shall be considered a right in rem.

4. Paragraph 1 shall not preclude the actions for voidness, voidability or unenforceability laid down in Article 4(2)(m).

Article 6 Set-off

1. The opening of insolvency proceedings shall not affect the right of creditors to demand the set-off of their claims against the claims of the debtor, where such a set-off is permitted by the law applicable to the insolvent debtor's claim.

2. Paragraph 1 shall not preclude the actions for voidness, voidability or unenforceability laid down in Article 4(2)(m).

Article 7 Reservation of title

1. The opening of insolvency proceedings against the purchaser of an asset shall not affect the seller's rights based on a reservation of title where at the time of the opening of proceedings the asset is situated within the territory of a Contracting State other than the State in which the proceedings were opened.

2. The opening of insolvency proceedings against the seller of an asset, after delivery of the asset, shall not constitute grounds for rescinding or terminating the sale and shall not prevent the purchaser from acquiring title where at the time of the opening of proceedings the asset sold is situated within the territory of a Contracting State other than the State of the opening of proceedings.

3. Paragraphs 1 and 2 shall not preclude the actions for voidness, voidability or unenforceability laid down in Article 4(2)(m).

Article 8 Contracts relating to immovable property

The effects of insolvency proceedings on a contract conferring the right to acquire or make use of immovable property shall be governed solely by the law of the Contracting State within the territory of which the immovable property is situated.

Article 9 Payment systems and financial markets

1. Without prejudice to Article 5, the effects of insolvency proceedings on the rights and obligations of the parties to a payment or settlement system or to a financial market shall be governed solely by the law of the Contracting State applicable to that system or market.

2. Paragraph 1 shall not preclude any action for voidness, voidability or unenforceability which may be taken to set aside payments or transactions under the law applicable to the relevant payment system or financial market.

Article 10 Contracts of employment

The effects of insolvency proceedings on employment contracts and relationships shall be governed solely by the law of the Contracting State applicable to the contract of employment.

Article 11 Effects on rights subject to registration

The effects of insolvency proceedings on the rights of the debtor in immovable property, a ship or an aircraft subject to registration in a public register shall be determined by the law of the Contracting State under the authority of which the register is kept.

Article 12 Community patents and trade marks

For the purposes of this Convention, a Community patent, a Community trade mark or any other similar right established by Community law may be included only in the proceedings referred to in Article 3(1).

Article 13 Detrimental acts

Article 4(2)(m) shall not apply where the person who benefited from a legal act detrimental to all the creditors provides proof that:

— the said act is subject to the law of a Contracting State other than that of the State of the opening of proceedings, and
— that law does not allow any means of challenging that act in the relevant case.

Article 14 Protection of third-party purchasers

Where, by an act concluded after the opening of insolvency proceedings, the debtor disposes, for consideration, of:

— an immovable asset or
— a ship or an aircraft subject to registration in a public register or
— securities whose existence presupposes registration in a register laid down by law,

the validity of that act shall be governed by the law of the State within the territory of which the immovable asset is situated or under the authority of which the register is kept.

Article 15 Effects of insolvency proceedings on lawsuits pending

The effects of insolvency proceedings on a lawsuit pending concerning an asset or a right of which the debtor has been divested shall be governed solely by the law of the Contracting State in which that lawsuit is pending.

Chapter II: Recognition of Insolvency proceedings

Article 16 Principle

1. Any judgment opening insolvency proceedings handed down by a court of a Contracting State which has jurisdiction pursuant to Article 3 shall be recognized in all the other Contracting States from the time that it becomes effective in the State of the opening of proceedings.

This rule shall also apply where, on account of his capacity, insolvency proceedings cannot be brought against the debtor in other Contracting States.

2. Recognition of the proceedings referred to in Article 3(1) shall not preclude the opening of the proceedings referred to in Article 3(2) by a court in another Contracting State. The latter proceedings shall be secondary proceedings within the meaning of Chapter III.

Article 17 Effects of recognition

1. The judgment opening the proceedings referred to in Article 3(1) shall, with no further formalities, produce the same effects in any other Contracting State as under the law of the State of the opening of proceedings, unless the Convention provides otherwise and as long as no proceedings referred to in Article 3(2) are opened in that other Contracting State.

2. The effects of the proceedings referred to in Article 3(2) may not be challenged in other Contracting States. Any restriction of the creditors' rights, in particular a stay or discharge, shall produce effects vis-à-vis assets situated within the territory of another Contracting State only in the case of those creditors who have given their consent.

Article 18 Powers of the liquidator

1. The liquidator appointed by a court which has jurisdiction pursuant to Article 3(1) may exercise all the powers conferred on him by the law of the State of the opening of proceedings in another Contracting State, as long as no other insolvency proceedings have been opened there nor any preservation measure to the contrary has been taken there further to a request for the opening of insolvency proceedings in that State. He may in particular remove the debtor's assets from the territory of the Contracting State in which they are situated, subject to Articles 5 and 7.

2. The liquidator appointed by a court which has jurisdiction pursuant to Article 3(2) may in any other Contracting State claim through the courts or out of court

that movable property was removed from the territory of the State of the opening of proceedings to the territory of that other Contracting State after the opening of the insolvency proceedings. He may also bring any action to set aside which is in the interests of the creditors.

3. In exercising his powers, the liquidator shall comply with the law of the Contracting State within the territory of which he intends to take action, in particular with regard to procedures for the realization of assets. Those powers may not include coercive measures or the right to rule on legal proceedings or disputes.

Article 19 Proof of the liquidator's appointment

The liquidator's appointment shall be evidenced by a certified copy of the original decision appointing him or by any other certificate issued by the court which has jurisdiction.

A translation into the official language or one of the official languages of the Contracting State within the territory of which he intends to act may be required. No legalization or other similar formality shall be required.

Article 20 Return and imputation

1. A creditor who, after the opening of the proceedings referred to in Article 3(1) obtains by any means, in particular through enforcement, total or partial satisfaction of his claim on the assets belonging to the debtor situated within the territory of another Contracting State, shall return what he has obtained to the liquidator, subject to Articles 5 and 7.

2. In order to ensure equal treatment of creditors a creditor who has, in the course of insolvency proceedings, obtained a dividend on his claim shall share in distributions made in other proceedings only where creditors of the same ranking or category have, in those other proceedings, obtained an equivalent dividend.

Article 21 Publication

1. The liquidator may request that notice of the judgment opening insolvency proceedings and, where appropriate, the decision appointing him be published in any other Contracting State in accordance with the publication procedures provided for in that State. Such publication shall also specify the liquidator appointed and whether the jurisdiction rule applied is that pursuant to Article 3(1) or Article 3(2).

2. However, any Contracting State within the territory of which the debtor has an establishment may require mandatory publication. In such cases, the liquidator or any authority empowered to that effect in the Contracting State where the proceedings referred to in Article 3(1) are opened shall take all necessary measures to ensure such publication.

Article 22 Registration in a public register

1. The liquidator may request that the judgment opening the proceedings referred to in Article 3(1) be registered in the land register, the trade register and any other public register kept in the other Contracting States.

2. However, any Contracting State may require mandatory registration. In such cases, the liquidator or any authority empowered to that effect in the Contracting

State where the proceedings referred to in Article 3(1) have been opened shall take all necessary measures to ensure such registration.

Article 23 Costs

The costs of the publication and registration provided for in Articles 21 and 22 shall be regarded as costs and expenses incurred in the proceedings.

Article 24 Honouring of an obligation to a debtor

1. Where an obligation has been honoured in a Contracting State for the benefit of a debtor who is subject to insolvency proceedings opened in another Contracting State, when it should have been honoured for the benefit of the liquidator in those proceedings, the person honouring the obligation shall be deemed to have discharged it if he was unaware of the opening of proceedings.

2. Where such an obligation is honoured before the publication provided for in Article 21 has been effected, the person honouring the obligation shall be presumed, in the absence of proof to the contrary, to have been unaware of the opening of insolvency proceedings; where the obligation is honoured after such publication has been effected, the person honouring the obligation shall be presumed, in the absence of proof to the contrary, to have been aware of the opening of proceedings.

Article 25 Recognition and enforceability of other judgments

1. Judgments handed down by a court whose judgment concerning the opening of proceedings is recognized in accordance with Article 16 and which concern the course and closure of insolvency proceedings, and compositions approved by that court shall also be recognized with no further formalities. Such judgments shall be enforced in accordance with Articles 31 to 51 of the Convention on Jurisdiction and the Enforcement of Judgments in Civil and Commercial Matters, with the exception of Article 34(2).

The first subparagraph shall also apply to judgments deriving directly from the insolvency proceedings and which are closely linked with them, even if they were handed down by another court.

The first subparagraph shall also apply to judgments relating to preservation measures taken after the request for the opening of insolvency proceedings.

2. The recognition and enforcement of judgments other than those referred to in paragraph 1 shall be governed by the Convention referred to in paragraph 1, provided that that Convention is applicable.

3. The Contracting States shall not be obliged to recognize or enforce a judgment referred to in paragraph 1 which might result in a limitation of personal freedom or postal secrecy.

Article 26 Public policy

Any Contracting State may refuse to recognize insolvency proceedings opened in another Contracting State or to enforce a judgment handed down in the context of such proceedings where the effects of such recognition or enforcement would be manifestly contrary to that State's public policy, in particular its fundamental principles or the constitutional rights and liberties of the individual.

Chapter III: Secondary Insolvency Proceedings

Article 27 Opening of proceedings

The opening of the proceedings referred to in Article 3(1) by a court of a Contracting State and which is recognized in another Contracting State (main proceedings) shall permit the opening, in that other Contracting State a court of which has jurisdiction pursuant to Article 3(2), of secondary insolvency proceedings without the debtor's insolvency being examined in that other State. These latter proceedings must be among the proceedings listed in Annex B. Their effects shall be restricted to the assets of the debtor situated within the territory of that other Contracting State.

Article 28 Applicable law

Save as otherwise provided in this Convention, the law applicable to secondary proceedings shall be that of the Contracting State within the territory of which the secondary proceedings are opened.

Article 29 Right to request the opening of proceedings

The opening of secondary proceedings may be requested by:

(a) the liquidator in the main proceedings;

(b) any other person or authority empowered to request the opening of insolvency proceedings under the law of the Contracting State within the territory of which the opening of secondary proceedings is requested.

Article 30 Advance payment of costs and expenses

Where the law of the Contracting State in which the opening of secondary proceedings is requested requires that the debtor's assets be sufficient to cover in whole or in part the costs and expenses of the proceedings, the court may, when it receives such a request, require the applicant to make an advance payment of costs or to provide appropriate security.

Article 31 Duty to cooperate and communicate information

1. Subject to the rules restricting the communication of information, the liquidator in the main proceedings and the liquidators in the secondary proceedings shall be duty bound to communicate information to each other. They shall immediately communicate any information which may be relevant to the other proceedings, in particular the progress made in lodging and verifying claims and all measures aimed at terminating the proceedings.

2. Subject to the rules applicable to each of the proceedings, the liquidator in the main proceedings and the liquidators in the secondary proceedings shall be duty bound to cooperate with each other.

3. The liquidator in secondary proceedings shall give the liquidator in the main proceedings an early opportunity of submitting proposals on the liquidation or use of the assets in the secondary proceedings.

Article 32 Exercise of creditors' rights

1. Any creditor may lodge his claim in the main proceedings and in any secondary proceedings.

2. The liquidators in the main and any secondary proceedings shall lodge in other proceedings claims which have already been lodged in the proceedings for which they were appointed, provided that the interests of creditors in the latter proceedings are served thereby, subject to the right of creditors to oppose that or to withdraw the lodgement of their claims where the law applicable so provides.

3. The liquidator in the main or secondary proceedings shall be empowered to participate in other proceedings on the same basis as a creditor, in particular by attending creditors' meetings.

Article 33 Stay of liquidation

1. The court, which opened the secondary proceedings, shall stay the process of liquidation in whole or in part on receipt of a request from the liquidator in the main proceedings, provided that in that event it may require the liquidator in the main proceedings to take any suitable measure to guarantee the interests of the creditors in the secondary proceedings and of individual classes of creditors. Such a request from the liquidator may be rejected only if it is manifestly of no interest to the creditors in the main proceedings. Such a stay of the process of liquidation may be ordered for up to three months. It may be continued or renewed for similar periods.

2. The court referred to in paragraph 1 shall terminate the stay of the process of liquidation:

— at the request of the liquidator in the main proceedings;

— of its own motion, at the request of a creditor or at the request of the liquidator in the secondary proceedings if that measure no longer appears justified, in particular, by the interests of creditors in the main proceedings or in the secondary proceedings.

Article 34 Measures ending secondary insolvency proceedings

1. Where the law applicable to secondary proceedings allows for such proceedings to be closed without liquidation by a rescue plan, a composition or a comparable measure, the liquidator in the main proceedings shall be empowered to propose such a measure himself.

Closure of the secondary proceedings by a measure referred to in the first subparagraph shall not become final without the consent of the liquidator in the main proceedings; failing his agreement, however, it may become final if the financial interests of the creditors in the main proceedings are not affected by the measure proposed.

2. Any restriction of creditors' rights arising from a measure referred to in paragraph 1 which is proposed in secondary proceedings, such as a stay of payment or discharge of debt, may not have effect in respect of the debtor's assets not covered by those proceedings without the consent of all the creditors having an interest.

3. During a stay of the process of liquidation ordered pursuant to Article 33, only the liquidator in the main proceedings or the debtor, with the former's consent, may propose measures laid down in paragraph 1 of this Article in the secondary

proceedings; no other proposal for such a measure shall be put to the vote or approved.

Article 35 Assets remaining in the secondary proceedings

If by the liquidation of assets in the secondary proceedings it is possible to meet all claims allowed under those proceedings, the liquidator appointed in those proceedings shall immediately transfer any assets remaining to the liquidator in the main proceedings.

Article 36 Subsequent opening of the main proceedings

Where the proceedings referred to in Article 3(1) are opened following the opening of the proceedings referred to in Article 3(2) in another Contracting State, Articles 31 to 35 shall apply to those opened first, in so far as the progress of those proceedings so permits.

Article 37 Conversion of earlier proceedings

The liquidator in the main proceedings may request that proceedings listed in Annex A previously opened in another Contracting State be converted into winding-up proceedings if this proves to be in the interests of the creditors in the main proceedings.

The court with jurisdiction under Article 3(2) shall order conversion into one of the proceedings listed in Annex B.

Article 38 Preservation measures

Where the court of a Contracting State which has jurisdiction pursuant to Article 3(1) appoints a temporary administrator in order to ensure the preservation of the debtor's assets, that temporary administrator shall be empowered to request any measures to secure and preserve any of the debtor's assets situated in another Contracting State, provided for under the law of that State, for the period between the request for the opening of insolvency proceedings and the judgment opening the proceedings.

Chapter IV: Provision of Information for Creditors and Lodgement of their Claims

Article 39 Right to lodge claims

Any creditor who has his habitual residence, domicile or registered office in a Contracting State other than the State of the opening of proceedings, including the tax authorities and social security authorities of Contracting States, shall have the right to lodge claims in the insolvency proceedings in writing.

Article 40 Duty to inform creditors

1. As soon as insolvency proceedings are opened in a Contracting State, the court of that State having jurisdiction or the liquidator appointed by it shall immediately inform known creditors who have their habitual residences, domiciles or registered offices in the other Contracting States.

2. That information, provided by an individual notice, shall in particular include time limits, the penalties laid down in regard to those time limits, the body or authority empowered to accept the lodgement of claims and the other measures laid down. Such notice shall also indicate whether creditors whose claims are preferential or secured in rem need lodge their claims.

Article 41 Content of the lodgement of a claim

A creditor shall send copies of supporting documents, if any, and shall indicate the nature of the claim, the date on which it arose and its amount, as well as whether he alleges preference, security in rem or a reservation of title in respect of the claim and what assets are covered by the guarantee he is invoking.

Article 42 Languages

1. The information provided for in Article 40 shall be provided in the official language or one of the official languages of the State of the opening of proceedings. For that purpose a form shall be used bearing the heading 'Invitation to lodge a claim. Time limits to be observed' in all the official languages of the European Union.

2. Any creditor who has his habitual residence, domicile or registered office in a Contracting State other than the State of the opening of proceedings may lodge his claim in the official language or one of the official languages of that other State. In that event, however, the lodgement of his claim shall bear the heading 'Lodgement of claim' in the official language or one of the official languages of the State of the opening of proceedings. In addition, he may be required to provide a translation, into that language, of the lodgement of claim.

Chapter V: Interpretation by the Court of Justice

Article 43 Jurisdiction of the Court of Justice

1. The Court of Justice of the European Communities shall have jurisdiction to give rulings on the interpretation of this Convention, including the Annexes thereto, and the Conventions on accession to this Convention by the States which become Members of the European Union after the date on which this Convention is closed for signature.

2. The Protocol on the Statute of the Court of Justice and the Rules of Procedure of the Court of Justice shall apply.

3. The Rules of Procedure of the Court of Justice shall, if necessary, be adjusted and supplemented in accordance with Article 188 of the Treaty establishing the European Community.

Article 44 Preliminary ruling proceedings

The following courts may request the Court of Justice to give a preliminary ruling on a question raised in a case pending before it and concerning interpretation of the provisions of the instruments referred to in Article 43(1) if that court considers that a decision on the question is necessary to enable it to give judgment:

(a) — in Belgium:

la Cour de Cassation/het Hof van Cassatie and le Conseil d'Etat/de Raad van State;

— in Denmark:
Højesteret;
— in the Federal Republic of Germany:
die obersten Gerichtshöfe des Bundes;
— in Greece:
'Αρειος Πάγος και Συμβούλιο της Επικρατείας;
— in Spain:
el Tribunal Supremo;
— in France:
la Cour de Cassation and le Conseil d'Etat;
— in Ireland:
the Supreme Court;
— in Italy:
la Corte suprema di cassazione and il Consiglio di Stato;
— in Luxembourg:
la Court Supérieure de Justice, when sitting as Cour de Cassation;
— in Austria:
= der Oberste Gerichtshof
= der Verfassungsgerichtshof
= der Verwaltungsgerichtshof;
— in the Netherlands:
de Hoge Raad;
— in Portugal:
o Supremo Tribunal de Justiça;
— in Finland:
Korkein oikeus/Högsta domstolen;
— in Sweden:
Högsta domstolen;
— in the United Kingdom:
the House of Lords and other courts from which no further appeal is possible;

(b) the courts of the Contracting States when acting as appeal courts.

Article 45 Proceedings brought by a competent authority

1. The competent authority of a Contracting State may request the Court of Justice to give a ruling on a question of interpretation of the instruments referred to in Article 43(1) if judgments given by courts of that State conflict with the interpretation given either by the Court of Justice or in a judgment of one of the courts of another Contracting State referred to in Article 44. The provisions of this paragraph shall apply only to judgments which have become *res judicata*.

2. The interpretation given by the Court of Justice in response to such a request shall not affect the judgments which gave rise to the request for interpretation.

3. The Procurators-General of the Supreme Courts of Appeal of the Contracting States, or any other authority designated by a Contracting State, shall be entitled

to ask the Court of Justice to give a ruling on interpretation in accordance with paragraph 1.

4. The Registrar of the Court of Justice shall give notice of the request to the Contracting States, to the Commission and to the Council of the European Union; they shall then be entitled within two months of the notification to submit statements of case or written observations to the Court.

5. No fees shall be levied nor any costs or expenses awarded in respect of the proceedings provided for in this Article.

Article 46 Reservations

1. Any signatory State which is unable to apply Article 44 for constitutional reasons may enter a reservation on that Article at the time of signing this Convention.

2. Any signatory State which has entered a reservation pursuant to paragraph 1 may withdraw all or part of that reservation by notifying the depositary.

Withdrawal shall take effect from the date on which the depositary receives the notification.

Chapter VI: Transitional and Final Provisions

Article 47 Applicability in time

The provisions of this Convention shall apply only to insolvency proceedings opened after its entry into force. Acts done by a debtor before the entry into force of this Convention shall continue to be governed by the law which was applicable to them at the time they were done.

Article 48 Relationship to other Conventions

1. When this Convention applies, it shall, in respect of the matters referred to therein, supersede, as between the States which are party to it, the following Conventions concluded between two or more of those States:

— the Convention between Belgium and France on Jurisdiction an the Validity and Enforcement of Judgments, Arbitration Awards and Authentic Instruments, signed at Paris on 8 July 1899;

— the Convention between Belgium and Austria on Bankruptcy, Winding-up, Arrangements, Compositions and Suspension of Payments (with Additional Protocol of 13 June 1973), signed at Brussels on 16 July 1969;

— the Convention between Belgium and the Netherlands on Territorial Jurisdiction, Bankruptcy and the Validity and Enforcement of Judgments, Arbitration Awards and Authentic Instruments, signed at Brussels on 28 March 1925;

— the Treaty between Germany and Austria on Bankruptcy, Winding-up, Arrangements and Compositions, signed at Vienna on 25 May 1979;

— the Convention between France and Austria on Jurisdiction, Recognition and Enforcement of Judgments on Bankruptcy, signed at Vienna on 27 February 1979;

— the Convention between France and Italy on the Enforcement of Judgments in Civil and Commercial Matters, signed at Rome on 3 June 1930;

— the Convention between Italy and Austria on Bankruptcy, Winding-up, Arrangements and Compositions, signed at Rome on 12 July 1977;
— the Convention between the Kingdom of the Netherlands and the Federal Republic of Germany on the Mutual Recognition and Enforcement of Judgments and other Enforceable Instruments in Civil and Commercial Matters, signed at The Hague on 30 August 1962;
— the Convention between the United Kingdom and the Kingdom of Belgium providing for the reciprocal enforcement of judgments in civil and commercial matters, with Protocol, signed at Brussels on 2 May 1934;
— the Convention between Denmark, Finland, Norway, Sweden and Iceland on Bankruptcy, signed at Copenhagen on 11 November 1933;
— the European Convention on Certain International Aspects of Bankruptcy, signed at Istanbul on 5 June 1990.

2. The Conventions referred to in paragraph 1 shall continue to have effect with regard to proceedings opened before the entry into force of this Convention.

3. This Convention shall not apply:
— in any Contracting State, to the extent that it is irreconcilable with the obligations arising in relation to bankruptcy from another convention concluded by that State with one or more non-contracting States before the entry into force of this Convention,
— in the United Kingdom of Great Britain and Northern Ireland, to the extent that it is irreconcilable with the obligations arising in relation to bankruptcy and the winding-up of insolvent companies from any arrangements with the Commonwealth existing at the time this Convention enters into force.

Article 49 Signature, ratification and entry into force

1. The Secretary-General of the Council of the European Union shall be the depositary of this Convention.

2. This Convention shall be open from 23 November 1995 up to and including 23 May 1996 for signature by the Member States of the European Union.

3. This Convention shall not enter into force until it has been ratified, accepted or approved by all the Member States of the European Union as constituted on the date on which this Convention is closed for signature. It shall enter into force on the first day of the sixth month following that of the deposit of the instrument of ratification, acceptance or approval by the last Member State of the European Union to take that step.

4. The instruments of ratification, acceptance or approval shall be deposited with the depositary.

Article 50 Accession to the Convention

1. The Contracting States recognize that any State which becomes a member of the European Union shall be required to accept this Convention as a basis for the negotiations between the Contracting States and that State necessary to ensure the implementation of the last indent of Article 220 of the Treaty establishing the European Community in relations between the Contracting States and that State.

2. The necessary adjustments may be the subject of a special Convention between the Contracting States and the new Member State.

Article 51 Notification by the Depositary

The depositary shall notify the signatory States of:

(a) the deposit of each instrument of ratification, acceptance or approval;

(b) the date of entry into force of this Convention;

(c) any other act, notification or communication relating to this Convention.

Article 52 Duration of the Convention

This Convention is concluded for an unlimited period.

Article 53 Revision or evaluation of the Convention

Any Contracting State may request the holding of a conference for the revision or evaluation of this Convention. In that event, the President of the Council of the European Union shall convene the conference.

If, within ten years of the entry into force of this Convention, no Contracting State has requested the holding of a conference for the evaluation of the Convention, such a conference shall be convened at the initiative of the Council of the European Union.

Article 54 Amendment of the Annexes

The Contracting States may at any time address to the depositary a declaration containing any amendment it wishes to make to the Annexes.

The depositary shall notify the signatory States and the Contracting States of the content of any such declaration. The desired amendment shall be deemed accepted if none of the States thus notified raises objections within three months of the date of notification. The amendment shall enter into force on the first day of the following month.

Article 55 Deposit of the Convention

This Convention, drawn up in a single original in the Danish, Dutch, English, Finnish, French, German, Greek, Irish, Italian, Portuguese, Spanish and Swedish languages, all twelve texts being equally authentic, shall be deposited in the archives of the General Secretariat of the Council of the European Union.

The depositary shall transmit a certified copy to the Government of each signatory State.

In witness whereof, the undersigned Plenipotentiaries have hereunto set their hands.

Annex A

Belgique/België

— La faillite/Het faillissement

— Concordat judiciaire/Het gerechtelijk akkoord

Danmark

— Konkurs

— Tvangsakkord
— Betalingsstandsning
— Insolvensbehandling

Deutschland
— Das Konkursverfahren
— Das gerichtliche Vergleichsverfahren
— Das Gesamtvollstreckungsverfahren
— Das Insolvenzverfahren

ΕΛΛΑΣ
— Πτώχευση
— Η ειδική εκκαθάριση
— Η προσωρινή διαχείριση εταιρίας. Η διοίκηση και η διαχείριση των πιστωτών
— Η υπαγωγή επιχείρησης υπό επίτροπο με σκοπό τη σύναψη συμβιβασμού με τους πιστωτές

España
— Concurso de acreedores
— Quiebra
— Suspensión de pagos

France
— Liquidation judiciaire
— Redressement judiciaire avec nomination d'un administrateur

Eire/Ireland
— Foirceannadh éigeantach/Compulsory winding-up
— Féimheacht/Bankruptcy
— Eastát daoine a d'éag agus iad dócmhainneach a riaradh i bhféimheacht/The administration in bankruptcy of the estate of persons dying insolvent
— Foirceannadh comhpháirtíochta i bhféimheacht/Winding-up in bankruptcy of partnerships
— Foirceannadh deonach creidiúnaithe (le deimhniú Cúirte)/Creditors' voluntary winding-up (with confirmation of a Court)
— Socruithe faoi rialú na Cúirte, lena ngabhann dílsiú mhaoin an fhéichiúnaí go hiomlán nó go páirteach don Sannaí Oifigiúil lena réadú agus lena himdháileadh/Arrangements under the control of the Court, which involve the vesting of all or part of the property of the debtor in the Official Assignee for realisation and distribution
— Scrúdaitheoireacht chuideachta/Company examinership

Italia
— Fallimento
— Concordato preventivo
— Liquidazione coatta amministrativa
— Amministrazione straordinaria
— Amministrazione controllata

Luxembourg
— Faillite
— Gestion contrôlée
— Concordat préventif de faillite (par abandon d'actif)
— Régime spécial de liquidation du notariat

Nederland
— Het faillissement
— De surséance van betaling

Österreich
— das Konkursverfahren
— das Ausgleichsverfahren
— das Vorverfahren

Portugal
— O processo de falência
— Os processos especiais de recuperação de empresa, ou seja:
 = A concordata
 = O acordo de credores
 = A reestruturação financeira
 = A gestáo controlada

Suomi/Finland
— konkurssi/konkurs
— yrityssaneeraus/företagssanering

Sverige
— Konkurs
— Offentligt ackord
— Företagsrekonstruktion

United Kingdom
— Winding-up by the Court (Compulsory Winding-up)
— Bankruptcy (England and Wales, Northern Ireland)
— Administration of the insolvent estate of a deceased person (England and Wales, Northern Ireland)
— Administration by a Judicial Factor of the insolvent estate of a deceased person (Scotland)
— Sequestration (Scotland)
— Creditors' Voluntary winding-up (with confirmation by the Court)
— Administration
— Voluntary Arrangements under the Insolvency Act 1986 or the Insolvent Partnerships Order 1994

Annex B

Belgique/België
— La faillite/Het faillissement

Danmark
— Konkurs
— Likvidationsakkord
— Insolvensbehandling

Deutschland
— Das Konkursverfahren
— Das Gesamtvollstreckungsverfahren
— Das Insolvenzverfahren

ΕΛΛΑΣ
— Πτώχευση
— Η ειδική εκκαθάριση

España
— Concurso de acreedores
— Quiebra
— Suspension de pagos basada en la insolvencia definitiva

France
— Liquidation judiciaire

Eire/Ireland
— Foirceannadh éigeantach/Compulsory winding-up
— Féimheacht/Bankruptcy
— Eastát daoine a d'éag agus iad dócmhainneach a riaradh i bhféimheacht/The administration in bankruptcy of the estate of persons dying insolvent
— Foirceannadh comhpháirtíochta i bhféimheacht/Winding-up in bankruptcy of partnerships
— Socruithe faoi rialú na Cúirte, lena ngabhann dílsiú mhaoin an fhéichiúnaí go hiomlán nó go páirteach don Sannaí Oifigiúil lena réadú agus lena himdháileadh/Arrangements under the control of the Court, which involve the vesting of all or part of the property of the debtor in the Official Assignee for realisation and distribution

Italia
— Fallimento
— Liquidazione coatta amministrativa

Luxembourg
— Faillite
— Régime spécial de liquidation du notariat

Nederland
— Het faillissement

Österreich
— das Konkursverfahren

Portugal
— O processo de falência

Suomi/Finland
— konkurssi/konkurs

Sverige
— Konkurs

United Kingdom
— Winding-up by the Court (Compulsory Winding-up)
— Bankruptcy (England and Wales, Northern Ireland)
— Administration of the insolvent estate of a deceased person (England and Wales, Northern Ireland)
— Administration by a Judicial Factor of the insolvent estate of a deceased person (Scotland)
— Sequestration (Scotland)

Annex C

Belgique/België
— Le curateur/De curator
— Le juge délégué/De rechter-commissaris

Danmark
— Kurator
— Midlertidig bestyrer
— Skifteretten
— Tilsyn
— Bobestyrer

Deutschland
— Konkursverwalter
— Vergleichsverwalter
— Sachwalter (nach der Vergleichsordnung)
— Verwalter
— Insolvenzverwalter
— Sachwalter (nach der Insolvenzordnung)
— Treuhänder

ΕΛΛΑΣ
— Σύνδικος
— Ο προσωρινός διαχειριστής. Η διοικούσα επιτροπή των πιστωτών
— Ο ειδικός εκκαθαριστής
— Ο επίτροπος

España
— Depositario-administrador
— Interventor o Interventores
— Síndicos
— Comisario

France
— Représentant des créanciers
— Mandataire liquidateur
— Administrateur judiciaire
— Commissaire à l'exécution de plan

Eire/Ireland
— Leachtaitheoir/Liquidator
— Sannaí Oifigiúil/Official Assignee
— Iontaobhaí i bhféimheacht/Trustee in bankruptcy
— Leachtaitheoir Sealadach/Provisional Liquidator
— Scrúdaitheoir/Examiner

Italia
— Curatore
— Commissario

Luxembourg
— Le curateur
— Le commissaire
— Le liquidateur
— Le conseil de gérance de la section d'assainissement du notariat

Nederland
— De curator in het faillissement
— De bewindvoerder in de surséance van betaling

Österreich
— Masseverwalter
— Ausgleichsverwalter
— Sachwalter
— Treuhänder
— Besonderer Verwalter
— Vorläufiger Verwalter
— das Konkursgericht

Portugal
— Gestor judicial
— Liquidatário judicial
— Comissáo de credores

Suomi/Finland
— pesänhoitaja/boförvaltare
— selvttäjä/utredare

Sverige
— Förvaltare
— God man
— Rekonstruktör

United Kingdom

- — Liquidator (England and Wales, Scotland, Northern Ireland)
- — Interim liquidator (Scotland)
- — Official Receiver (England and Wales, Northern Ireland)
- — Administrator (England and Wales, Scotland, Northern Ireland)
- — Trustee (England and Wales, Scotland, Northern Ireland)
- — Interim and Permanent Trustee in Sequestration (Scotland)
- — Judicial Factor (Scotland)
- — Supervisor of a voluntary arrangement

Appendix III

Council of Europe: Convention on Certain International Aspects of Bankruptcy[1]

Preamble

The member States of the Council of Europe, signatories hereto,

CONSIDERING that the aim of the Council of Europe is to achieve a greater unity between its members;

CONSIDERING that bankruptcy proceedings and similar proceedings more and more frequently concern persons who exercise activities outside the national territory;

CONSIDERING that it is necessary to guarantee a minimum of legal co-operation by dealing with certain international aspects of bankruptcy such as the power of administrators and liquidators in bankruptcy to act outside the national territory, the possibility of resorting to the opening of secondary bankruptcies in the territory of other Parties and the possibility for creditors to lodge their claims in the bankruptcies opened abroad,

HAVE AGREED AS FOLLOWS:

Chapter I: General Provisions

Article 1 Scope of the Convention

1. This Convention shall apply to collective insolvency proceedings which

Préambule

Les Etats membres du Conseil de l'Europe, signataires de la présente Convention,

CONSIDÉRANT que le but du Conseil de l'Europe est de réaliser une union plus étroite entre ses membres;

CONSIDÉRANT que les procédures de faillite et les procédures analogues concernent de plus en plus fréquemment des personnes qui exercent des activités en dehors du territoire national;

CONSIDÉRANT qu'il est nécessaire de garantir un minimum de coopération juridique en réglant certains aspects internationaux de la faillite, tels que le pouvoir des administrateurs et des syndics de faillite d'agir en dehors du territoire national, la possibilité de recourir à l'ouverture de faillites secondaires sur le territoire d'autres Parties et la possibilité pour les créanciers de produire leurs créances dans des faillites ouvertes à l'étranger,

SONT CONVENUS DE CE QUI SUIT:

Chapitre I: Dispositions générales

Article 1 Champ d'application de la Convention

1. La présente Convention s'applique aux procédures collectives fondées sur

[1] Signed at Istanbul, 5 June 1990.

entail a disinvestment of the debtor and the appointment of a liquidator and which may entail the liquidation of the assets.

Such proceedings, hereafter referred to as 'bankruptcy', are listed in Appendix A which is an integral part of this Convention.

Appendix A shall contain proceedings of the member States of the Council of Europe as well as of any State acceding to the Convention under the terms of Article 35.

This Convention shall not apply to proceedings relating to insurance companies or credit institutions.

2. When a bankruptcy is opened in a Party, this Convention shall govern:

a. the exercise in other Parties of certain powers of the liquidator concerning the administration of the debtor's assets;

b. the opening of secondary bankruptcies in other Parties;

c. the information to be given to creditors residing in other Parties and the lodgement of their claims.

3. For the purposes of this Convention:

a. 'liquidator' means any person or body whose function is to administer or liquidate the assets of the bankrupt or to supervise the activities of the debtor.
These persons and bodies are listed in Appendix B, which is an integral part of this Convention;

b. 'disinvestment of the debtor' means the placing of power to manage, control and dispose of the assets in the hands of a liquidator.

l'insolvabilité, qui entraînent un dessaisissement du débiteur et la désignation d'un syndic, et qui sont susceptibles d'entraîner la liquidation des biens.

De telles procédures, ci-après dénommées «faillite», sont énoncées à l'annexe A, qui fait partie intégrante de la présente Convention.

Figureront dans l'annexe A des procédures des Etats membres du Conseil de l'Europe ainsi que de tout Etat adhérent à la Convention conformément à l'article 35.

La présente Convention ne s'applique pas aux procédures relatives aux entreprises d'assurances et aux établissements de crédit.

2. Losqu'une faillite est ouverte dans une Partie, la présente Convention régit:

a. l'exercice dans d'autres Parties de certains pouvoirs du syndic relatifs à l'administration du patrimoine du débiteur;

b. l'ouverture de faillites secondaires dans d'autres Parties;

c. l'information à fournir aux créanciers résidant dans d'autres Parties et la production de leurs créances.

3. Aux fins de la présente Convention:

a. 'syndic' désigne toute personne ou tout organe dont la fonction est d'administrer ou de liquider le patrimoine du failli ou de surveiller la gestion des affaires du débiteur.
Ces personnes et organes sont énumérés à l'annexe B, qui fait partie intégrante de la présente Convention;

b. 'dessaisissement du débiteur' désigne le transfert à un syndic des pouvoirs d'administrer, de contrôler et de disposer du patrimoine.

Article 2 Proof of the appointment of the liquidator

The appointment of the liquidator shall be evidenced by a certified copy of the original decision appointing him or by an official certificate of appointment issued by the court or any other competent authority which has opened the bankruptcy. A translation in the official language or one of the official languages of the Party where the liquidator exercises his powers may be required. No legislation or other similar formality shall be required.

Article 2 Preuve de la nomination du syndic

La preuve de la nomination du syndic est donnée par la présentation d'une copie, certifiée conforme à l'original, de la décision qui le nomme ou d'un certificat officiel de nomination établi par la juridiction ou toute autre autorité compétente qui a ouvert la faillite. Une traduction dans la langue officielle ou l'une des langues officielles de la Partie où le syndic exerce ses pouvoirs peut être exigée. Aucune légalisation ou autre formalité analogue n'est requise.

Article 3 Opening of a bankruptcy

The decision to open the bankruptcy must:

a. emanate from a court or other authority having competence under Article 4;

b. be effective in the territory of the Party where the bankruptcy is opened; and

c. not be manifestly contrary to the public policy of the Party in which the liquidator intends to exercise his powers under the terms of Chapter II or in which the opening of a secondary bankruptcy is requested under the terms of Chapter III.

Article 3 Ouverture d'une faillite

La décision d'ouverture de la faillite doit:

a. émaner d'une juridiction ou autre autorité compétente selon l'article 4;

b. produire ses effets dans le territoire de la Partie où la faillite est ouverte; et

c. ne pas être manifestement contraire à l'ordre public de la Partie dans laquelle le syndic veut exercer ses pouvoirs conformément au chapitre II ou dans laquelle l'ouverture d'une faillite secondaire est demandée conformément au chapitre III.

Article 4 Indirect international competence

1. The courts or other authorities of the Party in which the debtor has the centre of his main interests shall be considered as being competent for opening the bankruptcy. For companies and legal persons, unless the contrary is proved, the place of the registered office shall be presumed to be the centre of their main interests.

2. The courts or other authorities of the Party in whose territory the debtor

Article 4 Compétence internationale indirecte

1. Sont considérées comme compétentes pour ouvrir la faillite les juridictions ou autres autorités de la Partie dans laquelle le débiteur a le centre de ses intérêts principaux. Pour les sociétés et les personnes morales, le centre des intérêts principaux est présumé, jusqu'à preuve du contraire, être le lieu du siège statutaire.

2. Sont également considérées comme compétentes les juridictions ou

has an establishment shall also be considered as being competent:

a. if the centre of the debtor's main interests is not located in the territory of any Party; or

b. if the bankruptcy cannot be opened by a court or other authority of the Party competent under paragraph 1 because of the provisions of its national law and of the capacity of the debtor. In this event, that Party shall not be obliged to apply this Convention.

However, when the bankruptcy of a debtor is opened under paragraph *a* or *b* by courts or other authorities in various Parties in which he has an establishment, the court or authority which first gave judgment shall alone be considered competent.

autres autorités de la Partie sur le territoire de laquelle le débiteur a un établissement:

a. si le débiteur n'a le centre de ses intérêts principaux sur le territoire d'aucune Partie; ou

b. si la faillite ne peut pas être ouverte par une juridiction ou autre autorité de la Partie compétente au sens du paragraphe 1, en raison de la loi de cette Partie et du fait de la qualité du débiteur. Dans ce cas, cette Partie n'est pas tenue d'appliquer la présente Convention.

Toutefois, lorsque la faillite d'un même débiteur est ouverte en application de l'alinéa *a* ou *b*, par des juridictions ou autres autorités de Parties différentes dans lesquelles le débiteur a un établissement, la juridiction ou l'autorité qui a statué en premier lieu est seule considérée comme compétente.

Article 5 Partial payment of the creditors

Without prejudice to claims guaranteed by securities or rights over land or other property, a creditor who has received part payment in respect of his claim in a bankruptcy opened in one Party may not participate in a dividend for the same claim in a bankruptcy opened with regard to the same debtor in another Party, so long as the dividend received by the other creditors in the bankruptcy opened in that other Party is less than the dividend he has already received.

Article 5 Désintéressement partiel des créanciers

Sans préjudice des créances assorties de sûretés réelles ou de droits réels, un créancier dont la créance a été partiellement payée dans une faillite ouverte dans une Partie ne peut prétendre à un dividende pour la même créance dans une faillite ouverte à l'égard du même débiteur dans une autre Partie tant que le dividende attribué aux autres créanciers dans la faillite ouverte dans cette autre Partie est inférieur au dividende qu'il a obtenu.

Chapter II: Exercise of Certain Powers of the Liquidator

Article 6 Scope of Chapter II

In addition to the proceedings provided for in Article 1, paragraph 1, this chapter shall also apply to proceedings ordered by a court or an authority upon a request for the opening of a collective procedure under Article 1, paragraph 1, and which aim at the provisional protection of the assets of the debtor.

Article 7 Capacity of the liquidator

The liquidator may exercise his powers under the conditions set out in this chapter on presentation of the document mentioned in Article 2 and under the conditions mentioned in Article 3.

Article 8 Measures of protection and preservation of the assets

From the date of his appointment, the liquidator may take or cause to be taken, in accordance with the law of the Party in which he intends to act, any necessary steps to protect or preserve the value of the assets of the debtor, including the seeking of assistance from competent authorities in that Party without, however, removing those assets from the territory of the Party where they are situated.

Article 9 Advertisement of the liquidator's powers

A summary of the decision appointing the liquidator as provided by Article 2 must, after any necessary authorisation given by the competent authority of the Party where the liquidator intends to act, be advertised pursuant to the method of publication determined by that Party.

Chapitre II: Exercice de Certains pouvoirs du Syndic

Article 6 Champ d'application du chapitre II

Outre les procédures prévues à l'article 1, paragraphe 1, le présent chapitre s'applique également aux procédures qui sont diligentées par une juridiction ou une autorité saisie d'une demande d'ouverture d'une procédure collective au sens de l'article 1, paragraphe 1, et qui ont pour objet la sauvegarde provisoire des biens du débiteur.

Article 7 Capacité du syndic

Le syndic peut exercer ses pouvoirs dans les conditions prévues par le présent chapitre sur présentation du document prévu à l'article 2 et selon les conditions mentionnées à l'article 3.

Article 8 Mesures de protection et de préservation des biens

Le syndic peut, dès sa nomination, prendre ou faire prendre, conformément à la loi nationale de la Partie dans laquelle il veut agir, toute mesure nécessaire permettant de protéger ou de préserver la valeur des biens du débiteur, y compris le recours à l'assistance des autorités compétentes de cette Partie, sans toutefois déplacer ces biens hors du territoire de la Partie où ils sont situés.

Article 9 Publicité des pouvoirs du syndic

Un extrait de la décision qui nomme le syndic prévue à l'article 2 doit, le cas échéant, après autorisation de l'autorité compétente de la Partie où le syndic veut agir, être publié selon le mode de publication déterminé par cette Partie.

Article 10 Acts of administration, management and disposal of the debtor's assets

1. Within the powers conferred on him under the law of the Party in which the bankruptcy is opened and under the conditions set out in the following articles of this chapter, the liquidator may take or cause to be taken any acts to administer, manage or dispose of the debtor's assets including removing them from the territory of the Party where they are situated.

2. The implementation of these measures shall be subject to the law of the Party in whose territory the assets are situated.

Article 11 Conditions of exercise of the liquidator's powers

1. The liquidator's powers as set out in Article 10, paragraph 1, shall be suspended during a two-month period commencing the day after the publication of the notice referred to in Article 9. If, during this period or at any later stage, any request for bankruptcy or for proceedings to prevent bankruptcy has been made against the debtor in the Party where the assets are located, the powers of the liquidator shall be suspended until any such requests are rejected.

The liquidator shall be empowered to lodge an application for bankruptcy if the conditions for opening a bankruptcy under the national law of the Party where he intends to act are met.

2. During the period mentioned in paragraph 1, only creditors who, in the Party where the liquidator intends to exercise his powers, enjoy a right to preferential payment or would have enjoyed such a right if the bankruptcy had been opened in that Party, creditors who have a public law claim or creditors who have a claim arising from

Article 10 Actes d'administration, de gestion et de disposition des biens du débiteur

1. Le syndic peut accomplir ou faire accomplir tout acte d'administration, de gestion et de disposition des biens du débiteur, y compris leur déplacement hors du territoire de la partie ou ils sont situés, dans le cadre des pouvoirs qui lui sont conférés selon la loi de la Partie dans laquelle la faillite est ouverte et selon les conditions énoncées aux articles suivants du présent chapitre.

2. La mise en œuvre de ces mesures est régie par la loi de la Partie dans le territoire de laquelle les biens sont situés.

Article 11 Conditions d'exercice des pouvoirs du syndic

1. Les pouvoirs du syndic tels que prévus à l'article 10, paragraphe 1, sont suspendus pendant une période de deux mois commençant le lendemain de la publication de l'acte de nomination mentionnée à l'article 9. Si, durant cette période ou à un stade ultérieur, des requêtes en faillite ou tendant à l'ouverture d'une procédure préventive de faillite ont été introduites à l'égard du débiteur dans la partie où les biens sont situés, les pouvoirs du syndic sont suspendus jusqu'à la décision rejetant de telles requêtes.

Le syndic est habilité à introduire une requête en faillite si les conditions d'ouverture d'une faillite prévues par la loi nationale de la Partie où il veut agir sont remplies.

2. Durant la période mentionnée au paragraphe 1, seuls peuvent engager ou continuer des poursuites individuelles à l'égard des biens du débiteur les créanciers qui, dans la Partie où le syndic veut exercer ses pouvoirs, jouissent d'un privilège ou auraient joui d'un

the operation of an establishment of the debtor or from employment in that Party, may commence or pursue individual legal action against the assets of the debtor.

3. On the expiration of the period mentioned in paragraph 1, the creditors may no longer commence individual legal action and only the liquidator shall have the power to take or cause to be taken the acts mentioned in Article 10, paragraph 1.

Article 12 Objections to the liquidator's powers

1. Where an objection is made to the exercise of his powers, it shall be for the liquidator to request the court of the Party in whose territory the act is to be performed to declare that he is entitled to exercise those powers under the Convention.

2. If the extent of his powers is contested, it is for the liquidator to establish the same.

Article 13 Effects of discharge of payment and delivery of assets

1. Payment or delivery of assets to the liquidator made in good faith shall constitute a valid discharge. They shall be presumed to be made in good faith if made after the advertisement mentioned in Article 9 or after presentation of the certificate mentioned in Article 2.

2. Without prejudice to Article 11, paragraph 2, payment or delivery of assets to the debtor shall not constitute a valid discharge if they have been made after the advertisement provided under Article 9, unless the person who made them establishes that he did not have knowledge of this advertisement.

privilège dans le cas d'une faillite ouverte dans cette Partie, les titulaires de créances de droit public, ainsi que les titulaires d'une créance liée à l'exploitation d'un établissement du débiteur ou résultant d'un emploi dans cette Partie.

3. Après la période mentionnée au paragraphe 1, les créanciers ne peuvent plus engager des poursuites individuelles et seul le syndic a le pouvoir d'accomplir ou de faire accomplir les actes mentionnés à l'article 10, paragraphe 1.

Article 12 Contestation des pouvoirs du syndic

1. En cas de contestation de l'exercice de ses pouvoirs, il appartient au syndic de demander à la juridiction de la Partie sur le territoire de laquelle l'acte doit être accompli de constater qu'aux termes de la Convention il est en droit de les exercer.

2. Lorsque l'étendue de ses pouvoirs est contestée, il appartient au syndic de l'établir.

Article 13 Effet libératoire des paiements et remises de biens

1. Les paiements ou remises de biens faits de bonne foi au syndic sont libératoires. Ils sont réputés accomplis de bonne foi s'ils sont faits après la publicité prévue à l'article 9 ou après la présentation du certificat mentionné dans l'article 2.

2. Sans préjudice de l'article 11, paragraphe 2, les paiements ou remises de biens faits au débiteur ne sont pas libératoires s'ils sont postérieurs à la publicité prévue à l'article 9, moins que la personne qui les a faits prouve qu'elle n'a pas eu connaissance de cette publicité.

Article 14 Limitations to the exercise of the liquidator's powers

1. The opening or recognition of bankruptcy proceedings or of proceedings which prevent bankruptcy in the Party in which the liquidator intends to exercise his powers provided for in this chapter shall prevent the exercise of his powers in that Party.

2. The liquidator cannot perform in another Party an act which is:

a. contrary to any security held by any person other than the debtor over land or other property established or recognised by the law of that Party; or

b. manifestly contrary to the public policy of that Party.

Article 15 Extension of the liquidator's powers

Any Party may permit the foreign liquidator to exercise on its territory wider powers than those laid down in this chapter.

Chapter III: Secondary Bankruptcies

Article 16 Secondary bankruptcy

Any debtor declared bankrupt by a court or any other competent authority under Article 4, paragraph 1 (main bankruptcy), may, by virtue of this fact alone, be declared bankrupt in any other Party (secondary bankruptcy), whether or not he is insolvent in that Party, provided that the decision declaring him bankrupt was made in accordance with Article 3, paragraphs *b* and *c*, and that no bankruptcy or proceedings to prevent bankruptcy have already been opened in that Party.

Article 14 Limitations à l'exercise des pouvoirs du syndic

1. L'ouverture ou la reconnaissance d'une procédure de faillite ou préventive de faillite dans la Partie où le syndic veut exercer ses pouvoirs prévus par le present chapitre fait obstacle à l'exercise de ses pouvoirs dans cette Partie.

2. Le syndic ne peut accomplir, dans une autre Partie, un acte qui est:

a. au détriment des sûretés réelles ou des droits réels des personnes autres que le débiteur et établis ou reconnus par la loi de cette Partie; ou

b. manifestement contraire à l'ordre public de cette Partie.

Article 15 Extension des pouvoirs du syndic

Toute Partie peut permettre au syndic étranger d'exercer sur son territoire des pouvoirs plus étendus que ceux prévus dans le présent chapitre.

Chapitre III: Faillites Secondaires

Article 16 Faillite secondaire

Tout débiteur déclaré en faillite par une juridiction ou toute autre autorité compétente selon l'article 4, paragraphe 1 (faillite principale), peut, de ce seul fait, être déclaré en faillite dans toute autre Partie (faillite secondaire), qu'il soit ou non insolvable dans cette Partie, pourvu que la décision en vertu de laquelle il a été déclaré en faillite ait été rendue conformément à l'article 3, alinéas *b* et *c*, et qu'une faillite ou une procédure préventive de faillite ne soit pas déjà ouverte dans cette Partie.

Article 17 International competence

Without prejudice to the other grounds of competence provided for by national law, the courts or authorities of any Party in which an establishment of the debtor is situated shall be competent to open a secondary bankruptcy. The courts or authorities of any Party in which assets of the debtor are situated shall be equally competent.

Article 18 Opening of the secondary bankruptcy

Upon production of the decision opening the main bankruptcy, the following shall be entitled to request the opening of the secondary bankruptcy:

a. the liquidator in the main bankruptcy; or

b. any other person or body granted the right to request the opening of a bankruptcy by the law of the Party where the opening of the secondary bankruptcy is requested.

Article 19 Applicable law

Except as otherwise provided in this Convention, the secondary bankruptcy shall be governed by the bankruptcy law of the Party where that bankruptcy is opened.

Article 20 Lodgement of claims

1. Any claim may be lodged in a secondary bankruptcy.

2. All claims lodged in the secondary bankruptcy shall, by means of copies, be notified to the liquidator or the competent authority of the main bankruptcy. Claims so notified shall be regarded as validly lodged in the main bankruptcy.

Article 17 Compétence internationale

Sans préjudice des autres chefs de compétence prévus par la loi nationale, sont compétentes pour l'ouverture d'une faillite secondaire les juridictions ou autorités des Parties dans lesquelles est situé un établissement du débiteur. Sont également compétentes les juridictions ou autorités de toute Partie dans laquelle sont situés des biens du débiteur.

Article 18 Ouverture de la faillite secondaire

Sont habilités à demander l'ouverture de la faillite secondaire, sur présentation de la décision prononçant la faillite principale:

a. le syndic de la faillite principale; ou

b. tout autre personne ou organe habilité à demander l'ouverture d'une faillite par la loi de la Partie où l'ouverture de la faillite secondaire est demandée.

Article 19 Loi applicable

Sauf disposition différente de la présente Convention, la faillite secondaire est régie par la loi sur les faillites de la Partie où cette faillite est ouverte.

Article 20 Production des créances

1. Toute créance peut être produite à la faillite secondaire.

2. Toutes les créances produites à la faillite secondaire sont communiquées, en copie, au syndic ou à l'autorité compétente de la faillite principale. Cette communication vaut production valable à la faillite principale.

Article 21 Payment of claims

Claims enjoying a right to preferential payment or a security over land or other property, public law claims and claims arising from the operation of an establishment of the debtor or from employment in the Party where the secondary bankruptcy is opened shall be verified and, when admitted, shall be paid from the proceeds of the liquidation of the assets of the secondary bankruptcy.

Article 22 Transfer of the remaining assets

Following the payment of claims in conformity with Article 21, the remaining assets shall form part of the assets in the main bankruptcy. Any administrative act necessary to this effect shall be performed forthwith by the liquidator of the secondary bankruptcy.

Article 23 Claims arising after the opening of the main bankruptcy

1. Without prejudice to remedies provided to creditors by the law of the main bankruptcy, claims arising before the opening of the secondary bankruptcy cannot be rejected in the main bankruptcy on the sole ground that they arose after the opening of the latter bankruptcy.

2. Without prejudice to the provisions of Article 21, the claims mentioned in paragraph 1 may participate in a dividend only on assets remaining in the secondary bankruptcy transferred under the conditions laid out in Article 22.

Article 24 Equality of creditors

Creditors in the main bankruptcy who are entitled to receive a dividend from assets coming from the secondary bankruptcy shall be treated equally, regardless of any privileges or other

Article 21 Désintéressement des créanciers

Les créances assorties d'un privilège ou d'une sûreté réelle, celles qui sont de droit public et celles liées à l'exploitation d'un établissement du débiteur ou résultant d'un emploi dans la Partie où est ouverte la faillite seondaire sont vérifiées, et, après leur admission, sont satisfaites par le produit de la liquidation de l'actif de la faillite secondaire.

Article 22 Transfert du surplus de l'actif

Après le paiement des créances prévu à l'article 21, le surplus de l'actif est ajouté à l'actif de la faillite principale. Le syndic de la faillite secondaire prend sans délai les mesures administratives nécessaires à cette fin.

Article 23 Créances nées après l'ouverture de la faillite principale

1. Sans préjudice des recours accordés aux créanciers par la loi de la faillite principale, les créances nées avant l'ouverture de la faillite secondaire ne peuvent être rejetées dans le cadre de la faillite principale du seul fait qu'elles sout nées après l'ouverture de cette faillite.

2. Sans préjudice des dispositions de l'article 21, les créances visées au paragraphe 1 ne donnent droit à dividende que sur le surplus de l'actif de la faillite secondaire transféré conformément à l'article 22.

Article 24 Egalité des créanciers

Les créanciers de la faillite principale habilités à recevoir un dividende sur la partie de l'actif provenant de la faillite secondaire sont traités de manière égale, sans tenir compte des privilèges

exceptions to the principle of equality between creditors provided by the law of the main bankruptcy.

ou autres exceptions au principe de l'égalité des créanciers prévus par la loi de la faillite principale.

Article 25 Duty to communicate information

The liquidators in the main and secondary bankruptcies shall promptly communicate to each other any information which might be relevant to the other proceedings, in particular all measures aimed at terminating the procedure.

Article 25 Devoir d'information

Les syndics de la faillite principale et de la faillite secondaire doivent se communiquer sans délai toute information pouvant être utile à l'autre procédure, et notamment toute mesure visant à mettre fin à la procédure.

Article 26 End of the secondary bankruptcy

Proceedings in a secondary bankruptcy cannot be terminated before an opinion has been obtained from the liquidator of the main bankruptcy, provided that such opinion is furnished within a reasonable period of time.

Article 26 Fin de la faillite secondaire

Il ne peut être mis fin à la procédure de faillite secondaire qu'après avis donné par le syndic de la faillite principale, à condition que cet avis soit donné dans un délai raisonnable.

Article 27 Composition in the secondary bankruptcy

A composition in the secondary bankruptcy, where such is provided for in the law applicable to that bankruptcy, cannot take place without the prior consent of the liquidator of the main bankruptcy. Such consent cannot be withheld if it is proved that the financial interests of the creditors of the main bankruptcy are not affected by that composition.

Article 27 Concordat dans la faillite secondaire

Si la loi applicable à la faillite secondaire prévoit la possibilité d'un concordat, ce concordat ne peut avoir lieu qu'avec l'accord du syndic de la faillite principale. Cet accord ne peut être refusé s'il est prouvé que ce concordat n'affecte pas les intérêts financiers des créanciers de la faillite principale.

Article 28 Plurality of bankruptcies

1. Any bankruptcy opened after the opening of a bankruptcy by a court or other authority which is competent in accordance with Article 4, paragraph 1, shall be a secondary bankruptcy.

2. The liquidator of a bankruptcy opened by a court or other authority which is competent in accordance with Article 4, paragraph 1, may request that the assets remaining from a bankruptcy

Article 28 Pluralité des faillites

1. Toute faillite ouverte après l'ouverture d'une faillite par une juridiction ou autre autorité compétente selon l'article 4, paragraphe 1, est une faillite secondaire.

2. Le syndic d'une faillite ouverte par une juridiction ou autre autorité compétente selon l'article 4, paragraphe 1, peut demander que le surplus de l'actif

opened previously in another Party be transferred to him after the end of that bankruptcy.

He may also request to be notified of any information provided for in Article 25.

d'une faillite ouverte antérieurement dans une autre Partie lui soit transféré après la fin de cette faillite.

Il peut en outre demander communication de toute information conformément à l'article 25.

Chapter IV: Information of the Creditors and Lodgement of their Claims

Article 29 Scope of Chapter IV

In addition to the proceedings provided for in Article 1, paragraph 1, this chapter shall also apply to proceedings which do not entail the disinvestment of the debtor or which cannot entail the liquidation of assets, as well as to secondary bankruptcy proceedings.

Article 30 Duty to inform the creditors

1. As soon as proceedings mentioned in Appendix A or secondary bankruptcy proceedings are opened in a Party, the competent authority of that Party or the liquidator appointed in it shall inform, promptly and individually, the known creditors residing in the other Parties.

2. This information shall be given by a notice containing the appropriate details, in particular as to time-limits and measures to be taken. Such a notice shall also indicate whether creditors whose claims are preferential or secured need lodge their claims.

Article 31 Lodgement of claims

Any creditor residing in a Party other than that in which the proceedings have been opened may lodge his claim in writing to the competent authority or

Chapitre IV: Information des Créanciers et Production de leurs Créances

Article 29 Champ d'application du chapitre IV

Outre les procédures prévues à l'article 1, paragraphe 1, le présent chapitre s'applique également aux procédures qui n'entraînent pas le dessaisissement du débiteur ou qui ne sont pas susceptibles d'entraîner la liquidation des biens, ainsi qu'aux procédures de faillite secondaire.

Article 30 Obligation d'informer les créanciers

1. Dès qu'une procédure visée à l'annexe A ou une procédure de faillite secondaire est ouverte dans une Partie, l'autorité compétente de cette Partie ou le syndic nommé dans celle-ci informe rapidement et individuellement les créanciers connus résidant dans les autres Parties.

2. Cette information est assurée par l'envoi d'une note contenant les renseignements appropriés, notamment quant aux délais à observer et aux mesures à prendre. Cette note indique aussi si les créanciers dont le créance est garantie par un privilège ou une sûreté réelle doivent produire leur créance.

Article 31 Production des créances

Tout créancier résidant dans une Partie autre que celle où la procédure a été ouverte peut produire sa créance par écrit en l'adressant à l'autorité

liquidator mentioned in Article 30. The creditor shall send copies of supporting documents, if any, and shall indicate the nature of the claim, the date on which it arose, its amount, as well as whether or not it is preferential and, if applicable, the assets affected by the preference.

comptétente ou au syndic mentionné à l'article 30. Le créancier envoie la copie des pièces justificatives, s'il en existe, et indique la nature de la créance, sa date de naissance, son montant, ainsi que le caractère privilégié ou non de cette créance et, éventuellement, les biens sur lesquels porte son privilège.

Article 32 Languages

1. Subject to the provisions of Article 39, the notice mentioned in Article 30 may be drawn up in the official language of the authority which has opened the procedure. If this language is neither one of the official languages of the Council of Europe nor that of the creditor nor that of the Party where he resides, a translation into one of these languages shall be attached to the notice.

2. Subject to the provisions of Article 39, the written claim mentioned in Article 31 may be drawn up in the language of the creditor. If this language is not that of the authority which has opened the procedure, a translation in that language or one of the official languages of the Council of Europe shall be attached to it.

Article 32 Langues

1. Sous réserve des dispositions de l'article 39, la note mentionnée à l'article 30 peut être rédigée dans la langue officielle de l'autorité qui a ouvert la procédure. Si cette langue n'est pas une des langues officielles du Conseil de l'Europe, ni celle du créancier, ni celle de la Partie où ce créancier réside, la note est accompagnée d'une traduction dans une de ces langues.

2. Sous réserve des dispositions de l'article 39, l'écrit mentionné à l'article 31 peut être rédigé dans la langue du créancier. Si cette langue n'est pas celle de l'autorité qui a ouvert la procédure, il est accompagné d'une traduction dans cette langue ou dans une des langues officielles du Conseil de l'Europe.

Chapter V: Final Provisions

Article 33 Signature, ratification, acceptance or approval

This Convention shall be open for signature by the member States of the Council of Europe. It is subject to ratification, acceptance or approval. Instruments of ratification, acceptance or approval shall be deposited with the Secretary General of the Council of Europe.

Chapitre V: Dispositions Finales

Article 33 Signature, ratification, acceptation ou approbation

La présente Convention est ouverte à la signature des Etats membres du Conseil de l'Europe. Elle sera soumise à ratification, acceptation ou approbation. Les instruments de ratification, d'acceptation ou d'approbation seront déposés près le Secrétaire Général du Conseil de l'Europe.

Article 34 Entry into force

1. This Convention shall enter into force on the first day of the month following the expiration of a period of three months after the date on which three member States of the Council of Europe have expressed their consent to be bound by the Convention in accordance with the provisions of Article 33.

2. In respect of any member State which subsequently expresses its consent to be bound by it, the Convention shall enter into force on the first day of the month following the expiration of a period of three months after the date of the deposit of the instrument of ratification, acceptance or approval.

Article 34 Entrée en vigueur

1. La présente Convention entrera en vigueur le premier jour du mois qui suit l'expiration d'une période de trois mois après la date à laquelle trois Etats membres du Conseil de l'Europe auront exprimé leur consentement à être liés par la Convention conformément aux dispositions de l'article 33.

2. Pour tout Etat membre qui exprimera ultérieurement son consentement à être lié par la Convention, celle-ci entrera en vigueur le premier jour du mois qui suit l'expiration d'une période de trois mois après la date du dépôt de l'instrument de ratification, d'acceptation ou d'approbation.

Article 35 Accession

1. After the entry into force of this Convention, the Committee of Ministers of the Council of Europe may invite any State not a member of the Council to accede to this Convention, by a decision taken by the majority provided for in Article 20.*d* of the Statute of the Council of Europe and by the unanimous vote of the representatives of the Contracting States entitled to sit on the Committee.

2. When a non-member State of the Council requests to be invited to accede to this Convention, it shall submit to the Secretary General of the Council of Europe the list of proceedings to be included in Appendix A and the persons or bodies to be included in Appendix B.

3. In respect of any acceding State, the Convention shall enter into force on the first day of the month following the expiration of a period of three months after the date of deposit of the instrument of accession with the Secretary General.

Article 35 Adhésion

1. Après l'entré en vigueur de la présente Convention, le Comité des Ministres du Conseil de l'Europe pourra inviter tout Etat non membre du Conseil à adhérer à la présente Convention, par une décision prise à la majorité prévue à l'article 20.*d* du Statut du Conseil de l'Europe, et à l'unanimité des représentants des Etats contractants ayant le droit de siéger au Comité.

2. Lorsqu'un Etat non membre du Conseil demande à être invité à adhérer à la présente Convention, il présente au Secrétaire Général du Conseil de l'Europe la liste des procédures devant figurer dans l'annexe A et des personnes ou organes devant figurer dans l'annexe B.

3. Pour tout Etat adhérent, la Convention entrera en vigueur le premier jour du mois qui suit l'expiration d'une période de trois mois après la date de dépôt de l'instrument d'adhésion près le Secrétaire Général.

Article 36 Appendices

1. Any Contracting State may, when depositing its instrument of ratification, acceptance, approval or accession or at any time thereafter, address to the Secretary General of the Council of Europe a declaration containing any change it wishes to make to Appendix A or Appendix B.

2. The Secretary General shall communicate such declaration to the signatory States and the Contracting States. The change shall be considered to be adopted if no objection is made by any State, thus notified, before the expiry of a period of three months from the date of notification. The change shall enter into force on the first day of the following month.

Article 37 Territorial application

1. Any State may, at the time of signature or deposit of its instrument of ratification, acceptance, approval or accession, specify the territory or territories to which this Convention shall apply.

2. Any State may at any later date, by a declaration addressed to the Secretary General of the Council of Europe, extend the application of this Convention to any other territory specified in the declaration. In respect of such territory, the Convention shall enter into force on the first day of the month following the expiration of a period of three months after the date of receipt of this declaration by the Secretary General.

3. Any declaration made under the two preceding paragraphs may, in respect of any territory specified in this declaration, be withdrawn by a notification addressed to the Secretary General. The withdrawal shall become effective on the first day of the month following the expiration of a period of

Article 36 Annexes

1. Tout Etat contractant pourra, lors du dépôt de son instrument de ratification, d'acceptation, d'approbation ou d'adhésion, ou à tout autre moment par la suite, adresser au Secrétaire Général du Conseil de l'Europe une déclaration contenant toute modification qu'il souhaite apporter à l'annexe A ou à l'annexe B.

2. Le Secrétaire Général notifie cette déclaration aux Etats signataires et aux Etats contractants. La modification est considérée comme adoptée si aucun Etat ainsi informé ne formule d'objection avant l'expiration d'une période de trois mois à partir de la date de la notification. La modification entre en vigueur le premier jour du mois qui suit.

Article 37 Portée territoriale

1. Tout Etat peut, au moment de la signature ou au moment du dépôt de son instrument de ratification, d'acceptation, d'approbation ou d'adhésion, désigner le ou les territoires auxquels s'appliquera le présente Convention.

2. Tout Etat peut, à tout autre moment par la suite, par une déclaration adressée au Secrétaire Général du Conseil de l'Europe, étendre l'application de la présente Convention à tout autre territoire désigné dans la déclaration. La Convention entrera en vigueur à l'égard de ce territoire le premier jour du mois qui suit l'expiration d'une période de trois mois après la date de réception de cette déclaration par le Secrétaire Général.

3. Toute déclaration faite en vertu des deux paragraphes précédents pourra être retirée, en ce qui concerne tout territoire désigné dans cette déclaration, par notification adressée au Secrétaire Général. Le retrait prendra effet le premier jour du mois qui suit l'expiration

three months after the date of receipt of this notification by the Secretary General.

Article 38 International conventions and arrangements

1. This Convention shall not prejudice the application of international conventions to which a Party is, or becomes, a party.

2. In their mutual relations, Parties which are members of the European Economic Community shall apply Community rules and shall therefore not apply the rules arising from this Convention, except in so far as there is no Community rule governing the particular subject concerned.

Article 39 Declarations on the use of languages

1. Any State may, at the time of signature or when depositing its instrument of ratification, acceptance, approval or accession, declare that the notice and written claim mentioned, respectively, in Articles 30 and 31 shall, by way of exception to the provisions of Article 32, be drawn up exclusively in its official language or one of its official languages.

2. Any State may, at the time of signature or when depositing its instrument of ratification, acceptance, approval or accession, declare that the written lodgement of claims mentioned in Article 31 may be drawn up in any language other than those mentioned in Article 32, paragraph 2.

Article 40 Reservations

1. Any State may, at the time of signature or when depositing its instrument of ratification, acceptance, approval or accession, declare that it will not apply either Chapter II or Chapter III of the Convention.

d'une période de trois mois après la date de réception de cette notification par le Secrétaire Général.

Article 38 Conventions et arrangements internationaux

1. La présente Convention ne porte pas atteinte à l'application des conventions internationales auxquelles une Partie est ou sera partie.

2. Dans leurs relations mutuelles, les Parties qui sont membres de la Communauté économique européenne appliquent les règles de la Communauté et n'appliquent donc les règles découlant de la présente Convention que dans la mesure où il n'existe aucune règle communautaire régissant le sujet particulier concerné.

Article 39 Déclarations sur l'usage des langues

1. Tout Etat peut, au moment de la signature ou au moment du dépôt de son instrument de ratification, d'acceptation, d'approbation ou d'adhésion, déclarer que la note et l'écrit visés, respectivement dans les articles 30 et 31, doivent, par dérogation aux dispositions de l'article 32, être exclusivement rédigés dans sa langue officielle ou dans une de ses langues officielles.

2. Tout Etat peut, au moment de la signature ou au moment du dépôt de son instrument de ratification, d'acceptation, d'approbation ou d'adhésion, déclarer que l'écrit visé à l'article 31 peut être rédigé dans toute autre langue que celles mentionnées à l'article 32, paragraphe 2.

Article 40 Réserves

1. Toute Partie peut, au moment de la signature ou au moment du dépôt de son instrument de ratification, d'acceptation, d'approbation ou d'adhésion, déclarer qu'elle n'appliquera pas soit le

2. A Party which has declared that it will not apply Chapter III shall nevertheless be bound, except where it has made an express declaration to the contrary, to apply Articles 20, paragraph 2, 23 and 24. Where a Party has made a declaration of non-application of these articles, the Party on whose territory a secondary bankruptcy is opened shall not be bound to apply Article 21 in its relations with the Party which made the said declaration.

3. No other reservation may be made in respect of the provisions of this Convention.

Article 41 Declaration on the information mentioned in Article 9

Any State shall, at the time of signature or when depositing its instrument of ratification, acceptance, approval or accession, designate the authority and the method of publication mentioned in Article 9 by a declaration addressed to the Secretary General of the Council of Europe.

Article 42 Implementation of the Convention

1. Following the entry into force of this Convention, a group of experts representing the Parties and the non-contracting member States of the Council of Europe shall meet at the request of at least two parties or on the initiative of the Secretary General of the Council of Europe.

2. The terms of reference of this group will be to assess the implementation of the Convention and to make any relevant suggestions.

chapitre II soit le chapitre III de la Convention.

2. Une Partie qui a déclaré qu'elle n'appliquerait pas le chapitre III sera néaumoins tenue, sauf déclaration expresse contraire, d'appliquer les articles, paragraphe 2, 23 et 24. En cas de déclaration de non-application de ces articles par une Partie, la Partie sur le territoire de laquelle sera ouverte une faillite secondaire ne sera pas tenue d'appliquer l'article 21 dans ses relations avec la Partie qui a fait ladite déclaration.

3. Aucune autre réserve n'est admise aux dispositions de la présente Convention.

Article 41 Déclaration sur les informations mentionnées à l'article 9

Tout Etat désigne, au moment de la signature ou au moment du dépôt de son instrument de ratification, d'acceptation, d'approbation ou d'adhésion, l'autorité et le mode de publication mentionnés à l'article 9 par une déclaration adressée au Secrétaire Général du Conseil de l'Europe.

Article 42 Mise en œuvre de la Convention

1. Après l'entrée en vigueur de la présente Convention, un groupe d'experts représentant les Parties à la Convention et les Etats membres du Conseil de l'Europe non Parties sera réuni à la demande d'au moins deux Parties ou à l'initiative du Secrétaire Général du Conseil de l'Europe.

2. Ce groupe a pour mandat de dresser un bilan de la mise en œuvre de la Convention et de faire toute suggestion utile.

Article 43 Denunciation

1. Any Party may at any time denounce this Convention by means of a notification addressed to the Secretary General of the Council of Europe.

2. Such denunciation shall become effective on the first day of the month following the expiration of a period of three months after the date of receipt of the notification by the Secretary General.

Article 44 Notifications

The Secretary General of the Council of Europe shall notify the member States of the Council and any State which has acceded or has been invited to accede to this Convention of:

a. any signature;
b. the deposit of any instrument of ratification, acceptance, approval or accession;
c. any date of entry into force of this Convention in accordance with Articles 34, 35 and 36;
d. any other act, notification or communication relating to this Convention.

Annex A

The proceedings provided for in Article 1 are the following, it being understood that category *a* concerns the application of Chapter II of the Convention, category *b* concerns the application of Chapter III and category *c* concerns the application of Chapter IV.

Article 43 Dénonciation

1. Toute Partie peut, à tout moment, dénoncer la présente Convention en adressant une notification au Secrétaire Général du Conseil de l'Europe.

2. La dénonciation prendra effet le premier jour du mois qui suit l'expiration d'une période de trois mois après la date de réception de la notification par le Secrétaire Général.

Article 44 Notifications

Le Secrétaire Général du Conseil de l'Europe notifiera aux Etats membres du Conseil de l'Europe et à tout Etat qui a adhéré à la présente Convention ou qui a été invité à y adhérer:

a. toute signature;
b. le dépôt de tout instrument de ratification, d'acceptation, d'approbation ou d'adhésion;
c. toute date d'entrée en vigueur de la présente Convention conformément à ses articles 34, 35 et 36;
d. tout autre acte, notification ou communication ayant trait à la présente Convention.

Annexe A

Les procédures mentionnées à l'article 1 sont les suivantes, étant entendu que la rubrique *a* concerne l'application du chapitre II de la Convention, que la rubrique *b* concerne l'application du chapitre III et que la rubrique *c* concerne l'application du chapitre IV.

Austria (Autriche)	a + b	Konkurs
	c	1. Konkurs 2. Ausgleichsverfahren
Belgium (Belgique)	a + b	La faillite/Het faillissement
	c	La faillite/Het faillissement Le concordat judiciaire/Het gerechtelijk akkoord
Cyprus (Chypre)	a + b + c	1. Bankruptcy 2. The administration in bankruptcy of the estate of persons dying insolvent 3. Compulsory winding-up 4. Creditors' voluntary winding-up 5. Winding-up subject to the supervision of the Court
Denmark (Danemark)	a + b	Konkurs
	c	1. Konkurs 2. Betalingsstandsning 3. Tvangsakkord 4. Gaeldssanening
Finland (Finlande)	a + b	Konkurssi/Konkurs
	c	1. Konkurssi/Konkurs 2. Akordi/Ackord
France	a + b	Liquidation judiciaire
	c	Redressement judiciaire Liquidation judiciaire
Federal Republic of Germany (République Fédérale d'Allemagne)	a + b	Konkurs
	c	1. Konkurs 2. Vergleichsverfahren
Greece (Grèce)	a + b	πτώχευση
	c	1. πτώχευση 2. ειδική εκκαθάριση εταιριών 3. προσωρινη διαχείριση εταιριών 4. διοίκηση χαι διαχείριση των πιστωιών
Iceland (Islande)	a + b	Eijaldtprotaskipti
	c	1. Gjaldtprotaskipti 2. Naujasamningar 3. Greijslustöjvun
Ireland (Irlande)	a + b	Compulsory winding up Creditors' voluntary winding-up Bankruptcy The administration in bankruptcy of the estate of persons dying insolvent Winding-up in bankruptcy of partnerships
	c	Arrangements under the control of the Court

Italy (Italie)	a + b	Fallimento
	c	1. Fallimento 2. Liquidazione coatta amministra-tiva 3. Amministrazione straordinaria 4. Concordato preventivo
Liechtenstein	a + b	Konkurs
	c	1. Konkurs 2. Nachlassvertrag
Luxembourg	a + b	Faillite
	c	1. Faillite 2. Condordat préventif de faillite 3. Régime spécial de liquidation des notaires 4. Gestion contrôlée (tendant à liquidation avec bonne réalisation de l'actif)
Malta (Malte)	a + b	Falliment/Bankruptcy
	c	1. Falliment/Bankruptcy 2. Akkordju/Composition
Netherlands (Pays-Bas)	a + b	Het faillissement
	c	1. Het faillisement 2. De surséance van betaling
Norway (Norvège)	a + b	Konkurs
	c	1. Konkurs 2. Gjeldsforhandling/tvangsakkord
Portugal	a + b	1. Falencia (comerciantes) 2. Insolvencia (não comerciantes)
	c	1. Falencia (comerciantes) 2. Insolvencia (não comerciantes) 3. Processo especial de recuperação da empresa e protecção dos credores 4. Meios preventivos da declaração da falencia
San Marino (Saint-Marin)	a + b	Concorso fra i creditori
	c	1. Concordato 2. Liquidazione coattiva 3. Moratoria
Spain (Espagne)	a + b	1. El concurso de acreedores (no comerciantes) 2. La quiebra (comerciantes)
	c	1. El concurso de acreedores (no comerciantes) 2. La quiebra (comerciantes) 3. El beneficio de quita y espera (no comerciantes)

		4. La suspensión de pagos (comerciantes) 5. La administración judicial de empresas (comerciantes)
Sweden (Suède)	a + b	Konkurs
	c	1. Konkurs 2. Ackordsförhandling
Switzerland (Suisse)	a + b	Faillite/Fallimento/Konkurs
	c	Faillite/Fallimento/Konkurs Procédure concordataire/Procedura concordatoria/Nachlassverfahren
Turkey (Turquie)	a + b	Iflas
	c	1. Iflas 2. Konkordato
United Kingdom (Royaume-Uni)	a + b	1. Winding-up by the Court (Compulsory Winding-up) 2. Creditors' voluntary winding-up 3. Bankruptcy (England and Wales, Northern Ireland) 4. Administration of the insolvent estate of deceased person (England and Wales, Northern Ireland) 5. Administration by a Judicial Factor of the insolvent estate of a deceased person (Scotland) 6. Sequestration (Scotland)
	c	1. Winding up by the Court (Compulsory Winding-up) 2. Creditors' voluntary winding-up 3. Bankruptcy (England and Wales, Northern Ireland) 4. Administration of the insolvent estate of deceased person (England and Wales, Northern Ireland) 5. Administration by a Judicial Factor of the insolvent estate of a deceased person (Scotland) 6. Sequestration (Scotland) 7. Administration 8. Corporate voluntary arrangements 9. Individual voluntary arrangements (England and Wales, Northern Ireland)

10. Trust Deed for Creditors (Scotland)
11. Composition Contract (Scotland)
12. Deeds of Arrangement

Annex B

The 'liquidators' in the member States, mentioned in Article 1, paragraph 3, are the following:

Annexe B

Les 'syndics' dans les Etats membres mentionnés au paragraphe 3 de l'article I, sont les suivants:

Austria (Autriche)	1. Masseverwalter 2. Ausgleichsverwalter 3. Sachwalter 4. Vorläufiger Verwalter
Belgium (Belique)	Le curateur/De kurator
Cyprus (Chypre)	1. The Liquidator 2. The Provisional Liquidator 3. The Official Receiver 4. The Trustee
Denmark (Danemark)	1. Kurator 2. Midlertidig bestyrer
Finland (Finlande)	1. Uskottu mies/God man 2. Toimitsijamies/Syssloman
France	1. Commissaire à l'exécution du plan 2. Représentant des créanciers 3. Liquidateur 4. Administrateur judiciaire
Federal Republic of Germany (République Fédérale d'Allemagne)	1. Konkursverwalter 2. Sequester 3. Vergleichsverwalter 4. Vorläufiger Vergleichsverwalter
Greece (Grèce)	1. σύνδιχος 2. εχχαθαριστής 3. διαχειριστής
Iceland (Islande)	1. Skiptarájandi 2. Skiptastjóri 3. Büstjóri
Ireland (Irlande)	1. Liquidator 2. Official Assignee
Italy (Italie)	1. Curatore 2. Commissario
Leichtenstein	Masseverwalter

Luxembourg	1. Curateur (faillite) 2. Liquidateur (concordat préventif de faillite) 3. Conseil de gérance de la section d'assainissement du notariat (liquidation d'une étude de notaire) 4. Commissaire (gestion contrôlée)
Malta (Malte)	Kurator/Curator
Netherlands (Pays-Bas)	1. De curator in het faillissement 2. De bewindvoerder in de surséance van betaling
Norway (Norvège)	1. Bostyrer 2. Midlertidig bostyrer 3. Gjeldsnemnda
Portugal	1. Sindico 2. Administrador da Falencia 3. Administrador judicial
San-Marino (Saint-Marin)	1. Procuratore 2. Liquidatore giudiziale
Spain (Espagne)	1. El Depositario 2. Los Síndicos 3. Los Interventores
Sweden (Suède)	1. Konkursförvaltare 2. God man enligt ackordslagen
Switzerland (Suisse)	Konkursverwaltung/L'administration des faillites/L'Amministrazione del Fallimento
Turkey (Turquie)	1. Iflas Idaresi 2. Komiser
United Kingdom (Royaume-Uni)	1. Liquidator 2. Provisional Liquidator 3. Official Receiver (England and Wales) 4. Interim Receiver (England and Wales, Northern Ireland) 5. Trustee (England and Wales, Scotland, Northern Ireland) 6. Official Assignee (Northern Ireland) 7. Interim and Permanent Trustee in Sequestration (Scotland) 8. Judicial Factor (Scotland)

Appendix IV

United Nations Commission on International Trade Law (UNCITRAL): Model Law on Cross-Border Insolvency, May 1997

Preamble

The purpose of this Law is to provide effective mechanisms for dealing with cases of cross-border insolvency so as to promote the objectives of:

(a) cooperation between the courts and other competent authorities of this State and foreign States involved in cases of cross-border insolvency;

(b) greater legal certainty for trade and investment;

(c) fair and efficient administration of cross-border insolvencies that protects the interests of all creditors and other interested persons, including the debtor;

(d) protection and maximization of the value of the debtor's assets; and

(e) facilitation of the rescue of financially troubled businesses, thereby protecting investment and preserving employment.

Chapter I: General Provisions

Article 1 Scope of application

(1) This Law applies where:

(a) assistance is sought in this State by a foreign court or a foreign representative in connection with a foreign proceedings; or

(b) assistance is sought in a foreign State in connection with a proceeding under [*identify laws of the enacting State relating to insolvency*]; or

(c) a foreign proceeding and a proceeding under [*identify laws of the enacting State relating to insolvency*] in respect of the same debtor are taking place concurrently; or

(d) creditors or other interested persons in a foreign State have an interest in requesting the commencement of, or participating in, a proceeding under [*identify laws of the enacting State relating to insolvency*].

(2) This Law does not apply to a proceeding concerning [*designate any types of entities, such as banks or insurance companies, that are subject to a special insolvency regime in this State and that this State wishes to exclude from this Law*].

Article 2 Definitions

For the purposes of this Law:

(a) 'foreign proceeding' means a collective judicial or administrative proceeding in a foreign State, including an interim proceeding, pursuant to a law relating to insolvency in which proceeding the assets and affairs of the debtor are subject to control or supervision by a foreign court, for the purpose of reorganization or liquidation;

(b) 'foreign main proceeding' means a foreign proceeding taking place in the State where the debtor has the centre of its main interests;

(c) 'foreign non-main proceeding' means a foreign proceeding, other than a foreign main proceeding, taking place in a State where the debtor has an establishment within the meaning of subparagraph (f) of this article;

(d) 'foreign representative' means a person or body, including one appointed on an interim basis, authorized in a foreign proceeding to administer the reorganization or the liquidation of the debtor's assets or affairs or to act as a representative of the foreign proceeding;

(e) 'foreign court' means a judicial or other authority competent to control or supervise a foreign proceeding;

(f) 'establishment' means any place of operations where the debtor carries out a non-transitory economic activity with human means and goods or services.

Article 3 International obligations of this State

To the extent that this Law conflicts with an obligation of this State arising out of any treaty or other form of agreement to which it is a party with one or more other States, the requirements of the treaty or agreement prevail.

Article 4 [*Competent court or authority*]*

The functions referred to in this Law relating to recognition of foreign proceedings and cooperation with foreign courts shall be performed by [*specify the court, courts, authority or authorities competent to perform those functions in the enacting State*].

Article 5 Authorization of [*insert the title of the person or body administering a reorganization or liquidation under the law of the enacting State*] to act in a foreign State

A [*insert the title of the person or body administering a reorganization or liquidation under the law of the enacting State*] is authorized to act in a foreign State on behalf of a proceeding under [*identify laws of the enacting State relating to insolvency*], as permitted by the applicable foreign law.

* A State where certain functions relating to insolvency proceedings have been conferred upon government-appointed officials or bodies might wish to include in article 4 or elsewhere in chapter I the following provision: 'Nothing in this Law affects the provisions in force in this State governing the authority of [*insert the title of the government-appointed person or body*]'.

Article 6 Public policy exception

Nothing in this Law prevents the court from refusing to take an action governed by this Law if the action would be manifestly contrary to the public policy of this State.

Article 7 Additional assistance under other laws

Nothing in this Law limits the power of a court or a [*insert the title of the person or body administering a reorganization or liquidation under the law of the enacting State*] to provide additional assistance to a foreign representative under other laws of this State.

Article 8 Interpretation

In the interpretation of this Law, regard is to be had to its international origin and to the need to promote uniformity in its application and the observance of good faith.

Chapter II: Access of Foreign Representatives and Creditors to Courts in this State

Article 9 Right of direct access

A foreign representative is entitled to apply directly to a court in this State.

Article 10 Limited jurisdiction

The sole fact that an application pursuant to this Law is made to a court in this State by a foreign representative does not subject the foreign representative or the foreign assets and affairs of the debtor to the jurisdiction of the courts of this State for any purpose other than the application.

Article 11 Application by a foreign representative to commence a proceeding under [*identify laws of the enacting State relating to insolvency*]

A foreign representative is entitled to apply to commence a proceeding under [identify laws of the enacting State relating to insolvency] if the conditions for commencing such a proceeding are otherwise met.

Article 12 Participation of a foreign representative in a proceeding under [*identify laws of the enacting State relating to insolvency*]

Upon recognition of a foreign proceeding, the foreign representative is entitled to participate in a proceeding regarding the debtor under [*identify laws of the enacting State relating to insolvency*].

Article 13 Access of foreign creditors to a proceeding under [*identify laws of the enacting State relating to insolvency*]

(1) Subject to paragraph (2) of this article, foreign creditors have the same rights regarding the commencement of, and participation in, a proceeding under [*identify laws of the enacting State relating to insolvency*] as creditors in this State.

(2) Paragraph (1) of this article does not affect the ranking of claims in a pro-

ceeding under [*identify laws of the enacting State relating to insolvency*], except that the claims of foreign creditors shall not be ranked lower than [*identify the class of general non-preference claims, while providing that a foreign claim is to be ranked lower than the general non-preference claims if an equivalent local claim (e.g. claim for a penalty or deferred-payment claim) has a rank lower than the general non-preference claims*].*

Article 14 Notification to foreign creditors of a proceeding under [*identify laws of the enacting State relating to insolvency*]

(1) Whenever under [*identify laws of the enacting State relating to insolvency*] notification is to be given to creditors in this State, such notification shall also be given to the known creditors that do not have addresses in this State. The court may order that appropriate steps be taken with a view to notifying any creditor whose address is not yet known.

(2) Such notification shall be made to the foreign creditors individually, unless the court considers that, under the circumstances, some other form of notification would be more appropriate. No letters rogatory or other, similar formality is required.

(3) When a notification of commencement of a proceeding is to be given to foreign creditors, the notification shall:

(a) indicate a reasonable time period for filing claims and specify the place for their filing;

(b) indicate whether secured creditors need to file their secured claims; and

(c) contain any other information required to be included in such a notification to creditors pursuant to the law of this State and the orders of the court.

Chapter III: Recognition of a Foreign Proceeding and Relief

Article 15 Application for recognition of a foreign proceeding

(1) A foreign representative may apply to the court for recognition of the foreign proceeding in which the foreign representative has been appointed.

(2) An application for recognition shall be accompanied by:

(a) a certified copy of the decision commencing the foreign proceeding and appointing the foreign representative; or

(b) a certificate from the foreign court affirming the existence of the foreign proceeding and of the appointment of the foreign representative; or

(c) in the absence of evidence referred to in subparagraphs (a) and (b), any other evidence acceptable to the court of the existence of the foreign proceeding and of the appointment of the foreign representative.

* The enacting State may wish to consider the following alternative wording to replace article 13(2): '(2) Paragraph (1) of this article does not affect the ranking of claims in a proceeding under [*identify laws of the enacting State relating to insolvency*] or the exclusion of foreign tax and social security claims from such a proceeding. Nevertheless, the claims of foreign creditors other than those concerning tax and social security obligations shall not be ranked lower than [*identify the class of general non-preference claims, while providing that a foreign claim is to be ranked lower than the general non-preference claims if an equivalent local claim (e.g. claim for a penalty or deferred-payment claim) has a rank lower than the general non-preference claims*]'.

(3) An application for recognition shall also be accompanied by a statement identifying all foreign proceedings in respect of the debtor that are known to the foreign representative.

(4) The court may require a translation of documents supplied in support of the application for recognition into an official language of this State.

Article 16 Presumptions concerning recognition

(1) If the decision or certificate referred to in article 15(2) indicates that the foreign proceeding is a proceeding within the meaning of article 2(a) and that the foreign representative is a person or body within the meaning of article 2(d), the court is entitled to so presume.

(2) The court is entitled to presume that documents submitted in support of the application for recognition are authentic, whether or not they have been legalized.

(3) In the absence of proof to the contrary, the debtor's registered office, or habitual residence in the case of an individual, is presumed to be the centre of the debtor's main interests.

Article 17 Decision to recognize a foreign proceeding

(1) Subject to article 6, a foreign proceeding shall be recognized if:

(a) the foreign proceeding is a proceeding within the meaning of article 2(a);
(b) the foreign representative applying for recognition is a person or body within the meaning of article 2(d);
(c) the application meets the requirements of article 15(2); and
(d) the application has been submitted to the court referred to in article 4.

(2) The foreign proceeding shall be recognized:

(a) as a foreign main proceeding if it is taking place in the State where the debtor has the centre of its main interests; or
(b) as a foreign non-main proceeding if the debtor has an establishment within the meaning of article 2(f) in the foreign State.

(3) An application for recognition of a foreign proceeding shall be decided upon at the earliest possible time.

(4) The provisions of articles 15, 16, 17 and 18 do not prevent modification or termination of recognition if it is shown that the grounds for granting it were fully or partially lacking or have ceased to exist.

Article 18 Subsequent information

From the time of filing the application for recognition of the foreign proceeding, the foreign representative shall inform the court promptly of:

(a) any substantial change in the status of the recognized foreign proceeding or the status of the foreign representative's appointment; and
(b) any other foreign proceeding regarding the same debtor that becomes known to the foreign representative.

Article 19 Relief that may be granted upon application for recognition of a foreign proceeding

(1) From the time of filing an application for recognition until the application is decided upon, the court may, at the request of the foreign representative, where

relief is urgently needed to protect the assets of the debtor or the interests of the creditors, grant relief of a provisional nature, including:

(a) staying execution against the debtor's assets;
(b) entrusting the administration or realization of all or part of the debtor's assets located in this State to the foreign representative or another person designated by the court, in order to protect and preserve the value of assets that, by their nature or because of other circumstances, are perishable, susceptible to devaluation or otherwise in jeopardy;
(c) any relief mentioned in article 21(1)(c), (d) and (g).

(2) [*Insert provisions (or refer to provisions in force in the enacting State) relating to notice.*]

(3) Unless extended under article 21(1)(f), the relief granted under this article terminates when the application for recognition is decided upon.

(4) The court may refuse to grant relief under this article if such relief would interfere with the administration of a foreign main proceeding.

Article 20 Effects of recognition of a foreign main proceeding

(1) Upon recognition of a foreign proceeding that is a foreign main proceeding,

(a) commencement or continuation of individual actions or individual proceedings concerning the debtor's assets, rights, obligations or liabilities is stayed;
(b) execution against the debtor's assets is stayed; and
(c) the right to transfer, encumber or otherwise dispose of any assets of the debtor is suspended.

(2) The scope, and the modification or termination, of the stay and suspension referred to in paragraph (1) of this article are subject to [*refer to any provisions of law of the enacting State relating to insolvency that apply to exceptions, limitations, modifications or termination in respect of the stay and suspension referred to in paragraph (1) of this article*].

(3) Paragraph (1) (a) of this article does not affect the right to commence individual actions or proceedings to the extent necessary to preserve a claim against the debtor.

(4) Paragraph (1) of this article does not affect the right to request the commencement of a proceeding under [*identify laws of the enacting State relating to insolvency*] or the right to file claims in such a proceeding.

Article 21 Relief that may be granted upon recognition of a foreign proceeding

(1) Upon recognition of a foreign proceeding, whether main or non-main, where necessary to protect the assets of the debtor or the interests of the creditors, the court may, at the request of the foreign representative, grant any appropriate relief, including:

(a) staying the commencement or continuation of individual actions or individual proceedings concerning the debtor's assets, rights, obligations or liabilities, to the extent they have not been stayed under article 20(1)(a);
(b) staying execution against the debtor's assets to the extent it has not been stayed under article 20(1)(b);

(c) suspending the right to transfer, encumber or otherwise dispose of any assets of the debtor to the extent this right has not been suspended under article 20(1)(c);
(d) providing for the examination of witnesses, the taking of evidence or the delivery of information concerning the debtor's assets, affairs, rights, obligations or liabilities;
(e) entrusting the administration or realization of all or part of the debtor's assets located in this State to the foreign representative or another person designated by the court;
(f) extending relief granted under article 19(1);
(g) granting any additional relief that may be available to [*insert the title of a person or body administering a reorganization or liquidation under the law of the enacting State*] under the laws of this State.

(2) Upon recognition of a foreign proceeding, whether main or non-main, the court may, at the request of the foreign representative, entrust the distribution of all or part of the debtor's assets located in this State to the foreign representative or another person designated by the court, provided that the court is satisfied that the interests of creditors in this State are adequately protected.

(3) In granting relief under this article to a representative of a foreign non-main proceeding, the court must be satisfied that the relief relates to assets that, under the law of this State, should be administered in the foreign non-main proceeding or concerns information required in that proceeding.

Article 22 Protection of creditors and other interested persons

(1) In granting or denying relief under article 19 or 21, or in modifying or terminating relief under paragraph (3) of this article, the court must be satisfied that the interests of the creditors and other interested persons, including the debtor, are adequately protected.

(2) The court may subject relief granted under article 19 or 21 to conditions it considers appropriate.

(3) The court may, at the request of the foreign representative or a person affected by relief granted under article 19 or 21, or at its own motion, modify or terminate such relief.

Article 23 Actions to avoid acts detrimental to creditors

(1) Upon recognition of a foreign proceeding, the foreign representative has standing to initiate [*refer to the types of actions to avoid or otherwise render ineffective acts detrimental to creditors that are available in this State to a person or body administering a reorganization or liquidation*].

(2) When the foreign proceeding is a foreign non-main proceeding, the court must be satisfied that the action relates to assets that, under the law of this State, should be administered in the foreign non-main proceeding.

Article 24 Intervention by a foreign representative in proceedings in this State

Upon recognition of a foreign proceeding, the foreign representative may, provided the requirements of the law of this State are met, intervene in any proceedings in which the debtor is a party.

Chapter IV: Cooperation with Foreign Courts and Foreign Representatives

Article 25 Cooperation and direct communication between a court of this State and foreign courts or foreign representatives

(1) In matters referred to in article 1, the court shall cooperate to the maximum extent possible with foreign courts or foreign representatives, either directly or through a [*insert the title of a person or body administering a reorganization or liquidation under the law of the enacting State*].

(2) The court is entitled to communicate directly with, or to request information or assistance directly from, foreign courts or foreign representatives.

Article 26 Cooperation and direct communication between the [*insert the title of a person or body administering a reorganization or liquidation under the law of the enacting State*] and foreign courts or foreign representatives

(1) In matters referred to in article 1, a [*insert the title of a person or body administering a reorganization or liquidation under the law of the enacting State*] shall, in the exercise of its functions and subject to the supervision of the court, cooperate to the maximum extent possible with foreign courts or foreign representatives.

(2) The [*insert the title of a person or body administering a reorganization or liquidation under the law of the enacting State*] is entitled, in the exercise of its functions and subject to the supervision of the court, to communicate directly with foreign courts or foreign representatives.

Article 27 Forms of cooperation

Cooperation referred to in articles 25 and 26 may be implemented by any appropriate means, including:

(a) appointment of a person or body to act at the direction of the court;
(b) communication of information by any means considered appropriate by the court;
(c) coordination of the administration and supervision of the debtor's assets and affairs;
(d) approval or implementation by courts of agreements concerning the coordination of proceedings;
(e) coordination of concurrent proceedings regarding the same debtor;
(f) [*the enacting State may wish to list additional forms or examples of cooperation*].

Chapter V: Concurrent Proceedings

Article 28 Commencement of a proceeding under [*identify laws of the enacting State relating to insolvency*] after recognition of a foreign main proceeding

After recognition of a foreign main proceeding, a proceeding under [*identify laws of the enacting State relating to insolvency*] may be commenced only if the debtor has assets in this State; the effects of that proceeding shall be restricted to the assets of the debtor that are located in this State and, to the extent necessary to implement cooperation and coordination under articles 25, 26 and 27, to other assets of the debtor that, under the law of this State, should be administered in that proceeding.

Article 29 Coordination of a proceeding under [*identify laws of the enacting State relating to insolvency*] and a foreign proceeding

Where a foreign proceeding and a proceeding under [*identify laws of the enacting State relating to insolvency*] are taking place concurrently regarding the same debtor, the court shall seek cooperation and coordination under articles 25, 26 and 27, and the following shall apply:

(a) when the proceeding in this State is taking place at the time the application for recognition of the foreign proceeding is filed,
  (i) any relief granted under article 19 or 21 must be consistent with the proceeding in this State; and
  (ii) if the foreign proceeding is recognized in this State as a foreign main proceeding, article 20 does not apply;
(b) when the proceeding in this State commences after recognition, or after the filing of the application for recognition, of the foreign proceeding,
  (i) any relief in effect under article 19 or 21 shall be reviewed by the court and shall be modified or terminated if inconsistent with the proceeding in this State; and
  (ii) if the foreign proceeding is a foreign main proceeding, the stay and suspension referred to in article 20(1) shall be modified or terminated pursuant to article 20(2) if inconsistent with the proceeding in this State;
(c) in granting, extending or modifying relief granted to a representative of a foreign non-main proceeding, the court must be satisfied that the relief relates to assets that, under the law of this State, should be administered in the foreign non-main proceeding or concerns information required in that proceeding.

Article 30 Coordination of more than one foreign proceeding

In matters referred to in article 1, in respect of more than one foreign proceeding regarding the same debtor, the court shall seek cooperation and coordination under articles 25, 26 and 27, and the following shall apply:

(a) any relief granted under article 19 or 21 to a representative of a foreign non-main proceeding after recognition of a foreign main proceeding must be consistent with the foreign main proceeding;
(b) if a foreign main proceeding is recognized after recognition, or after the filing of an application for recognition, of a foreign non-main proceeding, any relief in effect under article 19 or 21 shall be reviewed by the court and shall be modified or terminated if inconsistent with the foreign main proceeding;
(c) if, after recognition of a foreign non-main proceeding, another foreign non-main proceeding is recognized, the court shall grant, modify or terminate relief for the purpose of facilitating coordination of the proceedings.

Article 31 Presumption of insolvency based on recognition of a foreign main proceeding

In the absence of evidence to the contrary, recognition of a foreign main proceeding is, for the purpose of commencing a proceeding under [*identify laws of the enacting State relating to insolvency*], proof that the debtor is insolvent.

Article 32 Rule of payment in concurrent proceedings

Without prejudice to secured claims or rights *in rem*, a creditor who has received part payment in respect of its claim in a proceeding pursuant to a law relating to insolvency in a foreign State may not receive a payment for the same claim in a proceeding under [*identify laws of the enacting State relating to insolvency*] regarding the same debtor, so long as the payment to the other creditors of the same class is proportionately less than the payment the creditor has already received.

Appendix V
Latin American Treaties

(A) MONTEVIDEO TREATY ON INTERNATIONAL COMMERCIAL LAW, 12 MARCH, 1889 (extract)[1]

Title X: Bankruptcies

35. The judges competent to take jurisdiction in bankruptcy proceedings are those of the commercial domicile of the bankrupt, even when the person adjudged bankrupt occasionally engages in acts of commerce in another Country, or maintains agencies or branches there which operate on behalf, and on the responsibility, of the principal establishment.

36. If the bankrupt has two or more independent commercial houses in different territories, the courts of the respective domiciles shall be competent to take jurisdiction in the bankruptcy proceeding relative to each of the houses.

37. When bankruptcy has been declared in one country, in the case of the preceding Article, the precautionary measures prescribed in those proceedings shall also be enforced with respect to the property which the bankrupt possesses in other States, without prejudice to the rights which the following Articles confer upon the local creditors.

38. Once the precautionary measures have been taken by means of the appropriate letters rogatory, the judge to whom the letters are addressed shall order the publication for a period of sixty days of advertisements announcing both the adjudication of bankruptcy and the measures which have been prescribed.

39. Local creditors may, within the time limit fixed in the preceding Article, counting from the day following the publication of the advertisements, initiate a new bankruptcy proceeding against the bankrupt in their State; or, if circumstances do not permit an adjudication of bankruptcy, they may bring civil action against him.

In such a case, the various bankruptcy proceedings shall be conducted quite independently of one another, and the applicable law in the case of each of them shall be that of the country in which it is commenced.

40. The expression 'local creditors', in regard to a bankruptcy opened in a given country, shall be interpreted as referring to those whose claims should be satisfied in that place.

[1] Unofficial translation by the author.

41. In cases where more than one bankruptcy proceeding or action may be instituted, in accordance with the provisions in this Title, the balance that is left over for the account of the bankrupt in one State shall be placed at the disposal of the creditors in the other, and the respective judges should come to a mutual understanding with that end in view.

42. In cases where only one bankruptcy proceeding is instituted, either because only one is proper, according to the provisions contained in Article 35, or because the local creditors have not made use of the right conceded to them by Article 39, all of the creditors of the bankrupt shall present their claims and exercise their rights before the judge of the court which has pronounced the adjudication of bankruptcy.

43. Even when only one bankruptcy proceeding takes place, creditors who became mortgagees or pledgees prior to the declaration of the same may exercise their rights before the courts of the country in which the property mortgaged or pledged is located.

44. The preferential rights of local creditors in the country in which bankruptcy has been opened, if acquired prior to its declaration, shall be respected even in the case where the property over which the preferential right can be asserted has been removed to another State in which a bankruptcy proceeding or civil action against the same bankrupt is currently in progress.

The provision in the preceding paragraph shall only be applicable when the transfer of property took place within the period to which the bankruptcy has retroactive effect (i.e. during the 'suspect period').

45. The authority of the assignees or legal representatives of the bankruptcy shall be recognised in all the States, provided it is recognised by the law of the country in whose territory the proceeding in which they are acting was opened. They should be allowed in all places to exercise the functions which have been entrusted to them by the said law and by the present Treaty.

46. In cases where there is plurality of proceedings, the court in whose jurisdiction the bankrupt resides shall be competent to determine all the measures of a civil character which affect him personally.

47. Discharge (rehabilitation) of the bankrupt shall only take place when it has been pronounced in all the proceedings which involve him.

48. The provisions of this Treaty relating to bankruptcy shall apply to incorporated joint-stock companies, no matter what procedure for their liquidation is established by the laws of the Contracting States, in the case where they have ceased to pay their debts as they fall due.

(B) MONTEVIDEO TREATY ON INTERNATIONAL COMMERCIAL TERRESTRIAL LAW, 19 MARCH 1940 (extract)[2]

Title VIII: Of Bankruptcy

Article 40. The judges competent to formulate an adjudication of bankruptcy, are those of the domicile of the merchant or commercial partnership involved, even though the latter may incidentally be engaged in acts of commerce within another State or other States, or may have in one or more of these, agencies or branches which operate in behalf, and on the responsibility, of the principal establishment.

Article 41. If the bankrupt has two or more independent commercial houses in different territories, the judges or tribunals of the respective commercial domiciles shall be competent to take cognizance of the proceedings in bankruptcy relative to each of the said houses.

Article 42. Adjudication of bankruptcy, and other acts relative thereto, whose publication is required by the laws of the State where the adjudication took place, shall also be publicly announced in the States where the bankrupt has agencies, branches or establishments; and such publication shall be effected in accordance with the formalities prescribed by the local laws.

Article 43. When adjudication of bankruptcy has been pronounced in a given State, the precautionary measures of security and conservation prescribed in the corresponding bankruptcy proceedings, shall also be enforced in regard to the property which the bankrupt may possess in other States; and this enforcement shall be effected in conformity with the local laws.

Article 44. Once the precautionary measures have been duly taken by means of the appropriate letters rogatory, the judge to whom the letters are addressed shall order the publication during a thirty-day period, in the places where the bankrupt possesses property, of advertisements announcing both the adjudication of bankruptcy and the measures which have been prescribed.

Article 45. Local creditors may institute in their respective States, within a period of sixty days after the last of the notifications mentioned in the foregoing article, new proceedings in bankruptcy against the bankrupt; or, if the circumstances do not permit an adjudication of bankruptcy, they may bring civil action against him. In such cases, the several proceedings in bankruptcy shall be conducted quite independently of one another, and the law of the State where each particular proceeding is instituted shall be applied thereto. Likewise, the

[2] Translated from the Spanish by J. Irizarry y Puente and Gwladys L. Williams. Originally published in (1943) 37 A.J.I.L. Suppl., at 138–140. Reproduced with permission. © The American Society of International Law.

corresponding laws shall apply to each distinct and separate proceeding, in all matters relative to the conclusion of precautionary agreements or to other, analogous measures. All of the foregoing provisions shall be interpreted without prejudice to compliance with the measures specified in Article 43, to the provisions of Article 47 under this Title, or to the objections which may be interposed by the assignees or representatives of the whole body of creditors involved in the other proceedings.

Article 46. The expression 'local creditors', in regard to a bankruptcy case adjudicated in a given State, shall be interpreted as referring to those persons whose claims should be satisfied in the said State.

Article 47. In cases where more than one proceeding in bankruptcy may properly be instituted, according to the provisions set forth under this title, the balance left over in one State for the account of the bankrupt shall be placed at the disposal of the judge who has cognizance of the bankruptcy proceedings in another State, and the respective judges should come to a mutual understanding with that end in view.

Article 48. In cases where only one proceeding in bankruptcy is instituted, either because only one is proper under the provisions set forth in Article 40, or because the local creditors have not made use of the right conceded to them by Article 45, all of the creditors of the bankrupt shall present their claims and make use of their rights in conformity with the law, and before the judge or tribunal, of the State which has pronounced the adjudication of bankruptcy.

In such cases, the local claims existing in a particular State enjoy preference over those existing in other States, with respect to the sum total of the assets in the State where the former are located.

Article 49. The authority of the assignees or administrators, in cases involving a single bankruptcy proceeding, by whatsoever name they or their representatives may be designated, shall be recognized in all of the contracting States.

They may undertake measures of conservation or administration, appear in suits, and exercise the functions and rights accorded them by the laws of the State where the bankruptcy was adjudicated; but execution in regard to assets located outside of the jurisdiction of the judge who has cognizance of the proceeding must conform to the law of that location.

Article 50. Even when only one proceeding in bankruptcy is involved, mortgagees or pledgees constituted as such before the date of definitive stoppage of payment may exercise their rights before the judges of the State where the property mortgaged or pledged is located.

Article 51. In cases involving more than one proceeding in bankruptcy, property belonging to the debtor and located in the territory of another State where no proceeding in bankruptcy, civil action of insolvency, or other, analogous proceeding has been instituted, shall form part of the bankruptcy assets in the particular proceeding whose judge has been the first to act.

Article 52. When more than one proceeding in bankruptcy is involved, the judge or tribunal within whose jurisdiction the bankrupt is domiciled shall be competent to dictate all measures of a civil character which may concern the latter personally.

Article 53. The rules relative to bankruptcy shall apply, in so far as is suitable, to judicial liquidations, precautionary agreements, suspensions of payment, and other analogous measures provided for in the laws of the contracting States.

(C) MONTEVIDEO TREATY OF INTERNATIONAL PROCEDURAL LAW, 19 MARCH 1940 (extract)[3]

Title IV: Of Civil Meetings of Creditors

Article 16. Civil meetings of creditors are governed and conducted in accordance with the laws, and before the judges, of the country where the debtor has his domicile.

Article 17. In cases involving property located in one or more signatory States, other than property in the debtor's domicile, the creditors may institute independent proceedings in each of the said States.

Article 18. When the insolvency has been declared, and without prejudice to the right established in Article 17, each judge shall take the pertinent preventive steps with respect to the property located in other countries, and, in so doing, shall proceed according to the forms established for such cases in the preceding articles.

Article 19. When the preventive measures have been complied with, the judges to whom the letters requisitorial were addressed shall publish proclamations, throughout a thirty-day period, announcing the insolvency hearing, the appointment of the receiver and his domicile, the time-limit for submitting the evidence of claims, and the preventive measures which may have been taken.

Article 20. In the cases mentioned in Article 17, the local creditors, within a period of sixty days immediately after the last publication provided for in Article 19, may ask for insolvency proceedings against the debtor, with respect to property located in their own country. In these instances, just as in cases involving a single insolvency hearing which is held before the tribunals and according to the laws of the country of the debtor's domicile, the local creditors shall have preferential rights in regard to property located in the territory where their claims should be met.

Article 21. When several insolvency hearings are in order, any surplus which may be left over in favor of the debtor of one signatory State, shall be held to await the outcome of the other hearings, and shall preferably be handed over, through judicial channels, for the purposes of the hearing first announced.

[3] Translated from the Spanish by J. Irizarry y Puente and Gwladys L. Williams. Originally published in (1943) 37 A.J.I.L. Suppl., at 120–121. Reproduced with permission. © The American Society of International Law.

Article 22. Liens are determined exclusively by the law of the State where each proceeding is opened, subject to the following limitations:

(a) The special lien on immovables and the real right of mortgage, shall be subject to the law of the State where the property is located;

(b) The special lien on moveables is subject to the law of the State where those moveables are located, without prejudice to the rights of the State in regard to taxes due.

The same rule prevails with respect to rights based on possession or tenancy of moveable property, or on public registry, or on any other form of publicity.

Article 23. The authority of the receivers, or of the legal representatives of the creditors, shall be recognized in all of the States; and these shall permit in their territory the exercise of the functions allowed the said receivers and representatives by the insolvency law and by the present treaty.

Article 24. Incapacity affecting the debtor shall be decreed by the judge of his domicile, according to the law thereof. Incapacity relative to property located in other countries may be declared by the local tribunals in accordance with their own laws.

The rehabilitation of the insolvent party and the effects thereof shall be governed by the same rules.

Article 25. The rules relative to insolvency proceedings shall likewise be applicable to the judicial liquidations, precautionary agreements, suspensions of payment and other analogous measures which may be provided for in the laws of the contracting States.

(D) HAVANA CONVENTION ON PRIVATE INTERNATIONAL LAW, 20 FEBRUARY 1928 (extract)[4]

Title IX: Bankruptcy or Insolvency

Chapter I: Unity of Bankruptcy or Insolvency

Article 414

If the insolvent or bankrupt [*debtor*][5] has only one civil or commercial domicile, there can be only one preventive proceeding in insolvency or bankruptcy, or one suspension of payments, or a composition (*quita y espera*) in respect of all his assets and his liabilities in the contracting States.

[4] English translation as published in (1929) 86 L.N.T.S. No. 1950, at pp.362–364.

[5] In the English text of Art. 414, as published in 86 L.N.T.S. at p.362, the word 'creditor' is stated, although the context clearly requires the use of the word 'debtor', as inserted here. The Portuguese version of Art. 414, printed on p.363, uses the word '*credor*', equally erroneously. The Spanish and French versions of the Article, on pp. 226 and 227 respectively, employ the correct terms 'deudor' and 'débiteur'.

Article 415

If one and the same person or partnership should have in more than one contracting State various commercial establishments entirely separate economically, there may be as many suits for preventive proceeding in bankruptcy as there are commercial establishments.

Chapter II: Universality of Bankruptcy or Insolvency, and their Effects

Article 416

A decree establishing the capacity of the bankrupt or insolvent, has extraterritorial effect in each of the contracting States, upon the previous compliance with the formalities of registration or publication which may be required by the legislation of each State.

Article 417

A decree of bankruptcy or insolvency, rendered in one of the contracting States, shall be executed in others in the cases and manner established in this code in respect to judicial resolutions; but it shall have the effect of *res judicata* from the moment it is made final, as to the persons which it is to affect.

Article 418

The powers and functions of the trustees appointed in one of the contracting States in accordance with the provisions of this code shall have extraterritorial effect in the others, without the necessity of any local proceeding.

Article 419

The retroactive effect of a declaration of bankruptcy or insolvency and the annulment of certain acts in consequence of those judgments shall be determined by the law thereof and shall be applicable to the territory of all the other contracting States.

Article 420

Real actions and rights of the same nature shall continue to be subject, notwithstanding the declaration in bankruptcy or insolvency, to the law of the situation of the things affected thereby and to the competence of the judges of the place in which they are found.

Chapter III: Agreement and Rehabilitation

Article 421

The agreement among the creditors and the bankrupt or insolvent shall have extraterritorial effect in the other contracting States, saving the right to a real action by the creditors who may not have accepted.

Article 422

The rehabilitation of the bankrupt has also extraterritorial validity in the other contracting States, as soon as the judicial resolution by which it is ordered becomes final, and in conformity with its terms.

Appendix VI

Nordic Bankruptcy Convention[1]

His Majesty the King of Denmark and Iceland, the President of the Republic of Finland, His Majesty the King of Norway and His Majesty the King of Sweden, having agreed to conclude a Convention regarding bankruptcy, have appointed as their Plenipotentiaries: [names]

Who, being duly authorised for the purpose, have agreed on the following Articles:

Article 1

A declaration of bankruptcy in any of the contracting States shall also apply to the bankrupt's property in the territory of the other States.

Unless otherwise provided, the law of the country in which bankruptcy takes place shall determine the effects of such bankruptcy in the matter of divesting the bankrupt of the administration of his property; the extent of the assets and the property therein comprised or capable of being re-incorporated therein in consequence of annulment proceedings; the bankrupt's rights and obligations during bankruptcy; the administration of the bankrupt's property and transactions in respect thereof; the rights of creditors in respect of the payment of their claims; the allocation of the assets; the composition with creditors or other mode of settlement.

Such of the bankrupt's property as, under the law of the country in which it is situate, is not liable for seizure for any claim shall not be included in the assets.

Article 2

Should a declaration of bankruptcy in any of the States also apply to property situate in one of the other States, the bankruptcy officers shall be required forthwith to give notice of the bankruptcy by an announcement in the *Official Journal* of the said State and to take steps, in accordance with the rules in force in that State, for its entry in the Land Register, Shipping Register or any other public register.

A notification of the bankruptcy shall be sent as soon as possible to all known creditors in the other States, with the exception of those whose claims have been entered in the statement of assets and liabilities without specific application on their part. Creditors in the other State shall also be notified of any objections raised against their claims.

Article 3

The courts of the contracting States shall, at the request of the bankruptcy officers in one of the other States, make an inventory of the property situate in their

[1] No. 3574 of 1933 between Denmark, Finland, Iceland, Norway and Sweden, signed at Copenhagen on 7 November 1933. English translation as published in (1935), 155 L.N.T.S. No. 3574, at pp. 133–139.

territory and take the necessary steps for the provisional conservation of that property and for the sale of such property as is not suitable for conservation.

Moreover, the bankruptcy officers may, in respect of property situate in another State than that in which the bankruptcy is declared, request the assistance of the authorities in the same measure as if they were bankruptcy officers of that country.

This request may be addressed direct to the competent authority. If necessary, the costs may be required to be paid in advance.

Documents drawn up in Finnish or Icelandic shall be accompanied by a certified translation into Danish, Norwegian or Swedish.

Article 4

The question whether entry in the Land Register is a necessary condition in order that acts creating rights performed by the debtor previous to bankruptcy in respect of immovable property and accessories thereto may be valid as against the bankrupt estate and the question of the invalidation of such acts shall be settled in accordance with the law of the State in which the property is situate. The same applies to the question whether entry in the Land Register is necessary in order to prevent legal acts performed by the debtor during bankruptcy in respect of such property from having any effect on the estate. Similar questions regarding registered ships or aircraft or part shares therein shall be settled in accordance with the law of the country to which the ships or aircraft belong.

If, according to the law of one of the contracting States, entry in the Land Register, registration or any other form of publication is a necessary condition in order that the alienation or hypothication of movable property other than that mentioned in the first paragraph may be valid as against the bankrupt estate, the law in that State shall be applicable in deciding the question of the invalidity or invalidation of such legal act if the property is situate in that State at the beginning of the bankruptcy proceedings.

The question of the effect of bankruptcy on rights acquired in virtue of measures of execution shall be settled in accordance with the law of the State where execution has taken place.

Article 5

The right of creditors whose claims are secured by mortgage or pledge to take proceedings for the realisation of their claims, irrespective of the bankruptcy of the debtor, shall be governed by the law of the country in which the property mortgaged or pledged is situate when bankruptcy takes place. This rule shall apply *mutatis mutandis* to rights of retention.

The effect of the bankruptcy on the right to take proceedings for compulsory execution by measures of execution shall be determined by the law of the State in which execution takes place.

Article 6

The procedure for the sale of property forming part of the bankrupt estate shall be determined in accordance with the law of the State in which the property is situate.

Article 7

The rules applicable to preferential claims against particular assets and the question of priority as between such preferential claims, mortgages, pledges or other rights *in rem* attaching to the said assets shall be determined by the law of that country in which such property is situate when bankruptcy takes place. The specific preferential rights aforementioned shall have priority over all general preferential rights.

The extent to which preferential treatment shall be due to taxes and other public dues levied by a State other than that in which bankruptcy has been declared shall be governed by the law of the State to which such taxes and dues are payable. The extent to which preferential treatment shall be due to a lessor, the owner of premises in the territory of one of the other States, shall be determined by the law of the State in which the said premises are situate. Such preferential rights shall only apply to the property of the bankrupt in the State by which the aforesaid taxes and dues are levied or in whose territory are situate the premises in question. As between such preferential rights, priority shall be determined, when they are of a specific character, in accordance with the first paragraph of the present Article; when they are of a general character, they shall have priority over all other general preferential rights. The provisions of the first paragraph notwithstanding, priority as between general preferential rights of a fiscal character and the specific preferential rights referred to in the said paragraph shall be determined by the law of the State by which the taxes or dues are levied. It shall, however, be understood that the present Convention shall not affect the question of how far claims in respect of public taxes and dues levied by a State other than that in which bankruptcy is declared can be charged against the bankrupt estate.

Article 8

In so far as the application of the above provisions depends upon the situation of property, any claim possessed by the bankrupt shall be regarded as situate in the State in which bankruptcy is declared. If the claim is attested by a promissory note or other document the production of which is necessary in order to obtain payment, it is nevertheless considered as situate in the same State as the document in question.

Registered ships or aircraft are deemed to be situated in the State to which they belong, except as regards the application of Article 6.

Article 9

The provisions of the present Convention shall not apply to the question whether, and if so to what extent, the creditors of the bankrupt estate are entitled to exercise the rights of the bankrupt under a bilateral agreement the terms of which have not been fully carried out when bankruptcy takes place.

Article 10

The provisions of the Convention of March 16th, 1932, regarding jurisdiction shall apply to judicial decisions (including those confirming settlements) in annulment proceedings or those dealing with the extinguishment of rights in the case of bankruptcy declared in one of the States.

Judicial decisions given in any one of the States for the purpose of confirming a composition with creditors shall also apply in the other States.

The foregoing provisions shall apply irrespective of the fact that the bankrupt possesses property in the territory of only one of the contracting States.

Article 11

The present Convention shall only apply to the division of the bankrupt estates of deceased persons in so far as the liquidation of estates of deceased persons is dealt with by a Convention in force between the contracting States.

Article 12

The present Convention shall also apply to the public liquidation of banks in so far as such liquidation precludes bankruptcy proceedings in accordance with the law of the State in which the bank is situated.

The notification provided for in Article 2 must contain a statement to the effect that the liquidation is of such a kind as to be covered by the Convention.

Article 13

If in an adjudication in bankruptcy the court proposes to base its jurisdiction on a fact unconnected with the residence of a bankrupt individual or with the registered offices of a company, association or foundation which has been declared bankrupt, such fact shall be set forth in the judgment by which bankruptcy is declared. In such a case, the present Convention shall not apply to the bankruptcy in question. Proceedings in the latter may be continued irrespective of any subsequent bankruptcy proceedings in any of the other States.

Article 14

In the present Convention, the term 'bankruptcy officers' shall be deemed to include any legal authority competent in bankruptcy matters.

Article 15

Any procedure for compulsory composition opened in one of the contracting States shall preclude the declaration of bankruptcy and the procedure for compulsory composition in the other States, and shall involve therein the same restrictions in the application of compulsory execution as a procedure for composition in the country itself.

If the procedure for composition results in the confirmation of the composition, the latter shall be binding also in the other contracting States.

The provisions of Article 13 shall apply *mutatis mutandis*.

Article 16

The present Convention shall not apply to bankruptcies declared in consequence of petitions submitted or compositions proposed prior to its entry into force.

Article 17

The Convention shall be ratified and the ratifications shall be deposited in the archives of the Danish Ministry of Foreign Affairs as soon as possible.

The Convention shall come into force between the ratifying States on January 1st or on July 1st following the expiry of a period of three months after at least three of the contracting States have deposited their instruments of ratification. As regards States depositing their ratifications at a later date, the Convention shall come into force on January 1st or on July 1st following the expiry of a period of three months after the deposit of the instrument of ratification.

Any of the contracting States may denounce the Convention to any of the other States at one year's notice terminating on any January 1st or July 1st.

In faith whereof the respective Plenipotentiaries have signed the present Convention and have thereto affixed their seals.

Done at Copenhagen in one copy in each of the following languages: Danish, Finnish, Icelandic, Norwegian, and Swedish, there being two texts in Swedish, one for Finland and one for Sweden, on the 7th day of November, 1933.

Appendix VII
Select Bibliography

There is a vast literature relating to Private International Law (Conflict of Laws). The number of books and articles relating to the international aspects of Insolvency Law is also steadily growing. The following books may prove to be of particular interest to those in search of further information about the private international law aspects of insolvency.

A.E. ANTON, *Private International Law (from the standpoint of Scots law)*, 2nd edn. (1990)

J.-G. CASTEL, *Canadian Conflict of Laws*, 3rd edn. (1993), esp. chs. 30, 31

L. COLLINS (Gen. Ed.), *Dicey and Morris on the Conflict of Laws*, 12th edn. (1993, with supplements), esp. chs. 30, 31

J.H. DALHUISEN, *Dalhuisen on International Insolvency and Bankruptcy*, 2 vols (loose-leaf, 1979–1986)

I.F. FLETCHER, *Conflict of Laws and European Community Law* (1982)

—— *The Law of Insolvency*, 2nd edn. (1996), esp. Part III

—— (ed.), *Cross-Border Insolvency: Comparative Dimensions (The Aberystwyth Insolvency Papers)* (1990)

—— (ed.), *Cross-Border Insolvency: National and Comparative Studies (Reports delivered at the XIII International Congress of Comparative Law, Montreal 1990)* (1992)

R.M. GOODE, *Principles of Corporate Insolvency Law*, 2nd edn. (1997), esp. ch. 13

E.B. LEONARD and C.W. BESANT (eds.), *Current Issues in Cross-border Insolvency and Reorganisations* (1994)

J.G. MCLEOD, *The Conflict of Laws* (1983), esp. chs. 5, 6

B.H. MCPHERSON, *The Law of Company Liquidation*, 3rd edn. (1987), esp. ch. 16

K.H. NADELMANN, *Conflict of Laws, International and Interstate* (1972)

P.M. NORTH and J.J. FAWCETT, *Cheshire and North's Private International Law*, 12th edn. (1992), esp. Part VII

P.E. NYGH, *Conflict of Laws in Australia*, 6th edn. (1995), esp. Part VIII

F. PIGGOTT, *Foreign Judgments and Jurisdiction*, 3rd edn. (1910), esp. Part III, Book VI

H. RAJAK, P. HORROCKS and J. BANNISTER (eds.), *European Corporate Insolvency, A Practical Guide*, 2nd edn. (1995)

H. RAJAK (ed.), *Insolvency Law, Theory and Practice* (1993), esp. Part IV

E.F. SCOLES and P. HAY, *Conflict of Laws*, 2nd edn. (1992), esp. ch. 23

P. St. J. SMART, *Cross-Border Insolvency* (1991) (2nd edn. 1998). (References in this book are to the first edition)

E.I. SYKES and M.C. PRYLES, *Australian Private International Law*, 3rd edn. (1991), esp. chs. 9, 23

M. TROCHU, *Conflits de lois et conflits de juridictions en matière de faillite* (1967)

P.R. WOOD, *English and International Set-off* (1989)

—— *Principles of International Insolvency* (1995)

J.S. ZIEGEL (ed.), *Current Developments in International and Comparative Corporate Insolvency Law* (1994)

Additional reference sources:

Report of the Bankruptcy Convention Advisory Committee (Chairman, Kenneth Cork) (August 1976), Cmnd 6602. (See esp. Note of Reservations by A.E. Anton, at pp.105–128)

Report of the Review Committee on Insolvency Law and Practice (Chairman, Sir Kenneth Cork) (June 1982), Cmnd.8558, esp. chs. 1, 2, 49, 50 and 52

Report No. 45, General Insolvency Inquiry (Australian Law Reform Commission, Commissioner-in-charge, Mr. R.W. Harmer) (2 vols 1988), esp. ch. 19

Jonathan Pratter, *International insolvency bibliography: commentary in books and journals* (Austin, Texas: Tarlton legal bibliography series, No. 40, published by the Tarlton Law Library, Jamail Center for Legal Research, University of Texas at Austin). Supplementary bibliographical information for 1995–1997 is published in (1998) 33 *Texas International Law Journal* at 227–235 (compiled by Amy Pullen and Geralyn Trujillo)

Jean J. Davis and Victoria J. Szymczak, *Selected Insolvency and Bankruptcy Resources*, (1997) XXIII *Brooklyn Journal of International Law* at 183–202

Index